T0292754

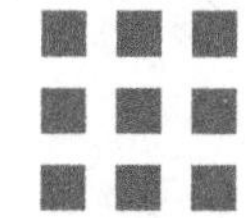

Artificial Intelligence in the Age of Neural Networks and Brain Computing

Artificial Intelligence in the Age of Neural Networks and Brain Computing

Second Edition

Edited by

Robert Kozma
Department of Mathematics, University of Memphis, Memphis, TN, United States and Research and Innovation Center, Óbuda University, Budapest, Hungary

Cesare Alippi
Politecnico di Milano, Milan, Italy and Università della Svizzera italiana, Lugano, Switzerland

Yoonsuck Choe
Department of Computer Science and Engineering, Texas A&M University, College Station, TX, United States

Francesco Carlo Morabito
AI_Lab-NeuroLab, Diceam, University Mediterranea of Reggio Calabria, Reggio Calabria, Italy

Academic Press is an imprint of Elsevier
125 London Wall, London EC2Y 5AS, United Kingdom
525 B Street, Suite 1650, San Diego, CA 92101, United States
50 Hampshire Street, 5th Floor, Cambridge, MA 02139, United States
The Boulevard, Langford Lane, Kidlington, Oxford OX5 1GB, United Kingdom

Copyright © 2024 Elsevier Inc. All rights reserved.

No part of this publication may be reproduced or transmitted in any form or by any means, electronic or mechanical, including photocopying, recording, or any information storage and retrieval system, without permission in writing from the publisher. Details on how to seek permission, further information about the Publisher's permissions policies and our arrangements with organizations such as the Copyright Clearance Center and the Copyright Licensing Agency, can be found at our website: www.elsevier.com/permissions.

This book and the individual contributions contained in it are protected under copyright by the Publisher (other than as may be noted herein).

Notices
Knowledge and best practice in this field are constantly changing. As new research and experience broaden our understanding, changes in research methods, professional practices, or medical treatment may become necessary.

Practitioners and researchers must always rely on their own experience and knowledge in evaluating and using any information, methods, compounds, or experiments described herein. In using such information or methods they should be mindful of their own safety and the safety of others, including parties for whom they have a professional responsibility.

To the fullest extent of the law, neither the Publisher nor the authors, contributors, or editors, assume any liability for any injury and/or damage to persons or property as a matter of products liability, negligence or otherwise, or from any use or operation of any methods, products, instructions, or ideas contained in the material herein.

ISBN 978-0-323-96104-2

For information on all Academic Press publications
visit our website at https://www.elsevier.com/books-and-journals

Publisher: Mara Conner
Acquisitions Editor: Chris Katsaropoulos
Editorial Project Manager: John Leonard
Production Project Manager: Prasanna Kalyanaraman
Cover Designer: Matthew Limbert

Typeset by STRAIVE, India

Contents

Contributors

Cesare Alippi Politecnico di Milano, Milan, Italy; Università della Svizzera Italiana, Lugano, Switzerland

David G. Brown US Food and Drug Administration, Silver Spring, MD, United States

Maurizio Campolo AI_Lab-NeuroLab, Diceam, University Mediterranea of Reggio Calabria, Reggio Calabria, Italy

Yoonsuck Choe Department of Computer Science and Engineering, Texas A&M University, College Station, TX, United States

Nigel Duffy Cynch AI, San Francisco, CA, United States

Péter Érdi Center for Complex Systems Studies, Kalamazoo College, Kalamazoo, MI, United States; Institute for Particle and Nuclear Physics, Wigner Research Centre for Physics, Hungarian Academy of Sciences, Budapest, Hungary

Dan Fink Cognizant AI Labs, San Francisco, CA, United States

Olivier Francon Cognizant AI Labs, San Francisco, CA, United States

Paola Galdi NeuRoNe Lab, DISA-MIS, University of Salerno, Fisciano, Salerno, Italy

Santiago Gonzalez The University of Texas at Austin, Austin, TX, United States

Marco Gori Department of Information Engineering and Mathematics, University of Siena, Siena, Italy

Stephen Grossberg Center for Adaptive Systems, Graduate Program in Cognitive and Neural Systems, Departments of Mathematics & Statistics, Psychological & Brain Sciences, and Biomedical Engineering, Boston University, Boston, MA, United States

Babak Hodjat Cognizant AI Labs, San Francisco, CA, United States

Cosimo Ieracitano AI_Lab-NeuroLab, Diceam, University Mediterranea of Reggio Calabria, Reggio Calabria, Italy

Mohak Kant Cognizant AI Labs, San Francisco, CA, United States

Nikola Kirilov Kasabov KEDRI, Auckland University of Technology, Auckland, New Zealand; Intelligent Systems Research Center, Ulster University, Derry, United Kingdom; IICT, Bulgarian Academy of Sciences, Sofia, Bulgaria; Dalian University, Dalian, China

Youngsik Kim Department of Electrical Engineering, Stanford University, Stanford, CA, United States

Robert Kozma Department of Mathematics, University of Memphis, Memphis, TN, United States; Research And Innovation Center, Óbuda University, Budapest, Hungary

Daniel S. Levine University of Texas at Arlington, Arlington, TX, United States

Qinbo Li Department of Computer Science and Engineering, Texas A&M University, College Station, TX; Meta Inc., Seattle, WA, United States

Jason Liang Cognizant AI Labs, San Francisco, CA, United States

Marco Maggini Department of Information Engineering and Mathematics, University of Siena, Siena, Italy

Nadia Mammone AI_Lab-NeuroLab, Diceam, University Mediterranea of Reggio Calabria, Reggio Calabria, Italy

Elliot Meyerson Cognizant AI Labs, San Francisco, CA, United States

Risto Miikkulainen Department of Computer Science, The University of Texas at Austin, Austin, TX; Cognizant AI Labs, San Francisco, CA, United States

Francesco Carlo Morabito AI_Lab-NeuroLab, Diceam, University Mediterranea of Reggio Calabria, Reggio Calabria, Italy

Arshak Navruzyan Launchpad, Inc., Kihei, HI, United States

Roman Ormandy R&D, Embody Corp, Los Gatos, CA, United States

Seiichi Ozawa Kobe University, Kobe, Japan

Dookun Park Department of Electrical Engineering, Stanford University, Stanford, CA, United States

Jose Krause Perin Department of Electrical Engineering, Stanford University, Stanford, CA, United States

Bala Raju Deiva AI, Palo Alto, CA, United States

Aditya Rawal Amazon AWS AI Labs, Santa Clara, CA, United States

Frank W. Samuelson US Food and Drug Administration, Silver Spring, MD, United States

Angela Serra NeuRoNe Lab, DISA-MIS, University of Salerno, Fisciano, Salerno, Italy

Hormoz Shahrzad Cognizant AI Labs, San Francisco, CA, United States

Roberto Tagliaferri NeuRoNe Lab, DISA-MIS, University of Salerno, Fisciano, Salerno, Italy

Matteo Tiezzi Department of Information Engineering and Mathematics, University of Siena, Siena, Italy

Paul J. Werbos US National Science Foundation (retired), Arlington, VA; Kummer Institute Center MST, Rolla, MO, United States

Bernard Widrow Department of Electrical Engineering, Stanford University, Stanford, CA, United States

Editors' brief biographies

Robert Kozma is Professor of Mathematics and Director of Center for Large-Scale Integrated Optimization and Networks, University of Memphis, TN, United States, and Professor of Obuda University, Budapest, Hungary; he is President of Kozmos Research Laboratories LLC, Boston, MA, United States. He is Fellow of IEEE and Fellow of the International Neural Network Society (INNS). He has been President of INNS and served on the Board of Governors of INNS, the IEEE Systems, Man, and Cybernetics Society, and on the AdCom of the IEEE Computational Intelligence Society. He has also served as Senior Fellow of US Air Force Research Laboratory. Dr. Kozma is the recipient of the INNS Gabor Award (2011) and the Alumni Association Distinguished Research Achievement Award (2010). He is Editor-In-Chief of *IEEE Transactions on Systems, Man, and Cybernetics: Systems*. His research includes robust decision support systems, autonomous robotics and navigation, distributed sensor networks, brain networks, and brain-computer interfaces.

Cesare Alippi is a professor at Politecnico di Milano, Milano, Italy, and Università della Svizzera italiana, Lugano, Switzerland. He is IEEE Fellow, ELLIS Fellow, Scientific Director of the Swiss AI Lab IDSIA, and Board of Governors member of the International Neural Network Society (INNS). In 2018, he received the IEEE CIS Outstanding Computational Intelligence Magazine Award, the 2016 Gabor award from the INNS, and the IEEE Computational Intelligence Society Outstanding Transactions on Neural Networks and Learning Systems Paper Award; in 2004, he received the IEEE Instrumentation and Measurement Society Young Engineer Award. Current research activity addresses adaptation and learning in nonstationary environments; graph learning; and intelligence for embedded, IoT, and cyber-physical systems.

Yoonsuck Choe is Professor and Director of the Brain Networks Laboratory at Texas A&M University (2001–present). He received his PhD in computer science from the University of Texas at Austin in 2001. His research interests are in neural networks and computational neuroscience, and he has published over 140 papers on these topics, including a research monograph on computations in the visual cortex. He serves on the International Neural Network Society (INNS) board of governors. He served as Program Chair and General Chair for IJCNN2015 and IJCNN2017, respectively, and serves on the editorial board of *IEEE Transactions on Cognitive and Developmental Systems.*

Francesco Carlo Morabito is Professor of Electrical and Neural Engineering with the University "Mediterranea" of Reggio Calabria, Italy, and the Former Dean of the Faculty of Engineering (2001–08) and Deputy Rector Vice-Rector for International Relations (2012–22). He is Foreign Member of the Royal Academy of Doctors, Spain (2004), and Member of the Institute of Spain, Barcelona Economic Network (2017). He served as the Governor of the International Neural Network Society for 12 years and now as VP for public relations. He was President of the Italian Society of Neural Networks (2008–14). He served in the organization of IJCNN conferences (Tutorial, International Liaison, European Link, Plenary). He has coauthored over 400 papers in various fields of engineering. He is the coauthor of 20 books and has 3 international patents. He is Associate Editor for *International Journal of Neural Systems, Neural Networks,* and *Renewable Energy.*

Introduction

We live in the era of artificial intelligence (AI), and AI is everywhere. It is on the front page of your favorite newspaper, in your pocket inside your smartphone, on your kitchen table, in your car, on the street, at your office, on trains and airplanes, and everywhere. The success of AI-based commercial products, proposed by many important companies, such as Google, IBM, Microsoft, Intel, Amazon, to name a few, can be interpreted as the coexistence of a successful synergism among what we call computational intelligence, natural intelligence, brain computing, and neural engineering.

The emergence of AI in many IT technologies happened almost overnight in the past couple of years. Recent developments in generative conversational agents like ChatGPT and its cousins rock the foundations of AI implementations. The blessing and the curse of AI are here. And all this is just the beginning, for the better or for the worse.

How did all this happen all of a sudden? Yes, it requires the powerful computing offered by advanced chips at a cheap cost. It also requires a massive amount of data available through the Internet and prolific communication resources, also called as Big Data. That is not all. Computational algorithms, called deep learning (DL), provide the framework of the programming approaches. DL was coined about a decade ago, but many experts employing these technologies do not realize that DL is rooted in the technology developed by the biologically motivated neural networks field in the 1960s.

Neural networks, thus, powerfully reemerged with different names and meanings in different, also unexpected, contexts within the current new wave of AI and DL. Neural networks represent a well-grounded paradigm rooted in many disciplines, including computer science, physics, psychology, information science, and engineering.

This volume is the second edition of the original volume published in 2018, which collected selected invited contributions from pioneers and experts in the field of neural networks. It has been designed to commemorate the 30th anniversary of International Neural Network Society (INNS), following the 2017 International Joint Conference on Neural Networks, in Anchorage, AK, United States, May 14–18, 2017. The conference is organized jointly by the INNS and the IEEE Computational Intelligence Society (CIS) and is the premiere international meeting for researchers and other professionals in neural networks and related areas, including neural network theory, DL, computational neuroscience, robotics, and distributed intelligence.

The present collection aims to show that the implications and applications of AI are nothing but a development of the endowed unique attributes of neural networks, namely, machine learning, distributed architectures, massively parallel processing, black-box inference, intrinsic nonlinearity, and a smart autonomous search engine. We strive to cover the major basic ideas of brain-like computing behind AI and to contribute to give a framework to DL as well as to launch novel intriguing paradigms as possible future alternatives.

The chapters included here are written by authors who are a blend of top experts; worldwide-recognized pioneers of the field; and researchers working on cutting-edge applications in signal processing, speech recognition, games, and adaptive control and decision-making. They include updated versions of chapters from the first edition and several new chapters marking the rapid development of the field in recent years. They describe topics such as Frontiers in Recurrent Neural Network Research; Big Science, Team Science, Open Science for Neuroscience; A Model-Based Approach for Bridging Scales of Cortical Activity; A Cognitive Architecture for Object Recognition in Video; How Brain Architecture Leads to Abstract Thought; DL-Based Speech Separation; and Advances in AI.

Our intent with the second edition is to demonstrate the importance of neural networks and brain science to produce AI that improves the quality of life of humanity. We present the relevant key concepts for our target audience, who are not a narrow group of specialists working in the field but rather a broad segment of the public intrigued by recent advances in AI.

Advances in AI, neural networks, and brain computing: An introduction

Francesco Carlo Morabito[a], Robert Kozma[b,c], Cesare Alippi[d,e], and Yoonsuck Choe[f]

[a]AI_LAB-NEUROLAB, DICEAM, UNIVERSITY MEDITERRANEA OF REGGIO CALABRIA, REGGIO CALABRIA, ITALY [b]DEPARTMENT OF MATHEMATICS, UNIVERSITY OF MEMPHIS, MEMPHIS, TN, UNITED STATES [c]RESEARCH AND INNOVATION CENTER, ÓBUDA UNIVERSITY, BUDAPEST, HUNGARY [d]POLITECNICO DI MILANO, MILAN, ITALY [e]UNIVERSITÀ DELLA SVIZZERA ITALIANA, LUGANO, SWITZERLAND [f]DEPARTMENT OF COMPUTER SCIENCE AND ENGINEERING, TEXAS A&M UNIVERSITY, COLLEGE STATION, TX, UNITED STATES

Chapter outline

1 Introduction

The present book is the second edition of the 2017 book "*Artificial Intelligence in the Age of Neural Networks and Brain Computing*". The original aim of this work was to analyze the exceptional growth of artificial intelligence (AI) we all experienced in recent years from the perspective of neurocomputing and neuroscience research as advocated from a group of pioneers within the International Neural Network Society (INNS) umbrella. That means trying to develop a general framework to constantly relate the conceptual equations and the brain model, looking at the practical applications of AI/neural systems. As the field rapidly developed in the last five years, we intend to introduce novel aspects emerged and to revise previous versions of the chapters.

Now, we live in the era of artificial intelligence (AI); and AI is everywhere. It is on the front page of your favorite newspaper, it is in your pocket inside your smartphone, on your kitchen table, in your car, on the street, at your office, on the trains and airplanes, on the smart farms, on the earth observation systems, on Mars, everywhere. The success of AI-based commercial products, proposed by many important companies, like Google, IBM, Microsoft, Intel, Amazon, just to name a few, can be interpreted as the coexistence of a successful synergism among what we call computational intelligence, natural intelligence, brain computing, and neural engineering.

The emergence of AI in many IT technologies happened almost overnight, in the past decade. The blessing and the curse of AI are here! And all this is just the beginning, for the

Artificial Intelligence in the Age of Neural Networks and Brain Computing. https://doi.org/10.1016/B978-0-323-96104-2.00016-6
Copyright © 2024 Elsevier Inc. All rights reserved.

better or for the worse. How all this happened all the sudden? Yes, it requires the powerful computing offered by advanced chips cheaply. It also requires massive amount of data available through the Internet and via prolific communication resources; also called as big data. That is not all. Computational algorithms called deep learning (DL) provide the framework of the programming approaches. Deep learning was coined about a decade ago, but many experts employing these technologies do not realize that DL is rooted in the technology developed in the biologically motivated neural networks field since the 1960s. The understanding of the general framework has also shown its importance in the last three years for answering to many relevant questions urged in many fields, including law and ethics, basically related to the real use of AI systems, e.g., in clinical applications. Here there is a need for explaining the underlying modalities of decisions of the black-box models, for augmenting human intelligence without risks, for combining information extraction from raw data and formal knowledge on the problems at hand.

Neural networks thus powerfully reemerged with different names and meanings in different, also unexpected, contexts within the current nouvelle vague of AI and DL. Neural networks represent a well-grounded paradigm rooted in many disciplines, including computer science, physics, psychology, information science, and engineering.

Along the three years from the publication date of the first edition of this book, there was a rapid growth of the field, particularly in the following direction lines, according to the view of these authors:

(1) Transformer Neural Networks: originally used in language processing tasks, these nonconvolutional architectures have been successfully proposed in visual tasks on large-scale image classification problems as "Vision Transformers"; here the convolution process of CNN is replaced by self-attention mechanisms as an automatic technique for aggregating information, again reminiscent of brain processing. Many ways to incorporate attention steps have been proposed, raising a basic question on how they develop novel representations from local and global spatial clues and how the developed features can effectively scale.

(2) Federated Learning and Edge Computing: in practical clinical and health problems, the need of big data is limited from many algorithmic and nontechnical aspects, i.e., data privacy, data exchange among different institutions, ...; federated learning is a novel learning paradigm recently emerged for addressing the problems raised from data governance, sharing, and privacy: it allows to train neural networks collaboratively without exchanging materially the data itself. The paradigm has been originally proposed in mobile and edge devices, recently becoming pervasive for healthcare applications, as a consensus model is used without moving patients' data beyond the firewalls of the hospitals where they are located. Local training is also important for reducing power consumption and cloud resources thus going toward a greener AI.

(3) Physically-Informed Neural Networks: in many scientific disciplines, among which nanotechnology, smart/soft materials and biological systems, to solve nontrivial time and rate dependent constitutive equations needed to have a full description of the underlying structured fluids under different protocols, neural network differentiation approach has been coupled with physical models. This approach can reduce the number of costly laboratory experiments needed to build direct and inverse models describing the kinematic and dynamic heterogeneities of complex systems' response under diverse stresses and operational conditions.

(4) Graph Neural Networks: Although DL (and CNN) showed significant successes in computer vision and related domains, the available architectures generally perform poorly in case of data with underlying structure, as it is in many social, biological, and robotic applications. Neural networks that are able to incorporate graph structures, like CNN extended to graphs, can yield generalized models that can improve model performance, in many tasks, particularly in DL of non-Euclidean data, as in geometric DL.

This volume collects selected invited contributions from pioneers and experts in the field of neural networks. This collection aims to show that the present implications and applications of AI is nothing but a development of the endowed unique attributes of neural networks, namely machine learning, distributed architectures, massively parallel processing, black-box inference, intrinsic nonlinearity, and smart autonomous search engine. We strive to cover the major basic ideas of brain-like computing behind AI and to contribute to give a framework to DL as well as to launch novel intriguing paradigms as possible future alternatives. The second edition is a reorganized version of the previous book that features some revised/updated versions of the earlier chapters, as well as four novel chapters on emerging topics.

Originally, this book has been designed to commemorate the 30th anniversary of International Neural Network Society (INNS), following the 2017 International Joint Conference on Neural Networks, in Anchorage, AK, USA, May 14–18, 2017. The conference is organized jointly by the INNS and the IEEE Computational Intelligence Society (CIS) and is the premiere international meeting for researchers and other professionals in neural networks and related areas, including neural network theory, DL, computational neuroscience, robotics, and distributed intelligence.

The chapters here included among which the new works are written by authors who form a blend from top experts, worldwide-recognized pioneers of the field, and researchers working on cutting-edge applications in signal processing, speech recognition, games, and adaptive control and decision-making. Our intent is to present the concepts involved to a target audience, who are not a narrow group of specialists working in the field but rather a broad segment of the public intrigued by recent advances in AI.

The volume presents an introduction and 17 peer-reviewed contributions, organized in three different parts (fundamentals, brain-inspired AI and cutting-edge developments in DL), briefly described in what follows.

This chapter is the present Introduction co-authored by the co-editors of the book.

The Part 1 of this second edition refers to "**Fundamentals of Neural Networks and Brain Computing**". It includes four chapters.

In Chapter 2, Widrow et al. reconsidered the Hebbian learning, originally proposed in the field of neurobiology as one of the basis of (unsupervised) adaptive algorithms directly derived from nature. Although the LMS algorithm was previously proposed by Widrow and Hoff as a supervised learning procedure, it can be implemented in an unsupervised fashion. The two algorithms can thus be combined to form the Hebbian-LMS unsupervised learning algorithm, which can be the key to interpret the nature's way to do learning at the neuron and synapse level.

In Chapter 3, Grossberg presents a survey of the main principles, architectures, and circuits proposed in a half century of researches in the field, whose aim was to develop a unified theory of brain and mind where the psychological perspective can be read through the emergence of brain mechanisms. The chapter describes novel revolutionary paradigms like complementary computing and laminar computing with reference to the autonomous adaptive intelligence characteristic of brains. The chapter reanalyzes the fundamental approach of Adaptive Resonance Theory (ART) as a core model for engineering and technology, as well as to abstract insights about mental disorders such as autism and Alzheimer's disease.

In Chapter 4, a revised chapter, Choe provides educated discussions and analyses about some key concepts central to brain science and AI, namely those associated with the dichotomies: meaning vs. information, prediction vs. memory, and question vs. answer. The author shows how a slightly different view on these concepts can help us move forward, beyond current limits of our understanding in these fields. In detail, the chapter elaborates over the intriguing definition of information as seen from different perspectives and its relationship with the concept of meaning. Then, it investigates the role of plasticity, that of memory, and how they relate to prediction. Finally, the focus moves on to the question vs. answer issue in AI algorithms and how it impacts on their ability to solve problems. This chapter has been substantially revised from the previous edition (Chapter 14), adding new illustrations to facilitate better conceptual understanding of the materials, and expanding on the discussion to include latest research in the field related to the subject matter.

In Chapter 5, Erdi presents an insightful review on the topic of hermeneutics applied to brain science. Brain-computer-mind trichotomy is discussed, where downward causality is discussed as a unique feature of brain-mind as opposed to computation. Hermeneutics is introduced next, applied to the brain, and it is argued that the brain is in principle a hermeneutic device. One application of this idea is the explanation of schizophrenia, which is argued to be due to a broken hermeneutic cycle. Finally, the chapter concludes with thoughts on how to achieve algorithms for neural/mental hermeneutics. This is a deep theoretical essay that touches upon fundamental issues in brain and neural sciences.

The Part 2 of this second edition refers to "**Brain-Inspired AI Systems**" that includes six chapters.

In Chapter 6, Werbos provides an impressive summary and a critical review of the reasons underlying today's wave of AI successes, including DL and the Internet of Things (IoT). As a major exponent both in research and research funding in the past decades, he provides an exciting insider's view of these developments, as well as points toward possible avenues in future research, neuroscience in particular. He also points out the key role researchers play in applying the novel technological development for the benefit of humanity.

In Chapter 7, Kozma touches a fundamental problem human have focused on for centuries, that of creating machines that act like them. The chapter investigates various aspects of biological and AI issues and introduces a balanced approach based on the concepts of complementarity and multistability as manifested in human brain operation and cognitive processing. As intelligence in human brains is the result of a delicate balance between fragmentation of local components and global dominance of coherent overall states, the chapter elaborates on how intelligence is manifested through the emergence of a sequence of coherent metastable amplitude patterns. This behavior leads to the cinematic theory of human cognition that both provides insights into key principles of intelligence in biological brains and helps in building more powerful artificially intelligent devices.

In Chapter 8, Kasabov presents an approach based on evolutionary connectionist systems (ECOS) that are able to evolve their architecture and functionality in adaptive data-driven modality. The evolving spiking neural networks (eSNN) are illustrated and proposed as a third generation of artificial neural networks (ANNs). eSNN can be used for future brain-like AI, and the NeuCube architecture is presented as a machine that can implement DL procedures. The chapter also proposes a combination of the AI and ANN approaches as a unique method derived from neuroscience.

In Chapter 9, Brown et al. focused on the pitfalls and opportunities of developing techniques of evaluation of AI systems. This is a cool topic, considering the relevant progresses that DL methodologies have introduced in the computational intelligence community. However, they rise the problem of measuring and comparing performance. The receiver operating characteristic (ROC) paradigm and the bootstrap method are considered as well-grounded approaches for performance metric in order to avoid overestimation that frequently limits the practical implementations of AI.

In Chapter 10, Levine reviews the history of neural networks as an artificial model of brain and mind. Neural networks are a paradigm that in principle link biology and technology: it thus comes as no surprise that the flagship journal of the International Neural Network Society is indeed neural networks. His chapter reconsiders the original ideas that motivate the nascence of this interdisciplinary society at the light of present developments.

In Chapter 11, Ormandy addresses crucial issues related to the limitations of mainstream AI and neural network technologies, especially in the context of the usefulness of the AI in developing new technologies to improve our quality of life. He describes the work started in collaboration with the late Walter Freeman in order to capture the dynamics of embodied human cognition and incorporate it to novel wearable personal assistants. The author reviews the literature from file theories through embodied cognition across species. The main thesis of this work is the critical importance of ephaptic interactions between neural populations, which produce neural fields measurable by noninvasive means, thus providing an opportunity for the development of wearable personal assistants in everyday life, including augmented memory, stress relief, fitness training, relaxation, and other applications.

The third part of this book refers to the "**Cutting-Edge Developments in Deep Learning and intelligent Systems**" and includes seven chapters.

In Chapter 12, Morabito et al. introduce a comprehensive investigation of DL applications in brain engineering and biomedical signal processing, with a particular focus on the processing of multivariate time-series coming from electrophysiology. Electroencephalography (EEG) and high-density EEG, magneto-encephalography technologies are reviewed, as they constitute the measurement systems yielding multivariate electrophysiological time-series. The use of DL methods for multivariate EEG time-series processing is then detailed to permit the reader to easily enter in this fascinating application framework. Future direction of research in DL, encompassing interpretability, architectures and learning procedures, and robustness aspects are then discussed, so as to provide the reader with some relevant open research topics. In addition, the present version of the chapter introduces the concept of explainability and interpretability of AI/DL systems, by proposing some of the basic approaches to explainable artificial intelligence (xAI).

In the revised version of this work, in Chapter 13, Alippi et al. present a timely and thorough review on the use of computational intelligence and machine learning methods in cyberphysical systems (CPS) and IoT. The review goes over four major research topics in this domain: (1) system architecture, (2) energy harvesting, conservation, and management, (3) fault detection and mitigation, and (4) cyberattack detection and countermeasures. Importantly, the authors challenge assumptions that are taken for granted, but do not apply anymore to the increasingly more complex CPS and IoT systems. These assumptions include high energy availability, stationarity, correct data availability, and security guarantees. This chapter provides an excellent review of the status of CPS and IoT and how to overcome the issues in these emerging fields.

In Chapter 14, Miikkulainen et al. present a novel automated method for designing deep neural network architecture. The main idea is based on neuroevolution to evolve the neural network topology and parameters. In the proposed work, neuroevolution is extended to evolve topology, components (modules), and hyperparameters. The method is applied to both feedforward architectures like CNN and also to recurrent neural networks (with LSTM units). The proposed method is tested on standard image tasks (object recognition) and natural language tasks (image captioning), demonstrating comparable results as state-of-the-art methods. This chapter provides a great overview of evolutionary methods developed at Sentient technologies for the design and optimization of deep neural networks.

In Chapter 15, a new chapter in this edition, Gonzalez et al. present TaylorGAN, a novel variant of the popular generative adversarial network (GAN). The key idea in TaylorGAN is to discover customized loss functions for the discriminator and the generator, to achieve higher-quality image synthesis compared to those based on fixed-loss functions. The main problem with automatically discovering loss functions is the diversity in the functional forms, and the difficulty in parameterizing these different functional forms. The authors present a novel approach to overcome this, through the use of multivariate Taylor expansion. This allows the parameterization of any arbitrary function, or, in reverse, the discovery of new functions by appropriate tuning of the Taylor expansion parameters. It is shown that these parameters can be found using evolutionary strategies, leading to superior performance compared to GAN variants with fixed-loss functions.

In Chapter 16, Tagliaferri et al. present an innovative approach of multiview learning as a branch of machine learning for the analysis of multimodal data in biomedical applications, among which, in particular, the authors focus on bioinformatics (i.e., gene expression, microRNA expression, protein–protein interactions, genome-wide association). The approach proposed allows capturing information regarding different aspects of the underlying principles governing complex biological systems. The authors also propose an example of how both clustering and classification can be combined in a multiview setting for the automated diagnosis of neurodegenerative disorders. They also show using some application examples how recent DL techniques can be applied to multimodal data to learn complex representations.

In Chapter 17, another new chapter in this edition, Choe and Li present their work on tool construction and use through hierarchical deep reinforcement learning. The authors first present a thoughtful review on the topic of tool construction and tool use, ranging from literature in animal behavior literature to AI and robotics applications, and its possible co-evolutionary relationship with the advancement of cognitive capacity in humans. For this chapter, the authors set up a simple physics-based simulation environment where two robotic arms are controlled to reach tool parts, and subsequently join them to be used as a composite tool for dragging objects. This turns out to be a nontrivial task, and the authors devised a hierarchical reinforcement learning approach, where a manager comes up with subtasks and several workers carry out the subtasks, toward the overall goal. This work is expected to serve as a meaningful first step toward tool-cognition co-evolution, greatly accelerating development in AI.

In the final chapter, Chapter 18, Gori et al. propose an alternative view of the neural network computational scheme based on the satisfaction of architectural constraints. The approach is inspired by the ideas of casting learning under the unifying notion of constraint, and it is also related to the theoretical framework for back-propagation formulated using Lagrangian optimization by LeCun et al. The introduction of the architectural constraints determines a solution which is based on a truly local propagation of signals for the back-propagation of the errors in the training phase. The Lagrangian formulation for constrained optimization is here applied to derive a constraint-based representation of neural network architectures. The case of graph neural networks, originally proposed by the authors, is considered, for which the learning process of both the transition function and the node states can be interpreted as the outcome of a joint process, in which the state computation on the input graph is expressed by a constraint satisfaction mechanism, that does not require an explicit iterative procedure and the network unfolding. The resulting training algorithm provides an efficient trade-off between the flexibility introduced by the Lagrangian-based formulation of the graph diffusion and the addition of new variables.

The field of neural networks inspired by the structure and operation of brains has been at the forefront of the recent progress in artificial intelligence and machine intelligence research, and it is expected to continue to be at the cutting edge in the years and decades ahead. The second edition of this volume provides a snapshot of the present status of the field and outlines multiple promising new directions for future development. It will be of benefit of researchers working on the theoretical and computational aspects, as well as engineering applications of this rapidly developing field.

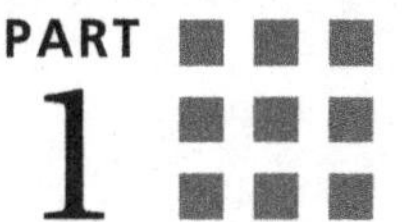

Fundamentals of neural networks and brain computing

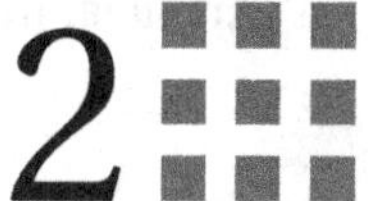

Nature's learning rule: The Hebbian-LMS algorithm

Bernard Widrow, Youngsik Kim, Dookun Park, and Jose Krause Perin
DEPARTMENT OF ELECTRICAL ENGINEERING, STANFORD UNIVERSITY, STANFORD, CA, UNITED STATES

Chapter outlines

1 Introduction

Donald O. Hebb has had considerable influence in the fields of psychology and neurobiology since the publication of his book *The Organization of Behavior* in 1949 [1]. Hebbian learning is often described as: "neurons that fire together wire together." Now imagine a

Artificial Intelligence in the Age of Neural Networks and Brain Computing. https://doi.org/10.1016/B978-0-323-96104-2.00012-9

Copyright © 2024 Elsevier Inc. All rights reserved.

large network of interconnected neurons whose synaptic weights are increased because the presynaptic neuron and the postsynaptic neuron fired together. This might seem strange. What purpose would nature fulfill with such a learning algorithm?

In his book, Hebb actually said: "When an axon of cell A is near enough to excite a cell B and repeatedly or persistently takes part in firing it, some growth process or metabolic change takes place in one or both cells such that A's efficiency, as one of the cells firing B, is increased."

"Fire together wire together" is a simplification of this. Wire together means increase the synaptic weight. Fire together is not exactly what Hebb said, but some researchers have taken this literally and believe that information is carried with the timing of each activation pulse. Some believe that the precise timing of presynaptic and postsynaptic firings has an effect on synaptic weight changes. There is some evidence for these ideas [2–4], but they remain controversial.

Neuron-to-neuron signaling in the brain is done with pulse trains. This is AC coupling and is one of nature's "good ideas," avoiding the effects of DC level drift that could be caused by the presence of fluids and electrolytes in the brain. We believe that the output signal of a neuron is the neuron's firing rate as a function of time.

Neuron-to-neuron signaling in computer-simulated artificial neural networks is done in most cases with DC levels. If a static input pattern vector is presented, the neuron's output is an analog DC level that remains constant as long as the input pattern vector is applied. That analog output can be weighted by a synapse and applied as an input to another neuron, a "postsynaptic" neuron, in a layered network or otherwise interconnected network.

The purpose of this chapter is to review a new learning algorithm that we call Hebbian-LMS [5]. It is an implementation of Hebb's teaching by means of the LMS algorithm of Widrow and Hoff. With the Hebbian LMS algorithm, unsupervised or autonomous learning takes place locally, in the individual neuron and its synapses, and when many such neurons are connected in a network, the entire network learns autonomously. One might ask, "what does it learn?" This question will be considered below where applications will be presented.

There is another question that can be asked: "Should we believe in Hebbian learning? Did Hebb arrive at this idea by doing definitive biological experiments, by 'getting his hands wet'?" The answer is no. The idea came to him by intuitive reasoning. Like Newton's theory of gravity, like Einstein's theory of relativity, like Darwin's theory of evolution, it was a thought experiment propounded long before modern knowledge and instrumentation could challenge it, refute it, or verify it. Hebb described synapses and synaptic plasticity, but how synapses and neurotransmitters worked was unknown in Hebb's time. So far, no one has contradicted Hebb, except for some details. For example, learning with "fire together wire together" would cause the synaptic weights to only increase until all of them reached saturation. That would make an uninteresting neural network, and nature would not do this. Gaps in the Hebbian learning rule will need to be filled, keeping in mind Hebb's basic idea, and well-working adaptive algorithms will be the result. The Hebbian-LMS algorithm will have engineering applications, and it may provide insight into learning in living neural networks.

The current thinking that led us to the Hebbian-LMS algorithm has its roots in a series of discoveries that were made since Hebb, from the late 1950s through the 1960s. These discoveries are reviewed in the next three sections. The sections beyond describe Hebbian-LMS and how this algorithm could be nature's algorithm for learning at the neuron and synapse level.

2 Adaline and the LMS algorithm, from the 1950s

Adaline is an acronym for "adaptive linear neuron." A block diagram of the original Adaline is shown in Fig. 1. Adaline was adaptive, but not really linear. It was more than a neuron since it also included the weights or synapses. Nevertheless, Adaline was the name given in 1959 by Widrow and Hoff.

Adaline was a trainable classifier. The input patterns, the vectors X_k, $k=1, 2, \ldots, N$, were weighted by the weight vector $W_k=[w_{1k}, w_{2k}, \ldots, w_{nk}]^T$, and their inner product was the sum $y_k=X_k^T W_k$. Each input pattern X_k was to be classified as $a+1$ or $a-1$ in accord with its assigned class, the "desired response." Adaline was trained to accomplish this by adjusting the weights to minimize mean square error. The error was the difference between the desired response d_k and the sum y_k, $e_k=d_k-y_k$. Adaline's final output q_k was taken as the sign of the sum y_k, that is, $q_k=SGN(y_k)$, where the function $SGN(\cdot)$ is the signum, take the sign of. The sum y_k will henceforth be referred to as $(\text{SUM})_k$.

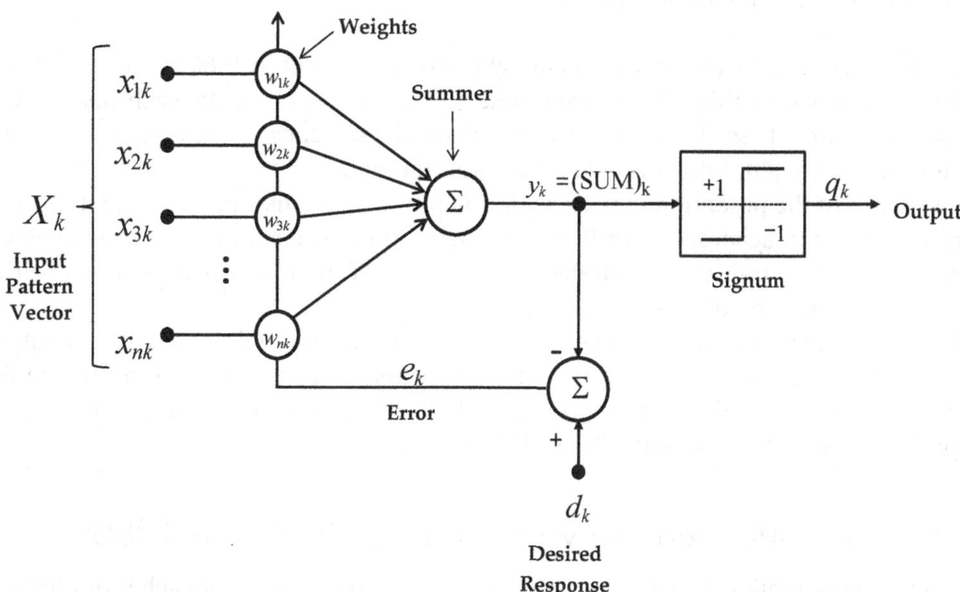

FIG. 1 Adaline (adaptive linear neuron).

The weights of Adaline were trained with the LMS algorithm, as follows:

$$W_{k+1} = W_k + 2\mu e_k X_k \tag{1}$$

$$e_k = d_k - X_k^T W_k \tag{2}$$

Averaged over the set of training patterns, the mean square error is a quadratic function of the weights, a quadratic "bowl." The LMS algorithm uses the methodology of steepest descent, a gradient method, for pulling the weights to the bottom of the bowl, thus minimizing mean square error.

The LMS algorithm was invented by Widrow and Hoff in 1959 [6], 10 years after the publication of Hebb's seminal book. The derivation of the LMS algorithm is given in many references. One such reference is the book *Adaptive Signal Processing* by Widrow and Stearns [7]. The LMS algorithm is the most widely used learning algorithm in the world today. It is used in adaptive filters that are key elements in all modems, for channel equalization and echo canceling. It is one of the basic technologies of the Internet and of wireless communications. It is basic to the field of digital signal processing.

The LMS learning rule is quite simple and intuitive. Eqs. (1) and (2) can be represented in words:

> *With the presentation of each input pattern vector and its associated desired response, the weight vector is changed slightly by adding the pattern vector to the weight vector, making the sum more positive, or subtracting the pattern vector from the weight vector, making the sum more negative, changing the sum in proportion to the error in a direction to make the error smaller.*

A photograph of a physical Adaline made by Widrow and Hoff in 1960 is shown in Fig. 2. The input patterns of this Adaline were binary, 4×4 arrays of pixels, each pixel having a value of +1 or −1, set by the 4×4 array of toggle switches. Each toggle switch was connected to a weight, implemented by a potentiometer.

The knobs of the potentiometers, seen in the photo, were manually rotated during the training process in accordance with the LMS algorithm. The sum (SUM) was displayed by the meter. Once trained, output decisions were +1 if the meter reading was positive, and −1 if the meter reading was negative.

The earliest learning experiments were done with this Adaline, training it as a pattern classifier. This was supervised learning, as the desired response for each input training pattern was given. A video showing Prof. Widrow training Adaline can be seen online (https://www.youtube.com/watch?v=skfNlwEbqck).

3 Unsupervised learning with Adaline, from the 1960s

In order to train Adaline, it is necessary to have a desired response for each input training pattern. The desired response indicated the class of the pattern. But what if one had only

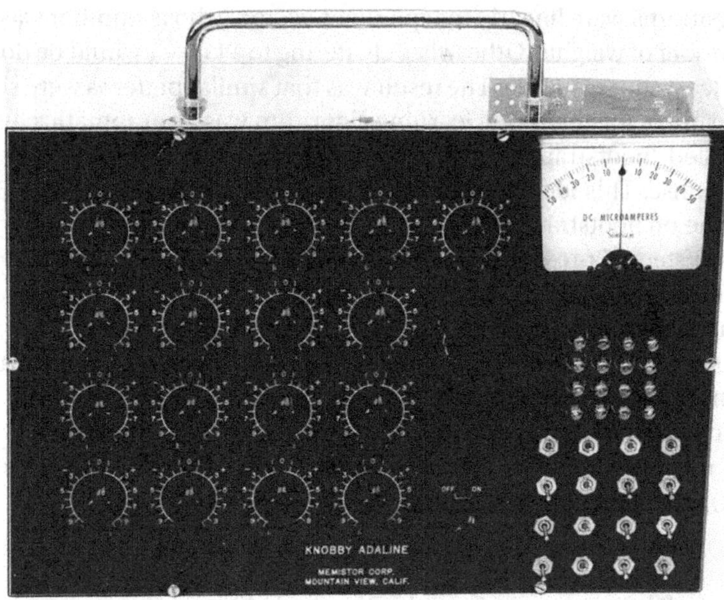

FIG. 2 Knobby Adaline.

input patterns and did not know their desired responses, their classes? Could learning still take place? If this were possible, this would be unsupervised learning.

In 1960, unsupervised learning experiments were made with the Adaline of Fig. 2 as follows. Initial conditions for the weights were randomly set and input patterns were presented without desired responses. If the response to a given input pattern was already positive (the meter reading to the right of zero), the desired response was taken to be exactly +1. A response of +1 was indicated by a meter reading half way on the right-hand side of the scale. If the response was less than +1, adaptation by LMS was performed to bring the response up toward +1. If the response was greater than +1, adaptation was performed by LMS to bring the response down toward +1.

If the response to another input pattern was negative (meter reading to the left of zero), the desired response was taken to be exactly −1 (meter reading half way on the left-hand side of the scale). If the negative response was more positive than −1, adaptation was performed to bring the response down toward −1. If the response was more negative than −1, adaptation was performed to bring the response up toward −1.

With adaptation taking place over many input patterns, some patterns that initially responded as positive could ultimately reverse and give negative responses, and vice versa. However, patterns that were initially responding as positive were more likely to remain positive, and vice versa. When the process converges and the responses stabilize, some responses would cluster about +1 and the rest would cluster about −1.

The objective was to achieve unsupervised learning with the analog responses at the output of the summer (SUM) clustered at +1 or −1. Perfect clustering could be achieved if the training patterns were linearly independent vectors whose number was less than or equal to the number of weights. Otherwise, clustering to +1 or −1 would be done as well as possible in the least squares sense. The result was that similar patterns were similarly classified, and this simple unsupervised learning algorithm was an automatic clustering algorithm. It was called "bootstrap learning" because Adaline's quantized output was used as the desired response. This idea is represented by the block diagram in Fig. 3.

Research done on bootstrap learning was reported in the paper "Bootstrap learning in threshold logic systems," presented by Bernard Widrow at an International Federation of Automatic Control conference in 1966 [8]. This work led to the 1967 Ph.D. thesis of William C. Miller, at the time a student of Professor Widrow, entitled "A modified mean square error criterion for use in unsupervised learning" [9]. These papers described and analyzed bootstrap learning as we understood it then.

Fig. 4 illustrates the formation of the error signal of bootstrap learning. The shaded areas of Fig. 4 represent the error, the difference between the quantized output q_k and the sum $(\text{SUM})_k$:

$$e_k = SGN((\text{SUM})_k) - (\text{SUM})_k \tag{3}$$

The polarities of the error are indicated in the shaded areas. This is unsupervised learning, comprised of the LMS algorithm of Eq. (1) and the error of Eq. (3).

When the error is zero, no adaptation takes place. In Fig. 4, one can see that there are three different values of (SUM) where the error is zero. These are the three equilibrium points. The point at the origin is an unstable equilibrium point. The other two equilibrium points are stable. Some of the input patterns will produce sums that gravitate toward the positive stable equilibrium point, while the other input patterns produce sums that gravitate toward the negative stable equilibrium point. The arrows indicate the directions of change to the sum that would occur as a result of adaptation. All input patterns will become classified as either positive or negative when the adaptation process converges. If the training patterns were linearly independent, the neuron outputs will be binary, +1 or −1.

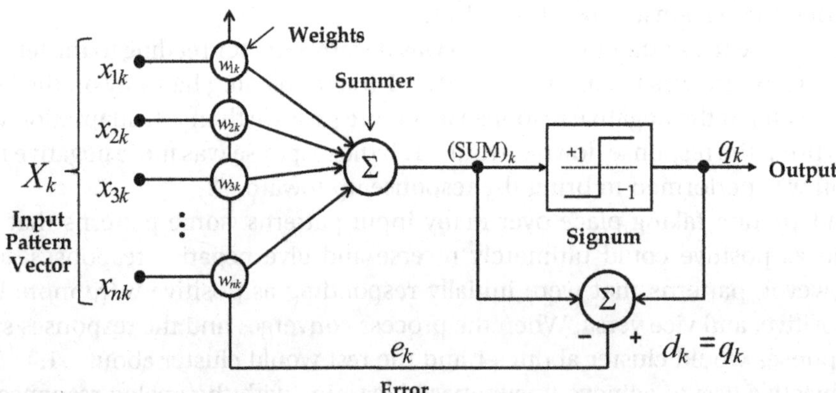

FIG. 3 Adaline with bootstrap learning.

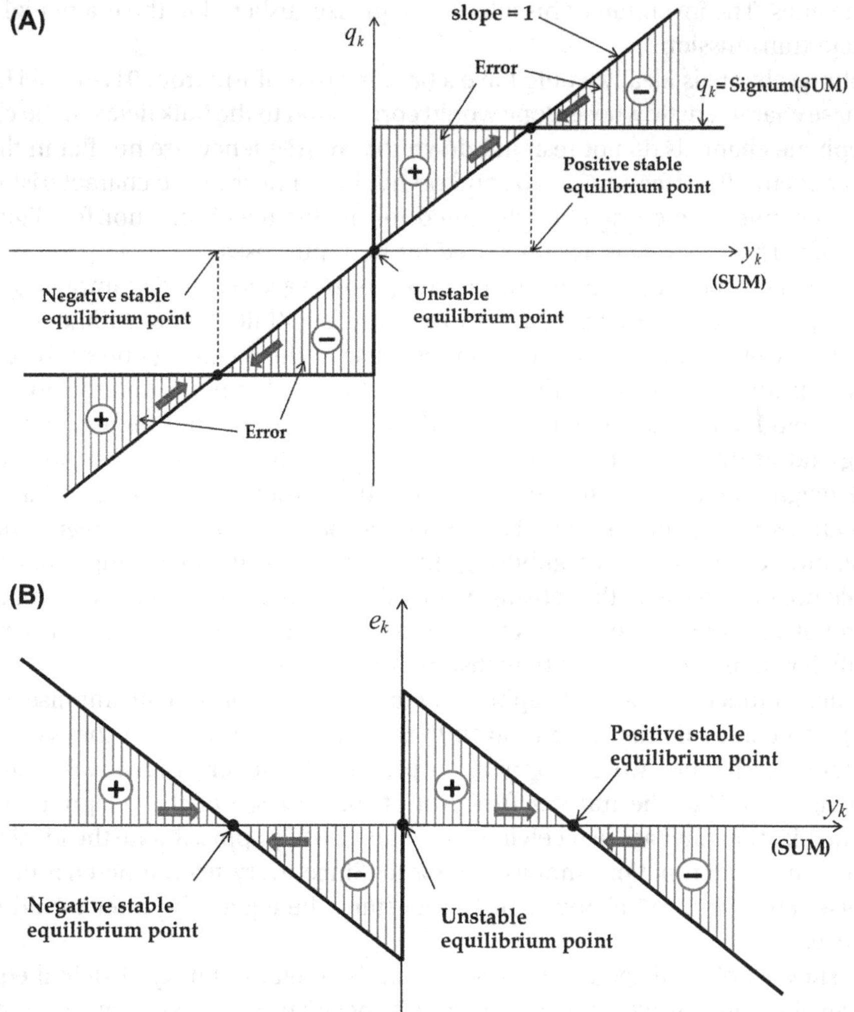

FIG. 4 Bootstrap learning. (A) The quantized output, the sum, and the error as a function of (SUM). (B) The error versus (SUM).

4 Robert Lucky's adaptive equalization, from the 1960s

In the early 1960s, as Widrow's group at Stanford was developing bootstrap learning, at the same time, independently, a project at Bell laboratories led by Robert W. Lucky was developing an adaptive equalizer for digital data transmission over telephone lines [10,11]. His adaptive algorithm incorporated what he called "decision-directed learning," which has similarities to bootstrap learning.

Lucky's work turned out to be of extraordinary significance. He was using an adaptive algorithm to adjust the weights of a transversal digital filter for data transmission over telephone lines. The invention of his adaptive equalizer ushered in the era of high-speed digital data transmission.

Telephone channels ideally would have a bandwidth uniform from 0 Hz to 3 kHz, and a linear phase characteristic whose slope would correspond to the bulk delay of the channel. Real telephone channels do not respond down to zero frequency, are not flat in the pass-band, do not cut off perfectly at 3 kHz, and do not have linear phase characteristics. Real telephone channels were originally designed for analog telephony, not for digital data transmission. These channels are now used for both purposes.

Binary data can be sent by transmitting sharp positive and negative impulses into the channel. A positive pulse is a ONE, a negative pulse is a ZERO. If the channel were ideal, each impulse would cause a sinc function response at the receiving end of the channel. When transmitting data pulses at the Nyquist rate for the channel, a superposition of sinc functions would appear at the receiving end. By sampling or strobing the signal at the receiving end at the Nyquist rate and adjusting the timing of the strobe to sample at the peak magnitude of a sinc function, it would be possible to recover the exact binary data stream as it was transmitted. The reason is that when one of the sinc functions has a magnitude peak, all the neighboring sinc functions would be having zero crossings and would not interfere with the sensing of an individual sinc function. There would be no "intersymbol interference," and perfect transmission at the Nyquist rate would be possible (assuming low noise, which is quite realistic for land lines).

The transfer function of a real telephone channel is not ideal, and the impulse response is not a perfect sinc function with uniformly spaced zero crossings. At the Nyquist rate, intersymbol interference would happen. To prevent this, Lucky's idea was to filter the received signal so that the transfer function of the cascade of the telephone channel and an equalization filter at the receiving end would closely approximate the ideal transfer function with a sinc-function impulse response. Since every telephone channel has its own "personality" and can change slowly over time, the equalizing filter would need to be adaptive.

Fig. 5 shows a block diagram of a system that is similar to Lucky's original equalizer. Binary data are transmitted at the Nyquist rate as positive and negative pulses into a telephone channel. At the receiving end, the channel output is inputted to a tapped delay line with variable weights connected to the taps. The weighted signals are summed. The delay line, weights, and summer comprise an adaptive transversal filter. The weights are given initial conditions. All weights are set to zero except for the first weight, which is set to the value of one. Initially, there is no filtering and, assuming that the telephone channel is not highly distorting, the summed signal will essentially be a superposition of sinc functions separated with Nyquist spacing. At the times when the sinc pulses have peak magnitudes, the quantized output of the signum will be a binary sequence that is a replica of the transmitted binary data. The quantized output will be the correct output sequence. The quantized output can accordingly be taken as the desired output, and the difference between the quantized output and the summed signal will be the error signal for adaptive purposes. This difference will only be usable as the error signal at times when the sinc

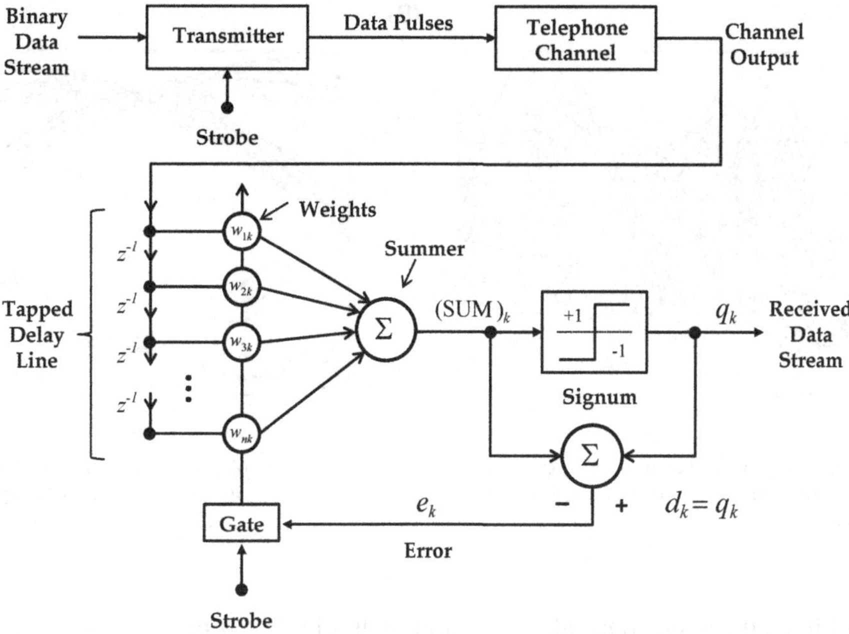

FIG. 5 Decision-directed learning for channel equalization.

functions are at their peak magnitudes. A strobe pulse samples the error signal at the Nyquist rate, timed to the sinc function peak, and the error samples are used to adapt the weights. The output decision is taken to be the desired response. Thus, decision-directed learning results.

With some channel distortion, the signum output will not always be correct, at peak times. The equalizer can start with an error rate of 25% and automatically converge to an error rate of perhaps 10^{-8}, depending on the noise level in the channel.

Fig. 6A shows the output of a telephone channel without equalization. Fig. 6B shows the same channel with the same dataflow after adaptive equalization. These patterns are created by overlaying cycles of the waveform before and after equalization. The effect of equalization is to make the impulse responses approximate sinc functions. When this is done, an "eye pattern" as in Fig. 6B results. Opening the eye is the purpose of adaptation. With the eye open and when sampling at the appropriate time, ones and zeros are easily discerned. The adaptive algorithm keeps the ones tightly clustered together and well separated from the zeros which are also tightly clustered together. The ones and zeros comprise two distinct clusters. This is decision-directed learning, similar to bootstrap learning.

In the present day, digital communication begins with a "handshake" by the transmitting and receiving parties. The transmitter begins with a known pseudorandom sequence of pulses, a world standard known to the receiver. During the handshake, the receiver knows the desired responses and adapts accordingly. This is supervised learning. The receiving adaptive filter converges, and now, actual data transmission can commence.

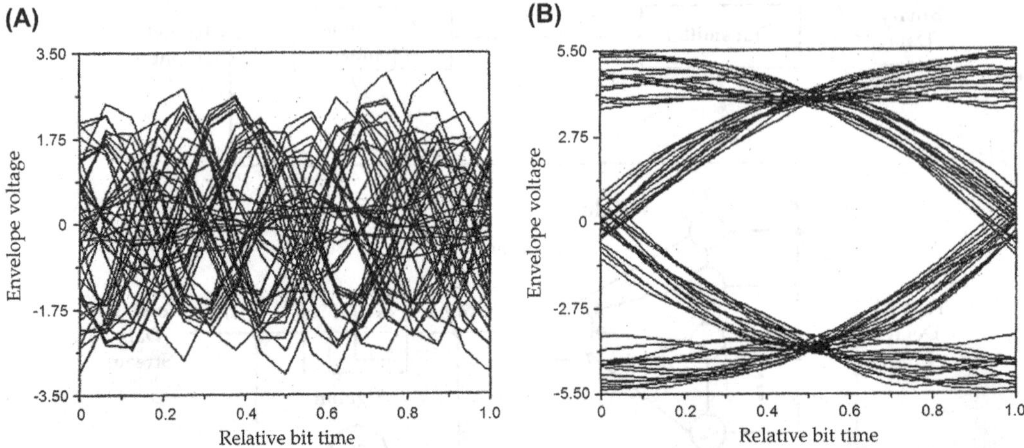

FIG. 6 Eye patterns produced by overlaying cycles of the received waveform. (A) Before equalization. (B) After equalization. *From Fig. 10.14 of B. Widrow, S.D. Stearns, Adaptive Signal Processing, Prentice-Hall, 1985, courtesy of Prentice Hall.*

Decision-directed equalization takes over and maintains the proper equalization for the channel by learning with the signals of the channel. This is unsupervised learning. If the channel is stationary or only changes slowly, the adaptive algorithm will maintain the equalization. However, fast changes could cause the adaptive filter to get out of lock. There will be a "dropout," and the transmission will need to be reinitiated.

Adaptive equalization has been the major application for unsupervised learning since the 1960s. The next section describes a new form of unsupervised learning, bootstrap learning for the weights of a single neuron with a sigmoidal activation function. The sigmoidal function is closer to being "biologically correct" than the signum function of Figs. 1, 3, and 5.

5 Bootstrap learning with a sigmoidal neuron

Fig. 7 is a diagram of a sigmoidal neuron whose weights are trained with bootstrap learning. The learning process of Fig. 7 is characterized by the following error signal:

$$\text{error} = e_k = SGM\left((\text{SUM})_k\right) - \gamma \cdot (\text{SUM})_k \tag{4}$$

The sigmoidal function is represented by $SGM(\cdot)$. Input pattern vectors are weighted, summed, and then applied to the sigmoidal function to provide the output signal $(\text{OUT})_k$. The weights are initially randomized; then adaptation is performed using the LMS algorithm Eq. (1), with an error signal given by Eq. (4).

Insight into the behavior of the form of bootstrap learning of Fig. 7 can be gained by inspection of Fig. 8. The shaded areas indicate the error, which is the difference between the sigmoidal output and the sum multiplied by the constant γ, in accordance with Eq. (4).

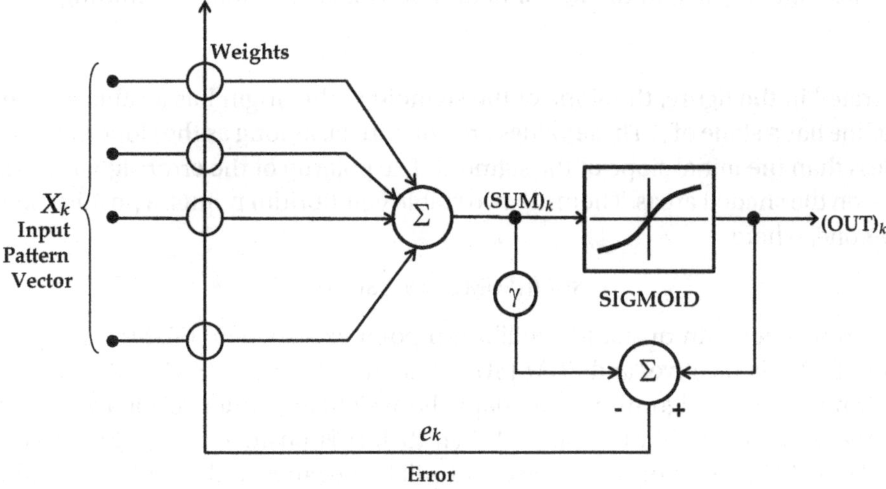

FIG. 7 A sigmoidal neuron trained with bootstrap learning.

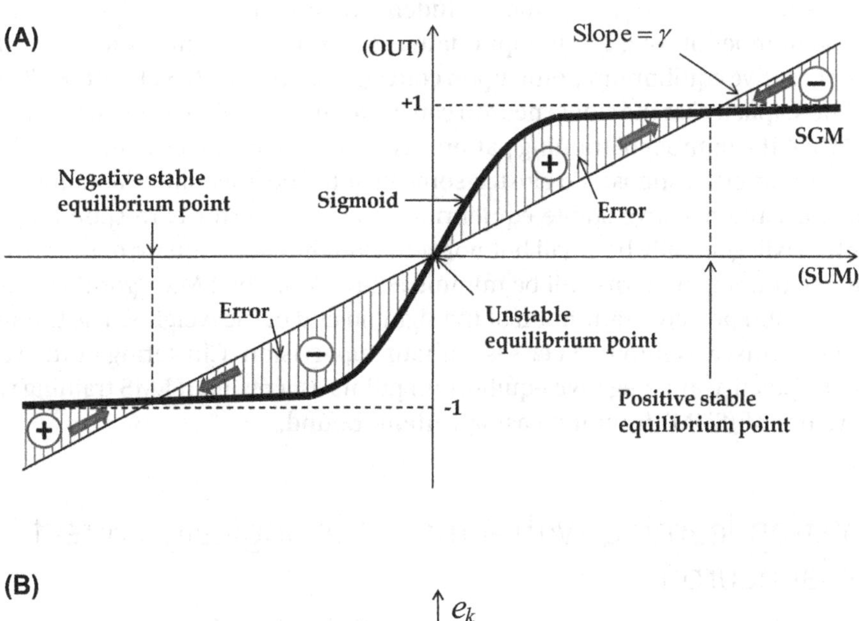

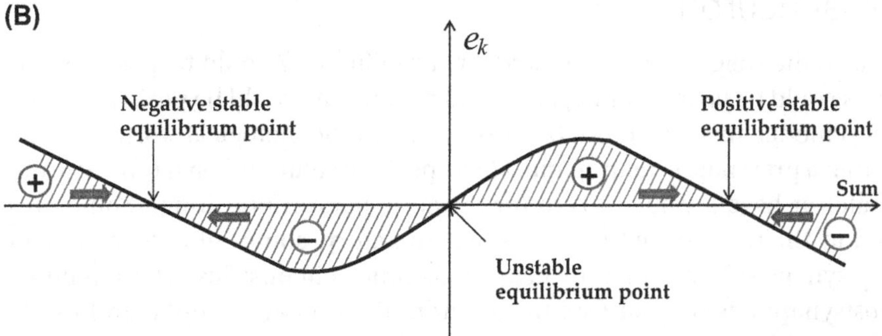

FIG. 8 The error of the sigmoidal neuron trained with bootstrap learning. (A) The output and error versus (SUM). (B) The error function.

As illustrated in the figure, the slope of the sigmoid at the origin has a value of 1, and the straight line has a slope of γ. These values are not critical, as long as the slope of the straight line is less than the initial slope of the sigmoid. The polarity of the error signal is indicated as + or – on the shaded areas. There are two stable equilibrium points, a positive one and a negative one, where

$$SGM((\text{SUM})) = \gamma \cdot (\text{SUM}) \tag{5}$$

and the error is zero. An unstable equilibrium point exists where (SUM) = 0.

When (SUM) is positive, and *SGM*((SUM)) is greater than $\gamma \cdot$ (SUM), the error will be positive and the LMS algorithm will adapt the weights in order to increase (SUM) up toward the positive equilibrium point. When (SUM) is positive and $\gamma \cdot$ (SUM) is greater than *SGM*((SUM)), the error will reverse and will be negative and the LMS algorithm will adapt the weights in order to decrease (SUM) toward the positive equilibrium point. The opposite of all these actions will take place when (SUM) is negative.

When the training patterns are linearly independent and their number is less than or equal to the number of weights, all input patterns will have outputs exactly at either the positive or negative equilibrium point, upon convergence of the LMS algorithm. The "LMS capacity" or "capacity" of the single neuron can be defined as being equal to the number of weights. When the number of training patterns is greater than capacity, the LMS algorithm will cause the pattern responses to cluster, some near the positive stable equilibrium point and some near the negative stable equilibrium point. The error corresponding to each input pattern will generally be small but not zero, and the mean square of the errors averaged over the training patterns will be minimized by LMS. The LMS algorithm maintains stable control and prevents saturation of the sigmoid and of the weights. The training patterns divide themselves into two classes without supervision. Clustering of the values of (SUM) at the positive and negative equilibrium points as a result of LMS training will prevent the values of (SUM) from increasing without bound.

6 Bootstrap learning with a more "biologically correct" sigmoidal neuron

The inputs to the weights of the sigmoidal neuron in Fig. 7 could be positive or negative, the weights could be positive or negative, and the outputs could be positive or negative. As a biological model, this would not be satisfactory. In the biological world, an input signal coming from a presynaptic neuron must have positive values (presynaptic neuron firing at a given rate) or have a value of zero (presynaptic neuron not firing). Some presynaptic neurons and their associated synapses are excitatory, some inhibitory. Excitatory and inhibitory synapses have different neurotransmitter chemistries. The inhibitory inputs to the postsynaptic neuron are subtracted from the excitatory inputs to form (SUM) in the cell body of the postsynaptic neuron. Biological weights or synapses behave like variable attenuators and can only have positive weight values. The output of the postsynaptic

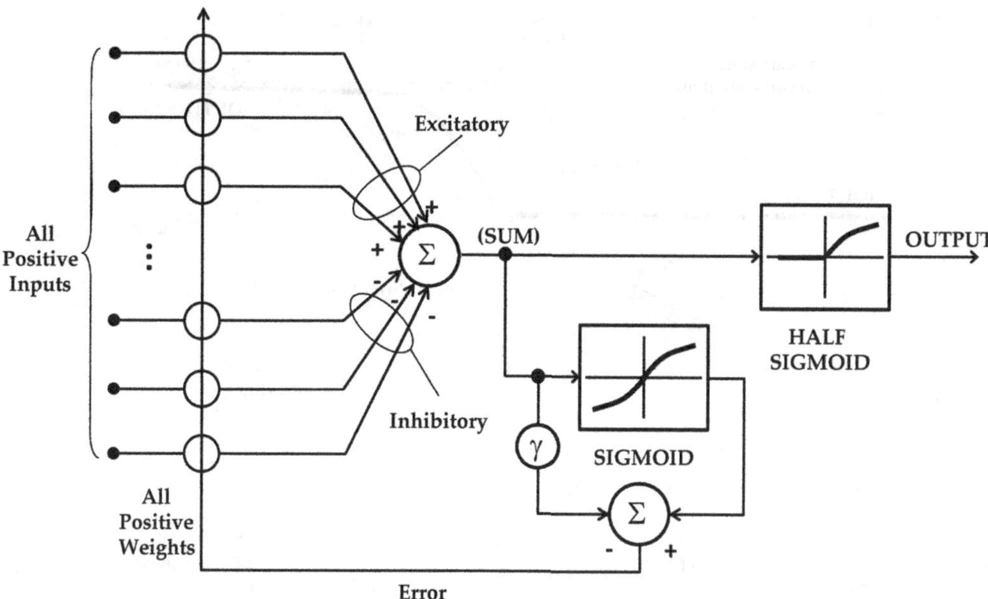

FIG. 9 A postsynaptic neuron with excitatory and inhibitory inputs and all positive weights trained with Hebbian-LMS learning. All outputs are positive. The (SUM) could be positive or negative.

neuron can only be zero (neuron not firing) or positive (neuron firing) corresponding to (SUM) being negative or positive. The postsynaptic neuron and its synapses diagrammed in Fig. 9 have the indicated properties and are capable of learning exactly like the neuron and synapses in Fig. 7. The LMS algorithm of Eq. (1) will operate as usual with positive excitatory inputs or negative inhibitory inputs. For LMS, these are equivalents of positive or negative components of the input pattern vector.

LMS will allow the weight values to remain within their natural positive range even if adaptation caused a weight value to be pushed to one of its limits. Subsequent adaptation could bring the weight value away from the limit and into its more normal range, or it could remain saturated. Saturation would not necessarily be permanent (as would occur with Hebb's original learning rule).

The neuron and its synapses in Fig. 9 are identical to those of Fig. 7, except that the final output is obtained from a "half sigmoid." So the output will be positive, the weights will be positive, and some of the weighted inputs will be excitatory, some inhibitory, equivalent to positive or negative inputs. The (SUM) could be negative or positive.

The training processes for the neurons and their synapses of Figs. 7 and 9 are identical, with identical stabilization points. The error signals are obtained in the same manner, and the formation of the error for the neuron and synapses of Fig. 9 is illustrated in Fig. 10. The error is once again given by Eq. (4). The final output, the output of the "half sigmoid," is indicated in Fig. 10. Fig. 10A shows the error and output. Fig. 10B shows the error function. When the (SUM) is negative, the neuron does not fire and the output is zero. When the

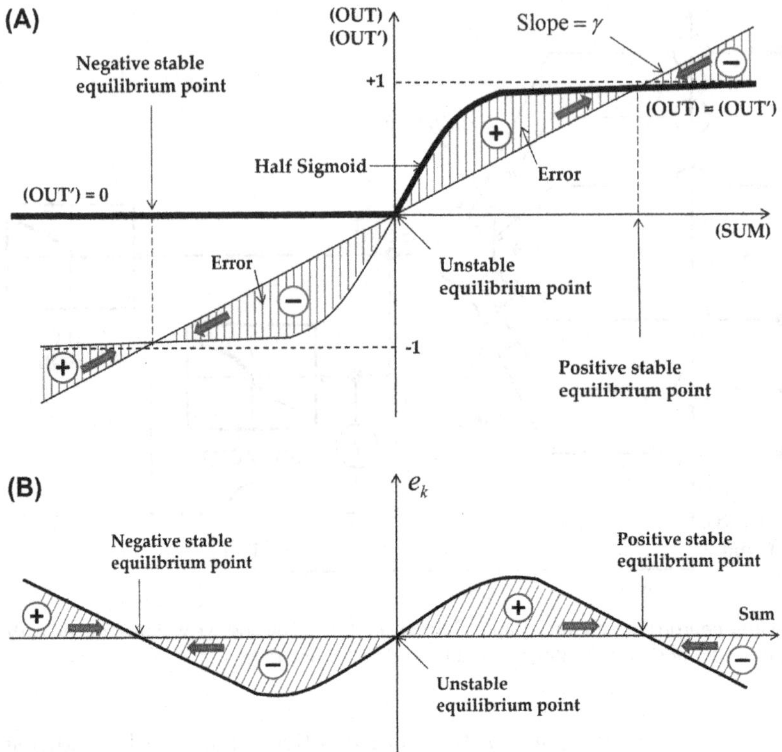

FIG. 10 The error of the sigmoidal neuron with rectified output, trained with bootstrap learning. (A) The output and error versus (SUM). (B) The error function.

(SUM) is positive, the firing rate, the neuron output, is a sigmoidal function of the (SUM) (note that with living neurons, the firing threshold is −70 mV, not zero).

The learning algorithm is

$$\begin{aligned} W_{k+1} &= W_k + 2\mu e_k X_k, \\ e_k &= SGM(X_k^T W_k) - \gamma X_k^T W_k \end{aligned} \tag{6}$$

Eq. (6) is a form of the Hebbian-LMS algorithm.

The LMS algorithm requires that all inputs to the summer be summed, not some added and some subtracted as in Fig. 9. Accordingly, when forming the X-vector, its excitatory components are taken directly as the outputs of the correspondingly connected presynaptic neurons while its inhibitory components are taken as the negative of the outputs of the correspondingly connected presynaptic neurons. Performing the Hebbian-LMS algorithm of Eq. (6), learning will then take place in accord with the diagram of Fig. 9.

With this algorithm, there is no inputted desired response with each input pattern X_k. Learning is unsupervised. The parameter μ controls stability and speed of convergence, as is the case for the LMS algorithm. The parameter γ has the value of 1/2 in the diagram of Fig. 10, but could have any positive value less than the initial slope of the sigmoid function

$$0 < \gamma < \frac{d}{d\xi} SGM(\xi) \bigg|_{\xi=0} \tag{7}$$

The neuron output signal is given by:

$$(\text{OUT})^k = \begin{cases} SGM(X_k^T W_k), & X_k^T W_k \geq 0 \\ 0, & X_k^T W_k < 0 \end{cases} \tag{8}$$

Eq. (6) represents the training procedure for the weights (synapses). Eq. (8) describes the signal flow through the neuron. Simulation results are represented in Fig. 11.

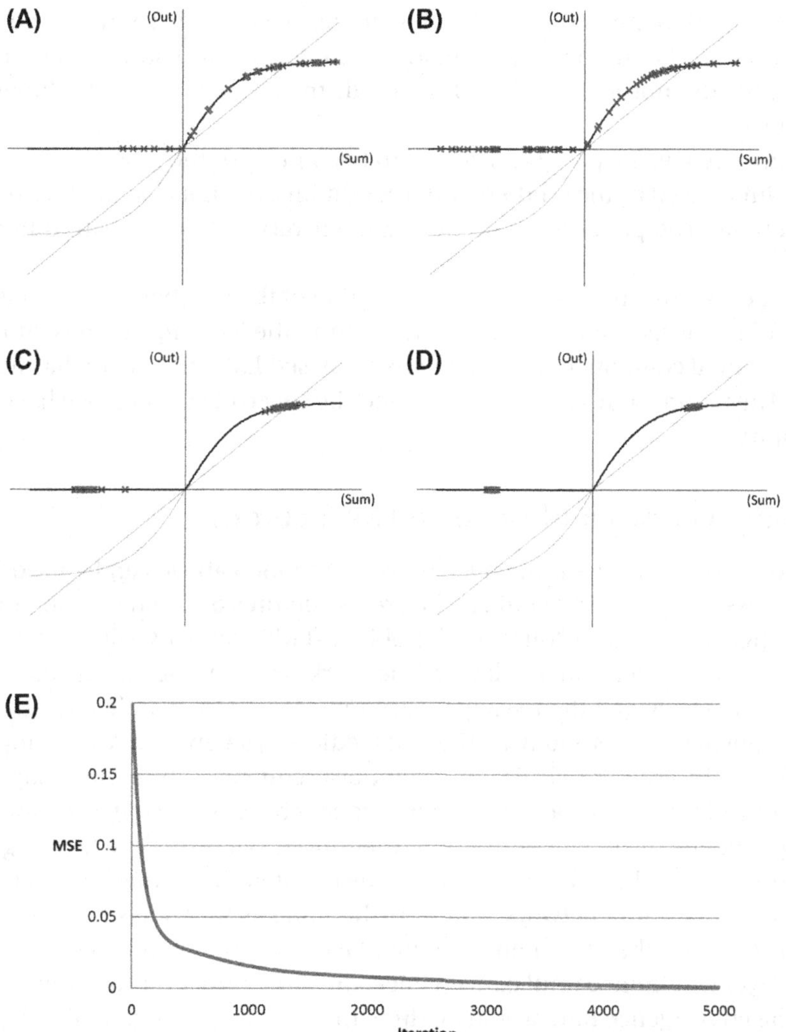

FIG. 11 A learning experiment with a single neuron. (A) Initial responses. (B) Responses after 100 iterations. (C) Responses after 2000 iterations. (D) Responses after 5000 iterations. (E) A learning curve.

Computer simulation was performed to demonstrate learning and clustering by the neuron and synapses of Fig. 9. Initial values for the weights were chosen randomly, independently, with uniform probability between 0 and 1. There were 50 excitatory and 50 inhibitory weights. There were 50 training patterns whose vector components were chosen randomly, independently, with uniform probability between 0 and 1. Initially, some of the input patterns produced positive (SUM) values, indicated in Fig. 11A by blue crosses (black in print version), and the remaining patterns produced negative (SUM) values, indicated in Fig. 11A by red crosses (gray in print version). After 100 iterations, some of the reds and blues (gray and black in print version) have changed sides, as seen in Fig. 11B. After 2000 iterations, as seen in Fig. 11C, clusters have begun to form and membership of the clusters has stabilized. There are no responses near zero. After 5000 iterations, tight clusters have formed as shown in Fig. 11D. At the neuron output, the output of the half sigmoid, the responses will be binary, 0s and approximate 1s.

Upon convergence, the patterns selected to become 1s or those selected to become 0s are strongly influenced by the random initial conditions, but not absolutely determined by initial conditions. The patterns would be classified very differently with different initial weights.

A learning curve, mean square error as a function of the number of iterations, is shown in Fig. 11E. When using a supervised LMS algorithm, the learning curve is known to be a sum of exponential components [7]. With unsupervised LMS, the theory has not yet been developed. The nature of this learning curve and the speed of convergence have only been studied empirically.

6.1 Training a network of Hebbian-LMS neurons

The method for training a neuron and synapses described above can be used in training neural networks. The networks could be layered structures or could be interconnected in random configurations like a "rat's nest." Hebbian-LMS will work with all such configurations. For simplicity, consider a layered network like the one shown in Fig. 12. The Hebbian-LMS neurons and their synapses are represented by double circles.

The example of Fig. 12 is a fully connected feedforward network. A set of input vectors are applied repetitively, periodically, or in random sequence. All of the synaptic weights are set randomly initially, and adaptation commences by applying the Hebbian-LMS algorithm independently to all the neurons and their input synapses. The learning process is totally decentralized. All of the synapses could be adapted simultaneously, so the speed of convergence for the entire network would be the same as that of a single neuron and its input synapses. If, on the other hand, the first layer was trained until convergence, then the second layer was trained until convergence, then the third layer was trained until convergence, the convergence time would be three times greater than that of a single neuron and its synapses. Training the network all at once would be faster with totally parallel operation.

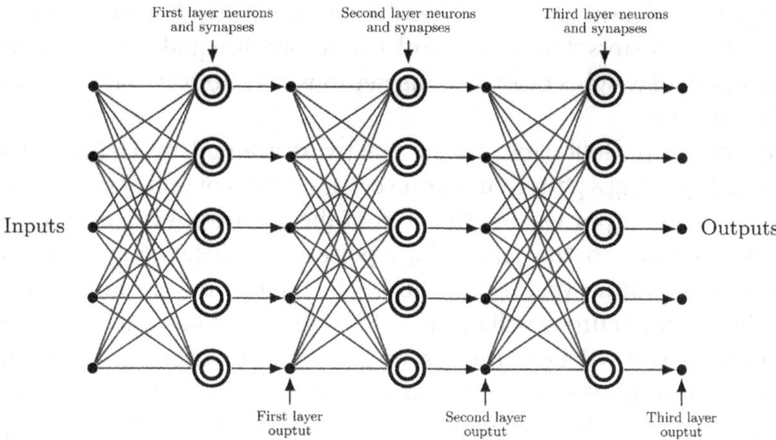

FIG. 12 An example of a layered neural network.

If the input patterns were linearly independent vectors, the output of the first-layer neurons would be binary after convergence. Since the input synapses of each of the first-layer neurons were set randomly and independently, the outputs of the first-layer neurons would be different from neuron to neuron. After convergence, the outputs of the second-layer neurons would also be binary, but different from the outputs of the first layer. The outputs of the third layer will also be binary after convergence.

If the input patterns were not linearly independent, the outputs of the first-layer neurons would not be purely binary. The outputs of the second layer would be closer to binary. The outputs of the third layer would be even closer to binary.

The number of training patterns equal to the number of synapses of the output layer neurons is the capacity of the network. It is shown in Ref. [12] that when applying patterns that are distinct but not necessarily linear independent to a nonlinear process such as layers of a neural network, the outputs of the layers would be distinct and linearly independent, if the number of training patterns were less than or equal to the network capacity. Then, the outputs of the output layer neurons will be perfectly binary. If the number of training patterns exceeds the network capacity, the network output will be 0s and "fuzzy" 1s, close to binary.

If one were to take one of the trained-in vectors and place a large cloud of vectors randomly disposed in a cluster about it, inputting all the vectors in the cluster without further training would result in identical binary output vectors at the output layer. This will be true as long as the diameter of the cluster is not "too large." How large this could be depending on the number and disposition of the other training vectors. Noisy or distorted input patterns in a cluster could be identified as equivalent to the associated training pattern. The network could determine a unique output pattern, a unique binary representation for training patterns in a cluster. This is a useful property for pattern classification.

With unsupervised learning, each cluster "chooses" its own binary output representation. The number of clusters that the network can resolve is equal to the network capacity, equal to the number of weights of each of the neurons of the output layer. Hebbian-LMS is a clustering algorithm.

An application is the following. Given a network trained by Hebbian-LMS, let the weights be fixed. Inputting a pattern from one of the clusters of one of the training patterns will result in a binary output vector. The sum of the squares of the errors of the output neurons will be close to zero. Now, inputting a pattern not close to any of the training patterns will result in an output vector that will not be binary and the sum of the squares of the errors of the output neurons will be large. So, if the input pattern is close to a training pattern, the output error will be close to zero. If the input pattern is distinct from all the training patterns, the output error will be large. One could use this when one is not asking the neural network to classify an input pattern, merely to indicate if the input pattern has been trained in, that is, seen before or not, deja vu, yes or no? This could be used as a critical element of a cognitive memory system [13].

In another application, a multilayer neural network could be trained using both supervised and unsupervised methods. The hidden layers could be trained with Hebbian-LMS, and the output layer could be trained with the original LMS algorithm. An individual input cluster would produce an individual binary "word" at the output of the final hidden layer. The output layer could be trained with a one-out-of-many code. The output neuron with the largest (SUM) would be identified as representing the class of the cluster of the input pattern.

A three-layer purely Hebbian-LMS network was simulated with 100 neurons in each layer. The input patterns were 50-dimensional, and the network outputs, binary after training, were 100-bit binary numbers. A set of training patterns was generated as follows. Ten random vectors were used as representing 10 clusters. Clusters were formed as clouds about the 10 original vectors. Each cloud contained 100 randomly disposed points. The ten 50-dimensional clusters are shown in Fig. 13A in two dimensions. The axes were chosen as the first two principal components.

All 1000 vectors were trained. The network was not "told" which vector belonged to which of the clusters. The 1000 input vectors were not labeled in any way. After convergence, the network produced 100-bit output words for each input vector. Ten distinct 100-bit output words were observed, each corresponding to one of the clouds. For a given 100-bit output word, all input vectors that caused that output word were given a specific color. The colored input points are shown in Fig. 13B. The colored points associate exactly as they did in the input clouds.

The uncolored points were trained into the network and they were "colored by the network." The network automatically produced unique representations for each of the clouds. This was a relatively easy problem since the number of clouds, 10, was much less than the network capacity, 100.

Fig. 14 illustrates how Hebbian-LMS creates binary outputs after the above training with the 1000 patterns. One of the neurons in the output layer was selected and

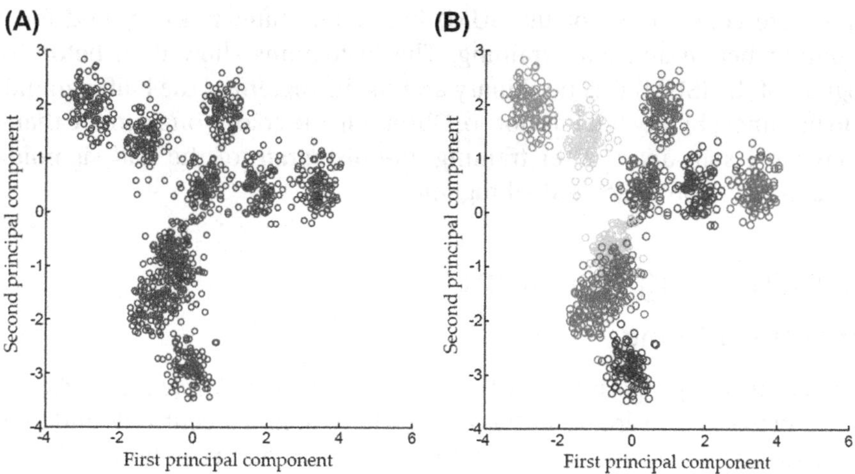

FIG. 13 Fifty-dimensional input vectors plotted along the first two principal components. (A) Before training. (B) After training.

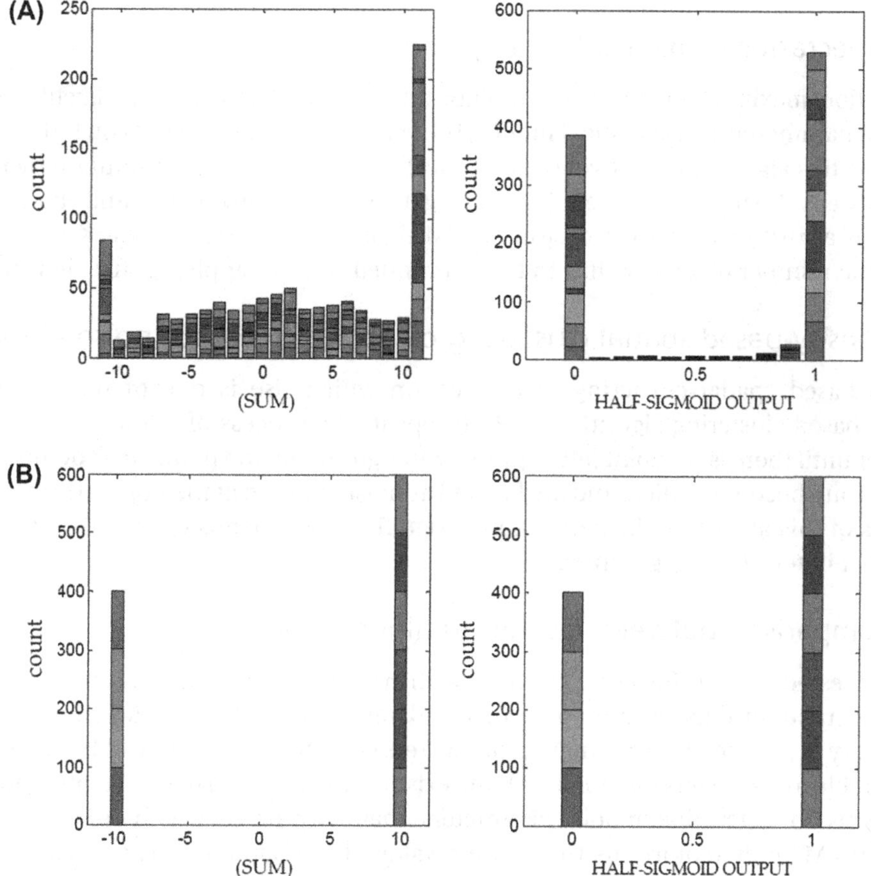

FIG. 14 Histogram of responses of a selected neuron in the output layer of a three-layer Hebbian-LMS network. (A) Before training and (B) after training.

histograms were constructed for its (SUM) before and after training, and for its half-sigmoid output before and after training. The histograms show that, before training, the histogram of the (SUM) was not binary and the histogram of the half-sigmoid output appears to be almost binary but it is not so. Observing the colors, one can see that some of the clusters were split apart. After training, the histogram of the half-sigmoid output shows the clusters to be intact and all together.

7 Other clustering algorithms

7.1 K-means clustering

The K-means clustering algorithm [14,15] is one of the most simple and basic clustering algorithms and has many variations. It is an algorithm to find K centroids and to partition an input dataset into K clusters based on the distances between each input instance and K centroids. This algorithm is usually fast to converge, relatively simple to compute, and effective in many cases. However, the number of clusters "K" is unknown in the beginning, and it has to be determined by heuristic methods.

7.2 Expectation-maximization algorithm

Expectation-maximization (EM) is an algorithm for finding maximum likelihood estimates of parameters in a statistical model [16]. When the model depends on hidden latent variables, this algorithm iteratively finds a local maximum likelihood solution by repeating two steps: E-step and M-step. Its convergence is well-known [17], and the K-means clustering algorithm is a special case of the EM algorithm. Same as with the K-means algorithm, the number of clusters has to be determined prior to applying this algorithm.

7.3 Density-based spatial clustering of application with noise algorithm

Density-based spatial clustering of application with noise is one of the well-known density-based clustering algorithms [18]. It repeats the process of grouping close points together until there is no point left to group. After grouping, the points that do not belong to any group become outliers and are labeled as noise. In spite of the popularity and effectiveness of this algorithm, its performance significantly depends on two threshold variables that determine the grouping.

7.4 Comparison between clustering algorithms

We have tested several clustering methods with artificial datasets such as the multivariate Gaussian random dataset and some of the datasets from the UCI Machine Learning Repository [19]. Overall performance of clustering with the Hebbian-LMS algorithm is comparable to the results obtained with the existing algorithms. These existing algorithms require us to determine model parameters manually or to use heuristic methods. Hebbian-LMS only requires us to choose a value of the parameter μ, the learning step.

In most cases, this choice is not critical and can be made like choosing μ for supervised LMS as described in detail in Ref. [7].

8 A general Hebbian-LMS algorithm

The Hebbian-LMS algorithm applied to the neuron and synapses of Fig. 9 results in a nicely working clustering algorithm, as demonstrated above, but its error signal, a function of (SUM), may not correspond exactly to nature's error signal. How nature generates the error signal will be discussed below.

It is possible to generate the error signal in many different ways as a function of the (SUM) signal. A most general form of Hebbian-LMS is diagrammed in Fig. 15. The learning algorithm can be expressed as

$$W_{k+1} = W_k + 2\mu e_k X_k \tag{9}$$

$$e_k = f(\text{SUM})_k = f(X_k^T W_k) \tag{10}$$

The neuron output can be expressed as

$$(\text{OUT})_k = \begin{cases} SGM((SUM)_k)|_{(SUM)_k} \geq 0 \\ 0|_{(SUM)_k} < 0 \end{cases} \tag{11}$$

For this neuron and its synapses to adapt and learn in a natural way, the error function *f*((SUM)) would need to be nature's error function. To pursue this further, it is necessary to incorporate knowledge of how synapses work, how they carry signals from one neuron to another, and how synaptic weight change is affected.

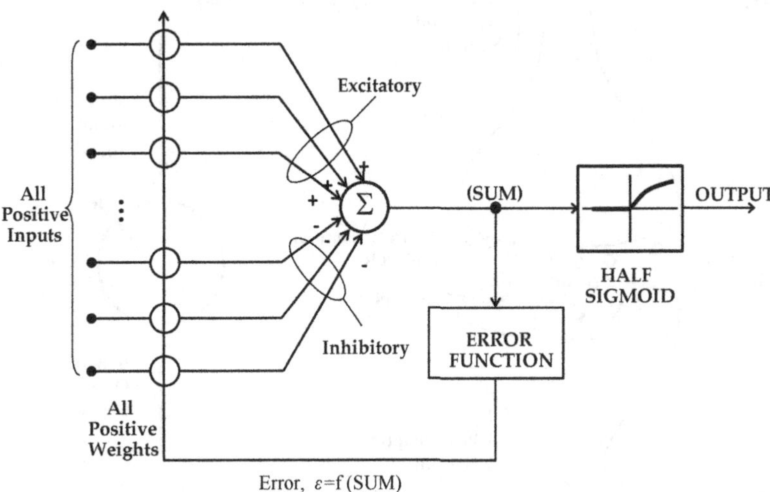

FIG. 15 A general form of Hebbian-LMS.

9 The synapse

The connection linking neuron to neuron is the synapse. Signal flows in one direction, from the presynaptic neuron to the postsynaptic neuron via the synapse which acts as a variable attenuator. A simplified diagram of a synapse is shown in Fig. 16A [20]. As an element of neural circuits, it is a "two-terminal device."

There is a 0.02 μ gap between the presynaptic side and the postsynaptic side of the synapse which is called the synaptic cleft. When the presynaptic neuron fires, a protein called a neurotransmitter is injected into the cleft. Each activation pulse generated by the presynaptic neuron causes a finite amount of neurotransmitter to be injected into the cleft. The neurotransmitter lasts only for a very short time, some being reabsorbed and some diffusing away. The average concentration of neurotransmitter in the cleft is proportional to the presynaptic neuron's firing rate.

Some of the neurotransmitter molecules attach to receptors located on the postsynaptic side of the cleft. The effect of this on the postsynaptic neuron is either excitatory or inhibitory, depending on the nature of the synapse and its neurotransmitter chemistry [20–24]. A synaptic effect results when neurotransmitter molecules attach to the receptors. The effect is proportional to the average amount of neurotransmitter present and the number of receptors. Thus, the effect of the presynaptic neuron on the postsynaptic neuron is proportional to the product of the presynaptic firing rate and the number of receptors present. The input signal to the synapse is the presynaptic firing rate, and the synaptic weight is proportional to the number of receptors. The weight or the synaptic "efficiency" described by Hebb is increased or decreased by increasing or decreasing the number of receptors. This can only occur when neurotransmitter is present [20]. Neurotransmitter

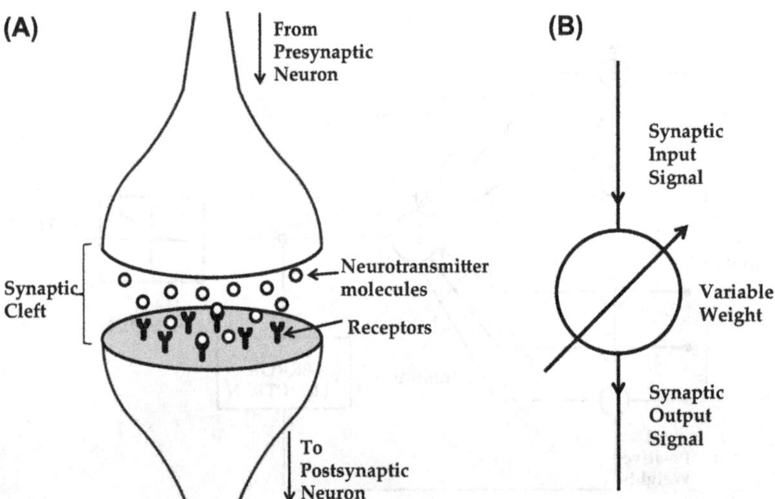

FIG. 16 A synapse corresponding to a variable weight. (A) Synapse. (B) A variable weight.

is essential both as a signal carrier and as a facilitator for weight changing. A symbolic representation of the synapse is shown in Fig. 16B.

The effect of the action of a single synapse upon the postsynaptic neuron is actually quite small. Signals from thousands of synapses, some excitatory, some inhibitory, add in the postsynaptic neuron to create the (SUM) [20,25]. If the (SUM) of both the positive and negative inputs is below a threshold, the postsynaptic neuron will not fire and its output will be zero. If the (SUM) is greater than the threshold, the postsynaptic neuron will fire at a rate that increases with the magnitude of the (SUM) above the threshold. The threshold voltage within the postsynaptic neuron is a "resting potential" close to −70 mV. Summing in the postsynaptic neuron is accomplished by Kirchhoff's addition.

Learning and weight changing can only be done in the presence of neurotransmitter in the synaptic cleft. Thus, there will be no weight changing if the presynaptic neuron is not firing, that is, if the input signal to the synapse is zero. If the presynaptic neuron is firing, there will be weight change. The number of receptors will gradually increase (up to a limit) if the postsynaptic neuron is firing, that is, when the (SUM) of the postsynaptic neuron has a voltage above threshold. Then, the synaptic membrane that the receptors are attached to will have a voltage above threshold since this membrane is part of the postsynaptic neuron. See Fig. 17. All this corresponds to Hebbian learning, firing together wiring together. Extending Hebb's rule, if the presynaptic neuron is firing and the postsynaptic neuron is not firing, the postsynaptic (SUM) will be negative and below the threshold, the membrane voltage will be negative and below the threshold, and the number of receptors will gradually decrease.

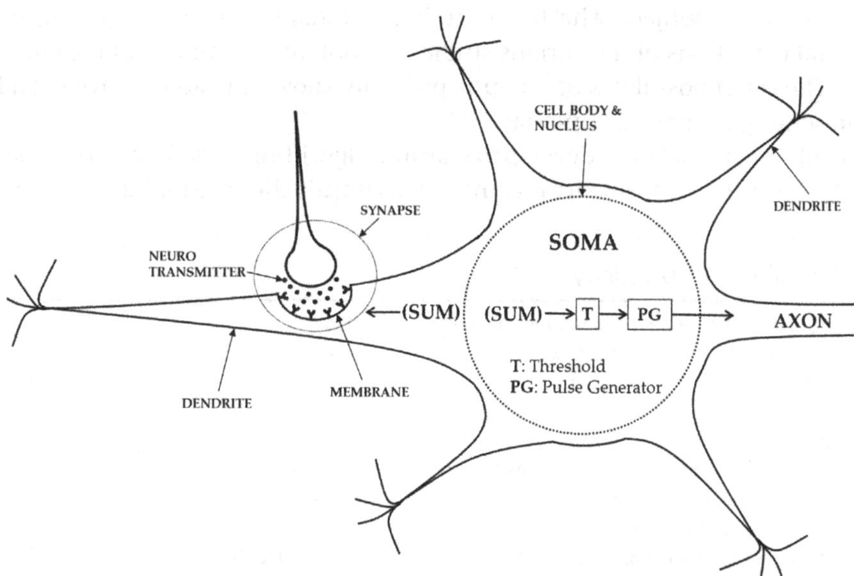

FIG. 17 A neuron, dendrites, and a synapse.

There is another mechanism having further control over the synaptic weight values, and it is called synaptic scaling [26–30]. This natural mechanism is implemented chemically for stability, to maintain the voltage of (SUM) within an approximate range about two set points. This is done by scaling up or down all of the synapses supplying signal to a given neuron. There is a positive set point and a negative one, and they turn out to be analogous to the equilibrium points shown in Fig. 8. This kind of stabilization is called homeostasis and is a phenomenon of regularization that takes place over all living systems. The Hebbian-LMS algorithm exhibits homeostasis about the two equilibrium points, caused by reversal of the error signal at these equilibrium points. See Fig. 8. Slow adaptation over thousands of adapt cycles, over hours of real time, results in homeostasis of the (SUM).

Fig. 17 shows an exaggerated diagram of a neuron, dendrites, and a synapse. This diagram suggests how the voltage of the (SUM) in the soma of the postsynaptic neuron can by ohmic conduction determine the voltage of the membrane.

Activation pulses are generated by a pulse generator in the soma of the postsynaptic neuron. The pulse generator is energized when the (SUM) exceeds the threshold. The pulse generator triggers the axon to generate electrochemical waves that carry the neuron's output signal. The firing rate of the pulse generator is controlled by the (SUM). The output signal of the neuron is its firing rate.

10 Postulates of synaptic plasticity

The above description of the synapse and its variability or plasticity is based on a study of the literature of the subject. The literature is not totally clear or consistent, however. Experimental conditions of the various studies are not all the same, and the conclusions can differ. The set of postulates of synaptic plasticity shown in Table 1 have been formulated representing a "majority opinion."

A group of researchers have developed learning algorithms called "anti-Hebbian learning [31–33]": "Fire together, unwire together." This is truly the case for inhibitory synapses.

Table 1 Postulates of plasticity.

1. Presynaptic neurons not firing: no neurotransmitter in synaptic gap
   (a) Excitatory synapse—no weight change
   (b) Inhibitory synapse—no weight change
2. Presynaptic neuron firing
   (a) Excitatory synapse
      - Postsynaptic neuron firing, synaptic weight increases (Hebb's rule)
      - Postsynaptic neuron not firing, synaptic weight decreases (extended Hebb's rule)
   (b) Inhibitory synapse
      - Postsynaptic neuron firing, synaptic weight decreases (extended Hebb's rule)
      - Postsynaptic neuron not firing, synaptic weight increases (extended Hebb's rule)
3. Homeostasis keeps (SUM) close to one or the other equilibrium point, stabilizing firing rate of postsynaptic neuron

We call this in the above postulates an extension of Hebb's rule. Anti-Hebbian learning fits the postulates and is therefore essentially incorporated in the Hebbian-LMS algorithm.

11 The postulates and the Hebbian-LMS algorithm

The Hebbian-LMS algorithm of Eqs. (6)–(8) and diagrams in Figs. 9 and 10 as applied to both excitatory and inhibitory inputs perform in complete accord with the biological postulates of synaptic plasticity.

An algorithm based on Hebb's original rule would cause all the weights to converge and saturate at their maximum values after many adaptive cycles. Weights would only increase, never decrease. A neural network with all equal weights would not be useful. Accordingly, Hebb's rule is extended to apply to both excitatory and inhibitory synapses and to the case where the presynaptic neuron fires and the postsynaptic neuron does not fire. Synaptic scaling to maintain stability also needs to be taken into account. The Hebbian-LMS algorithm does all this.

12 Nature's Hebbian-LMS algorithm

The Hebbian-LMS algorithm performs in accord with the synaptic postulates. These postulates indicate the direction of synaptic weight change, increase or decrease, but not the rate of change. On the other hand, the Hebbian-LMS algorithm of Eq. (6) not only specifies direction of weight change but also specifies rate of change. The question is could nature be implementing something like Hebbian-LMS at the level of the individual neuron and its synapses and in a full-blown neural network?

The Hebbian-LMS algorithm changes the individual weights at a rate proportional to the product of the input signal and the error signal. The Hebbian-LMS error signal is roughly proportional to the (SUM) signal for a range of values about zero. The error drops off and the rate of adaptation slows as (SUM) approaches either equilibrium point. The direction of adaptation reverses as (SUM) goes beyond the equilibrium point, creating homeostasis.

In the synaptic cleft, the amount of neurotransmitter present is proportional to the firing rate of the presynaptic neuron, that is, the input signal to the synapse. By ohmic conduction, the synaptic membrane voltage is proportional to the voltage of the postsynaptic soma, the (SUM), which determines the error signal. The rate of change in the number of neurotransmitter receptors is approximately proportional to the product of the amount of neurotransmitter present and the voltage of the synaptic membrane, negative or positive. This is all in agreement with the Hebbian-LMS algorithm. It is instructive to compare the drawings of Fig. 17 with those of Figs. 9 and 15. In a functional sense, they are very similar. Figs. 9 and 15 show weight changing being dependent on the error signal, a function of the (SUM), and the input signals to the individual weights. Fig. 17 indicates that the (SUM) signal is available to the synaptic membrane by linear ohmic conduction and the input signal is available in the synaptic cleft as the concentration of neurotransmitter.

The above description of synaptic plasticity is highly simplified. The reality is much more complicated. The literature on the subject is very complicated. The above description is a simplified high-level picture of what occurs with adaptation and learning in neural networks.

The question remains: When nature performs learning in neural networks, is this done with an algorithm similar to Hebbian-LMS? No one knows for sure, but "*if it walks like a duck, quacks like a duck, and looks like a duck, maybe it is a duck.*"

13 Conclusion

The Hebbian learning rule of 1949, "fire together wire together," has stood the test of time in the field of neurobiology. The LMS learning rule of 1959 has also stood in the test of time in the field of signal processing and telecommunications. This chapter has reviewed several forms of a Hebbian-LMS algorithm that implements Hebbian-learning by means of the LMS algorithm. Hebbian-LMS extends the Hebbian rule to cover inhibitory as well as excitatory neuronal inputs, making Hebbian learning more "biologically correct." At the same time, Hebbian-LMS is an unsupervised clustering algorithm that is very useful for automatic pattern classification.

Given the available parts of nature's neural networks, namely neurons, synapses, and their interconnections and wiring configurations, what kind of learning algorithms could be implemented? There may not be a unique answer to this question. But it may be possible that nature is performing Hebbian-LMS in at least some parts of the brain.

The basic building blocks of modern-day computers are flip-flops and logic gates. By analogy, is it possible that clustering is a basic building block of living neural systems?

Appendix: Trainable neural network incorporating Hebbian-LMS learning

Trainable neural networks can be constructed with several Hebbian-LMS layers followed by a supervised output layer. An example of such network is shown in Fig. A.1.

The unsupervised hidden layers serve as a preprocessor for the output layer. Clustering with the hidden layers aids the output layer in making final classification decisions. The Hebbian-LMS neurons train independently but are in communication with their neighbors, like the cells in living tissue. They work independently yet all work together for the common goal of pattern clustering.

A four-layer network like that of Fig. A.1 has been simulated. The neurons had symmetric sigmoids. Input signals and weights could be either positive or negative. This would be more typical for engineering applications. Adaptation is demonstrated by the learning curves of Fig. A.2. The hidden layers of the network were trained with Hebbian-LMS. The output layer was trained with LMS to implement a one-out-of-many code. The learning curves are plots of output error versus the number of training cycles, each cycle being a training sequence including the entire set of training patterns. The output error is a count

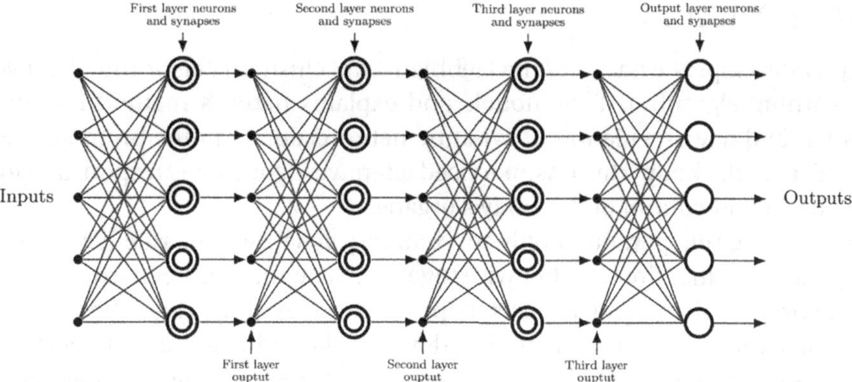

FIG. A.1 A network with three Hebbian-LMS hidden layers and a trainable LMS output layer with a one-out-of-many code.

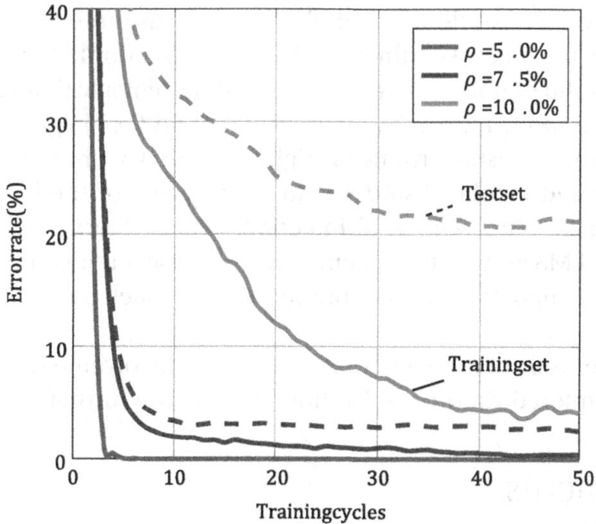

FIG. A.2 Learning curves obtained in statistical classification experiments with a Hebbian-LMS neural network similar to the one illustrated in Fig. A.1.

of number of errors or misclassifications. Plots were given for both training and testing datasets.

The network had 150 neurons per hidden layer. The input patterns had 50 components. The input training patterns were of 100 clusters, each cluster having 20 vectors randomly distributed about a centroid, with centroids randomly distributed in the 50-dimensional input space. The parameter ρ is defined as the ratio between the standard deviation of the samples about a centroid and the average distance between centroids. The bigger the value of ρ, the more difficult the problem. This is evident from the plots of Fig. A.2.

Chapter postscript

This chapter develops the basics of the Hebbian-LMS clustering algorithm, believed to be nature's learning algorithm. This models and explains nature's method for controlling upregulation and downregulation of synaptic neuroreceptors in the brain and hormone receptors all over the body. This unsupervised adaptive algorithm is responsible for learning in the brain and control of the body's organs.

Hebb's learning rule pertained only to excitatory synapses. His rule has been characterized by "neurons that fire together wire together." The rule has been extended. If a presynaptic neuron is firing and a postsynaptic neuron is not firing, then the synaptic coupling that connects them weakens, i.e., downregulates the number of neuroreceptors. If the synapse is inhibitory, the rule reverses so that neurons that fire together unwire together. Evidence from petri dish experiments confirm the extended Hebbian rule.

When thinking about this rule, I realized that extended Hebbian learning is precisely the unsupervised version of the LMS algorithm that I was experimenting with in the early 1960's. The name I gave this rule was Hebbian-LMS. I was quite excited.

I began to dig deeper and was influenced by several Stanford Medical School publications and articles in the popular press that reported on biological phenomena related to neuroreceptors or hormone receptors. An example is COVID. I began to study brain phenomena such as pain/pleasure, runner's high, addiction/withdrawal, mood disorders such as depression and bipolar disorder, and phenomena of the body such as control of blood salinity, kidney function, viral infection, cancer, thermoregulation, and many more. The Hebbian-LMS algorithm is deeply involved in all of these phenomena. In some cases, remedies are proposed that are counterintuitive, such as for viral infections and breast cancer.

A comprehensive study of these phenomena and the involvement of the Hebbian-LMS algorithm can be explored via the publication listed in the further reading.

Acknowledgments

We would like to acknowledge the help that we have received from Neil Gallagher, Naren Krishna, and Adrian Alabi. This chapter is based on B. Widrow, Y. Kim, and D. Park, "The Hebbian-LMS Learning Algorithm," in *IEEE Computational Intelligence Magazine*, vol. 10, no. 4, pp. 37–53, Nov. 2015.

References

[1] D.O. Hebb, The Organization of Behavior, Wiley & Sons, 1949.

[2] G.-Q. Bi, M.-M. Poo, Synaptic modifications in cultured hippocampal neurons: dependence on spike timing, synaptic strength, and postsynaptic cell type, J. Neurosci. 18 (24) (1998) 10464–10472.

[3] G.-Q. Bi, M.-M. Poo, Synaptic modifications by correlated activity: Hebb's postulate revisited, Annu. Rev. Neurosci. 24 (2001) 139–166.

[4] S. Song, K.D. Miller, L.F. Abbott, Competitive Hebbian learning through spike-timing-dependent synaptic plasticity, Nat. Neurosci. 3 (9) (2000) 919–925.

[5] B. Widrow, Y. Kim, D. Park, The Hebbian-LMS learning algorithm, IEEE Comput. Intell. Mag. 10 (4) (2015) 37–53.

[6] B. Widrow, M.E. Hoff Jr., Adaptive switching circuits, in: IRE WESCON Convention Record, 1960, pp. 96–104.

[7] B. Widrow, S.D. Stearns, Adaptive Signal Processing, Prentice-Hall, 1985.

[8] B. Widrow, Bootstrap learning in threshold logic systems, in: International Federation of Automatic Control, 1966, pp. 96–104.

[9] W.C. Miller, A Modified Mean Square Error Criterion for Use in Unsupervised Learning (Ph.D. thesis), Stanford University, 1967.

[10] R.W. Lucky, Automatic equalization for digital communication, Bell Syst. Tech. J. 44 (4) (1965) 547–588.

[11] R.W. Lucky, Techniques for adaptive equalization for digital communication, Bell Syst. Tech. J. 45 (2) (1966) 255–286.

[12] B. Widrow, A. Greenblatt, Y. Kim, D. Park, The no-prop algorithm: a new learning algorithm for multilayer neural networks, Neural Netw. 37 (2012) 182–188.

[13] B. Widrow, J.C. Aragon, Cognitive memory, Neural Netw. 41 (2013) 3–14.

[14] J.A. Hartigan, M.A. Wong, Algorithm AS 136: a K-means clustering algorithm, J. R. Stat. Soc.: Ser. C: Appl. Stat. 28 (1) (1979) 100–108.

[15] J. MacQueen, Some methods for classification and analysis of multivariate observations, in: Proceedings of the Fifth Berkeley Symposium on Mathematical Statistics and Probability, vol. 1 (14), 1967, pp. 281–297.

[16] A.P. Dempster, N.M. Laird, D.B. Rubin, Maximum likelihood from incomplete data via the EM algorithm, J. R. Stat. Soc. Ser. B Methodol. 39 (1) (1977) 1–38.

[17] C.F.J. Wu, On the convergence properties of the EM algorithm, Ann. Stat. 11 (1) (1983) 95–103.

[18] M. Ester, H.-P. Kriegel, J. Sander, X. Xu, A density-based algorithm for discovering clusters in large spatial databases with noise, in: Proceedings of Second International Conference on Knowledge Discovery and Data Mining (KDD), vol. 96 (34), 1996, pp. 226–231.

[19] M. Lichman, UCI Machine Learning Repository, 2013. http://archive.ics.uci.edu/ml.

[20] D. Purves, G.J. Augustine, D. Fitzpatrick, A.-S. LaMantia, J.O. McNamara, S.M. Wiliams, Neuroscience, Sinauer Associates, Inc, 2008.

[21] H.R. Wilson, J.D. Cowan, Excitatory and inhibitory interactions in localized populations of model neurons, Biophys. J. 12 (1) (1972) 1–24.

[22] C. van Vreeswijk, H. Sompolinsky, Chaos in neural networks with balanced excitatory and inhibitory activity, Science 274 (5293) (1996) 1724–1726.

[23] C. Luscher, R.C. Malenka, NMDA receptor-dependent long-term potentiation and long-term depression (LTP/LTD), Cold Spring Harb. Perspect. Biol. 4 (2012) 1–15.

[24] M.A. Lynch, Long-term potentiation and memory, Physiol. Rev. 84 (1) (2004) 87–136.

[25] J.F. Prather, R.K. Powers, T.C. Cope, Amplification and linear summation of synaptic effects on motoneuron firing rate, J. Neurophysiol. 85 (1) (2001) 43–53.

[26] G.G. Turrigano, K.R. Leslie, N.S. Desai, N.C. Rutherford, S.B. Nelson, Activity dependent scaling of quantal amplitude in neocortical neurons, Nature 391 (1998) 892–896.

[27] G.G. Turrigano, S.B. Nelson, Hebb and homeostasis in neuronal plasticity, Curr. Opin. Neurobiol. 10 (3) (2000) 358–364.

[28] G.G. Turrigano, The self-tuning neuron: synaptic scaling of excitatory synapses, Cell 135 (3) (2008) 422–435.

[29] N. Virtureira, Y. Goda, The interplay between Hebbian and homeostasis synaptic plasticity, J. Cell Biol. 203 (2) (2013) 175–186.

[30] D. Stellwagen, R.C. Malenka, Synaptic scaling mediated by glial TNF-α, Nature 440 (2006) 1054–1059.

[31] V.R. Kompella, M. Luciw, J. Schmidhuber, Incremental slow feature analysis: adaptive low-complexity slow feature updating from high-dimensional input streams, Neural Comput. 24 (11) (2012) 2994–3024.

[32] Z.K. Malik, A. Hussain, J. Wu, Novel biologically inspired approaches to extracting online information from temporal data, Cogn. Comput. 6 (3) (2014) 595–607.

[33] Y. Choe, Anti-Hebbian learning, in: Encyclopedia of Computational Neuroscience, 2014, pp. 1–4.

Further reading

B. Widrow, Cybernetics 2.0: A General Theory of Adaptivity and Homeostasis In the Brain and in the Body, Springer, 2022.

3

A half century of progress toward a unified neural theory of mind and brain with applications to autonomous adaptive agents and mental disorders

Stephen Grossberg

CENTER FOR ADAPTIVE SYSTEMS, GRADUATE PROGRAM IN COGNITIVE AND NEURAL SYSTEMS, DEPARTMENTS OF MATHEMATICS & STATISTICS, PSYCHOLOGICAL & BRAIN SCIENCES, AND BIOMEDICAL ENGINEERING, BOSTON UNIVERSITY, BOSTON, MA, UNITED STATES

Chapter outlines

1 Toward a unified theory of mind and brain

A major scientific and technological revolution in understanding autonomous adaptive intelligence is currently underway. How the brain works provides a critical example of such intelligence. This revolution has been supported, in part, by publications over the past 50 years of design principles, mechanisms, circuits, and architectures that are part of an emerging unified theory of biological intelligence. This emerging theory explains

Artificial Intelligence in the Age of Neural Networks and Brain Computing. https://doi.org/10.1016/B978-0-323-96104-2.00009-9

Copyright © 2024 Elsevier Inc. All rights reserved.

and predicts how brain mechanisms give rise to mental functions as emergent properties. A self-contained, nontechnical exposition of this theory can be found in Grossberg [1].

This theory has clarified how advanced brains are designed to enable individuals to autonomously adapt in real time in response to complex changing environments that are filled with unexpected events. Its results hereby provide a blueprint for designing increasingly autonomous adaptive agents for future applications in engineering and technology. Many large-scale applications in engineering and technology have already been developed, for example, http://techlab.bu.edu/resources/articles/C5.

As part of the development of the biological theory, the data from thousands of psychological and neurobiological experiments have been explained and predicted in a unified way, including data about perception, cognition, cognitive-emotional dynamics, and action. These results include an emerging unified theory of what happens in an individual brain when it consciously sees, hears, feels, or knows something; how seeing, hearing, feeling, and knowing can be integrated into unified moments of conscious experience; and how unconscious processes can influence a brain's decision-making [2].

As sufficiently mature models of typical, or normal, behaviors became understood, it also became possible to increasingly explain brain mechanisms and behavioral symptoms of mental disorders. Applications to autism, schizophrenia, and medial temporal amnesia were among the first to be made, for example, Carpenter and Grossberg [3], Grossberg [4], and Grossberg and Seidman [5]. Additional applications have been recently made toward explaining how the dynamics of learning, memory, and cognition may break down during Alzheimer's disease, why slow wave sleep disorders are often correlated with Alzheimer's disease and other mental disorders, and how symptoms of Fragile X syndrome and autistic repetitive behaviors may arise [6,7], and how these insights may help to guide new clinical therapies.

How did a theory that was developed to explain data about the learning and performance of typical, or normal, behaviors lead to explanations of data about mental disorders? This happened when it began to be noticed that, when various model brain mechanisms become imbalanced in prescribed ways, then formal analogs of behavioral symptoms of different mental disorders emerged. In autism, these imbalances include underaroused emotional depression in the drive representations of regions like the amygdala, hypervigilant learning and narrowing of attention in the recognition learning circuits of brain regions like the temporal and prefrontal cortices, and a failure of adaptively timed learning in brain regions like the hippocampus, basal ganglia, and cerebellum [5]. In this way, one could begin to understand the neural mechanisms and behavioral symptoms of mental disorders on a continuum with neural mechanisms and behavioral properties of typical behaviors.

Said in another way, after one does due diligence in discovering and characterizing the brain mechanisms of normal behaviors, then mechanistic explanations of clinical data *automatically* emerge from these theories. In a similar way, the discovery of key brain mechanisms, circuits, and architectures to explain one kind of data has often thrust me into explanations of other, seemingly quite different, kinds of data where variations and specialization of these mechanisms, circuits, and architectures are also operative. In this sense, by getting the theoretical foundations of biological intelligence right, one can then begin to reap the benefits of the gift that never stops giving.

2 A theoretical method for linking brain to mind: The method of minimal anatomies

One cannot hope to derive a unified theory of an entire brain in one step, and one should not try to do so. Rather, this grand goal can be achieved incrementally, in stages, starting with a large behavioral database that excites a theorist's imagination (Fig. 1). The derivation begins with behavioral data because *brain* evolution needs to achieve *behavioral* success. Starting with behavioral data enables models to be derived whose brain mechanisms have been shaped during evolution by behavioral success. Starting with a large database helps to rule out incorrect, but otherwise seemingly plausible, models of how a brain works.

Such a derivation has always led in the past to the discovery of novel design principles and mechanisms (Fig. 1) with which to explain how an individual, behaving in real time, can generate the behavioral data as emergent properties. This conceptual leap from data to design is the art of modeling. Once derived, despite being based on psychological constraints, the minimal mathematical model that realizes the behavioral design principles has always looked like part of a brain (Fig. 1). I first experienced such a derivation of brain mechanisms from psychological hypotheses when I was a Freshman at Dartmouth College in 1957–58. It was a transformative experience that shaped the rest of my life https://youtu.be/9n5AnvFur7I.

The past 60 years of modeling have abundantly supported the hypothesis that brains look the way that they do because they embody natural computational designs whereby

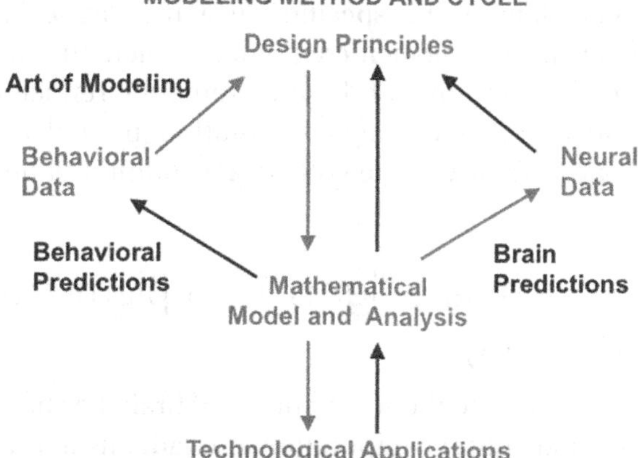

FIG. 1 A modeling method and cycle that clarifies how increasingly refined neural models can explain and predict increasingly large interdisciplinary behavioral and neurobiological databases.

individuals autonomously adapt to changing environments in real time. The revolution in understanding biological intelligence is thus, more specifically, a revolution in understanding *autonomous adaptive intelligence*. The link from behavior-to-principle-to-model-to-brain has, in addition, often disclosed unexpected functional roles of the derived brain mechanisms that are not clear from neural data alone.

At any stage of this modeling cycle, the goal is to first derive the *minimal model* that embodies the psychological hypotheses that drive the model derivation. Such a "minimal" model is one for which, if any model mechanism is removed, or "lesioned," then the remaining model can no longer explain a key set of previously explained data. A wise theorist should, I believe, strongly resist "throwing in" known neural mechanisms that are not yet in the minimal model if there is no functional understanding of why they are needed. Once the link between mechanism and function is broken in this way, the ability of the current minimal model to drive further model refinements will be lost.

In particular, once a connection is made top-down from behavior to brain by such a minimal model, mathematical and computational analysis discloses what data the minimal model, and its individual and species variations, can and cannot explain. The data that cannot be explained are as important as those that can be explained, because they demarcate a "boundary between the known and the unknown." Analysis of this boundary focuses a theorist's attention upon design principles that the current model does not yet embody. These new design principles and their mechanistic realizations are then consistently incorporated into the model to generate a more realistic model, and one that has always been able to explain and predict a lot more psychological and neurobiological data. If the model cannot be refined, or unlumped, in this way, then that is strong evidence that the current model contains a serious error and must be discarded.

This theoretical cycle has been successfully repeated multiple times, and has led to models with an increasingly broad explanatory and predictive range, including models that can individually explain psychological, neurophysiological, neuroanatomical, biophysical, and biochemical data. In this specific sense, the classical mind/body problem is being solved through principled, albeit incremental, refinements and expansions of theoretical understanding. One can think of these incremental refinements as a way that a theory can try to carry out a kind of "conceptual evolution" by analyzing how various environmental pressures may have driven the biological evolution of our brains.

3 Revolutionary brain paradigms: Complementary computing and laminar computing

The possibility of deriving a unified theory of mind and brain has built upon the discovery that advanced brains embody novel computational paradigms in order to achieve autonomous adaptive intelligence. Two of these paradigms are complementary computing and laminar computing.

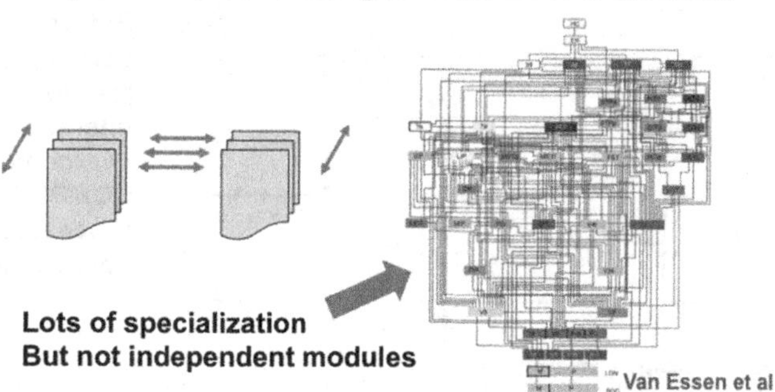
COMPLEMENTARY COMPUTING
New principles of
UNCERTAINTY and COMPLEMENTARITY
clarify why
Multiple Parallel Processing Streams Exist in the Brain
Lots of specialization
But not independent modules
Van Essen et al

FIG. 2 Complementary computing clarifies why there are multiple parallel processing streams in the brain, each with multiple processing stages to resolve computational uncertainties that cannot be overcome by just one processing stream or stage. The anatomical macrocircuit of the visual system dramatically illustrates this state of affairs.

Complementary computing [8] describes how the brain is organized into complementary parallel processing streams whose interactions generate biologically intelligent behaviors (Fig. 2). A single cortical processing stream can individually compute some properties well, but cannot, by itself, process other computationally complementary properties. Pairs of complementary cortical processing streams interact to generate emergent properties that overcome their complementary deficiencies to compute complete information with which to represent or control some faculty of intelligent behavior. Complementary computing hereby clarifies how different brain regions can achieve a great deal of specialization without being independent modules.

Fig. 2 includes an anatomical macrocircuit of the monkey visual system that illustrates its multiple brain regions, and the dense connections between them [9]. Fig. 3 summarizes a macrocircuit of some of the main brain regions that are modeled in an emerging unified theory of visual intelligence, and the perceptual processes that they carry out. This macrocircuit also includes bottom-up, horizontal, and top-down connections that are needed to overcome computational weaknesses due to Complementary computing that each brain region would experience if it acted alone.

4 The What and Where cortical streams are complementary

The category learning, attention, recognition, and prediction circuits of the ventral, or What, cortical processing stream for perception and cognition [10,11] are computationally complementary to those of the dorsal, or Where and How, cortical processing steam for spatial representation and action [10–12]. One reason for this What-Where complementarity is that the What stream learns object recognition categories that are substantially

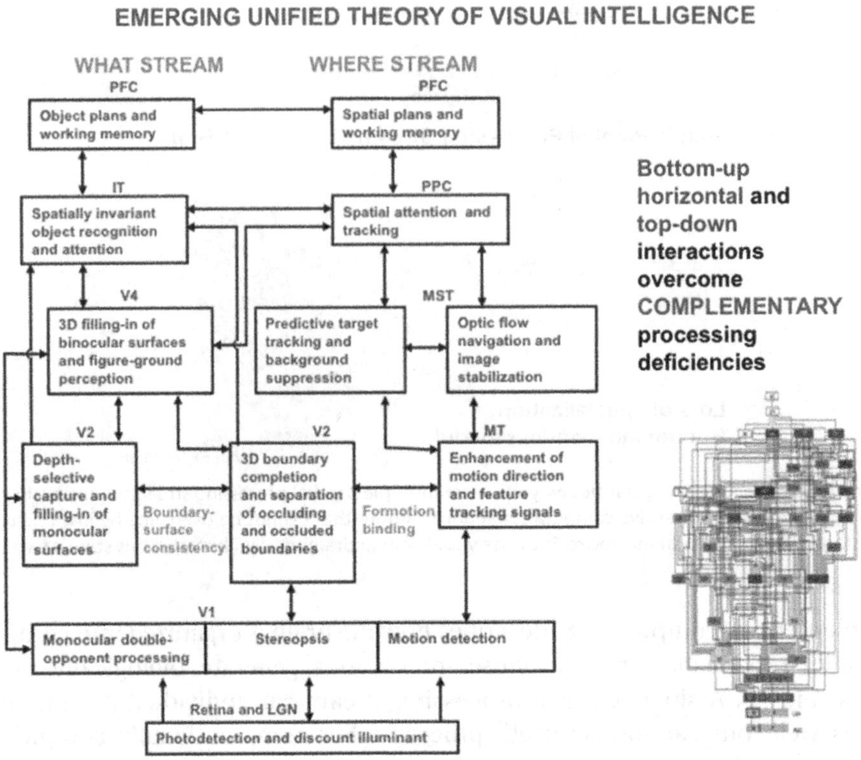

FIG. 3 A model macrocircuit of an emerging unified theory of visual intelligence. Its processing stages begin at the retina and end in the prefrontal cortex, and include both the What and the Where cortical processing streams. The bottom-up, horizontal, and top-down interactions between model processing stages are needed to overcome the computational weaknesses that each processing stage would experience if it acted alone, due to complementary computing.

invariant under changes in an object's view, size, and position. These invariant object categories enable our brains to recognize valued objects without experiencing a combinatorial explosion. They cannot, however, locate and act upon a desired object in space. Cortical Where stream spatial and motor representations can locate objects and trigger actions toward them, but cannot recognize them. By interacting together, the What and Where streams can recognize valued objects and direct appropriate goal-oriented actions toward them.

5 Adaptive resonance theory

Abundant psychological and neurobiological data have confirmed all of the foundational predictions concerning how perceptual/cognitive processes in the What stream use excitatory matching and match-based learning to create self-stabilizing categorical representations of objects and events, notably recognition categories that can be learned quickly without experiencing catastrophic forgetting during subsequent learning. In other words, this learning process solves the *stability-plasticity dilemma*. They thereby enable increasing expertise, and an ever-expanding sense of self, to emerge throughout life. See Grossberg [2,13,14] for reviews.

Excitatory matching by object attention is embodied by the ART matching rule (Fig. 4). This type of attentional circuit enables us to prime our expectations to anticipate objects and events before they occur, and to focus attention upon expected objects and events when they do occur. Good enough matches between expected and actual events trigger resonant states that can support learning of new recognition categories and refinement of old ones, while also triggering conscious recognition of the *critical feature patterns* that are attended and enable recognition to occur. Excitatory matching also controls reset of the attentional focus when bottom-up inputs significantly mismatch currently active top-down expectations. Cycles of resonance and reset underlie much of the brain's perceptual and cognitive dynamics (Fig. 5).

These matching and learning laws have been articulated as part of adaptive resonance theory, or ART, which has been systematically developed since it was first reported in 1976 [15,16]. ART is a cognitive and neural theory of how the brain autonomously learns to attend, recognize, and predict objects and events in a changing world. ART is currently the most highly developed cognitive and neural theory available, with the broadest explanatory and predictive range. Central to ART's predictive power is its ability to carry out fast, incremental, and stable unsupervised and supervised learning in response to a changing world. ART specifies mechanistic links between processes of consciousness, learning, expectation, attention, resonance, and synchrony (the CLEARS processes) during both unsupervised and supervised learning. I have predicted that all brains that can solve the stability-plasticity dilemma do so using these predicted links between CLEARS processes. Indeed, my 41-year-old prediction that "all conscious states are resonant

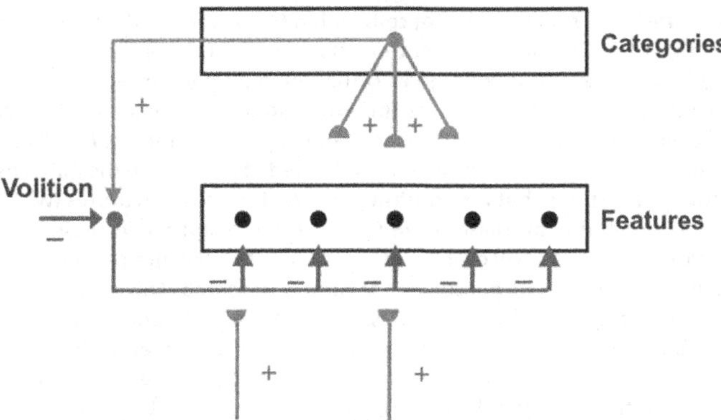

FIG. 4 ART matching rule. Bottom-up inputs can activate their target featural cells, other things being equal. A top-down expectation, by itself, can only modulate, prime, or sensitize cells in its excitatory on-center (*green* pathways (*gray* in print version) with hemicircular adaptive synapses) because of the wider off-surround (*red* pathways; *black* in print version) that tends to balance the top-down excitation ("one-against-one") within the on-center, while causing driving inhibition in the off-surround. When bottom-up inputs and a top-down expectation are both active, only cells where bottom-up excitation and the top-down excitatory prime converge in the on-center can fire ("two-against-one"), while other featural cells are inhibited.

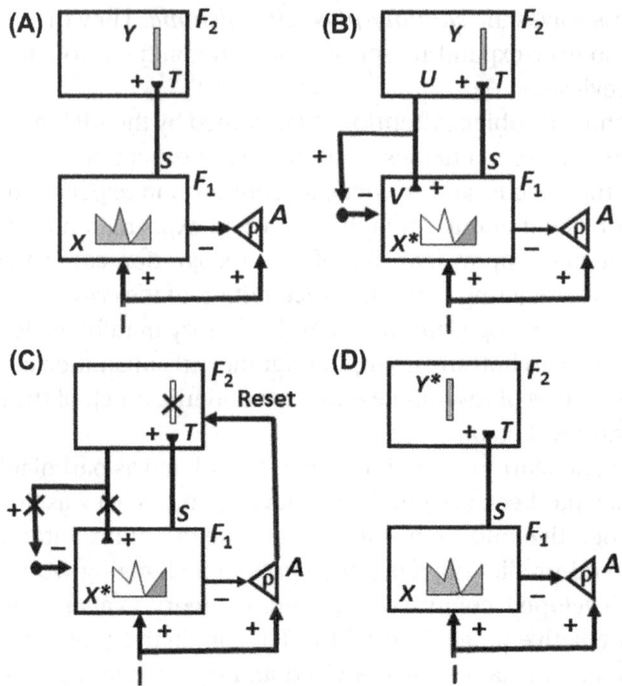

FIG. 5 How ART searches for and learns a new recognition category using cycles of match-induced resonance and mismatch-induced reset. (A) Input pattern I is instated across feature detectors at level F_1 as an activity pattern X, at the same time that it generates excitatory signals to the orienting system A with a gain ρ that is called the *vigilance* parameter. Activity pattern X generates inhibitory signals to the orienting system A as it generates a bottom-up input pattern S to the category level F_2. A dynamic balance within A between excitatory inputs from I and inhibitory inputs from S keeps S quiet. The bottom-up signals in S are multiplied by learned adaptive weights to form the input pattern T to F_2. The inputs T are contrast-enhanced and normalized within F_2 by recurrent lateral inhibitory signals that obey the membrane equations of neurophysiology, otherwise called shunting interactions. This competition leads to selection and activation of a small number of cells within F_2 that receive the largest inputs. The chosen cells represent the category Y that codes for the feature pattern at F_1. In this figure, a winner-take-all category is shown. (B) The category activity Y generates top-down signals U that are multiplied by adaptive weights to form a prototype, or critical feature pattern, V that encodes the expectation that the active F_2 category has learned for what feature pattern to expect at F_1. This top-down expectation input V is added at F_1 cells. If V mismatches I at F_1, then a new STM activity pattern X^* (the hatched pattern) is selected at cells where the patterns match well enough. In other words, X^* is active at I features that are confirmed by V. Mismatched features (*white* area) are inhibited. When X changes to X^*, total inhibition decreases from F_1 to A. (C) If inhibition decreases sufficiently, A releases a nonspecific arousal burst to F_2; that is, "novel events are arousing." The vigilance parameter ρ determines how bad a match will be tolerated before a burst of nonspecific arousal is triggered. This arousal burst triggers a memory search for a better-matching category, as follows: Arousal resets F_2 by inhibiting Y. (D) After Y is inhibited, X is reinstated and Y stays inhibited as X activates a different category, that is represented by a different activity pattern Y^*, at F_2. Search continues until a better matching, or novel, category is selected. When search ends, an attentive resonance triggers learning of the attended data in adaptive weights within both the bottom-up and top-down pathways. As learning stabilizes, inputs I can activate their globally best-matching categories directly through the adaptive filter, without activating the orienting system. *Adopted and reproduced with permission from G. Carpenter, S. Grossberg, Normal and amnesic learning, recognition, and memory by a neural model of cortico-hippocampal interactions, Trends Neurosci. 16 (1993) 131–137.*

states" is consistent with all the data that I know, and has helped to explain many data about consciousness, as will be briefly noted below.

ART hereby contributes to functional and mechanistic explanations of such diverse topics as 3D vision and figure-ground perception in natural scenes; optic-flow-based navigation in natural scenes toward goals around obstacles and spatial navigation in the dark; invariant object and scenic gist learning, recognition, and search; prototype, surface, and boundary attention; gamma and beta oscillations during cognitive dynamics; learning of entorhinal grid cells and hippocampal place cells, including the use of homologous spatial and temporal mechanisms in the medial entorhinal-hippocampal system for spatial navigation and the lateral stream for adaptively timed cognitive-emotional learning; breakdowns in attentive vigilance during autism, medial temporal amnesia, and Alzheimer's disease; social cognitive abilities such as the learning of joint attention and the use of tools from a teacher, despite the different coordinate systems of the teacher and learner; a unified circuit design for all item-order-rank working memories that enable stable learning of recognition categories, plans, and expectations for the representation and control of sequences of linguistic, spatial, and motor information; conscious speech percepts that are influenced by future context; auditory streaming in noise during source segregation; and speaker normalization that enables language learning from adults after a critical period of babbled sounds by a child; cognitive-emotional dynamics that direct motivated attention toward valued goals; and adaptive sensory-motor control circuits, such as those that coordinate predictive smooth pursuit and saccadic eye movements, and coordinate looking and reaching movements. Brain regions that are functionally described include visual and auditory neocortex; specific and nonspecific thalamic nuclei; inferotemporal, parietal, prefrontal, entorhinal, hippocampal, parahippocampal, perirhinal, and motor cortices; frontal eye fields; supplementary eye fields; amygdala; basal ganglia: cerebellum; and superior colliculus.

ART does not, however, describe many spatial and motor behaviors. These processes typically use different matching and learning laws. ART is thus not "a theory of everything."

6 Vector associative maps for spatial representation and action

Complementary spatial/motor processes in the Where stream often use inhibitory matching and mismatch-based learning to continually update spatial maps and sensory-motor gains that can effectively control our changing bodies throughout life. Inhibitory matching can take place between representations of where we want to move and where we are now (Fig. 6), so that when we arrive at where we want to be, the match equals zero. Inhibitory matching by the Vector Associative Map, or VAM, Matching Rule thus cannot solve the stability-plasticity dilemma [17,18]. That is why spatial and motor representations cannot support conscious qualia. Instead, spatial maps and motor gains experience catastrophic forgetting as they learn how to accurately control our changing bodies throughout life.

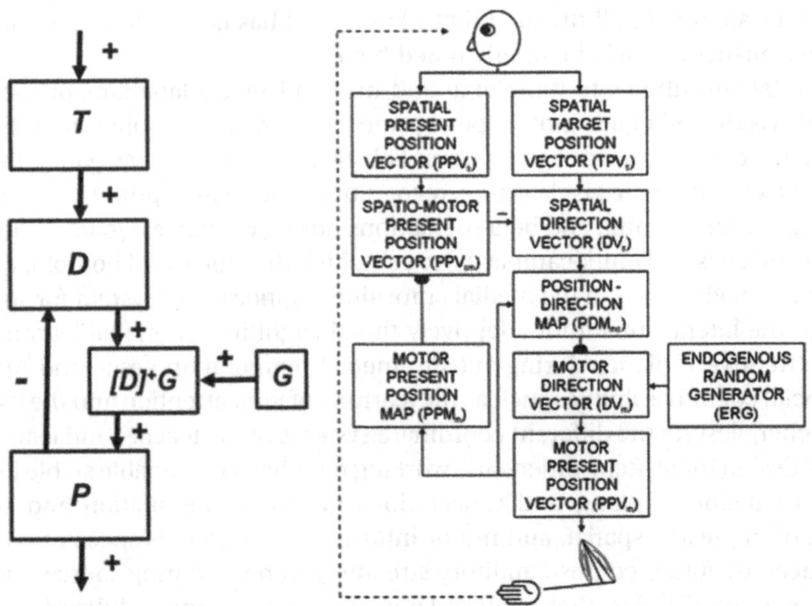

FIG. 6 *Left panel*: Vector integration to endpoint, or VITE, model circuit for reaching. A present position vector (P) is subtracted from a target position vector (T) to compute a difference vector (D) that represents the distance and direction in which the arm must move. The rectified difference vector ([D]) is multiplied by a volitional GO signal (G) before the velocity vector [D]G is integrated by P until P equals T, hence the model name vector integration to endpoint. *Right panel*: DIRECT model circuit. This refinement of VITE processing enables the brain to carry out what is called motor equivalent reaching, in particular to move a tool under visual guidance to its correct endpoint position on the first try, without measuring the dimensions of the tool or the angle that it makes with the hand. DIRECT hereby clarifies how a spatial affordance for tool use may have arisen from the ability of the brain to learn how to reach during infant development. In DIRECT, this developmental process uses an endogenous random generator, or ERG, to provide the "energy" during a critical period of motor babbling to activate a motor direction vector (DV_m) that moves the hand/arm via the motor present position vector (PPV_m). As the hand/arm moves, the eyes reactively track the position of the moving hand, giving rise to the visually-activated spatial target position vector (TPV_s) and spatial present position vector (PPV_s), which coincide during reactive tracking. These vectors are used to compute the spatial difference vector (DV_s). It is this spatial transformation, along with the mapping from spatial directions into motor directions, that gives the model its motor equivalent reaching capabilities. To compute these transformations, the PPV_s first activates the spatio-motor present position vector (PPV_{sm}), which is then subtracted from the TPV_s. As a result, the PPV_s signal that reaches the TPV_s is slightly delayed, thereby enabling the DV_s computation to occur. The PPV_{sm} stage is one of two stages in the model where spatial and motor representations are combined. The subscripts "s" and "m" denote spatial and motor, respectively. A transformation, called a *circular reaction* [19–21], is learned from spatial-to-motor and motor-to-spatial representations at the two adaptive pathways in the model, which are denoted by hemispherical synapses. In particular, the spatial direction vector (DV_s) is adaptively mapped into the motor direction vector (DV_m), thereby carrying out the transformation from visual *Direction Into* joint *Rotation* that gives the DIRECT model its name. *Left panel: Adopted and reproduced with permission from D. Bullock, S. Grossberg, Neural dynamics of planned arm movements: emergent invariants and speed-accuracy properties during trajectory formation, Psychol. Rev. 95 (1988) 49–90. Right panel: Reproduced with permission from D. Bullock, S. Grossberg, F.H. Guenther, A self-organizing neural model of motor equivalent reaching and tool use by a multijoint arm, J. Cogn. Neurosci. 5 (1993) 408–435.*

Together these complementary processes create a self-stabilizing perceptual/cognitive front end in the What stream for learning about the world and becoming conscious of it, while it intelligently commands more labile spatial/motor processes in the Where stream that control our changing bodies.

7 Homologous laminar cortical circuits for all biological intelligence: Beyond Bayes

The second computational paradigm is called laminar computing [2,14,22,23]. Laminar computing describes how the cerebral cortex is organized into layered circuits whose specializations support all higher-order biological intelligence. Indeed, the laminar circuits of cerebral cortex seem to realize a revolutionary computational synthesis of the best properties of feedforward and feedback processing, digital and analog processing, and data-driven bottom-up processing and hypothesis-driven top-down processing [14,24]. For example, in response to an unambiguous scene, a fast feedforward sweep can occur through the entire visual hierarchy, leading to rapid recognition, as reported by Thorpe et al. [25]. Such a feedforward sweep can occur, for example, in the LAMINART architecture [26,27] that is shown in Fig. 7 by leaping from retina to the lateral geniculate nucleus

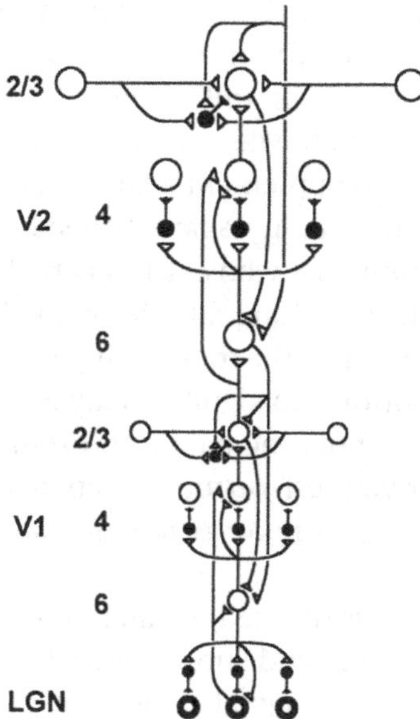

FIG. 7 The LAMINART model clarifies how bottom-up, horizontal, and top-down interactions within and across cortical layers in V1 and V2 interblob and pale stripe regions, respectively, carry out bottom-up adaptive filtering, horizontal grouping, and top-down attention to carry out perceptual grouping, including boundary completion. Similar interactions seem to occur in all six-layered cortices. See text for details. *Reproduced with permission from R. Raizada, S. Grossberg, Context-sensitive bindings by the laminar circuits of V1 and V2: a unified model of perceptual grouping, attention, and orientation contrast, Vis. Cogn. 8 (2001) 431–466.*

(LGN), then through layers 6, 4, and 2/3 in cortical area V1 to layers 6, 4, and 2/3 in cortical area V2, and beyond.

If, however, a scene contains ambiguous information, for example in the form of multiple possible groupings of the same sets of features in a complex textured scene, then the network can automatically use its feedback loops to make the best decision in the face of this uncertainty. In particular, competition among these groupings can occur due to inhibitory interneurons in layers 4 and 2/3 (black cells and synapses in Fig. 7). This competition can cause all cell activities to become smaller because the competitive circuits in the model are *self-normalizing*; that is, they tend to conserve the total activity of the circuit. This self-normalizing property arises from the ability of the shunting on-center off-surround networks that realize the competitive circuits to process input contrasts over a large dynamic range without saturation, and thereby solve what I have called the *noise-saturation dilemma* [28,29].

Self-normalizing competition among alternative cortical interpretations of the data may hereby reduce the activation amplitude and coherence of each grouping alternative, thereby slowing down its processing. This slowing down of processing rate occurs as interlaminar, but intracortical, feedback between layers 2/3-to-6-to-4-to-2/3 (Fig. 7), among other feedback pathways, contrast-enhances and amplifies the grouping that is supported by the most evidence. The amplification of the winning grouping's activity automatically speeds up its ability to send output signals to the next cortical region.

This example illustrates an important sense in which the cortex "runs as fast as it can" in response to the degree of uncertainty in the data, automatically switching from fast feedforward processing in response to unambiguous data to slower feedback processing to resolve uncertainties in the data to the degree that the data allow. Our brains hereby go beyond current Bayesian models to implement a kind of real-time probability theory and hypothesis testing that trades uncertainty against speed to make the best decisions in response to probabilistic environments whose rules can change rapidly through time.

Fig. 7 also depicts how the ART matching rule circuit in Fig. 4 is realized within the laminar circuits of neocortex. For example, the top-down pathway from layer 6 in V2 projects to layer 6 in V1, which sends bottom-up signals to layer 4. These bottom-up signals are sent via a modulatory on-center (note the balanced excitatory and inhibitory pathways to layer 4) surrounded by a driving off-surround network. The top-down signals from V2 are hereby "folded" at layer 6 in V1 in order to reach layer 4. I have accordingly called this property *folded feedback*.

Because the ART matching rule is realized within laminar neocortical circuits, they can solve the stability-plasticity dilemma and support rapid learning and stable memory.

Fig. 7 also shows that bottom-up signals from the LGN use the same modulatory on-center, off-surround network to activate layer 4 in V1 that is used by the top-down attentional feedback pathway. In addition, there is a direct bottom-up excitatory pathway from LGN to layer 4 so that the LGN can activate V1 in response to inputs from the retina. Taken together the direct LGN-to-4 pathway and the LGN-to-6-to-4 modulatory on-center, off-surround network ensures that bottom-up inputs from the LGN to V1 are contrast-normalized at layer 4 cells.

The sharing of the layer 6-to-4 modulatory on-center, off-surround network by bottom-up and top-down pathways converts this network into a decision interface where preattentive automatic bottom-up processing and attentive task-selective top-down processing can cooperate and compete to choose the combination of signals that is most salient at any given moment.

Such a cooperative-competitive decision interface exists in every granular neocortical area. As a result, a top-down task-selective priming signal from a higher cortical area can propagate through multiple lower cortical areas via their layers 6, which can then activate their layer 6-to-4 modulatory on-center, off-surround networks. In this way, an entire cortical hierarchy may get ready to process incoming bottom-up signals to accommodate the bias imposed by the prime.

Fig. 7 also shows that layer 2/3 in each cortical area also projects back to layer 6, and then up to layer 4 via the folded feedback network. The horizontal connections in layer 2/3 carry out a variety of functions in different cortical areas. In V2, they carry out perceptual grouping and boundary completion [30], a process whose so-called *bipole grouping* properties were predicted before the neurophysiological data of von der Heydt et al. were reported [31,32] and which were subsequently extensively modeled by LAMINART (e.g., [26,27,33,34]). In cognitive processing regions, such as the ventrolateral prefrontal cortex, it has been suggested that such horizontal connections enable learning of categories, also called *list chunks*, that respond selectively to sequences of items that are stored in working memory [35,36].

The development of these horizontal connections begins before birth and continues in response to the statistics of visual environments after birth. The fact that the layer 2/3-to-6-to-4-to-2/3 pathway satisfies the ART Matching Rule enables this development, as well as that of other cortical circuits, to dynamically self-stabilize even before higher cortical areas are developed enough to send reliable top-down intercortical attentional signals with which to further stabilize it. Thus "cells that fire together can wire together" without risking catastrophic forgetting in these laminar cortical circuits. I like to describe this property by saying that "the preattentive perceptual grouping is its own attentional prime" [22].

The above combination of properties illustrates how parsimoniously and elegantly laminar cortical circuits carry out their multifaceted functions.

The same canonical laminar design models vision, speech, and cognition: VLSI! Even elegant model designs must also support intelligent behavioral functions in order to provide compelling explanations of how brains work, and a guide for new technological developments. In fact, variations of the LAMINART cortical design have, to the present, been naturally embodied in laminar cortical models of vision, speech, and cognition that explain and predict psychological and neurobiological data that other models have not yet handled. These models include the 3D LAMINART model of 3D vision and figure-ground separation (e.g., [33,34,37–42]), the cARTWORD model of conscious speech perception [36,43], and the LIST PARSE model of cognitive working memory and chunking [35,44].

These models illustrate how *all* neocortical areas combine bottom-up, horizontal, and top-down interactions that embody variations of the same canonical laminar cortical circuitry that is illustrated by Fig. 7. These specialized laminar architectures hereby provide a blueprint for a general-purpose VLSI chip set whose specializations may be used to embody different kinds of biological intelligence as part of an autonomous adaptive agent. From the perspective of ART as a biological theory, they also illustrate how different resonances may use similar circuits to support different conscious experiences, as I will note in greater detail below.

8 Why a unified theory is possible: Equations, modules, and architectures

There are several fundamental mathematical reasons why it is possible for human scientists to discover a unified mind-brain theory that links brain mechanisms and psychological functions, and to demonstrate how similar organizational principles and mechanisms, suitably specialized, can support conscious qualia across modalities.

One reason for such intermodality unity is that a small number of equations suffices to model all modalities. These include equations for short-term memory, or STM; medium-term memory, or MTM; and long-term memory, or LTM, that I published in *The Proceedings of the National Academy of Sciences* in 1968. See Grossberg [13,14] for recent reviews of these equations.

These equations are used to define a somewhat larger number of modules, or microcircuits, that are also used in multiple modalities where they can carry out different functions within each modality. These modules include shunting on-center off-surround networks, gated dipole opponent processing networks, associative learning networks, spectral adaptively-timed learning networks, and the like. Each of these types of modules exhibits a rich, but not universal, set of useful computational properties. For example, shunting on-center off-surround networks can carry out properties like contrast-normalization, including discounting the illuminant; contrast-enhancement, noise suppression, and winner-take-all choice; short-term memory and working memory storage; attentive matching of bottom-up input patterns and top-down learned expectations; and synchronous oscillations and traveling waves.

Finally, these equations and modules are specialized and assembled into modal architectures, where "modal" stands for different modalities of biological intelligence, including architectures for vision, audition, cognition, cognitive-emotional interactions, and sensory-motor control.

An integrated self or agent, with autonomous adaptive capabilities, is possible because it builds on a shared set of equations and modules within modal architectures that can interact seamlessly together.

Modal architectures are *general-purpose,* in the sense that they can process any kind of inputs to that modality, whether from the external world or from other modal architectures. They are also *self-organizing,* in the sense that they can autonomously develop and learn in response to these inputs. Modal architectures are thus less general than the von Neumann architecture that provides the mathematical foundation of modern computers, but much more general than a traditional AI algorithm. ART networks form part of several different modal architectures, including modal architectures that enable seeing, hearing, feeling, and knowing.

9 All conscious states are resonant states

ART resonances clarify questions such as the following, which have been raised by distinguished philosophers [2]: What kind of "event" occurs in the brain during a conscious experience that is anything more than just a "whir of information-processing?" What happens when conscious mental states "light up" and directly appear to the subject? ART explains that, over and above "just" information processing, our brains sometimes go into a context-sensitive *resonant state* that can involve multiple brain regions. Abundant experimental evidence supports the ART prediction that "all conscious states are resonant states." Not all brain dynamics are "resonant," and thus consciousness is not just a "whir of information-processing."

Second, when does a resonant state embody a conscious experience? And how do different resonant states support different kinds of conscious qualia? The other side of the coin is equally important: When does a resonant state fail to embody a conscious experience? ART explains [2] how various evolutionary challenges that advanced brains face in order to adapt to changing environments in real time have been met with particular conscious states, which form part of larger adaptive behavioral capabilities. ART sheds new mechanistic light on the fact that humans are not conscious just to Platonically contemplate the beauty of the world. Rather, humans are conscious in order to enable them to better adapt to the world's changing demands. To illustrate these claims, ART explains how resonances for conscious seeing help to ensure effective looking and reaching, resonances for conscious hearing help to ensure effective speaking, and resonances for conscious feeling help to ensure effective goal-directed action.

10 The varieties of brain resonances and the conscious experiences that they support

Toward this end, ART has explained six different types of neural representations of conscious qualia and has provided enough theoretical background and data explanations based on these representations to illustrate their explanatory and predictive power [2]. These explanations also suggest multiple kinds of experiments to deepen our mechanistic understanding of the brain mechanisms for generating conscious resonances.

For example, *surface-shroud resonances* are predicted to support conscious percepts of visual qualia. *Feature-category resonances* are predicted to support conscious recognition of visual objects and scenes. Both kinds of resonances may synchronize during conscious seeing and recognition, so that we know what a familiar object is when we consciously see it. *Stream-shroud resonances* are predicted to support conscious percepts of auditory qualia. *Spectral-pitch-and-timbre resonances* are predicted to support conscious recognition of sources in auditory streams. Stream-shroud and spectral-pitch-and-timbre resonances may synchronize during conscious hearing and recognition of auditory streams, so that we know what the familiar sounds are that are segregated in a stream. *Item-list resonances* are predicted to support recognition of speech and language. They may synchronize with stream-shroud and spectral-pitch-and-timbre resonances during conscious hearing of speech and language, and build upon the selection of auditory sources by spectral-pitch-and-timbre resonances in order to recognize the acoustical signals that are grouped together within these streams. *Cognitive-emotional resonances* are predicted to support conscious percepts of feelings, as well as recognition of the source of these feelings. Cognitive-emotional resonances can also synchronize with resonances that support conscious qualia and knowledge about them. All of these resonances have distinct anatomical substrates that are explained in Grossberg [2], which also explains various psychological and neurobiological data from typical and clinical individuals.

11 Why does resonance trigger consciousness?

Detailed analyses of psychological and neurobiological data by ART clarify why resonance is necessary for consciousness. As one example: In order to fully compute visual boundaries and surfaces whereby to see the world, the brain computes three pairs of complementary computational properties of boundaries and surfaces (Fig. 8), along with three hierarchical resolutions of uncertainty that require multiple processing stages to overcome. This example illustrates that there is a great deal of uncertainty in the early stages of visual processing by the brain. Only after all three hierarchical resolutions of uncertainty are complete, and after boundaries are completed and surfaces filled-in, has the brain constructed a contextually informative and temporally stable enough representation of scenic objects on which to base adaptive behaviors.

If this is indeed the case, then why do not the earlier stages undermine behavior? The proposed answer is that *brain resonance, and with it conscious awareness, is triggered at the processing stage that represents visual boundary and surface representations, after they are complete and stable enough to control visually-based behaviors like attentive looking and reaching.* ART also explains how, after such a resonance is triggered between prestriate visual cortex and parietal cortex, it can propagate bottom-up to higher cortical areas, such as prefrontal cortex, and top-down to earlier cortical and LGN processing areas, using the ART matching rule (Fig. 4) to select data that consistent with the triggering resonance and to suppress inconsistent information.

12 Toward autonomous adaptive intelligent agents and clinical therapies in society

The above summary suggests that a firm foundation has been built over the past 50 years whereby discoveries about mind and brain can greatly influence the development of technologies that can have a profound impact on society, and can facilitate a deeper mechanistic understanding of several major mental disorders. The technological developments

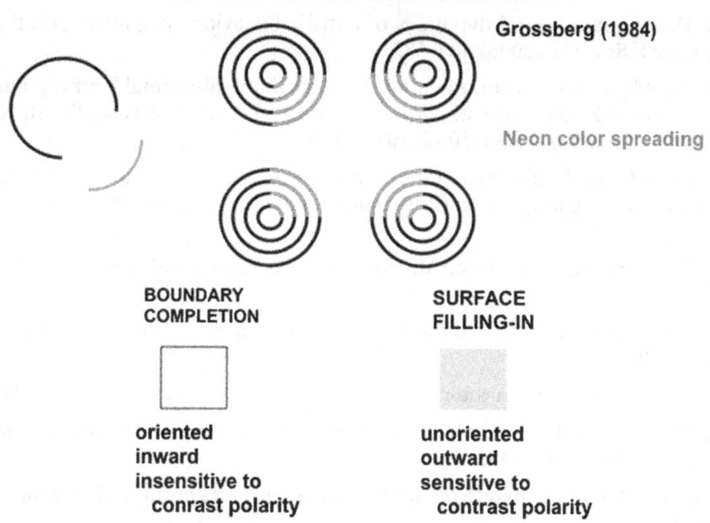

FIG. 8 Complementary computational properties of visual boundaries and surfaces. Visual boundaries and surfaces are computed by the interblob and blob cortical processing streams, respectively, that occur within and between cortical areas V1, V2, and V4. An illusory square is completed in response to the configuration of *black* and *blue* (*light gray* in print version) arcs that form the image. When this happens, breaks, called end gaps, occur in the boundaries where the *black* arcs touch the *blue* (*light gray* in print version) arcs. *Blue* (*light gray* in print version) color can then flow out of the *blue* (*light gray* in print version) arcs to fill-in the interior of the illusory square. The resulting percept of *neon* (*light gray* in print version) color spreading illustrates complementary properties of boundary completion and surface filling-in [32,45], namely: Boundaries are completed in an *oriented* way, *inward* between pairs or greater numbers of inducers with similar orientational preferences, and are *insensitive* to contrast polarity, in the sense that they pool over opposite contrast polarities using V1 complex cells at each position. In contrast, surfaces fill-in brightness and surface color in an *unoriented* way, *outward* from individual contrastive inducers, and are *sensitive* to contrast polarity, indeed support the visible qualia that observers can consciously see. These three pairs of boundary and surface properties (oriented vs unoriented, inward vs outward, insensitive vs sensitive to contrast polarity) are manifestly complementary. Properties that are needed to complete a boundary cannot be used to fill-in a surface, and conversely. On the other hand, boundaries and surfaces need to reciprocally interact across the interblob and blob stream for either of them to generate a useful percept.

will include increasingly autonomous adaptive agents, whereas new clinical therapies for mental disorders will benefit from understanding the neural mechanisms can cause their behavioral symptoms.

References

[1] S. Grossberg, Conscious Mind, Resonant Brain: How Each Brain Makes a Mind, Oxford University Press, New York, 2021.

[2] S. Grossberg, Towards solving the hard problem of consciousness: the varieties of brain resonances and the conscious experiences that they support, Neural Netw. 87 (2017) 38–95.

[3] G. Carpenter, S. Grossberg, Normal and amnesic learning, recognition, and memory by a neural model of cortico-hippocampal interactions, Trends Neurosci. 16 (1993) 131–137.

[4] S. Grossberg, The imbalanced brain: from normal behavior to schizophrenia, Biol. Psychiatry 48 (2000) 81–98.

[5] S. Grossberg, D. Seidman, Neural dynamics of autistic behaviors: cognitive, emotional, and timing substrates, Psychol. Rev. 113 (2006) 483–525.

[6] S. Grossberg, Acetylcholine neuromodulation in normal and abnormal learning and memory: vigilance control in waking, sleep, autism, amnesia, and Alzheimer's disease, Front. Neural Circuits 2 (2017) 2017, https://doi.org/10.3389/fncir.2017.00082.

[7] S. Grossberg, D. Kishnan, Neural dynamics of autistic repetitive behaviors and Fragile X syndrome: basal ganglia movement gating and mGluR-modulated adaptively timed learning, Front. Psychol. 9 (2018) 269.

[8] S. Grossberg, The complementary brain: unifying brain dynamics and modularity, Trends Cogn. Sci. 4 (2000) 233–246.

[9] D.J. Felleman, D.C. Van Essen, Distributed hierarchical processing by the primate cerebral cortex, Cereb. Cortex 1 (1991) 1–47.

[10] M. Mishkin, A memory system in the monkey, Philos. Trans. R. Soc. Lond. B 298 (1982) 85–95.

[11] M. Mishkin, L.G. Ungerleider, K.A. Macko, Object vision and spatial vision: two cortical pathways, Trends Neurosci. 6 (1983) 414–417.

[12] M.A. Goodale, A.D. Milner, Separate visual pathways for perception and action, Trends Neurosci. 15 (1992) 20–25.

[13] S. Grossberg, Adaptive Resonance Theory, Scholarpedia, 2013. http://www.scholarpedia.org/article/Adaptive_resonance_theory.

[14] S. Grossberg, Adaptive resonance theory: How a brain learns to consciously attend, learn, and recognize a changing world, Neural Netw. 37 (2013) 1–47.

[15] S. Grossberg, Adaptive pattern classification and universal recoding, I: parallel development and coding of neural feature detectors, Biol. Cybern. 23 (1976) 121–134.

[16] S. Grossberg, Adaptive pattern classification and universal recoding, II: feedback, expectation, olfaction, and illusions, Biol. Cybern. 23 (1976) 187–202.

[17] P. Gaudiano, S. Grossberg, Vector associative maps: unsupervised real-time error-based learning and control of movement trajectories, Neural Netw. 4 (1991) 147–183.

[18] P. Gaudiano, S. Grossberg, Adaptive vector integration to endpoint: self-organizing neural circuits for control of planned movement trajectories, Hum. Mov. Sci. 11 (1992) 141–155.

[19] J. Piaget, La Formation du Symbole Chez L'enfant, Delachaux Niestle, S.A, Paris, 1945.

[20] J. Piaget, Play, Dreams and Imitation in Childhood (C. Gattegno and C.F.M. Hodgson, Transl.), Roudedge and Kegan Paul, London, 1951.

[21] J. Piaget, The Origins of Intelligence in Children, International Universities Press, New York, 1952.

[22] S. Grossberg, How does the cerebral cortex work? Learning, attention and grouping by the laminar circuits of visual cortex, Spat. Vis. 12 (1999) 163–186.

[23] S. Grossberg, E. Mingolla, W.D. Ross, Visual brain and visual perception: how does the cortex do perceptual grouping? Trends Neurosci. 20 (1997) 106–111.

[24] S. Grossberg, Consciousness CLEARS the mind, Neural Netw. 20 (2007) 1040–1053.

[25] S. Thorpe, D. Fize, C. Marlot, Speed of processing in the human visual system, Nature 381 (1996) 520–522.

[26] S. Grossberg, R. Raizada, Contrast-sensitive perceptual grouping and object-based attention in the laminar circuits of primary visual cortex, Vis. Res. 40 (2000) 1413–1432.

[27] R. Raizada, S. Grossberg, Context-sensitive bindings by the laminar circuits of V1 and V2: a unified model of perceptual grouping, attention, and orientation contrast, Vis. Cogn. 8 (2001) 431–466.

[28] S. Grossberg, Contour enhancement, short term memory, and constancies in reverberating neural networks, Stud. Appl. Math. 52 (1973) 213–257.

[29] S. Grossberg, Intracellular mechanisms of adaptation and self-regulation in self-organizing networks: the role of chemical transducers, Bull. Math. Biol. 42 (3) (1980) 365–396.

[30] R. von der Heydt, E. Peterhans, G. Baumgartner, Illusory contours and cortical neuron responses, Science 224 (1984) 1260–1262.

[31] M.A. Cohen, S. Grossberg, Neural dynamics of brightness perception: features, boundaries, diffusion, and resonance, Percept. Psychophys. 36 (1984) 428–456.

[32] S. Grossberg, Outline of a theory of brightness, color, and form perception, in: E. Degreef, J. van Buggenhaut (Eds.), Trends in Mathematical Psychology, North-Holland, Amsterdam, 1984, pp. 59–86.

[33] S. Grossberg, A. Yazdanbakhsh, Laminar cortical dynamics of 3D surface perception: stratification, transparency, and neon color spreading, Vis. Res. 45 (2005) 1725–1743.

[34] J. Leveille, M. Versace, S. Grossberg, Running as fast as it can: how spiking dynamics form object groupings in the laminar circuits of visual cortex, J. Comput. Neurosci. 28 (2010) 323–346.

[35] S. Grossberg, L. Pearson, Laminar cortical dynamics of cognitive and motor working memory, sequence learning and performance: toward a unified theory of how the cerebral cortex works, Psychol. Rev. 115 (2008) 677–732.

[36] S. Kazerounian, S. Grossberg, Real-time learning of predictive recognition categories that chunk sequences of items stored in working memory, Front. Psychol. (2014), https://doi.org/10.3389/fpsyg.2014.01053.

[37] Y. Cao, S. Grossberg, A laminar cortical model of stereopsis and 3D surface perception: closure and da Vinci stereopsis, Spat. Vis. 18 (2005) 515–578.

[38] Y. Cao, S. Grossberg, Stereopsis and 3D surface perception by spiking neurons in laminar cortical circuits: a method of converting neural rate models into spiking models, Neural Netw. 26 (2012) 75–98.

[39] L. Fang, S. Grossberg, From stereogram to surface: how the brain sees the world in depth, Spat. Vis. 22 (2009) 45–82.

[40] S. Grossberg, P.D.L. Howe, A laminar cortical model of stereopsis and three-dimensional surface perception, Vis. Res. 43 (2003) 801–829.

[41] S. Grossberg, G. Swaminathan, A laminar cortical model for 3D perception of slanted and curved surfaces and of 2D images: development, attention and bistability, Vis. Res. 44 (2004) 1147–1187.

[42] S. Grossberg, A. Yazdanbakhsh, Y. Cao, G. Swaminathan, How does binocular rivalry emerge from cortical mechanisms of 3-D vision? Vis. Res. 48 (2008) 2232–2250.

[43] S. Grossberg, S. Kazerounian, Laminar cortical dynamics of conscious speech perception: a neural model of phonemic restoration using subsequent context in noise, J. Acoust. Soc. Am. 130 (2011) 440–460.

[44] M.R. Silver, S. Grossberg, D. Bullock, M.H. Histed, E.K. Miller, A neural model of sequential movement planning and control of eye movements: item-order-rank working memory and saccade selection by the supplementary eye fields, Neural Netw. 26 (2011) 29–58.

[45] S. Grossberg, E. Mingolla, Neural dynamics of form perception: boundary completion, illusory figures, and neon color spreading, Psychol. Rev. 92 (1985) 173–211.

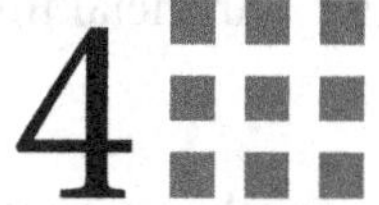

Meaning versus information, prediction versus memory, and question versus answer

Yoonsuck Choe
DEPARTMENT OF COMPUTER SCIENCE AND ENGINEERING, TEXAS A&M UNIVERSITY, COLLEGE STATION, TX, UNITED STATES

Chapter outlines

1 Introduction

Brain and neuroscience, psychology, artificial intelligence, all strive to understand and replicate the functioning of the human mind. Advanced methods for imaging, monitoring, and altering the activity of the brain at the whole-brain scale are now available, allowing us to probe the brain in unprecedented detail. These methods include high-resolution 3D imaging (using both physical [serial] sectioning and optical sectioning), monitoring ongoing neural activity (e.g., calcium imaging), and selective activation of genetically specific neurons (optogenetics). On the other hand, in artificial intelligence, deep learning based on decades-old neural networks research made exponential progress, and it is now routinely beating human performance in many areas including object recognition and game playing.

However, despite such progress in both fields, there are still many open questions. In brain science, one of the main questions is how to put together the many detailed experimental results into a system-level understanding of brain function. Also, there is the ultimate question to understand the phenomenon of consciousness. In artificial intelligence research, especially in deep learning, there are lingering issues of robustness (e.g., deep

Artificial Intelligence in the Age of Neural Networks and Brain Computing. https://doi.org/10.1016/B978-0-323-96104-2.00003-8
Copyright © 2024 Elsevier Inc. All rights reserved.

neural networks are easily fooled by slightly altered inputs such as adversarial inputs), and interpretability (deep neural networks are basically a black box, and humans do not understand why or how they work so well).

In this essay, I will talk about some of the concepts that are central to brain science and artificial intelligence, such as information and memory, and discuss how a slightly different view on these concepts can help us move forward, beyond current limits of our understanding in these fields.

The rest of this chapter is organized as follows. In Section 2, I will discuss meaning vs information, with an emphasis on the need to consider the sensorimotor nature of brain function. In Section 3, I will talk about prediction and memory, in the context of synaptic plasticity and brain dynamics. In Section 4, I will move on to a broader topic of question vs answer, and discuss how this dichotomy is relevant to both brain science and artificial intelligence. Section 5 will include some further discussions, followed by conclusions (Section 6).

2 Meaning vs information

The concepts of computing and information have fundamentally altered the way we think about everything, including brain function and artificial intelligence. In analyzing the brain and in building and interpreting intelligent artifacts, computing has become a powerful metaphor, and information has become the fundamental unit of processing and measurement. We think about the brain and artificial neural networks in terms of computing and information processing and measure their information content. In this section, I will talk mostly about information.

First of all, what is information? We tend to use this word in a very loose sense, and information defined in this way is imbued with meaning (or semantic content). In a scientific/engineering discussion, information usually refers to the definition given in Claude Shannon's information theory [1]. In information theory, information is based on the probability of occurrence of each piece of message, and the concept is used to derive optimal bounds on the transmission of data.

However, there can be an issue if we try to use Shannon's definition of information in our everyday sense, since as Shannon explicitly stated in his primary work on information theory, information defined as such does not have any meaning attached to it. So, for example, in an engineered information system, when we store information or transmit information, the data themselves do not have meaning. The meaning only resides in the human who accesses and views the information. All the processing and transmission in the information system is at a symbolic level, not at a semantic level.

Philosopher John Searle's paper on the "Chinese room argument" [2] made clear of the limitation of the computational/information processing view of cognition. Inside the Chinese room, there is an English monolingual person with all the instructions for processing Chinese language. The room has two mail slots, one for input, and one for output.

A Chinese speaker standing outside the room writes down something (in Chinese) on a piece of paper and deposits it in the input slot, and the English speaker inside will process the information based on the instructions present in the room and meticulously draw (not write) the answer on a piece of paper and returns it through the output slot. From the outside, the Chinese room speaks and understands perfect Chinese, but there is no true understanding of Chinese in this system. The main problem is that the information within the room lacks meaning, and this is why grounding is necessary; grounding in the sense that information is grounded in reality, not hovering above in an abstract realm of symbols (see Stevan Harnad's concept of symbol grounding [3]). Many current artificial intelligence systems including deep learning tend to lack such grounding, and this can lead to brittleness, since these systems simply learn the input output mapping, without understanding.

Thus, we need to think in terms of the meaning of the information, how semantic grounding is to be done: How does the brain ground information within itself? (See [4] for a similar approach, the "inside-out" approach, in neuroscience.) How can artificial intelligence systems ground information within itself? What is the nature of such grounding? Perceptual? Referential? This can be a very complex problem, so let us consider a greatly simplified scenario.

Suppose you are sitting inside a totally dark room, and you only observe the occasional blinking of some light bulbs (Fig. 1). You count the bulbs, and it looks like there are four of them. Each of these bulbs seem to be representing some information, but you are unsure what they mean. So, here you have a classic symbol grounding problem. The light bulbs are like symbols, and they represent something. However, sitting inside this room, it seems that there is no way you can figure out the meaning of these blinking lights. Now consider that the dark room is the primary visual cortex (V1), and the four light bulbs are neurons that represent something, and in place of you, we put inside the room the downstream visual areas (Fig. 2A). With our reasoning above, it would suggest that the downstream visual areas have no way to understand the meaning of V1 activities. Paradoxically, the problem seems to be trivial, if seen from the outside (Fig. 2B). This is absurd, since humans have no problem with visual understanding, even without any knowledge of how the orientation-tuned neurons in the visual cortex work!

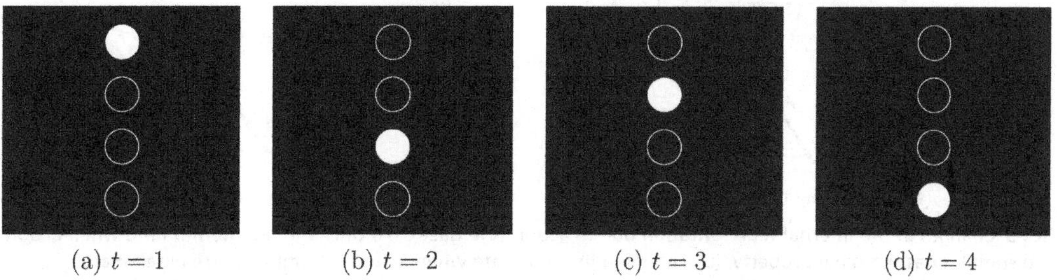

(a) $t = 1$ (b) $t = 2$ (c) $t = 3$ (d) $t = 4$

FIG. 1 Inside a black box. There are four lights that blink at different times. What do they mean?

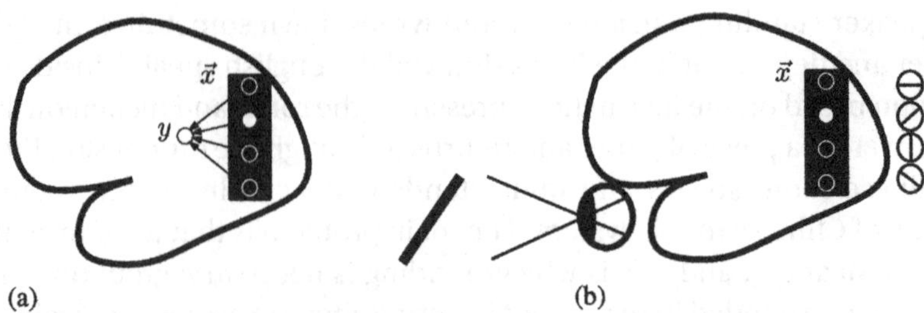

FIG. 2 Brain, from the inside and from the outside. (A) From the inside, the neural activity in the simple visual cortex $\vec{x}$ cannot be deciphered by the downstream neuron y, just by looking at $\vec{x}$. (B) From the outside, by presenting different input stimuli in the environment (e.g., a 45-degree diagonal line), and observing which neurons are activated in $\vec{x}$ (e.g., the second neuron from the top) when that input is presented, we can tell what the neurons in $\vec{x}$ represent (the four angles shown to the right).

It turns out that this problem can only be solved if we allow motor interaction from within the system. Inside the dark room, we can install a joystick connected to an external camera, and the person sitting inside can move it around and see how the joystick movement relates to the changes in the blinking light in a systematic manner. Consider the case where the four light bulbs represent four different orientations 0 degrees, 45 degrees, 90 degrees, and 135 degrees, respectively. How can movement of the joystick reveal the meaning of these light bulbs? We can map this scenario into the brain (Fig. 2A), and consider the joystick as the eye movement signal in the motor cortex (Fig. 3).

Let us first consider what is happening inside the brain (Fig. 3A, "Inside," top row). The second neuron is turned on, and the eye movement (dashed arrow) is along 45 degrees. In the next step (Fig. 3A, "Inside," bottom row), the eye movement is along 225 degrees. The two states can alternate, and curiously the second neuron keeps on firing and all other neurons are silent. Now, let us see what's happening in the environment. There is a long 45-degree line in the external environment, and the gaze (circle) is tracing along this line

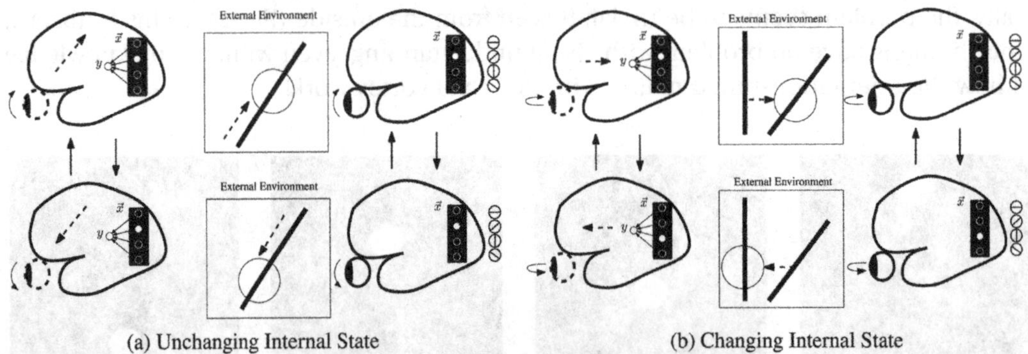

FIG. 3 Changes in the internal representation due to action (eye gaze). (A) Unchanging internal state when action and stimulus has the same property. (B) Changing internal state when action and stimulus are misaligned.

in the 45-degree direction (Fig. 3A, "Outside," top row). In the next step (Fig. 3A, "Outside," bottom row), the gaze is tracing backward in the 225-degree direction. Of course, this "outside" perspective is not known to the observer "inside." However, by discovering a specific type of action (45–225-degree back-and-forth movement) that keeps the internal state invariant (the second neuron), the property of the internal representation (45-degree orientation) can be inferred.

This kind of internal state invariance breaks down when the property of the action is not aligned with the property of the internal representation, as we can see in Fig. 3B. In this case, back-and-forth horizontal movement (top row to bottom row, etc.) leads to alternating internal states (second neuron is active, then the third neuron is active, and the same sequence repeats).

Through this kind of sensorimotor exploration, the property of the internal representation can be recovered, from within the system without direct perceptual access to the external environment, thus the meaning can remain intrinsic to the system.

In our lab, we explored these ideas in a reinforcement learning setting (learn a policy p that maps from state S [orientation] to action A [gaze direction]), where we showed that the internal state invariance criterion can be used as a reward for motor grounding of internal sensory representations in a simple visuomotor agent. See [5] and subsequent works for more details.

To sum up, meaning is central to brain science and artificial intelligence, and to provide meaning to information (i.e., grounding), it is critical to consider the sensorimotor aspect of the information system, whether natural or artificial.

3 Prediction vs memory

Many questions in brain and neuroscience focus on the concept of plasticity, how the brain changes and adapts due to experience, and this leads to the question of memory. Connections between neurons adapt over time (synaptic plasticity: long term, short term, etc.), and ongoing neural dynamic of the brain can also be altered by the immediate input stimulus. On a higher level, plasticity is usually considered in relation to various forms of memory: long-term memory, short-term memory, working memory, episodic memory, implicit memory, explicit memory, etc. Also, in a commonsense way, people ask how the brain remembers, and what constitutes memory in the brain. In artificial intelligence, the same is true: How information should be represented, stored, and retrieved; how connection weights should be adapted in artificial neural networks to store knowledge; and how neural networks can be used to utilize external memory, etc.

What is memory, and how is it related to prediction, and why should we think more about prediction than memory? Memory is backward looking, directed toward the past, while prediction is forward looking, and is directed toward the future. Memory enables prediction, since without memory, the system will be purely reactive, living in the eternal present. So, again, why should we direct our attention toward prediction? In terms of brain function and artifacts that try to mimic it, prediction is of prime importance. In our everyday life, moment to moment prediction and long-term prediction play a critical role. Simple tasks as walking, navigating, and many daily activities involving interaction with the environment and with other humans require prediction. Long-term predictions of phenomena such as seasonal changes enable planning and improved productivity. So, in a sense, prediction is an important brain function, and it is increasingly being recognized as a central function of the brain as well as a key ingredient in intelligent machines (for an overview of related ideas, see Andy Clark's paper [6], and various papers on the use of predicted future states in reinforcement learning [7]).

In this section, I will talk about how such predictive function could have emerged in the brain, how it is related to synaptic plasticity mechanisms (memory), how it is relevant to the study of neural networks, and how predictive properties in the brain can be linked to higher-level phenomena such as consciousness.

First, consider delay in the nervous system. Neurons send their signals to their receiving neurons via elongated wires called axons. Transmission through these axons can take few milliseconds (ms), the duration depending on various factors such as the length, diameter, and whether the axon is insulated with myelin or not. When you add up the delay, it comes to a significant amount of time: about 180–260 ms from stimulus presentation to behavioral reaction [8]. This kind of delay may be considered bad for the system, since it can be a matter of life and death, especially for fast moving animals. Also, in engineering systems, delay is considered a great hindrance. However, delay can be useful in two ways: (1) in a reactive system such as a feedforward neural network, addition of delay in the input can effectively add memory, and (2) mechanisms evolved to counteract the adverse effects of delay can naturally lead to predictive capabilities.

In [9], we showed that addition of delay in feedforward neural network controller can solve a 2D pole balancing problem that does not include velocity input. Also, in a series of works we showed that certain forms of synaptic plasticity (dynamic synapses) can be considered as a delay compensation mechanism, and how it relates to curious perceptual phenomena such as the flash lag effect (see [10] for an overview). In flash lag effect, a moving object is perceived as being ahead of a statically flashed object that is spatially aligned (Fig. 4). One explanation for this phenomenon is that the brain is compensating for the delay in its system, by generating an illusion that is aligned, in real time, with the current state of the external environment. For example, image of the two aligned objects hit the retina (Fig. 4, $t=3$). The information takes several milliseconds to reach the visual area in the brain (Fig. 4, $t=4$, bottom row). In the meanwhile, the gray object moves ahead (Fig. 4, $t=4$, top row, gray box), so by the time the two objects are perceived (when the information arrives in the visual area at $t=4$), in the environment, they are misaligned because the moving object has moved on. The argument is that flash lag effect allows the brain to perceive this as misaligned objects, which is more in line with the actual environmental state at the time of perception ($t=4$). We showed that facilitating neural dynamics, based on dynamic synapses (the facilitating kind, not the depressing kind: See Markram and colleagues' works cited in [10]) can replicate this phenomenon, and furthermore, the use

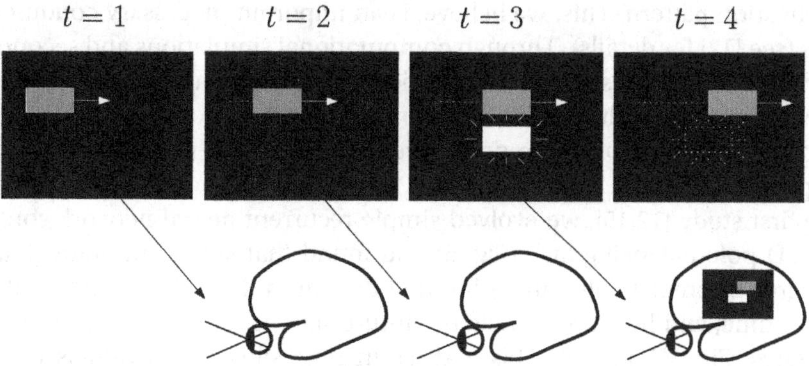

FIG. 4 Flash lag effect. The *white* bar is flashed briefly ($t = 3$) when the moving bar *(gray)* passes its location. This event is perceived as staggered (as shown inside the brain in the bottom right, $t = 4$), not vertically aligned (as shown in $t = 3$).

of spike-timing-dependent plasticity (STDP) can help explain more complex phenomena such as orientation flash lag effect (see [10] and references within).

Second, we will consider predictive properties in brain dynamics and how it can be related to higher-level phenomena such as consciousness. As we discussed above, prediction seems to be a key function of the brain. How can it also be used to gain insights into phenomena such as consciousness? In consciousness studies, the neural correlate is highly sought after, where neural correlates of consciousness refer to the "… neural events and structures … sufficient for conscious percept or conscious memory" [11]. This view is somewhat static (of course it depends on the definition of "event"), and its dependence on sufficient conditions can lead to issues relating to the hard problem of consciousness—how and why it "feels" like it. In our view, it would be better to first consider the necessary conditions of consciousness, and this led us to the realization that the property of brain dynamics, not just isolated "events," need to be considered. We also found that predictive property in brain dynamics has an important role to play in consciousness, and this is how the discussion of consciousness comes into the picture in this section [12].

Let us consider necessary conditions of consciousness. We begin by considering consciousness and its subject. There cannot be a consciousness without a subject, since consciousness, being a subjective phenomenon, cannot be subjective without a subject (see [13] pp 191–193, on how sensations "belonging to a subject" is a major property of consciousness). Next, consider the property of the subject (or let us say "self"). Self is the author of its own actions, and there is a very peculiar property about these actions authored by the self—that it is 100% predictable. When I say "I will clap my hands in 5 seconds", in 5 s, I will make sure that happens, so that my behavior in such a case is 100% predictable, by myself but not by others. This is quite unlike most phenomena in the world that are not so much the case. In order to support such a prediction, some part of the brain has to have a dynamic pattern that has a predictable property. That is, based on past activation patterns in the neural dynamic trajectory, it needs to be possible to predict the current activation pattern. This, we believe, is an important necessary condition of consciousness (see [12] for details). Through computational simulations and secondary analysis of public EEG data, we showed that predictive dynamics can emerge and have fitness advantage in synthetic evolution [12], and conscious states such as awake condition and REM sleep condition exhibit more predictive dynamics than unconscious states (slow-wave sleep) [14].

For the first study [12,15], we evolved simple recurrent neural network controllers to tackle the 2D pole-balancing task (Fig. 5) and found that successful individuals have a varying degree of predictability in its internal dynamics (how the hidden unit activities change over time, and how predictable the future state is, given a short time window in the past states: Fig. 5C and D). This is discouraging, since if individuals with internal dynamics with high (Fig. 5C) or low predictability (Fig. 5D) are equally good in behavioral performance, predictive dynamics may not evolve to dominate. However, a slight change in the environment made individuals with high predictive dynamics to proliferate. The only change necessary was to make the task a little harder (make the initial random tilt of the pole to be more). This suggests that predictive internal dynamics have a fitness advantage when the environment changes over time, and this happens to be how the nature is, thus predictive dynamics will become dominant. Not the strongest or the fastest species survive: The most adaptable species survive, where prediction seems to be the key, and this helps satisfy the necessary condition for consciousness.

In the second study [14], we analyzed publicly available brain EEG data collected during awake, rapid eye movement (REM) sleep, and slow-wave sleep. Since awake and vivid dreaming (REM sleep) are associated with consciousness while deep sleep (slow-wave sleep) with unconsciousness, we measured the predictability in these EEG signal wave forms. We preprocessed the raw EEG signal, computed the interpeak interval (IPI), the time distance between peaks in the EEG signal, and measured how easy it is to predict

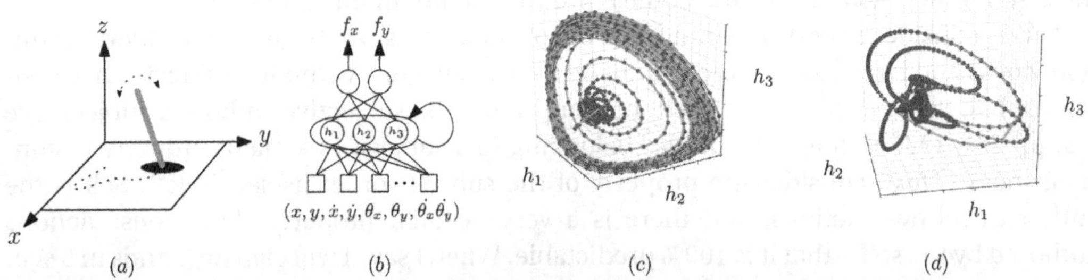

FIG. 5 2D pole balancing. (A) The 2D pole balancing task. (B) Recurrent neural network controller. Inputs are the location of the cart and angles of the pole and their respective velocities, and the outputs are the force to be applied in the x and the y direction. (C) Internal dynamics example 1 (hidden states h_1, h_2, h_3 plotted over time in 3D). (D) Internal dynamics example 2. Both (C) and (D) are from successful controllers. *(C and D) Based on J. Kwon, Y. Choe, Internal state predictability as an evolutionary precursor of self-awareness and agency, in: Conference Proceedings of the Seventh International Conference on Development and Learning, 2008, with permission from IEEE.*

the next IPI based on previous IPI data points. We found that awake and REM EEG signals have higher IPI predictability than that of slow-wave sleep, suggesting that IPI predictability and consciousness may be correlated.

In this section, I discussed how synaptic plasticity mechanisms can be directly linked to prediction, how delay in the nervous system may have led to predictive capabilities, and how predictive dynamics can serve as a precursor of consciousness. In sum, prediction is a key aspect of the brain, and it should also be considered when designing intelligent artifacts.

4 Question vs answer

In both brain science and artificial intelligence, the general focus is to understand how the brain solves problems relating to perceptual, cognitive, and motor tasks, or how to make artificial intelligence algorithms solve problems in vision, natural language processing, game playing, robot control, etc. That is, we are focused on mechanisms that produce answers, and less on mechanisms that pose the questions. Of course, we know the importance of asking the right questions, and any researcher is well aware of the importance of picking the right research question. Often times, research involves finding new ways to conceive of the problem, rather than finding new ways of solving problems as conceived [16], and this is especially essential when the conceived problem itself is ill-formed so as to be unsolvable (e.g., "how can we prove Euclid's 5th postulate" [unsolvable], vs "can we prove Euclid's 5th postulate" [solvable]).

In 2012, Mann and I discussed in [17] the need to start paying attention to problem posing, as opposed to (or in addition to) problem solving, in artificial intelligence. It turns out that problem posing has been an active topic in the education literature (see [18] and many subsequent publications), and these works show that learning and problem posing are intricately related. However, this angle is not explored much in artificial intelligence, except for rare exceptions, and I strongly believe integrating learning and problem posing can lead to a much more robust and more general artificial intelligence. Some of those rare exceptions is Schmidhuber's study, which explicitly addresses this issue. In his Powerplay algorithm, both problems and solvers are parameterized and the algorithm seeks specific problems that are solvable with the current capability of the solver, and loop through this to train an increasingly general problem solver [19]. More recently, question asking has been employed in interactive problem solving in robotics [20] and vision problems [21]. However, these are done within a strict task framework, so open-ended questions or questions that question the validity of existing questions cannot be generated. See [21] for a bit more open-ended approach called inverse Visual Question Answering. More recent works include goal generation and goal selection, where agents come up with their own goals and select from the candidate goals [22,23]. Some ideas we discussed in [17] for problem posing include: (1) recognizing events in the environment that can be potentially become a problem to be solved, (2) checking if existing problems are ill-posed, and

(3) given an overarching goal, come up with smaller problems that may be of different kind than the original goal (if they are of the same kind, straight-forward divide-and-conquer algorithms can be used). For an intelligent agent posing new questions, inventing new tasks, and creating new goals will become increasingly important, as the current learning algorithms cannot easily go beyond its defined task context.

How can the idea of question vs answer be relevant to brain science? I think it is relevant since the topic has not received attention that it deserves, and question asking (or problem posing) is an important function of the brain. There are many papers on decision making, but not much on how the brain asks questions that requires subsequent decision making. Understanding the brain mechanism of question asking can lead to new discoveries regarding core brain function, and in turn the insight can help us build better intelligent artifacts.

In sum, question asking needs more attention from brain science and artificial intelligence, in order for us to gain a deeper understanding of brain function and to build more intelligent artifacts. Furthermore, we can ask a metaquestion: Are we asking the right questions when trying to solve the problem of intelligence, artificial or natural? The pairs of contrasting concepts I discussed in this chapter are largely based on asking this meta question.

5 Discussion

In this chapter, I talked about several dichotomies of concepts that are important to brain science and artificial intelligence: meaning vs information, prediction vs memory, and question vs answer, with an emphasis on the first concept in each pair. Below, I will discuss additional related works that have relevance to the topics I discussed in the preceding sections.

In terms of meaning, deep neural network research commonly approaches the issue from a different angle than the one presented in this chapter—that of embedding, for example, word and sentence embedding [24] (see [25] for an extensive review on word meaning in minds and machines, which includes a detailed survey on word embedding). The main idea of embedding is to map words or sentences (or other raw input) into a vector space where concepts can be manipulated algebraically based on their meaning. For example, when vector representations of "Germany" and "capital" are added, the resulting vector represents "Berlin" (example from [24]). The main idea in this case is to train a neural network to map the input word to a series of words that appear before or after the input word in a sentence. The hidden layer representation then tends to take on this desired semantic property. This is one step toward meaningful information. However, whether the meaning in this case is intrinsic to the system, that is, interpretable from within the system, is an open question. A large body of work on huge language models that appeared in recent years based on transformers such as GPT-3 [26], although very powerful, may still suffer from lack of meaning.

As we saw in Section 2, the motor aspect is important for semantic grounding of meaning. In a related context, philosopher Ludwig Wittgenstein proposed that the meaning of language is in its use [27]. Basically, this is a departure from meaning based on what it (e.g., a word) represents (see [28] for various views on representation in neuroscience). A more recent thesis in this general direction comes from Glenberg and Robertson [29], where they emphasized that "what gives meaning to a situation is grounded in actions particularized for that situation," thus taking an action-oriented view of grounding (on a more general note, see [30–32], on the importance of embodiment). There are more notable works in this direction, which all put emphasis on the sensorimotor aspect of meaning [33–37]. Recent works in deep learning are also exploring grounding based on learning of physical commonsense knowledge through interaction with environmental objects. See [38], for example.

One interesting question is, does the range of possible motor behavior somehow limit the degree of understanding? That is, can organisms with higher degree of freedom and richer repertoire of actions gain higher level of understanding? I believe this is true. For example, recall the orientation perception thought experiment in Section 2. If the visuomotor agent was only able to move horizontally or vertically, but not diagonally, it would never be able to figure out what the 45 and 135 degrees light bulbs (the neurons) mean. Intelligence is generally associated with the brain size or brain/body ratio, but what may also be very important is how rich the behavioral repertoire of the animal is. For example, all the animals we consider to be intelligent have such flexibility in behavior: primates, elephants, dolphins, corvids, and even octopuses. An extension of this idea is, can an agent extend its behavioral repertoire? This is possible by learning new moves, but it is also possible by using tools. The degree of understanding can exponentially grow if the agent can also construct increasingly more complex tools. This I think is one of the keys to human's superior intelligence. See [39] for our latest work on tool construction and tool use in a simple neuroevolution agent, and our earlier work on tool use referenced within. On a related note, also consider the works by Zhao et al. [40], where they showed how novel robot morphology and controllers can be discovered through graph heuristic search. Although this is not strictly tool construction, the same methodology could be extended to tool construction and use.

In Section 2, I proposed the internal state invariance criterion, within the context of reinforcement learning. This raises an interesting idea regarding rewards in reinforcement learning. In traditional reinforcement learning, the reward comes from the external environment. However, research in reinforcement learning started to explore the importance of rewards generated from within the learning agent. This is called "intrinsic motivation" [22,41], and the internal state invariance criterion could be a good candidate for this. In this view, intrinsic motivation also seems to be an important ingredient for meaning that is intrinsic to the learning system. Another related work in this direction is [42], based on the criterion of independently controllable features (also see [43] on "empowerment"). The main idea is to look for good internal representations where "good" is defined by whether an action can independently control these internal representations or not. With this, both the perceptual representations and the motor policy are learned. This kind of criterion can be internal to the agent, thus, keeping things intrinsic, while allowing the agent to understand the external environment. Also see [44] for our earlier work on codevelopment of visual receptive fields (perceptual representations) and the motor policy.

Next, I would like to discuss various mechanisms that can serve as memory, and how, in the end, they all lead to prediction. In neural networks, there are several ways to make the network responsive to input from the past. Delayed input line is one, which allows a reactive feedforward network to take input from the past into consideration when processing the current input (see, e.g., [9]). Another approach is to include recurrent connections, connections that form a loop. More sophisticated methods exist such as long short-term memory (LSTM), etc., but generally they all fall under the same banner of recurrent neural networks. Finally, there is a third category that can serve as a memory mechanism, which is to allow feed forward neural networks to drop and detect token-like objects in the environment (a form of stigmergy). We have shown that this strategy can be used in tasks that require memory, just using feed forward neural networks [45]. From an evolutionary point of view, reactive feedforward neural networks may have appeared first, and subsequently, delay and ability to utilize external materials may have evolved (note that this is different with systems that have an integrated external memory, e.g., differentiable neural computers [46]). Further development or internalization of some of these methods (especially the external material interaction mechanism) may have led to a fully internalized memory. These memory mechanisms involve some kind of recurrent loop (perhaps except for the delayed input case), thus giving rise to dynamic internal state (see [45] for a more detailed discussion on this, in relation to olfaction and hippocampal function). As we have seen in Section 3, in such a system, networks with predictive dynamics have a fitness advantage, and thus such phenotypes will proliferate.

Continuing with the discussion on prediction, let us consider the ideas by Jun Tani. In his book [47] (pp. 161–172), he also talks about predictive dynamics and self-consciousness. In his work, prediction is mostly about the sensory consequence of action, and about the error in this prediction (also see O'Regan and Noë's notion of sensorimotor contingencies [48] and related ideas in Hawkins [49] pp. 139). Tani argues that self-consciousness arises when this prediction error is high. This may be counter to my notion of high predictability correlating with consciousness. However, Tani's formulation and my formulation are not directly comparable, since in Tani's case, the prediction error is computed by directly comparing the incoming sensory stimuli and the predicted sensory stimuli, while in my case, prediction is based purely on the internal state (the hidden state). I think these two views may be complementary. Further research into this may be needed, and the outcomes are expected to be synergistic. Lastly, I would like to mention that some recent advances in machine learning are benefitting from the use of prediction as a learning objective/criterion. In machine learning situations where explicit target values are rare or task-specific rewards are very sparse, it is a challenge to train effectively the learning model. Recent work by Finn and Levine [7] (and others) showed that learning motor tasks in a completely self-supervised manner is possible without detailed rewards, by using a deep predictive model, which uses a large data set of robotic pushing experiment. This shows a concrete example where prediction can be helpful to the agent. See [7] for more references on related approaches that utilize prediction.

Finally, let us examine question asking. As briefly hinted in Section 4 (citing [17]), generating questions or posing problems can be viewed as generating new goals. Similar in spirit with Schmidhuber's Powerplay [19], Florensa et al. proposed an algorithm for automatic goal generation in a reinforcement learning setting [50] (also see the works by Stanley et al. [51]). The algorithm is used to generate a range of tasks that the agent can currently perform. A generator network is used to propose a new task to the agent, where the task is drawn from a parameterized subset of the state space. A significant finding based on this approach is that the agent can efficiently and automatically learn a large range of different tasks without much prior knowledge. There have since been several different works on this topic. In [52], Misra et al. proposed learning by asking questions and applied it to a visual question answering domain for automated curriculum discovery, and Akakzia et al. showed the connection between grounding and autonomously acquiring skills through goal generation [53]. These results show the powerful role of question asking in learning agents.

6 Conclusion

In this chapter, I talked about meaning vs information, prediction vs memory, and question vs answer. These ideas challenge our ingrained views of brain function and intelligence (information, memory, and problem solving), and we saw how the momentum is building up to support the alternative views. In summary, we should pay attention to (1) meaning, and how it can be recovered through action, (2) prediction as a central function of the brain and artificial intelligence agents, and (3) question asking (or problem posing) as an important requirement for robust artificial intelligence, and the need to understand question asking mechanisms in brain science. In all three cases, we also learned that taking the "internal" perspective is important, and that this can lead to different perspectives that can give us new insights.

Acknowledgments

In this revised chapter, most notably, figures were added for a better explanation of the concepts discussed in the text, the discussion section was greatly expanded to include relevant references that were omitted, and latest references that appeared in the meanwhile were added. I would like to thank Asim Roy and Robert Kozma, who, together with myself, chaired a panel discussion on "Cutting Edge Neural Networks Research" at the 30th anniversary International Joint Conference on Neural Networks in Anchorage, Alaska in 2017, where I had the opportunity to refine many of my previous ideas, especially on meaning vs information. I would also like to thank the panelists Peter Erdi, Alex Graves, Henry Markram, Leonid Perlovsky, Jose Principe, and Hava Siegelmann, and those in the audience who participated in the discussion. The full transcript of the panel discussion is available at https://github.com/yschoe/ijcnn2017-panel-cutting-edge-nnet-research. Fig. 5C and D were reproduced from [15] by permission from IEEE (license #5310531004085). Finally, I would like to thank my current and former students who helped develop and test the ideas in this chapter, and Takashi Yamauchi for his thoughtful feedback.

References

[1] C.E. Shannon, A mathematical theory of communication, Bell Syst. Tech. J. 27 (3) (1948) 379–423.

[2] J.R. Searle, et al., Minds, Brains, and Programs, 1980, pp. 201–224.

[3] S. Harnad, The symbol grounding problem, Phys. D: Nonlinear Phenom. 42 (1-3) (1990) 335–346.

[4] G. Buzsáki, The Brain From Inside Out, Oxford University Press, 2019.

[5] Y. Choe, N.H. Smith, Motion-based autonomous grounding: inferring external world properties from internal sensory states alone, in: Conference Proceedings of the 21st National Conference on Artificial Intelligence (AAAI 2006), 2006.

[6] A. Clark, Whatever next? Predictive brains, situated agents, and the future of cognitive science, Behav. Brain Sci. 36 (3) (2013) 181–204.

[7] C. Finn, S. Levine, Deep visual foresight for planning robot motion, in: 2017 IEEE International Conference on Robotics and Automation (ICRA), 2017.

[8] S.J. Thorpe, M. Fabre-Thorpe, Seeking categories in the brain, Science 291 (5502) (2001) 260–263.

[9] K. Nguyen, Y. Choe, Dynamic control using feedforward networks with adaptive delay and facilitating neural dynamics, in: Conference Proceedings of the International Joint Conference on Neural Networks, 2017.

[10] H. Lim, Y. Choe, Extrapolative delay compensation through facilitating synapses and its relation to the flash-lag effect, IEEE Trans. Neural Netw. 19 (2008) 1678–1688.

[11] F. Mormann, C. Koch, Neural correlates of consciousness, Scholarpedia 2 (12) (2007) 1740.

[12] Y. Choe, J. Kwon, J.R. Chung, Time, consciousness, and mind uploading, Int. J. Mach. Conscious. 4 (2012) 257–274.

[13] N. Humphrey, A History of the Mind, HarperCollins, New York, 1992.

[14] J. Yoo, J. Kwon, Y. Choe, Predictable internal brain dynamics in EEG and its relation to conscious states, Front. Neurorobot. 8 (2014) (00018).

[15] J. Kwon, Y. Choe, Internal state predictability as an evolutionary precursor of self-awareness and agency, in: Conference Proceedings of the Seventh International Conference on Development and Learning, 2008.

[16] G. Claxton, Hare Brain, Tortoise Mind: Why Intelligence Increases When You Think Less, The Ecco Press, Hopewell, NJ, 1999.

[17] Y. Choe, T.A. Mann, From problem solving to problem posing, Brain-Mind Mag. 1 (2012) 7–8.

[18] E.A. Silver, On mathematical problem posing, For Learn. Math. 14 (1) (1994) 19–28.

[19] J. Schmidhuber, POWERPLAY: training an increasingly general problem solver by continually searching for the simplest still unsolvable problem, Front. Psychol. 4 (313) (2013).

[20] M. Cakmak, A.L. Thomaz, Designing robot learners that ask good questions, in: Conference Proceedings of the 7th ACM/IEEE International Conference on Human-Robot Interaction, 2012.

[21] F. Liu, T. Xiang, T.M. Hospedales, W. Yang, C. Sun, iVQA: Inverse visual question answering, in: Conference Proceedings of the IEEE Conference on Computer Vision and Pattern Recognition, 2018.

[22] S. Forestier, R. Portelas, Y. Mollard, P.-Y. Oudeyer, Intrinsically motivated goal exploration processes with automatic curriculum learning, *arXiv preprint arXiv:1708.02190*, 2017.

[23] C. Colas, T. Karch, N. Lair, J.-M. Dussoux, C. Moulin-Frier, P.F. Dominey, P.-Y. Oudeyer, Language as a cognitive tool to imagine goals in curiosity-driven exploration, *arXiv preprint arXiv:2002.09253*, 2020.

[24] T. Mikolov, I. Sutskever, K. Chen, G. Corrado, J. Dean, Distributed representations of words and phrases and their compositionality, *arXiv preprint arXiv:1310.4546*, 2013.

[25] B.M. Lake, G.L. Murphy, Word meaning in minds and machines, *arXiv preprint arXiv:2008.01766*, 2020.

[26] T.B. Brown, B. Mann, N. Ryder, M. Subbiah, J. Kaplan, P. Dhariwal, A. Neelakantan, P. Shyam, G. Sastry, A. Askell, et al., Language models are few-shot learners, *arXiv preprint arXiv:2005.14165*, 2020.

[27] L. Wittgenstein, Philosophical Investigations, Blackwell, Oxford, 1953.

[28] B. Baker, B. Lansdell, K. Kording, A philosophical understanding of representation in neuroscience, *arXiv preprint*, p. arXiv:2102.06592, 2021.

[29] A.M. Glenberg, D.A. Robertson, Symbol grounding and meaning: a comparison of high-dimensional and embodied theories of meaning, J. Mem. Lang. 43 (3) (2000) 379–401.

[30] M. Mitchell, Why AI is harder than we think, *arXiv preprint arXiv:2104.12871*, 2021.

[31] F.J. Varela, E. Thompson, E. Rosch, The Embodied Mind: Cognitive Science and Human Experience, MIT Press, Cambridge, MA, 1991.

[32] H.J. Chiel, R.D. Beer, The brain has a body: adaptive behavior emerges from interactions of nervous system, body and environment, Trends Neurosci. 20 (12) (1997) 553–557.

[33] R.A. Téllez, C. Angulo, Acquisition of meaning through distributed robot control, in: Conference Proceedings of the ICRA Workshop on Semantic information in robotics, 2007.

[34] A. Laflaquière, J.K. O'Regan, B. Gas, A. Terekhov, Discovering space—grounding spatial topology and metric regularity in a naive agent's sensorimotor experience, Neural Netw. 105 (2018) 371–392.

[35] A.K. Engel, A. Maye, M. Kurthen, P. König, Where's the action? The pragmatic turn in cognitive science, Trends Cogn. Sci. 17 (5) (2013) 202–209.

[36] J. Modayil, B. Kuipers, Autonomous development of a grounded object ontology by a learning robot, in: Conference Proceedings of the National Conference on Artificial Intelligence, 2007.

[37] J.M. Stober, Sensorimotor Embedding: A Developmental Approach to Learning Geometry, 2015.

[38] R. Zellers, A. Holtzman, M. Peters, R. Mottaghi, A. Kembhavi, A. Farhadi, Y. Choi, PIGLeT: Language grounding through neuro-symbolic interaction in a 3D world, *arXiv preprint arXiv:2106.00188*, 2021.

[39] R. Reams, Y. Choe, Emergence of tool construction in an articulated limb controlled by evolved neural circuits, in: Conference Proceedings of the International Joint Conference on Neural Networks, 2017.

[40] A. Zhao, J. Xu, M. Konaković-Luković, J. Hughes, A. Spielberg, D. Rus, W. Matusik, RoboGrammar: graph grammar for terrain-optimized robot design, ACM Trans. Graph. 39 (6) (2020) 1–16.

[41] A.G. Barto, S. Singh, N. Chentanez, Intrinsically motivated learning of hierarchical collections of skills, in: Conference Proceedings of the 3rd International Conference on Development and Learning, 2004.

[42] V. Thomas, J. Pondard, E. Bengio, M. Sarfati, P. Beaudoin, M.-J. Meurs, J. Pineau, D. Precup, Y. Bengio, Independently controllable features, *arXiv preprint arXiv:1708.01289*, 2017.

[43] N.C. Volpi, D. Polani, Goal-directed empowerment: combining intrinsic motivation and task-oriented behaviour, IEEE Trans. Cogn. Develop. Syst. (2020).

[44] H.-F. Yang, Y. Choe, Co-development of visual receptive fields and their motor-primitive-based decoding scheme, in: Conference Proceedings of the International Joint Conference on Neural Networks 2007 Post Conference Workshop on Biologically-Inspired Computational Vision (BCV) 2007, 2007.

[45] J.R. Chung, Y. Choe, Emergence of memory in reactive agents equipped with environmental markers, IEEE Trans. Auton. Ment. Dev. 3 (2011) 257–271.

[46] A. Graves, G. Wayne, M. Reynolds, T. Harley, I. Danihelka, A. Grabska-Barwińska, S.G. Colmenarejo, E. Grefenstette, T. Ramalho, J. Agapiou, et al., Hybrid computing using a neural network with dynamic external memory, Nature 538 (7626) (2016) 471–476.

[47] J. Tani, Exploring Robotic Minds: Actions, Symbols, and Consciousness as Self-organizing Dynamic Phenomena, Oxford University Press, 2016.

[48] J.K. O'Regan, A. Noë, A sensorimotor account of vision and visual consciousness, Behav. Brain Sci. 24 (2001) 939–973.

[49] J. Hawkins, A Thousand Brains: A New Theory of Intelligence, Basic Books, New York, NY, 2021.

[50] C. Florensa, D. Held, X. Geng, P. Abbeel, Automatic goal generation for reinforcement learning agents, in: International Conference on Machine Learning, 2018.

[51] R. Wang, J. Lehman, J. Clune, K.O. Stanley, Paired open-ended trailblazer (POET): Endlessly generating increasingly complex and diverse learning environments and their solutions, *arXiv preprint arXiv:1901.01753*, 2019.

[52] I. Misra, R. Girshick, R. Fergus, M. Hebert, A. Gupta, L. Van Der Maaten, Learning by asking questions, in: Conference Proceedings of the IEEE Conference on Computer Vision and Pattern Recognition, 2018.

[53] A. Akakzia, C. Colas, P.-Y. Oudeyer, M. Chetouani, O. Sigaud, Grounding Language to Autonomously-Acquired Skills via Goal Generation, *arXiv preprint arXiv:2006.07185*, 2020.

The brain-mind-computer trichotomy: Hermeneutic approach

Péter Érdi[a,b]

[a]CENTER FOR COMPLEX SYSTEMS STUDIES, KALAMAZOO COLLEGE, KALAMAZOO, MI, UNITED STATES [b]INSTITUTE FOR PARTICLE AND NUCLEAR PHYSICS, WIGNER RESEARCH CENTRE FOR PHYSICS, HUNGARIAN ACADEMY OF SCIENCES, BUDAPEST, HUNGARY

Chapter outlines

1 Dichotomies

The term “brain” is often associated with the notions of “mind” and of “computer.” The brain-mind-computer problem has been treated within the framework of three separate dichotomies, that is, the brain-mind problem, the brain-computer analogy/disanalogy, and the computational theory of mind. Fig. 1 visualizes the skeleton of a unified approach.

Artificial Intelligence in the Age of Neural Networks and Brain Computing. https://doi.org/10.1016/B978-0-323-96104-2.00019-1
Copyright © 2024 Elsevier Inc. All rights reserved.

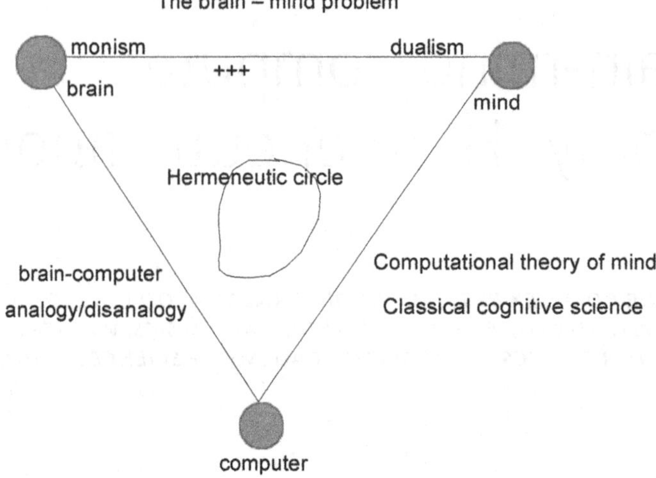

FIG. 1 The brain-mind-computer trichotomy.

1.1 The brain-mind problem

First, the brain-mind problem is related to the age-old philosophical debate between monists and dualists. Attempts to "solve" the brain-mind problem can be classified into two basic categories:

1. materialistic monism, leading in its ultimate consequences to some kind of reductionism; and
2. interactionist dualism, which is more or less some type of Neo-Cartesian philosophy.

The classification is, obviously, a crude oversimplification: A wide spectrum of monistic theories exist from Skinner's radical behaviorism [1] and Patricia.

Churchland's eliminative materialism [2] through Smart's physicalism [3] to Bunge's emergent materialism [4] (see also the controversial book of Deacon [5]):

- monism versus dualism
- reductionism
- emergentism
- functionalism
- downward causation

Interactionist dualism has always been an influential viewpoint since Descartes defined the interaction between the spatially extended body and a noncorporeal mind. Though its modern version was elaborated by two intellectual heroes of the 20th century (Sir Karl Popper and Sir John Eccles [6]), it has been criticized or even ignored by the representatives of the "main stream" of the philosophy of mind, mostly as functionalists, as well as by biologically oriented thinkers. Bickle [7] suggested that philosophers should adopt a "ruthless reductionist" approach by learning molecular and cellular neurobiology. The multiple realizability thesis (say Ref. [8]) emphasizes the importance of hierarchical organization from molecules to social interactions. Any nonreductionist physicalist theory should tell something about "downward causation."

"Downward causation" is a notion which suggests that higher level systems influence lower level configurations. Classical molecular biology deals exclusively with upward mechanisms of causation (from simple events to more complicated ones) and neglects completely the explanatory role of downward causation. Since we know that both molecules and genes form complicated networks or feedback loops, it is difficult to defend the concept that there is nothing else in science than a linear chain of elementary steps leading from cause to effect [9].

The methodologically successful reductionism is never complete, as Popper suggested: there is always some "residue" to be explained.

"Downward causation," that is, the mental agents can influence the neural functioning was suggested by Sperry [10,11]. Sperry was criticized for stating that the postulate that physiological mechanisms of the brain are directly influenced by conscious processes is unclear [12,13]. Alternatively, it was cautiously suggested by János Szentágothai in a somewhat overlooked paper that the nervous system can be considered as being open to various kinds of information, and that there would be no valid scientific reason to deny the existence of downward causation, or more precisely, a two-way causal relationship between brain and mind [14], see Fig. 2.

In some similar way, Campbell and Bickhard [15] argue that "organization principles" should have some priorities since our best physics tells us that there are no basic particulars, only fields in process." The relationship among free will, downward causation, and the emergence of complexity is discussed in an edited book from a broad perspective [16].

Twenty years ago it was argued [17] that the philosophical tradition of hermeneutics, that is, the "art of interpretation," which is a priori neither monist nor dualist, can be applied to the brain. Even more is stated: on one side, the brain is an "object" of interpretation, on the other side, it is itself an interpreter: the brain is a hermeneutic device. In a similar vein, in *The Metaphorical Brain 2*, Michael Arbib [18] argued that our theories of the brain are metaphors, while the brain itself represents the world through schemas, which may themselves be viewed as metaphors.

1.2 The brain-computer analogy/disanalogy

Second, the problem of the brain-computer analogy/disanalogy was a central issue of early cybernetics, in a sense revived by the neurocomputer boom. More precisely, the two sides of the metaphor ("computational brain" vs "neural computer") should be the subject of a brief discussion. There are several different roots of the early optimism related to the power of the brain-computer analogy. We recall two of them. First, both elementary computing units and neurons were characterized as digital input-output devices, suggesting an analogy at even the elementary hardware level. Second, the (more or less)

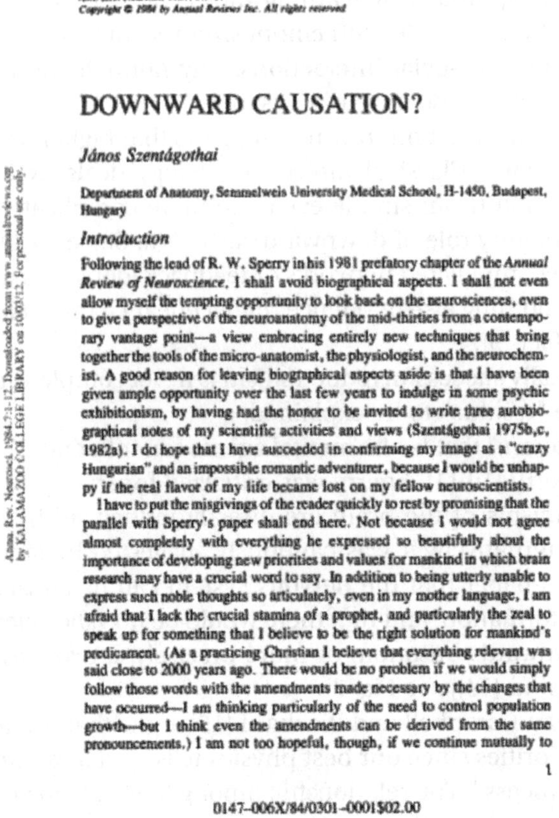

Ann. Rev. Neurosci. 1984. 7:1–11
Copyright © 1984 by Annual Reviews Inc. All rights reserved

DOWNWARD CAUSATION?

János Szentágothai

Department of Anatomy, Semmelweis University Medical School, H-1450, Budapest, Hungary

Annu. Rev. Neurosci. 1984.7:1-12. Downloaded from www.annualreviews.org by KALAMAZOO COLLEGE LIBRARY on 10/03/12. For personal use only.

Introduction

Following the lead of R. W. Sperry in his 1981 prefatory chapter of the *Annual Review of Neuroscience*, I shall avoid biographical aspects. I shall not even allow myself the tempting opportunity to look back on the neurosciences, even to give a perspective of the neuroanatomy of the mid-thirties from a contemporary vantage point—a view embracing entirely new techniques that bring together the tools of the micro-anatomist, the physiologist, and the neurochemist. A good reason for leaving biographical aspects aside is that I have been given ample opportunity over the last few years to indulge in some psychic exhibitionism, by having had the honor to be invited to write three autobiographical notes of my scientific activities and views (Szentágothai 1975b,c, 1982a). I do hope that I have succeeded in confirming my image as a "crazy Hungarian" and an impossible romantic adventurer, because I would be unhappy if the real flavor of my life became lost on my fellow neuroscientists.

I have to put the misgivings of the reader quickly to rest by promising that the parallel with Sperry's paper shall end here. Not because I would not agree almost completely with everything he expressed so beautifully about the importance of developing new priorities and values for mankind in which brain research may have a crucial word to say. In addition to being utterly unable to express such noble thoughts so articulately, even in my mother language, I am afraid that I lack the crucial stamina of a prophet, and particularly the zeal to speak up for something that I believe to be the right solution for mankind's predicament. (As a practicing Christian I believe that everything relevant was said close to 2000 years ago. There would be no problem if we would simply follow those words with the amendments made necessary by the changes that have occurred—I am thinking particularly of the need to control population growth—but I think even the amendments can be derived from the same pronouncements.) I am not too hopeful, though, if we continue mutually to

1

0147-006X/84/0301-0001$02.00

FIG. 2 Downward causation.

equivalence had been demonstrated between the mathematical model of the "control box" of a computer as represented by the state-transition rules for a Turing machine, and of the nervous system as represented by the McCulloch-Pitts model. Binary vectors of "0" and "1" represented the state of the computer and of the brain, and their temporal behavior was described by the updating of these vectors. In his posthumously published book *The Computer and the Brain*, John von Neumann [19] famously emphasized the particular character of "neural mathematics": "…The logics and mathematics in the central nervous system, when viewed as languages, must structurally be essentially different from those languages to which our common experience refers…."

Arguments for the computer-brain disanalogy were listed by Conrad [20]. Digital computers are programmed from outside; are structurally programmable; have low adaptability; and work by discrete dynamics. Their physical implementation is irrelevant in principle; they exhibit sequential processing and the information processing happens mostly at the network level. Brains are self-organizing devices; they are structurally nonprogrammable; they work by both discrete and continuous dynamics; their functions depend strongly on the physical (i.e., biological) substrate; the processing is parallel; and processing occurs for both network and intraneuronal information.

Inspiration from the brain leads away from an emphasis on a single universal machine toward a device composed of different structures, just as the brain may be divided into the cerebellum, hippocampus, motor cortex, and so on. Thus we can expect to contribute to neural computing as we come to chart better the special power of each structure. The brain may be considered a metaphor for sixth generation computing, where the latter is characterized by cooperative computation, perceptual robotics, and learning [21].

We now know that (mostly part of now the collective wisdom, but see, for example, also Ref. [22]): (1) brains are not digital computers; (2) brain does not have a central processing unit, but rather uses cooperative, distributed computation; (3) memory organization is based on dynamical (as opposed to static) principles, (4) brain uses the combination of discrete and continuous time dynamics, and (5) the synaptic organization of the brain is very unique, and may be the key element of the biological substrate of human intelligence.

1.3 The computational theory of mind

Third, the computational theory of mind holds that the computational metaphor is the final explanation of mental processes. The classical version of the theory suggests that the mind executes Turing style computation. As is well-known, the birth of the formal AI was the Dartmouth Conference held in the summer of 1956 (an important year, in many respects) and organized by John McCarthy. The goal was to discuss the possibilities to simulate human intelligent activities (use of language, concept formation, problem solving). The perspectives of cyberneticians and AI researchers have not been separated immediately. Some of McCulloch's papers also belong to the early AI works, as the article titles reflect: "Toward Some Circuitry of Ethical Robots or an Observational Science of the Genesis of Social Evaluation in the Mind-like Behavior of Artifacts" or "Machines That Think and Want."

"Connectionism" [23] emerged an ambitious conceptual framework for a general brain-mind-computer theory movement, but it is based on principles of "brain-style computation" that ignore many of the "real brain" data. The connectionist movement is thus directed more to the engineers of near-future generation computer systems and toward cognitive psychologists.

There are recent debates about the meaning of the term "mind computes," and "embodied cognition" seems to be a radical alternative [24]. The central hypothesis of embodied cognitive science is that cognition emerges from the interaction of brain, the whole body, and of its environment. What does it mean to understand a phenomenon? A pragmatic answer is to synthesize the behavior from elements. Many scientists believe if they are able to build a mathematical model based on the knowledge of the mechanism to reproduce a phenomenon and predict some other phenomena by using the same model framework, they understand what is happening in their system. Alternatively, instead of building a mathematical model one may wish to construct a robot. Embodied cognitive science now seems to be an interface between neuroscience and robotics: the features of embodied cognitive systems should be built both into neural models, and robots, and the goal is to integrate sensory, cognitive, and motor processes.

It is not yet clear whether there is any reason that a more general framework of computational framework would not be able to integrate the dynamic interaction of mind with its environment, but there to build neuromorphic and brain-based robots by combining computational neuroscience and traditional robotics [25].

2 Hermeneutics

Hermeneutics is a branch of continental philosophy which treats the understanding and interpretation of texts. For an introduction for nonphilosophers, please see Ref. [26]. One of the most important concepts in hermeneutics is the hermeneutic circle. This notion means that the definition or understanding of something employs attributes which already presuppose a definition or understanding of that thing. The method is in strong opposition to the classical methods of science, which do not allow such circular explanations. Hans-Georg Gadamer (1900–2002) writes [27]: "Understanding always implies a *pre-understanding* which is in turn prefigured by the determinate tradition in which the interpreter lives and that shapes his prejudices." (The Nobel Prize winner physicist Steven Weinberg [28] wrote: "... A physicist friend of mine once said that in facing death, he drew some consolation from the reflection that he would never again have to look up the word 'hermeneutic' in the dictionary.")

2.1 Second-order cybernetics

The "second-order cybernetics" (initiated by Heinz von Foerster and Roger Ashby) considered that the observer and the observed are the parts of the same system, and the result of the observation depends on the nature of their interaction.

Heinz von Foerster (1911–2002), born and raised in Vienna, served as the secretary of the last five Macy conferences. (Between 1958 and 1975, he directed the very influential Biological Computer Laboratory at the University of Illinois at Urbana-Champaign.) He constructed and defended the concept of second-order cybernetics. As opposed to the new computer science and control engineering, which became independent fields, second-order cybernetics emphasized the concepts of autonomy, self-organization, cognition, and the role of the observer in modeling a system. Cybernetic systems, such as organisms and social systems, are studied by another cybernetic system, namely the observer [29]. Von Foerster was a radical constructivist. According to this view, knowledge about the external world is obtained by preparing models on it. The observer constructs a model of the observed system; therefore, their interactions should be understood "by cybernetics of cybernetics," or "second-order" cybernetics. It is difficult to reconstruct the story, but it might be true that a set of cyberneticians, who felt the irreducible complexity of the system-observer interactions, abandoned building and test formal models, and used verbal language using metaphors. They were the subjects of well-founded critics for not studying specific phenomena. Constructivism is an important element of new cognitive systems. About the history of second-order cybernetics see Ref. [30].

2.2 Hermeneutics of the brain

Ichiro Tsuda [31,32] applied the principles of hermeneutics to the brain by using chaos as a mechanism of interpretation. He suggested that (1) a particular chaotic phenomenon, namely chaotic itinerancy, may be identified with what he calls a hermeneutic process; (2) in opposition to the idea that "the brain is a computer, the mind is a programmer," "... the brain can create even a programmer through the interpretation process expressed by chaotic itinerancy ..." [32].

In Ref. [17] it was asked: how, if at all, two extreme approaches, the "device approach" and the "philosophical approach" could be reconciled. It was suggested by turning to the philosophical tradition that hermeneutics, that is, the "art of interpretation," which is neither monist nor dualist a priori, can be applied to the brain. Further, it was stated that the brain is both the "object" of interpretation as well as the interpreter: therefore the brain is itself a hermeneutic device. For our own dialog with Tsuda, see Ref. [33].

The preunderstanding in hermeneutics might be related to the "Bayesian brain" hypothesis [34]. The prior probability distribution often called the prior, is the probability distribution that would express one's beliefs about this quantity before some evidence is taken into account, and might play the role of the preunderstanding. There seems to be an interesting analogy that action-perception cycle was analyzed in a Bayesian framework [35].

2.3 The brain as a hermeneutic device

The brain can be considered a different type of devices. Among these: the brain can be seen as a thermodynamic device; a control device; a computational device; an information storing, processing, and creating device; or a self-organizing device. The device approach is strongly related to the *dynamic metaphor* of the brain [36]. Dynamic systems theory offers a conceptual and mathematical framework to analyze spatiotemporal neural phenomena occurring at different levels of organization. These include oscillatory and chaotic activity both in single neurons and in (often synchronized) neural networks, the self-organizing development and plasticity of ordered neural structures, and learning and memory phenomena associated with synaptic modification. Systems exhibiting high structural and dynamic complexity may be candidates of being thought of as hermeneutic devices. The human brain, which is structurally and dynamically complex, thus qualifies as a hermeneutic device. One of the characteristic features of a hermeneutic device is that its operation is determined by circular causality. Circular causality was analyzed to establish self-organized neural patterns related to intentional behavior [37].

The world of systems determined by linear (and only linear) causal relationships belongs to the class of "simple systems" or mechanisms. The alternative is not a "subjective" world, immune to science, but a world of complex systems, that is, one which contains closed causal loops.

Systems with feedback connections and connected loops can be understood based on the concepts of circular and network causality. Leaving aside the clear and well-organized world of linear causal domains characterizing "simple systems," we find ourselves in the jungle of complex systems [38].

As we know from engineering control theory, large systems consist of both controller and controlled units. The controller discharges control signals toward the controlled system. The output of the controlled system is often sent back to the controller ("feedback control") forming a closed loop. Negative feedback control mechanisms serve to reduce the difference between the actual and the desired behavior of the system. In many cases, specific neural circuits implement feedback control loops which regulate specific functions.

Analyzing the question of whether the technical or "device approach" to the brain and the "philosophical approach" can be reconciled, it was concluded that the brain is a physical structure which is controlled and also controls, learns, and teaches; processes and creates information; recognizes and generates patterns; and organizes its environment and is organized by it. It is an "object" of interpretation, but also it is itself an interpreter. The brain not only perceives but also creates a new reality: it is a hermeneutic device [17].

2.4 Neural hermeneutics

Frith [39] is working on establishing a scientific discipline "neural hermeneutics" dealing with the neural basis of social interaction. The key element of this approach is the assumption that the representations of the external world can be shared with others, and this shared representation may be the basis of predicting other's actions during interactions. Recently active inference and predictive coding were offered [35] as the basic mechanisms/algorithms of social communication.

3 Schizophrenia: A broken hermeneutic cycle

3.1 Hermeneutics, cognitive science, schizophrenia

Gallagher's analysis implies: (1) Hermeneutics and cognitive science are in agreement on a number of things. An example is the way we know objects. The interpretation of objects needs "schema theory" given by Michael Arbib [40]; (2) Hermeneutics can contribute to cognitive science. The basis of the argument is that understanding situations needs hermeneutic interpretation. The usual critique is that logic, rule-based algorithms, and other similar computational methods are too rigid to interpret ill-defined situations, but hermeneutics "the art of interpretation" can do it. ("Mental models," which also help to analyze situations also should have been mentioned. Mental models have played a fundamental role in thinking and reasoning and were proposed in a revolutionary suggestion by Kenneth Craik (191445) [41]. The idea that people rely on mental models can be traced back to Craik's suggestion that the mind constructs "small-scale models" of reality that it uses to predict events.) (3) Cognitive science also has something to offer to hermeneutics, particularly to understand other minds. The most popular notion today is the *theory of mind* or more precisely "theory of other's minds." The most effective method of cognitive science to understand other minds, that is, to show empathy is to simulate other minds by using analogical thinking [42]. The neural basis of theory of mind now seems to be related to mirror neurons, which is the key structure of imitation, and possibly language evolution [43]. For a possible mechanism for internal interpretation through action, see Ref. [44]. A failure of attributing self-generated action generated by the patient himself (what we may label as the lack of ability to close the hermeneutic circle) can be a characteristic of schizophrenic patients [45].

Independently from our interest in hermeneutics, we have started to work on combined behavioral, brain imaging, and computational approaches to associative learning in healthy and schizophrenia patients to explain their normal and reduced performance. The working hypothesis we adopt is that schizophrenia is a "disconnection syndrome," as was suggested among others by Friston and Frith [46] and our aim is to qualitatively and quantitatively understand the functional bases of these disconnections. Schizophrenia and connectivity research are historically related, see Fig. 3.

Rethinking these studies from the perspective of the hermeneutic approach together with the preliminary results of our combined experimental and computational studies [47,48] leads us to believe that the hermeneutic circle necessary for associative learning is broken in schizophrenic patients. Specifically, significant impairments in the prefronto-hippocampal and hippocampal-inferior temporal pathways have been found. These findings imply that the lack of cognitive control over the processes of associative learning may underlie the decreased performance of schizophrenia patients in related tasks. Therapeutic strategies should act to repair this circle. For details [49–51].

4 Toward the algorithms of neural/mental hermeneutics

4.1 Understanding situations: Needs hermeneutic interpretation

- Logic, rule-based algorithms, and similar computational methods are too rigid to interpret ill-defined situations,
- Hermeneutics, "the art of interpretation" can do it,
- Hermeneutics: emphasize the necessity of self-reflexive interpretation and adopts circular causality.

Biological systems contain their own descriptions, and therefore they need special methods. Hermeneutics emphasizes the necessity of self-reflexive interpretation. Both

FIG. 3 Pioneers of schizophrenia and connectivity. *From G. Collin, E. Turk and M.P. van den Heuvel, Connectomics in schizophrenia: from early pioneers to recent brain network findings, Biol. Psychiatry Cogn. Neurosci. Neuroimaging 1 (2016) 199–208.*

natural science as "objective analyzer" and (post)modern art reiterate the old philosophical question: What is reality? The human brain is not only able to perceive what is called objective reality but also can create new reality. It is a hermeneutic device.

"Can complexity scientists bridge, in the words of C. P. Snow, the two cultures of academia—the humanities and the sciences—to create a more thoroughgoing explanation of human cognition? Can the tools of hermeneutics, mathematics, and computer simulation be integrated to assemble better and more useful models of human social understanding than that currently exist? These are the two provocative and ambitious questions—the former the broader, and the latter the more specific—that frame the intent and focus of Klüver and Klüver's recent book *Social Understanding*," see Refs. [52,53].

Somewhat parallelly with the arguments of this paper—the action-perception cycle—having been motivated by Walter Freeman's findings and theory [37,54] Robert Kozma is working on understanding the neural mechanisms, the intentional perception-action cycle [55,56]. It is stated that knowledge and meaning is created in the brain by circular intentional dynamics, where "meaningful stimulus is selected by the subject and the cerebral cortex creates the structures and dynamics necessary for intentional behavior and decision-making."

What we see is that the mathematics of hermeneutics and of the intentional must be somewhat different from what we use to describe the physical world. Frameworks of mathematical models of complex systems and of cognitive systems should be unified by elaborating algorithms of neural and mental hermeneutics [57]. But this will be a different story.

Acknowledgments

A preliminary version of this chapter has been published as a CEUR-WS.org paper. PE thanks the Henry Luce Foundation to let him to be a Henry R Luce Professor. "Thank you" for the reviewer for the constructive comments.

References

[1] B.F. Skinner, About Behaviorism, Knopf, New York, 1974.

[2] P.S. Churchland, Neurophilosophy: Toward a Unified Science of the Mind-Brain, The MIT Press, Cambridge, MA, 1986.

[3] J.J. Smart, Physicalism and emergence, Neuroscience 6 (1981) 109–113.

[4] M. Bunge, The Mind-body Problem, Pergamon Press, 1980.

[5] T.W. Deacon, Incomplete Nature: How Mind Emerged from Matter, W.W. Norton & Company, New York, 2011.

[6] K.R. Popper, J.C. Eccles, The Self and Its Brain, Springer Verlag, Berlin, 1977.

[7] J. Bickle, Philosophy and Neuroscience: A Ruthlessly Reductive Account, Kluwer Acad/Publ, 2003.

[8] K. Aizawa, C. Gillett, Levels, individual variation, and massive multiple realization in neurobiology, in: J. Bickle (Ed.), Oxford Hand-Book of Philosophy and Neuroscience, Oxford University Press, New York, 2009, p. 529581.

[9] M.H.V. Van Regenmortel, Reductionism and complexity in molecular biology, EMBO Rep. 5 (11) (2004) 1016–1020, https://doi.org/10.1038/sj.embor.7400284.

[10] R.W. Sperry, A modified concept of consciousness, Psychol. Rev. 76 (6) (1969) 532.

[11] R.W. Sperry, Mind-brain interaction: mentalism yes; dualism, no, Neuroscience 5 (1980) 195–206.

[12] G.M. Edelman, G.M. Edelman, V.B. Mount-Castle (Eds.), Group selection and phasic reentrant signalling: a theory of higher brain function, in: The Mindful Brain: Cortical Organization and the Group-Selective Theory of Higher Brain Function, The MIT Press, Cambridge, MA, 1978, pp. 55–100.

[13] J. Szentágothai, P. Érdi, Outline of a general brain theory, KFKI-1983-117, Centr. Res. Inst. Phys. Hung. Acad. Sci., Budapest, 1983.

[14] J. Szentágothai, Downward causation? Annu. Rev. Neurosci. 7 (1984) 1e11.

[15] R. Campbell, M.H. Bickhard, Physicalism, emergence and downward causation, Axiomathes 21 (1) (2011) 33–56.

[16] N. Murphy, G. Ellis, T. O'Connor, Downward Causation and the Neurobiology of Free Will, Springer Verlag, Berlin and Heidelberg, 2009.

[17] P. Érdi, The brain as a hermeneutic device, Biosystems 38 (2–3) (1996) 179–189.

[18] M.A. Arbib, The Metaphorical Brain, John Wiley & Sons, New York, 1989.

[19] J. von Neumann, The Computer and the Brain, Yale Univ. Press, New Haven, 1958.

[20] M. Conrad, The brain-machine disanalogy, Biosystems 22 (1989) 197–213.

[21] M.A. Arbib, The brain as a metaphor for sixth generation computing, in: R. Paton (Ed.), Computing With Biological Metaphors, Chapman and Hall, 1994.

[22] S.M. Potter, What can artificial intelligence get from neuroscience? in: M. Lungarella, J. Bongard, R. Pfeifer (Eds.), 50 Years of Artificial Intelligence: Essays Dedicated to the 50th Anniversary of Artificial Intelligence, Springer-Verlag, Berlin, 2007, pp. 174–185.

[23] D.E. Rumelhart, J.L. McClelland, Parallel Distributed Processing: Explo-Rations in the Microstructure of Cognition, vols. 1, 2, MIT Press, Cambridge, MA, 1986.

[24] A. Chemero, Radical Embodied Cognitive Science, MIT Press, Cambridge, 2009.

[25] L. Krichmar, H. Wagatsuma (Eds.), Neuromorphic and Brain-based Robots, Cambridge University Press, 2011.

[26] J.C. Mallery, R. Hurwitz, G. Duffy, Hermeneutics: from textual explication to computer understanding? in: S.C. Shapiro (Ed.), The Encyclopedia of Artificial Intelligence, John Wiley & Sons, New York, 1987.

[27] H.-G. Gadamer, Truth and Method, Sheed and Ward, London, 1976.

[28] S. Weinberg, Sokal's hoax, in: The New York Review of Books, vol. XLIII, August 8, 1996, pp. 11–15. No. 13.

[29] H. Von Foerester, Observing Systems (Systems Inquiry Series), Inter-systems Publications, 1982.

[30] A. Muller, K.H. Muller, An Unfinished Revolution?: Heinz von Foerster and the Biological Computer Laboratory/BCL 1958-1976, Edition Echoraum, 2007.

[31] I. Tsuda, A hermeneutic process of the brain, Prog. Theor. Phys. Suppl. 79 (1984) 241–259.

[32] I. Tsuda, Chaotic itineracy as a dynamical basis of hermeneutics in brain and mind, World Futures 32 (1991) 167–184.

[33] P. Érdi, I. Tsuda, Hermeneutic approach to the brain: process versus device, Theor. Hist. Sci. VI (2) (2002) 307–321.

[34] K.J. Friston, The history of the future of the Bayesian brain, NeuroImage 15 (2) (2012) 62–248. 12301233.

[35] K.J. Friston, C.D. Frith, Active inference, communication and hermeneutics, Cortex 68 (2015) 129–143.

[36] P. Érdi, On the 'dynamic brain' metaphor, Brain Mind 1 (2000) 119–145.

[37] W.J. Freeman, Consciousness, intentionality, and causality, J. Conscious. Stud. 6 (1999) 143–172.

[38] P. Érdi, Complexity Explained, Springer Publ, 2007.

[39] C. Frith, Making Up the Mind: How the Brain Creates Our Mental World, Blackwell Publ, 2007.

[40] M.A. Arbib, P. Érdi, J. Szentágothai, Neural Organization: Structure, Function, Dynamics, The MIT Press, Cambridge, MA, 1997.

[41] K. Craik, The Nature of Explanation, Cambridge Univ. Press, 1943.

[42] A. Barnes, P. Thagard, Empathy and analogy, Dialogue Can. Philos. Rev. 36 (1997) 705–720.

[43] M.A. Arbib, The mirror system, imitation, and the evolution of language, in: C. Nehaniv, K. Dautenhahn (Eds.), Imitation in Animals and Artefacts, MIT Press, Cambridge, MA, 2002, pp. 229–280.

[44] Y. Choe, N.H. Smith, Motion-based Autonomous Grounding: Inferring External World Properties from Encoded Internal Sensory States Alone, 2006.

[45] M.A. Arbib, T.N. Mundhenk, Schizophrenia and the mirror system: an essay, Neuropsychologia 43 (2005) 268–280.

[46] K.J. Friston, C.D. Frith, Schizophrenia: a disconnection syndrome? Clin. Neurosci. 3 (1995) 88–97.

[47] V. Diwadkar, B. Flaugher, T. Jones, L. Zalányi, M.S. Keshavan, P. Érdi, Impaired associative learning in schizophrenia: behavioral and computational studies, Cogn. Neurodyn. 2 (2008) 207–219.

[48] P. Érdi, B. Ujfalussy, L. Zalányi, V.A. Diwadkar, Computational approach to schizophrenia: disconnection syndrome and dynamical pharmacology, in: L.M. Ricciardi (Ed.), A Selection of Papers of the BIOCOMP 2007 International Conference, Proceedings of the American Institute of Physics, 2007, pp. 65–87. 1028.

[49] P. Érdi, M. Bányai, B. Ujfalussy, V. Diwadkar, The schizophrenic brain: a broken hermeneutic circle, in: Some New Insights and Results the 2011 International Joint Conference on Neural Networks (IJCNN). San Jos, CA, USA, 2011, pp. 3024–3027.

[50] V. Diwadkar, The schizophrenic brain: a broken hermeneutic circle, Neural Netw. World 19 (2009) 413–427.

[51] M. Bányai, V. Diwadkar, P. Érdi, Model-based dynamical analysis of functional disconnection in schizophrenia, NeuroImage 58 (3) (2011) 870–877.

[52] J. Klüver, C. Klüver, Castellani B: Review: Social Understanding: On Hermeneutics, Geometrical Models and Artificial Intelligence, 2010.

[53] J. Klüver, C. Klüver, Social Understanding: On Hermeneutics, Geometrical Models and Artificial Intelligence, Springer-Verlag, Berlin, 2010.

[54] W.J. Freeman, How and why brains create meaning from sensory information, Int. J. Bifurcat. Chaos 14 (2) (2004) 515530.

[55] R. Kozma, Intentional systems: review of neurodynamics, modeling, and robotics implementations, Phys Life Rev 5 (1) (2007) 121.

[56] J.J. Davis, G. Gillett, R. Kozma, Revisiting Brentano on consciousness: a striking correlation with ECoG findings about the action-perception cycle and the emergence of knowledge and meaning, Mind Matter 13 (1) (2015) 45–69.

[57] G. Collin, E. Turk, M.P. van den Heuvel, Connectomics in schizophrenia: from early pioneers to recent brain network findings, Biol. Psychiatry Cogn. Neurosci. Neuroimaging 1 (2016) 199–208.

Further reading

P. Érdi, Neurobiological approach to computing devices, Biosystems 21 (1988) 125–133.

P. Érdi, The brain-mind-computer trichotomy, in: G.J. Dalenoort, E. Scheerer (Eds.), Connectionism: Bridge between Mind and Brain? ZIF, Bielefeld, 1990. p. 7.

S. Gallagher, Hermeneutics and the cognitive sciences, J. Conscious. Stud. 10–11 (2004) 162–174.

R. Rosen, Drawing the boundary between subject and object: comments on the mind-brain problem, Theor. Med. 14 (1993) 89–100.

O.E. Rössler, Endophysics, in: J. Casti, A. Karlquist (Eds.), Real Brains—Artificial Minds, North-Holland, New York, 1987.

J. Szentágothai, P. Érdi, Self-organization in the nervous system, J. Soc. Biol. Struct. 12 (1989) 367–384.

PART 2

Brain-inspired AI systems

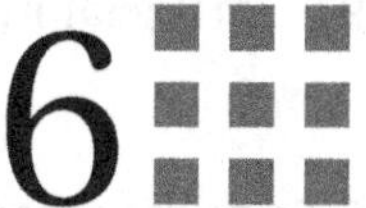

The new AI: Basic concepts, and urgent risks and opportunities in the internet of things

Paul J. Werbos[a,b]

[a]US NATIONAL SCIENCE FOUNDATION (RETIRED), ARLINGTON, VA, UNITED STATES [b]KUMMER INSTITUTE CENTER MST, ROLLA, MO, UNITED STATES

Chapter outlines

Artificial Intelligence in the Age of Neural Networks and Brain Computing. https://doi.org/10.1016/B978-0-323-96104-2.00006-3

Copyright © 2024 Elsevier Inc. All rights reserved.

1 Introduction and overview

1.1 Deep learning and neural networks before 2009–11

For many years, the majority of computer scientists believed that the field of artificial intelligence would never live up to its initial promise, or have a major impact on technology or the economy. There were periodic efforts to abolish research programs in that area at the National Science Foundation, based on the view that all those lines of research never panned out and that other stakeholders should get the money. Even within artificial intelligence, the field of machine learning was mostly viewed with disdain until the US National Science Foundation (NSF) mounted a major cross-cutting initiative to support it [1] as part of a larger initiative which grew still larger for a few years [2]. Sergey Brin, cofounder of Google, has reported [3] that the leaders of computer science assured him that neural networks could never do anything very interesting.

From 1988 to 2008, mathematical neural network research was led primarily by a partnership between engineers (IEEE) and the International Neural Network Society (INNS), who organized the International Joint Conferences on Neural Networks (IJCNN). Another important conference, smaller in that period, was the Neural Information Processing Systems (NIPS) conference, led by Terry Sejnowski, a prominent neuroscientist. Substantial advances and substantial applications in real-world engineering challenges were made in this work [4], but because of tribalism and vested interests the progress was not well reported in general education in computer science. The number of inaccurate statements made about the field outside the field was far too numerous and extreme for us to address directly. Even today, much of the information sent to high-level policy makers and to the press comes from the same type of "expert" who provided false information in the past.

1.2 The deep learning cultural revolution and new opportunities

The deep learning revolution of 2009–11 changed the story dramatically. At the 2014 World Congress in Computational Intelligence (WCCI) in Beijing, LeCun called this revolution "the second rebirth of neural networks," as important as the first dramatic rebirth back in 1986–88 which crystallized in the first IEEE International Conference on Neural Networks in 1988 in San Diego, California. Immediately after his talks and mine at that conference, at a time when I still ran the neural network research at NSF, some people at Beijing whisked me to the office of a very powerful dean at Tsinghua University and from there to the National

Science Foundation of China (NSFC), which proposed a dramatic new research push for joint US-China research. I was deeply disappointed when new management at NSF did not respond well to the proposal, but China did create a major research push on its own, and I submitted retirement papers to NSF effective on Valentine's day, 2015.

But the purpose of this paper is not to relitigate the past. Section 2 will explain a few of the key concepts of deep learning, starting from the recent industry interest and working back to what underlies it. The methods which have become widely used in the computer industry since 2011 validate the idea of trying to learn fundamental principles from the brain, but they still fall far short of fully exploiting the fundamental design capabilities which can be found even in the brain of the mouse. We now have a solid mathematical path for how to build such a high level of intelligence [5], including many powerful methods which have been applied in engineering but not yet widely disseminated in computer science; Section 3 will discuss a few examples, with pointers to where you can learn the all-important technical details.

1.3 Need and opportunity for a deep learning revolution in neuroscience

The deep learning cultural revolution in computer science was a great advance, but in my view, we still need another cultural revolution in the field of computational neuroscience, which has yet to assimilate new findings about how intelligence works at a systems level in the brain, despite a series of NSF efforts to build bridges between the relevant disciplines [1,2,6], and great efforts by systems neuroscientists like Karl Pribram and Walter Freeman [7] to broaden the paradigm. Section 4 will review recent research opening the door to a whole new paradigm here [8,9], and some of the important previous work leading up to it.

Fig. 1 illustrates the research goals and strategy of the cross-cutting NSF initiative in cognitive optimization and prediction which I proposed and led in 2008, and did my best to continue funding as part of my core program in the Engineering Directorate after that.

FIG. 1 Vision of the NSF COPN research initiative of 2008 [6].

I accepted the neural network job at NSF in 1988, mainly because of the arrow on the lower right here: the hope that better mathematical understanding of intelligence in general would help us to understand not only the brain but also the mind, on the deepest possible level, and help expand our ability to develop the deepest human potential more effectively. At the recent conference of the Asia-Pacific Neural Network Society (APNNS), I responded to the last question of the entire conference by giving my personal view: "I personally agree that the human mind is more than just the brain of a mouse, but any true Daoist master would understand that we cannot truly, fully understand the consciousness and soul of a human before can understand the brain intelligence of the mouse. It is a crucial step along the path." Section 4 will also say more about these issues.

1.4 Risks of human extinction, need for new paradigm for internet of things

But at the end of the day, the end of the day might be coming. More and more, we can actually understand why humans tend to underestimate the possibilities of massive changes for the better or for the worse. There is a growing community of people who believe that there is a serious possibility that the human species might well deploy new technologies in a way which results in total extinction of the species, maybe sooner and maybe later, and that we really should be working more effectively to understand what the threats are and what could be done to reduce them.

Misuse of artificial intelligence, as in the *Terminator* movies, is one of those threats. Yet as the Internet of Things (IoT) grows very quickly to control every vehicle (civilian or military) on earth, every generator, every home, every city and every medical device, in a coordinated way, perhaps from physically hardened physical servers, the threat of artificial stupidity (AS) is almost as large, and far more imminent, than the threat of AI. A new relation is being built very quickly between humans and the web of computer software which will be controlling them and their economy. It is a matter of life or death that this new relation not start off on a bad foot, fatal to all sides. That requires development of a new paradigm for the IoT which includes not only a focus on safer forms of deep learning, but also better interfaces and coordination with unbreakable operating systems, market-like distributed control, teleautonomy, advanced quantum technology, and, above all, new energy to make sure that deep human collaboration and deeper human potential are enhanced and empowered in ways that allow humans to keep up with it all. Section 5 will give my current groping thoughts about these life or death challenges (see Fig. 2).

2 Brief history and foundations of the deep learning revolution

2.1 Overview of the current landscape

All of the big firms in information technology (IT) now have substantial activities in "the new AI" based on deep learning and neural networks. The *New York Times* has posted an

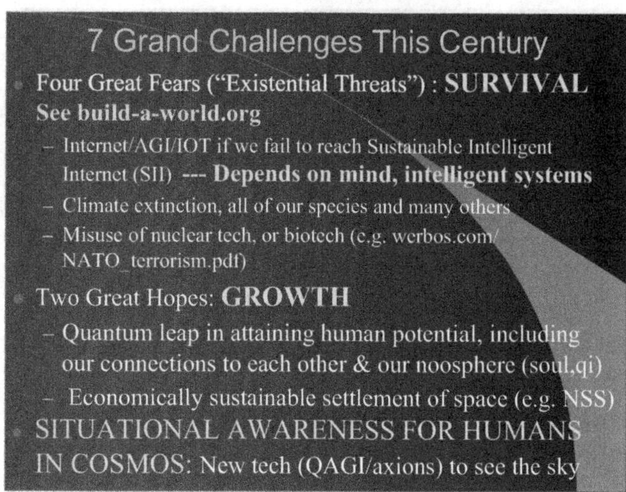

FIG. 2 Four of the three to six most serious ultimate threats of human extinction, as depicted at www.werbos.com/IT_big_picture.pdf.

excellent story on what is happening now in the mainstream of that industry, describing many of the key players [10]. The largest technical conference on the real cutting edge of AI research in those companies at that time was held in Barcelona, a research symposium organized by Juergen Schmidhuber; the website for that symposium [11] is a good source of further information.

Not so long after that conference, I am grateful to have had a chance to be one of the first people invited to the long-term futures conference of one of the most important leading companies from outside the company. They expressed the general sentiment of the industry: "How was it that Google saw all this first and got the jump on us so completely?" And in more detail: "The new AI based on deep learning is remaking the world here and now. We need to jump to CNN and RNN, the next big thing." At the time, I assumed that "CNN" meant cellular neural networks, a very important breakthrough on the computer hardware side [12]; however, they meant convolutional neural networks, a particular type of mathematical neural network design which could be implemented either as a program for an ordinary PC, as a program for special hardware like Game Processing Units (GPU) which offer much more throughput in implementing neural networks, or even as an actual chip architecture. Here I will use the acronyms CeNN and CoNN for cellular and CNNs, respectively, to avoid confusion. The company's interest in recurrent neural networks (RNNs) was recent, seen as "the next new big thing."

The term "deep learning" is one of those cultural terms which is defined mainly by what it means to a large group of people. Generally, it means some combination of neural network learning exploiting three tools new to much of the world: (1) CoNNs; (2) neural networks with many layers (deep, after all); (3) autoencoder or bottleneck networks. But all three of these design capabilities were used and known many decades ago. The deep

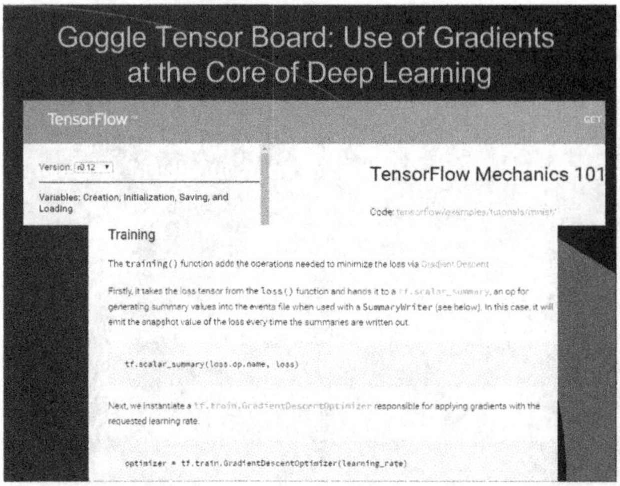

FIG. 3 Core page of Google open tensor flow system.

learning revolution was not about a new underlying technology, but about a cultural revolution, an appreciation of what the tools could do, and development of new groups and procedures for using them.

The core of the "new AI" is the idea of complex systems developed by learning rather than programming. For the first few years of the deep learning revolution, the market was dominated by the tensor flow open software package developed by Google. Fig. 3 depicts the core page of the tensor flow system, the page which addresses how the learning is done for whatever network design or data the user may choose:

The core of the learning is based on optimizer routines which rely on gradients, on vectors of derivatives, which tell the optimizer whether changing any parameter of the system leads to more error or less error.

Must gradients really be at the core of any complex system for learning or for general purpose optimization in a nonlinear world? Many, many theorists have hoped to avoid them, and many attempts have been made, but at the end of the day gradients are central to any really effective system for these purposes [13]. Competitors to Google, like Amazon Cloud Services, have been attracting more market share lately, especially as computer hardware is deployed which exploits the special parallel structure of all these neural network designs, but the effective and exact calculation of gradients by the general method we call "backpropagation" remains at the very center here, as it was at the center of the first rebirth of the neural network field.

2.2 How the deep revolution actually happened

Why and how did the deep learning revolution occur when it did? It is amazing at times to hear the varieties of creative stories which people swear by on these topics—but certainly we know that Google's big investment and energy were the start of the big new wave, and

Sergey Brin himself has told us how that happened [3]. It was not a matter of strange politics or impulses, but of solid breakthrough results which came to his attention. From the *New York Times* investigation of these events [10], we know that Andrew Ng came to Google with solid proof that neural networks could solve problems in computer technology which people had believed impossible before he came to them with proof. But how did that happen?

In the year 2008, it was "generally known" that artificial neural networks could not possibly perform well on tasks requiring pattern recognition over images with a large number of pixels, or natural language processing, etc. It was also well-known that CoNNs, bottleneck networks, and networks with many layers had been in existence for many decades (e.g., see my 1988 paper in the flagship journal of IEEE [14] citing early breakthrough success of CoNNs on small but challenging tasks in ZIP code recognition, describing how to train a generalized network design which effectively has N layers where N is the number of neurons). The new NSF initiative depicted in Fig. 1 was intended to break down many of the cultural barriers between disciplines which had limited progress in all these fields, so it was only natural that Yan LeCun (like me, one of the early pioneers in using backpropagation) expressed interest in submitting a proposal to obtain the funding necessary to disprove the conventional wisdom and break the logjam. Because I did have to follow the rules of NSF, I told him this would be fine, if he could find a card-carrying engineer to act as PI, with him as co-PI. The final proposal from Ng and LeCun then came to the usual NSF panel review.

After the panel review, I was under incredible pressure not to fund that proposal. After all, many more prominent people swore that this simply could not work, so we should not waste money on bothering to find out. They could think of other uses for the $2 million. Fortunately, Dr. Sohi Rastegar, head of the Emerging Frontiers Research and Innovation(EFRI) office, stood by the great corporate culture which had guided NSF ever since its creation by Vannevar Bush, and he did authorize me to use my judgment and fund the proposal anyway, despite threats of lawsuits. Once Ng and LeCun had enough funds to really attack big outstanding challenge problems in computer technology, they reported breakthrough results defying all conventional wisdom within just 1 year, as depicted in Fig. 4. This was just one of the success reports from one of the four projects funded under the initiative depicted in Fig. 1.

In summary, it was a solid demonstration of empirical results on widely used competitions which really created this cultural revolution. Of course, the availability of Game Processing Units (GPUs) also was important in making these demonstrations possible. The open source culture of Google also was essential in having a much bigger impact on university culture than the earlier success of neural networks in equally challenging real-world applications, such as vehicle control and missile interception [4] whose leaders do not work so hard to make their best technology well-known.

2.3 Backpropagation: The foundation which made this possible

When I began work in the neural network field in the 1960s, it was widely "known" that neural networks were an old discredited heresy. Anyone still working in that field was

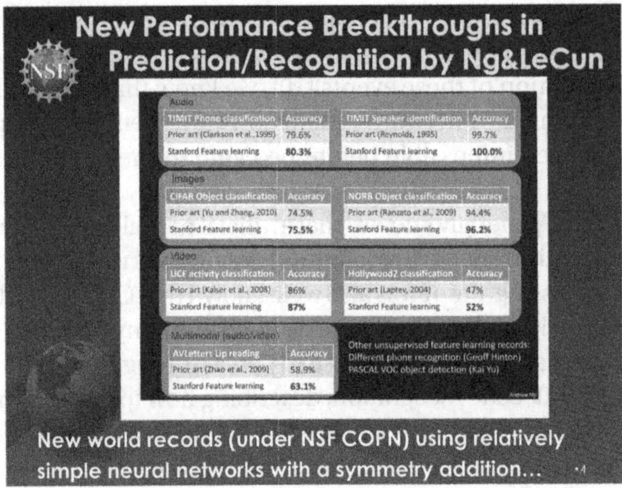

FIG. 4 Key slide from first year "grant results" report from Ng and LeCun to COPN/NSF.

generally treated as a crackpot. The theoretical rules of the scientific method [15] and the rational quest for truth are generally not upheld so strictly for the work of those labeled as crackpots, regardless of the logic of the work.

The belief that ANNs could never do anything useful (letalone explain how brains do so) was solidified by a seminal book from Marvin Minsky [16], who is deeply revered for his insight in traditional AI to this day. The most powerful argument against ANNs in that book had two parts: (1) the observation that ANNs could not even solve a minimal example of a classification task, the XOR problem (see Fig. 5A), unless they had at least one hidden layer (see Fig. 5B); and (2) even after years of effort, no one had found a reasonably effective way to train such a network to perform such classification tasks.

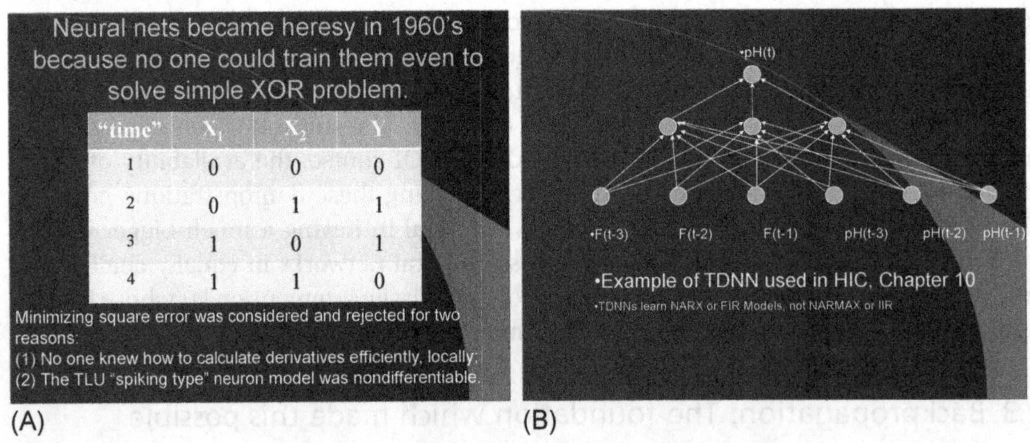

FIG. 5 (A) The XOR task; (B) example of 3-layer ANN with one hidden layer [17].

Amari had previously mentioned the possibility of trying steepest descent methods to train such networks, but dismissed them as unworkable and did not give solutions to the obvious problems [18].

Circa 1970, when I was a student at Harvard, I found a way to solve these problems and suggested to Minsky that we could share the credit by writing a joint paper. There were two key elements to my solution: (1) replacing the old "Threshold Logic Unit" model of the neuron with a new differentiable model of the neuron; and (2) using a new way to calculate derivatives by a new kind of dynamic feedback procedure, which seemed intuitively obvious and which actually was a translation into mathematics of Freud's theory of psychodynamics.

Minsky stated that he could not get away with using such a model of the neuron, since it was holy writ in computational neuroscience that the brain is a modern digital device relying on ones and zeroes—spikes—for its computations. But then I showed them some actual time-series recordings from the brain, shown in Fig. 6, similar to much of what we still see today:

I argued that the true "neural code" for the highest level neurons is not just ones and zeros, but bursts of volleys of continuous intensity, at regular intervals. However, Minsky stated that he simply could not get away with that, and history has shown that his political strategy worked better than mine.

At about the same time, I wrote this up as a request for computer time from my Department at Harvard. Professor Larry Ho, who controlled computer time that year, rejected the request on grounds that he did not think that this kind of backpropagation could possibly work. However, when I asked to use this as the basis for my Harvard Ph.D. thesis [20], the department said that they would allow it, so long as neural networks were not a major part of the thesis and so long as I could prove that the new method for calculating derivatives

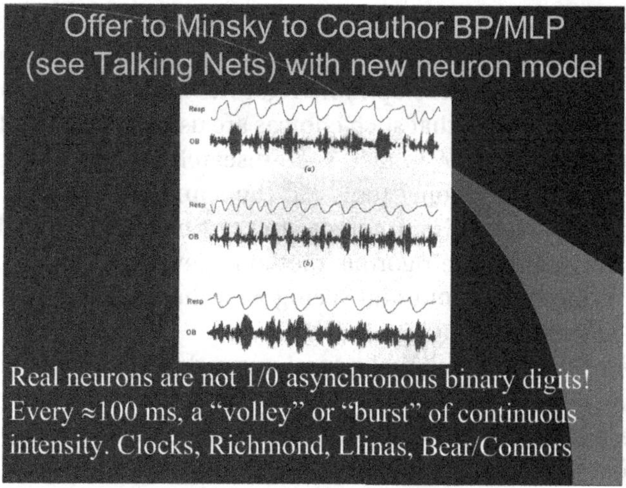

FIG. 6 Recordings from actual neurons [19] and some updated sources.

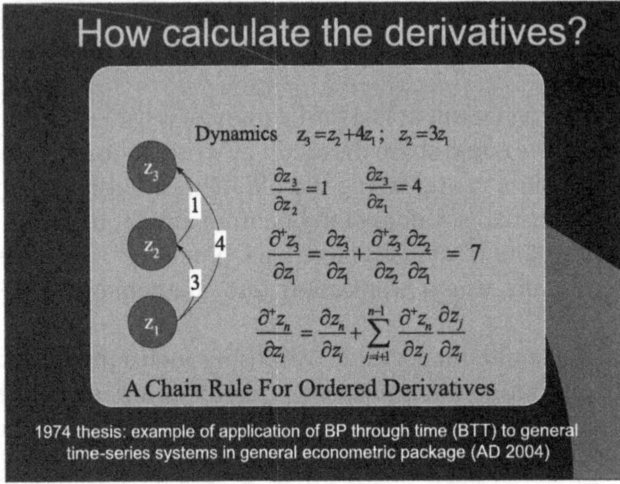

FIG. 7 General backpropagation as formulated and proven in 1974.

would really work. This was an excellent piece of guidance from them, which led to my proving the general chain rule for ordered derivatives illustrated in Fig. 7.

Note that this method for calculating gradients can be applied to any large sparse differentiable nonlinear system, and not just the type of ANN illustrated in Fig. 5A. In 1988, I generalized the method for use on implicit, simultaneous-equation types of model; for a review of the history, and of ways to use this method not only in neural networks but in other applications, see my paper on automatic differentiation [21].

2.4 CoNNs, >3 layers, and autoencoders: The three main tools of today's deep learning

Many people argue that the phrase "deep learning" simply means adding more layers to an ANN, beyond the traditional popular three you see in Fig. 5B. But many have said that someone should do research to develop more rigorous ways to decide on the number of layers, and so on. They complain that such choices are usually based on trying things out, and seeing what happens to error. In fact, such research was done long ago, and many tools exist which implement rational tools. All the standard methods of statistics also work. People planning to use ANNs in forecasting or time-series modeling applications should be sure to understand the rigorous methods developed in statistics [22], which are also based on trying models out and seeing what happens to error, in a systematic way. Section 3 will say more about numbers of layers.

Widespread use of the convolutional neural network (CoNN) was arguably the most important new direction in the new wave of deep learning which started in 2009–11. The basic CoNN is a variation of the simple feedforward ANN shown in Fig. 5B, varied in a way which makes it possible to handle a much larger number of inputs. The key idea is illustrated in Fig. 8.

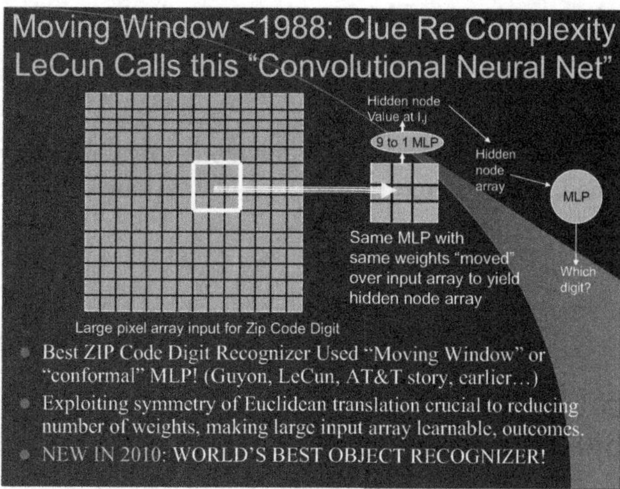

FIG. 8 Schematic of what a CoNN is. See LeCun's tutorial [23] for more details.

The CoNN addresses the special case where the inputs to the neural network are organized in a regular Euclidean grid, like what we often see in camera images. In a naïve ANN, each of the many, many hidden neurons would take inputs from different regions of the image. That would require estimating many, many parameters to train the network (millions, if there are millions of pixels in the image). From statistical theory, we know that this would require really huge amounts of data, even by the standards of big data, to achieve reasonable accuracy.

The key idea in CoNNs is to "reuse" the same hidden neuron "in different locations." Equivalently, we could phrase this as "sharing weights" between all the sibling hidden neurons of the same type handling different parts of the image. In terms of basic mathematics, the CoNN is exploiting the idea of invariance with respect to Euclidean translations in order to drastically reduce the number of weights which must be estimated or trained, and improve accuracy when one only has a finite amount of data. Note however that this trick only works when the input data do possess Euclidean symmetry; the cells of our retina do not. Of course, it is easy enough to apply this same principle to a feedforward ANN with many layers, as LeCun and others have many times.

A simpler design which has also been crucial to the success of LeCun and others is the autoencoder or bottleneck network, developed and popularized by Cottrell long ago [24]. The idea is to train an ordinary feedforward ANN with N layers, just like the example of Fig. 5B (but with more layers sometimes), but to train it to try to output predictions of the same data which it uses as input. This would be a trivial prediction task (just set the outputs to equal the known inputs), except when the hidden neurons on one or more layer are much fewer than the number of inputs, making it impossible to learn to setall the outputs to equal all the inputs. The hidden layer (bottleneck layer) of such a network learns to be a kind of compressed representation of the image. By developing layers and layers of such compression, by training over a large set of images, LeCun develops a kind of preprocessing which improves the performance of later stages of prediction and classification, as basic statistics easily explains.

A neat trick here is that one can train the autoencoders over millions of images which have not been classified, and use a more limited set of data labeled for the prediction task itself.

3 From RNNs to mouse-level computational intelligence: Next big things and beyond

3.1 Two types of recurrent neural network

The greater use of recurrent neural networks can give a very substantial improvement in neural network performance, but it is extremely important to distinguish between two types of recurrence—time-lagged recurrence versus simultaneous recurrence. Applications which do not distinguish between these two tend to use training procedures which are inconsistent either in mathematics or in addressing the tasks which the developer imagines they might address.

The easiest type of recurrent network to understand and use is the time-lagged recurrent network (TLRN), depicted in Fig. 9.

The key idea is that one can augment any input-output network, such as an N-layer ANN or a CoNN, by designing it to output additional variables forming a vector R, which are used only as additional inputs (a kind of memory) for the next time period.

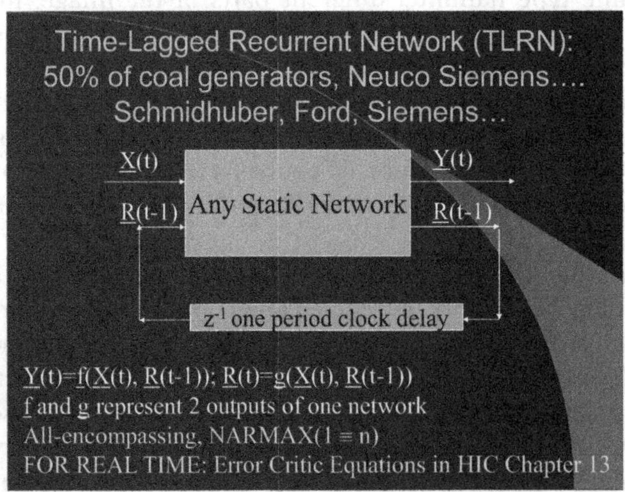

FIG. 9 The time-lagged recurrent network (TLRN) [14,17].

I still remember the major time-series forecasting competition led by Sven Crone, which was presented at several major conferences in statistics, forecasting, neural networks, and computer science, including IJCNN 2007 in Orlando, Florida. Most of the way through the competition, Sven informed me that the students of statistics, using 22 old well-established methods, were doing much better than the teams from the other fields, despite enormous amounts of effort, cleverness, and creativity.

When I heard that, I remembered how many students even in the neural network field were using simple popularized methods like naïve feedforward networks or Vapnik methods or clever kludges, and simply had not studied the solid mathematics of TLRNs. And so I mentioned the situation to friends in Ford Motor Research, which was then the world's leader in advanced practical neural network research and applications (and had allowed its people like Feldkamp, Puskorius, Marko, and Prokhorov to publish extensively). After many years of careful fair comparisons, that group had settled on TLRNs trained by backpropagation through time for all its mission-critical applications, like minimum cost compliance with stiff new EPA Clean Air rules. They had developed practical procedures for "multistreaming" to use their in-house general TLRN package effectively in safety-critical large general applications. Without a lot of effort and with no tweaking, they input Crone's challenge into their system, and quickly turned out the clear number one winner. Later, at IJCNN 2011, Ford was a lead sponsor of the time-series competition—and did not enter, perhaps because the rules required full disclosure by all contestants, but quietly verified that their system still outperformed all the competition.

It is important to understand why the standard, basic general TLRN has a firm foundation in statistics [25]. Mathematicians such as Andrew Barron [26] and Eduardo Sontag have proven that standard feedforward ANNs can approximate smooth nonlinear functions much more accurately than other approximators like Taylor series as the number of inputs grows, and that the universal approximation property applies to dynamical systems over time. The TLRN format here, assuming Gaussian noise at each time interval, therefore gives us a strict universal generalization of the vectorized general form of the standard ARMA models and methods of time-series analysis.

Despite the strict dominance of the TLRN over traditional and widely known designs for prediction, for dynamic modeling, and for reconstructing the true state of the world (like autoencoders but more rigorous and powerful), there are extensions of the general TLRN which have performed much better in tests in simulation and on real data from the chemical process industry [17], and room for further development of even more powerful extensions [25]. The company Deep Mind (a major leader in today's deep learning, now owned by Google) has been developing ways to approximate backpropagation through time in feedforward real-time computations, but as the figure indicates a more general approximation was described in detail in the *Handbook of Intelligent Control* in 1992 (and shown to work well enough in tests by Prokhorov for control applications).

But what of recurrence without a time delay or a clock? Is it good for applications other than associative memory (an area studied to great exhaustion decades ago, building on classic work by Grossberg and Kohonen)?

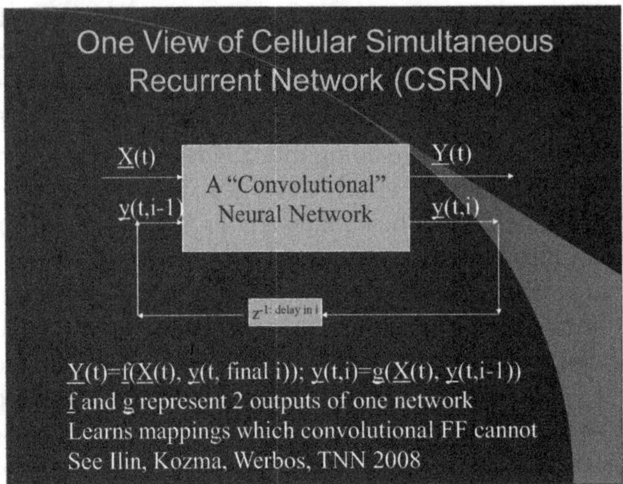

FIG. 10 The CSRN, an example of simultaneous recurrence [27].

Indeed it is. See Fig. 10 for an example.

The recurrence in Fig. 10 looks exactly like the recurrence in Fig. 9 to the untrained eye. However, notice that there are two time indices here, "*t*" and "*i*." This kind of design implies a kind of cinematic processing, in which new input vectors arrive from time to time (indexed by the integer *t*, the big clock index) but in which many iterations of processing (indexed by *i*, a kind of inner loop index) try to attain some kind of convergence in the inner loop. Simultaneous recurrence is the kind of recurrence one would use to represent models like simultaneous equation models in economics, or implicit models defined by some kind of relaxation to equilibrium. Feedforward CoNNs can approximate a wide range of *smooth* functions, but for effective intelligent control and true brain-like intelligence it is important to have a more general capability to approximate *nonsmooth* functions. Our 2008 paper gave an example of a simple learning problem which arises in learning how to navigate a cluttered space, as a general skill (not just learning a particular maze). The usual CoNN simply could not learn such a difficult task, but the CSRN could. The paper also described a further extension beyond CSRN suitable for exploiting non-Euclidean symmetries, which is essential for true brain-like capabilities.

For an even more powerful universal learning system able to capture all the benefits of the most advanced TLRN design and extensions of CSRN, one would simply combine both types of recurrence in a single system (as does the brain). See the *Handbook of Intelligent Control* [17] for discussion of how to combine both types together.

3.2 Deep versus broad: A few practical issues

Philip Chen, a recent president of the IEEE Society for Systems, Man and Cybernetics, has argued [28] that "broad" neural networks could perform just as well as "deep" (many layered) neural networks. In actuality, debates about the number of layers were already

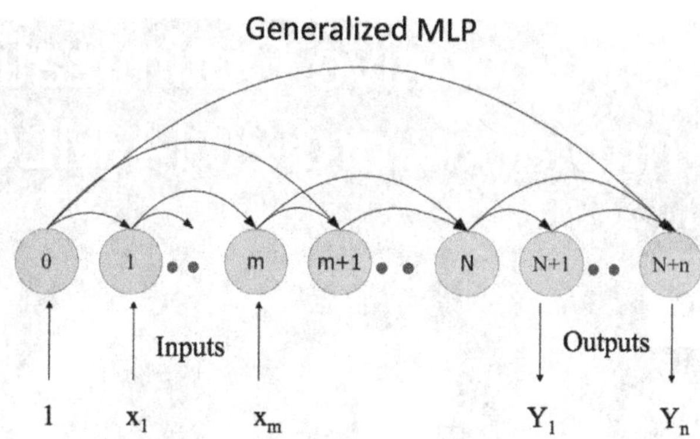

FIG. 11 Generalized MLP design.

resolved in principle by 1990, when I explained [14] how to use the more general static ANN design illustrated in Fig. 11:

Formally, this is the deepest possible feedforward network possible with N neurons and implementation on a sequential computer. Each neuron is a layer unto itself, making it all broad as well as deep. All possible feedforward network structures with N neurons are a special case of this general structure. The key is to use rational, statistically grounded learning (using penalty functions, pruning and growing methods) to learn the exact details. Such general methods have been developed extensively over many years by many authors, though the more formal strategy which I proposed in 2011 [25] could be useful in consolidating and strengthening that literature.

On the other hand, an ANN with just two layers (not even a hidden layer) and simultaneous recurrence would be able to learn even deeper relations than Fig. 11; in that design, "breadth" actually creates depth automatically, by learning. In fact, this is how the brain achieves depth, by using a cerebral cortex which only has six layers but which uses recurrent connections between layers to learn structures which seem like many, many functional layers of processing after the fact.

3.3 Roadmap for mouse-level computational intelligence (MLCI)

At its start, the neural network field hoped to uncover simple, basic laws of learning, powerful enough that all the complexities of higher intelligence could be understood as emergent phenomena, as things which can be learned and need not be assumed a priori. This vision emanated in great part from the great vision of Donald Hebb [29].

By about 1990, however, I understood that there are fundamental reasons why learning and accounting for symmetries in a general way, and some kind of principled chunking of time, really is a crucial tool, even for a general-purpose learning system like a brain. I was inspired in part by a close consideration of work by Albus [30], but also by understanding how the mathematics really does allow much greater capability when such principles are fully exploited. This led me to a workable new framework for trying to build brain-like

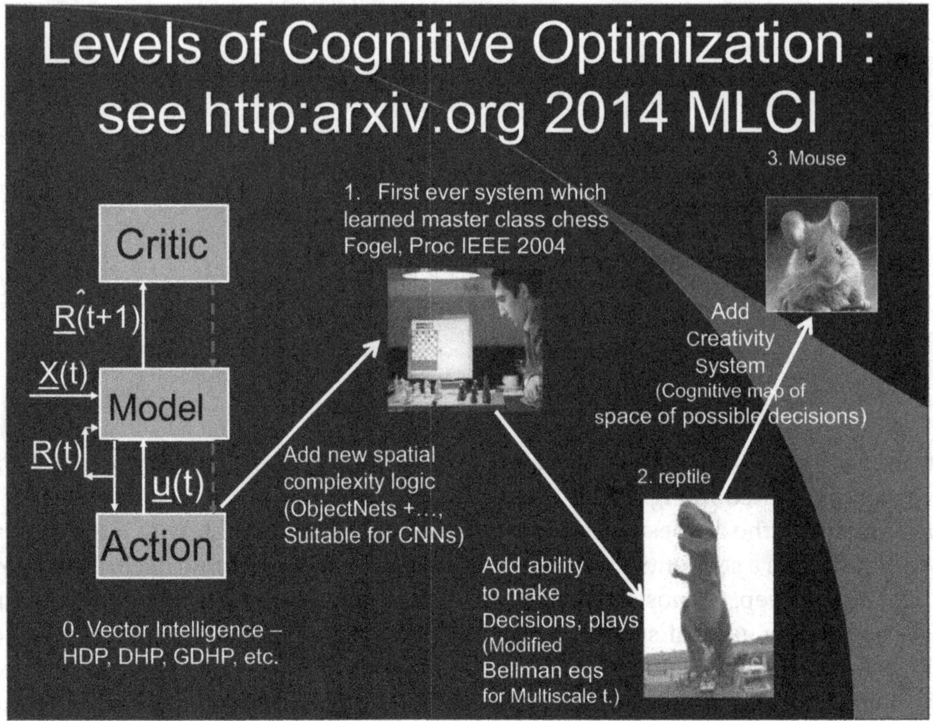

FIG. 12 Roadmap for cognitive optimization.

neural networks [31], including substantial new algorithms. There were certain gaps, particularly on how to go from the temporal intelligence stage to the full creative mouse-level stage, generally filled in at least conceptually by 2009 [32]. This led to the two connected roadmaps for cognitive prediction and cognitive optimization summarized in my main talk at WCCI2014 [5] and in Fig. 12.

3.4 Emerging new hardware to enhance capability by orders of magnitude

True neural network designs are inherently parallel, like the brain. They are designed to be capable of fully exploiting any computer hardware which allows thousands or billions of calculations to be done in parallel. Section 2 mentioned how GPUs played an important role in the deep learning revolution, but GPUs (like feedforward CoNNs) are just the first step on a path which can go much further.

One major landmark in recent years was the discovery of memristors in actual electronics, as proposed many decades before by Leon Chua. Memristors are uniquely well-suited to more efficient hardware implementation of neural networks and are opening the door to many commercial opportunities [33].

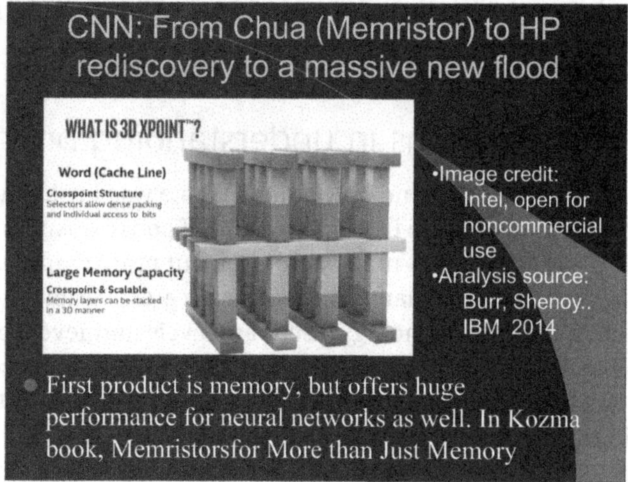

FIG. 13 Newly emerging computer hardware which might be adapted to give us breakthrough throughput in implementing neural networks.

Many years ago, GPUs were designed and marketed simply for use in playing games on a computer, or for video card kinds of applications. Dan Hammerstrom began to study how parallel chips intended for one purpose could be used for neural networks as well, even though they were not initially sold that way.

In a similar way, memory applications have been driving a massive development of memristive-type computer hardware, as illustrated in Fig. 13.

There is a reason to expect that orders of magnitude more capability will be possible here, beyond the GPU generation.

Even beyond that is the kind of capability which a new kind of electronic/photonic hardware might offer, if we combine the capabilities of neural networks and of quantum computing in the most powerful way which is technically possible [34]. But do we really want to do that?

Back at the time of the first rebirth of neural networks, Jasper Lupo, who presided over the $100 million DARPA research in this area, said at the large meetings: "This is bigger than the atomic bomb." At the time, this seemed like just another example of the hype which was confusing people with a kind of misdirected optimism. But as time goes on, there are more and more hints that he might have been right after all. As with most dramatic new technologies, it could be used for good or ill.

Years ago, someone asked me: "Are humans really mature enough to use this technology for the good? Shouldn't we wait until they know themselves better?" But in this case, the serious mathematical principles involved are a key part of what we need to know *in order to* know ourselves better. We are walking a tightrope between risks, on the one hand (as Section 5 will discuss), and the need for humans as a whole to understand themselves better and achieve the level of integrity (mental integration) necessary even to survive as a species. There are times when that seems like an impossible goal, but the experience of the last many years has shown me clearly that "impossible" problems can at times be solved in the end, if one has the discipline to really remember the larger goal.

4 Need for new directions in understanding brain and mind

The deep learning revolution in AI and computer science was basically a cultural revolution. In the understanding of brain intelligence and of consciousness in the mind, the obstacles to greater progress are also mainly cultural, but more complex, because many cultures are involved, and because many cultures have a great variety of misleading conventional wisdoms. As with AI technology, there are levels and levels of understanding and progress possible. Painful as it is, I will narrow my scope here (except at the end of this section), and say just a little on a few simple questions: "Could it be that there is backpropagation in the brain, and that the brain actually uses the kind of clocks shown in Fig. 9 as *it* learns to predict its environment better and better over time? Could it even be that the higher intelligence of the entire brain really is evolved to '*try*' to maximize its expected future utility, just as the rational expectations people in economics say, and falls short only because it takes time to learn and because the optimization problem is a difficult one requiring levels and levels of approximation? Is life a game of probabilities in the end?"

4.1 Toward a cultural revolution in hard neuroscience

There have been hopes that politically correct clock-free models of learning based only on bottom-up research in neuroscience could lead to chip designs which somehow would be able to learn to predict, classify, and solve complex decision problems better than the new mathematics being developed for ANNs. Many millions of dollars have been spent using that philosophy, with questionable success at best. It was very interesting to see how and why HP pulled out of the great DARPA SYNAPS program [33]. That program did achieve some great things, but the outcome reinforced the question: if bottom-up modeling of how the brain learns to predict and to act has not really worked, why not try a top-down approach, moving from the actual learning powers we see in the brain down to the circuits in the brain which may implement them somehow? Since we now know that the calculations of derivatives (exact or modulated) are crucial to AI, why not look to see how and where these calculations might be implemented in the brain?

Back in 1993, when Simon Haykin arranged for Wiley to reprint my Ph.D. thesis in its entirety [35] (reformatted to be more readable) along with a few new papers to put it into context, the great neuropsychologist Karl Pribram wrote an endorsement which appears on the back: "What a delight it was to see Paul Werbos rediscover Freud's version of 'backpropagation.' Freud was adamant (in The Project for a Scientific Psychology) that selective learning could only take place if the presynaptic neuron was as influenced as the postsynaptic neuron during excitation. Such activation of both sides of the contact barrier (Freud's name for the synapse) was accomplished by reducing synaptic resistance by the absorption of 'energy' at the synaptic membranes. Not bad for 1895! But Werbos 1993 is even better."

Freud's work itself is incredibly complicated and variegated. Backpropagation was developed as a kind of mathematical explanation and embodiment of the specific ideas discussed very clearly, and attacked by a pair of modernist social scientists attacking psychoanalysis in general [36]. Pribram himself probed much deeper into Freud's efforts to understand brain learning and intelligence in general [37], but the details are beyond the scope of this simple chapter.

How does the brain actually implement a universal ability to learn to predict? Here is a figure from my theory [32] of how it works:

If you compare Figs. 9–14, you will see that the big picture on the right here matches easily, but the cutout picture on the left is more complicated than anything in Fig. 9. That is because my theory assumes a kind of more advanced version ofautoencoder network taken from my work on mouse-level computational intelligence (Section 3.3). The cutout on the left is an actual photograph of the famous "six layers" of the higher mammal cerebral cortex, which has the same basic cutaway structure in humans, mice, and rats.

If you look closely at Figs. 6 and 9, you will see reference to a number of very important leading researchers whose work led me to this theory. I apologize that I cannot say more here about that work, for reasons of length, but the papers I do cite here give more details. I am also grateful that every one of these great people (except for Scheibel, Connors, and Bliss) took the time at least once to try to explain to me the real intuitive content of what they saw in their data.

It will take a lot of new effort by many new researchers to test out all the details of my theory, or to update it in a way which still fits the kind of neural network mathematics which has a sound mathematical and engineering foundation. For that reason,

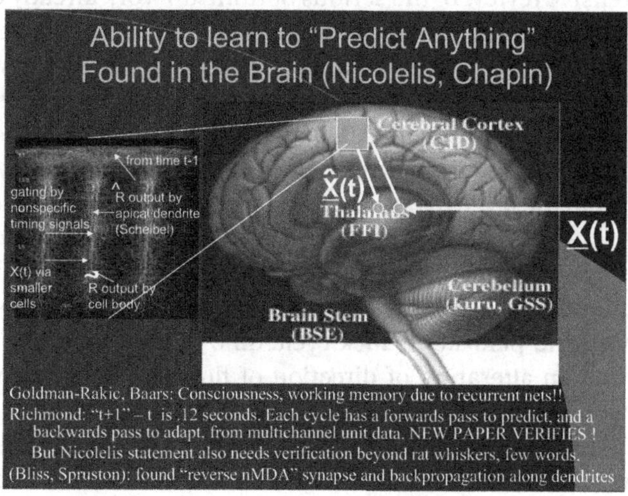

FIG. 14 Brain circuit corresponding to Fig. 9.

I recently decided to extract just two key hypotheses from the theory for further testing: Does the brain really implement a kind of discrete time "cinematic processing" (as in Fig. 10), which requires a kind of hard-wired regular clock to control the overall learning process? Does the cerebral cortex of the brain actually employ a regular alternation of a forward pass to compute its outputs, in the first part of a clock cycle, followed by a backward pass to calculate modulated derivatives and to adapt the main synapses used to generate coherent predictions of its environment? Except for the word "derivatives," this is exactly what Barry Richmond of NIH said to me in a long discussion as we walked to or from a meeting at the Dana Foundation, but I could not find it in print in the published paper he sent me. (Of course, these are just two of the predictions of the theory I published long before.)

Why argue about forward and backward passes in the fast calculations of the brain, when we can simply look directly at real-time data on brain activity with enough resolution in time to test what Richmond asserted? Two major studies did exactly that in 2016, and both support these two hypotheses.

The beautiful figure in the middle captures exactly what Richmond said he saw in his data as well: alternating windows of processing, which seem to go in alternating directions, separated by windows of relative quiet. These results came from a state-of-the-art use of "eCog" technology, a cousin of EEG technology which is far more precise in recording activity in the dendrites (the top level of what you see in Fig. 14) at similar high sampling rate (kilohertz). They are explained further in the final joint paper with Freeman [8].

For my own study [9], in collaboration with Yeshua Davis (who also did much of the computer analysis for Freeman's recent studies), I used existing data—the best data I could find for this purpose. I used the data from a groundbreaking study by Buzsáki's group [38] which was perhaps the most important mainstream study done by then on how general learning actually takes place at a systems level in the brain. Their paper started from an intensive review of the serious bottom-up work already done on learning in the brain, and asked whether that small-scale work is actually reflected in what we see in a systems-level study of changes in the whole brain when it learns new tasks. Buzsáki's group took data from more than 100 channels from microelectrodes deep in the cerebral cortex and hippocampus, at a rate of 20,000 measurements per second. This data estimated the actual firing levels of the neurons, the outputs from the bodies of the neurons, including outputs from the large pyramid cells you see in Fig. 9, from the bottom layer of the cortex.

The graphics in our paper are not so impressive as Fig. 15, but the paper contains a number of hard quantitative measures directly testing the two key questions: Do we see a regular, precise, and persistent clock cycle time in the data from an individual rat over time? Do we see an alteration of direction of flow of information (like the mirror image impression you see in the top panels of Fig. 15) or does flow just keep going from the input side of the cortex to the output side as older computational theories would suggest? The paper gives extensive details of many new measures, all of which agreed that the clock cycle time can be measured with high precision in this kind of data, and that the

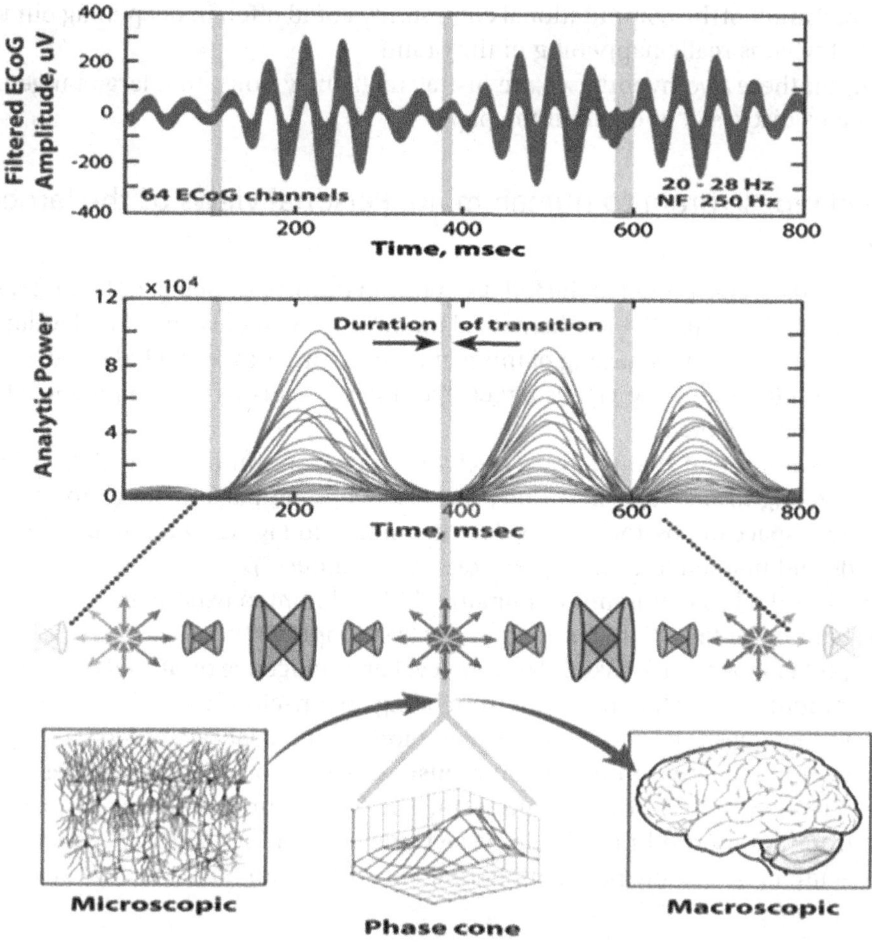

FIG. 15 Empirical results summarized in Kozma and Freeman [7] (used with permission).

"mirror image" hypothesis fits the data with about 40% less error than the error with more conventional theories of biological neural network dynamics.

Of course, there are lots of caveats here, and I would urge the reader to click on the link to the paper itself for a more complete picture. Backpropagation does not predict that the backwards pass is a precise mirror image of the forward pass, but on the whole it does predict a reverse flow of information in the pass which calculates derivatives (locally, of course). The results in our new paper are hopefully just a beginning of a whole new direction, and not an end. If I were still at NSF, I would try to organize a new forecasting competition to predict the Buzsáki data (perhaps even funding Buzsáki group to collect more data, to allow fair blind testing). I would inform the competitors of several resources, including our paper, which may be as important to forecasting of that data as seasonal effects are to predicting things like monthly or weekly economic data. Who knows what a full mobilization of the computational community could offer, in deepening our understanding of what is really happening in the brain?

But again, these two hypotheses are just a small entry point to a large range of new opportunities discussed in detail in the paper.

4.2 From mouse brain to human mind: Personal views of the larger picture

Even as scientists, committed to the full discipline of third-party science [15] and the even narrower discipline of precise mathematical modeling [35], we also need to develop some kind of first-person understanding of mind and life, in order to lead a balanced, sane and even rational life, respecting values larger than the subgoals which we pursue when we wear our hats as scientists.

It really is important that we learn to change hats from time to time [39], using very focused thinking in one area at a time, but also stepping back at times to try to map out the larger space of possibilities (as does the mouse in Fig. 12, but also using our skills with words and mathematics to support our "inner mouse").

As I look at the broader issues of human mind and human experience, I see a picture more and more like Fig. 16, adapted from my 2009 paper [32]:

Some philosophers have asked: "at what level of intelligence or of soul does an organism or a computer make the transition from being unconscious to not being conscious?" In my view, that question itself is grossly naïve and reflects a lack of understanding of any of the many forms or definitions of consciousness. Consciousness is a matter of degree or of level [40], not a "yes" or "no" question. The human brain is basically just a half a level up from the mouse brain, as discussed briefly in my 2011 IJCNN paper [41] and in more detail in one of my papers in neural networks from 2012 [42]. We are not born

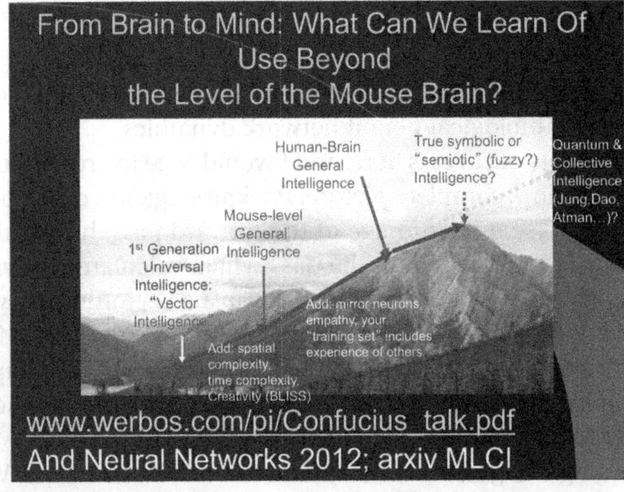

FIG. 16 Big picture of levels of consciousness.

The Biggest Picture
Is the dark cosmos a dark forest or an ocean of life?
Is the primitive village earth surrounded only by hungry tigers or by an ancient civilization like China 1500AD?
Who of us will respect our true ancestors and pass the serious examinations?

FIG. 17 Photograph of distribution of dark matter, a vast network connecting (*orange* (*light gray* in print version) dots) (galaxies).

with a complete ability to use symbolic reasoning and logic and mathematics, or even to use language itself in a completely sane manner; we can learn to emulate sanity or integrity (zhengqi) [43], but it does not come naturally. All we are born with, beyond the kind of learning we see in the mouse brain, are "mirror" neurons and the machinery which supports them: machinery which allows us to include vicarious experience in our own database of memories which we learn from, and to "dance out" our own past experience in ways which other people can assimilate. True natural language is just a kind of dance with words. The core challenge in developing human potential is for us to learn to fully emulate sanity and then to emulate the higher levels of consciousness which sanity opens up [44].

In the end, I view human consciousness as just one small village within a larger cosmos, as depicted in Fig. 17.

Fig. 17 was developed to support a discussion in China of the classic "Three Body" trilogy by Cixin Liu. In my view, dark matter and dark energy (which form more than 90% of the mass-energy of our universe) look like a vast and ancient connected ocean of pulsing energy, which we should expect to form a vast ocean of life. In my view, the answer to the classic "Fermi Paradox [45]" is that we ourselves are connected to that ocean of life. Our possibilities are much better than one might expect, based only on the risks to be discussed in Section 5 or on the possibilities discussed by Cixin Liu (or in CNN news); however, not all teenagers survive to adulthood in the natural world, and the survival of our particular small village is not at all guaranteed.

5 Information technology (IT) for human survival: An urgent unmet challenge

AI is only one of several new developments in technology and in the world situation which threaten the very existence of the human species, depending on how they play out. As the IoT pushes to organize, control, and coordinate every vehicle (civilian or military), every generator, every home, every city, every factory, and every medical device in the world, the real challenge is how to design general frameworks or platforms which can effectively address all of the major threats in a consistent, integrated, and intelligent way. Good systems designers know what a nightmare it can be if different pieces are developed separately, without enough serious thought about what the future interfaces could be.

Well-informed traditional IT people have developed many excellent descriptions of some of the properties which new global, integrating IT platforms should have [46,47], but no one on earth, including me, has found concrete systems answers to the key systems design questions [48] necessary to actually achieve these desired properties.

Because most of the readers of this chapter have already heard about the Terminator risk from AI (which is quite serious), I will focus instead here on a few examples of other threats.

5.1 Examples of the threat from artificial stupidity

Most Americans already understand how impossible life would be if there were no humans available on the telephone, and if one had to navigate traditional dumb voicemail systems to do anything at all. From observing such systems, and from certain outsourced help lines systems, we already understand that corporations sometimes deploy such systems because of the beliefs and culture of their management, even when they don't really improve total system productivity at all. Many of us are already familiar with systems which save the government or a corporation a few dollars, by creating pains and hassles which waste a lot more dollars and value outside the narrow books of the group making the change. We know about the risks of police profiling systems which are not intelligent or accurate enough to spot people who are truly likely to commit a crime, and end up causing problems and waste for totally innocent people.

But even so, a more graphic example of what AS could do may be helpful.

In the year 2000, I led the creation of a joint NSF-NASA workshop to evaluate the possibilities for machine learning and neural nets to make it possible and economic to generate energy in space and beam it down to earth [49,50]. The chair, George Bekey, was not only a leader in robotics research, but also the brother of Ivan Bekey, who for many years was NASA's top planner for long-term future possibilities in space.

As part of the workshop, top roboticists were asked: Is it possible, as the Space Sciences Institute once proposed, to design a 50 ton payload which could be dropped on the moon, designed to make use of resources on the moon to expand and grow and export material up to lunar orbit for use in construction of power stations and cities in orbit? The experts generally agreed it could be done, simply by extending technologies already emerging for robots to make robots. There would be no need for these robots to outsmart humans; they would need only to reproduce, swarm, and adapt. But with large numbers, it would be impossible to effectively guarantee no natural Darwinian selection.

So try to picture in your mind what this would really look like. An entire planet swarming with energetic, aggressive "metal cockroaches," no more intelligent than earth cockroaches, but far more capable physically. In essence, robots do not have to be as smart as humans to become a threat to human life.

5.2 Cyber and EMP threats to the power grid

A few years ago, I attended a talk by Texas Republican Congressman Trent Franks, where he described what it was like to become chair of that committee of the House which receives all of the secret information from all sources on the most serious threats to life in the United States. "You all are only worried because you don't have all the information. If you did, the way I do, you would be terrified out of your minds." Actually, thanks to NSF and IEEE, I have had access to some information he did not have, which pushes in the same direction, but what he said was important anyway.

Franks said that of all the threats he knew of, the threat from large electromagnetic pulses (EMP) is the most serious and immediate. EMPs from solar flares or from credible possible attacks might well take down enough of the power grid to bring the United States back to the Stone Age, except for the obvious possibility of nuclear or biological warfare then taking down what is left. The EMP attack is serious and is discussed further in my recent paper for NATO on risks from terrorism and how to deal with them [51].

Equally important, however, is the threat of a coordinated attack to take down half the generators in the country, which would have very similar effects. In the past, operators of the critical power infrastructure have been far more secure than other infrastructures, in part because they would use operating systems like SE-Linux, backed up by support from Red Hat and NSA, using technology derived from the provably unbreakable "Orange Book" technology first developed for the Honeywell Multics system. (As it happens, the first implementation of backpropagation ran on that system [20], and that gave me a chance to see some of the innards; see http://multicians.org/.) But backdoors have been a major part of that system, and recent leaks have made it more and more clear that our situation is ever riskier. Neural network intrusion detection can help, as can the "sandboxing" being developed by Bromium, but neither should not be oversold as a complete solution. In fact, it may be that the most urgent need for new developments in all of the IT sector is a need for new directions in unbreakable operating systems [51].

One of the major cultural problems here is that risk assessments often assume that risks are independent events, and underestimate rare but catastrophic "correlated risks." More and more, other critical infrastructures need the same level of additional security which the power grid does.

5.3 Threats from underemployment of humans

Many people in the IT field believe, with reason, that the coming massive loss of jobs worldwide will lead to conflicts so severe that we might not survive them [52]. Underemployment in the United States has already started to cause serious political conflicts, as people worry more and more about jobs, but it seems that what is coming will dwarf all that. The Millennium Project has compiled and unified dozens of studies of future employment from all over the world, and the scenarios for the next few decades are not reassuring [53]. Cultural problems and conflicting views about human potential are part of the reason for disturbing world conflicts [51] growing recently, but the sheer rise in unemployment of young males in the Middle East is thought to be just as important by many. It will not help if new IT happens to centralize power in a way which is all too tempting to certain groups both in the West and in the Middle East, both of the Kurzweil persuasion and of the back-to-Abbasid persuasion, to aggravate future conflicts just as it did in France in the 1770s when aristocrats strengthened inequalities in French society. But how can we design IT systems which actually make better use of the inner potential of all humans, in a realistic way?

5.4 Preliminary vision of the overall problem, and of the way out

Fig. 18 gives my view of the big picture of the growing pains of IT today. In traditional thinking, people have assumed that money and biology would be the ultimate arbiters of human life, calling the shots. IT was just one more new means of production—important enough to cause massive changes, but not to change the basic nature of the system. But with the IoT coming on fast, we are entering a new era where IT rules over

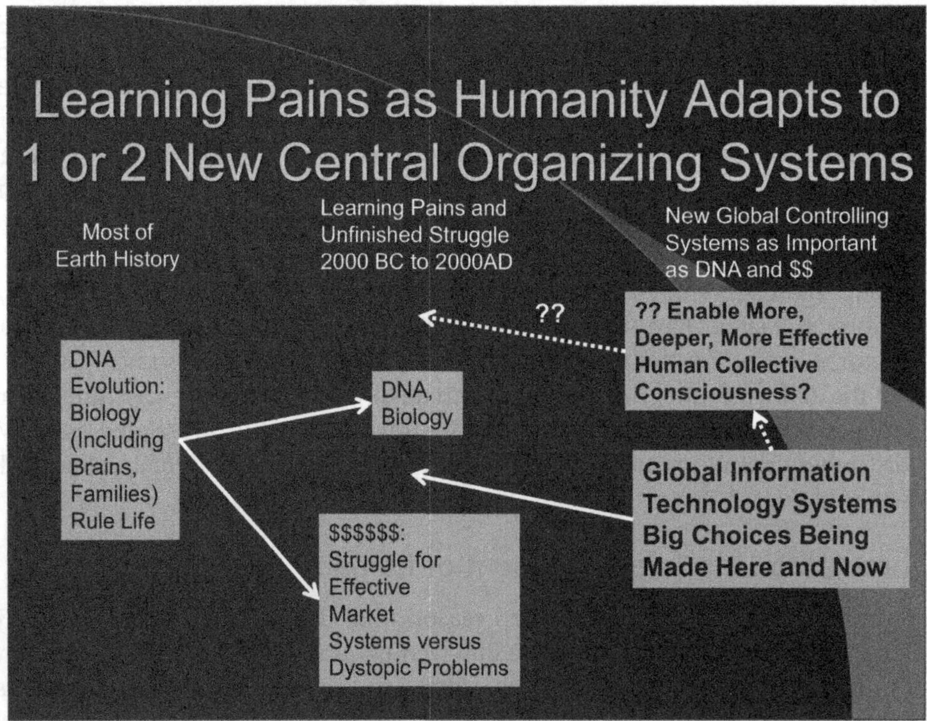

FIG. 18 IT as part of the big picture.

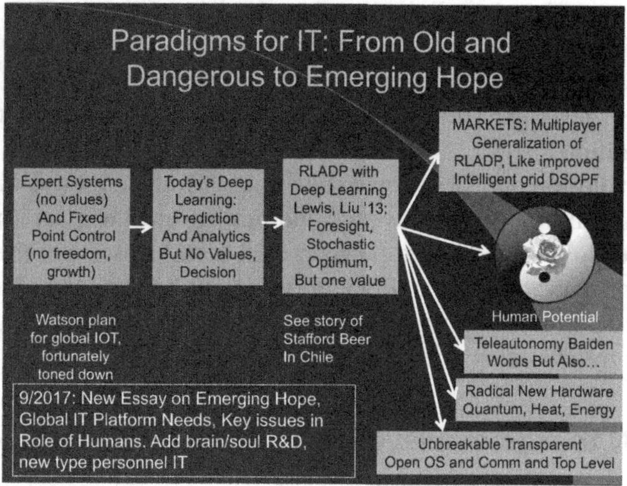

FIG. 19 Hope for a new paradigm.

money, not vice versa, and we desperately need new paradigms to hold things together. It may be very important that human potential also be accelerated, somehow, to keep things from going totally crazy and unsustainable.

Fig. 19 summarizes my view of the massive change in paradigms we will need, in order to survive the challenges ahead. Somehow we need to progress to the right-hand side of this figure, and integrate and support all five of the more hopeful new directions on the right. It is not yet obvious exactly how to do this, but that just adds to the urgency of pushing hard not only to deploy new systems but to think through the concrete possibilities.

This past paragraph already summarizes the global conclusions from all of this work.

6 From deep learning to the future: How to build and use true quantum artificial general intelligence

6.1 The deep learning revolution

Before 2008, mainstream computer science did not believe that neural networks or deep learning would ever be relevant to challenges like speech recognition, face recognition or pattern recognition important to the growth of the internet. (For example, see the older edition of the standard textbook on AI by Stuart Russell et al.) That changed dramatically after Google demonstrated a new product, an open access product letting users define systems containing neural networks, and training them based on gradients.

Sergey Brin of Google explained how this happened in a major talk he gave at the World Economic Forum. (See links at werbos.com/Mind.htm.) Like others in the IT industry, he had believed the mainstream view. But Andrew Ng and Yann LeCun showed him real performance results from neural networks applied to a wide variety of standard difficult challenges in AI, outperforming all the best standard AI used on those challenges. Those results came a grant I awarded them under the NSF COPN activity [54]. The COPN research plan is still relevant and important today, more advanced in those areas than any funding efforts I gave seen since. That plan built heavily on other chapters of this book, from the earlier edition.

By 2017, the revolution had swept over the entire IT industry. I was invited that year to represent the Millennium Project (www.millenium-project.org) at the global futures meeting at Intel headquarters. Their top expert said that the future of their entire industry was with recurrent neural networks RNN and convolutional networks CNN. They had made great progress in developing multicore ritual chips but were worried about new competition from more analog and adaptive chips like GPU.

6.2 From COPN to mammal level artificial general intelligence AGI

The term AGI, for artificial general intelligence, has become more useful and more important in recent years, because the older term AI allows for systems which few of us would call truly intelligent. In the past, many of us defined an " intelligent system" as a system which learns to do better and better in maximizing some measure of value or utility U over time, in general, "in any environment." When I refer to AGI here, I will be referring to that kind of capability.

When we build AGI, or try to understand how intelligence works in biological brains, it is important to remember that there are levels and levels of design. Some AGI are more general than others [55,56]. The more powerful general designs all contain at least two major components, as suggested in Fig. 1:

(1) The optimization system proper, defining the overall architecture of the optimization system. Before 2000, we generally called this kind of design "reinforcement learning," "adaptive critics" or adaptive dynamic programming [57,58] (Chapter 13). Modern accounts integrating what we know across many fields refer to this kind of design as RLADP, reinforcement learning and approximate dynamic programming [59,60].

(2) The major subsystem used to model or predict the stream of inputs coming to the system as a function of its actions u(t). The most general treatment of how to design such a system, up to the mammal brain level, may be found in www.werbos.com/Erdos.pdf.

By 2014, we understood the mathematical principles necessary to "climb" the ladder, up from the early types of neural network design to the mammal brain level. The roadmap for building such systems was given in Werbos [5], presented at the World Congress in Computational Intelligence held that year in China. In Beijing, it was also discussed at Tsinghua University and with the NSF of China, both of which followed up, even as the key connections were terminated in the US due to exogenous political forces. A patent search for "Werbos" gives implementation details for many of the key steps, going beyond the simpler types of neural networks most popular today.

FIG. 20 Pathway to mammal brain level of generality in RLADP.

The roadmap was actually two roadmaps, one for the steps necessary to reach the mammalian level in RLADP, and the other for prediction/modeling/state estimation. These are illustrated in Figs. 20 and 21.

Werbos and Davis [61] tested key predictions of this theory of mammal brain intelligence against real-time multielectrode data from rat brains, using the best data then available from the Buzsaki lab. These predictions fit far better than predictions from older computational models which did not address how to solve difficult general problems in prediction and optimization.

In previous work, Ilin et al. [27] described how spatial complexity can be handled by "ObjectNets," a neural network design which can be implemented in part by the hippocampus encoding memories in terms of traces of objects in the field of view, exploiting the symmetries across different objects. This is far more general and powerful than the simple Euclidean symmetry assumed in convolutional neural networks. But interesting new information has become available about the parahippocampal and paralimbic structures in cetacean brains, and perhaps to a lesser extent in some human brains, implementing the additional power available from exploiting more completely the symmetries between different actors, which can be useful among other things in making better use of mirror neurons, the progenitor of "natural languages" containing subjects (actors) as well as verbs (decision blocks) and objects.

6.3 From classical artificial general intelligence to QAGI

Almost all quantum computing in the US today is based on ways of using the Quantum Turing Machine (QTM), invented by David Deutsch of Oxford. Deutsch proved that QTMs are a universal superset of what can be done with an ordinary Turing machine computer.

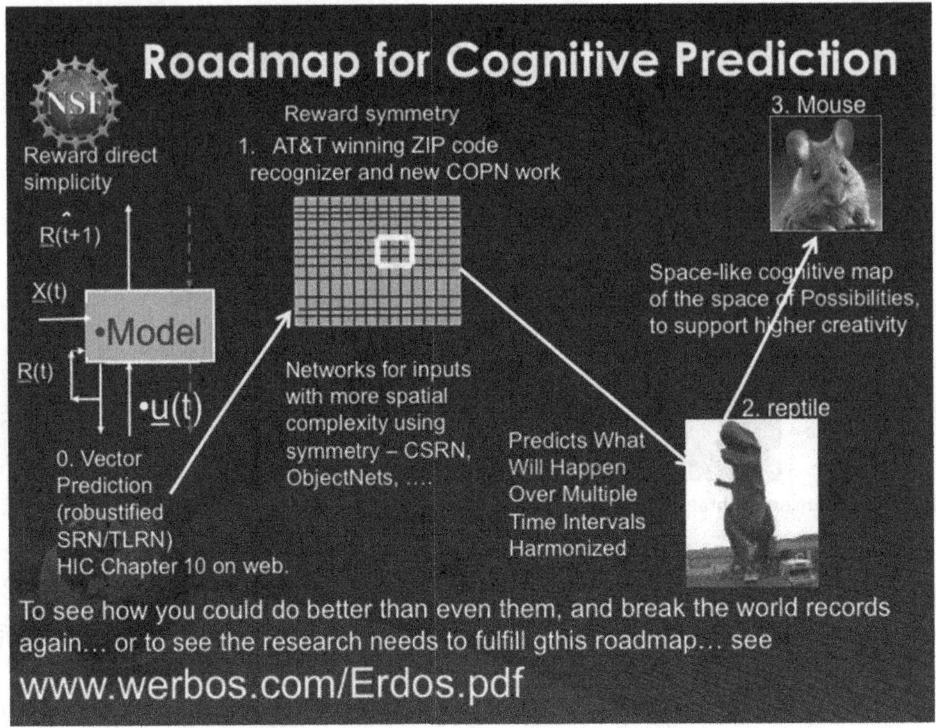

FIG. 21 Pathway to mammal brain level of generality in prediction.

By raising the capabilities up from classical computing to true quantum computing, exploiting the physics of macroscopic Schrodinger cats," it can raise the power of digital computing by orders of magnitude in theory.

However, when QTMS are applied to optimization tasks, like those which underlie advanced neural networks, the benefits have been relatively small compared to what the physics would seem to allow. Werbos and Dolmatova [62] discussed how the greatest computational power may be had by combining the greatest powers of analog, neural network designs and the powers available from quantum superposition. The Canadian company D-Wave did a magnificent job of showing many possible applications, including applications to neural networks, but it did not achieve so much as was hoped.

In 2022, Werbos [63] reviewed this history in some detail and explained how the original vision from D-Wave can be upgraded by using true quantum annealing instead of the methods used in the past by D-Wave for the kind of quadratic optimization task at the core of their system. A provisional patent has been filed with additional material on the details of the crucial initial quadratic optimization task, of hardware options which should be explored, and of many possible early applications. For example, wherever RLADP can be used, true quantum annealing (tQuA) can be used to upgrade its performance, especially in addressing "needle in a haystack" optimization problems suitable for massively parallel searches performed by Schrodinger cats. When AGI is upgraded to use quantum

RLADP instead of classical RLADP, it becomes quantum AGI, a superset of anything which can be done with classical AGI. By 2023, Quantum AI was becoming a popular buzzword used for marketing crude hacks; for a discussion of how AGI based on true, thermal quantum annealing (tQuA) can revolutionize the Internet and global security, see Werbos [64]. See extra content in a one page summary on the deep learning revolutions past and future from my WCCI2022 plenary talk. In addition, please see my patent description "Thermal Quantum Annealing", # US 2023/0252334 A1, https://image-ppubs.uspto.gov/dirsearch-public/print/downloadPdf/20230252334, which includes new details of how to implement and embody the technology, and use it to create orders of magnitude better results in seeing objects far away in the sky.

Appendix: Neural network revolutions, past and future: From BP (neural and fuzzy) to quantum artificial general intelligence (QAGI)[a]

The neural network field has experienced three massive revolutions, starting from 1987, when IEEE held the first International Conference on Neural Networks (ICNN), leading the National Science Foundation (NSF) to create the Neuroengineering research program, which I ran and expanded from 1988 to 2014. This first period of growth already saw a huge proliferation of important new applications in engineering such as vehicle control, manufacturing, and partnerships with biology; see Werbos [65]. IEEE conferences were the primary intellectual center of the new technology, relying mostly on generalized backpropagation (including backpropagation over time and backpropagation for deep learning) and on a ladder of neural network control designs, rising up to "reinforcement learning" (a.k.a. "adaptive critics" or "adaptive dynamic programming").

The second great revolution resulted from a paradigm shifting research program, COPN, which resulted from deep dialog and voting across research program directors at NSF [6]. In that program, I funded Andrew Ng and Yann LeCun to test neural networks on crucial benchmark challenges in artificial intelligence (AI) and computer science. After they demonstrated to Google that neural networks could outperform classical methods in AI, Google announced a new product that set off a massive wave of "new AI" in industry and in computer science.

In computer science, this added momentum to the movement for artificial general intelligence (AGI), which our reinforcement learning designs already aimed at. However, there are levels and levels of generality, even in "general intelligence" [55]. We now speak of reinforcement learning and approximate dynamic programming (RLADP).

In WCCI 2014, held in Beijing, I presented detailed roadmaps of how to rise up from the most powerful methods popular in computer science even today, up to intelligence as general as that of the basic mammal brain (see [5]). This led to intense discussions at

[a]This is a summary of a keynote talk given by Paul J. Werbos at IEEE World Congress of Computational Intelligence (WCCI2022), Padua, Italy, June 12, 2022, https://wcci2022.org/invited-speakers/.

Tsinghua and at the NSF of China, which led to new research directions in China where there have been massive new applications beyond what most researchers in the west consider possible. (See http://1dddas.org/ for the diverse and fragmented communities in the west. Also do a patent search on Werbos for details of how to implement higher level classical AGI.) Werbos and Davis [9] show how this view of intelligence fits real-time data from rat brains better than older paradigms for brain modeling.

This year, we have opened the door to a new revolution. Just as adaptive analog networks, neural networks, massively and provably open up capabilities beyond old sequential Turing machines, the quantum extension of RLADP offers power far beyond what the usual Quantum Turing Machines (invented by David Deutsch) can offer. It offers true quantum AGI (QAGI), which can multiply capabilities by orders of magnitude in an application domain that requires higher intelligence such as observing the sky, management of complex power grids, and "quantum bromium" (hard cybersecurity). See [63] and links on internet issues at build-a-world.org.

References

[1] NSF, Learning and Intelligent Systems. www.nsf.gov/pubs/1998/nsf97132/nsf97132.htm.

[2] NSF, KDI: Knowledge and Distributed Intelligence. www.nsf.gov/pubs/1999/nsf9929/nsf9929.pdf.

[3] www.weforum.org/agenda/2017/01/google-sergey-brin-i-didn-t-see-ai-coming.

[4] P.J. Werbos, Computational intelligence from AI to BI to NI, in: SPIE Sensing Technology+Applications, International Society for Optics and Photonics, 2015. www.werbos.com/SPIE2015_NN.pdf.

[5] P.J. Werbos, From ADP to the brain: foundations, roadmap, challenges and research priorities, in: 2014 International Joint Conference on Neural Networks (IJCNN), IEEE, 2014. https://arxiv.org/abs/1404.0554.

[6] NSF, Emerging Frontiers in Research and Innovation, 2008. www.nsf.gov/pubs/2007/nsf07579/nsf07579.htm.

[7] R. Kozma, W.J. Freeman, Cognitive Phase Transitions in the Cerebral Cortex-enhancing the Neuron Doctrine by Modeling Neural Fields, Springer, 2016.

[8] R. Kozma, W.J. Freeman, Cinematic operation of the cerebral cortex interpreted via critical transitions in self-organized dynamic systems, Front. Syst. Neurosci. 11 (2017). www.ncbi.nlm.nih.gov/pmc/articles/PMC5348494/.

[9] P.J. Werbos, J.J.J. Davis, Regular cycles of forward and backward signal propagation in prefrontal cortex and in consciousness, Front. Syst. Neurosci. 10 (2016). www.ncbi.nlm.nih.gov/pmc/articles/PMC5125075/.

[10] G. Lewis-Kraus, The great AI awakening, New York Times (2016). https://nyti.ms/2hMtKOn.

[11] Recurrent Neural Networks and Other Machines that Learn Algorithms. http://people.idsia.ch/~rupesh/rnnsymposium2016/.

[12] A. Adamatzky, G. Chen, Chaos, CNN, Memristors and Beyond: A Festschrift for Leon Chua with DVD-ROM, 2013, Composed by Eleonora Bilotta, World Scientific https://pdfs.semanticscholar.org/3b5e/916a8d8897de46bdfcd945b6119b761f1913.pdf.

[13] D. Luenberger, Y. Ye, Linear and Nonlinear Programming, fourth ed., Springer, 2016.

[14] P.J. Werbos, Backpropagation through time: what it does and how to do it, Proc. IEEE 78 (10) (1990) 1550–1560. http://mail.werbos.com/Neural/BTT.pdf.

[15] T.S. Kuhn, The Structure of Scientific Revolutions, second ed., University of Chicago Press, 1970.

[16] M. Minsky, S. Papert, Perceptrons, MIT Press, Cambridge, MA, 1969, pp. 18–19.

[17] V. Nostrand, in: D.A. White, D.A. Sofge (Eds.), Handbook of Intelligent Control: Neural, Fuzzy, and Adaptive Approaches, 1992. Chapter 10 www.werbos.com/HIC_Chapter10.pdf.

[18] S. Amari, A theory of adaptive pattern classifiers, IEEE Trans. Electronic Comp. 3 (1967) 299–307.

[19] W.A. Rosenblith, Sensory Communication: Contributions to the Symposium on Principles of Sensory Communications, Jul. 19–Aug. 1, 1959, MIT Press, 1961.

[20] P.J. Werbos, Beyond Regression: New Tools for Prediction and Analysis in the Behavioral Sciences, Doctoral Dissertation, Applied Mathematics, Harvard University, MA, 1974.

[21] P. Werbos, Backwards differentiation in AD and neural nets: past links and new opportunities, in: Automatic Differentiation: Applications, Theory, and Implementations, 2006, pp. 15–34. http://mail.werbos.com/AD2004.pdf.

[22] G.E. Box, G.M. Jenkins, Time series analysis, control, and forecasting, Holden Day, San Francisco, CA 3226 (3228) (1976) 10.

[23] Y. LeCun, Convolutional Neural Networks, 2023. http://deeplearning.net/tutorial/lenet.html.

[24] G.W. Cottrell, Extracting features from faces using compression networks: face, identity, emotion and gender recognition using holons, in: Connectionist Models: Proceedings of the 1990 Summer School, 1990, pp. 328–337. http://cseweb.ucsd.edu/~gary/pubs/connectionist-models-1990.pdf.

[25] P. Werbos, Mathematical foundations of prediction under complexity, in: Erdos Lecture Series, 2011. www.werbos.com/Neural/Erdos.pdf.

[26] A.R. Barron, Approximation and estimation bounds for artificial neural networks, Mach. Learn. 14 (1) (1994) 113–143.

[27] R. Ilin, R. Kozma, P.J. Werbos, Beyond feedforward models trained by backpropagation: a practical training tool for a more efficient universal approximator, IEEE Trans. Neural Netw. 19 (6) (2008) 929–937. https://arxiv.org/abs/0710.4182.

[28] C.P. Chen, Z. Liu, Broad learning system: an effective and efficient incremental learning system without the need for deep architecture, IEEE Trans. Neural Networks Learning Syst. (2018) 10–24.

[29] D.O. Hebb, The Organization of Behavior: A Neuropsychological Theory, Wiley Science Editions, 1952. http://14.139.56.90/bitstream/1/2027513/1/HS1199.pdf.

[30] J.S. Albus, Outline for a theory of intelligence, IEEE Trans. Syst. Man Cybernet. 21 (3) (1991) 473–509. ftp://calhau.dca.fee.unicamp.br/pub/docs/ia005/Albus-outline.pdf.

[31] P.J. Werbos, 3-Brain Architecture for an Intelligent Decision and Control System, 2001, U.S. Patent 6,169,981 http://www.freepatentsonline.com/6169981.html.

[32] P.J. Werbos, Intelligence in the brain: a theory of how it works and how to build it, Neural Netw. 22 (3) (2009) 200–212. https://www.iospress.nl/book/identification-of-potential-terrorists-and-adversary-planning/.

[33] R. Kozma, R.E. Pino, G.E. Pazienza (Eds.), Advances in Neuromorphic Memristor Science and Applications, vol. 4, Springer Science & Business Media, 2012.

[34] P.J. Werbos, L. Dolmatova, Analog quantum computing (AQC) and the need for time-symmetric physics, Quantum Inf. Process 15 (3) (2016) 1273–1287. www.werbos.com/triphoton.pdf.

[35] P.J. Werbos, The Roots of Backpropagation: From Ordered Derivatives to Neural Networks and Political Forecasting, John Wiley & Sons, 1994.

[36] Y.D. Barrett, Ego and Instinct: The Psychoanalytic View of Human Nature-Revised, No. 154.22 Y23, Random House, 1970.

[37] K.H. Pribram, M.M. Gill, Freud's "Project" Re-assessed: Preface to Contemporary Cognitive Theory and Neuropsychology, Basic Books, 1976.

[38] S. Fujisawa, A. Amarasingham, M.T. Harrison, G. Buzsáki, Behavior-dependent short-term assembly dynamics in the medial prefrontal cortex, Nat. Neurosci. 11 (7) (2008) 823–833.

[39] D.J. Levitin, The Organized Mind: Thinking Straight in the Age of Information Overload, Penguin Random House, 2014.

[40] P.J. Werbos, What do neural nets and quantum theory tell us about mind and reality, in: No Matter, Never Mind: Proceedings of toward a Science of Consciousness: Fundamental Approaches, Tokyo, 1999, pp. 63–87. https://arxiv.org/abs/q-bio/0311006.

[41] P. Werbos, Neural networks as a path to self-awareness, in: Neural Networks (IJCNN), The 2011 International Joint Conference on IEEE, IEEE, 2011, pp. 3264–3271. http://werbos.com/pi/NNs_As_Path_IJCNN11_Mar28.pdf.

[42] P.J. Werbos, Neural networks and the experience and cultivation of mind, Neural Netw. 32 (2012) 86–95.

[43] P.J. Werbos, Links between consciousness and the physics of time, in: International IFNA-ANS Journal "Problems of Nonlinear Analysis in Engineering Systems", 2015. http://www.kcn.ru/tat_en/science/ans/journals. http://www.werbos.com/Mind_in_Time.pdf.

[44] P. Werbos, Unification of Objective Realism and Spiritual Development, 2017. http://scsiscs.org/conference/index.php/scienceandscientist/2017/paper/view/166/53. www.facebook.com/paul.werbos/posts/1924099547620453.

[45] D. Brin, Existence, Tor Books, 2012.

[46] D. Tapscott, A. Tapscott, Blockchain Revolution, Penguin, 2016.

[47] https://webfoundation.org/.

[48] http://drpauljohn.blogspot.com/2017/10/questions-needing-addressing-as-iot.html.

[49] https://www.nsf.gov/awardsearch/showAward?AWD_ID=0075691.

[50] http://www.werbos.com/SSP2000/SSP.htm.

[51] P. Werbos, New technology options and threats to detect and combat terrorism, in: T.J. Gordon, E. Florescu, J.C. Glenn, Y. Sharan (Eds.), Identification of Potential Terrorists and Adversary Planning: Emerging Technologies and New Counter-Terror Strategies, IOP Press, 2017. https://www.iospress.nl/book/identification-of-potential-terrorists-and-adversary-planning/. www.werbos.com/NAT_terrorism.pdf.

[52] www.theatlantic.com/magazine/archive/2015/07/world-without-work/395294/.

[53] Millennium Project, Future Work/Technology 2050. http://107.22.164.43/millennium/AI-Work.html.

[54] National Science Foundation, Emerging Frontiers in Research and Innovation 2008, 2007. https://www.nsf.gov/pubs/2007/nsf07579/nsf07579.htm.

[55] P.J. Werbos, What do neural nets and quantum theory tell us about mind and reality? Adv. Conscious. Res. 33 (2001) 63–88. https://arxiv.org/pdf/q-bio/0311006.pdf.

[56] M.E. Bitterman, The evolution of intelligence, Sci. Am. 212 (1) (1965) 92–101.

[57] W.T. Miller III, R.S. Sutton, P.J. Werbos (Eds.), Neural Networks for Control, MIT Press, 1990.

[58] D.A. White, D.A. Sofge (Eds.), Handbook of Intelligent Control: Neural, Fuzzy, and Adaptive Approaches, Van Nostrand Reinhold Company, 1992. Chapter 13 http://www.werbos.com/HICChapter13.pdf.

[59] F.L. Lewis, D. Liu (Eds.), Reinforcement Learning and Approximate Dynamic Programming for Feedback Control, vol. 17, John Wiley & Sons, 2013.

[60] P.J. Werbos, Approximate dynamic programming (ADP), in: J. Baillieul, T. Samad (Eds.), Encyclopedia of Systems and Control, second ed., Springer, 2021.

[61] P.J. Werbos, J.J. Davis, Regular cycles of forward and backward signal propagation in prefrontal cortex and in consciousness, Front. Syst. Neurosci. 97 (2016). https://www.frontiersin.org/articles/10.3389/fnsys.2016.00097/.

[62] P.J. Werbos, L. Dolmatova, Analog quantum computing (AQC) and the need for time-symmetric physics, Quantum Inf. Process 15 (3) (2016) 1273–1287. See the extended version at Werbos.com/triphoton.pdf, owing thanks to discussions with Tsinghua University, building on their collaborations with Wilczek.

[63] P.J. Werbos, Quantum technology to expand soft computing, Syst. Soft Comp. 4 (2022) 200031. https://www.sciencedirect.com/science/article/pii/S2772941922000011.

[64] P.J. Werbos, Response submitted to NSF/TIP request for guidance on new roadmap, 2023. http://drpauljohn.blogspot.com/2023/06/draft-response-nsftip-request-for.html. (Accessed 26 June 2023).

[65] P.J. Werbos, Computational intelligence from AI to BI to NI, in: Independent Component Analyses, Compressive Sampling, Large Data Analyses (LDA), Neural Networks, Biosystems, and Nanoengineering XIII, vol. 9496, pp. 149–157. SPIE, 2015.

7

Computers versus brains: Challenges of sustainable artificial and biological intelligence

Robert Kozma[a,b]

[a]DEPARTMENT OF MATHEMATICS, UNIVERSITY OF MEMPHIS, MEMPHIS, TN, UNITED STATES

[b]RESEARCH AND INNOVATION CENTER, ÓBUDA UNIVERSITY, BUDAPEST, HUNGARY

Chapter outlines

1 The dream of creating artificial intelligence

1.1 From ancient Greeks to digital computers

Our greatest thinkers through millennia had a never-ending quest to understand and mimic human behavior. Ancient Greek philosophers pondered about the nature of human intelligence and the potential of man-made devices to reproduce human behaviors. Tangible technical progress has been achieved only after the proliferation of the ideas of the

Artificial Intelligence in the Age of Neural Networks and Brain Computing. https://doi.org/10.1016/B978-0-323-96104-2.00013-0

Copyright © 2024 Elsevier Inc. All rights reserved.

Renaissance, including the artistic and scientific genius of Leonardo da Vinci in the 15th to 16th centuries. In addition to being an unparalleled artist of all times, Leonardo was an outstanding scientist too who designed flying machines, automatic weapons, as well as a mechanic humanoid robot knight [1]. Although there is no surviving implementation of Leonardo's robot, its designs show Leonardo's deep understanding of the human body and his ingenuity in early engineering designs.

From the 17th century, mechanical toys and machines became popular. A prominent example is Farkas Kempelen's chess-playing machine the "Turk." According to the available documentation, Kempelen built the "Turk" in 1795, which has been phenomenally popular for many years [2]. Kempelen traveled with the "Turk" in the European courts, defeating many human challengers, including Catherine the Great and Napoleon Bonaparte. As it turned out, the "Turk" chess machine was a fake; a human was hiding inside the machine who was an expert chess player. In spite of this disappointing revelation, the very fact that the "Turk" has been an advanced machine with moving body parts imitating human behaviors was a great engineering feat at that age.

Much technological advancement has been made in the following centuries as the result of the industrial revolution, but it was not until the invention of digital computers in the mid-20th century when the human dream of creating machines equaling human intelligence can be realized. The invention of electronic digital computers created a new playfield for the development of intelligent machines.

1.2 The birth of artificial intelligence and machine intelligence

Dominated by the proliferation of digital computers, symbolic approaches have been prominent in the new research discipline of AI, which rapidly progressed during the 60s to 80s, following Minsky's footsteps [3,4]. As the computational power of computers expanded, the sophistication of symbol manipulations increased tremendously. A leading AI paradigm explicitly declared that advanced manipulation of a physical symbol system has all the sufficient and necessary means of intelligent behavior in man and machine [5,6]. Accordingly, external events and perceptions are transformed into inner symbols to represent the state of the world. There is a set of rules describing possible deductions and actions through logical inferences using these rules. The rules are part of an inference engine; together with a knowledge base and corresponding data, they constitute an expert system. The knowledge base may become huge to account for the intricate specifics of the real-life problem domain. In expert systems, problem-solving takes the form of a search through the space of symbols using inferences, such as Laird and colleagues' SOAR and many extensions [7,8].

Symbolic AI approaches produced many successful implementations. However, symbolic models may become rigid and they may not be able to fully accommodate the many changes inevitable in real-life situations. Dreyfus' situated intelligence approach is a prominent example of a philosophical alternative to symbolism [9]. Dreyfus ascertains that intelligence is defined in the context of the environment, and a fixed symbol system cannot fully grasp the essence of intelligence [9]. Situated intelligence finds its successful applications in embodied intelligence and robotics; see e.g., [10,11].

Neural networks represent an alternative to symbolic approaches [12]. They employ massive data to build AI classifiers without the need for preset symbolic rule base. Neural networks can be viewed as bottom-up methods starting from data and moving toward abstractions at higher levels, while symbolic AI implements top-down processing by employing a broad existing knowledge base to make inferences applicable to the specific problem at hand. Neural networks emphasize parallel-distributed processing over adaptive structures and they are robust and flexible. Knowledge-based neural networks are devoted to combine the advantages of symbolic and neural approaches [13].

1.3 New AI with super-human performance, and the deep learning frontier

The human dream of building machines that parallel or even exceed human intelligence became a reality 25 years ago and led to the development of AI with super-human performance in many practical tasks. The spectacular successes of AI have attracted great interest and also cautionary views not only in the technical community but also in the broad public [14]; see Fig. 1 for a chronology.

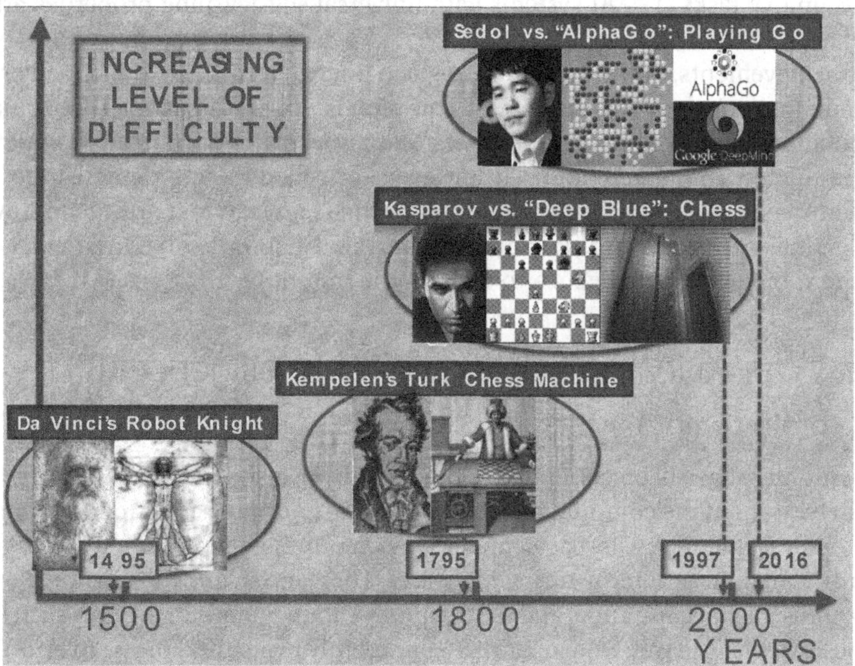

FIG. 1 Examples of mimicking human performance and intelligence during the past 500 years; from Leonardo Da Vinci's mechanical knight design (1495), through Kempelen Farkas' chess-playing robot the "Turk" (1795), to IBM Deep Blue defeating the world chess champion Garry Kasparov in 1997, and Google Alpha-Go defeating the Go world champion Lee Sedol in 2016.

A crucial breakthrough happened in 1997 when IBM's Deep Blue supercomputer defeated the reigning world chess champion Gary Kasparov in six matches [15]. This has been a widely applauded breakthrough, although some skeptics remarked that Deep Blue used brute force to defeat Kasparov, and it was not really intelligent, rather it exercised overwhelming computational power against its human counterpart. The chess played by Deep Blue still resembled the concept of "man hidden in the machine." Although no actual human was being hidden in the machine, still the computer operations were based on incorporating a great many human players' expertize in the game.

The critics of Deep Blue's performance predicted that AI would not be a real match to human intelligence in the foreseeable future in various more challenging mental tasks. However, recent events showed that AI systems did rise to the challenge. In 2011, the IBM computer system Watson beat the best human players in the television quiz show Jeopardy. This was followed in 2016 by the stunning win of Google's Alpha-Go over the world's best Go player Lee Sedol in a contest organized in Seoul, S. Korea according to the strictest world Go competition regulations [16]. Alpha-Go represented a significant advancement with respect to Deep Blue because it was based on learning from examples, rather than using only a priori rules.

It is clear that by today's highest standards, humans are of no match to the best AI algorithms in chess, Go, shogi, card games, and many other challenging computer games and specific cognitive tasks [17]. AI systems with universal self-learning properties are dominating the field [18].

These achievements, however, come at a steep price in terms of exponentially increasing demand for computational resources. This path is not sustainable as the demand for AI computational power raises real conflict among various societal needs competing for limited resources. Implementations using event-driven domains demonstrate further progress in Deep Q-Learning applications [18], which can lead to a drastic improvement in energy-efficient neuromorphic platforms. In this Chapter, we analyze what can be learned from biological intelligence to address the mounting challenges AI faces.

2 What can AI learn from biological intelligence (BI)?

2.1 The brain-computer metaphor

Digital computers have been compared to brains starting from their very inception [19,20] and the debate about the computer-brain relationship continues until today. Digital computers employ sequential, rule-based operations on numbers represented in digital form, which are the manifestations of Turing machines. There are scientists insisting that brains are in fact huge digital computers and the computer-brain metaphor is to be taken literally. Others observe that the wet-ware of brains is inherently messy and prone to errors, so the real wonder to be learned from brains is how it is possible to achieve robust functioning and high-level cognitive performance in spite of the noisy operation of brain tissues. Insights gained in the past more than half a century using increasingly sophisticated brain imaging techniques indicate that brains implement massively parallel and distributed operating principles with complex dynamic interactions between billions of brain components, which likely differ from the operation of a postulated digital Turing machine [19,21].

2.2 Neural networks and deep learning

Describing today's groundbreaking AI achievements, we have to realize that the underlying powerful deep learning approaches are based on neural network research conducted for many decades, motivated by the knowledge accumulated on the operation and functions of biological neural systems. Artificial neural networks appeared first in the 1940s in McCulloch and Pitts' pioneering work [22] and in Wiener's cybernetics [23]. Mathematical guarantees of their functional approximation properties were provided by Kolmogorov and Arnold [24,25], with many developments in the following decades. Werbos' backpropagation presented the first constructive algorithm to build such an approximation [26], but it was not until the late 80s that neural networks became mainstream through parallel and distributed processing [27–29].

The first edition of the present book marked the 30th anniversary of the foundation of the International Neural Network Society (INNS), which provided the forum for many pioneers of the field to develop neuromorphic computational theories and practical implementations [12]. Indeed, deep learning uses multilayer neural network architectures trained by the backpropagation learning algorithm, which has been developed over 40 years ago [26]. These results provide firm theoretical foundations for a new wave of AI with deep learning neural networks.

We do not aim at providing an overview of the massive work on neural networks in the past decades. Some prominent examples include LeCun's LeNet convolutional networks [30] and Schmidhuber's long short-term memories [31], illustrating the fundamental work that leads to the deep learning revolution of AI at the turn of the century [32]. The successes of deep learning were facilitated by several main factors, including easy access to vast amounts of data, often referred to as "Big Data," and the availability of cheap computing technology based on very powerful chips: Graphical Processing Units (GPU), Tensor Processing Units (TPU), and neuromorphic chips. Deep learning can efficiently adjust billions of parameters on massively parallel computer hardware, leading to superior performance in various applications, such as image processing and speech recognition.

3 Always at the edge—The miracle of life and intelligence

3.1 Multistability in physics and biology

Multistability has been described in physical and biological processes. Physical systems consisting of many parts may exhibit various dynamical regimes depending on the dynamics of their parts and the nature of the interactions among the components. If the interaction among the parts is strong, the overall behavior may become a synchronized regime. Synchronization can be either amplitude or phase synchrony [33]. In the case of amplitude synchrony, the amplitudes of the various components are the same across the system, which is a strong case of synchrony. In some other conditions, the amplitudes of the individual components may differ, but they are in the same phase, i.e., they wake and wane simultaneously. This more relaxed occurrence of synchrony is called phase synchrony. An even more complex behavior may occur when different parts of the system show amplitude or phase synchrony for some time, but the synchrony diminishes for other periods, at least in parts of the system. This is the case of multistability when the system is intermittently stable (metastable) for some time and space and it switches to another state as the dynamics evolve [34–36]. As described by the complementarity principle, such switching between metastable states is the result of spontaneous symmetry breaking in self-organizing dynamical systems [37–39].

Coupled map lattices (CML) give a convenient mathematical model of metastable behaviors. In CMLs, the dynamics of each part of the system are described by some nonlinear mapping function, while the parts are connected according to lattice geometry. Examples of a CML over a one-dimensional lattice (circle) with periodic boundary conditions are shown in Fig. 2. Various types of coupling are considered, including *local,*

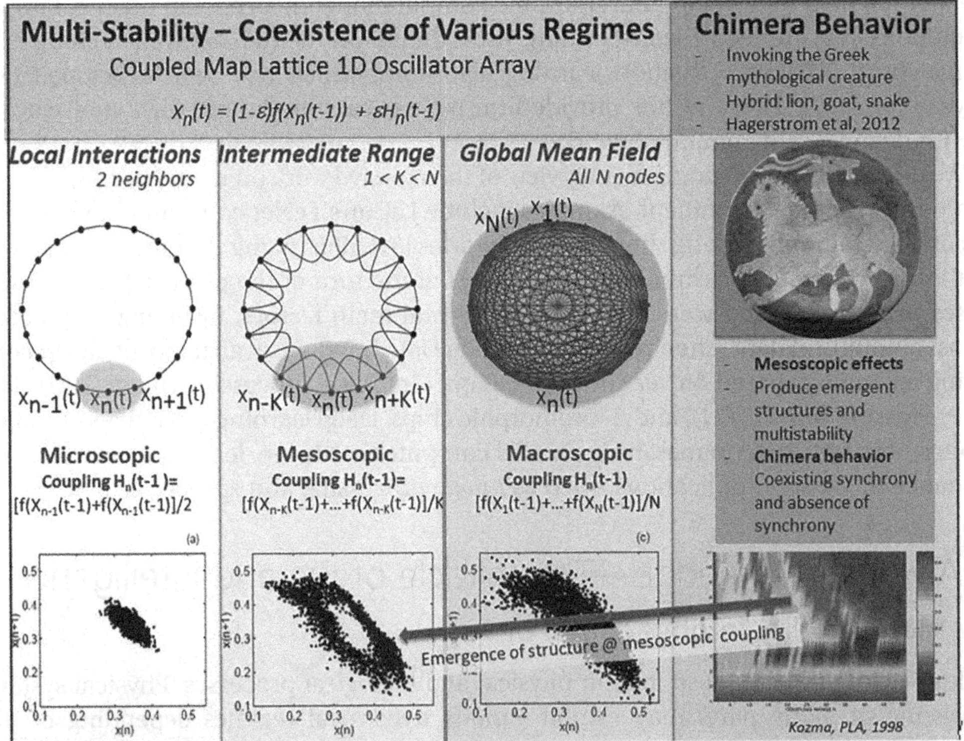

FIG. 2 Multistability effects due to mesoscopic/intermediate-range interactions. Coupled map lattices with local, intermediate, and global (mean-field) interactions. The emergence of low-dimensional attractor structures is demonstrated for mesoscopic coupling; based on [35]. The phase diagram with regions of high synchrony and low synchrony identifies chimera states with co-existing nonsynchronous and coherent states.

mesoscopic, and *global* coupling, respectively [35]. In the case of *local* coupling, a node interacts only with its direct neighbors on the lattice, which means two neighbors (left and right) over the 1D lattice. The other extreme case is *global* or mean field coupling when each node interacts with all other nodes of the lattice. Note that in mean field models, the actual lattice geometry becomes irrelevant due to the all-to-all interactions.

Mesoscopic or intermediate-range effects are of particular interest when a node interacts with some nodes beyond its immediate neighbors but not the whole lattice. Intermediate-range coupling can produce peculiar resonance effects when oscillations emerge in a narrow frequency band. Detailed analysis showed that mesoscopic coupling produces the so-called *chimera* effect with the mixture of qualitatively different behaviors identified, e.g., in laser systems [40]. In chimera dynamics, the array of identical oscillators splits into two domains: one coherent with phase synchrony, while the other lacks coherence and is desynchronized. Chimera states in oscillatory systems of physics are named after mythological beasts with multiple heads and identities joined in one body [41].

3.2 Metastability in cognition and brain dynamics

Our subjective perceptions suggest that conscious experiences are continuous processes with typically smooth variation in time. Decades-long studies pioneered by Freeman, however, indicate that the perception of continuity and smoothness is an illusion and our cognitive processing contains frequent switches and rapid transitions between relatively stable periods of cognitive processing [42,43]. In cognitive science, this behavior is referred to as metastability and multistability, which are important manifestations of consciousness and human intelligence [44]. Further analysis indicates that discontinuities are not merely important aspects of cognition; rather they are key attributes of intelligent behavior representing the cognitive "Aha" moment of sudden insight and deep understanding in humans and animals [45].

Behavioral manifestations of metastability are described by Kelso as the complementarity principle [38]. For example, the reader is encouraged to look at the Necker cube in Fig. 3A. After some period of time, you will experience a switching between two mental

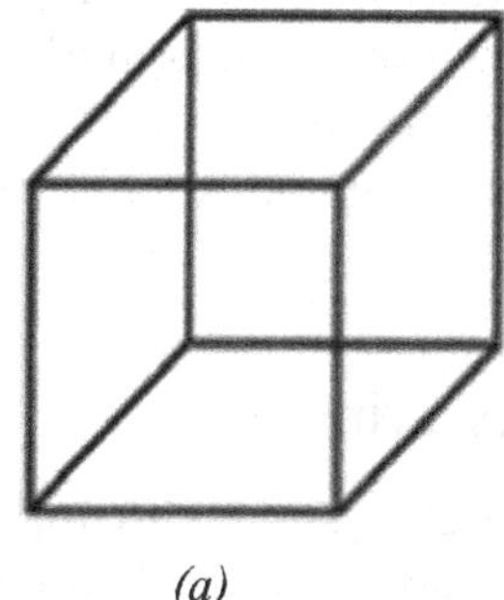

(a)

(b)

FIG. 3 Illustration of bistability in visual perception: (A) Necker cube; (B) vase versus two faces. *Graphics are courtesy of A. de Smet.*

representations with the front side of the cube being the lower or higher square, respectively. A similar effect is induced by inspecting the "vase" in Fig. 3B which, after some time, spontaneously switches to the percept of two faces and vice versa. Such spontaneous switching between metastable perceptual representations is interpreted according to the complementarity principle as the result of symmetry breaking in self-organizing dynamical systems. The emergence of patterns and pattern switching occurs spontaneously, solely as a result of the dynamics of the system: no specific ordering influence from the outside and no homunculus-like agent or program inside is responsible for the behavior observed [37,39].

The concept of metastable patterns and intermittent transients has been extended to neurodynamics [46–48]. Note that in the foregoing discussions, we do not claim that perceptual switching with the Necker cube and switches observed in neurodynamics are the same phenomena. Rather we point out that switches may occur in different forms and at different time scales in cognition and neural processes. Freeman's neurodynamics describes the brain state through a trajectory across a high-dimensional space. The trajectory evolves through a sequence of metastable states [34,46]. These metastable states may be viewed as intermittent symbolic representations of the stimuli in the context of the individual's past experiences and present desires. However, these metastable symbols are transient and disintegrate soon after they emerge [36,48].

This leads to the cinematic theory of human cognition [42,43]. Human intelligence is manifested through the emergence of a sequence of coherent metastable amplitude patterns. Any particular metastable pattern exists only for a brief period of 0.1–0.2 s; this is why it is called metastable. The pattern ultimately collapses in a rapid desynchronization effect, followed by the emergence of a new metastable pattern. According to the cinematic theory of cognition, the metastable patterns represent the movie frame, and the brief desynchronization period corresponds to the shutter. The collapse of the states signifies the shutter and it takes about 10–20 ms. This collapse is the manifestation of a spatial bottleneck in neural processing that produces repeated singularities in time in the form of the shutter.

Fig. 4 illustrates experimental findings on metastability in brain dynamics using electrocorticograms (ECoGs) from an array of 8×8 electrodes in the rabbit sensory cortex [36]. The top plot with the ECoG signals shows beating patterns of relatively high synchrony for about 150–200 ms, interrupted by brief desynchronization periods marked by blue bars. The bottom plots in Fig. 4 show the complementary aspects of microscopic and macroscopic neural processes in rabbit brains, interacting through phase cones emerging at the mesoscopic scales.

3.3 Metastability and the complementarity principle

The co-existence of multiple dynamical states in a single system is an important behavior that bears relevance to many fields of science, including biological and artificial intelligence. In the case of the CML physical model, the bistable/multistable dynamics became

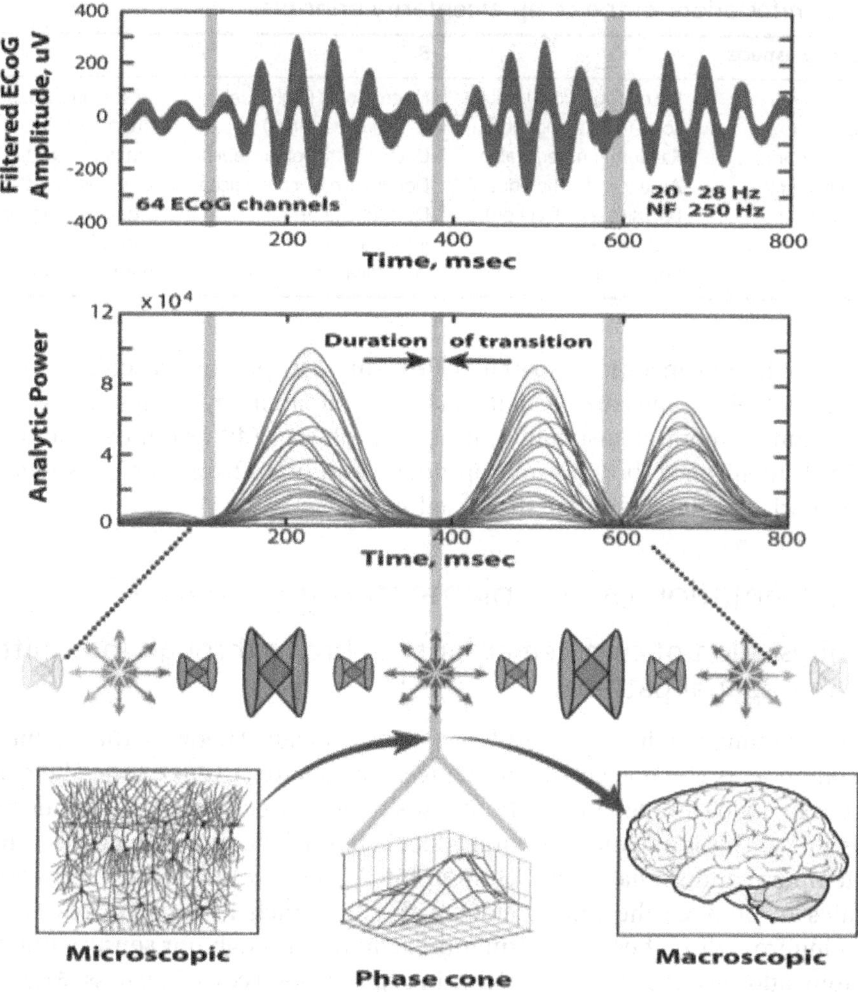

FIG. 4 Metastability of brain dynamics manifested in electrocorticograms (ECoGs); top plot: filtered ECoG signals from an array of 8×8 electrodes in rabbit sensory cortex; beating patterns of relatively high synchrony have a duration of 150–200 ms, interrupted by brief periods (10–20 ms) of desynchronization marked by blue bars; bottom plot shows the complementary aspects of microscopic (0.1 mm) and macroscopic (50 mm) neural processes in rabbit brain, interacting through phase cones emerging at the mesoscopic scales (6–8 mm). *Adopted from R. Kozma, W.J. Freeman, Cognitive Phase Transitions in the Cerebral Cortex—Enhancing the Neuron Doctrine by Modeling Neural Fields, Springer, New York, 2016.*

prominent in the case of mesoscopic coupling, which represents an intermediate-range effect between the extremes of microscopic and macroscopic connectivity in the physical space. Kelso's complementary principle provides a conceptual framework for such processes [38]. Accordingly, let "~" denote the complementary relationship between two opposing aspects A and B of a specific phenomenon. Examples of complementarity in various domains of science and technology are given in Table 1, such as system hierarchy

Table 1 Manifestations of the complementarity principle.

Complementary aspects	A	B	~
Hierarchy level	Microscopic (low level)	Macroscopic (high level)	Mesoscopic (medium level)
Spatial scale	Local (direct neighbor)	Global (mean-field)	Intermediate-range
Predictability over time	Random (unpredictable)	Deterministic (predictable)	Partially predictable
Coordination dynamics	Absence of coherence	Dominance of coherence	Chimera metastable states
Process evolution	Diffusive (no direction)	Drift (directed)	Mixed (space/time)
Physics	Entropy	Information	Knowledge
Artificial intelligence	Bottom-up (emergence)	Top-down (inference)	Integrated (brain-like)

levels (low, high, and medium), spatial scales (microscopic, macroscopic, and mesoscopic), predictability and stochasticity [49], coordination dynamics (no coherence, coherence, and chimera metastability), process evolution (diffusion, drift, and mixed), and artificial intelligence (bottom-up, top-down, and brain-like). The consequences of complementarity in building AI are discussed next.

4 Implementation of complementarity for new AI

4.1 Manifestation of complementarity in brains through intermittent local-global spatial patterns

Intelligence in human brains is the result of a delicate balance between the fragmentation of local components and the global dominance of a coherent overall state. The balancing act happens in brains through intermittent transitions between synchronous and nonsynchronous states. This is a spatio-temporal effect in brain dynamics with nonlocal interference of temporal and spatial scales. Human intelligence works through these repeated singularities to produce the brain's clockwork [50], which in turn creates knowledge and meaning from disembodied information acquired through our sensory organs. The desynchronization event plays a crucial role in cognition and consciousness [51,52]; it corresponds to the "Aha" moment of deep insight and understanding.

Neither top-down symbolic AI approaches, nor pure bottom-up, deep learning neural networks can grasp this complex balancing process in its entirety. In the spirit of the complementarity principle, the two aspects of intelligence must be integrated in a unified approach. Brains tell us that this integration can happen through the sequence of metastable patterns, separated by phase transitions in the singular spatio-temporal brain dynamics. These transitions are not prescribed by an external agency; rather they emerge as the result of the brain's neurodynamics.

4.2 Brain-inspired integration of top-down and bottom-up AI

Here, we summarize the important lessons learned from the operation of human brains and human intelligence, which can be incorporated in next generation AI algorithms and hardware implementations. Fig. 5 illustrates the relationship between symbolic AI and

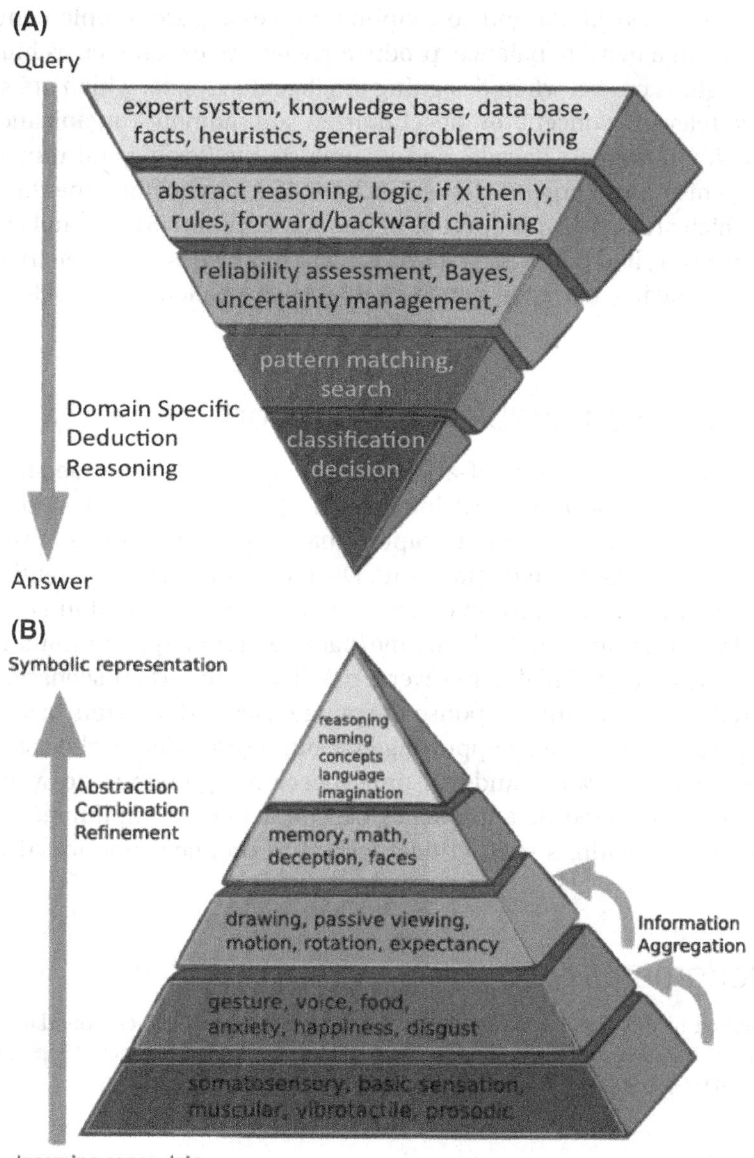

FIG. 5 Illustration of complementary approaches to develop artificial intelligence: (A) expert system with sequential specification and deduction, in the form of top-down inference shown here as an inverted pyramid; (B) data-based, bottom-up pyramid of cognition with sequential layers of abstraction and refinement. *Adopted from P. Taylor, J.N. Hobbs, J. Burroni, H.T. Siegelmann, The global landscape of cognition: hierarchical aggregation as an organizational principle of human cortical networks and functions, Sci. Rep. 5 (2015) 18112.*

nonsymbolic neural network approaches. Fig. 5A corresponds to an expert system with sequential specification and deduction, in the form of top-down inference; it is shown here as an inverted pyramid. Fig. 5B shows a bottom-up pyramid of cognition with sequential layers of abstraction and refinement [53].

Brains teach us that symbolic and nonsymbolic processing are complementary aspects and they co-exist in a delicate balance, producing what we experience as human intelligence. This insight is crucial when designing intelligent systems, which are sustainable.

The highly relevant concept of decentralized autonomous organizations (DAOs) gained popularity in the past decade, and it supports the flexible and robust operation of complex organisms and organizations. DAO manifests the complementary aspects of intelligence, which are inherent properties of human cognition [51,52], and extends them to social, engineering, and financial systems [54,55]. It provides a feasible framework and technologies for solving the governance problems in challenging problems faced by humanity.

5 Conclusion: Sustainable AI to support humanity

To substantially advance the state-of-art of AI, we can rely on our understanding of the mechanisms that underlie biological intelligence. Many current AI systems give the appearance of intelligence, but cannot adapt to changing circumstances or truly interpret and make decisions based on dynamic input. Deep learning has the potential of moving towards these goals, however, resource constraints are often ignored in DL settings. DL typically requires a huge amount of data/time/parameters/energy/computational power, which may not be readily available in several practically important scenarios [56]. Relevant task domains include rapid response to emergencies and disasters based on incomplete and disparate information, supporting graceful degradation in the case of physical damage or resource constraints, and real-time speech recognition in noisy and cluttered backgrounds. Brain-inspired AI approaches can implement complimentary aspects of intelligent systems to address such critical tasks and produce superior AI in the years ahead.

Acknowledgments

The work presented in this chapter is supported in part by National Science Foundation Grant NSF-CRCNS-DMS-13-11165 and by Defense Advanced Research Project Agency "Superior AI" Grant, DARPA/MTO HR0011-16-1-0006.

References

[1] L. Da Vinci, A renaissance robot: Designed a sophisticated robot to mimic the motions of an armored knight, Mech. Eng., New York 120 (1998) 80–83.

[2] T. Standage, The Turk: The Life and Times of the Famous Eighteenth-Century Chess-Playing Machine, Walker & Company, 2002.

[3] M.L. Minsky, S. Papert, Perceptrons: An Introduction to Computational Geometry, MIT Press, Cambridge, MA, 1969.

[4] M. Minsky, A Framework for Representing Knowledge, MIT, AI Lab, Cambridge, MA, 1974.

[5] A. Newell, H.A. Simon, Human Problem Solving, Prentice-Hall, Englewood Cliffs, NJ, 1972, p. 1972.

[6] Newell, A. (1980). Physical symbol systems, Cognit. Sci., vol. 4, pp. 135–183, 1980.

[7] J.A. Anderson, J.W. Silverstein, S.A. Ritz, R.S. Jones, Distinctive features, categorical perception, and probability learning: Some applications of a neural model, Psychol. Rev. 84 (1977) 413–451.

[8] J.E. Laird, A. Newell, P.S. Rosenbloom, SOAR: An architecture for general intelligence, Artif. Intell. 33 (1987) 1–64.

[9] H.L. Dreyfus, Why Heideggerian AI failed and how fixing it would require making it more Heideggerian, Artif. Intell. 171 (18) (2007) 1137–1160.

[10] R.A. Brooks, Cambrian Intelligence: The Early History of the New AI, vol. 97, MIT Press, Cambridge, MA, 1999.

[11] R. Kozma, H. Aghazarian, T. Huntsberger, E. Tunstel, W.J. Freeman, Computational aspects of cognition and consciousness in intelligent devices, Comput. Intell. Mag., IEEE 2 (3) (2007) 53–64.

[12] J.A. Anderson, E. Rosenfeld (Eds.), Talking Nets: An Oral History of Neural Networks, MIT Press, 2000.

[13] G.G. Towell, J.W. Shavlik, Knowledge-based artificial neural networks, Artif. Intell. 70 (1994) 119–165.

[14] S. Hawking, S. Russell, M. Tegmark, F. Wilczek, Stephen Hawking: "Transcendence looks at the implications of artificial intelligence-but are we taking AI seriously enough?", The Independent 2014 (05-01) (2014) 9313474.

[15] D.G. Stork (Ed.), HAL's Legacy: 2001's Computer as Dream and Reality, MIT Press, 1997.

[16] D. Silver, J. Schrittwieser, K. Simonyan, I. Antonoglou, A. Huang, A. Guez, T. Hubert, L. Baker, M. Lai, A. Bolton, Y. Chen, Mastering the game of go without human knowledge, Nature 550 (7676) (2017) 354.

[17] V. Mnih, K. Kavukcuoglu, D. Silver, A.A. Rusu, J. Veness, M.G. Bellemare, A. Graves, M. Riedmiller, A.K. Fidjeland, G. Ostrovski, S. Petersen, Human-level control through deep reinforcement learning, Nature 518 (7540) (2015) 529–533.

[18] J. Schrittwieser, I. Antonoglou, T. Hubert, K. Simonyan, L. Sifre, S. Schmitt, A. Guez, E. Lockhart, D. Hassabis, T. Graepel, T. Lillicrap, Mastering atari, go, chess and shogi by planning with a learned model, Nature 588 (7839) (2020) 604–609.

[19] J. Von Neumann, The Computer and the Brain, Yale Univ. Press, New Haven, CT, 1958.

[20] A.M. Turing, Computing machinery and intelligence, Mind 59 (236) (1950) 433–460.

[21] R. Kozma, M. Puljic, Neuropercolation model of pattern-based computing in brains through cognitive phase transitions, Theoret. Comput. Sci. C – Nat. Comput. 633 (2015) 54–70.

[22] W.S. McCulloch, W. Pitts, A logical calculus of the idea immanent in nervous activity, Bull. Math. Biophys. 5 (1943) 115–133.

[23] N. Wiener, Cybernetics: Control and Communication in the Animal and the Machine, Wiley, New York, 1948, p. 194.

[24] A.N. Kolmogorov, On the representation of continuous functions of many variables by superposition of continuous functions of one variable and addition, Dokl. Akad. Nauk USSR 144 (1957) 679–681. American Mathematical Society Translation, 28, 55-59 [1963].

[25] V.I. Arnold, On functions of three variables, Dokl. Akad. Nauk USSR 114 (1957) 679–681.

[26] P.J. Werbos, Beyond regression: new tools for prediction and analysis in the behavioral sciences, 1974. Doctoral Dissertation, Applied Mathematics, Harvard University, MA.

[27] Rumelhart, D.E., Hinton, G.E., & Williams, R.J. (1986). Learning representations by error propagation. In D.E. Ru-Melhart, J.L. McClelland and the PDP Research Group (Eds.), Parallel Distributed Processing (vol. 1, pp. 318-362). Cambridge, MA: MIT Press.

[28] R. Hecht-Nielsen, Kolmogorov mapping neural network existence theorem, IEEE First Int. Conf. Neural Networks 3 (1987) 11–13.

[29] S. Grossberg, Nonlinear neural networks: Principles, mechanisms, and architectures, Neural Netw. 1 (1) (1988) 17–61.

[30] Y. LeCun, L. Bottou, Y. Bengio, P. Haffner, Gradient-based learning applied to document recognition, Proc. IEEE 86 (11) (1998) 2278–2324.

[31] S. Hochreiter, J. Schmidhuber, Long short-term memory, Neural Comput. 9 (8) (1997) 1735–1780.

[32] Y. LeCun, Y. Bengio, G. Hinton, Deep learning, Nature 521 (7553) (2015) 436–444.

[33] A. Pikovsky, M. Rosenblum, J. Kurths, Synchronization a Universal Concept Non-linear Science, Cambridge University Press, Cambridge, U.K., 2001.

[34] W.J. Freeman, How and why brains create meaning from sensory information, Int. J. Bifurcat. Chaos 14 (02) (2004) 515–530.

[35] R. Kozma, Intermediate-range coupling generates low-dimensional attractors deeply in the chaotic region of one-dimensional lattices, Phys. Lett. A 244 (1–3) (1998) 85–91.

[36] R. Kozma, W.J. Freeman, Cognitive Phase Transitions in the Cerebral Cortex—Enhancing the Neuron Doctrine by Modeling Neural Fields, Springer, New York, 2016.

[37] J.S. Kelso, Dynamic Patterns: The Self-organization of Brain and Behavior, MIT Press, 1997.

[38] J.S. Kelso, D.A. Engstrom, The Complementary Nature, MIT Press, Cambridge, MA, 2006.

[39] E. Tognoli, J.S. Kelso, The metastable brain, Neuron 81 (1) (2014) 35–48.

[40] A.M. Hagerstrom, T.E. Murphy, R. Roy, P. Hovel, I. Omelchenko, E. Scholl, Experimental observation of chimeras in coupled-map lattices, Nat. Phys. 8 (9) (2012) 658–661.

[41] D.M. Abrams, S.H. Strogatz, Chimera states for coupled oscillators, Phys. Rev. Lett. 93 (2004) 174102.

[42] W.J. Freeman, Proposed cortical "shutter" mechanism in cinematographic perception, in: Neurodynamics of Cognition and Consciousness, Springer, Berlin Heidelberg, 2007, pp. 11–38.

[43] R. Kozma, W.J. Freeman, Cinematic operation of the cerebral cortex interpreted via critical transitions in self-organized dynamic systems, Front. Syst. Neurosci. 11 (10) (2017), https://doi.org/10.3389/fnsys.2017.00010.

[44] H. Mercier, D. Sperber, Why do humans reason? Arguments for an argumentative theory, Behav. Brain Sci. 34 (2011) 57–111.

[45] R. Kozma, J.J.J. Davis, Why do phase transitions matter in minds? J. Conscious. Stud. 25 (1–2) (2017) 131–150.

[46] W.J. Freeman, Mass Action in the Nervous System, Academic Press, New York, 1975.

[47] W.J. Freeman, R.Q. Quiroga, Imaging Brain Function with EEG: Advanced Temporal and Spatial Analysis of Electroencephalographic Signals, Springer Verlag, Berlin, 2012.

[48] R. Kozma, W.J. Freeman, Intermittent spatio-temporal de-synchronization and sequenced synchrony in ECoG signals, Chaos 18 (2008) 037131.

[49] P.J. Werbos, Approximate dynamic programming for real-time control and neural modeling, Chapter 13, in: D.A. White, D.A. Sofge (Eds.), Handbook of Intelligent Control, Van Nostrand Reinhold Co., New York, 1992, pp. 493–525.

[50] P.J. Werbos, J.J. Davis, Regular cycles of forward and backward signal propagation in prefrontal cortex and in consciousness, Front. Syst. Neurosci. 10 (97) (2016) 1–12.

[51] B.J. Baars, N. Geld, R. Kozma, Global workspace theory (GWT) and prefrontal cortex: Recent developments, Front. Psychol. (2021), https://doi.org/10.3389/fpsyg.2021.749868. Nov 10:5163. vol. 12 749868. 10 Nov. 2021.

[52] R. Kozma, B.J. Baars, N. Geld, Evolutionary advantages of stimulus-driven EEG phase transitions in the upper cortical layers, Front. Syst. Neurosci. 15 (2021) 784404.

[53] P. Taylor, J.N. Hobbs, J. Burroni, H.T. Siegelmann, The global landscape of cognition: hierarchical aggregation as an organizational principle of human cortical networks and functions, Sci. Rep. 5 (2015) 18112.

[54] R. Qin, W. Ding, J. Li, S. Guan, G. Wang, Y. Ren, Z. Qu, Web3-based decentralized autonomous organizations and operations: architectures, models, and mechanisms, IEEE Trans. Syst. Man Cybernet: Syst. 53 (4) (2023) 2073–2082.

[55] W. Ding, J. Hou, J. Li, C. Guo, J. Qin, R. Kozma, F.Y. Wang, DeSci based on Web3 and DAO: A comprehensive overview and reference model, IEEE Trans. Comput. Social Syst. 9 (5) (2022) 1563–1573.

[56] D. Patel, H. Hazan, D.J. Saunders, H.T. Siegelmann, R. Kozma, Improved robustness of reinforcement learning policies upon conversion to spiking neuronal network platforms applied to Atari Breakout game, Neural Netw. 120 (2019) 108–115.

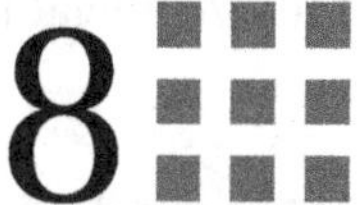

Brain-inspired evolving and spiking connectionist systems

Nikola Kirilov Kasabov[a,b,c,d]

[a]KEDRI, AUCKLAND UNIVERSITY OF TECHNOLOGY, AUCKLAND, NEW ZEALAND [b]INTELLIGENT SYSTEMS RESEARCH CENTER, ULSTER UNIVERSITY, DERRY, UNITED KINGDOM [c]IICT, BULGARIAN ACADEMY OF SCIENCES, SOFIA, BULGARIA [d]DALIAN UNIVERSITY, DALIAN, CHINA

Chapter outlines

1 The historic merge of artificial neural networks and fuzzy logic

The section introduces first how neural networks and fuzzy logic can be merged for the development of intelligent adaptive systems. The following Section 2 presents principles, methods and their applications of evolving connectionist systems (ECOS), that allow a system to evolve its knowledge from data through incremental and life-long learning.

Copyright © 2024 Elsevier Inc. All rights reserved.

Two models, namely EFuNN and DENFIS, that evolve fuzzy rules incrementally are described and illustrated with a wide range of applications.

Methods of artificial intelligence (AI) were incrementally created over a long history, based on exact number and strict rules, starting from propositional logic of **Aristotle (384–322 BC)** to the current days (e.g., [1–10]). However, human cognitive behavior and reasoning is not always based on exact numbers and fixed rules. In 1965, Lotfi Zadeh introduced fuzzy logic [11,12] that represents information uncertainties and tolerance in a linguistic form. He introduced fuzzy rules, containing fuzzy propositions and fuzzy inference.

Fuzzy propositions can have truth values between true (1) and false (0), for example, the proposition "washing time is short" is true to a degree of 0.8 if the time is 4.9 min, where *Short* is represented as a fuzzy set with its membership function—see Fig. 1. Fuzzy rules can be used to represent human knowledge and reasoning, for example,

```
IF washing load is small THEN washing time is short.
```

Fuzzy systems (FS) calculate exact outputs based on input data and a set of fuzzy rules. However, fuzzy rules need to be articulated in the first instance, they need to change, adapt, evolve through learning, possibly, life-long learning to reflect the way human knowledge evolves. And that is why FS were merged with artificial neural networks (ANN).

ANNs are computational models that mimic the nervous system in its main function of adaptive learning and generalization. ANNs are universal computational models. One of the most popular artificial neuron models is the McCulloch and Pitts neuron developed in 1943 (Fig. 2A). It was used in early ANNs, such as Rosenblatt's Perceptron [13] and multilayer perceptron [14–17]. A simple example is given in Fig. 2B.

Various types of ANN architectures and learning algorithms have been developed, for example, multilayer perceptrons and backpropagation supervised learning algorithm [16,17]; self-organizing maps (SOM) and unsupervised learning algorithms [18]; adaptive resonance theory (ART) [19]; recurrent ANN and reinforcement learning [20]; other [21].

The MLP model was extended to multiple (e.g., hundreds) layers of neurons, using the error backpropagation learning algorithm, that led to the development of the deep neural networks (DNN) [22,23]. DNNs are ANN that have several layers of neurons and connections in their structures (rather than 3 as shown in Fig. 2B). A class of DNN is the

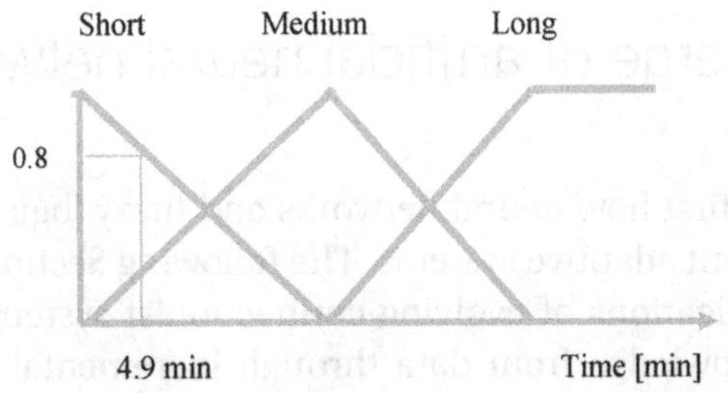

FIG. 1 An example of fuzzy sets, here representing fuzzy terms of short, medium and long washing time.

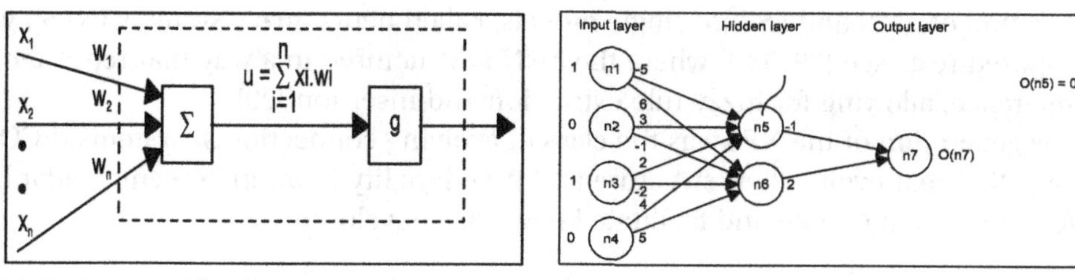

(a) A simple artificial neuron. (b) An example of a simple feedforward ANN.

FIG. 2 Examples of: (A) a single neuron mode; (B) a multilayer perceptron of three layers.

convolutional DNN, where neurons at the first layer learn features only within a small subsection of the input vector data (e.g., a small square of pixels from an image). These neurons are connected to the next layer where features are combined, until the output classification layer, where output classes are determined [22,24–28]. DNNs are excellent for vector- or frame-based data, but not much for temporal (or spatio-/spectro-temporal data). There is no *time of asynchronous events* learned in the model. They are difficult to adapt to new data, and the structures are not flexible. While DNNs were powerful to learn large amount of data in a batch mode type of learning, they were not suitable for incremental and life-long learning and knowledge representation.

Integration of ANN and FS was first achieved in multimodel systems, where an ANN model and a fuzzy rule-based system are developed separately using complementary data of the same problem and then weighted output is calculated. An example is given in Fig. 3 [29,30]. If the ANN modules allow for incremental learning, then updated rules can be extracted incrementally, or in a life-long learning mode. Such ANN are the ECOS, described below.

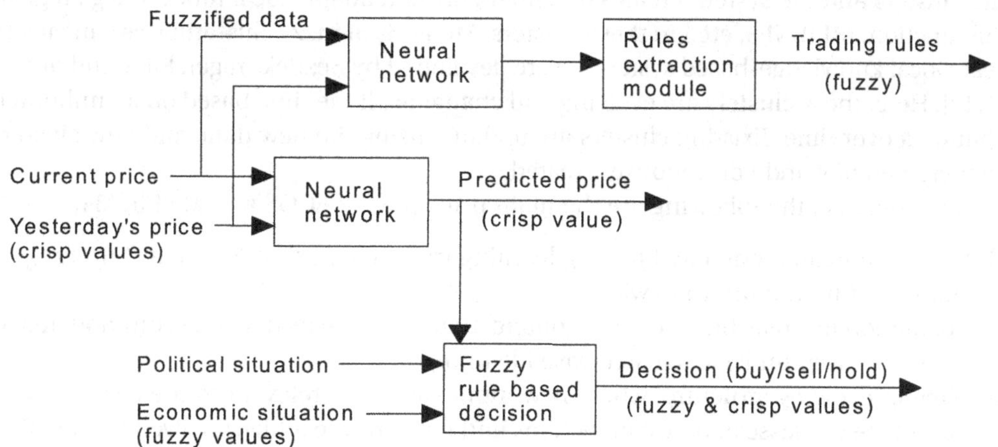

FIG. 3 A hybrid ANN-fuzzy rule-based expert system for financial decision support [29]. The neural network modules can learn incrementally and fuzzy rules can be extracted incrementally as well for the understanding of the dynamical changes in the incoming data.

Integration of ANN and FS into single models, called neuro-fuzzy systems (NFS), was also proposed (e.g., see [29–33]), where the ANN is structured in a way that represents a fuzzy inference, allowing for fuzzy rule extraction and insertion [29].

A new generation of the NFS was the class of evolving connectionist systems (ECOS), which are NFS that evolve their structure and functionality in an incremental, adaptive and life-long learning mode and facilitate knowledge development.

2 Evolving connectionist systems (ECOS)

2.1 Principles of ECOS

In ECOS, instead of training a fixed ANN, such as DNN, or NFS, through changing its connection weights based on an existing dataset over many iterations and fixing these connections for future data, an ECOS structure and its functionality are always evolving from incoming data, often in an online, one-pass, life-long learning mode [34–37].

ECOS are connectionist systems that evolve their structure and functionality in a continuous, self-organized, online, adaptive, interactive way from incoming data over unlimited time [34]. They can process both data and insert/extract knowledge in a supervised and/or unsupervised way. ECOS learn local models from data through clustering of the data and associating a neuron to represent the cluster center and a local function for each cluster. They can change incrementally their input features as well [36,38]. Some principles of ECOS have been proposed as part of the classical neural network models, such as self-organizing maps, radial basis functions, Fuzzy ARTMap, growing neural gas, neuro-fuzzy systems, resource allocation network (for a review see [29]). Other ECOS models, along with their applications, have been reported in [39,40].

The principle of ECOS is based on *local learning*—neurons are allocated as centers of data clusters and the system creates incrementally and adapts local models (e.g., regression function, MLP, NFS, etc.) in these clusters. Methods of fuzzy clustering, as a means to create local knowledge-based systems, were developed by Bezdek, Yager, Filev and others [41,42]. Here, these clusters are evolving and changing all the time based on an unlimited input data over time. Existing clusters are updated using the new data, and new clusters are incrementally and continuously created.

To summarize, the following are the main principles of ECOS as stated in [34]:

(1) Fast incremental, possibly life-long learning from data, using "one-pass" training, starting with little prior knowledge;

(2) Adaptation in a real-time and in an online mode where new data is accommodated as it comes based on local, cluster-based learning;

(3) "Open," evolving structure, where new input variables (relevant to the task), new outputs (e.g., classes), new connections and neurons are added/evolved "on the fly";

(4) Both data learning and knowledge representation is facilitated in a comprehensive and flexible way, for example, supervised learning, unsupervised learning, evolving clustering, "sleep" learning, forgetting/pruning, fuzzy rule insertion and extraction, thus allowing for *transfer learning*;

(5) Active interaction with other ECOSs and with the environment in a multimodal fashion;

(6) Representing both space and time in their different scales, for example, clusters of data, short- and long-term memory, age of data, forgetting, etc.;

(7) System's self-evaluation in terms of behavior, global error and success, and related knowledge representation.

2.2 EFuNN and DENFIS

Here, the concept of ECOS is illustrated on two implementations: the evolving fuzzy neural network (EFuNN) [35] and the dynamic evolving neuro-fuzzy inference system (DENFIS) [37]. Examples of EFuNN and DENFIS are shown in Figs. 4 and 5, respectively.

In ECOS, clusters of data are created based on similarity between data samples either in the input space (this is the case in some of the ECOS models, e.g., DENFIS), or in both the input and output space (this is the case, e.g., in the EFuNN models). Samples (examples) that have a distance to an existing node (cluster center, rule node) less than a certain threshold are allocated to the same cluster and the cluster changes its center. Samples that do not fit into existing clusters form new clusters. Cluster centers are continuously adjusted according to new data samples, and new clusters are created incrementally. ECOS learn from data and automatically create or update a local fuzzy model/function to approximate the data in the corresponding cluster, for example:

IF <*data is in a fuzzy cluster* C_i> *THEN* <*the model is* F_i>

where F_i can be a fuzzy value, a logistic or linear regression function (Fig. 5) or ANN model [37,38].

The ECOS methods are realized as software modules as part of a free-to-use development system NeuCom (www.theneucom.com).

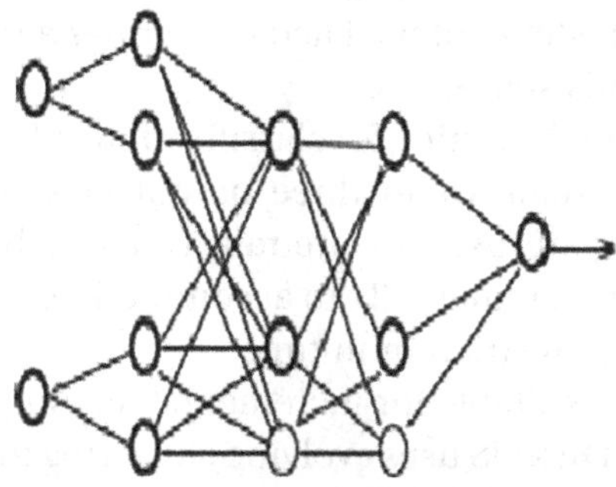

FIG. 4 An example of EFuNN model. *From N.K. Kasabov, Evolving fuzzy neural networks for on-line supervised/unsupervised, knowledge-based learning, IEEE Trans. Syst. Man Cybern. B Cybern. 31 (6) (2001) 902–918.*

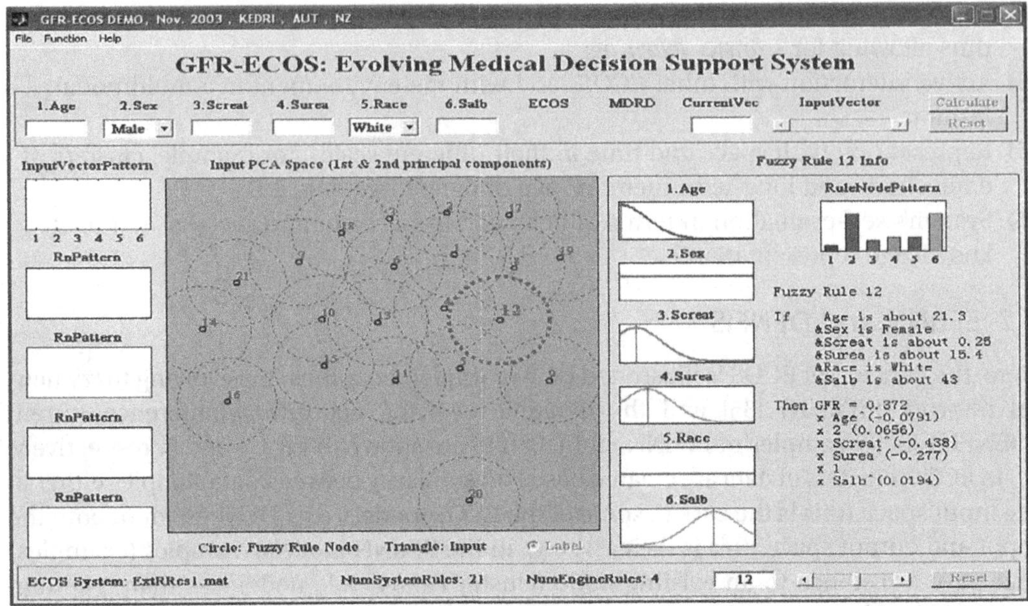

FIG. 5 An example of DENFIS model. *From N.K. Kasabov, Evolving Connectionist Systems: Methods and Applications in Bioinformatics, Brain Study and Intelligent Machines, Springer-Verlag, London, 2002 and N.K. Kasabov, Evolving Connectionist Systems: The Knowledge Engineering Approach, second ed., Springer-Verlag, London, 2007.*

2.3 Incremental and life-long learning in EFuNN and DENFIS

Here, incremental and life-long learning capabilities of EFuNN and DENFIS are discussed and illustrated.

The EFuNN model [35] is suitable for supervised, incremental learning and classification of vector-based data as for every new input-output vector, an existing hidden neuron, representing an existing cluster from previous data, is either changed its connection weights meaning changing the cluster center according to the new data vector, or a new hidden neuron is created in case of the new input data vector being different above a threshold from previous cluster centers. Each cluster has a defined class output, so the clustering is supervised in this sense.

Fig. 6 represents incremental learning for classification in EFuNN using the benchmark Iris dataset of four input variables and three output class variables, when randomly selected 30 samples/vectors are used to pretrain in a batch mode an EFuNN model, and then this model evolved incrementally to accommodate another 120 samples, which process can continue without restriction in time.

The DENFIS model [37] is suitable for incremental learning of time series data represented as a series of vectors. DENFIS uses evolving clustering method (ECM) to incrementally evolve clusters in an unsupervised way as shown in Fig. 7. For each cluster, at a current time of learning, a function is created and updated to approximate the data in this

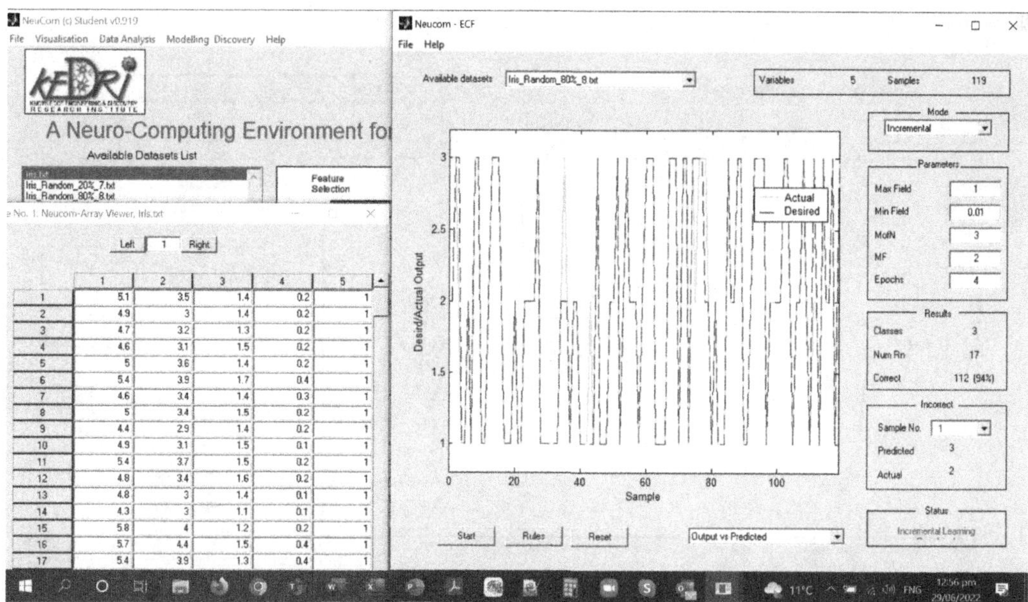

FIG. 6 Incremental learning and classification in an EFuNN model to classify a stream of input vectors belonging to 3 classes. On the left side is a subset of the input data and on the right side is classification output as a result of incremental training. There are 17 rule/cluster neurons/nodes evolved and overall accuracy is 94%. *The free NeuCom software is used from https://theneucom.com.*

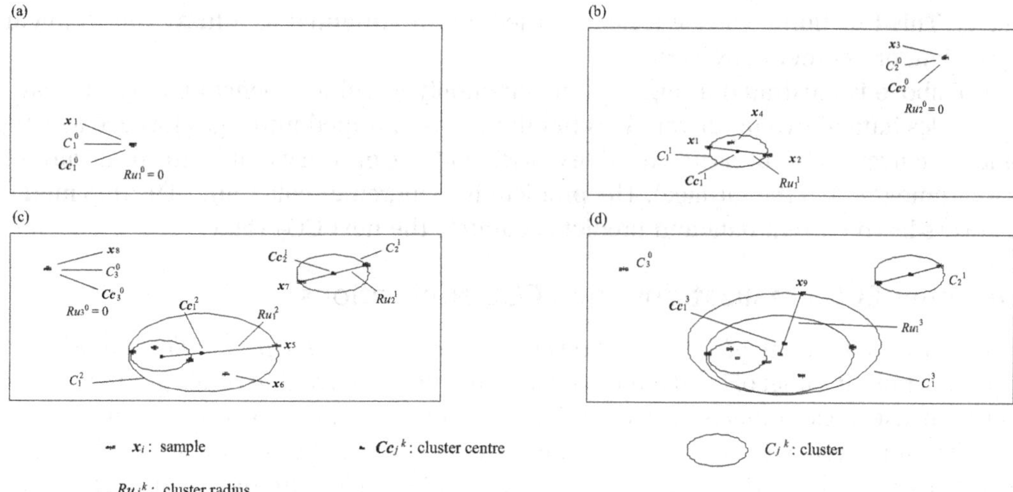

FIG. 7 An illustration of the incremental and life-long evolution of clusters in DENFIS over incoming data, here represented for simplicity in a 2D space. *From N.K. Kasabov, Q. Song, DENFIS: dynamic evolving neural-fuzzy inference system and its application for time-series prediction, IEEE Trans. Fuzzy Syst. 10 (2) (2002) 144–154.*

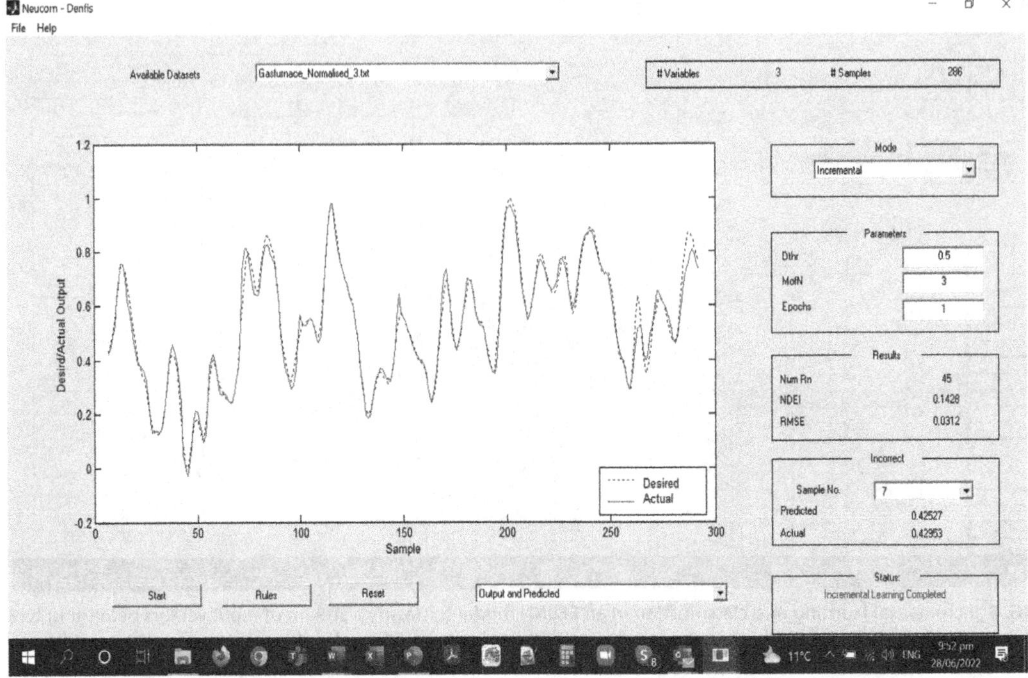

FIG. 8 Incremental learning of a time series in DENFIS. During learning of 296 vectors representing the time series at consecutive time points, the model has evolved 45 clusters and the overall RMSE is 0.0312.

cluster. This function could be locally learned and represented as a fuzzy rule, a linear regression, or another ANN/NFS.

The above is illustrated in Fig. 8 of incrementally learning a benchmark gas furnace time series data of two input variables (methane gas, pumped into a gas furnace at time t and the current value of carbon dioxide $CO_2(t)$) and one output variable (the next value of CO_2 at time $(t+4)$ in the furnace). The problem is to incrementally train a DENFIS model to always learn current data and predict accurately the next CO_2 value.

2.4 Other ECOS realizations and ECOS applications

A special development of ECOS is *transductive reasoning and personalized modeling.* Instead of building a set of local models (i.e., prototypes) to cover the whole problem space and then use these models to classify/predict any new input vector, in transductive modeling for every new input vector, a new model is created based on selected nearest neighbor vectors from the available data. Such ECOS models are the neuro-fuzzy inference system (NFI) and the transductive weighted NFI (TWNFI) [43]. In TWNFI, for every new input vector the neighborhood of closets data vectors is optimized using both the distance between the new vector and the neighboring ones and the weighted importance of the input variables, so that the error of the model is minimized in the neighborhood area [44].

Transductive reasoning is a type of life-long learning, as for every new data, at any time, a new model for this data is created using already stored past data.

The following are examples of methods, systems and applications that use all or some of the principles of ECOS from above:

- Evolving self-organized maps (ESOM) [45];
- Evolving clustering method (ECM) [46];
- Incremental feature learning in ECOS [47];
- Online ECOS optimization [48];
- Assessment of EFuNN accuracy for pattern recognition using data with different statistical distributions [49];
- Recursive clustering based on a Gustafson-Kessel algorithm [50];
- Using a map-based encoding to evolve plastic neural networks [51];
- Evolving Takagi-Sugeno fuzzy model based on switching to neighboring models [52];
- A soft computing-based approach for modeling of chaotic time series [53];
- Uninorm-based evolving neural networks and approximation capabilities [54];
- Global, local and personalized modeling and profile discovery in bioinformatics: An integrated approach [55];
- FLEXFIS: a robust incremental learning approach for evolving Takagi-Sugeno fuzzy models [56];
- Evolving fuzzy classifiers using different model architectures [57];
- RSPOP: Rough set-based pseudo-outer-product fuzzy rule identification algorithm [58];
- SOFMLS: Online self-organizing fuzzy modified least-squares network [59];
- Online sequential extreme learning machine [60];
- Finding features for real-time premature ventricular contraction detection using a fuzzy neural network system [61];
- Evolving fuzzy rule-based classifiers [62];
- A novel generic Hebbian ordering-based fuzzy rule base reduction approach to Mamdani neuro-fuzzy system [63];
- Implementation of fuzzy cognitive maps based on fuzzy neural network and application in prediction of time series [64];
- Backpropagation to train an evolving radial basis function neural network [65];
- Smooth transition autoregressive models and fuzzy rule-based systems: Functional equivalence and consequences [66];
- Development of an adaptive neuro-fuzzy classifier using linguistic hedges [67];
- A metacognitive sequential learning algorithm for neuro-fuzzy inference system [68];
- Metacognitive RBF network and its projection-based learning algorithm for classification problems [69];

- SaFIN: A self-adaptive fuzzy inference network [70];
- A sequential learning algorithm for metacognitive neuro-fuzzy inference system for classification problems [71];
- Architecture for development of adaptive online prediction models [72];
- Clustering and coevolution to construct neural network ensembles: An experimental study [73];
- Algorithms for real-time clustering and generation of rules from data [74];
- SAKM: Self-adaptive kernel machine—A kernel-based algorithm for online clustering [75];
- A BCM theory of metaplasticity for online self-reorganizing fuzzy-associative learning [76];
- Evolutionary strategies and genetic algorithms for dynamic parameter optimization of evolving fuzzy neural networks [77];
- Incremental leaning and model selection for radial basis function network through sleep learning [78];
- Interval-based evolving modeling [79];
- Evolving granular classification neural networks [80];
- Stability analysis for an online evolving neuro-fuzzy recurrent network [81];
- A TSK fuzzy inference algorithm for online identification [82];
- Design of experiments in neuro-fuzzy systems [83];
- EFuNNs ensembles construction using a clustering method and a coevolutionary genetic algorithm [84];
- eT2FIS: An evolving type-2 neural fuzzy inference system [85];
- Designing radial basis function networks for classification using differential evolution [86];
- A metacognitive neuro-fuzzy inference system (McFIS) for sequential classification problems [8];
- An evolving fuzzy neural network based on the mapping of similarities [87];
- Incremental learning by heterogeneous bagging ensemble [88];
- Fuzzy associative conjuncted maps network [89];
- EFuNN ensembles construction using CONE with multiobjective GA [90];
- Risk analysis and discovery of evolving economic clusters in Europe [91];
- Adaptive time series prediction for financial applications [92];
- Adaptive speech recognition [93];
- and others [38].

ECOS methods and systems presented above use predominantly the McCulloch and Pitts model of a neuron (Fig. 2A). They have been efficiently used for wide range of applications as some of them listed above. A next generation of ANN and ECOS models are based on more biologically plausible models of neurons, called spiking neural networks (SNN). An ECOS realization of SNN, called evolving SNN (eSNN), is presented in the next section.

3 Spiking neural networks (SNNs)

3.1 Main principles, methods and examples of SNN and evolving SNN (eSNN)

Spiking neural network (SNN) architectures use a spiking neuron model and spike information representation. Spike information representation accounts for time in the data and for changes in the data over time. This is where SNN can be chosen as preferred methods and used efficiently.

A spiking neuron model receives input information represented as trains of spikes over time from many inputs. When sufficient input information is accumulated in the membrane of the neuron, the neuron's postsynaptic potential exceeds a threshold and the neuron emits a spike at its axon (Fig. 9).

Some of the state-of-the-art models of a spiking neuron include: early models by Hodgkin and Huxley [94]; spike response models (SRM); integrate-and-fire models (IFM) (Fig. 6); Izhikevich models [95]; adaptive IFM; probabilistic IFM [95,96].

Based on the ECOS principles, an evolving spiking neural network architecture (eSNN) was proposed in [38]. It was initially designed as a visual pattern recognition system. The first eSNNs were based on Thorpe's neural model [97], in which the importance of early spikes (after the onset of a certain stimulus) is boosted, called rank-order coding and learning. Synaptic plasticity is employed by a fast supervised one-pass learning algorithm. Output neurons evolve in an incremental, online mode, to capture new data samples. These nodes can merge based on similarity. The eSNN models use spike information representation, spiking neuron models and spike learning and encoding rules, and the structure is evolving to capture spatio-temporal relationship from data.

Different eSNN models are developed, including:

- Reservoir-based eSNN for spatio- and spectro-temporal pattern recognition (Fig. 10) [98];
- Dynamic eSNN (deSNN) [99]—a model that uses both rank-order (RO) and spike-time-dependent plasticity (STDP) learning rules [100] to account for spatio-temporal data. The incremental learning algorithm for deSNN is shown in Fig. 11.

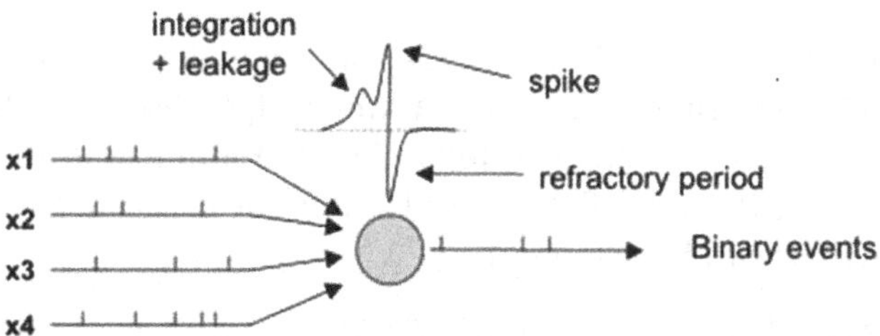

FIG. 9 The structure of the LIFM of a spiking neuron.

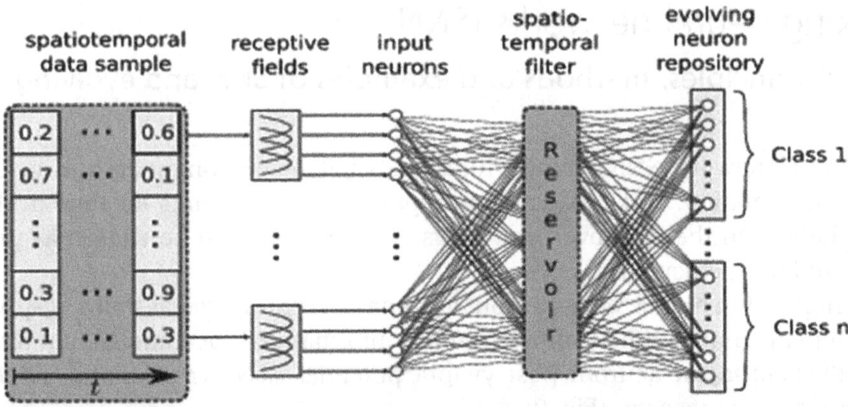

FIG. 10 A reservoir-based eSNN for spatio-temporal data classification. Output nodes evolve over time for each class through incremental supervised learning from input stream data.

The deSNN incremental learning algorithm.

1: Set deSNN parameters (including: Mod, C, Sim, and the SDSP parameters)

2: FOR every input spatio-temporal spiking pattern Pi (using time window T, t=0,1,..., t_{max}) from a data stream

DO

2a. Create a new output neuron i for this pattern and calculate the initial values of connection weights wi(0) using the RO learning rule.

FOR every time point from the time window T, t=1,...,tmax

DO

2b. Adjust the connection weights w_i for consecutive spikes on the corresponding synapses using a drift parameter D (a new spike at time *t* will increase the w_i (t) and no spike will decrease it with the drift D)

END (FOR)

2c. Calculate PSPimax using the spiking neuron (e.g. LIF) formula.

2d. Calculate the spiking threshold of the ith neuron.

2e. IF the new neuron weight vector wi is similar to the weight vector of an already trained output neuron (using Euclidean distance to measure similarity and a threshold Sim), then merge the two neurons.

ELSE

Add the new neuron to the output neurons repository.

END IF

END FOR (Repeat for every incoming spatio-temporal pattern from the data stream)

FIG. 11 The deSNN incremental learning algorithm [99].

Extracting fuzzy rules from an eSNN and deSNN would make the eSNN not only an efficient incremental learning model, but also a knowledge-based developmental model. A method was proposed [101] and illustrated in Fig. 12A and B. Based on the connection weights (W) between the receptive field layer (L1) and the class output neuron layer (L2), the following fuzzy rules can be extracted:

IF (input variable v is SMALL) THEN class C_i;
IF(v is LARGE) THEN class C_j

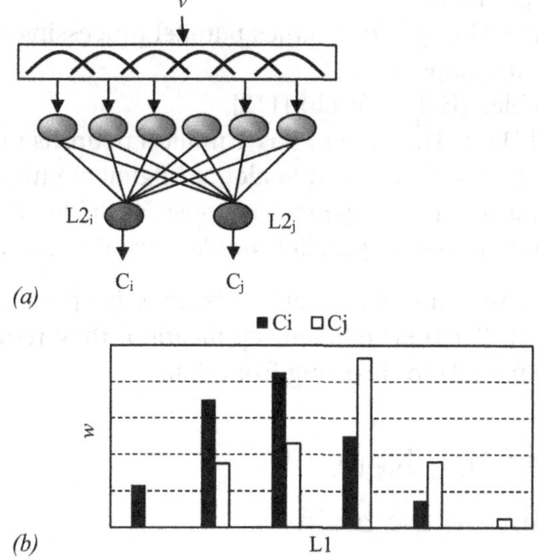

FIG. 12 Rule representation from a trained eSNN: (A) a simple structure of an eSNN for two-class classification based on one input variable using six receptive fields to convert the input values into spike trains; (B) the connection weights of the connections to class C_i and C_j output neurons respectively are interpreted as fuzzy rules.

3.2 Applications and hardware implementations of SNN and eSNN

Numerous applications based on different SNN and more specifically, on eSNN, are developed, for example:

- Advanced spiking neural network technologies for neurorehabilitation [102];
- Object movement recognition [103];
- Multimodal audio and visual information processing [104];
- Ecological data modeling and prediction of the establishment of invasive species [105];
- Integrated brain data analysis [106];
- Predictive modeling method and case study on personalized stroke occurrence prediction [107].

The full advantage of SNN in terms of speed and low computational cost can be achieved when SNNs are implemented in neuromorphic hardware platforms. Opposite to the traditional von Neumann computational architecture, where memory, control and ALU are separated, in neuromorphic systems all these modules are integrated together as they are integrated in the brain.

To make the implementation of SNN models more efficient, specialized neuromorphic hardware are developed, including:

- A hardware model of an integrate-and-fire neuron [108];
- A silicon retina [109];

- INI Zürich SNN chips [110,111];
- IBM True North [112]. The system enables parallel processing of 1 million spiking neurons and 1 billion synapses;
- DVS and silicon cochlea (ETH, Zurich) [113];
- Stanford NeuroGrid [114]. The system has 1 million neurons on a board, 63 billion connections, and is realized as hybrid analogue/digital circuits;
- SpiNNaker [115]. The system is a general-purpose, scalable, multichip multicore platform for real-time massively parallel simulations of large-scale SNN.

The neuromorphic platforms are characterized by massive parallelism, high-speed and low power consumption. For their efficient application, they require the development of SNN computational models for learning from data.

4 Brain-inspired SNN. NeuCube

4.1 Life-long learning in the brain

The best example of a life-long learning system is the human brain. It learns all the time new data, related to new actions and categories. The learned knowledge is in the form of spatially distributed and connected clusters of neurons through connections that are activated in time based on stimuli. So, the brain is the ultimate spatio-temporal life learning system. For example, when actions to grasp and lift objects are learned incrementally, trajectories are created from the visual cortex to the motor cortex (Fig. 13). These trajectories are updated, and new ones are formed in a life-long learning way.

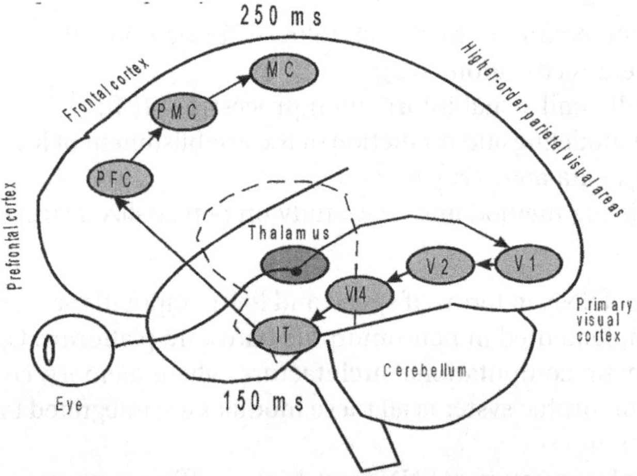

FIG. 13 A learned trajectory of activated neuronal clusters when a person has learned to see an object and to grasp it. When the person is learning to grasp another object, part of the already learned trajectory is used in a transfer learning way. Learning in the brain is incremental, life-long and the developed knowledge is represented as trajectories of connected neuronal clusters. *From L. Benuskova, N. Kasabov, Computational Neurogenetic Modelling, Springer, 2007.*

4.2 Brain-inspired SNN architectures. NeuCube

Inspired by the structure and the functions of the human brain, a SNN learning machine was developed, named NeuCube [106]. It was initially designed for spatio-temporal brain data modeling, but then it was also used for climate data modeling and stroke occurrence prediction and other applications [107] (Fig. 14).

The NeuCube framework is depicted in Fig. 14. It consists of the following modules:

- Input information encoding module;
- 3D SNN reservoir module (SNNr);
- Output (e.g., classification) module;
- Gene regulatory network (GRN) module (optional);
- Optimization module (optional).

The input module transforms input data into trains of spikes. Spatio-temporal data (such as EEG, climate, cybersecurity, financial, etc.) is entered after the encoding into the main module—the 3D SNN neurogenetic brain cube, or simply the SNNcube. Input data is entered into *predesignated spatially distributed* areas of the SNNcube that correspond to the spatial location in the origin where data was collected.

Learning in the SNN is performed in two stages:

- Unsupervised training, where spatio-temporal data is entered into relevant areas of the SNNcube over time. Unsupervised learning is performed to modify the initially set connection weights. The SNNcuber will learn to activate the same groups of spiking neurons when similar input stimuli are presented, also known as a *polychronization* effect [95].

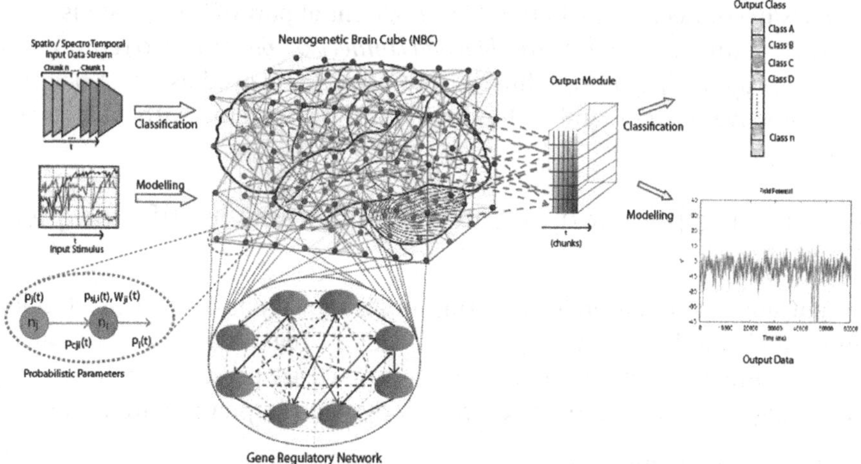

FIG. 14 A block diagram of the brain-inspired SNN system NeuCube with an evolving output module for classification or regression [106].

- Evolving supervised training of the spiking neurons in the output classification module, where the same data that was used for unsupervised training is now propagated again through the trained SNN and the output neurons are trained to classify the spatio-temporal spiking pattern of the SNNcube into predefined classes (or output spike sequences). As a special case, all neurons from the SNNcube are connected to every output neuron. Feedback connections from output neurons to neurons in the SNN can be created for reinforcement learning. Different SNN methods can be used to learn and classify spiking patterns from the SNNcube, including the deSNN [99] and SPAN models [116]. The latter is suitable for generating motor control spike trains in response to certain patterns of activity of the SNNr.

Memory in the NeuCube architecture is represented as a combination of the three types of memory described below, which are mutually interacting:

- Short-term memory, represented as changes of the PSP and temporary changes of synaptic efficacy;
- Long-term memory, represented as a stable establishment of synaptic efficacy—long-term potentiation (LTP) and long-term depression (LTD);
- Genetic memory, represented as a genetic code.

In NeuCube, similar activation patterns (called "polychronous waves") can be generated in the SNNcube with recurrent connections to represent short-term memory. When using STDP learning, connection weights change to form LTP or LTD, which constitute long-term memory.

Results of the use of the NeuCube suggest that the NeuCube architecture can be explored for learning long (spatio-) temporal patterns and to be used as associative memory. Once data is learned, the SNNcube retains the connections as a long-term memory. Since the SNNcube learns functional pathways of spiking activities represented as structural pathways of connections, when only a small initial part of input data is entered the SNNcube will "synfire" and "chain-fire" *learned connection pathways* to reproduce *learned functional pathways (trajectories)*. Thus, a NeuCube can be used as an associative memory, as a predictive system and a life-long learning system, with a wide scope of applications.

4.3 Developing application-oriented SNN systems for life-long learning using NeuCube

Using a NeuCube computational platform, application systems can be developed for incremental and life-long learning, classification, regression or data analysis of temporal- or spatio-/spectro-temporal data. Examples are presented in [117–120].

The following steps need to be taken as a design and implementation process:

(a) Input data encoding into spike sequences;
(b) Mapping input variables into input spiking neurons;

(c) Unsupervised learning spatio-temporal spike sequences in a scalable 3D SNN reservoir;
(d) Ongoing learning and classification of data over time;
(e) Dynamic parameter optimization;
(f) Evaluating the time for predictive modeling;
(g) Adaptation on new data, possibly in an online/real-time mode;
(h) Model visualization and interpretation for a better understanding of the data and the processes that generated it;
(i) Implementation of the SNN model as both software and a neuromorphic hardware system (if necessary).

A NeuCube development system, that allows for the above steps to be explored for an efficient application system development, is available from: http://www.kedri.aut.ac.nz/neucube/.

A wide range of applications of NeuCube are described in [116]. In [121], a method for using SNN for efficient data compression is introduced, with wide range of applications in telecommunication.

In [122], a survey of applications using NeuCube SNN machine can be found. They include: temporal data compression [121]; bio- and neuroinformatics applications [123]; personal assistance [124,125]; brain data analysis [126]; automated financial, banking and trading systems [127]; traffic streaming data modeling [128]; neuro-rehabilitation [129–131]. A review of applications can be found in [132].

Examples of application NeuCube models are shown in Figs. 15 and 16 (see also [122,125,133,134]).

5 What role can evolutionary computation (EC) methods play for life-long learning in evolving connectionist systems (ECOS)?

This is an interesting question, as the ECOS principles apply to a *single individual system*, that develops its structure, functions and knowledge during a life-span, while evolutionary computation (EC) methods deal with *populations of individuals over generations.*

In order to answer the above question, we should first answer the biological equivalent of this question, namely: What is the role of evolution for the life-long learning of an individual brain?

And the answer is simple, evolution sets the genetic code of an individual before they start the journey of life-long learning. And this journey stops when the individual dies. The accumulated knowledge of this individual during their learning journey is passed to the next generation of individuals through communication during their life span and through passing their genes to the off-springs.

However, during the life span of an individual, genes can change for a better adaptation of the individuals, and this small changes are passed to the next generations with a

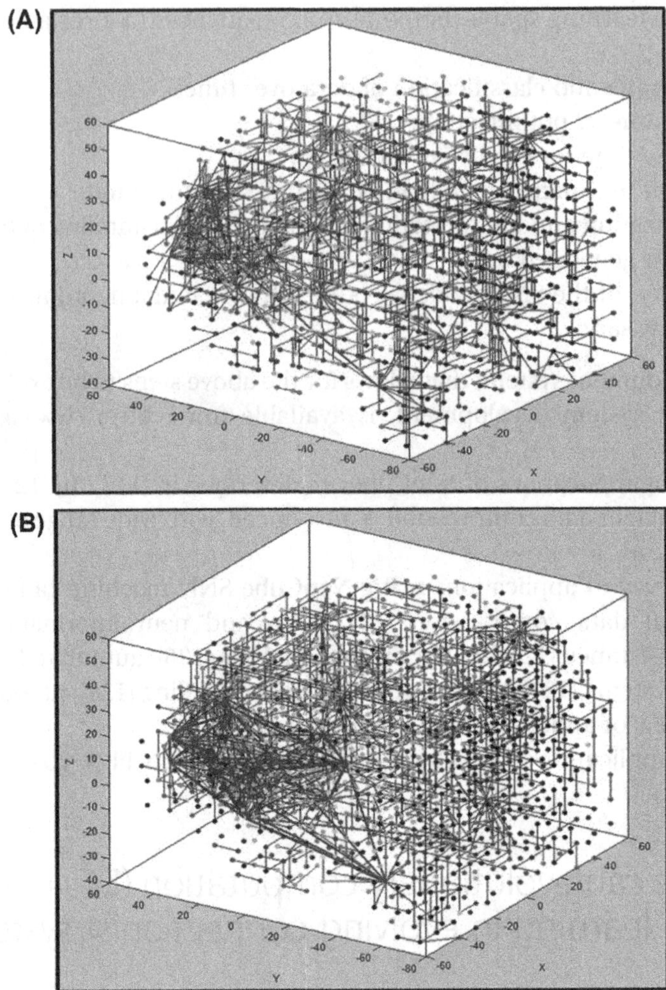

FIG. 15 (A and B) Deep learning of fMRI data in a NeuCube BI-SNN. Voxels are mapped into a SNNcube using Talairach template: (A) learned connections after STDP unsupervised learning using affirmative sentence fMRI data represented by 20 selected voxels; (B) using negative sentence data [125,133]. These models are able to continue learning new data in an incremental, life-long learning mode.

multiplicative effect over many generations. And this is a principle first suggested by **Jean Baptiste Lamarck (1744–1829)** and further developed as the Lamarckism theory, which states that "*…an organism can pass on to its offspring physical characteristics that the parent organism acquired through use or disuse during its lifetime. It is also called the inheritance of acquired characteristics, or more recently soft inheritance*" (Wikipedia).

Translated in the language of ECOS, it means that before the "life-long learning journey" of an ECOS begins, the parameters (genes) of an ECOS model can be initialized optimally through evolutionary computation (EC), based on previous data or previous

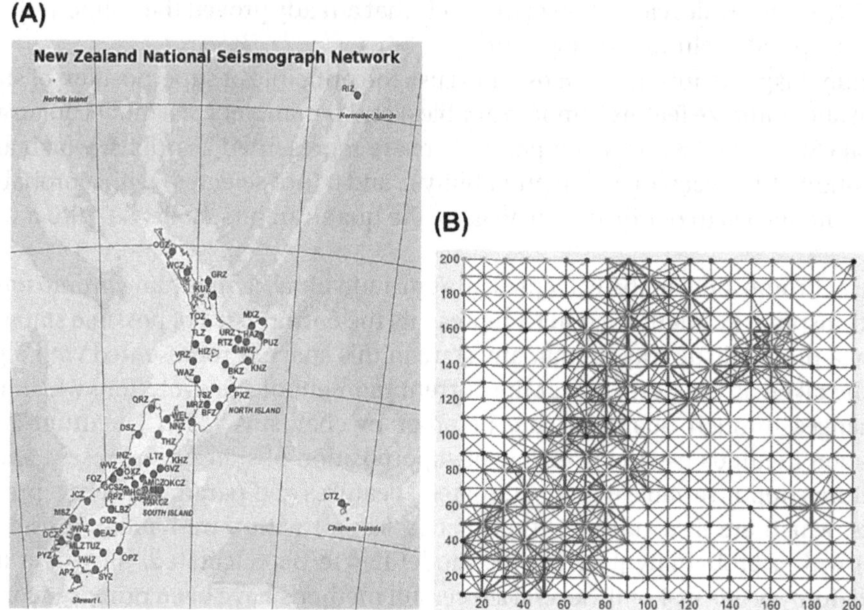

FIG. 16 Incremental learning of seismic data in a NeuCube model: (A) A map of the seismic stations in New Zealand; (B) connectivity of part of a trained SNNcube on seismic data from New Zealand stations [122,134]. The model can be incrementally trained on incoming data ate a high rate.

performance of similar models. In 1998, **Walter Freeman** commented on ECOS "*...throw the chemicals and let the system grow...*" And during this learning and growing, the model parameters can also change for a better performance.

EC adopts principles of natural evolution introduced by **Charles Darwin** [135,136], such as:

- Genes are carrier of information that realize both stability and plasticity;
- A chromosome defines an individual;
- Individuals create a new generation of individuals through crossover;
- Only the fittest individuals survive in a population to create the next generation;
- Selection criteria are based on ranking principles;
- Mutation is applied when there is no improvement of individuals over generations.

EC is a population/generation-based optimization method used in the past to optimize and fix model parameters (e.g., connection weights, number of neurons, learning rate, etc.) in order to select the best performing model (e.g., higher classification accuracy; minimum predicting error) [137,138]. However, ECOS are not fixed models, but developing during their life-time learning.

ECOS have several parameters that need to be optimized for an optimal performance. And this is crucial for the BI-SNN, such as NeuCube, that has many such parameters. Several successful EC methods have been proposed and used for this purpose (for a review, see [36,133]). A newly developed set of methods that already proved their superiority is the quantum-inspired evolutionary algorithms.

Quantum inspired optimization methods use the principle of superposition of states to represent and optimize features (input variables) and parameters of a model, for example, ECOS and eSNN [38]. Features and parameters are represented as qubits, which are in a superposition of 1 (selected) with a probability α, and 0 (not selected) with a probability β. When the model has to perform on new data, the quantum bits "collapse" into a value of 1 or 0.

While a chromosome in the EC represents one individual, a quantum chromosome in a quantum-inspired EC methods (QiEC) represents the entire space of possible states of the system in a probabilistic way, so that any state in this space is represented with a probability to be taken as the best state at the current moment of the evolution, which probability changes through quantum gate or other mechanisms [133]. Quantum-inspired optimization methods use the principle of superposition of states to represent and optimize features (input variables) and parameters. Features and parameters are represented as qubits, which are in a superposition of 1 (selected) with a probability α, and 0 (not selected) with a probability β. When the model has to be calculated, the quantum bits "collapse" into a value of 1 or 0. Several successful methods have been proposed for quantum inspired EC, among them are quantum-inspired evolutionary algorithm (QiEA) [139], quantum-inspired particle swarm optimization method (QiPSO) [140], and also applied for the optimization of the parameters of evolving spiking neural networks (eSNN) and NeuCube [133].

6 Conclusion

The chapter presents principles of ECOS and SNN and then surveys their use for practical applications. The chapter specifically addresses the problem of designing evolving systems for incremental and life-long learning and knowledge discovery from complex data. Different types of ECOS methods are suitable for different applications as discussed in the chapter. Spiking neural networks (SNNs) are discussed as promising brain-inspired techniques for brain-like AI applications. One of the SNN platform NeuCube is presented for deep, incremental and life-long learning of temporal or spatio-temporal data with some case study applications on fMRI and seismic data. The chapter advocates that integrating principles derived from brain science [141,142] and from computational intelligence (neural networks, fuzzy systems, evolutionary computation, quantum computing) could lead to more efficient information technologies, leading to brain-like AI [123,133].

Acknowledgment

The work on this paper is supported by the Knowledge Engineering and Discovery Research Institute (KEDRI, http://www.kedri.aut.ac.nz) under a SRIFT AUT grant. A video presentation supporting this chapter and giving more details can be found on: https://www.youtube.com/watch?v=fphrAVA_GbY&t=1988s.

The described NeuCom and NeuCube development software environments are available from https://www.theneucom.com and from https://www.kedri.aut.ac.nz/neucube. Several people took part in the development of the NeuCom and the NeuCube software systems: Qun Song, Peter Hwang, James Hu, Yunshi Li, Enmei Tu, Neelava Sengupta, Nathan Scott, Stefan Schliebs and others.

This chapter touches some of the topics I have been working in the last 40+years. I am grateful to many people who have shared ideas with me, such as Shun-ichi Amari, Teuvo Kohonen, Walter Freeman, John Taylor, Lotfi Zadeh, Takeshi Yamakawa, Steve Grossberg, John Andreae, Janus Kacprzyk, Steve Furber, Robert Kozma, Lubica Benuskova, Michail Defoin-Platel, Zeng-Guang Hou, Giacomo Indiveri, Carlo Morabito, Marley Vellasco, Andreas Koenig, Mario Fedrizzi, Plamen Angelov, Dimitar Filev, Seiichi Ozawa, Cesare Alippi and many others.

References

[1] D. Dennett, From Bacteria to Bach and Back. The Evolution of Minds, W. W. Norton & Co, 2017.

[2] S. Russell, P. Norvig, Artificial Intelligence: A Modern Approach, third ed., Prentice Hall, Upper Saddle River, NJ, 2009.

[3] N.J. Nilsson, The Quest for Artificial Intelligence: A History of Ideas and Achievements, Cambridge University Press, Cambridge, 2010.

[4] P. McCorduck, Machines Who Think: A Personal Inquiry into the History and Prospects of Artificial Intelligence, second ed., A.K. Peters, Ltd, Natick, MA, 2004.

[5] N. Kasabov (Ed.), Springer Handbook of Bio-/Neuroinformatics, Springer, 2014, p. 1230. https://www.springer.com/gp/book/9783642305733.

[6] C. Muller (Ed.), Fundamental Issues of Artificial Intelligence, Synthese Library/Springer, Berlin, 2016. at 553.

[7] J.H. Andreae (Ed.), Man-Machine Studies, 1974. ISSN 0110 1188, nos. UC-DSE/4 and 5.

[8] J.H. Andreae, Thinking with the Teachable Machine, Academic Press, 1977.

[9] J. Ferguson, Aristotle, Twayne Publishers, New York, 1972.

[10] J. De Groot, Aristotle's Empiricism: Experience and Mechanics in the 4th Century BC, Parmenides Publishing, 2014, ISBN: 978-1-930972-83-4.

[11] L.A. Zadeh, Fuzzy sets, Inf. Control 8 (3) (1965) 338–353.

[12] L.A. Zadeh, Fuzzy logic, IEEE Comput. 21 (4) (1988) 83–93.

[13] F. Rosenblatt, The perceptron: a probabilistic model for information storage and organization in the brain, Psychol. Rev. 65 (1958) 386–402.

[14] S. Amari, A theory of adaptive pattern classifiers, IEEE Trans. Electron. Comput. EC-16 (3) (1967) 299–307.

[15] S. Amari, Mathematical foundations of neurocomputing, Proc. IEEE 78 (9) (1990) 1443–1463.

[16] D. Rumelhart, J. McLelland (Eds.), Parallel and Distributed Processing, MIT Press, 1986.

[17] P. Werbos, Backpropagation through time, Proc. IEEE 78 (10) (1990).

[18] T. Kohonen, Self-Organising Maps, Springer, 1992.

[19] G.A. Carpenter, S. Grossberg, Adaptive Resonance Theory, MIT Press, 1991.

[20] R.S. Sutton, A.G. Barto, Reinforcement Learning, MIT Press, 1998.

[21] C.M. Bishop, Pattern Recognition and Machine Learning, Springer, 2006.

[22] Y. Bengio, Y. LeCun, G. Hinton, Deep learning, Nature 521 (7553) (2015) 436–444.

[23] W.Q. Yan, Computational Methods for Deep Learning, Springer, 2022.

[24] I. Goodfellow, Y. Bengio, A. Courville, Deep Learning, MIT Press, 2016.

[25] J. Schmidthuber, Deep learning in neural networks: an overview, Neural Netw. 61 (2014) 85–117.

[26] Y. Bengio, Learning deep architectures for AI, Found. Trends Mach. Learn. 2 (1) (2009) 1–127, https://doi.org/10.1561/2200000006.

[27] A. Esteva, B. Kuprel, R.A. Novoa, J. Ko, S. Swetter, H. Blau, S. Thrun, Dermatologist-level classification of skin cancer with deep neural networks, Nature 542 (2001) 115–118.

[28] A. Krizhevsky, I. Sutskever, G. Hinton, ImageNet classification with deep convolutional neural networks, in: Proc. NIPS 2012, MIT Press, 2012.

[29] N.K. Kasabov, Foundations of Neural Networks, Fuzzy Systems and Knowledge Engineering, MIT Press, Cambridge, MA, 1996.

[30] N.K. Kasabov, S.I. Shishkov, A connectionist production system with partial match and its use for approximate reasoning, Connect. Sci. 5 (3-4) (1993) 275–305.

[31] T. Yamakawa, E. Uchino, T. Miki, H. Kusanagi, A neo fuzzy neuron and its application to system identification and prediction of the system behavior, in: Proc. 2nd Int. Conf. on Fuzzy Logic and Neural Networks, Japan, July 1992, pp. 477–483.

[32] T. Furuhashi, T. Hasegawa, S. Horikawa, Y. Uchikawa, An adaptive fuzzy controller using fuzzy neural networks, in: Proc. of 5th Int'l Fuzzy System Association World Congress, Korea, July 1993, pp. 769–772.

[33] N.K. Kasabov, J.S. Kim, M.J. Watts, A.R. Gray, FuNN/2—a fuzzy neural network architecture for adaptive learning and knowledge acquisition, Inf. Sci.s 101 (3-4) (1997) 155–175.

[34] N.K. Kasabov, Evolving fuzzy neural networks—algorithms, applications and biological motivation, in: T. Yamakawa, G. Matsumoto (Eds.), Methodologies for the Conception, Design and Application of Soft Computing, World Scientific, 1998, pp. 271–274.

[35] N.K. Kasabov, Evolving fuzzy neural networks for on-line supervised/unsupervised, knowledge-based learning, IEEE Trans. Syst. Man Cybern. B Cybern. 31 (6) (2001) 902–918.

[36] N.K. Kasabov, Evolving Connectionist Systems: Methods and Applications in Bioinformatics, Brain Study and Intelligent Machines, Springer-Verlag, London, 2002.

[37] N.K. Kasabov, Q. Song, DENFIS: dynamic evolving neural-fuzzy inference system and its application for time-series prediction, IEEE Trans. Fuzzy Syst. 10 (2) (2002) 144–154.

[38] N.K. Kasabov, Evolving Connectionist Systems: The Knowledge Engineering Approach, second ed., Springer-Verlag, London, 2007.

[39] M.E. Futschik, N.K. Kasabov, Fuzzy clustering in gene expression data analysis, in: Proc. of the IEEE Int'l Conf. on Fuzzy Systems, USA, 2002, pp. 414–419.

[40] M.J. Watts, A decade of Kasabov's evolving connectionist systems: a review, IEEE Trans. Syst. Man Cybern. C Appl. Rev. 39 (3) (2009) 253–269.

[41] J.C. Bezdek, Analysis of Fuzzy Information, CRC Press, Boca Raton, FL, 1987.

[42] R.R. Yager, D.P. Filev, Generation of fuzzy rules by mountain clustering, J. Intell. Fuzzy Syst. Appl. Eng. Technol. 2 (3) (1994) 209–219.

[43] Q. Song, N.K. Kasabov, TWNFI—a transductive neuro-fuzzy inference system with weighted data normalization for personalized modelling, Neural Netw. 19 (10) (2006) 1591–1596.

[44] N.K. Kasabov, Y. Hu, Integrated optimisation method for personalised modelling and case study applications, Int. J. Funct. Inform. Personal. Med. 3 (3) (2010) 236–256.

[45] D. Deng, N.K. Kasabov, On-line pattern analysis by evolving self-organizing maps, Neurocomputing 51 (2003) 87–103.

[46] Q. Song, N. Kasabov, NFI: a neuro-fuzzy inference method for transductive reasoning, IEEE Trans. Fuzzy Syst. 13 (6) (2005) 799–808.

[47] S. Ozawa, S. Too, S. Abe, S. Pang, N. Kasabov, Incremental learning of feature space and classifier for online face recognition, Neural Netw. (2005) 575–584.

[48] Z. Chan, N. Kasabov, Evolutionary computation for on-line and off-line parameter tuning of evolving fuzzy neural networks, Int. J. Comput. Intell. Appl. 4 (3) (2004) 309–319. Imperial College Press.

[49] R.M. de Moraes, Assessment of EFuNN accuracy for pattern recognition using data with different statistical distributions, in: Proc. of the 2nd Brazilian Congress on Fuzzy Systems, Brazil, November 2012, pp. 672–685.

[50] D. Dovžan, I. Škrjanc, Recursive clustering based on a Gustafson–Kessel algorithm, Evol. Syst. 2 (1) (2011) 15–24.

[51] P. Tonelli, J.-B. Mouret, Using a map-based encoding to evolve plastic neural networks, in: Proc. of the IEEE Workshop on Evolving and Adaptive Intelligent Systems, France, April 2011, pp. 9–16.

[52] A. Kalhor, B.N. Araabi, C. Lucas, Evolving Takagi–Sugeno fuzzy model based on switching to neighboring models, Appl. Soft Comput. 13 (2) (2013) 939–946.

[53] J. Vajpai, J.B. Arun, A soft computing based approach for modeling of chaotic time series, in: Proc. of the 13th Int'l Conf. on Neural Information Processing, China, October 2006, pp. 505–512.

[54] F. Bordignon, F. Gomide, Uninorm based evolving neural networks and approximation capabilities, Neurocomputing 127 (2014) 13–20.

[55] N. Kasabov, Global, local and personalised modelling and profile discovery in bioinformatics: an integrated approach, Pattern Recognit. Lett. 28 (6) (2007) 673–685.

[56] E.D. Lughofer, FLEXFIS: a robust incremental learning approach for evolving Takagi–Sugeno fuzzy models, IEEE Trans. Fuzzy Syst. 16 (6) (2008) 1393–1410.

[57] P.P. Angelov, E.D. Lughofer, X. Zhou, Evolving fuzzy classifiers using different model architectures, Fuzzy Sets Syst. 159 (23) (2008) 3160–3182.

[58] K.K. Ang, C. Quek, RSPOP: rough set-based pseudo outer-product fuzzy rule identification algorithm, Neural Comput. 17 (1) (2005) 205–243.

[59] J. de Jesús Rubio, SOFMLS: online self-organizing fuzzy modified least-squares network, IEEE Trans. Fuzzy Syst. 17 (6) (2009) 1296–1309.

[60] G.B. Huang, N.Y. Liang, H.J. Rong, On-line sequential extreme learning machine, in: Proc. of the IASTED Int'l Conf. on Computational Intelligence, Canada, July 2005, pp. 232–237.

[61] J.S. Lim, Finding features for real-time premature ventricular contraction detection using a fuzzy neural network system, IEEE Trans. Neural Netw. 20 (3) (2009) 522–527.

[62] P.P. Angelov, X. Zhou, F. Klawonn, Evolving fuzzy rule-based classifiers, in: Proc. of the IEEE Symposium on Computational Intelligence in Image and Signal Processing, USA, April 2007, pp. 220–225.

[63] F. Liu, C. Quek, G.S. Ng, A novel generic Hebbian ordering-based fuzzy rule base reduction approach to Mamdani neuro-fuzzy system, Neural Comput. 19 (6) (2007) 1656–1680.

[64] H. Song, C. Miao, W. Roel, Z. Shen, F. Catthoor, Implementation of fuzzy cognitive maps based on fuzzy neural network and application in prediction of time series, IEEE Trans. Fuzzy Syst. 18 (2) (2010) 233–250.

[65] J. de Jesús Rubio, D.M. Vázquez, J. Pacheco, Backpropagation to train an evolving radial basis function neural network, Evol. Syst. 1 (3) (2010) 173–180.

[66] J.L. Aznarte, J.M. Benítez, J.L. Castro, Smooth transition autoregressive models and fuzzy rule-based systems: functional equivalence and consequences, Fuzzy Sets Syst. 158 (24) (2007) 2734–2745.

[67] B. Cetisli, Development of an adaptive neuro-fuzzy classifier using linguistic hedges, Expert Syst. Appl. 37 (8) (2010) 6093–6101.

[68] K. Subramanian, S. Suresh, A meta-cognitive sequential learning algorithm for neuro-fuzzy inference system, Appl. Soft Comput. 12 (11) (2012) 3603–3614.

[69] G.S. Babu, S. Suresh, Meta-cognitive RBF network and its projection based learning algorithm for classification problems, Appl. Soft Comput. 13 (1) (2013) 654–666.

[70] S.W. Tung, C. Quek, C. Guan, SaFIN: a self-adaptive fuzzy inference network, IEEE Trans. Neural Netw. 22 (12) (2011) 1928–1940.

[71] S. Suresh, K. Subramanian, A sequential learning algorithm for meta-cognitive neuro-fuzzy inference system for classification problems, in: Proc. of the Int'l Joint Conf. on Neural Networks, USA, August 2011, pp. 2507–2512.

[72] P. Kadlec, B. Gabrys, Architecture for development of adaptive on-line prediction models, Memetic Comput. 1 (4) (2009) 241–269.

[73] F.L. Minku, T.B. Ludemir, Clustering and co-evolution to construct neural network ensembles: an experimental study, Neural Netw. 21 (9) (2008) 1363–1379.

[74] D.P. Filev, P.P. Angelov, Algorithms for real-time clustering and generation of rules from data, in: J. Valente di Oliveira, W. Pedrycz (Eds.), Advances in Fuzzy Clustering and its Applications, John Wiley & Sons, Chichester, 2007.

[75] H. Amadou Boubacar, S. Lecoeuche, S. Maouche, SAKM: self-adaptive kernel machine: a kernel-based algorithm for online clustering, Neural Netw. 21 (9) (2008) 1287–1301.

[76] J. Tan, C. Quek, A BCM theory of meta-plasticity for online self-reorganizing fuzzy-associative learning, IEEE Trans. Neural Netw. 21 (6) (2010) 985–1003.

[77] F.L. Minku, T.B. Ludermir, Evolutionary strategies and genetic algorithms for dynamic parameter optimization of evolving fuzzy neural networks, in: Proc. of the IEEE Congress on Evolutionary Computation, Scotland, 2005, pp. 1951–1958.

[78] K. Yamauchi, J. Hayami, Incremental leaning and model selection for radial basis function network through sleep, IEICE Trans. Inf. Syst. e90-d (4) (2007) 722–735.

[79] D.F. Leite, P. Costa, F. Gomide, Interval-based evolving modeling, in: Proc. of the IEEE Workshop on Evolving and Self-Developing Intelligent Systems, USA, March 2009, pp. 1–8.

[80] D.F. Leite, P. Costa, F. Gomide, Evolving granular neural networks from fuzzy data streams, Neural Netw. 38 (2013) 1–16.

[81] J. de Jesús Rubio, Stability analysis for an online evolving neuro-fuzzy recurrent network, in: P.P. Angelov, D.P. Filev, N.K. Kasabov (Eds.), Evolving Intelligent Systems: Methodology and Applications, John Wiley & Sons, Hoboken, NJ, 2010.

[82] K. Kim, E.J. Whang, C.W. Park, E. Kim, M. Park, A TSK fuzzy inference algorithm for online identification, in: Proc. of the 2nd Int'l Conf. on Fuzzy Systems and Knowledge Discovery, China, August 2005, pp. 179–188.

[83] C. Zanchettin, L.L. Minku, T.B. Ludermir, Design of experiments in neuro-fuzzy systems, Int. J. Comput. Intell. Appl. 9 (2) (2010) 137–152.

[84] F.L. Minku, T.B. Ludermir, EFuNNs ensembles construction using a clustering method and a coevolutionary genetic algorithm, in: Proc. of the IEEE Congress on Evolutionary Computation, Canada, July 2006, pp. 1399–1406.

[85] S.W. Tung, C. Quek, C. Guan, eT2FIS: an evolving type-2 neural fuzzy inference system, Inf. Sci. 220 (2013) 124–148.

[86] B. O'Hara, J. Perera, A. Brabazon, Designing radial basis function networks for classification using differential evolution, in: Proc. of the Int'l Joint Conf. on Neural Networks, Canada, July 2006, pp. 2932–2937.

[87] J.A.M. Hernández, F.G. Castañeda, J.A.M. Cadenas, An evolving fuzzy neural network based on the mapping of similarities, IEEE Trans. Fuzzy Syst. 17 (6) (2009) 1379–1396.

[88] Q.L. Zhao, Y.H. Jiang, M. Xu, Incremental learning by heterogeneous bagging ensemble, in: Proc. of the Int'l Conf. on Advanced Data Mining and Applications, China, November 2010, pp. 1–12.

[89] H. Goh, J.H. Lim, C. Quek, Fuzzy associative conjuncted maps network, IEEE Tran. Neural Netw. 20 (8) (2009) 1302–1319.

[90] F.L. Minku, T.B. Ludermir, EFuNN ensembles construction using CONE with multi-objective GA, in: Proc. of the 9th Brazilian Symposium on Neural Networks, Brazil, October 2006, pp. 48–53.

[91] N. Kasabov, Adaptation and interaction in dynamical systems: modelling and rule discovery through evolving connectionist systems, Appl. Soft Comput. 6 (3) (2006) 307–322.

[92] H. Widiputra, R. Pears, N. Kasabov, Dynamic interaction network versus localized trends model for multiple time-series prediction, Cybern. Syst. 42 (2) (2011) 100–123.

[93] A. Ghobakhlou, M. Watts, N. Kasabov, Adaptive speech recognition with evolving connectionist systems, Inf. Sci. 156 (2003) 71–83.

[94] A.L. Hodgkin, A.F. Huxley, A quantitative description of membrane current and its application to conduction and excitation in nerve, J. Physiol. 117 (4) (1952) 500–544.

[95] E.M. Izhikevich, Which model to use for cortical spiking neurons? IEEE Trans. Neural Netw. 5 (vol. 15) (2004) 1063–1070.

[96] J.J. Hopfield, Pattern recognition computation using action potential timing for stimulus representation, Nature 376 (6535) (1995) 33–36.

[97] S. Thorpe, A. Delorme, R. van Rullen, Spike-based strategies for rapid processing, Neural Netw. 14 (6-7) (2001) 715–725.

[98] D. Verstraeten, B. Schrauwen, M. D'Haene, D. Stroobandt, An experimental unification of reservoir computing methods, Neural Netw. 20 (3) (2007) 391–403.

[99] N.K. Kasabov, K. Dhoble, N. Nuntalid, G. Indiveri, Dynamic evolving spiking neural networks for on-line spatio- and spectro-temporal pattern recognition, Neural Netw. 41 (2013) 188–201.

[100] S. Song, K.D. Miller, L.F. Abbott, Competitive Hebbian learning through spike-timing-dependent synaptic plasticity, Nat. Neurosci. 3 (9) (2000) 919–926.

[101] S. Soltic, N.K. Kasabov, Knowledge extraction from evolving spiking neural networks with rank order population coding, Int. J. Neural Syst. 20 (6) (2010) 437–445.

[102] Y. Chen, J. Hu, N.K. Kasabov, Z. Hou, L. Cheng, NeuroCubeRehab: a pilot study for EEG classification in rehabilitation practice based on spiking neural networks, in: Proc. of the 20th Int'l Conf. on Neural Information Processing, South Korea, November 2013, pp. 70–77.

[103] EU FP7 Marie Curie EvoSpike Project, INI/ETH/UZH, 2011-2012. https://cordis.europa.eu/project/id/272006.

[104] S.G. Wysoski, L. Benuskova, N.K. Kasabov, Evolving spiking neural networks for audiovisual information processing, Neural Netw. 23 (7) (2010) 819–835.

[105] S. Schliebs, M. Defoin-Platel, S. Worner, N.K. Kasabov, Integrated feature and parameter optimization for evolving spiking neural networks: exploring heterogeneous probabilistic models, Neural Netw. 22 (5-6) (2009) 623–632.

[106] N.K. Kasabov, NeuCube: a spiking neural network architecture for mapping, learning and understanding of spatio-temporal brain data, Neural Netw. 52 (2014) 62–76.

[107] N.K. Kasabov, V.L. Feigin, Z.-G. Hou, Y. Chen, L. Liang, R. Krishnamurthi, M. Othman, P. Parmar, Evolving spiking neural networks for personalized modelling of spatio-temporal data and early prediction of events: a case study on stroke, Neurocomputing 134 (2014) 269–279.

[108] C. Mead, Analog VLSI and Neural Systems, Addison-Wesley Longman Publishing Co, Boston, MA, 1989.

[109] M. Mahowald, C. Mead, The Silicon Retina, Sci. Am. 264 (5) (1991) 76–82.

[110] F. Corradi, G. Indiveri, A neuromorphic event-based neural recording system for smart brain-machine-interfaces, IEEE Trans. Biomed. Circuits Syst. 9 (5) (2015) 699–709.

[111] J. Binas, U. Rutishauser, G. Indiveri, M. Pfeiffer, Learning and stabilization of winner-take-all dynamics through interacting excitatory and inhibitory plasticity, Front. Comput. Neurosci. 8 (2014) 68.

[112] J. Sawada, et al., TrueNorth ecosystem for brain-inspired computing: scalable systems, software, and applications, in: Proc. of the Int'l Conf. for High Performance Computing, Networking, Storage and Analysis, USA, November 2016, pp. 130–141.

[113] INI Labs. http://inilabs.com.

[114] B.V. Benjamin, et al., Neurogrid: a mixed-analog-digital multichip system for large-scale neural simulations, Proc. IEEE 102 (5) (2014) 699–716.

[115] S.B. Furber, D.R. Lester, L.A. Plana, J.D. Garside, E. Painkras, S. Temple, A.D. Brown, Overview of the SpiNNaker system architecture, IEEE Trans. Comput. 62 (12) (2012) 2454–2467.

[116] A. Mohemmed, S. Schliebs, S. Matsuda, N.K. Kasabov, Training spiking neural networks to associate spatio-temporal input–output spike patterns, Neurocomputing 107 (2013) 3–10.

[117] K. Subramanian, S. Sundaram, N. Sundararajan, A metacognitive neuro-fuzzy inference system (McFIS) for sequential classification problems, IEEE Trans. Fuzzy Syst. 21 (6) (2013) 1080–1095.

[118] F. Alvi, R. Pears, N. Kasabov, An Evolving Spatio-Temporal Approach for Gender and Age Group Classification With Spiking Neural Networks, Evolving Systems, Springer, 2017.

[119] K. Kumarasinghe, N. Kasabov, D. Taylor, Deep learning and deep knowledge representation in spiking neural networks for brain-computer interfaces, Neural Netw. 121 (2019) 169–185, https://doi.org/10.1016/j.neunet.2019.08.029. Jan 2020.

[120] M. Doborjeh, Z. Doborjeh, N. Kasabov, M. Barati, G.Y. Wang, Deep learning of explainable EEG patterns as dynamic spatiotemporal clusters and rules in a brain-inspired spiking neural network, Sensors 21 (2021) 4900, https://doi.org/10.3390/s21144900.

[121] N. Sengupta, N.K. Kasabov, Spike-time encoding as a data compression technique for pattern recognition of temporal data, Inf. Sci. 406–407 (2017) 133–145.

[122] N.K. Kasabov, N. Scott, E. Tu, S. Marks, N. Sengupta, E. Capecci, M. Othman, M. Doborjeh, N. Murli, R. Hartono, J.I. Espinosa-Ramos, L. Zhou, F. Alvi, G. Wang, D. Taylor, V.L. Feigin, S. Gulyaev, M. Mahmoudh, Z.-G. Hou, J. Yang, Design methodology and selected applications of evolving spatio-temporal data machines in the NeuCube neuromorphic framework, Neural Networks 78 (2016) 1–14.

[123] N. Kasabov (Ed.), The Springer Handbook of Bio- and Neuroinformatics, Springer, 2014. 1230 pp.

[124] N. Kasabov, From multilayer perceptrons and neuro-fuzzy systems to deep learning machines: which method to use?—a survey, Int. J. Inf. Technol. Security 9 (20) (2017) 3–24.

[125] N. Kasabov, M. Doborjeh, Z. Doborjeh, Mapping, learning, visualisation, classification and understanding of fMRI data in the NeuCube spatio temporal data machine, IEEE Trans. Neural Netw. Learn. Syst. 28 (4) (2017) 887–899, https://doi.org/10.1109/TNNLS.2016.2612890.

[126] C. Ge, N. Kasabov, Z. Liu, J. Yang, A spiking neural network model for obstacle avoidance in simulated prosthetic vision, Inf. Sci. 399 (2017) 30–42.

[127] R.R. Khansama, V. Ravi, A. Gollahalli, N. Sengupta, N.K. Kasabov, I. Bilbao-Quintana, Stock market movement prediction using evolving spiking neural networks, in: Handbook of Big Data Analytics, Applications in ICT, Security and Business Analytics, vol. 2, July 2021, pp. 285–312, https://doi.org/10.1049/PBPC037G (Chapter doi:10.1049/PBPC037G_ch14, ISBN: 9781839530593, e-ISBN: 9781839530609).

[128] E. Tu, N. Kasabov, J. Yang, Mapping temporal variables into the NeuCube spiking neural network architecture for improved pattern recognition and predictive modelling, IEEE Trans. Neural Netw. Learn. Syst. 28 (6) (2017) 1305–1317, https://doi.org/10.1109/TNNLS.2016.2536742.

[129] A.L. Benabid, et al., An exoskeleton controlled by an epidural wireless brain–machine interface in a tetraplegic patient: a proof-of-concept demonstration, Lancet Neurol. (2019), https://doi.org/10.1016/S1474-4422 (19) 30321-7.

[130] F.B. Wagner, et al., Targeted neurotechnology restores walking in humans with spinal cord injury, Nature 563 (7729) (2018) 7729, https://doi.org/10.1038/s41586-018-0649-2.

[131] K. Kumarasinghe, N. Kasabov, D. Taylor, Brain-inspired spiking neural networks for decoding and understanding muscle activity and kinematics from electroencephalography signals during hand movements, Sci. Rep. 11 (1) (2021) 1–15.

[132] S. Dora, N. Kasabov, Spiking neural networks for computational intelligence: an overview, Big Data Cogn. Comput. 5 (4) (2021) 67, https://doi.org/10.3390/bdcc5040067.

[133] N. Kasabov, Time-Space, Spiking Neural Networks and Brain-Inspired Artificial Intelligence, Springer, 2019. 750 p https://www.springer.com/gp/book/9783662577134.

[134] http://geonet.co.nz..

[135] C. Darwin, On the Origin of Species by Means of Natural Selection, or the Preservation of Favoured Races in the Struggle for Life, first ed., John Murray, London, 1859, p. 502. retrieved 1 March 2011.

[136] C. Darwin, On the Origin of Species by Means of Natural Selection, or the Preservation of Favoured Races in the Struggle for Life, second ed., John Murray, London, 1860. retrieved 9 January 2009.

[137] T. Bäck, D.B. Fogel, Z. Michalewicz (Eds.), Handbook of Evolutionary Computation, 1997, ISBN: 0750303921.

[138] D.E. Goldberg, Genetic Algorithms in Search, Optimization and Machine Learning, Addison Wesley, 1989.

[139] M. Defoin-Platel, S. Schliebs, N.K. Kasabov, Quantum-inspired evolutionary algorithm: a multimodel EDA, IEEE Trans. Evol. Comput. 13 (6) (2009) 1218–1232.

[140] H.N.A. Hamed, N.K. Kasabov, S. Shamsuddin, Probabilistic evolving spiking neural network optimization using dynamic quantum inspired particle swarm optimization, Aust. J. Intell. Inf. Process. Syst. 11 (1) (2010) 23–28.

[141] D. Kudithipudi, M. Aguilar-Simon, J. Babb, et al., Biological underpinnings for lifelong learning machines, Nat. Mach. Intell. 4 (2022) 196–210, https://doi.org/10.1038/s42256-022-00452-0.

[142] T.L. Hayes, G.P. Krishnan, M. Bazhenov, H. Siegelmann, T. Sejnowski, C. Kanan, Replay in deep learning: current approaches and missing biological elements, 2021. arXiv:2104.04132v2 [q-bio.NC].

Pitfalls and opportunities in the development and evaluation of artificial intelligence systems

David G. Brown and Frank W. Samuelson

US FOOD AND DRUG ADMINISTRATION, SILVER SPRING, MD, UNITED STATES

Chapter outlines

1 Introduction

Sergei, my appliance repairman, tells me my washing machine needs a new motherboard. I guess it does the crossword puzzle between loads. I look over at the car with the funny hat in the next lane and there's no driver. I read that it has no audio sensor and can't hear me honk at it. What else can't it do? Does it understand that if a ball rolls across the road a child may be in pursuit? This is the century of artificial intelligence (AI), when computational intelligence (CI) algorithms show great promise to tremendously improve the quality of our lives. Unfortunately, of course, it is also the age of AI hype, in which systems without the intelligence of a cockroach (Fig. 1) are touted as marvelous advances and cavalierly ceded the authority over life-and-death decisions. We are warned that AI may be an existential threat to our species; however, the dangers of AI at least for the foreseeable future pale in comparison with those of AS (artificial stupidity), whereby CI algorithms are used

Artificial Intelligence in the Age of Neural Networks and Brain Computing. https://doi.org/10.1016/B978-0-323-96104-2.00017-8
Copyright © 2024 Elsevier Inc. All rights reserved.

FIG. 1 Of course, this is unfair to the cockroach, a highly intelligent critter with neurological complexity far beyond any AI system yet developed [1,2]. You should appreciate how hard it was to hold the little fella down while we wrote on its back. *Original image ArtyuStock | Dreamstime.*

that are confusing, dysfunctional, and, yes, dangerous. In order not to become road kill on the AI superhighway, we need adherence to "rules of the road" in their development and deployment—maybe even a hefty dose of common sense.

"Just whom are you calling stupid, buster?" Now I've offended my refrigerator, and she's threatening an ice cream melt down. I'd better clarify: The algorithm is not at fault, it is just inadequate for the task at hand—and we use it anyway. The stupidity is thus closer to home: it is the developer's and our own (mis)understanding of CI capabilities versus the requirements of the job we task it to perform that is to blame and leads us to use AI systems in inappropriate ways. AI system developers are like parents everywhere: they love their children and tend to have inflated views of their capabilities (even leaving out the developer's natural incentive of avarice). Similarly, AI users are generally a gullible lot, moving from the last "next big thing" to its successor with fond hopes of miraculous results. So how do we get the most out of AI? There are some good common sense rules that should be followed in the CI development process, and much more attention needs to be paid to the evaluation phase. Fortunately, there is already a mature field of performance assessment methodology ready to assist in this undertaking. In what follows we will try to provide a road map of this field.

Fig. 2 illustrates our paradigm for the AI development and implementation process. The first requirement is for a well-defined task, such as the identification of an approaching vehicle or detection of a malignant tumor, possibly in conjunction with a human decision maker or as a component of a larger AI system. A CI agent or "observer," call it "Hal," is developed to address this task using a collection of data from which it can abstract certain relevant features and use these features to make a decision. We will make the simplifying assumption that this is a binary task for each of a number of cases, for example, patients or scenes. For example, either a patient is abnormal (A) or is not (B); either an approaching object in a scene is a bicycle (A) or a pedestrian (B). Our world of binary decisions is admittedly a great oversimplification; however, simplification helps ease of comprehension and here represents a nontrivial introduction to the field. Thus, each case will be of class A or class B, and Hal must calculate the odds of each. During the developmental or training

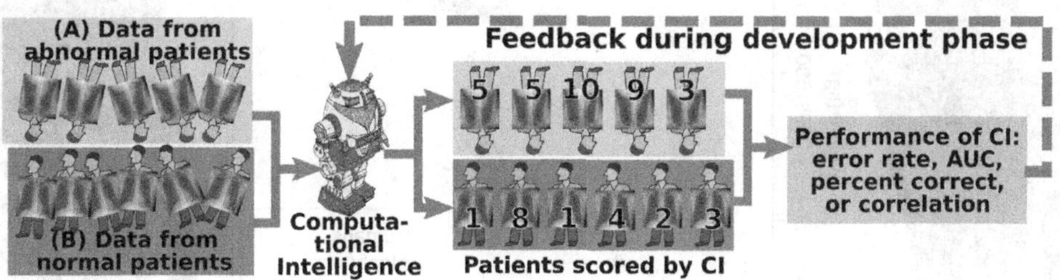

FIG. 2 Samples of data, such as X-ray images, from different classes, are fed to the CI, and it outputs a score for each patient, as shown. Higher output scores indicate a higher likelihood of being abnormal or other signals being present. The CI has imperfect performance because it does not rate all abnormal patients higher than all normal patients. Using these ratings, we can generate summary statistics to evaluate the performance of the CI. During the training phase of the CI, this performance is fed back to adjust the CI such that its performance on the training set will increase. *Robot by John Olsen, Openclipart.*

phase, we use cases of known class to quantify the quality of Hal's decisions and improve them through a feedback mechanism (*dashed line* in Fig. 2). For example, Hal could be trained on a collection of mammograms with known pathology status to identify patients with breast cancer. This information could be used by a radiologist in combination with other patient data to determine the course of patient management (or we can provide the information from Hal together with all other patient data to a Super Hal and dispense with the radiologist completely).

Each datum or each mathematical construct of the data from a case is a "feature" of that case. For example, body temperature, blood pressure, pulse rate, height, and weight are typical features recorded on a visit to the doctor's office. Similarly, wavelet coefficients can be features used to characterize an image. Hal uses these features to make its decision. A useful concept in this regard is "feature space." Each individual observation, or case, is represented by a point in the space for which each feature serves as a different dimension. This is illustrated in Fig. 3 for the problem of distinguishing between people and elephants. The features used are height and weight, and Hal's job is to estimate for each location in feature space the probability that an object with that combination of height and weight is humanoid rather than pachydermal. Then based on the cost/benefit of making the correct decision, a decision surface can be selected along one of the probability contours determined. As you can see from the figure, that is not a difficult task for this dataset—almost everywhere "of interest" for these features there is a good separation between the two types of cases. A decision surface for this problem could be any line drawn separating the two clusters of points. Also, we are fudging by calling it a "probability": the decision variable can be any function strictly monotonic with that probability.

If the locations of the respective cases were to overlap in feature space, as for men and women, for example, then much greater ambiguity arises, Fig. 4. Say the task is to determine which individuals are women. Given an infinite amount of data in the training set, the requisite probability would be easy to determine. At height H and weight W (or within some infinitesimal region surrounding that point) how many women are there relative to

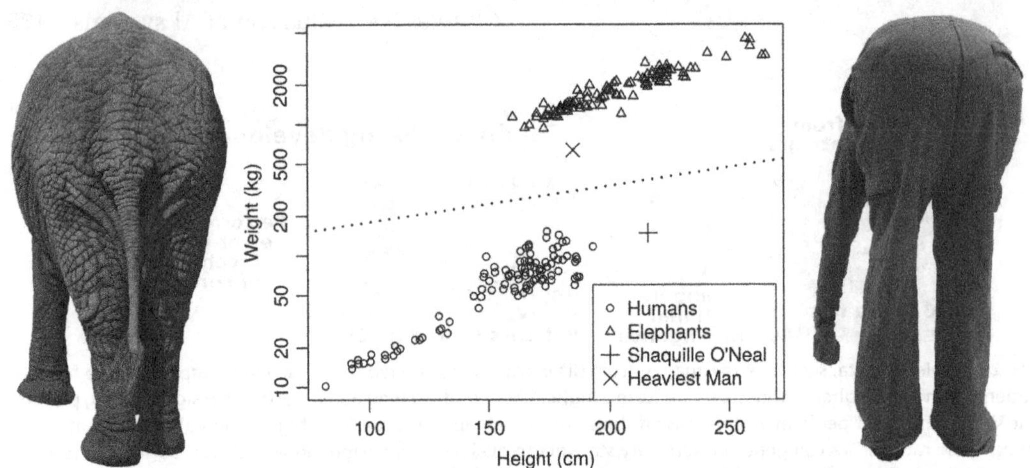

FIG. 3 Plot showing the heights and weights of random samples of 100 Asian elephants [3] and 100 humans from the United States [4], flanked by a true pachydermal posterior (Wisconsinart | Dreamstime) and the remarkably similar one of an author. The plot also shows the heights and weights of basketball player Shaquille O'Neal and the heaviest man ever recorded (Guinness world records). The *dotted line* is a possible decision surface in the feature space separating the two classes. Only extreme obesity (X) causes any overlap between classes.

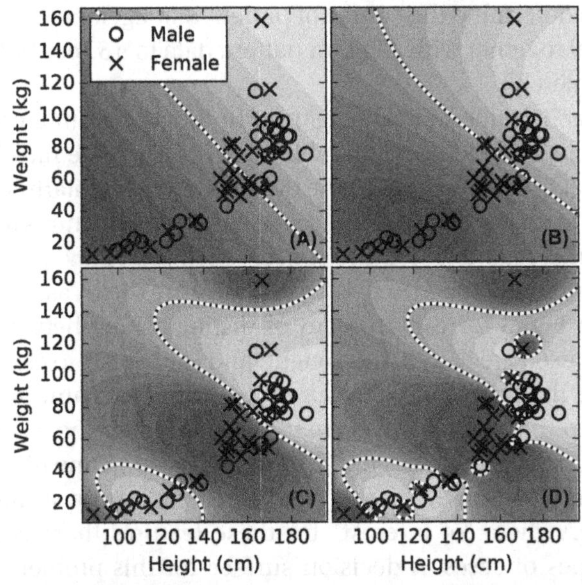

FIG. 4 The plotted points indicate the height and weight of 55 randomly selected male and female people from the NHANES study [4]. The shaded contours show the output values t of a kernel discriminator (our CI) derived from the data with four decreasing levels of smoothing (A, B, C, and D). Lighter shades and lower values of t indicate a higher probability of the observation being a male. Darker shades indicate a higher probability of being female. The dotted curves make up decision surfaces delineating regions of greater than 50% probability that an individual with a given height and weight would be a female. The first discriminator (A) used extremely large smoothing, effectively yielding a linear discriminator. Discriminator B used medium-sized smoothing and appears similar to a quadratic discriminator. Discriminator C uses smaller smoothing, yielding a discriminator that is somewhat overtrained. D shows a highly overtrained discriminator with very small smoothing that performs perfectly on the data used to train it, but poorly on new samples of data.

the total population in that volume (here area) of feature space? With finite datasets, the calculation is more ambiguous. Fig. 4 shows probability curves for our limited dataset given a variety of different reasonable statistical models. This is indicative of the difficulty in training Hal in real-world problems with limited data. For each model, the decision surface is shown assuming that we require at least a 50% chance that an individual is a woman to make that decision.

2 AI development

2.1 Our data are crap

Our first duty is to validate and characterize our data. The sage aphorism "garbage in: garbage out" is applicable to the CI development process. Our algorithm will be no better than the data used in its development. This is especially important because the data are usually not generated by the algorithm developer. How was our dataset collected? when? where? using what measurement tools? and with what accuracy? Is it representative of the data universe that is the domain of our task? Below are some of the data concerns that we may experience.

The data aren't relevant to our problem. Doubtless, there is a lot of information in our data, but does any of it pertain to our task? We are trying to use information in our data to separate two classes of cases. If that information is lacking, then no matter what kind of CI observer we develop, it just won't perform well. We lack discriminability. Perhaps we are using low-resolution images to try to solve a high-resolution task. Perhaps we are using imaging data for prostate cancer detection when the amateur neighborhood proctologist (Fig. 5) is right in suggesting that olfactory data would lead to superior performance.

Our data aren't internally consistent. Large datasets are often composed of "meta data" consisting of many chunks of data from different sources. For example, large-scale NIH clinical trials are frequently criticized for being based on an agglomeration of data from different institutions using different medical equipment and following different clinical protocols. Or, the data may simply be out of date. Sensors are continually being improved and made more sensitive and less noisy, with better spatial, spectral, and/or temporal resolution.

Our dataset isn't representative of the universe on which our CI observer will be used. The data are fine but not directly relevant to our task. Perhaps our algorithm will be used for facial recognition purposes by the police in the inner city, but our data is mainly of Caucasian subjects. Again, in medical terms, data from a diagnostic study (performed on sick people) may not be applicable to a device used in the screening of an asymptomatic population. Or in the CGI world, it is composed of views of normal human landscapes, but it will be used for the development of a navigation aide for Dr. Strange in his bizarre world. Our data must accord with the task we are using it for.

We don't know "ground truth" for our cases—we never do. Unless our data are simulated—and thereby not directly applicable to real-world problems—we always have

FIG. 5 Human modesty has largely robbed modern medicine of the use of the olfactory sense. We generally view it as offensive to sniff or be sniffed. Dobie, however, does not feel that constraint. There have been numerous studies touting canine abilities in cancer detection [5], and there is a very active field of development of artificial noses [6]. *Image Garosha | Dreamstime.*

a problem knowing the validity of the assignment of cases to our classes. Well, perhaps that's not much of a problem for distinguishing elephants from people; however, I'll bet that for pet images from the internet, some of our dogs would meow. In the medical context, we often use human experts for ground truth, and most people would readily agree that radiologists can make mistakes in the assignment of normal versus lesion-present cases from radiographs. What is more startling is the propensity for disagreement among pathologists, see Fig. 6. If we use pathology to determine ground truth, then for the sake of our equanimity we might prefer using one pathologist rather than a panel; because, if we do the latter, we'll discover how frequently they disagree. Of course, this is not an actual recommendation, because we need to use the best possible estimate for our ground truth.

This leads to a second "ground truth" concern. Obviously, there are easier and tougher cases for any discrimination task, and clearly, the uncertainty in ground truth is directly correlated with the degree of case difficulty.

Our data are noisy. All data are noisy, especially if they come from sensors of some kind. This at least should be quantifiable. If the data are mediated by human intervention, then additional variation is to be expected. We must try to identify and where possible minimize the noise in our data to avoid propagating error in our features and final outcome.

Our data are incomplete. Images can be misplaced; questionnaire items can be left blank; data items can be "out of range" and nonsensical. For each of our data points or

FIG. 6 A panel of three typical pathologists. We are particularly concerned by the results reported by the one on the right. For pathology discordance see, for example, Elmore et al. [7], finding that "Among the 3 consensus panel members, unanimous agreement of their independent diagnoses was 75%." *Image Ka2shka | Dreamstime.*

cases, we need to be sure that all appropriate data are present or we must have a justifiable procedure in place to handle any deficits.

We don't have enough data. We never do. We need data to develop our CI classifier, including feature identification, architecture selection, parameter tuning (including when to stop training), and finally performance evaluation. In particular, the amount of data directly limits the complexity of the classifier that we can utilize. There is a famous theorem popularized by the eminent information theorist Thomas Cover which bears on this point. Unless the number of our training cases is at least twice the number of features we are trying to use for our classifier, we are practically guaranteed perfect performance for any arbitrary assignment of class labels to our cases [8]. We revisit this point again under algorithm development.

One valuable method for overcoming a lack of sufficient data for our task is to utilize "similar" data, either simulated or natural in a pretraining phase of our algorithm development (as is of course natural for the human brain). Deep learning techniques, in particular, require vast amounts of data, so that a boost from training on a related dataset may enable us to overcome our own insufficiencies. For example, if we want to identify dogs, we might train our network on the universe of cats out there on the internet. Just don't be surprised if later our CI is much better with chihuahuas than Doberman pinschers. Inevitably we are still stuck with the limitations of our own particular data, with the same perils of overtraining on any limited set plus the biases introduced by the pretraining.

Life is hard, but we move on. Our data are crap: Get over it.

2.2 Our algorithm is crap

Our feature selection is wrong. It is always wrong. Our chances (or those of our deep learning machine, no matter how deep) of wringing the ideal features from a massive database are miniscule. That doesn't mean we shouldn't try; however, it means it's a much tougher problem than we think it is, and we aren't going to ever (totally) succeed. Chen and Brown [9] show what happens when simulated microarray data with 30 known true features out of 1000 features are used to discriminate between two groups of patients. For this problem, out of 30 features selected as "sticking farthest out of the noise" on average only three were valid discriminatory features for low intrinsic separation and nine for high separation conditions.

This problem is not alleviated when our CI observer is choosing its own features. Azriel Rosenfeld was a prominent AI researcher at the University of Maryland who did a lot of interesting work on object recognition (and self-driving vehicles). He used to tell a story about one of his early successes. He had a contract with the army to develop an algorithm to identify battle tanks. He had data for scenes with and without tanks and was enthusiastic and then puzzled when his CI performed brilliantly—too brilliantly. Even if only a very small portion of a tank were visible in a scene, his CI observer would say a tank was there. Upon reflection, he saw that the tankless scenes had been shot on a cloudy day and the with-tank ones on a sunny day. That was the sole feature his CI had needed. Our CI observer may not be very smart, but it is smarter than we are, in its own sly way.

We cheated in our feature selection, and we will pay for it. Actually we may not pay for it at all. Our cheating will give us better (more publishable) results, we will be much sought after and awarded tenure at an early age; whereas our more honest colleagues will have worse results and end their lives flipping burgers. No, no, forget that, and let's try to clean up our act. We cheated by using cases for feature selection that we later very fastidiously separated into sets for training and for testing. This is a common failing. Very frequently the entire dataset is used during the feature selection stage as though this were not an integral part of training [10]. Table 1 illustrates how this can lead to a very significant but false increase in perceived performance.

In Table 1, the true ideal AUC value is 0.70, due to 30 truly useful features out of 1000. Method 1, which is honest CI development, is overwhelmed by the 970 noisy features due to a limited training set. Knowing the truly useful features a priori (method 2) is helpful (but completely unrealistic), but variability in the training and testing datasets still limits CI performance. Using the entire dataset (training and testing datasets together) for either the feature selection or training (methods 3, 4) yields significant positive bias and an undeserved paper in Nature.

Our architecture is wrong. It is too complicated for the task and for the data we have. We want perfection but have yet to accept the fact that perfection is evil. We should want generalizability. It is always possible to achieve perfection on the training set: just follow Tom Cover [8] who demonstrated that we can increase the size of the feature space, until any

Table 1 The measured AUC performance of four different methods of developing our CI [9].

	Method 1	Method 2	Method 3	Method 4
Features selected on	Training set	Predetermined	Entire set	Entire set
CI trained on	Training set	Training set	Training set	Entire set
CI tested on	Testing set	Testing set	Testing set	Entire set
Tested AUC	0.52	0.63	0.83	0.91

small child could pass a (hyper)plane through it, separating the two classes perfectly. Or, we could equivalently encase each type A case in a sphere of vanishingly small radius, for example, by letting a smoothness parameter go to zero as in Fig. 4D. Once again we would have perfect separation in the training set with the added benefit of having produced a classifier with perfect specificity, but unfortunately, zero sensitivity for the entire universe of cases outside of the training set. Very complex algorithms with large feature spaces are prone to failure when presented with cases that were outside their training set. For example, Su, Vargas, and Kouichi show that changing a single pixel in an image can completely change the discrimination of a complex CI such as a deep neural network [11].

Given the task and the type of data available to us, we have only so much inherent discriminability—even for the ideal observer. If we have perfection on our training set, then we either are working on a task not worth doing or we've got to use a less complex algorithm or ease up on the throttle and halt training earlier.

Our algorithm is too simple for the task at hand. Some tasks require complicated classifiers. We may need to acquire more data, or as suggested above, do pretraining on some kind of similar data, for example, to allow a deep network to learn a feature space pertinent to our problem.

We'll train our CI algorithm as well as we can. Still, our algorithm is crap: get over it.

3 AI evaluation

Now we reach the heart of our subject. Having worked through the defects of our data and potential problems of our methodology, we have a finished product: Is it any good? If our evaluation is crap, we can't get over it. Many CI developers seem exhausted by the birthing process and only cursorily treat the assessment of their proud creation. How well does it work? How does it compare with other algorithms for its assigned task? Finally, how well do we understand its behavior? Always remember that no technological result is credible without accompanying error bars. Open any AI conference proceedings and scan the articles' evaluation sections. This will not take a long time; because, on average there just isn't much to see. We can do better.

3.1 Use of data

Before creating a CI, we must consider how we will use our limited set of data to train the CI and evaluate its performance after it is trained. There are several ways to do this, and below we discuss using resubstitution, cross-validation, and a separate testing set.

Resubstitution: We can use all our data to train our CI, and then apply that CI to the same set of data to test it, as in Method 4 of Table 1. This is called resubstitution. It will give an overly optimistic estimate of performance on the general population, particularly if there are a large number of features or a large number of parameters to be fit in our algorithm. Indeed this method can give a perfect measure of performance on a CI that achieves only random performance on the overall population, as discussed above. Essentially resubstitution only demonstrates that our model fits the training set data.

Cross-Validation: In cross-validation, we evaluate the performance of our CI by training it on some large fraction of the data, such as 90% of the cases, and testing the CI on the remaining 10% of the cases. We then repeat the process a number of times, each time selecting a different 90% of the cases, and testing on the unincluded 10%. The average of the testing performance across the 10% hold-out sets is used as our estimate of the performance on the population of a CI trained with 100% of the data.

In theory, this estimate should be slightly pessimistic because we are training the CI with only 90% of the data rather than 100%. However, in practice we have regularly seen performance estimates from cross-validation that are substantially positively biased with respect to a CI's true performance on the population for the following reasons:

(1) Users perform the entire above cross-validation repeatedly, tweaking the CI each time until they find a CI architecture that works very well on their particular data.
(2) Users have data with large batch effects, such as the tank example in the previous section.
(3) Some steps of CI training, such as feature selection, were not included in the cross-validation, such as Method 3 of Table 1.

Separate Testing Set: Before starting the training of the CI, we can set aside a portion of the data on which we will later test our CI, as in Method 1 of Table 1. Developers won't have access to this testing set, and the application of the CI to the testing set will only happen once before the results of the test are reported. When selecting the test set, we should be prepared to handle data that is much different from the training data. At a minimum, they contain different cases. Ideally, the cases in the training and testing sets should have been collected on different days, in different batches, with different cameras or collection devices. This truly tests the ability of our CI to generalize to the entire population, and the performance on the test set will provide an unbiased estimate of the performance of the whole intended use population. Note that this method of evaluating performance may be required by regulatory bodies.

3.2 Performance measures

There are many possible performance measures to choose from for CI observers. Recall what our CI observer is doing. From the data for a particular case, it computes a rating t. We want to use this rating to help us discriminate between cases of class A (called here "abnormal") and class B ("normal"). A larger value of t should indicate a higher probability of being abnormal. If t is greater than some threshold T, then we say the case is "positive" by our CI; otherwise, it is "negative." Canned CI packages may just return a binary yes/no classification. However, somewhere those algorithms are making calculations on continuous or ordinal input features, and later make an implicit or explicit binary decision. Our rating t is the underlying value on which this decision is based. During training, our

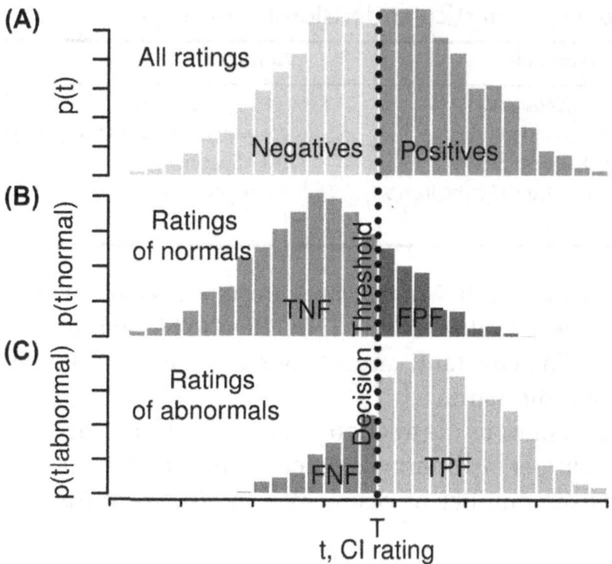

FIG. 7 Probability densities of CI output t for all cases (A), normal cases (B), and abnormal cases (C).

observer establishes a mapping of t values in a feature space as we showed in Fig. 4. The contours of constant t illustrated there correspond to possible thresholds *T* and delineate the corresponding decision surfaces.

We assume that the cases we are using to test the CI were selected at random from a larger population of cases. The output ratings of the CI are a random sample from some probability distribution. The probability density of t, $p(t)$, over our dataset, is shown in Fig. 7A. The area under the curve $p(t)$ to the right of T is the fraction of cases we call "positive" based on the CI ratings, and the area to the left is the fraction of cases we call "negative."

As discussed above we can divide our dataset into two subsets, "normal" and "abnormal." Fig. 7B and C shows the normalized conditional probability densities p-$(t|\text{normal})$ and $p(t|\text{abnormal})$. The decision threshold T is indicated by the dotted vertical line, with everything to the right a positive decision and everything to the left a negative decision. The area of $p(t|\text{abnormal})$ to the right of T is the fraction of abnormals that will be successfully classified as positive and is the true positive fraction (TPF) or sensitivity. To the left of T is the false negative fraction (FNF). Similarly, for $p(t|\text{normal})$, the area to the right of T is the false positive fraction (FPF), and that to the left of T is the fraction of normals correctly classified as negative, known as the true negative fraction (TNF) or specificity. The resulting truth table, Table 2, is used by statisticians to illustrate the results of our binary decisions.

Note that these fractions are specific to the normal and abnormal subpopulations and are not affected by the fraction of cases that are abnormal, known as the prevalence. If we

Table 2 Truth table for a particular decision threshold *T*.

Truth table	Abnormal	Normal	Sum
Result positive	TPF=Sensitivity We found it!	FPF=1−Specificity We worry wrongly! (type I error)	1 + (Sens-Spec)
Result negative	FNF=1−Sensitivity We missed it! (type II error)	TNF=Specificity We ruled it out!	1 − (Sens-Spec)
Sum	1	1	2

test our CI on a dataset where 20% of the cases are abnormal or on a dataset with the prevalence of 80%, the expected values of TPF, TNF, FPF, and FNF will be the same as long as (1) the threshold *T* remains constant, and (2) our methods of sampling data from each subpopulation remain the same.

Accuracy is often defined as the fraction of cases that were correctly assigned by the CI. It is the sum of the number of abnormals called positive and the number of normal called negative divided by the number of cases. We can also write this fraction in the terms presented above:

$$\text{Accuracy} = \text{Prevalence} \times \text{TPF} + (1 - \text{Prevalence}) \times \text{TNF}.$$

Two less common measures, the positive predictive value (PPV), the fraction of all positive results that are true positives, and the negative predictive value (NPV), the fraction of negative results that are true negatives, are also prevalence dependent. These are helpful for their explanatory value of the real significance of test results. For example, for serious diseases with very low prevalence, positive CI results can cause needless worry. Even for a very sensitive CI, say sensitivity of 0.99, and quite good specificity of 0.90, given a low prevalence of disease 0.01 for the general population, fewer than 10% (PPV) of those told they tested positive are actually positive, and the great majority are needlessly distraught.

Accuracy, PPV, and NPV strongly depend upon the prevalence of abnormal cases in the sample of data we use to test our CI (Fig. 8). Therefore, we should not use these metrics if the prevalence of our test sample does not match that of the true population in which the CI algorithm will be used. For example, if we test our above CI on data seeded with extra cases of a rare serious disease, then measured accuracy, PPV, and NPV will be meaningless for the actual low prevalence population. Furthermore, as we show later, the optimal classifier decision threshold (*T* value) usually does not correspond to the one yielding maximum accuracy.

Consider the CI from Fig. 2 designed to discriminate between two classes of patients, abnormal (shown upside down) and normal (shown right side up). In Fig. 9, we order those patients using the ratings that were assigned by the CI. Ideally, every truly abnormal patient would have been given a rating higher than every normal patient, and we could assign every abnormal patient as positive, and every normal patient as negative. However, due to our imperfect CI, or perhaps due to the noisy images themselves, the normal and abnormal patients are not perfectly separable given the ratings.

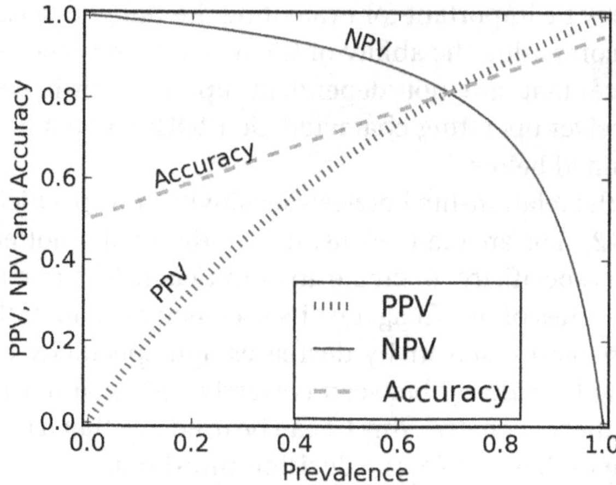

FIG. 8 Accuracy, PPV, and NPV as functions of the fraction of abnormals (prevalence) in an example dataset with sensitivity 0.95 and specificity 0.50.

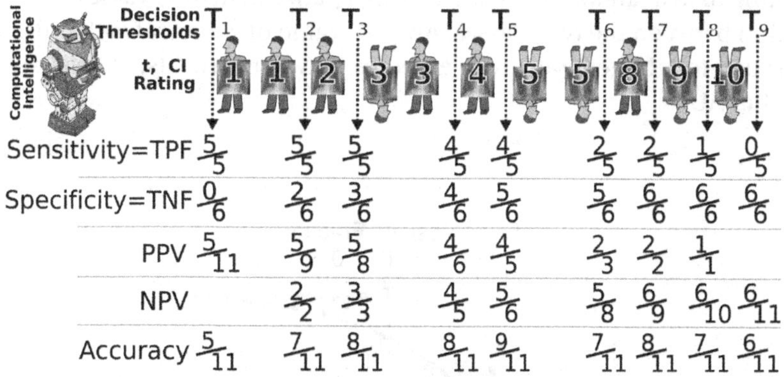

FIG. 9 This figure gives threshold-dependent performance measures TPF, TNF, PPV, NPV, and accuracy, at all thresholds for a small dataset.

Now what happens if we change our threshold T on the CI rating? Of course we can calculate TPF, TNF, PPV, NPV, and accuracy for any decision threshold. For example, in Fig. 9 if we use threshold T_5 and declare that all patients with a CI rating greater than 4.5 tested positive, then 4/5 of the diseased patients will be correctly declared positive (TPF = 80%), 5/6 of the nondiseased patients will be correctly declared negative (TNF = 83%), 4/5 of the patients that we called positive really have the disease (PPV = 80%), 5/6 of the patients that we called negative are truly normal (NPV = 83%), and 9/11 of the patients were correctly assigned (accuracy = 82%).

Note that all of these measures change when we change our decision threshold for testing positive. For example, if we use threshold T_3, and declare that all patients with a CI rating greater than 2.5 tested positive, all the above measures will be different. While a decision threshold may be important for evaluating the utility of a CI in a particular scenario, usually when comparing the ability of CIs to separate two classes we prefer measures of performance that are not dependent upon a particular threshold. These measures are the receiver operating characteristic (ROC) curve and the area under that curve (AUC) as explained below.

The ROC curve is the relationship between sensitivity and specificity as we change our decision threshold [12]. For arcane reasons, it is traditionally plotted as sensitivity as a function of one minus specificity. To create an empirical ROC curve (Fig. 10) we can plot the sensitivity (TPF) values of our CI against its specificity (TNF) both from Fig. 9. As the decision threshold increases, sensitivity decreases and specificity increases. The curve represents the inevitable trade-off between correctly calling abnormal patients positive and calling normal patients negative. Any CI can be used at either a high sensitivity or high specificity depending on how we set the decision threshold.

The area under a ROC curve (AUC) is an overall measure of the performance of our CI. It can be considered the integral of sensitivity over specificity, the integral of specificity over sensitivity, or the probability that a randomly chosen abnormal patient will have a higher CI rating than a randomly selected normal patient. An AUC value of 1 indicates perfect separation between the two classes. An AUC value of ½ indicates that the two classes cannot be separated. In general, given a choice between two CIs, we will select the one with the higher AUC.

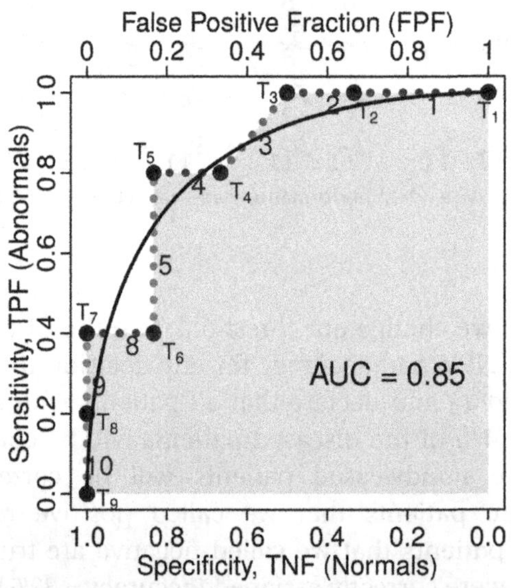

FIG. 10 Two ROC curves. The *dotted line* is an empirical ROC curve of the data in Fig. 9. Each point is labeled with the threshold *T* at which that point is measured. *Each dotted line* segment is labeled with the ratings of the patients that the segment represents. Note that by convention the specificity axis increases to the left. The area under the curve (AUC) is 0.85 for this dataset. The continuous *black line* is a parametric model of this ROC data [13].

3.3 Decision thresholds

In its final implementation, we have to choose a decision threshold T for our CI or equivalently some operating point on our ROC curve. Above what rating value should our CI tell its users that a case is positive? Frequently CI developers choose a threshold that maximizes the accuracy of the CI on some test sets. For example, such a developer would choose threshold T_5 ($t=4.5$) in Fig. 9. This choice maximizes the number of correct calls by the CI on our dataset, but it makes two dubious assumptions. It assumes that the prevalence of abnormal cases in our test sample is the same as for the population on which the CI will be implemented, and it assumes that all correct/incorrect decisions have the same benefits/costs. If calling an abnormal case positive (true positive) has a greater benefit or utility than calling a normal case negative, then maximizing accuracy is the wrong choice to make. For example, by studying the decisions of radiologists, Abbey et al. [14] estimated that the benefit of a true positive decision in breast cancer screening is about 162 times greater than the benefit of a true negative, and therefore, the false positive fraction in screening is about 450 times larger than that which would maximize accuracy.

The choice of threshold T should be the one that maximizes the expected utility of all the decisions that a CI will make, where the utility is the sum of the benefits from true results minus the costs of false ones [15,16]. Different decision thresholds yield different numbers of true positives and true negatives, as in Fig. 9, and therefore different total expected utilities. While these expected utilities are difficult to calculate with any degree of accuracy, experiments show that all of us set decision thresholds in everyday practice as though we are attempting to maximize the benefits and minimize the costs of our decisions.

As an example of decision thresholds and utilities in real-world practice, we present data from Elmore et al. [17]. The circles in Fig. 11 show the sensitivities and specificities

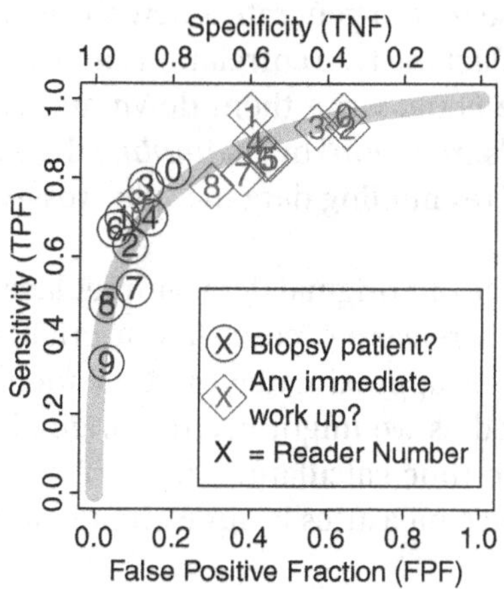

FIG. 11 Sensitivities and specificities of 10 readers making two types of decisions. The wide line is a parametric model of their average ROC curve.

of 10 HI (human intelligence) readers when deciding if 150 patients should be sent for biopsy. The diamonds in the plot show how the same 10 readers decided whether to send the same 150 patients to different diagnostics. Note that all these decisions are consistent with a single ROC curve, which is modeled by the *wide solid line.* All the readers processed the same image data, and all the readers had roughly the same AUC and the same ability to separate normal patients from abnormal patients. However, many of these decisions were made at very different decision thresholds. Different readers operated at different decision thresholds. All readers attempted to maximize the utility of their decisions by having a higher threshold for sending people to biopsy because the cost of a biopsy is higher than for other diagnostics [18].

4 Variability and bias in our performance estimates

It is important that we report a measure of uncertainty or provide confidence intervals on any performance measurement that we report. Our measurement is based on one set of data used to train and test the CI. If someone else were to attempt to reproduce our results, they would probably use different training and testing data, and they would get a performance measure different from ours. Is this number consistent with our measure of CI performance? Or is their performance *significantly* different? To make statements of statistical significance, we need to know the statistical uncertainty for these performance measures. Our uncertainty estimates should reflect how much variation there would be if others tried to reproduce our results with new data. If we properly calculate our uncertainties, the results from about 83% of the reproductions of the study will fall within our calculated 95% confidence interval.

Generally, we do not have the data, time, or money to reproduce the study repeatedly, but we may simulate the reproduction of the experiment and use the variation in our performance statistic in that simulation as an estimate of our uncertainty. While we could create simulated data and use that to generate a new CI version and test it, our simulated data might not accurately reflect the true correlations in real data. Indeed if we knew what all the correlations were, we could write them down and create an ideal discriminator. Therefore, we often create a "simulation" by *resampling* the existing data. This idea is illustrated in Fig. 12. Methods of resampling data include cross-validation, the jackknife, and the bootstrap [19].

In the bootstrap, we sample our original data with replacement to create another sample of the same size [20]. If there were N cases in our original dataset, the resampled set would also have N cases, but approximately 37% of them would be duplicates. This resampled data are then used as we might use the original data, to train or test our CI. We do this many times, each time calculating the performance of our CI. The standard deviation of these performance measures is our estimate of the uncertainty in the performance of the CI.

We can validate our CI at different levels. If we know that the parameters of our CI are fixed and we want to know our uncertainty of its performance on the population, then just

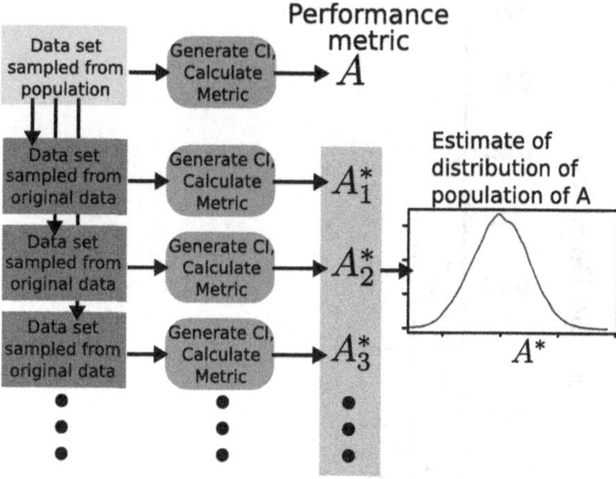

FIG. 12 An illustration of resampling. Using the original dataset, we create and/or test our AI with a sample of data, yielding an estimate of performance such as A=AUC. That set is then resampled, and the process is repeated. We may use the variance of these reproduced performance metrics as an estimate of the true variance of the metric.

a first level of assessment may be warranted [21]. Here, we would repeatedly resample (bootstrap) the testing set, keeping the same CI and CI output t for each case (no retraining), and recalculate the performance metric for each resample. The standard deviation of these recalculated metrics is our estimate of the variation that we would see if we repeatedly selected new testing sets, applied the same fixed CI to those sets, and calculated our metric. It is our estimate of the uncertainty of the performance of our CI on the population. Alternatively, we can use equations by Hanley and McNeil [22] to estimate the uncertainty of the AUC.

However, if we want to compare the performance of our CI with someone else who is attempting to duplicate our results, then we also need to estimate the uncertainty of the performance of our CI due to the finite set of data used to train the CI. In this case, we need to repeatedly resample the training dataset, and retrain our CI, as well as resample the testing set. A plot of the variability in the performance of CI due to the training sample is shown in Fig. 13. The plot also shows the mean bootstrap and jackknife estimates of this variability.

5 Conclusion

In the development of AI systems, there are many traps for the unwary. We have outlined our concerns about the data used to train and test these systems, the architecture of the systems themselves, and the techniques used in their evaluation. The data used should be chosen to be the most internally consistent, least noisy, highest quality, and most relevant to your task. Our algorithm should not be driven too hard to achieve the best possible result on the training set: the benefits from this are illusory, as generalizability is being

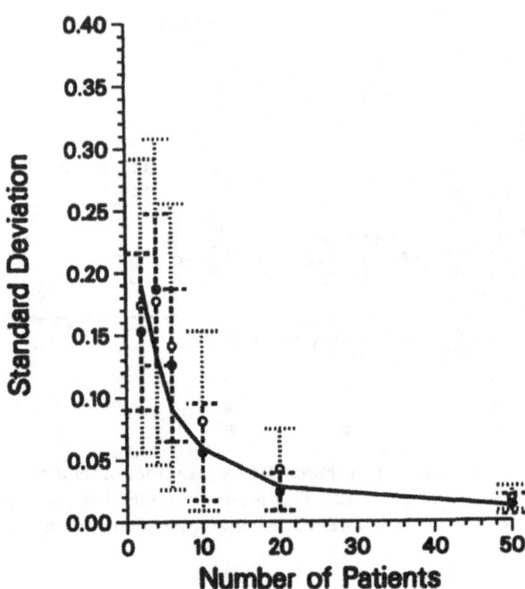

FIG. 13 Uncertainty estimates of our CI's performance as a function of the training sample size [23]. Mean jackknife estimates are *open circles* and *solid circles* are the mean bootstrap estimates of uncertainty due to the variation in the training dataset. The *solid line* is the true standard deviation of performance. As the number of patients in the training sample increases, the variability of the CI's performance on the population decreases, and the jackknife and bootstrap are good methods of estimating this uncertainty.

sacrificed. In addition, good data hygiene must be maintained by not reusing data for testing that has already been employed during the training phase. These facets should all be examined carefully and either remediated or fully disclosed. We should do what we can and disclose the rest.

With regard to the performance evaluation of AI systems, we have stressed the necessity of rigorous evaluation methodology and the importance of the provision of uncertainty along with performance metrics. We have also pointed to the defects in prevalence-dependent measures such as accuracy and the advantages of prevalence-independent measures such as sensitivity, specificity, ROC, and AUC. Further, we have noted that emphasis on performance at any one particular operating point on the ROC curve is misguided. Research has shown that operating points can change radically between the development and implementation stages for AI systems, but that AUC, for example, remains remarkably constant. For further information on the AI development/evaluation process consult the appended bibliography. Please note the extended tutorial on performance evaluation on our website: davidgbrown.co [24].

It is not easy to participate in the responsible development and deployment of AI systems; however, through rigorous attention to detail, honest evaluation, and dedication to transparency, we can improve the present state of the process. If we can improve AI and diminish AS, we can make the world a little less crappy place. Go for it.

Acknowledgment

We thank Eugene O'Bryan for assisting us with his digital art skills.

References

[1] N. Strausfeld, Arthropod Brains: Evolution, Functional Elegance, and Historical Significance, Belknap Press, 2012.

[2] D. Fox, Consciousness in a cockroach, Discover Mag. (2007).

[3] H.S. Mumby, S.N. Chapman, J.A. Crawley, K.U. Mar, W. Htut, A.T. Soe, et al., Distinguishing between determinate and indeterminate growth in a long-lived mammal, BMC Evol. Biol. 15 (2015) 214.

[4] National Health and Nutrition Examination Survey, 2013. Cited 2017 08 15. Available from: https://wwwn.cdc.gov/Nchs/Nhanes/2013-2014/BMX_H.htm.

[5] E. Cohen, J. Conifield, 2016. Cited 2017 12 3. Available from: http://www.cnn.com/2015/11/20/health/cancer-smelling-dogs/index.html.

[6] J. Fitzgerald, Artificial nose technology: status and prospects in diagnostics, Am. J. Hum. Genet. 35 (1) (2017) 33–42.

[7] J. Elmore, G. Longton, P. Carney, et al., Diagnostic concordance among pathologists interpreting breast biopsy specimens, J. Am. Med. Assoc. 313 (11) (2015) 1122–1132.

[8] T. Cover, Geometrical and Statistical properties of systems of linear inequalities with applications in pattern recognition, EC-14, IEEE Trans. Electronic Comput. (1965) 326–334.

[9] W. Chen, D.G. Brown, Optimistic bias in the assessment of high dimensional classifiers with a limited dataset, in: Proceedings of International Joint Conference on Neural Networks, International Neural Network Society, San Jose, CA, 2011, pp. 2698–2703.

[10] R. Simon, M.D. Radmacher, K. Dobbin, L.M. McShane, Pitfalls in the use of DNA microarray data for diagnostic and prognostic classification, J. Natl. Cancer Inst. 95 (1) (2003) 14–18.

[11] J. Su, D.V. Vargas, S. Kouichi, One Pixel Attack for Fooling Deep Neural Networks, 2017.

[12] J.P. Egan, Signal Detection Theory and ROC Analysis, Harcourt Brace Jovanovich, New York, 1975.

[13] J.C. Ogilvie, C.D. Creelman, Maximum-likelihood estimation of receiver operating characteristic curve parameters, J. Math. Psychol. 5 (1968) 377–391.

[14] C.K. Abbey, M.P. Eckstein, J.M. Boone, Estimating the relative utility of screening mammography, Med. Decis. Mak. 33 (2013) 510–520.

[15] C.E. Metz, Basic principles of ROC analysis, Semin. Nucl. Med. 7 (4) (1978) 283–298.

[16] J. von Neumann, O. Morgenstern, Theory of Games and Economic Behavior, Princeton University Press, 1953.

[17] J.G. Elmore, C.K. Wells, C.H. Lee, et al., Variability in radiologists' interpretations of mammograms, N. Engl. J. Med. 331 (22) (1994) 1493–1499.

[18] F.W. Samuelson, Inference Based on Diagnostic Measures From Studies of New Imaging Devices, vol. 20, Academic Radiology, 2013, pp. 816–824.

[19] T. Hastie, R. Tibshirani, J. Friedman, The Elements of Statistical Learning, Springer, New York, 2001.

[20] B.J. Efron, R. Tibshirani, Introduction to the Bootstrap, Chapman & Hall, Boca Raton, 1993.

[21] W. Chen, B.G. Gallas, W.A. Yousef, Classifier variability: accounting for training and testing, Pattern Recogn. 45 (2012) 2661–2671.

[22] J.A. Hanley, B.J. McNeil, The meaning and use of the area under the receiver operating characteristic curve, Radiology 143 (1) (1982) 29–36.

[23] D.G. Brown, A.C. Schneider, M.P. Anderson, R.F. Wagner, Effects of finite sample size and correlated/noisy input features on neural network pattern classification, in: Proceedings of the SPIE Medical Imaging, SPIE, Newport Beach, 1994, p. 642.

[24] D.G. Brown, Evaluation of Computational Intelligence Decision Makers, Cited 2017 11 03. Available from: http://davidgbrown.co/.

Theory of the brain and mind: Visions and history

Daniel S. Levine

UNIVERSITY OF TEXAS AT ARLINGTON, ARLINGTON, TX, UNITED STATES

Chapter outlines

The International Neural Network Society (INNS) was founded in 1987 by a group of scientists interested in pursuing fundamental problems about the mind and imbued with a highly interdisciplinary vision. Many of these scientists had been laboring for over 20 years at the fringes of their respective disciplines and now saw an opportunity to bring their outlook to a larger audience, based on renewed interest both in the artificial intelligence and the basic science communities. The vision is well described in this mission statement:

> *The International Neural Network Society is the premiere organization for individuals interested in a theoretical and computational understanding of the brain and applying that knowledge to develop new and more effective forms of machine intelligence. (https://www.linkedin.com/company/international-neural-network-society-inns)*

In other words, INNS, along with its flagship journal, *Neural Networks*, was conceived as a home for researchers and students interested in the theory of brain and mind, whether their primary interest was in understanding neuroscience or in applying brain-like computation in industry. This chapter discusses some of the history and current trends in neural networks and computational neuroscience, with the aim of exploring how well INNS's primary vision has been fulfilled over the years. My focus will be on the modeling of neuroscientific and psychological data, which I know best, more than on engineering applications.

Artificial Intelligence in the Age of Neural Networks and Brain Computing. https://doi.org/10.1016/B978-0-323-96104-2.00004-X
Copyright © 2024 Elsevier Inc. All rights reserved.

1 Early history

The early history of the neural network field is discussed thoroughly in Chapter 2 of [1] and will be summarized here. It began essentially in the 1940s when advances in neuroscience converged with the early development of digital computers. Many scientists and engineers in that period were taken with an analogy between computers and real brains, based on the fact that neurons are all-or-none, either firing or not firing, just as binary switches in a digital computer are either on or off. This analogy stimulated the development of the science of cybernetics [2] and the first significant article about the logic of networks of neurons [3].

McCulloch and Pitts [3] proved mathematically that a network of all-or-none neurons could be constructed so that one neuron in the network fires selectively in response to any given spatiotemporal array of firings of other neurons in the network. While the all-or-none nature of the network units and the focus on single neurons were oversimplifications, some of McCulloch and Pitts' constructions anticipated themes that are common in more recent neural networks. For example, some of their networks presage the distinction developed in popular later models between input, output, and hidden units [4]. The input units react to particular data features from the environment (e.g., "cold object on skin," "black dot in upper left corner," "loud noise to the right"). The output units generate particular organismic responses (e.g., "I feel cold," "the pattern is a letter A," "walk to the right"). The hidden units are neither input nor output units themselves but, via network connections, influence output units to respond to prescribed patterns of input unit firings or activities. The input-output-hidden trilogy can at times be seen as analogous to the distinction between sensory neurons, motor neurons, and all other neurons (interneurons) in the brain.

Also, one of McCulloch and Pitts' examples involved constructing a network to feel the heat when a cold object is removed. This is an example of a contrast effect, which has been modeled more recently using either opponent processing via transmitter depletion [5,6], or temporal differences based on reward prediction errors [7–11].

Networks of the McCulloch-Pitts type do not include learning: their responses remain uniform over time, although some of them store a memory of previous stimulation via reverberation. Yet under the influence of psychology, other researchers drew the distinction between mechanisms for short-term memory (STM) and for long-term memory (LTM; [12,13]). Hebb [12] expressed the emerging consensus in the field that reverberatory loops (say, between cortex and thalamus in the brain) could be a mechanism for STM, but that LTM required structural or biochemical changes in synapses or neurons.

Hebb sought a neural basis for classical conditioning. He predicted that paired presynaptic and postsynaptic stimuli would lead to increases in the strength of a synapse, anticipating later findings in neuroscience about synaptic plasticity [14,15]. His idea was widely accepted in both neuroscience and neural modeling, but some neuroscientists and modelers expressed concern that Hebb's law could lead to instability and needed to be counteracted by a law for reducing synaptic strength if stimuli were unpaired [16]. In fact, the findings on long-term potentiation at synapses were shortly followed by other findings on long-term depression [17–19].

A synthesis of Hebb and McCulloch-Pitts occurred in various versions of the perceptrons due to Rosenblatt [20] whose multilayer perceptrons were *trained* to respond selectively to specific patterns of sensory stimuli. Perceptrons formed the basis for the widely used backpropagation networks [4,21], which in turn form the basis for the currently popular deep learning methods [22–24].

The mathematics employed in the McCulloch-Pitts and Rosenblatt models was discrete, as befits a network of all-or-none neurons. Yet the biophysics of neurons, like other physical processes, points to the importance of variables that can take on a continuum of possible values. Rashevsky [25] and other pioneers showed that the discrete processes in a network of neurons could be averaged over a large number of neurons to generate continuous processes in networks whose units are populations rather than individual neurons.

2 Emergence of some neural network principles

From about the mid-1960s to the mid-1980s, when much less-detailed cognitive neuroscience results were available than are now, several pioneering neural modelers developed network architectures based largely on abstract principles, though incorporating some of that period's state of the art in neuroscience (cf. Ref. [1], Chapters 3 and 4). This led to the development of some "building blocks" that could be incorporated into larger and more complex networks. Since different building blocks were used to model different functions, this was not a "one size fits all" approach to neural modeling.

One of these principles, inspired both by Hebb and by psychologists such as Hull [13], was associative learning. Associative learning was a prominent feature in the work of Grossberg, Anderson, Kohonen, and Kosko [26–39]. Grossberg's early networks, such as the outstar, were particularly notable for including conditioned decreases as well as increases in synaptic strength, in order that a network could learn the proportions between activations of different units in a stimulus pattern.

Just as associative learning is important in models of long-term memory, lateral inhibition or competition plays a crucial role in models of short-term memory. This principle is particularly important in models of perception [40–44]. Competitive interactions capture data, showing that the visual system does not store every stimulus it receives equally but sharpens contrast and reduces noise.

Opponent processing is a psychological principle that captures the fact that people and animals often perceive contrasts rather than absolute amounts of variables. Contrast effects were first observed in the realm of emotion: the absence of electric shock when one has just been shocked is rewarding, and the absence of food when one is hungry and expecting food is punishing. Grossberg [5] explained these effects using the gated dipole model with neural transmitter accumulation and depletion, and in later articles extended the idea both to visual perception and motor control. The method of temporal differences [10,11] was later applied to similar phenomena.

The temporal difference method is closely related to networks that incorporate error correction. Motor control, for example, involves comparing the current position of muscles with a target position (e.g., Ref. [45]). Error correction has been applied to cognitive information processing in backpropagation networks [4]. In fact [21] initially developed what came to be known as backpropagation to control the parameters in time-series models.

In the 1970s, several modelers combined lateral inhibition and associative learning in various ways to develop early multilevel networks for perceptual coding (e.g., Refs. [46–50]). These models usually included a retinal and a cortical level, with the cortical level learning a categorization of stimulus patterns impinging on the retina. The categorization was based on learned retinal-to-cortical (bottom-up) connections that learned to encode commonly presented patterns. Grossberg [51] showed that for the categorization to be stable over time, the learned bottom-up connections needed to be supplemented by learned top-down feedback. This combination of bottom-up and top-down connections was the origin of what became known as adaptive resonance theory (ART; [52]).

All of these principles were first suggested on psychological grounds but verified many years later by data from neuroscience. The results that emerged from neuroscience led in this century to refinements and extensions of the earlier models, and the newer models increasingly incorporated explicit representations of brain regions.

3 Neural networks enter mainstream science

Yet the scientists who labored in the neural network field between the 1960s and 1980s were not widely known and had to find academic appointments in more traditional fields. Many have labeled that period the dark ages in the field, but Stephen Grossberg at one plenary talk at the International Joint Conference on Neural Networks (IJCNN) said it should instead be called a golden age because it was creative and spawned many of the key ideas of the field that are still in use.

This state of affairs changed in the 1980s with a surge of interest in the relationships between neuroscience and artificial intelligence, at a more sophisticated level than had occurred in the 1940s. Artificial intelligence researchers increasingly found that the methods of symbolic heuristic programming that had dominated their field were inadequate to handle situations that involved processing imprecise information. Hence, after having abandoned interest in the brain for nearly 30 years, they started turning back to neuroscience and psychology for possible answers to their problems. At the same time, several specific publications in neural modeling, such as the article of Hopfield [53] and the two-volume book edited by Rumelhart and McClelland [4], caught the attention of psychologists and neuroscientists by showing that simple networks could reproduce some of their data.

These developments led to the alliance between engineering and neuroscience that spawned INNS, the IJCNN conferences, and a host of smaller neural network conferences across the world. They also led to a rediscovery of the work of researchers who had started in the "dark ages," such as Grossberg, Anderson, and Kohonen.

Yet the popularization of neural networks within academia has often been accompanied by a restricted view of the nature and explanatory capabilities of neural networks. Because of the influence of the PDP approach developed by Rumelhart and McClelland [4], many neuroscientists, psychologists, and even philosophers (e.g., Bechtel [54]) write with a view of all or most neural networks as requiring extensive training to achieve a predetermined goal. This means that between the sensory and effector ends of the network, the inner components start out with little or no intrinsic structure and emerge out of the wash as "internal representations." Also, many authors seem to believe that the three-layer back propagation network with input, output, and hidden layers is the standard "neural network."

By contrast, an overview of the neural network field [1] shows the great diversity of neural network architectures, of which PDP networks are just a fraction. Also, while the PDP approach emphasizes development over genetics, both innate and learned processes are of evolutionary importance to organisms, and the richest neural networks incorporate and integrate both types of processes.

Most importantly, different neural and psychological functions often require different architectures, even if those functions are integrated together into a larger network. This means that any "one size fits all" approach to neural network modeling is bound to have limitations. For example, Gaudiano and Grossberg [55] discuss the different requirements for sensory pattern processing and motor control. Motor control involves comparing the present position with a target position and inhibiting movement if the present and target positions match. In sensory pattern processing, by contrast, the pattern recognizer is excited if present and expected patterns match. The different requirements suggest different architectures for the two subprocesses, and these two architectures can be concatenated into a larger system architecture that generates motion in response to appropriate sensory events.

Buoyed by early successes in modeling perception and motor control, the neural network field has expanded in the last 30 years into processes several synapses away from the sensory and motor ends, such as conditioning, attention, cognitive control, and executive function. Some models of those processes have been built on and refined earlier, more abstract models of simpler processes. Others have started from data about the complex processes and used simple equations for neural interactions to simulate those data without reference to simpler processes. Because of the unity of the brain and mind, it is my contention that those models that build on the models of simpler processes are more likely to have staying power.

4 Is computational neuroscience separate from neural network theory?

The growth of the neural modeling field in the 1990s and early 2000s led to the formation of different research niches. Since then, an increasing number of researchers have taken up the challenge of modeling complex data from neuropsychology and cognitive neuroscience. Many of these researchers seldom if ever attend IJCNN conferences or publish in *Neural Networks*, and they are not part of the INNS community (although some of them attend other conferences that cut across engineering and neuroscience concerns, such as Neural Information Processing Systems or NeurIPS, formerly NIPS).

In particular, computational neuroscience since the 1990s has become a field with its own meetings that are largely disconnected from the neural network or artificial intelligence meetings. The concern of many computational neuroscientists has been about processes at the level of neurons and small neural ensembles without relating those processes to cognitive or behavioral functions (see, e.g., Ref. [56]). Yet more recently Ashby and Hélie [57] have proposed that the best computational models of brain function are based on a synthesis of these fields that they call *computational cognitive neuroscience*:

> *Computational Cognitive Neuroscience (CCN) is a new field that lies at the intersection of computational neuroscience, machine learning, and neural network theory (i.e., connectionism).*

The advantages that Ashby and Hélie posit for CCN models as opposed to purely cognitive models include the ability to make predictions about neural processes such as fMRI, EEG, and single-unit responses, as well as behavioral data. Yet CCN is really not new but has been a gradual development over 20–30 years, in part as an outgrowth of previous neural models that were more abstract and cognitive and had less neuroscientific detail. The third edition of my textbook [1] uses "Computational Cognitive Neuroscience" as the title for its second half and emphasizes the roots of those models in the more introductory models of the book's first half.

Current models which can be considered CCN come from a variety of intellectual sources. One of those sources is the backpropagation algorithm. One of the earliest models in this tradition was a network theory of the Stroop task, which involves naming the color of ink in a word that represents either the same color or a different color [58,59]. This model included a simulation of poor performance on this task by schizophrenics, based on "lesioning" of a particular neural network connection. Subsequently, O'Reilly [60] set out to mimic the effects of the backpropagation algorithm using the LEABRA equations which were purportedly more biologically realistic.

O'Reilly [61] followed up this work by proposing six principles for computational modeling of the cortex. This approach led to a sophisticated set of interrelated models which simulated such processes as working memory [62,63] and Pavlovian conditioning [64]. Yet this modeling approach in some ways betrays its one-size-fits-all origins. It is based on distributed representations of concepts when there is a basis for making some models use more localized representations (see Ref. [65] for discussion). Also, the LEABRA equations use both associative learning and error-driven learning at *every synapse*, rather than using different types of learning for different processes.

A second source of many CCN models, particularly in the area of conditioning, is the temporal difference (TD) model of Sutton and Barto [10,11]. The TD idea that learning occurs when there is an error in reward prediction (i.e., a previously neutral stimulus becomes rewarding or a previously rewarding stimulus becomes unrewarding) obtained experimental support from results on responses of dopamine neurons in the midbrain [66–68]. Reward prediction was thought to be implemented via dopamine neuron connections to the basal ganglia, and several later variants of the TD model exploited this connection [69–71]. These models are built on the notion of reinforcement learning with an actor and a critic, a design that is also popular in control engineering (e.g., Ref. [72]).

The TD approach is popular with conditioning researchers because it is built around a single and easily understandable principle, namely, maximization of predicted future reward. Yet its very simplicity, with the implication that there is a unique locus in the brain that controls Pavlovian learning, limits the predictive applicability of this approach unless it is extended to incorporate principles that suggest roles for regions not included in these articles, such as the amygdala and prefrontal cortex (see Ref. [73]; for a review).

Other CCN models come not from previous simpler neural models but from neural elaborations of previous nonneural models from mathematical psychology. This approach has been particularly fruitful in the area of category learning [74–76]. Interestingly Love and Gureckis [76] noted the kinship of their model with the adaptive resonance theory of categorization [52], which was based on associative learning combined with lateral inhibition and opponent processing.

Finally, there are a number of CCN models which are refinements or extensions of more abstract models that arose before current data were available but embodied network principles based on cognitive requirements. The cognitive requirements these networks were designed to fulfill are frequently based on complementary pairs, such as learning new inputs without forgetting old ones, or processing both boundaries and interiors of visual scenes (e.g., Ref. [77]). One example of this type of CCN model is Grossberg and Versace [78], which extends the previously more abstract adaptive resonance model to incorporate neural data about corticothalamic interactions and the role of acetylcholine. The model of [78] explicitly incorporates neuronal spiking, as does a recent model of emotional effects on memory via pathways from the amygdala to the hippocampus [79]. Another example is Ref. [80] which is built on previously more abstract conditioning models and incorporates neural data about dopaminergic prediction error and different roles for the amygdala and orbitofrontal cortex. Other examples are described in a recent book [81].

My answer to the question posed by the title of this section is, no, computational neuroscience, or at least computational cognitive neuroscience, is not separate from neural network theory. That is, CCN is not a fundamental conceptual break from earlier neural network models. Rather CCN is simply the biological side of what those of us who were involved in the founding of INNS and related institution envisioned decades ago. It is the type of modeling we expected as more neuroscience data became available due to technical advances such as fMRI, and as the models themselves evolved.

5 Discussion

My bias is toward the type of models based both on neuroscience and on principles that embody cognitive requirements. These include my own work (e.g., Refs. [82–86]). Yet all of the researchers discussed in the last section are dedicated scientists who have made serious efforts to model important cognitive and behavioral phenomena while incorporating sophisticated neural data. Sometimes models generated from two or more different intellectual sources converge enough to differ mainly in details about the network roles of specific brain regions, an example being the discussion by O'Reilly, Frank, Hazy, and Watts [64] of the similarities and differences between their model of the basal ganglia in conditioning and a model of the same process by Brown, Bullock, and Grossberg [7].

Hence, it is in the interests of the field that different modeling groups interact more than they have. In particular, there need to be more conferences that encompass all these different modeling communities and thereby facilitate dialogue about the comparative merits of different models.

The other development that would advance the field is for the scientific community to accept the existence of a "theoretical cognitive neuroscience" or "theoretical neuropsychology" that has a life of its own, interacting with but partially separate from experimental cognitive neuroscience. There should be more centers devoted to the theoretical understanding of mind and brain. The Center for Cognitive and Neural Systems at Boston University is such a place, being over 30 years old and spanning the biological and engineering components of neural network theory, but I am not aware of another center like it anywhere in the world. This development would be analogous to the separate, independent, and interacting existence of theoretical and experimental physics. Theoretical physics has been a respected subfield at least since the late nineteenth century with the status achieved in Germany by Hermann von Helmholtz, Gustav Kirchhoff, and Max Planck [87].

So some changes still need to be made in the cultures of various scientific subcommunities for INNS's primary vision to be fully realized. Changes in the reward structure of science, particularly in the United States, would facilitate this development. The all-or-none, almost casino-like, nature of grant funding in my country discourages dialogue between advocates of competing models and drains resources that might be available for more of the right kind of conferences. Yet a great deal of good work linking the biological and technological sides of the field has already taken place, along with an explosion of relevant journals and both large and small conferences. So the future of the field has a good chance to be bright.

References

[1] D.S. Levine, Introduction to Neural and Cognitive Modeling, third ed., Taylor & Francis, New York, 2019.

[2] N. Wiener, Cybernetics, Wiley, New York, 1948.

[3] W.S. McCulloch, W. Pitts, A logical calculus of the ideas immanent in nervous activity, Bull. Math. Biophys. 5 (1943) 115–133.

[4] D.E. Rumelhart, J.L. McClelland, Parallel Distributed Processing, vols. 1 and 2, MIT Press, Cambridge, MA, 1986.

[5] S. Grossberg, A neural theory of punishment and avoidance. I. Qualitative theory, Math. Biosci. 15 (1972) 39–67.

[6] S. Grossberg, N.A. Schmajuk, Neural dynamics of attentionally-modulated Pavlovian conditioning: conditioned reinforcement, inhibition, and opponent processing, Psychobiology 15 (1987) 195–240.

[7] J.W. Brown, D. Bullock, S. Grossberg, How the basal ganglia use parallel excitatory and inhibitory learning pathways to selectively respond to unexpected rewarding cues, J. Neurosci. 19 (1999) 10502–10511.

[8] R.E. Suri, W. Schultz, A neural network model with dopamine-like reinforcement signal that learns a spatial delayed response task, Neuroscience 91 (1999) 871–890.

[9] R.E. Suri, W. Schultz, Temporal difference model reproduces anticipatory neural activity, Neural Comput. 13 (2001) 841–862.

[10] R.S. Sutton, A.G. Barto, Toward a modern theory of adaptive networks: expectation and prediction, Psychol. Rev. 88 (1981) 135–170.

[11] R.S. Sutton, A.G. Barto, Reinforcement Learning: An Introduction, MIT Press, Cambridge, MA, 1998.

[12] D.O. Hebb, The Organization of Behavior, Wiley, New York, 1949.

[13] C.L. Hull, Principles of Behavior, Appleton, New York, 1943.

[14] T.V.P. Bliss, T. Lømo, Long-lasting potentiation of synaptic transmission in the dentate area of the anaesthetized rabbit following stimulation of the perforant path, J. Physiol. Lond. 232 (1973) 331–356.

[15] E.R. Kandel, L. Tauc, Heterosynaptic facilitation in neurones of the abdominal ganglion of Aplysia depilans, J. Physiol. Lond. 181 (1965) 1–27.

[16] G.S. Stent, A physiological mechanism for Hebb's postulate of learning, Proc. Natl. Acad. Sci. 70 (1973) 997–1001.

[17] M.F. Bear, Bidirectional synaptic plasticity: from theory to reality, Philos. Trans. R. Soc.: Biol. Sci. 358 (2003) 649–655.

[18] M.F. Bear, L.N. Cooper, F.F. Ebner, A physiological basis for a theory of synapse modification, Science 237 (1987) 42–48.

[19] A. Kirkwood, M.F. Bear, Hebbian synapses in visual cortex, J. Neurosci. 14 (1994) 1634–1645.

[20] F. Rosenblatt, Principles of Neurodynamics, Spartan Books, Washington, DC, 1962.

[21] P.J. Werbos, Beyond Regression: New Tools for Prediction and Analysis in the Behavioral Sciences, Unpublished doctoral dissertation, Harvard University, 1974.

[22] G.E. Hinton, S. Osindero, Y.-W. Teh, A fast learning algorithm for deep belief nets, Neural Comput. 18 (2006) 1527–1554.

[23] Y. LeCun, Y. Bengio, G.E. Hinton, Deep learning, Nature 521 (2015) 436–444, https://doi.org/10.1038/nature14539.

[24] J. Schmidhuber, Deep learning in neural networks: an overview, Neural Netw. 61 (2015) 85–117.

[25] N. Rashevsky, Mathematical Biophysics, vol. II, Dover, New York, 1960.

[26] J.A. Anderson, A memory storage model utilizing spatial correlation functions, Kybernetika 5 (1968) 113–119.

[27] J.A. Anderson, Two models for memory organization using interacting traces, Math. Biosci. 8 (1970) 137–160.

[28] J.A. Anderson, A simple neural network generating an interactive memory, Math. Biosci. 14 (1972) 197–220.

[29] J.A. Anderson, A theory for the recognition of items from short memorized lists, Psychol. Rev. 80 (1973) 417–438.

[30] S. Grossberg, A prediction theory for some non-linear functional-differential equations, I. Learning of lists, J. Math. Anal. Appl. 21 (1968) 643–694.

[31] S. Grossberg, A prediction theory for some non-linear functional-differential equations, II. Learning of patterns, J. Math. Anal. Appl. 22 (1968) 490–522.

[32] S. Grossberg, Embedding fields: a theory of learning with physiological implications, J. Math. Psychol. 6 (1969) 209–239.

[33] S. Grossberg, On learning and energy-entropy dependence in recurrent and nonrecurrent signed networks, J. Stat. Phys. 1 (1969) 319–350.

[34] T. Kohonen, Associative Memory—A System-Theoretical Approach, Springer, New York, 1977.

[35] T. Kohonen, P. Lehtio, J. Rovamo, J. Hyvarinen, K. Bry, L. Vainio, A principle of neural associative memory, Neuroscience 2 (1977) 1065–1076.

[36] T. Kohonen, Self-Organization and Associative Memory, Springer-Verlag, Berlin, 1984/1995. Reprinted in 1988, 1989, and 1995.

[37] B. Kosko, Adaptive bidirectional associative memories, Appl. Opt. 26 (1987) 4947–4960.

[38] B. Kosko, Competitive adaptive bidirectional associative memories, in: IEEE First International Conference on Neural Networks, vol. II, IEEE/ICNN, San Diego, 1987, pp. 759–766.

[39] B. Kosko, Bidirectional associative memories, IEEE Trans. Syst. Man Cybern. 18 (1988) 49–60.

[40] S.A. Ellias, S. Grossberg, Pattern formation, contrast control, and oscillations in the short-term memory of shunting on-center off-surround networks, Biol. Cybern. 20 (1975) 69–98.

[41] S. Grossberg, Contour enhancement, short term memory, and constancies in reverberating neural networks, Stud. Appl. Math. 52 (1973) 213–257.

[42] S. Grossberg, D.S. Levine, Some developmental and attentional biases in the contrast enhancement and short-term memory of recurrent neural networks, J. Theor. Biol. 53 (1975) 341–380.

[43] H.R. Wilson, J.D. Cowan, Excitatory and inhibitory interactions in localized populations of model neurons, Biophys. J. 12 (1972) 1–24.

[44] H.R. Wilson, J.D. Cowan, A mathematical theory of the functional dynamics of cortical and thalamic nervous tissue, Kybernetika 13 (1973) 55–80.

[45] D. Bullock, S. Grossberg, Neural dynamics of planned arm movements: emergent invariants and speed-accuracy properties during trajectory formation, Psychol. Rev. 95 (1988) 49–90.

[46] S. Grossberg, On the development of feature detectors in the visual cortex with applications to learning and reaction-diffusion systems, Biol. Cybern. 21 (1976) 145–159.

[47] S. Grossberg, Adaptive pattern classification and universal recoding: parallel development and coding of neural feature detectors, Biol. Cybern. 23 (1976) 121–134.

[48] C. von der Malsburg, Self-organization of orientation sensitive cells in the striate cortex, Kybernetika 14 (1973) 85–100.

[49] R. Perez, L. Glass, R. Shlaer, Development of specificity in the cat visual cortex, J. Math. Biol. 1 (1974) 275–288.

[50] H.R. Wilson, A synaptic model for spatial frequency adaptation, J. Theor. Biol. 50 (1975) 327–352.

[51] S. Grossberg, Adaptive pattern classification and universal recoding: feedback, expectation, olfaction, and illusions, Biol. Cybern. 23 (1976) 187–202.

[52] G.A. Carpenter, S. Grossberg, A massively parallel architecture for a self-organizing neural pattern recognition machine, Computer Vision Graph. Image Process. 37 (1987) 54–115.

[53] J.J. Hopfield, Neural networks and physical systems with emergent collective computational abilities, Proc. Natl. Acad. Sci. 79 (1982) 2554–2558.

[54] W. Bechtel, Mental Mechanisms: Philosophical Perspectives on Cognitive Neuroscience, Taylor & Francis, New York, 2008.

[55] P. Gaudiano, S. Grossberg, Vector associative maps: unsupervised real time error-based learning and control of movement trajectories, Neural Netw. 4 (1991) 147–183.

[56] P. Dayan, L.F. Abbott, Theoretical Neuroscience: Computational and Mathematical Modeling of Neural Systems, MIT Press, Cambridge, MA, 2005.

[57] F.G. Ashby, S. Hélie, A tutorial on computational cognitive neuroscience: modeling the neurodynamics of cognition, J. Math. Psychol. 55 (2011) 273–289.

[58] J.D. Cohen, K. Dunbar, J.L. McClelland, On the control of automatic processes: a parallel distributed processing account of the Stroop effect, Psychol. Rev. 97 (1990) 332–361.

[59] J.D. Cohen, D. Servan-Schreiber, Context, cortex and dopamine: a connectionist approach to behavior and biology in schizophrenia, Psychol. Rev. 99 (1992) 45–77.

[60] R.C. O'Reilly, Biologically plausible error-driven learning using local activation differences: the Generalized Recirculation Algorithm, Neural Comput. 8 (1996) 895–938.

[61] R.C. O'Reilly, Six principles for biologically based computational models of cortical cognition, Trends Cogn. Sci. 2 (1998) 455–462.

[62] M.J. Frank, B. Loughry, R.C. O'Reilly, Interactions between the frontal cortex and basal ganglia in working memory: a computational model, Cogn. Affect. Behav. Neurosci. 1 (2001) 137–160.

[63] R.C. O'Reilly, M.J. Frank, Making working memory work: a computational model of learning in the prefrontal cortex and basal ganglia, Neural Comput. 18 (2006) 283–328.

[64] R.C. O'Reilly, M.J. Frank, T.E. Hazy, B. Watz, PVLV: the primary value and learned value Pavlovian learning algorithm, Behav. Neurosci. 121 (2007) 31–49.

[65] J.S. Bowers, Grandmother cells and localist representations: a review of current thinking, Lang. Cogn. Neurosci. 32 (2017) 257–273.

[66] T. Ljungberg, P. Apicella, W. Schultz, Responses of monkey dopamine neurons during learning of behavioral reactions, J. Neurophysiol. 67 (1992) 145–163.

[67] J. Mirenowicz, W. Schultz, Importance of unpredictability for reward responses in primate dopamine neurons, J. Neurophysiol. 72 (1994) 1024–1027.

[68] W. Schultz, P. Apicella, T. Ljungberg, Responses of monkey dopamine neurons to reward and conditioned stimuli during successive steps of learning a delayed response task, J. Neurosci. 13 (1993) 900–913.

[69] D. Joel, Y. Niv, E. Ruppin, Actor-critic models of the basal ganglia: new anatomical and computational perspectives, Neural Netw. 15 (2002) 535–547.

[70] Y. Niv, Reinforcement learning in the brain, J. Math. Psychol. 53 (2009) 139–154.

[71] Y. Niv, M.O. Duff, P. Dayan, Dopamine, uncertainty and TD learning, Behav. Brain Funct. 1 (2005) 6 (Ch. 6).

[72] P.J. Werbos, Approximate dynamic programming for real-time control and neural modeling, in: D.A. White, D.A. Sofge (Eds.), Handbook of Intelligent Control: Neural, Fuzzy and Adaptive Approaches, Van Nostrand Reinhold, New York, 1992, pp. 493–525.

[73] E.A. Ludvig, R.S. Sutton, E.J. Kehoe, Evaluating the TD model of classical conditioning, Learn. Behav. 40 (2012) 305–319.

[74] F.G. Ashby, L.A. Alfonso-Reese, A.U. Turken, E.M. Waldron, A neuropsychological theory of multiple systems in category learning, Psychol. Rev. 105 (1998) 442–481.

[75] F.G. Ashby, J.M. Ennis, B.J. Spiering, A neurobiological theory of automaticity in perceptual categorization, Psychol. Rev. 114 (2007) 632–656 (Ch. 8).

[76] B.C. Love, T.M. Gureckis, Models in search of a brain, Cogn. Affect. Behav. Neurosci. 7 (2007) 90–108.

[77] S. Grossberg, The complementary brain: unifying brain dynamics and modularity, Trends Cogn. Sci. 4 (2000) 233–246.

[78] S. Grossberg, M. Versace, Spikes, synchrony, and attentive learning by laminar thalamocortical circuits, Brain Res. 1218 (2008) 278–312.

[79] Y.J. John, J. Wang, D. Bullock, H. Barbas, Emotional intensity can enrich or degrade memories: impact of the amygdalar pathway on hippocampus through inhibitory neurons, bioRxiv (2022), https://doi.org/10.1101/2022.03.17.484812. preprint.

[80] M. Dranias, S. Grossberg, D. Bullock, Dopaminergic and non-dopaminergic value systems in conditioning and outcome-specific revaluation, Brain Res. 1238 (2008) 239–287.

[81] S. Grossberg, Conscious Mind, Resonant Brain: How Each Brain Makes a Mind, Oxford University Press, New York, 2021.

[82] S. Grossberg, D.S. Levine, Neural dynamics of attentionally modulated Pavlovian conditioning: blocking, interstimulus interval, and secondary reinforcement, Appl. Opt. 26 (1987) 5015–5030.

[83] N.G. Jani, D.S. Levine, Aneural network theory of proportional analogy-making, Neural Netw. 13 (2000) 149–183.

[84] D.S. Levine, Neural dynamics of affect, gist, probability, and choice, Cogn. Syst. Res. 15–16 (2012) 57–72, https://doi.org/10.1016/j.Cogsys.2011.07.002.

[85] D.S. Levine, N.G. Jani, D.G. Gilbert, Modeling the effects of nicotine on a continuous performance task, Neurocomputing 52–54 (2003) 573–582.

[86] D.S. Levine, P.S. Prueitt, Modeling some effects of frontal lobe damage: novelty and perseveration, Neural Netw. 2 (1989) 103–116.

[87] C. Jungnickel, R. McCormmach, The Second Physicist, Springer, Berlin, 2017.

From synapses to ephapsis: Embodied cognition and wearable personal assistants

Roman Ormandy
R&D, EMBODY CORP, LOS GATOS, CA, UNITED STATES

Chapter outlines

1 Neural networks and neural fields

A large class of neural networks is designed to perform Hebbian learning, changing weights on synapses according to the principle "*neurons which fire together, wire together.*" The end result, after a period of training, is a static circuit optimized for the recognition of a specific pattern. There is plenty of evidence that the mammal neocortex indeed performs Hebbian learning. It turns out, however, that the mammal neocortex does much more than simply change the weights of individual neurons. Populations of interacting neurons are behaving quite differently than individual neurons or static neural networks. Theory for the role of neuron populations and ephapsis in human cognition comes from the seminal work of Walter Freeman, and Robert Kozma [1] as well as the ideas of Gerald Edelman [2], Gyorgy Buzsaki [3], and many others.

In his 1975 book, *Mass Action in the Nervous system,* Walter Freeman [4] starts with a measurement of the population of neurons (by EEG) rather than individual neurons (in-neuron electrode). While an individual neuron generates *transmembrane potential,* a group of neurons generates an *extracellular potential field.* Whereas the path inside the dendrites is private for the neuron, the path outside is very public. The same path is shared via ion channels for the loop currents of all neurons in the neighborhood so that electrodes placed outside the neurons measure the cortical potential of the whole neighborhood.

Artificial Intelligence in the Age of Neural Networks and Brain Computing. https://doi.org/10.1016/B978-0-323-96104-2.00005-1
Copyright © 2024 Elsevier Inc. All rights reserved.

While electrodes inside the neuron measure microscopic activity, electrodes outside the neuron measure the mesoscopic activity of a group of neurons.

Freeman chose the olfactory perception for a detailed study because it is dominant in most animals. Freeman's team implanted 8 × 8 electrode arrays arranged in a 4 × 4 mm spatial layout on top of a small section of the olfactory bulb in several rabbits. It is known that even if most of the bulb has been surgically removed, animals can still discriminate odors regardless of which part remains. This holographic-like encoding enabled Freeman to detect the pattern of activity covering an entire bulb, even though the 4 × 4 mm sensor window covers only a fraction of it. The common wave has a different amplitude at each location of the bulb so the wave serves as a carrier wave in the gamma range with a spatial pattern of amplitude modulation (AM) throughout the bulb. Freeman was surprised to find a spatial pattern of bulbar activity that was nearly invariant with the same odorant. Remarkably, the oscillations of the dendritic potential have the same waveform over the whole bulb. This must mean that the common wave is due to the interactions of neurons throughout the entire bulb. The patterns are therefore created by the neuron population, not imposed from outside. The conclusion is that neural populations form fields, not networks.

Each pattern is as *unique for each rabbit* as is the individual history of the animal. Information processing view would require the brain to store, accumulate, and average sets of AM patterns in a training period and then retrieve the average pattern as a standard template against which to compare all incoming patterns during a test period, not only with one average AM pattern but also with all other average patterns, to find the best match. Freeman's data shows that brains do not have the neural machinery to perform these engineering operations and even if they did, they would not have the time needed to run them. For Freeman, Hebbian assemblies modeled by neural networks are a mere ignition mechanism for the sustained ephapsis (e-field created by oscillating neurons) which provides continuous fuel for real-time embodied cognition.

Initially, mainstream researchers did not pay much attention to Freeman's findings. More recently, however, the discovery of place cells for which Edward and May-Britt Moser and John O'Keefe were awarded the Nobel Prize in 2014, provides empirical confirmation of Freeman's insight. O'Keefe and his student, Michael Recce, provided experimental support showing that the spikes of place cells shift systematically relative to the phase of the ongoing theta oscillation. They called the phenomenon "phase precession." Thus, the phase of spikes and the animal's position on a track are correlated. Hippocampus seems to employ a gain control mechanism to assure that the relationship between the position and spike phase is independent of the firing rate or the speed of the animal and depends only on the size of the place field. The phase-precession is the first convincing example of the critical role of oscillations in brain function.

Buzsaki [3] rejected the idea of place cells forming a simple map and concluded that the current position of the animal is embedded in the representation of the past and the expected future in terms of both location and time. The currently coded item is placed into a spatiotemporal context by the theta oscillation mechanism. There is a relation between gamma activity and slower theta oscillations. The slow carrier wave can serve to combine and segregate cell assemblies, nested within gamma waves. Buzsaki postulates that it is the brain's interaction with the body and the physical-social environment that provide meaning to the subset of spontaneous states of the brain. Echoing philosopher George Mead, he wrote: "The brain gradually acquires self-awareness by learning to predict neural performance of other brains. Acquisition of self-consciousness requires feedback from other brains."

Despite his profound insight into the oscillatory nature of the workings of the brain, Buzsaki remains, like most scientists, a dualist, sending "information" between neuronal groups, using oscillations as a novel way to explain "binding problem" and finding cognitive maps in the hippocampus. Howard Eichenbaum [5] interpreted the same observations differently, for him hippocampus does not create a cognitive map, i.e., a representation, rather it integrates temporal events in any modality, not just a locomotion, and converts them into a spatially organized "personal story book" via path integration. Similarly, McNaughton concluded that place cells are formed by dead reckoning and distance is calculated based on self-motion clues.

2 Ephapsis

In 1975, Freeman did not yet have a clear understanding of the mechanism, which could bring the billions of neurons that make up each human cerebral hemisphere into global order within a few thousandths of a second. In 2006, however, he published with Vitiello's seminal paper [6], which offers an answer. Freeman and Vitiello start with an observation:

> *"The dominant mechanism for neural interactions by axodendritic synaptic transmission should impose distance-dependent delays on the EEG oscillations owing to finite propagation velocities and sequential synaptic delays. It does not. Neural populations have a low velocity information and energy transfers and high velocity of spread of phase transitions."*

The answer to this puzzle may be provided by Carver Mead's *Collective Electrodynamics* [7] or Giuseppe Vitiello's *Quantum Field Theory* (QFT) [8] both of which differ drastically from *Quantum Mechanics.* Freeman speculates that wave packets he observed act as a bridge from quantum dynamics at the atomic level through the microscopic pulse trains of neurons to macroscopic properties of large populations of neurons. The field theory of many-body systems allows for phase transition by *spontaneous break of symmetry* (SBS) or event-related potential (ERP). SBS is always accompanied by the dynamical formation of collective waves (Nambu-Goldstone modes or bosons), that span the whole system. These ordering waves (bosons) condense in the system ground state and ordering is a result of this boson condensation. Examples of macroscopically observed patterns are *phonons* (elastic waves) in crystals and *magnons* (spin waves) in magnets.

Freeman and Vitiello propose that the physical nature of the SBS carrier wave is a dipole wave in which the 3D-rotational (electric) axis is spontaneously broken. They believe that cortical boson condensate or its wave packet may explain the rapid course of perception: how the neocortex can respond to the impact of photons from a face in a crowd on a handful of retinal neurons mixed among many impulses elicited by light from the crowd. Phase transition of order from disorder emerges suddenly: the neural vapor as it were, condenses into neural droplets, the first step in recognition within a few tens of milliseconds, which is insufficient for classical models.

Boson condensate enables an orderly description of the phase transition that includes all levels of macroscopic, mesoscopic, and microscopic organization of the cerebral patterns that mediate the integration of an animal with its environment. Dendritic trees may interact by ephapsis of the ionic currents from their neighbors densely packed in the neuropil. No one knows how ephaptic transmission works but the candidate mechanism may include coupling through water dipoles, because both the intracellular and extracellular compartments are weak ionic solutions, comprised of more than 80% water, with high electrical conductivity on either side of the lipid layers. This is in good agreement with Carver Mead's observation in *Collective Electrodynamics*, that electric dipoles coupling is a million times stronger than coupling of magnetic dipoles. NG theorem predicts that the quanta have zero mass and thus they can span the whole system volume without inertia.

According to Freeman, cognitivists assign the starting point for analysis to the sensory receptors in the skin. Bundles of axons serve as channels to carry the information to the brainstem and eventually, information converges in the thalamus where it is already subdivided and classified by the receptors with respect to its features such as color, motion, or tonal modulation. These researchers view the thalamus as acting like a postmaster to deliver the bits of information to destinations that have already been assigned by the sensory receptors. They think that stimulus salience selects the information for transmission to the cortex. Pulses represent primitive elements of sensation or features. The primary cortex combines these representations of features into representations of objects and transmits them into adjacent association areas; a combination of lines and colors might make up a face, a set of phonemes might form a sentence, and a sequence of joint angles might represent a gesture after a "binding" process is executed. The problem is that so far cognitivists have not been able to show where that happens, or in what way perception differs from sensation, or where the information in perception changes into information for action.

Freeman assigns the starting point to the limbic system, not the sensory receptors. Hippocampus is a part of the surface of each cerebral hemisphere, only buried deep inside the medial temporal lobe. It is more like the hub of a spider web than the memory bank or CPU of a computer. The entorhinal cortex, which interacts with so many other parts of the brain, is the main source of input and output from the hippocampus and it, rather than the thalamus, performs multisensory convergence, followed by spatial localization of events and temporal sequencing of them into the hippocampus, which cooperates with other areas to form multisensory perceptions and coordinates learning, remembering, and recall. Perception starts with attention and expectations in the limbic system (indicated in the following picture by the asterisk) and is transmitted from there by corollary

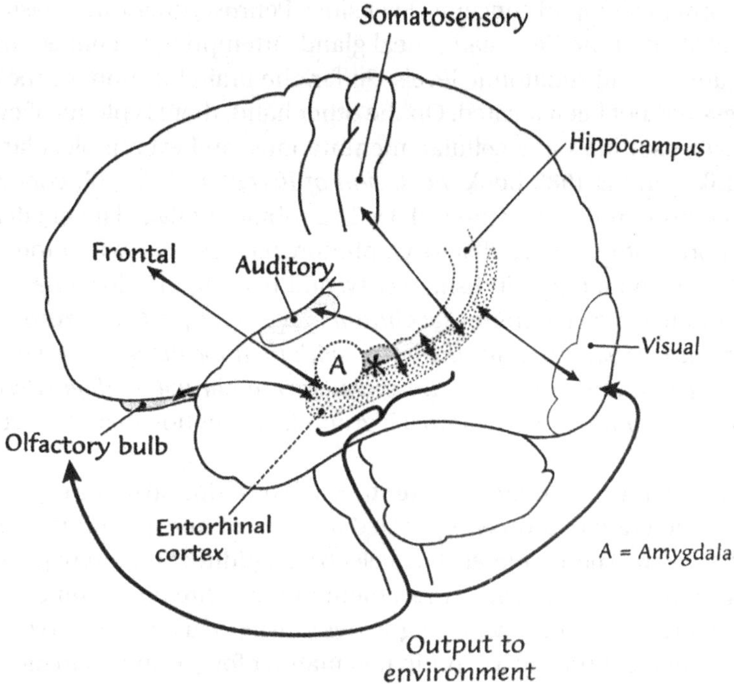

FIG. 1 Starting point for perception is the limbic system, not the sensory receptors (Freeman 2001).

discharges to all sensory cortices in the process of preafference. A new hypothesis forms and it is confirmed or denied by modified sensory input resulting from anticipatory organism action (Fig. 1).

3 Embodied cognition

In addition to ephapsis, Freeman concluded [9] that the biology of meaning includes the entire brain and body, with the history built by experience into bones, muscles, endocrine glands, and neural connections "*Meaningful states consist of pulses and waves in brain, the contraction of the muscles, the joint angles of skeletal system, and the secretion of cells in the autonomic and neuroendocrine systems.... The skills of athletes, dancers and musicians, live not only in their synapses but also in their limbs, fingers and torsos. Cognitive scientists and biologists who study the molecular basis of learning in synapses tend to overlook the fact that enlarged muscles and honed immune systems have also learned to do their jobs. The strengths of connections between the neurons and the properties of the body are continually shaped by learning and exercise throughout a lifetime.*"

Most cognitive scientists and AI researchers are dualists, implicitly assuming the separation of body and mind. Consequently, cognitive scientists are on a never-ending quest to find in the brain the seat of "binding" where formerly meaningless features are combined to form meaningful concepts. Ever since Penrose, quantum physicists are looking for an equivalent of the Cartesian pineal gland, attempting to connect the mind with matter at the atomic and subatomic levels. So far, the brain location for the hypothetical binding process has not been located. On the other hand, there is plenty of evidence however for motor/sensor links at a cellular, membranous, and even molecular level.

Yakov Vinnikov in his 1982 book, *Evolution of Receptor Cells* [10], concluded that all sensors evolved from motor structures of $9 \times 2 + 2$ tubules of flagellate or ciliate cells. This includes chemoreceptors (taste, olfactory), photoreceptors (cones and rods), and mechanoreceptors (the lateral organ in fish, gravity, and hearing). He formulates a molecular theory of reception, which combines "*evolution of receptive proteins transforming certain types of energy into biopotentials for the brain, with their localization in the plasma membranes forming a 'maximum grip,' positioning these membranes with greatest adequacy to the direction of the stimulus.*" This approach grounds perception in motor action Merleau-Ponty style.

Edward Tsien on the Slideshare website starts the description of the evolution of neural systems with a depiction of loosely organized systems of nerves with no central control, like Hydra or Starfish. These animals have electrical, bidirectional synapses where stimulation at any point spreads to cause movement of the entire body. Some cnidarians, like jellyfish, can coordinate their swimming activity using clusters of nerve cells. Jellyfish skirts must open and contract in a coordinated manner for the animal to move. Flatworms have a ladder-like nervous system with a greater concentration of neurons in the anterior part. Enlargement of the anterior ganglia that receive sensory input coming also from the anterior portion of animal gives rise to the first brains. The anterior brain connected to a nerve cord is the basic design for all organisms with a central nervous system. Circular worms have a more complicated nervous system, but even with the brain removed, worms can still move, mate, burrow, feed, and even learn a maze. Most sophisticated invertebrates, like octopuses, have a large brain and "image" forming eyes. The neural system of insects divides neuron groups into three segments. The concentration of a variety of sensory organs on the head provides for rapid communication with the brain (Fig. 2).

Vertebrates have larger brains and the spinal cord is protected by the vertebrae with ascending sensory pathways and descending motor pathways. Attaching muscles to the

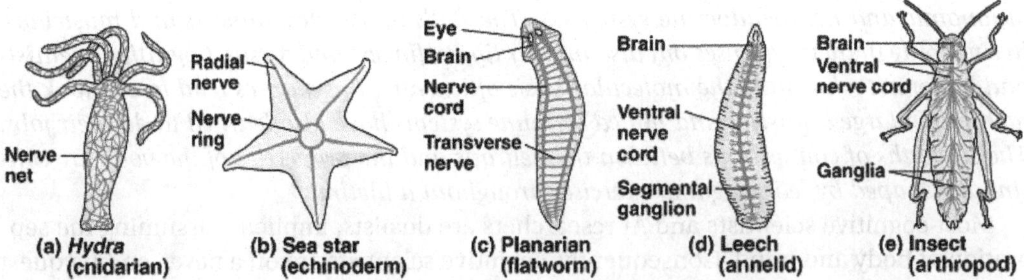

FIG. 2 Primitive neural systems; (A) Hydra (cnidarian), (B) Sea star (echinoderm), (C) Planarian (flatworm), (D) Leech (annelid), and (E) Insect (arthropod).

internal framework in Chordata greatly improves movement. Vertebrates have a vertebral column, a well-differentiated head, and a bony skeleton. Finally, mammals developed the neocortex and neocerebellum, which are both prominent in primates. The longer one studies the evolution of neural systems, the more it becomes apparent that *all* innovations of neural systems were tightly coupled to changes in organism motor control. Lampreys, the most primitive of vertebrates, are the only fish species without a cerebellum. The reason is simple; lampreys do not have jaws, nor "real" vertebrae. With jaws and better muscles, modern fish not only acquired the cerebellum but also developed larger cortexes. The transition from an aquatic environment to terrestrial habitats afforded organisms new means of locomotion as illustrated by the elaboration of basal ganglia during the evolutionary transition from amphibians to reptiles. Reptiles also gained better vision. The emergence of mammals was accompanied by an explosion in special senses, as well as the arrival of the neocortex as the major target of the basal ganglia circuitry, devoted to executing and inhibiting the basal ganglia-mediated control of movement. Eventually, the liberation of front limbs in primates for object manipulation resulted in the use of these limbs for meaningful, signifying social gestures in one species of primates and thus the emergence of speech. It is quite illuminating to observe the growth and interplay of sensor and motor parts of the brain in the process of vertebrate evolution (Fig. 3):

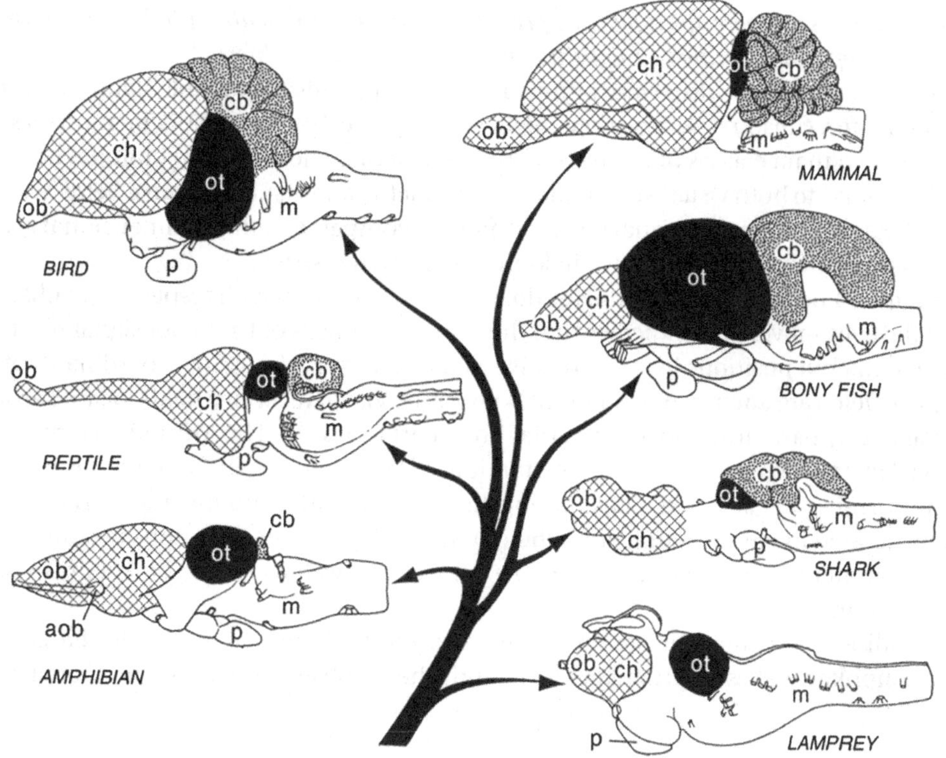

FIG. 3 Evolution of vertebrate brains.

The picture above, taken from Glenn Northcutt's 2002 paper [11], shows the evolution of the brain in vertebrates. Crosshatched (*ch*) area is the cortex, stippled (*cb*) area is the motor cerebellum, and the black (*ot*) area shows the sensor optic tectum. The lowest vertebrate, lamprey, has virtually no cerebellum due to the lack of a structured skeleton that the cerebellum could control, but it does have a sizable optic tectum which, fed by visual stimuli from large eyes, takes over the control of lampreys' lower motor actions. Optical tectum continues to form larger portions of the brain in higher vertebrates such as amphibians, bony fish, and birds, which all show enlarged cerebellum due to increasingly elaborate skeletons and muscles, all the way up to mammals, under the name of the superior colliculus, where it is overshadowed by a large cortex and prominent basal ganglia with profuse projections in and out of the cortex. The moral of the story is that the cerebellum evolved to coordinate feedback from proprioceptors, while the cortex evolved to coordinate feedback from exteroceptors.

It turns out that even the highest reaches of the cognitive realm in the form of vision and speech are solidly grounded in motor action. Merleau-Ponty [12] called vision "*palpation with the eyes,*" as "*we move our eyes around the scene the way we move the hands about the body of our lover. We enact our perceptual content through activity of skillful looking.*" Gibson [13] was very clear about the motor aspect of vision: "*We must perceive in order to move, but we must move in order to perceive. The perception is constrained by manipulation, and the manipulation is constrained by perception. To perceive something is also to perceive how to approach it and what to do about it. Visual control of hands is inseparably connected with the visual perception of objects.*"

Giacomo Rizzolatti's discovery of mirror neurons provides a possible neuronal implementation for Gibson's observation. In describing the VIP-F4 circuit in monkeys, he observed two main classes of neurons: visual and tactile. There are also bimodal neurons, which respond to both visual and tactile stimuli. Tactile and visual receptive fields are usually in "register," that is the visual receptive field encompasses a three-dimensional spatial region around the tactile receptive field in peri-personal space.

In most F4 neurons, receptive fields do not change position with respect to an observer when the eyes move. This indicates that the visual responses of F4 do not signal positions on the retina but positions in space relative to the observer. The spatial coordinates of the receptive fields are anchored to different body parts. Visual receptive fields located around a certain body part (arm) move when that body part is moved. The AIP and F5 circuits are involved in grasping and "action understanding." Data suggest that this circuit is involved in transforming the size and shape of objects (coded in AIP) into the appropriate motor schema (coded in F5) for acting upon them. Further, F5 canonical neurons become active during the mere observation of "graspable" objects, as well as during object grasping or manipulation.

In addition to canonical neurons, there are *mirror* neurons, which discharge both when a monkey makes a particular *action*, and when it observes another individual doing a similar action. Mirror neurons do not respond to object presentation. Actions most effective in triggering mirror neurons are *grasping, holding, manipulating,* and *placing.* The majority of neurons are active during the observation of one action only.

Rizzolatti and Matteli [14] conclude that both space perception and action recognition derive from *preceding* motor knowledge concerning the external world and actions. Support for this notion comes from the demonstration of the existence of peri-personal space. Peri-personal space is an extension of space on the body surface. It is anchored to the body and moves when the body and body parts move. From a physical point of view, there is no reason whatsoever why eyes should select light stimuli coming exclusively from space located around the body of the perceiver.

The motor hypothesis implies that F4 neurons code potential motor actions directed toward a particular spatial location. When a visual stimulus is presented in the peri-personal space, it evokes automatically a "potential motor action" which maps the spatial stimulus position in motor terms. The results showed that in a large majority of the neurons, the receptive field expanded in depth with the increase of stimulus velocity. These results are not compatible with a geometrical space representation. In contrast, if the space is coded in motor terms since time is inherent to movement, the spatial map must have dynamic properties and vary, therefore, according to the change in time of the object's spatial location. Supporting evidence is in the finding that movement plays an essential role in establishing ocular dominance. Signals from the retina are not enough; if kittens are paralyzed when exposed to visual patterns or when visual signals are not used to control behavior (gondola-driven kittens), they do not lead to changes in cortical function.

Actions that do not belong to the motor repertoire of the observer (e.g., barking) are recognized based on their visual properties. In contrast, actions that do belong to the motor repertoire of the observer, activate the parietal-frontal circuits that are involved in action programming. These actions are understood through the mirror neuron system. The visual representation of the observed actions evokes the corresponding action representation whose outcome is known to the acting individual (Liberman). Personal knowledge is based not on a visual description of observed events, but on the *resonance of the observer's motor system.* Thus, perception is not a process categorically distinct from action, but, on the contrary, our fundamental knowledge, our personal knowledge of the other, is based on the motor system. These findings strongly support Merleau-Ponty's concept of intentional arc.

A.M. Liberman in the 2000 paper coauthored with Whalen [15], conceived a *motor theory of speech,* which is compatible with Rizzolatti's and Gibson's views. The traditional theory of speech identifies sounds (phonemes) as the primitives that are exchanged when linguistic communication occurs. The Liberman motor theory of speech claims on the other hand, that the phonetic elements of speech, the true primitives that underlie linguistic communications, are not sounds but rather, the articulatory gestures that generate those sounds.

The gestures are changes in the cavities of the vocal tract—opening or closing, widening or narrowing, lengthening or shortening. Liberman states that these gestures are phonetic ab initio, requiring no cognitive translation to make them so. Particulation of the vocal tract, that is, the division of the vocal tract action into independently controllable components (the lips, the blade, the body and root of tongue, the vellum, and the larynx), unique to our species, opened the way for the selection of gestures that could be overlapped, interleaved, and merged, that is, coarticulated. The assumption is that the coarticulation of gestures is controlled by species-specific specialization for language—a phonetic module. The listener effortlessly perceives gestures the speaker produced, not because the process is simple, but because the phonetic module is so well adapted to its complex task.

The traditional theory of speech cannot explain how production and perception developed together in evolution. George H Mead's [16] requirement for parity means that language communication can succeed only if two parties have a common understanding of what counts—what counts for the speaker, must count for the listener. From a motor theory point of view, the speaker produces gestures that are managed by machinery that evolved in connection with a specifically communicative (linguistic) function, from which it follows that gestures are phonetic by their very nature. They are recovered from the acoustic signal by the phonetic component of the larger specialization for language. There is no need to appeal to cognitive connections between an initial auditory representation and some more abstract phonetic unit to which it is somehow linked (bound) because the initial representation is already phonetic.

In a two-way communication, where the speaker and listener exchange roles, motor theory stipulates that parties conduct their business in a common currency of phonetic gestures; the gesture that is the unit of production for the speaker is the unit of perception for the listener. In contrast, traditional theory needs to explain how representations of the speaker (motor) and representations of the listener (auditory) which are not alike, marched through evolutionary development in perfect step. The motor theory holds that the primary representations of the speaker and listener are exactly the same; accordingly, a change in one is inevitably mirrored by the same changes in the other.

Motor theory, unlike traditional theory, explains clearly the gulf, which separates speech from reading and writing. The preliterate child is a prodigy of phonologic development, commanding thousands of words; he readily produces their phonological structures when speaking, and just as readily, parses them when listening. He exploits the particulate principle quite naturally when speaking; it is enough to be a member of the human race and to have been exposed to the mother tongue. By contrast, applying the particular principle to the task of reading and writing is an achievement of a distinctly intellectual kind. The relationship between the alphabet and speech is entirely arbitrary and reading is always a translation. From the traditional view, one might expect that reading and writing would be easier than speech. After all, alphabetic characters are clearer signals than sounds of speech.

According to Liberman, evolution came up with a distinct phonetic module, not in the higher reaches of cognitive machinery, but down among the "nuts and bolts" of action and perception, that is, motor structures. By creating distinctly *phonetic motor structures* to serve as the ultimate constituents of language, the phonetic specialization enables speech to meet requirements for parity, as well as those for particulate communication, while also giving it a biological advantage over the reading and writing of its alphabetic transcription.

Once again, Rizzolatti and Arbib in *Language within our grasp* [17] provide the empirical evidence, which supports Liberman's views. This time they find it in mirror neurons located in Broca's area. These neurons, they claim, represent the link between sender and receiver that Liberman postulated in his theory.

Broca's area is most commonly thought of as an area for speech. PET data indicate that Broca's area might also become active during the execution of hand or arm movement, during mental imagery of hand grasping movement, and during tasks involving hand-mental rotations. They find further evidence indicating, that individuals recognize actions made by others because the neural pattern elicited in their premotor areas during action observation is similar to that which is internally generated to produce that action.

In the case of action observation, there is a strong spinal cord inhibition that selectively blocks motoneurons involved in the observed action execution. Sometimes, however, for example, when the observed action is of particular interest, the premotor system will allow a brief prefix of the movement to be exhibited. This prefix will be recognized by the other individual. This fact will affect both the actor and the observer. The actor will recognize an intention in the observer, and the observer will notice that its involuntary response affects the behavior of the actor. When this occurs, a primitive dialogue between observer and actor is established. This dialogue forms the core of the language. The advertising industry recognized the importance of these motor prefixes, as evidenced by their use of an electric field sensor attached to the thumb muscle to indicate a buyer's interest in a product. It turns out that the "grabbing" reflex betrays the buyer even if he pretends to display a lack of interest with his disinterested facial expression.

Rizzolatti and Arbib argue that: (1) the mimetic capability inherent to F5 and Broca's area had the potential to produce various types of closed systems related to the different types of motor fields present in that area (hand, mouth, and larynx); (2) the first open system to evolve en route to human speech was a manual gestural system that exploited the observation and execution matching system described earlier; and (3) this paved the way for the evolution of the open vocalization system we know as speech. Congruent with this view is the fact that mimetic capacity, a natural extension of action recognition, is central to human cultures such as dances, games, and tribal rituals and that the evolution of this capacity was a necessary precursor to the evolution of language. It has been shown that a newborn can mimic her mother's facial expression as early as an hour after birth.

Finally, Esther Thelen [18] claims that in principle there is no difference between the processes engendering walking, reaching, and looking for hidden objects and those resulting in mathematics and poetry. In her pioneering psychological studies of reaching, grasping, and walking, she dismisses the accepted theory that phylogenetically old "central pattern generators" (CPG) in the brain guide the child's acquisition of these motor skills. She then proceeds to dismantle the concept of central pattern generators in the brain with a series of elegant experiments, starting with walking. A normal infant transitions to weight-supporting stepping behaviors at 8–10 months. Thelen discovered that 7-month-old infants, who normally did not step, performed highly coordinated, alternating steps when they were supported with their feet on a slowly moving motorized treadmill.

She proposes that development is the outcome of the self-organizing processes of continually active living systems, without the need for programming and rules. Self-organization is not magic; it occurs because of inherent nonlinearities in nearly all of our physical and biological universe. In dynamic terminology, behavioral development may be envisioned as sequences of system attractors of varying stability, evolving and dissolving over time. Pattern emerges through the cooperativity of the components alone. New forms appear during development as a series of *phase shifts* engendered by the loss of stability of current forms. An example is the disappearance of newborn stepping. At birth, infants can produce reliable cyclic kicking and stepping, but they soon lose this ability. When the stepping pattern is envisioned as a product of a dedicated reflex network, this loss is difficult to understand, resulting in ad hoc explanations such as cortical inhibition. Thelen argues that loss of stepping is closely paralleled by weight gain from subcutaneous fat, necessary for postnatal temperature regulation. Here, changes in the nervous system may well reflect and not engender changes in the periphery.

Cognitive scientists see cognitive development as flowing in only one direction—from percepts to concepts to language in a classical reductionist approach. Thelen sees instead continuous interactions in both directions—from perception to language and from language to perception. It makes no sense to ask whether one determines the other, the entrainment is mutual.

Thelen compares this to Watt's centrifugal governor, stabilizing the speed of steam engine rotation in a variable environment. It does a near-perfect job because, at every point in time, everything depends on everything else. The raising of the arms, the motion of the throttle valve, and the speed of the flywheel are not connected in linear progress. No behavior of the system is prior to, or a progenitor, to another; rather, all are mutually entrained, simultaneously products and causes in a complex stream of activity in time (Fig. 4).

Of course, we could build a digital equivalent of a governor from electronic components. It may seem that a computational model offers an easy solution to the problem of metacognition and symbolic thought. The computational governor, unlike the centrifugal one, consists of structures that measure (represent) things. To explain how such a device might think about keeping the flywheel steady or invent a system of symbols to stand for various steps in the procedure, we need only to explain how the device looks down on its own cognitive processes and makes them accessible to consciousness. In this view, metacognition and explicitly symbolic thoughts are built out of the very same representations that do the job of more ordinary cognition.

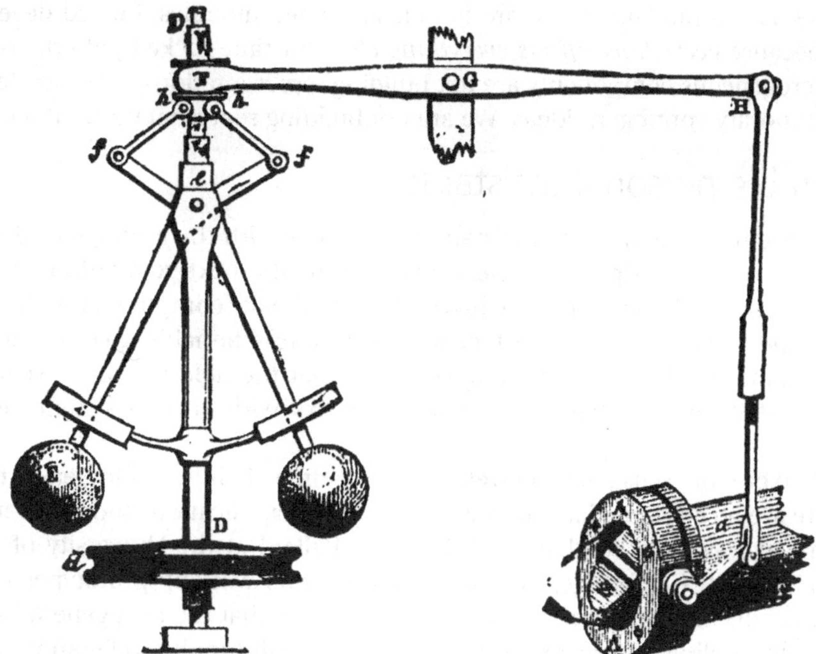

FIG. 4 Governor and throttle valve.

This kind of explanation is pervasive in cognitive science today. Phonemes are postulated to be the representational units of speech perception and speech production. Phonemes are also, more or less explicitly, represented by the letters of the alphabet. Alphabets thus can be viewed as the external representations of internal symbols and their invention as evidence for phonemes' internal reality. Teaching reading, writing poetry, theorizing about phonology, and talking pig Latin can also be viewed as using the very same representations that underlie the perception and productions of speech. Thus, all cognition is one kind of thing: the explicit symbolic manipulation of doing logic, drawing maps, and counting are overt versions of what all cognitive process is. As Liberman has shown, representational entities such as phonemes do not exist in palpable forms, like flywheels or letters on a piece of paper. If we were to look into the brain, we would not see symbols.

Thelen proposes that symbolic thought, like walking up and down slopes, like interpreting novel words, is emergent in activities and in the products of those activities in the physical world and on us. As we act and explore our world, our actions will produce concrete physical changes in that world that we may perceive. By perceiving the products of activity and the reentrant mapping of that perceiving onto the ongoing activity from which it emerged, we create *external* symbols and discover their value. This is another description of Merleau-Ponty's action/perception arc.

In Thelen's view, development does not unfold according to some prespecified plan, there is no plan. Developmental change is caused by the interacting influences of heterogeneous components, these are not encapsulated modules; indeed development happens because *everything affects everything else.* But time-locked patterns of activity across heterogeneous components are not building representations of the world by connecting temporary contingent ideas. We are not building representations at all.

4 Wearable personal assistants

If we combine the field approach of neural resonance with the motor-based theory of cognition, we arrive at a powerful new platform for the next generation of wearable personal assistants. Unlike pure AI, which is trying to make computers intelligent, neurally based personal assistants are focused on a more attainable goal of augmenting existing human intelligence and memory. Given that the field approach scales easily to larger spatial levels, integrating social networks with such assistants is almost frictionless.

When two or more sensors are correlated in real-time, their power increases exponentially. There are no commercially available multimodal applications today but university researchers such as Alex Pentland at MIT, Dana Ballard at the University of Texas, or researchers at MSR Cambridge, produced experimental working prototypes delivering promising results in a laboratory environment. I believe that the next generation of personal assistants will augment text-based user profiles with multimodal and motor data from our hands, arms, legs, feet, torso, neck, and head, as well as internal organs such as the heart and lungs.

The key to usable personal assistants lies in the embodied approach, grounded in neural science [19]. It will start with a minimally acceptable amount of body sensors in multiple modalities, eventually reaching critical mass, resulting in a phase shift and the emergence of new chaotic attractors augmenting the existing landscape of user's knowledge. Neurally based personal assistants will thus build this knowledge landscape and, at the same time, travel through it in itinerant trajectories formed by the user experience. There are numerous applications for such technology:

Augmented memory. Human memory is fallible, and it gets worse as we age. Anyone over forty was probably in a situation when he would appreciate quick help in attaching a name to a face, movie, or a context to a meeting he attended some time ago. Over time, the personal assistant will detect the user's intentions and become his trusted advisor, able to assist without prompting, such as to remind him to take a medicine at the usual time or suggest a restaurant menu selection based on his likes and recorded allergies. A personal assistant can take on a different role as the user ages and experiences greater memory loss. As the personal assistant learns the user's personality better, it can offer more active guidance for the user throughout the day.

Stress relief. Stress relief can be accomplished through relaxation techniques and meditation. Both rely on the entrainment between neural activity and the body, including breathing lungs and beating heart. Embodied assistants can integrate motor and EEG sensors with these techniques. First, motor and EMG sensors will be used to provide additional user feedback during meditation, which should minimize the tendency of EMG artifacts to pollute EEG readings. Second, controlled motor activities, such as breathing or simple motor exercise (e.g., Qi-Gong), can drive the user to the desired state directly by combining EEG and motor feedback into a single solution.

Health and fitness. While most wearable sensors today are focused on health and fitness, they are hardwired to a specific activity such as walking or swimming. Neurally based assistants capable of capturing the meaning of user actions and their intentions can provide advice and real-time monitoring of any fitness activity, from a simple exercise to meditation, and suggest dietary regimes optimal for the user's current intent and long-term goals.

Media guide. The personal assistant could also suggest to his user news articles, videos, movies, or music based on user history and current preferences, which he could then stream to any user's device. Unlike the existing media assistants, which push the services of a proprietary manufacturer or content provider, it would always act on the user's behalf and keep his confidential information protected from prying eyes.

Lifestyle and transactions. Finally, neural assistants could suggest to the user suitable activity and even perform many types of transactions online, from renting a room on Airbnb and hiring a plumber on TaskRabbit to investing in electronic currencies such as bitcoin. In fact, blockchain technology and Ethereum smart contracts are a perfect match for wearable assistants in their never ceasing effort to protect user data. Over time, they become their user's alter egos.

I conclude this chapter with some principles of the design for neural-based wearable personal assistants I developed over the years. Taken together, they offer a glimpse of a new way of not only looking at AI and personal assistants, but perhaps they also offer a new view of how our brains and bodies think and act in our world:

1. *Neural populations form fields, not structures.* Structures, like neural networks, are static spatial patterns, frozen in time. Resonant neural populations form and reform dynamically, in real-time, over the entire brain via AM carrier waves.
2. *Meaning is embodied.* Meanings reside in the mutually entrained ecosystem of the brain, body, and environment. They are not representations; meanings arise from the global resonance of large neuron populations in the cortex. They are assembled from already meaningful local multimodal sensor streams, which are combined to form context-dependent attractor basins. Meanings do not reside in the outside world, but symbols, and other artifacts such as a knife, traffic signs, gestures, alphabet, and grammar, do.
3. *Meaning is context based.* When learning to walk, infants will produce walking behavior earlier when placed in an inductive context, that is, buoyed by water, or put on the treadmill. The meaning of the word "bank" in "I sat on a river bank," differs from its meaning in "I walked into Citi bank." The same color swatch will look different on different colored backgrounds, and the same music phrase will sound different depending on what notes preceded or followed it.

4. *The brain does not represent, it assimilates.* It does not "store processed input signals," or stimuli, there are no representations inside the brain, i.e., no links between the internal world of symbols and the external world of objects. The body does not "absorb" stimuli, but changes its own form to become similar to aspects of stimuli that are relevant to the intent that emerged within the brain.
5. *Categorization is perceptual.* Concepts form when two or more percepts temporally correlate. The meaning of a concept is not based on its link to the outside world, but on its usefulness to the user, planning actions in different environmental contexts. World objects do not have prearranged labels, and there is no homunculus in the brain supervising perception and cognition.
6. *There is no central control.* There are no symbols, rules, logic, computations, programming, or algorithms stored in the brain. Central Process is the hidden homunculus of the computing paradigm. When an infant learns to walk or speak, no one process has to coordinate the emergence of walking or speaking behavior, it emerges, like in all open systems, through the entrainment of internal components, i.e., sensor neurons, interneurons, motor neurons, and muscle structures, and external components such as objects, forces, and other people.
7. *Action guides perception.* Stimuli do not "arrive" in the brain, action precedes and guides perception. The frontal lobes of the cortex form a plan first and then instruct senses to confirm or deny the presence of data needed for the current action. There is a context for each percept.
8. *Multimodality is grounded in motor action.* Every perceptual concept requires a motor action plus one or more correlated percepts, like speech, sight, or touch. When we eat an apple, we execute an action with our teeth, lips, and jaw, and at the same time, we also perceive through our eyes, nose, lips, and taste buds. Most perception occurs within our body. Re-afference, proprioception, and even exteroception consist mostly of an organism observing itself and its actions.

Recent developments with merging large language model AI (LLM AI) and 3D making movies from chat, open fascinating opportunities. At the same time, all virtual reality (VR) headsets do not live up to the expectations. Future progress in this field should be based on AI using neural science. Personal assistants, metaverse, AI, and AR are coming together in the most surprising ways [20,21].

Humans love metaphors. According to George Lakoff and Mark Johnson [22], "*Metaphor is not just a matter of language, human thought processes are largely metaphorical.*" It matters which metaphors we use. During 400 years of Cartesian dualism, we went from the brain as a clock metaphor to the brain as a computer metaphor. It may be the time for a new metaphor, one based not on static structures, modularity, and syntax, but on dynamic fields where the brain is seen more like a vast ocean of waves forming and reforming in real-time in never ceasing maelstroms ignited by chaotic but nonrandom attractors such as the Lorenz attractor illustrated below (Fig. 5).

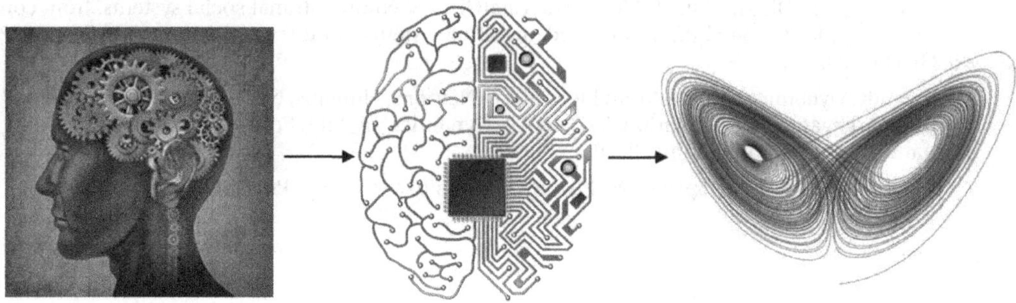

FIG. 5 From brain as a clock, to brain as a computer. to brain as a field of waves.

References

[1] R. Kozma, W.J. Freeman, Cognitive Phase Transitions in the Cerebral Cortex-Enhancing the Neuron Doctrine by Modeling Neural Fields, Springer Verlag, 2016.

[2] G. Edelman, Neural Darwinism, Basic Books, 1987.

[3] G. Buzsaki, Rhythms of the Brain, Oxford Press, 2006.

[4] W. Freeman, Mass Action in the Nervous system, Academic Press, 1975.

[5] H. Eichenbaum, The Cognitive Neuroscience of Memory, Oxford, 2002.

[6] W. Freeman, G. Vitiello, Nonlinear brain dynamics as macroscopic manifestation of underlying many-body field dynamics, Phys. Life Rev. (2006).

[7] C. Mead, Collective Electrodynamics, M.I.T. Press, 2000.

[8] G. Vitiello, Quantum Field Theory, Wiley, 2010.

[9] W.J. Freeman, How Brains Make Up Their Minds, Columbia University Press, 2000.

[10] V. Yakov, Evolution of Receptor Cells, Springer Verlag, 1982.

[11] N. Glenn, Understanding Vertebrae Brain Evolution, Symposium: Recent Advances in Neurobiology, 2002.

[12] Merleau-Ponty, Phenomenology of Perception, Gallimard, 1945.

[13] J.J. Gibson, The Ecological Approach to Visual Perception, Psychology Press, 1986.

[14] M. Rizzolatti, Two Different Streams form the Dorsal Visual System: Anatomy and Functions, Springer Verlag, 2003.

[15] A.M. Liberman, D. Whalen, On the relation of speech to language, Trends Cogn. Sci. 4 (2000).

[16] G.H. Mead, Mind, Self, & Society, University of Chicago, 1934.

[17] G. Rizzolatti, M.A. Arbib, Language within our grasp, Trends Neurosci. (1998).

[18] E. Thelen, L. Smith, A Dynamic Systems Approach to the Development of Cognition and Action, MIT Press, 1994.

[19] D.H. Heck, S.S. McAfee, Y. Liu, A. Babajani-Feremi, R. Rezaie, W.J. Freeman, J.W. Wheless, A.C. Papanicolaou, M. Ruszinkó, Y. Sokolov, R. Kozma, Breathing as a fundamental rhythm of brain function, Front. Neural Circuits 10 (2017) 115.

[20] F.Y. Wang, J. Li, R. Qin, J. Zhu, H. Mo, B. Hu, ChatGPT for computational social systems: from conversational applications to human-oriented operating systems, IEEE Trans. Comput. Soc. Syst. 10 (2) (2023) 414–425.

[21] R. Ormandy, Dynamics of Life—From Electrons to Neurons, Humans, Nations and Bitcoins, https://www.researchgate.net/publication/337548019_Dynamics_of_Life_From_Electrons_to_Neurons_Humans_Nations_and_Bitcoins, 2020.

[22] G. Lakoff, M. Johnson, Metaphors We Live By, University of Chicago Press, 1980.

PART 3

Cutting-edge developments in deep learning and intelligent systems

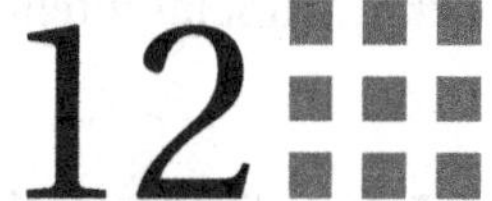

Explainable deep learning to information extraction in diagnostics and electrophysiological multivariate time series☆

Francesco Carlo Morabito, Maurizio Campolo, Cosimo Ieracitano, and Nadia Mammone

AI_LAB-NEUROLAB, DICEAM, UNIVERSITY MEDITERRANEA OF REGGIO CALABRIA, REGGIO CALABRIA, ITALY

Chapter outlines

☆To my loved daughter, Valeria.

Artificial Intelligence in the Age of Neural Networks and Brain Computing. https://doi.org/10.1016/B978-0-323-96104-2.00011-7

Copyright © 2024 Elsevier Inc. All rights reserved.

1 Introduction

The processing of multivariate time series for identification, classification, and prediction problems or information extraction is a research and application topic spanning many different science domains. The strong impact of digitalization, information, and communication technology as well as the prevalence of sensor networks for the emergence of the Internet of Things (IoT) have strongly motivated a resurgence of interest in machine learning (ML) for multivariate time-series analysis. deep learning (DL) techniques are a variant of ML well founded in classical neural network theory. They use deep architectures where many hidden layers or maps of neurons generate a lower-dimensional projection of the input space that corresponds, for example, to the signals generated by the network of sensors in monitoring applications. The successive hidden layers are able to build an effective high-level abstraction of the raw data. State-of-the-art DL processors present architectural advantages and benefits of novel training paradigms synergistic with other approaches, like compressive sensing and sparsity methods. The high number of neurons and links is reminiscent of brain networks and allows the storage of the essential features of the underlying input-output mapping. In biomedical signal processing, many diagnostic systems produce multivariate time series, and the automatic extraction of features without human intervention is of high interest for supporting clinical diagnoses and for highlighting latent aspects hidden in standard visual interpretation. For example, in medical imaging, small irregularities in tissues from prodromal to tumors can be detected in the successive levels of abstractions of the DL network. The development of efficient DL systems can have a significant impact on public health also because of the possibility of incorporating real-time information in the existing computational models. DL is indeed data-driven model endowed with the ability of generalization. In this chapter, DL methods are briefly presented from the historical perspective of neural network studies. Electroencephalographic (EEG) multivariate data are considered as many application domains spanning from brain-computer interface (BCI) to neuroscience take advantage of this noninvasive and cheap technique as the basis of brain studies. Two different DL architectures will be proposed that successfully solve difficult neurology problems.

2 The neural network approach

ML has the objective to yield computers the ability to autonomously learn and interact with their environment by exploiting data to learn optimal behaviors without the need for a specific programming step. Neural networks (NN) are machines explicitly designed to possess this ability. NNs are a collection of elementary processing nodes suitably arranged in various topological architectures. The elementary node of the network is referred to as a neuron and includes a linear part taking a weighted linear combination of its inputs and a nonlinear part where a selected nonlinear function transforms the net input in the final output of the node. The inputs of the neuron come from other neurons and its output is distributed to other nodes. The organization of the neurons is hierarchical if the nodes are structured in layers. This kind of topology is somehow reminiscent of the organization of pyramidal neurons in the mammalian brain. Other kinds of topologies have been considered, in particular the maps and the grids, where the neurons are organized in 2D or 3D distributions. The most typical neural network architecture is referred to as multilayer perceptron (MLP): here the neurons are organized in successive layers. The input layer is linear and just distributes the inputs (possibly deriving from a network of sensors) to the successive layer; the output layer gives the final output of the processing chain; in between there is a layer of nodes that are not linked to inputs and outputs and for this reason is called "hidden." A pictorial illustration of the MLP NN is reported in Fig. 1A. The MLP is quite similar to the ADALINE previously proposed in signal processing literature apart from the presence of the nonlinearities at least in the hidden layer's nodes.

Various nonlinear functions have been proposed for approximation, pattern recognition, and classification problems. In MLP, the nodes in successive layers are connected and the connections are weighted. Among them, monotonic saturating functions (i.e., sigmoids) are a favorite choice. In dynamical problems, nonmonotonic functions have been proposed. The weights are typically randomly initialized.

Thus, the MLP is of a feedforward type. However, in recursive networks, there are also feedback links and this enriches the dynamical behavior of NNs.

The relevance of MLP in approximating input-output mappings has been increased by the proofs of some theorems, demonstrating that any continuous mapping can be approximately by MLP with at least one hidden layer whose output functions are sigmoid (or

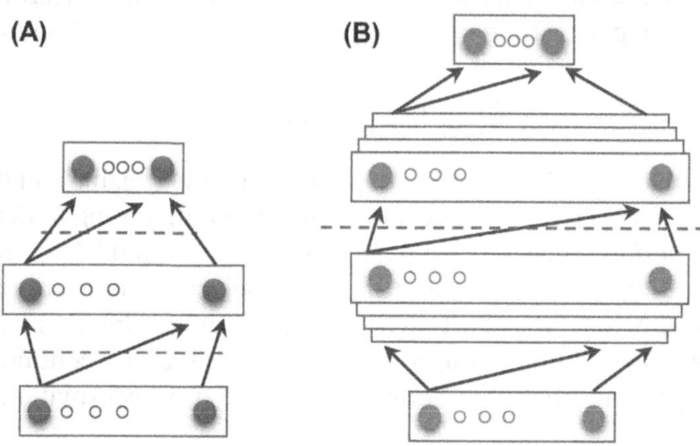

FIG. 1 (A) A shallow (one hidden layer) and (B) a deep (multiple hidden layers) neural network.

monotonic) functions. It is worth mentioning that this notion of universal approximation just states that the NN can learn, not what in practice it really does learn.

NNs are adaptive systems that are trained aiming to derive an optimal representation of the weights' matrices. The training is carried out through a specific "learning" procedure. The learning can be supervised (SL), unsupervised (UL), semisupervised (SSL), or reinforced (RL). In SL, NNs are forced to associate their outputs to real (or complex) valued targets fixed by a "teacher," through a procedure (typically gradient-based) that optimizes approximation errors (a "cost" function). The goal of SL is to derive optimal weights' matrices that minimize or achieve a small error. However, NNs are asked to generalize well in unseen input vectors, i.e., generating small errors also testing cases. In UL, there is no teacher, and the NN is asked to autonomously extract some underlying statistical regularities from the available data. In SSL, a prestage of UL is used to facilitate the following SL procedure. In the case of the availability of both labeled and unlabeled data, these procedures can help to extract additional information on the problem under analysis. In some applications, i.e., image "semantic" segmentation, an additional form of learning is considered, referred to as weakly supervised learning, where the relevant labels are weakly annotated in the training data because of the heavy annotation cost. In RL, the machine interacts with the surrounding environment and, following the observation of the consequences of its actions, it learns how to modify its own behavior in response to some form of "reward" received.

The different approximation theorems imply a "sufficient" number of hidden nodes to satisfy the universal approximation properties. However, this in turn implies a high number of degrees of freedom in the optimization procedure. The capacity of the NN is statistically bounded and underlies a relation between the number of weights to be determined and the number of "examples" available to train them. A high number of free parameters increases the descriptive complexity of NN, approximately related to the number of bits of information required to describe a NN. The complexity of NN limits generalization ability. Unsuccessful generalization performance reduced the impact of the NN approach, after an initial enthusiastic acceptance. Some techniques have been proposed to reduce the complexity of NNs, among which some concepts relevant to deep learning (DL) are the weight sharing, the regularization, and the forced introduction of data invariances.

3 Deep architectures and learning

DL methods iteratively modify more sets of parameters (the weights and the biases of the layer-to-layer matrices) by minimizing a loss/cost function aiming to define an optimal set. However, the performance of DL, and more generally, ML and NN approaches strongly depend on the quality of available data or the careful selection of a representation suitable for the task at hand. Most of the efforts in designing the processing chain are thus devoted to data preprocessing or domain transformation. Time series are commonly analyzed in time, frequency, or time-frequency domain. The related transformation constitutes an engineering way to extract features from data that are apparent in a specific domain. DL represents the most significant and successful advance in ML over the last decade. A large part of the current appeal of DL techniques derives from the possibility of acquiring data representations that are not model-based but totally data-driven. This circumvents the need to hand-designed features. The hierarchically organized learned features are often richer and more powerful than the ones suitably engineered. DL is indeed an emerging methodology firmly rooted within the traditional ML community whose main objective is to design learning algorithms and architectures for extracting multiple-level representations from data. The representation is both hierarchical and distributed, as the relevant characteristics of a problem emerge gradually in successive levels (or layers) and are the collective result of weighting multiple nodes similarly to shallow NNs. These representations facilitate the pattern recognition tasks sometimes without the need for any feature engineering but just autonomously extracting them from the available data. This is because the multiple layers of successive latent representations are able to disentangle potential confounding factors in the input data, also reducing their complexity. Fig. 1B shows a deep architecture. The huge amount of researches recently carried out in the field by a large number of academic and industrial groups are motivated by the surprising successes achieved also in precommercial competitions and applications. AlphaGo and Watson are some relevant examples. Major IT companies (e.g., Google, IBM, Intel, Facebook, Baidu, and Microsoft) hold a large extent of patents in the field; they also made DL their core business. This resurgence of interest in the NN approach is related to the following evidences:

(1) General availability of large database (big data) coming from international initiatives and worldwide collaboration on projects;
(2) Availability of big computing power mainly associated with cloud computing and novel GPU extensions;
(3) Availability of novel algorithms and processing architectures, or advanced paradigms of computation, like quantum computing and memristor-based network implementations.

Indeed, as previously noted, the capacity of a NN chain is related to the number of free parameters whose estimation calls for large datasets. In turn, to process big data, powerful computing is needed.

Some of the DL schemes are biologically motivated. In essence, the brain visual cortex inspired hierarchical DL architectures. In particular, neurons found in the visual cortex of cats respond to specific properties of visual sensory inputs, like lines, edges, colors, and the successive layers extract combinations of such low-level features to derive higher-level features resulting in objects' recognition [1].

Several DL models have been proposed in the literature. In what follows, the most known are presented: deep belief networks (DBNs), stacked autoencoders (SAEs), and deep convolution neural networks (CNN).

3.1 Deep belief networks

DBN is a probabilistic generative model, composed of stacked modules of restricted Boltzmann machines (RBMs) (Fig. 2) [2]. An RBM is an undirected energy-based model with two layers of visible (v) and hidden (h) units, respectively, with connections only between layers. Each RBM module is trained one at a time in an unsupervised manner and using a contrastive divergence procedure [3]. The output (learned features) of each stage is used as input for the subsequent RBM stage. After, the whole network is commonly trained with supervised learning to improve classification performance (fine-tuning method).

3.2 Stacked autoencoders

The *Stacked Autoencoders* architecture is similar to DBNs, where the main component is the autoencoder (Fig. 3) [4]. An autoencoder (AE) is a NN trained with unsupervised learning whose attempt is to reproduce at its output the same configuration of input. A single hidden layer with the same number of inputs and outputs implements it. AE consists of two main stages: compression of the input space into a lower dimension space (encoding) and reconstruction of the input data from the compressed representation (decoding). In a stacked architecture, the encoded pattern is used as input for training the successive AEs. The SAE ends with an output layer trained with a supervised criterion. As DBN, the whole network can be fine-tuned to improve classification performance.

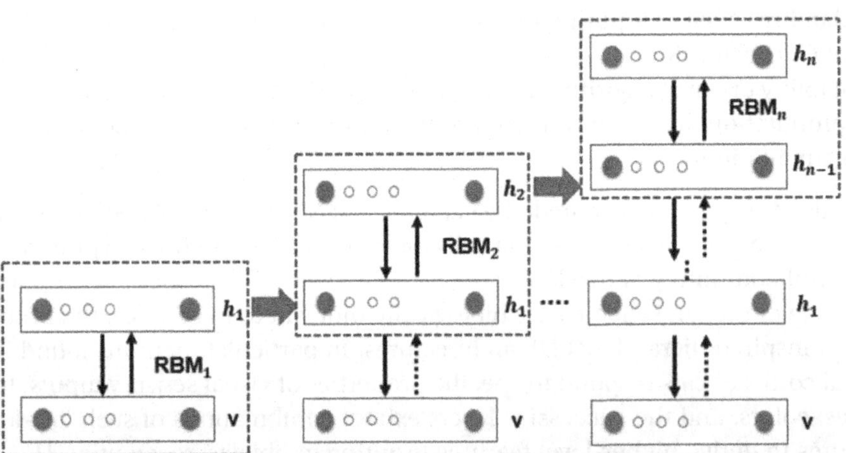

FIG. 2 Deep belief network (DBN) architecture composed of stacked restricted Boltzmann machines (RBMs). Each RBM consists of a visible layer **v** and a single hidden layer $\mathbf{h}_n$. RBM$_1$ is trained using the input data as visible units. The hidden layer $\mathbf{h}_2$ of RBM$_2$ is trained using the output of the previous trained layer $\mathbf{h}_1$ of the RBM$_1$. The output of $\mathbf{h}_2$ is the input of the next RBM$_3$ and so on. The trained layers $\mathbf{h}_1$, $\mathbf{h}_2$, ..., $\mathbf{h}_n$ form the stacked architecture. Finally, the whole DBN is fine-tuned with a standard backpropagation algorithm.

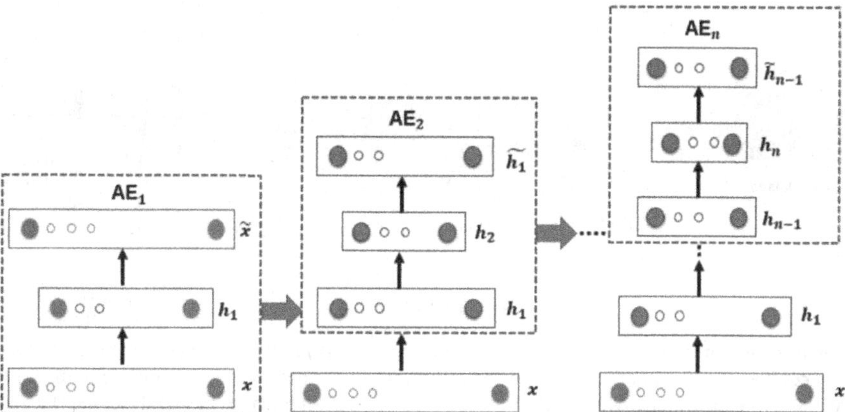

FIG. 3 Stacked autoencoders architecture. The first autoencoder (AE$_1$) maps the input instance $\mathbf{x}$ into a compressed representation $\mathbf{h_1}$ (coding operation) which is used to reconstruct the input data (decoding operation). After training AE$_1$, the *code* $\mathbf{h_1}$ is used as input to train AE$_2$, providing the *code* vector $\mathbf{h_2}$ and so on. The procedure is repeated for all AE$_n$ autoencoders. The compressed representations $\mathbf{h_1}, \mathbf{h_2}, \ldots, \mathbf{h_n}$ form the stacked architecture (SAE) which is typically fine-tuned using a conventional backpropagation algorithm.

3.3 Convolutional neural networks

Convolutional neural networks (CNN) are an alternative type of DNN that allow to model both time and space correlations in multivariate signals. They are attractive as they explicitly consider and take advantage of input topology. In SAE, for example, the inputs can be organized in any order without affecting the performance of the model. In biomedical signal processing, however, spectral and time-frequency representations of the original signals show strong correlations: modeling local correlations is easy with CNNs through weight sharing. CNNs are inspired by the visual cortex of the brain and have been widely applied in image and speech recognition. A CNN includes an automatic feature extractor (composed of multiple stages of convolution and pooling layers) and a standard MLP-NN which processes the features learned before for classification tasks (Fig. 4) [5]. The convolutional layer computes the dot product between the input image X and a set of K_j learnable filters. Each filter K_j sized $k_1 \times k_2$ moves across the input space performing the convolution with local subblocks of inputs, providing Y_j *feature maps* ($Y_j = \sum X^*K_j + B_j$, where B is the bias term). A rectified linear unit (ReLU) activation function is commonly applied to each feature map, to improve computational efficiency by inducing sparsity and to reduce the effect of the vanishing gradient problem [6,7]. The nonlinear convolutional layer is followed by the pooling layer which performs a maximum or average subsampling of the feature maps previously obtained in the previous step: a filter sized $\overline{k}_1 + \overline{k}_2$ moves across the input feature map taking the maximum (max pooling) or the average (average pooling) of the neighbor values selected by the filter. Finally, the learned feature maps are the input of a standard NN that performs classification tasks.

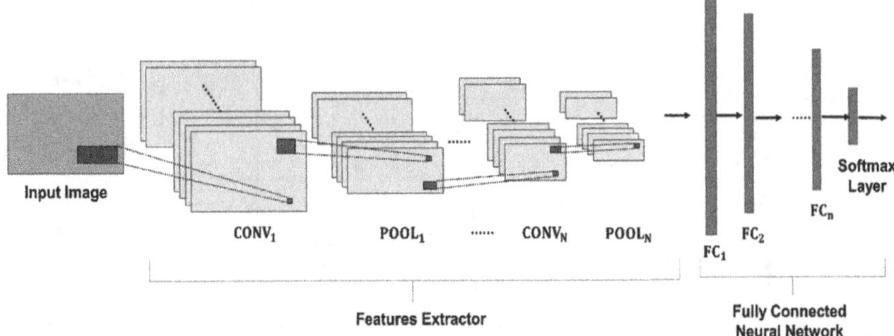

FIG. 4 CNN architecture. It includes a sequence of convolution (CONV) and pooling (POOL) layers followed by a standard fully connected neural network. In the convolutional layer, the input map convolves with *K* filters (or kernels), providing *K* feature maps. After applying a nonlinear activation function (sigmoidal or ReLU) to each feature map, the pooling layer is performed. The features learned are the input of a fully connected neural network followed by a softmax layer, which performs the classification tasks.

4 Electrophysiological time series

4.1 Multichannel neurophysiological measurements of the activity of the brain

The brain generates bio-electromagnetic fields related to the activity and the synaptic action of interacting neurons. This activity can be detected through sensors yielding neurophysiological measurements like electroencephalography (EEG) and magnetoencephalography (MEG).

4.2 Electroencephalography (EEG)

The EEG collects the measurements of the brain's electrical activity. It consists of recording and displaying, over the time, the voltage difference between two scalp sites: the location of interest and the "reference" location. Since its discovery in 1924 by Berger, EEG has become a routine examination in neurology [8] and the basic neurophysiological measurement of many brain-computer interface (BCI) applications [9].

EEG electrodes are located at the surface of the scalp (Fig. 5) and collect the electrical activity generated by networks of neurons. Extracellular current flow is generated because of the excitatory and inhibitory postsynaptic potentials produced by cell bodies and dendrites of pyramidal neurons. The *EEG waveforms* are mainly produced by layers of pyramidal neurons whose synchronous activity produces a bioelectromagnetic field, that propagates from the sources to the recording scalp electrodes. Fields propagate through tissues that have different conduction properties and overlap with the fields generated by other neuronal populations. As a result, the potentials recorded at a specific electrode site will reflect the combination of the contributions of different cortical sources (volume

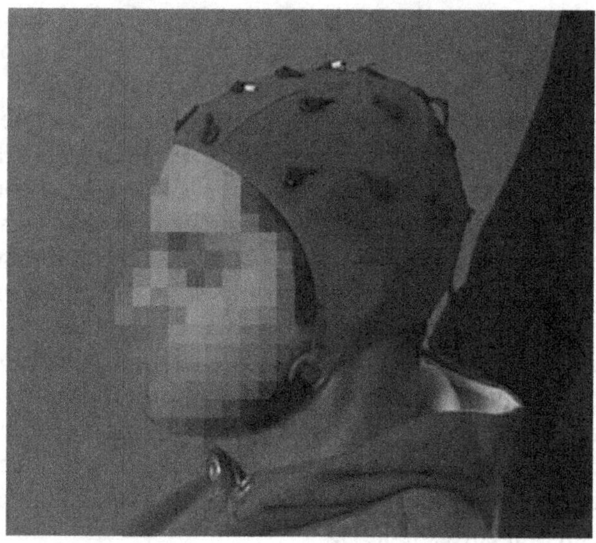

FIG. 5 Standard EEG recording cap.

conduction effect). The issue of volume conduction is not trivial in EEG analysis as it can result in apparently high functional connectivity between channels thus leading to a wrong neurophysiological interpretation of the results. It has long been discussed in the literature and all of the proposed approaches (Laplacian filtering, source estimation, and the use of connectivity measures not sensitive to phase interactions, among others) introduce various limitations and may cancel relevant source activity at low spatial frequencies [10].

EEG waveforms are characterized by amplitude, shape, morphology, and frequency. Four major rhythms are commonly investigated when analyzing EEG signals: delta (0–4 Hz), theta (4–8 Hz), alpha (8–13 Hz), and beta (13–30 Hz) bands, which are associated with specific physiological and mental processes [11]. Alpha is the main resting rhythm of the brain, it is commonly observed in awake adults, especially in the occipital electrodes. In healthy subjects, theta rhythm appears at the early stages of sleep and the delta appears at deep-sleep stages. Beta waves appear because of anxiety or intense mental activity. The brain wave components of EEG signals can be investigated by frequency analysis or, when keeping track of the temporal evolution of EEG frequencies necessary, by time-frequency analysis [12].

The EEG electrode placement was standardized in a 10–20 system, which is a method to describe the location of electrodes over the scalp. This system is based on the relationship between the location of the electrode and underlying brain lobes. The distances between adjacent electrodes are either 10% or 20% of the total front-back (nasion-inion) or right-left distance of the skull.

EEG signals are important in the study of many neurological diseases. For example, Alzheimer's disease (AD) is a neurodegenerative disorder with a subtle, asymptomatic onset and a gradual progression toward the full-blown stage of the disease, when the clinical symptoms become noticeable [13]. AD affects the neuronal metabolic processes and leads to a loss of connections between nerve cells. Three main characteristics can be commonly observed in AD patients' EEG signals, compared to healthy controls: the slowing effect (the power at low frequencies increases, whereas the power at high frequencies decreases), the reduction of complexity and of synchrony between pairs of EEG signals [14,15]. Such effects come with the functional disconnection caused by the death of neurons [16,17].

In Creutzfeldt-Jakob disease (CJD), a progressive transmissible form of encephalopathy, patients develop dementia and a peculiar spongiform degeneration of cortical and subcortical gray matter [18]. EEG helps in diagnosing CJD, particularly in the middle/late stages of the disease when periodic sharp wave complexes (PSWC) become clearly visible [19]. PSWC may disappear at the later stages of the disease when spongiform changes involve the whole cerebral cortex [20,21].

Fig. 6 (top) shows the EEG traces of a patient affected by CJD, a patient affected by AD, and a Healthy Control (HC), recorded by the occipital channel O_1. The EEG was recorded in a comfortable eye-closed resting state. The signals were band-pass filtered at 0.5–32 Hz and sampled at 256 Hz. The CJD EEG (Fig. 6, top) exhibits the typical aforementioned PSWC sharp and wave complexes. The AD EEG (Fig. 6, middle) shows the "slowing effect," peculiar to cerebral degeneration due to AD.

The AD slowing effect is evident in Fig. 6 (middle) and Fig. 7A (middle). The dominant peak in the alpha band (8–13 Hz), peculiar of healthy subjects (HC) in an eye-closed resting state, is indeed present in the power spectral densities (PSD) of the HC, whereas it slowed and reduced in the AD patient as well as in the CJD patient. Delta band (0–4 Hz) looks prominent in both AD and CJD patients, as rather expected from clinical considerations. In Dl approaches, this clinical behavior can be automatically extracted and represented in suitable features.

4.3 High-density electroencephalography

EEG signals have very good temporal resolution but poor spatial resolution, because of both volume conduction effects and large interelectrode distance. Biophysical analyses reported that some information on the scalp electrical potentials is lost unless an intersensor distance of 1 to 2 cm is used [22–25]. With a standard 10–20 system, the average intersensor distance is 7 cm. Achieving a 1 to 2 cm sampling density would require 500 EEG channels distributed uniformly over the scalp. High-density-EEG (HD-EEG) offers a high temporal resolution, typical of EEG, in conjunction with a high spatial resolution (Fig. 8). HD-EEG with 256 channels provides adequate approximate spatial sampling [23,24]. An example of high-density EEG recording is shown in Fig. 9.

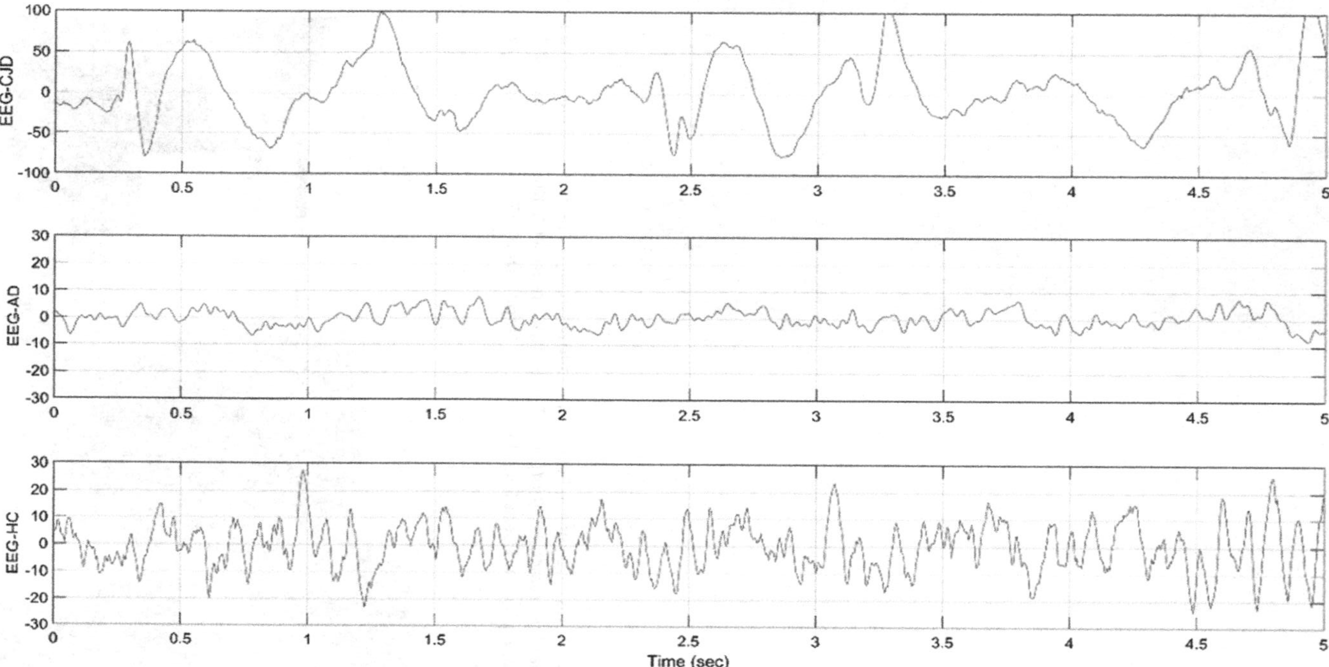

FIG. 6 EEG was recorded at location O1 (occipital) from a CJD patient *(top)*, an AD patient *(middle)*, and a healthy subject *(bottom)*.

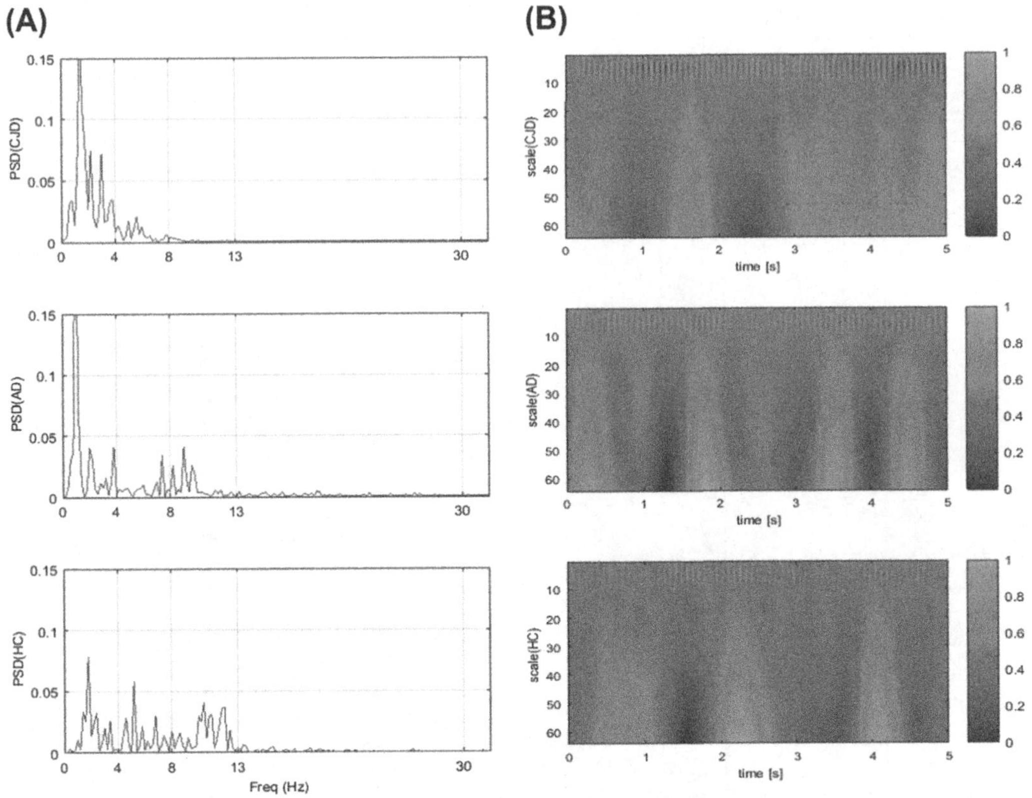

FIG. 7 (A) Power spectral densities (PSD) of the EEG signals (shown in Fig. 6) recorded from a CJD patient *(top)*, an AD patient *(middle)*, and a healthy subject, HC *(bottom)*. The abscissa represents the frequency and the ranges of the brain rhythms (delta, theta, alpha, and beta EEG rhythms are emphasized). (B) Time-frequency maps (TFM) for the same signals.

FIG. 8 High-density 256 channels EEG recording system.

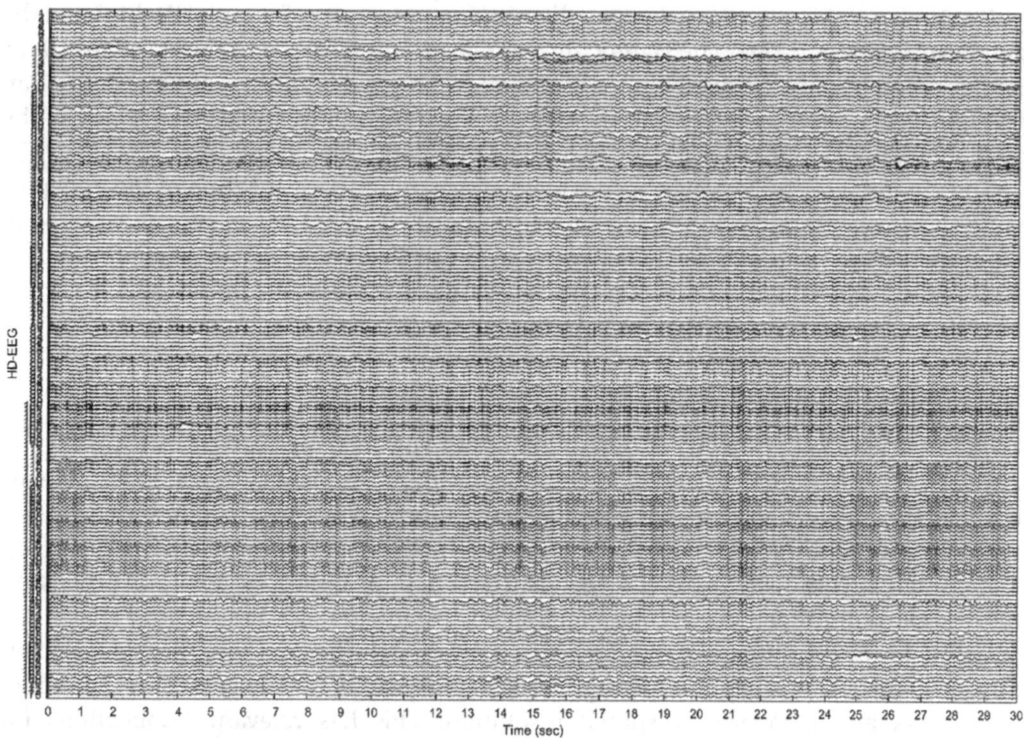

FIG. 9 A 30 s sample of high-density 256 channels EEG recording.

Fig. 10 depicts the 3D scalp topography of the power of the EEG recording shown in Fig. 9. The signal power was estimated for every EEG epoch, and then averaged over the time giving the average power value per channel. The obtained values were then mapped over the scalp, where the coloration of intersensor areas was estimated by interpolation [26].

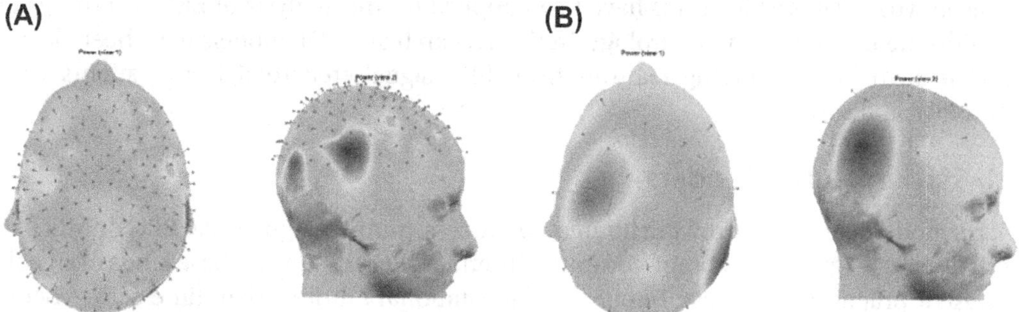

FIG. 10 3D scalp topography of the power of the EEG recording is shown in Fig. 9. (A) Topographic reconstruction was achieved by taking into account all the available scalp channels. (B) Topographic reconstruction was achieved by taking into account only the standard 19 channels.

Fig. 10 shows the interpolated power distribution topography for both HD-EEG and the standard 19-channel EEG. The significant interelectrodes distance in the standard 10–20 configuration implies the need for interpolation with unavoidable loss of precision. As an example, because of the interpolation effect, the two high-power areas (red areas) in the right parietal-occipital zone in Fig. 10A are clustered into one in Fig. 10B.

The potential of HD-EEG has been widely proven in the identification of the epileptogenic onset zone through electrical source imaging [27–29], but it is mostly unexplored in many other fields of application, like dementia. However, it requires a high computational effort and generates huge amounts of data, particularly in long-time monitoring. It is clear that DL approaches can be of great help to manage this kind of data.

4.4 Magnetoencephalography

Magnetoencephalography (MEG) is a functional neuroimaging technique for mapping brain activity by recording magnetic fields produced by electrical currents occurring naturally in the brain, using very sensitive magnetometers. Arrays of superconducting quantum interference devices (SQUIDs) are currently the most common magnetometer.

Although EEG and MEG signals originate from the same neurophysiological processes, many important differences can be highlighted. Magnetic fields are less distorted than electric fields by the different conductivity properties of the head tissues (the skull is insulating, whereas the scalp is conducting), resulting in a mild sensitivity to volume conduction effects and in a greater spatial resolution. This has relevant implications for connectivity analyses and source modeling. Furthermore, MEG measurements are absolute as they are independent of the reference choice.

However, EEG is far more affordable, manageable, and cheap than MEG, which caused its widespread availability, as compared to MEG technology, both in research and clinical practice.

5 Deep learning models for EEG signal processing

In recent years, DL architectures have been applied for the analysis of EEG recordings in cognitive neuroscience and neurology. In this research area, DL models have been developed to learn discriminating features from EEG signals recorded from patients with neurological disorders.

5.1 Stacked auto-encoders

DL methodologies are of growing interest to process complex signals like EEG or MEG, in both disease diagnosis and brain-computer interface (BCI) systems. These kinds of signals represent practical examples of noisy and nonstationary multivariate time series, being acquired simultaneously on multiple channels. Typically, EEG is acquired during a long time for diagnosis purposes and it presents some artefactual and noise activity that may reduce its reliability and visual interpretability. The DL approach to EEG/MEG signal

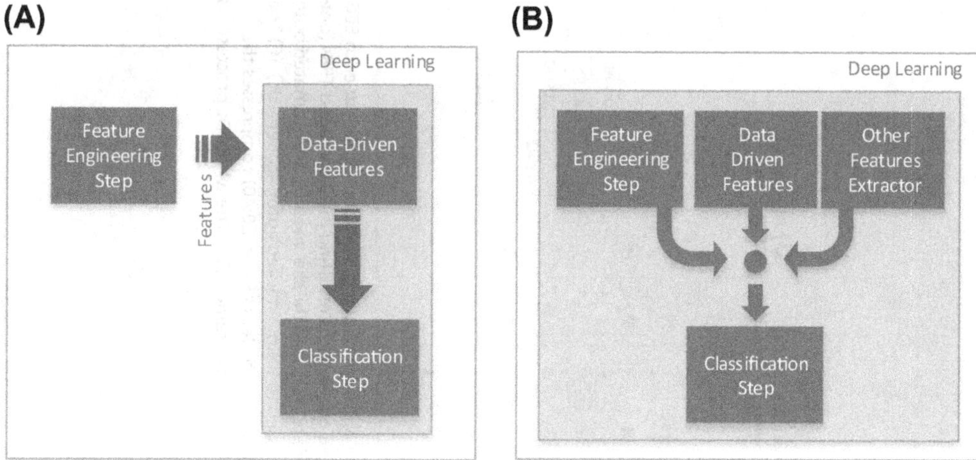

FIG. 11 (A) Serial and (B) parallel DL schemes.

processing can be proposed in two basic ways (see Fig. 11): (1) *in series*, in which a feature engineering step yields a high number of features that are then combined and reduced by a DL network before using them for classification; (2) *in parallel*, where the data-driven features and the engineered features form a unique input vector for the classification step. The serial step is preferred for reducing the information redundancy of the features. In a recent paper [30], a serial scheme based on SAEs has been proposed that includes a time-frequency transform of the input recordings, an intermediate step of data-driven feature combination, and a final classification stage. The SAE model has been proposed for discriminating EEGs of subjects affected by early stage CJD from other forms of rapidly progressive dementia (RPD).

Each AE is implemented by an MLP-NN that includes an encoding stage followed by a decoder. Higher-order features have been obtained by stacking two levels of nonlinear (sigmoidal) nodes. The output of the deepest hidden layer is the final feature vector used as input for the classification step. The processing chain is depicted in Fig. 12. It is worth noting that while the "engineered" features are extracted channel by channel, the higher-order features generated by the SAE are mixing information pertaining to all of the channels. This procedure can be limited to selected areas, i.e., frontal or parietal channels, to gain information on brain areas mostly relevant for the classification.

The output of each hidden layer of the SAE is given by:

$$\underline{h} = \underline{\sigma}\left(\underline{\underline{\Phi}}\,\underline{x}\right),$$

where $\underline{s}$ is the node nonlinearity, for example, the standard sigmoidal function:

$$\sigma = (1 + e^{-z})^{-1}.$$

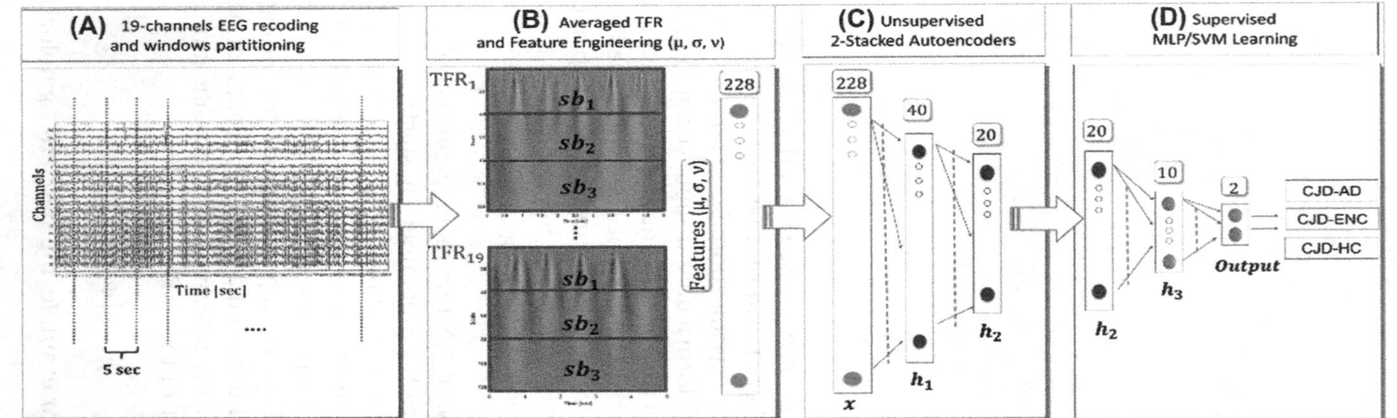

FIG. 12 Flowchart of the method proposed in Ref. [30]. (A) The 19-channel EEG recording is partitioned into *N* nonoverlapping 5s windows. (B) For each EEG epoch, and for every EEG channel a time-frequency representation (TFR) is computed. The TFRs are averaged over epochs resulting in 19 averaged TFRs (one per channel). Each averaged TFR is subdivided into three subbands, and then, the mean (μ), the standard deviation (σ), and the skewness (v) are estimated both for the subbands and for the whole TFR. Therefore, $12 \times 19 = 228$ engineered features are extracted and are used to train 2 stacked autoencoders (UL). (C) The first autoencoder (AE_1, 228:40:228) compresses the input representation in 40 parameters ($\mathbf{h_1}$). The second autoencoder (AE_2, 40:20:40) compresses the 40 learned features in 20 higher-level paraments ($\mathbf{h_2}$). Finally, a classifier with a single hidden layer ($\mathbf{h_3}$) of 10 neurons is trained (SL). The whole DL processor is possibly fine-tuned to improve the performance of the classification tasks: CJD-AD, CJD-ENC, CJD-HC.

$\underline{\underline{\Phi}}$ is the learned matrix of the encoding layer of the MLP-NN. The loss/cost function to be minimized through learning is given by:

$$\mathcal{L} = \|\underline{\widetilde{x}} - \underline{x}\|^2 + \lambda\left\|\underline{\underline{\varphi}}\right\|^2$$

where λ is the regularization coefficient, $\underline{\underline{\varphi}}$ is the matrices' weights, $\underline{x}$ is the input vector, and $\underline{\widetilde{x}}$ is the approximate (learned) output that reconstructs $\underline{x}$ through the training of the AE, i.e.,

$$\underline{\widetilde{x}} = \underline{\sigma}\left[\underline{\underline{\Psi}}\left(\sigma\left(\underline{\underline{\Phi}}\,\underline{x}\right)\right)\right]$$

Here, the aim of the MLP-NN is to learn a suitable representation of the input vector and it can be traded off with the quality of reconstruction of the input; accordingly, the choice of an optimal λ is not a strong constraint.

5.2 Summary of the proposed method for EEG classification

The DL approach can solve a binary classification problem (0: healthy subjects, 1: patient with disease) or a multiclass problem (i.e., either different stages of a degenerative brain disease or differentiation between diseases). This approach can include both feature-engineering and data-driven steps aiming to represent discriminative information from the available data hardly emerging from the visual inspection of the EEG recordings. The available EEG database (including all of the considered categories of subjects) passes through a processing chain that can be resumed as follows:

(1) Artifact rejection by clinical (visual) inspection: the segments of signal affected by evident artefactual components are cut from all the recording channels;
(2) The residual recordings are subdivided into nonoverlapping epochs of 5 s duration through a moving window procedure;
(3) A time-frequency analysis of the signals is carried out: the continuous wavelet transform (CWT) with Mexican Hat mother wavelet has been used in Ref. [30] but other time-frequency representations can be used; in particular, the empirical mode decomposition (EMD) can yield the advantage of being fully data-driven [31];
(4) Extraction of the relevant "engineered" features from the TFMs possibly taking into account the relevant brain rhythms (as an example, mean values standard deviations and skewness of the wavelet coefficients);
(5) Detection of evident outliers in the features; these values may be generated by segments of artifacts that have not been detected in step 1 and can be dropped out.

According to this procedure, [30], a vector of features has been generated from the TFMs; the resulting input vector includes 228 elements. The successive steps, based on the DL approach, combine the single-channel features, thus exploiting the multivariate nature of the EEG signal. A final classification stage, based on support vector machines (SVM) trained by SL, outputs the classification result. The DL-based system, after global

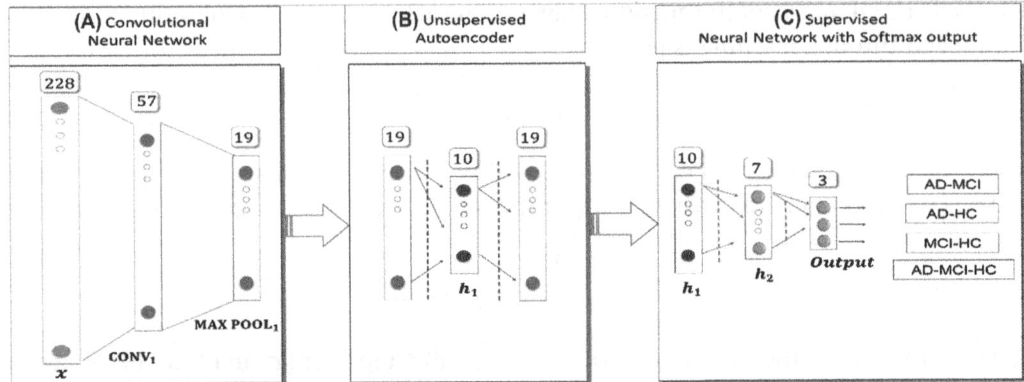

FIG. 13 Flowchart of the method presented in Ref. [32]. Extraction of the 228 features vector as shown in Fig. 12A and B. DL architecture: in the first stage, a convolutional layer (CONV1) performs the convolution operation between the 228 input features and 19 masks of 12 elements, outputting a vector of 57 features. Then, a max pooling layer (MAX POOL$_1$) reduces the feature vector size to 19. An autoencoder compresses the 19 outputs to 10 latent variables that form the input to the final fully connected MLP-NN with 7 hidden neurons, for binary (ADMCI, AD-HC, MCI-HC) and 3-way classification (AD-MCI-HC) tasks. In the figure, the output layer is specialized for the 3-way classification.

fine-tuning of the network by backpropagation, provided an average classification accuracy of around 90%, with similar sensitivity and specificity.

5.3 Deep convolutional neural networks

A second approach to DL-EEG has been introduced by [32]. It is based on a customized CNN for discriminating EEG recordings of subjects with Alzheimer's disease (AD), mild cognitive impairment (MCI), an early form of dementia, and healthy controls (HC). Fig. 13 shows the flowchart of the method. The EEG recordings have been transformed in the time-frequency domain, on an epoch by-epoch basis. Then, a grand total of 228 time-frequency features have been extracted and used as input vectors to the deep network. The DL model includes a convolutional layer followed by a sigmoidal nonlinearity, a max pooling layer, an autoencoder, and a classification single hidden layer MLP-NN. More than one convolutional-pooling stage can be used to generate higher-level features. The combined DL processor globally reduced the dimensionality of the input feature space from 228 to 10 latent features, providing very good performance in both binary (83% accuracy) and 3-way classification (82% accuracy) as reported in Table II of Ref. [32].

5.4 Other DL approaches

Other researchers have faced the problem of DL-EEG pattern classification. In particular, Zhao and He [33] proposed a 3-stacked restricted Boltzmann machines (RBM) structure for the classification of AD patients. They claimed to reach 92% of accuracy.

Other papers focused on the detection of epileptic seizures in EEG recordings. [34] modeled a DBN model for the classification and anomaly detection of epileptic patterns.

[35] developed a CNN for seizure prediction achieving zero-false alarm on 95% of patients analyzed, whereas Turner et al. [36] proved the effectiveness of the DBN algorithm in seizure detection (*F*-measure up to 0.9). Recently, DL networks have been also applied in the fast-growing field of brain-computer interface (BCI) as a rapid serial visual presentation (RSVP) task [37], steady-state visual evoked potential (SSVEP) classification [38], and P300 waves detection [39].

6 Future directions of research

The examples presented in this chapter aimed to show that DL can be a powerful tool to assist the solution of difficult biomedical signal processing problems like discriminating brain states to differentiate brain pathological conditions or to interpret tasks in BCI applications, like the classification of the left and right hand in motor imagery. The use of EEG is the gold standard in both cases. It is cheap and noninvasive and can be repeated easily being commonly well accepted by patients. Furthermore, the relevant data can be acquired through the increasingly popular wearable devices that allow capturing continuously physiological and functional data in both well-being and healthcare applications. This potentially rich information content can be transmitted through Bluetooth and smartphone channels for remote monitoring. This opens relevant possibilities in the immediate care of patients, for example, in life-threatening situations like epileptic absences. However, it also raises novel challenges to DL, like the resource-constrained use of low-power devices. The EEG is a complex signal, i.e., a multivariate nonstationary time series, which is inherently high-dimensional taking into account time, spectral, and spatial (channel) dynamic evolution. Recently, various DL architectures have been proposed to decode disease- or task-related information from the raw EEG recording with and without handcrafted features. Higher-level features extracted from DL can be analyzed, visualized, and interpreted to yield a different perspective with respect to conventional engineered features. Despite the exponential growth of research papers in DL, in most cases, a black-box approach is yet provided. In what follows, some of the critical issues of presently investigated DL are briefly summarized.

6.1 DL Explainability/interpretability

General methods to interpret how DL networks take decisions are basically lacking. There is no full theoretical understanding of how learning evolves in DL networks and how it generates their inner organization. This unsolved lack of ability to explain decisions to clinicians prevents the practical use of any predictive outcome. Some information-theoretic-based model has been proposed to "open the black box": in particular, it has been suggested that the network optimize the information bottleneck trade-off between prediction and compression in the successive layers [40]. Essentially, it has been shown that DL spends most of the information available in the database of training for learning efficient representations instead of fitting the labels. This consideration seems to confirm the importance of UL techniques, for which unsatisfactory algorithms have been devised so far [41]. Future advances in UL will focus on finding structural information on the input signals and in building generative models: generative adversarial networks are indeed highly promising directions of research [42].

6.1.1 explainable artificial intelligence (xAI)

The opaqueness of DL (AI)-models is denoted as *black-box behavior.* It has been recently explored by the so-called *explainable artificial intelligence (xAI).* Explainability refers to the development of computational methodologies able to guarantee transparency in AI systems; for example, they can show which input area mostly contributed to achieve a specific performance and explaining how [43]. Some common xAI techniques are described in the following paragraphs.

6.1.2 Occlusion sensitivity analysis

Occlusion sensitivity analysis (OSA) is used to measure the *sensitivity* of a trained CNN to different regions of an input image [44]. OSA procedure consists of systematically occluding areas of the input data by using a moving grey mask and evaluating the related effect on the network output. For each position of the occluding mask, the occluded image is fed into the trained CNN to estimate the deterioration of the discrimination performance. Such modifications are used to plot the *heatmap* or *saliency maps,* which can reveal the most relevant regions of the input image for the classification task. In this representation, the areas mostly involved in recognizing a class are depicted with red coloration; in contrast, the areas less relevant for the discrimination task are depicted with a blue coloration.

6.1.3 Gradient-weighted class activation mapping (Grad-CAM)

The gradient-weighted class activation mapping (GradCAM) is one of the most employed xAI techniques typically used to better understand the CNN-based models [45]. Indeed, Grad-CAM allows to detect which input area is most significant for predictions. Let o^c the score of a certain class c. The gradient $\frac{\partial o^c}{\partial R^n}$ of the last convolutional layer is first calculated, where R^n are the features maps (with n number of features representations). Then, the global average pooling is evaluated to estimate the neuron importance weights $\widehat{w}_n^c$, defined as:

$$\widehat{w}_n^c = \frac{1}{Z}\sum_i \sum_j \frac{\partial o^c}{\partial R_{i,j}^n}$$

where Z denotes the number of pixels in a feature map and (i, j) identifies the pixels. Finally, a weighted combination of R^n is computed:

$$\widehat{w}_n^c = ReLU\left(\sum_n \widehat{w}_n^c R^n\right)$$

where *ReLU* is the rectified linear unit transfer function. The result of this operation is known as the *Grad-CAM map* or *importance map* where the most important input areas for the classification are detected with coloration from blue (low importance) to red (high importance).

6.1.4 xAI approaches in biomedical engineering applications

In Ref. [46], the authors proposed an xAI approach for EEG-based brain-computer interface systems. Fig. 14 shows the flowchart of the method. In particular, the explainability of the developed CNN-based system was investigated to provide a better understanding of cortical sources activation when the brain is planning the hand's close/open (HC/HO) movement. To this end, an occlusion sensitivity analysis was performed to explore which cortical areas were mostly involved in the classification process and a *k*-means clustering technique was also employed to detect the highest saliency region. The cortical sources were then mapped to the cortical representation. Results showed that the central region

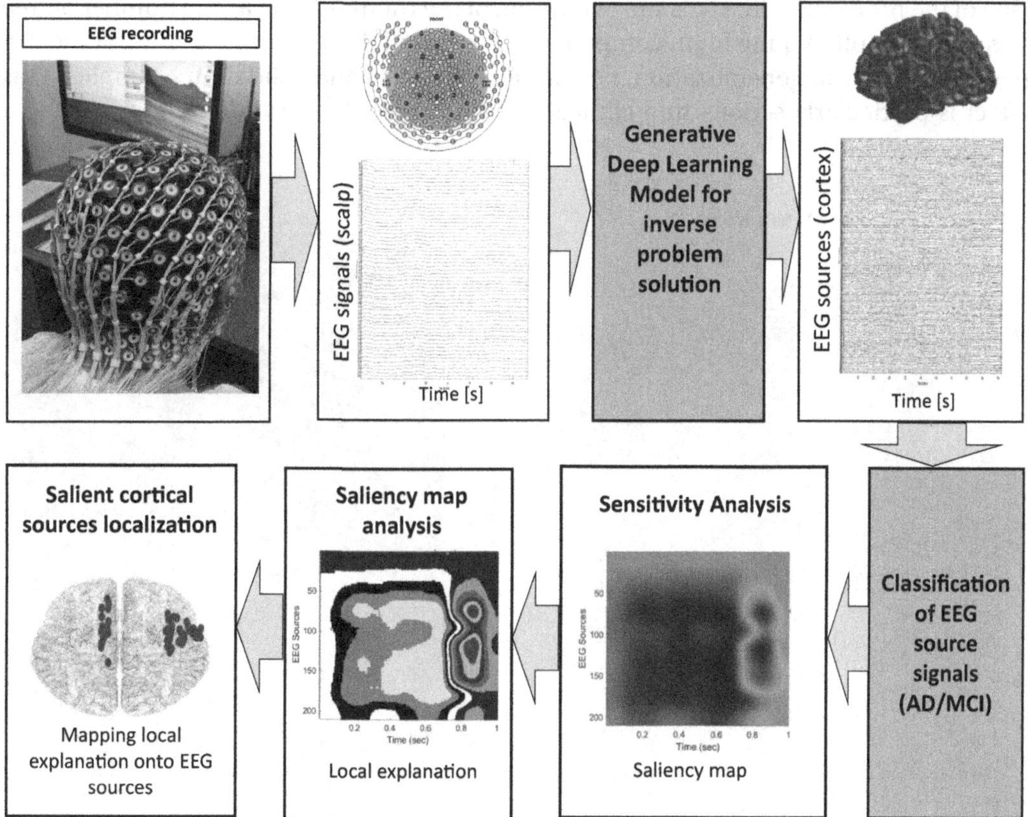

FIG. 14 Flowchart of the method presented in Ref. [46].

(close to the longitudinal fissure) and the right temporal zone of the premotor together with the primary motor cortex appear to be primarily involved.

Another approach based on xAI was introduced by Ref. [47] to longitudinally monitor subjects affected by mild cognitive impairment (MCI) by using high-density electroencephalography (HD-EEG). In particular, the proposed method consisted in mapping windows of HD-EEG into channel-frequency (HD-CF) representations using the power spectral density (PSD) estimation, subsequently used as input to a custom CNN, trained to classify the HD-CF maps as "T0" (MCI state) or "T1" (AD state). The Grad-CAM approach was applied to "explain" the approach taken by CNN. The methodology was capable of detecting which EEG channels (i.e., head region) and range of frequencies (i.e., subbands) resulted in more active in the progression to AD. Results showed that the activation of different EEG channels observed the main information that was included only in the subband. As an example, Fig. 15 reports the Grad-CAM maps of Subject 01 at time T0 (MCI state) and at time T1 (AD state).

6.2 Advanced learning approaches in DL

One of the problems with DL is the overfitting of the training data, as the number of free parameters is often quite high, compared to the size of the training set; in this case, DL performs poorly in generalization, i.e., on held-out tests and validation examples. This effect is particularly serious in a clinical setting, where the fresh data often refer to a

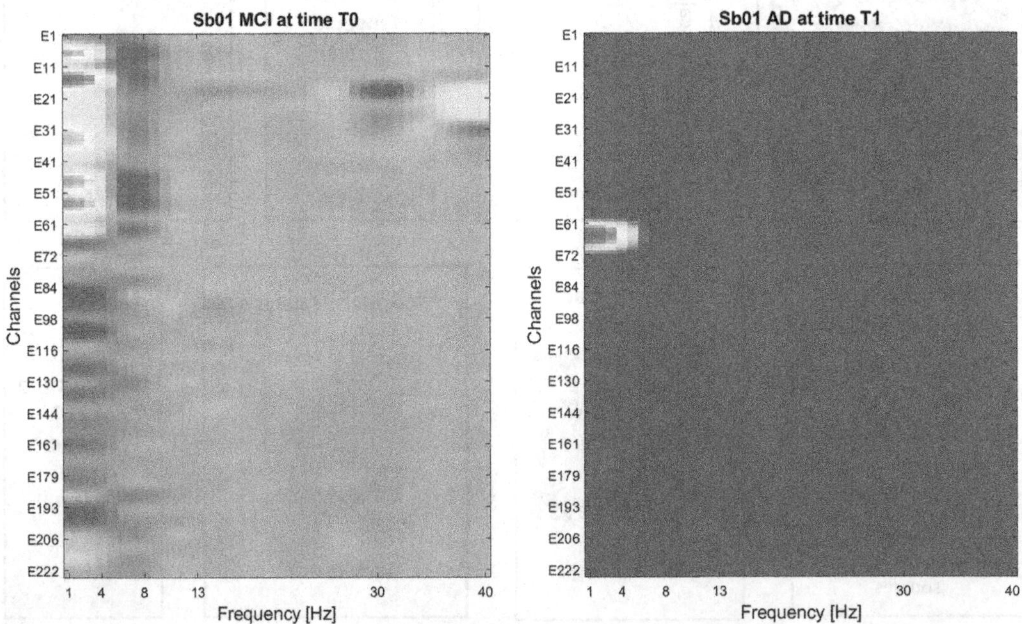

FIG. 15 Grad-CAM maps of Subject 01 at time T0 (MCI state) and at time T1 (AD state). *Red* color denotes areas with the highest relevance; vice-versa, *blue* color denotes areas with the lowest relevance [47].

novel patient. Several strategies for reducing the impact of overfitting have been proposed in the literature. One of these suggests randomly omitting half of the feature detectors on each training example [48]. The use of AEs with UL is also quite beneficial, particularly when the learning cost functions involve regularization terms, as in the dropout method. SAEs face the problem of vanishing gradients that become negligible during training; therefore, the DL network tends to learn the average of all the training examples. Furthermore, the AE treats all inputs equally and its representational capability aims to minimize the reconstruction error of each input. This is a shortcoming in the presence of noisy data. In addition, being trained without knowing the labels, the AE cannot discriminate between task-irrelevant and task-relevant information in the dataset. One of the approaches to deal with these problems is to make a pretraining of DL networks and to evaluate the architectural design (i.e., the number of layers and the related nodes) by means of information theoretical quantities, like entropy and mutual information [49]. In other works, the impact of the hidden nodes is measured simply by the variance of the output of the nodes. Indeed, any node with constant activation across different inputs fails to convey discriminative information about the input vectors. This observation can help reduce the size of the hidden layers during or posttraining. Another way proposed to minimize the limitations of deep architectures is to change the standard, biologically plausible, sigmoidal neuron nonlinearity, by substituting it with a strong nonlinear rectifier that helps to create a sparse representation with true zeros. The EEG is not sparse per se, but interchannel and intrachannel redundancy can be exploited to generate a block-sparse representation in suitable domains [50]. An evident advantage of rectifying neurons is that they allow the DL network to better disentangle information with respect to dense DL. In addition, by varying the number of active hidden neurons, and thus giving a variable-size flexible data structure, they allow to represent the effective dimensionality of the input data vectors.

6.3 Robustness of DL networks

DL is rapidly becoming a standard approach for the processing of medical and health data. In particular, DL provides the opportunity to automate the extraction of relevant features (as a difference with highly subjective interpretation of diagnostic data), integrate multimodal data, and combine the extraction stage with classification procedures. The classification performance is often limited as the available databases are typically small and incomplete, and preprocessing of data remains commonly a rather crucial step. The designed classifiers sometimes do not satisfy a check of robustness: it happens that trained models reduce their performance if small perturbations are applied to the examples. Adversarial perturbations are a relevant example. A rectifier-based sparse representation is typically robust to small input changes, as the set of nonzero features is well conserved. From geometric considerations, it has been shown that the high instability of DL networks is related to data points that reside very close to the classifier's decision boundary. As the robustness of DL is a critical requirement in a clinical setting, novel strategies for designing and training of DL schemes should be devised by the community in the years to come.

7 Conclusions

DL can yield appropriate tools for analyzing multivariate time-series data from a genuinely new perspective, which is both fully data-driven and automatic but can also take advantage of engineered features derived from standard signal processing methods, like frequency and time-frequency transforms. In recent years, the international community has shown enormous interest in DL and artificial intelligence, by funding several programs, in the public and private sectors. It is foreseen that these programs will favor a relevant growth of the economy and national gross value added (GVA). However, in this chapter it has been shown that DL is just a contingent development of ML and NN techniques originally proposed decades ago. This chapter focused on a rather limited aspect of DL, namely the processing of multivariate time series that is relevant for biomedical applications but also pertinent to the future development of IoT systems. The techniques here described can support a significant leap forward in the real-time processing of unstructured data and in clinical diagnosis. Open problems and limitations of DL have been discussed.

References

[1] Y. LeCun, Y. Bengio, G. Hinton, Deep learning, Nature 521 (7553) (2015) 436–444.

[2] G.E. Hinton, S. Osindero, Y.W. Teh, A fast learning algorithm for deep belief nets, Neural Comput. 18 (7) (2006) 1527–1554.

[3] G.E. Hinton, Training products of experts by minimizing contrastive divergence, Training 14 (8) (2006).

[4] D. Erhan, Y. Bengio, A. Courville, P.A. Manzagol, P. Vincent, S. Bengio, Why does unsupervised pre-training help deep learning? J. Mach. Learn. Res. 11 (Feb) (2010) 625–660.

[5] A. Krizhevsky, I. Sutskever, G.E. Hinton, Image-net classification with deep convolutional neural networks, in: Advances in Neural Information Processing Systems, 2012, pp. 1097–s.

[6] V. Nair, G.E. Hinton, Rectified linear units improve restricted Boltzmann machines, in: Proceedings of the 27th international conference on machine learning (ICML-10), 2010, pp. 807–814.

[7] M.D. Zeiler, M. Ranzato, R. Monga, M. Mao, K. Yang, Q.V. Le, P. Nguyen, A. Senior, V. Vanhoucke, J. Dean, et al., On rectified linear units for speech processing, in: 2013 IEEE International Conference on Acoustics, Speech and Signal Processing (ICASSP), IEEE, 2013, pp. 3517–3521.

[8] P.L. Nunez, R. Srinivasan, Electric Fields of the Brain: The Neurophysics of EEG, Oxford University Press, USA, 2006.

[9] S. Vaid, P. Singh, C. Kaur, EEG signal analysis for BCI interface: a review, in: 2015 Fifth International Conference on Advanced Computing Communication Technologies (ACCT), IEEE, 2015, pp. 143–147.

[10] G.R. Philips, J.J. Daly, J.C. Principe, Topographical measures of functional connectivity as biomarkers for post-stroke motor recovery, J. Neuroeng. Rehabil. 14 (1) (2017) 67.

[11] W.O. Tatum IV, Handbook of EEG Interpretation, Demos Medical Publishing, 2014.

[12] C.S. Herrmann, M. Grigutsch, N.A. Busch, EEG oscillations and wavelet analysis, in: T.C. Handy (Ed.), Event-Related Potentials: A Methods Handbook, MIT Press, 2005, pp. 229–259.

[13] F. Vecchio, C. Babiloni, R. Lizio, F.V. Fallani, K. Blinowska, G. Verrienti, G. Frisoni, P.M. Rossini, Resting state cortical EEG rhythms in Alzheimer's disease: toward EEG markers for clinical applications: a review, Suppl. Clin. Neurophysiol. 62 (2013) 223–236.

[14] J. Dauwels, S. Kannan, Diagnosis of Alzheimer's disease using electric signals of the brain. A grand challenge, Asia-Pac. Biotech News 16 (10n11) (2012) 22–38.

[15] J. Dauwels, K. Srinivasan, M. Ramasubba Reddy, T. Musha, F.B. Vialatte, C. Latchoumane, et al., Slowing and loss of complexity in Alzheimer's EEG: two sides of the same coin? Int. J. Alzheimer's Dis. 2011 (2011).

[16] F. Hatz, M. Hardmeier, N. Benz, M. Ehrensperger, U. Gschwandtner, S. Ruegg, C. Schindler, A.U. Monsch, P. Fuhr, Microstate connectivity alterations in patients with early Alzheimer's disease, Alzheimers Res. Ther. 7 (1) (2015) 78.

[17] J. Jeong, EEG dynamics in patients with Alzheimer's disease, Clin. Neurophysiol. 115 (7) (2004) 1490–1505.

[18] P. Parchi, A. Giese, S. Capellari, P. Brown, W. Schulz-Schaeffer, O. Windl, I. Zerr, H. Budka, N. Kopp, P. Piccardo, et al., Classification of sporadic Creutzfeldt-Jakob disease based on molecular and phenotypic analysis of 300 subjects, Ann. Neurol. 46 (2) (1999) 224–233.

[19] H.G. Wieser, K. Schindler, D. Zumsteg, EEG in Creutzfeldt–Jakob disease, Clin. Neurophysiol. 117 (5) (2006) 935–951.

[20] U. Aguglia, A. Gambardella, E. Le Piane, D. Messina, G. Farnarier, R. Oliveri, M. Zappia, A. Quattrone, Disappearance of periodic sharp wave complexes in Creutzfeldt-Jakob disease, Clin. Neurophys. 27 (4) (1997) 277–282.

[21] S. Gasparini, E. Ferlazzo, D. Branca, A. Labate, V. Cianci, M.A. Latella, U. Aguglia, Teaching neuroimages: pseudohypertrophic cerebral cortex in end-stage Creutzfeldt-Jakob Disease, Neurology 80 (2) (2013) e21.

[22] J. Malmivuo, R. Plonsey, Bioelectromagnetism: Principles and Applications of Bioelectric and Biomagnetic Fields, Oxford University Press, USA, 1995.

[23] O.R. Ryynanen, J.A. Hyttinen, P.H. Laarne, J.A. Malmivuo, Effect of electrode density and measurement noise on the spatial resolution of cortical potential distribution, IEEE Trans. Biomed. Eng. 51 (9) (2004) 1547–1554.

[24] O.R. Ryynanen, J.A. Hyttinen, J.A. Malmivuo, Effect of measurement noise and electrode density on the spatial resolution of cortical potential distribution with different resistivity values for the skull, IEEE Trans. Biomed. Eng. 53 (9) (2006) 1851–1858.

[25] R. Srinivasan, D.M. Tucker, M. Murias, Estimating the spatial Nyquist of the human EEG, Behav. Res. Methods 30 (1) (1998) 8–19.

[26] A. Delorme, S. Makeig, EEGLab: an open source toolbox for analysis of single-trial EEG dynamics including independent component analysis, J. Neurosci. Methods 134 (1) (2004) 9–21.

[27] V. Brodbeck, L. Spinelli, A.M. Lascano, M. Wissmeier, M.I. Vargas, S. Vulliemoz, C. Pollo, K. Schaller, C.-M. Michel, M. Seeck, Electroencephalographic source imaging: a prospective study of 152 operated epileptic patients, Brain 134 (10) (2011) 2887–2897.

[28] P. Mégevand, L. Spinelli, M. Genetti, V. Brodbeck, S. Momjian, K. Schaller, C.M. Michel, S. Vulliemoz, M. Seeck, Electric source imaging of interictal activity accurately localises the seizure onset zone, J. Neurol. Neurosurg. Psychiatry 85 (1) (2014) 38–43.

[29] S.F. Storti, I.B. Galazzo, A. Del Felice, F.B. Pizzini, C. Arcaro, E. Formaggio, R. Mai, P. Manganotti, Combining ESI, ASL and PET for quantitative assessment of drug-resistant focal epilepsy, NeuroImage 102 (2014) 49–59.

[30] F.C. Morabito, M. Campolo, N. Mammone, M. Versaci, S. Franceschetti, F. Tagliavini, et al., Deep learning representation from electroencephalography of early-stage Creutzfeldt-Jakob disease and features for differentiation from rapidly progressive dementia, Int. J. Neural Syst. 27 (02) (2017) 1650039.

[31] A. Zahra, N. Kanwal, N. Rehman, S. Ehsan, M.D.-M. KD, Seizure detection from EEG signals using multivariate empirical mode decomposition, Comput. Biol. Med. 88 (2017) 132–141.

[32] F.C. Morabito, M. Campolo, C. Ieracitano, J.M. Ebadi, L. Bonanno, A. Bramanti, S. De Salvo, N. Mammone, P. Bramanti, Deep convolutional neural networks for classification of mild cognitive impaired and Alzheimer's disease patients from scalp EEG recordings, in: Research and Technologies for Society and Industry Leveraging a better tomorrow (RTSI), 2016 IEEE 2nd International Forum on, IEEE, 2016, pp. 1–6.

[33] Y. Zhao, L. He, Deep learning in the EEG diagnosis of Alzheimer's disease, in: Asian Conference on Computer Vision, Springer, 2014, pp. 340–353.

[34] D. Wulsin, J. Gupta, R. Mani, J. Blanco, B. Litt, Modeling electroencephalography waveforms with semi-supervised deep belief nets: fast classification and anomaly measurement, J. Neural Eng. 8 (3) (2011) 036015.

[35] P. Mirowski, D. Madhavan, Y. LeCun, R. Kuzniecky, Classification of patterns of EEG synchronization for seizure prediction, Clin. Neurophysiol. 120 (11) (2009) 1927–1940.

[36] J. Turner, A. Page, T. Mohsenin, T. Oates, Deep belief networks used on high-resolution multichannel electroencephalography data for seizure detection, in: 2014 AAAI Spring Symposium Series, 2014.

[37] R. Manor, A.B. Geva, Convolutional neural network for multi-category rapid serial visual presentation BCI, Front. Comput. Neurosci. 9 (2015).

[38] H. Cecotti, A. Graeser, Convolutional neural network with embedded Fourier transform for EEG classification, in: 19th International Conference on Pattern Recognition, ICPR 2008, IEEE, 2008, pp. 1–4.

[39] H. Cecotti, A. Graser, Convolutional neural networks for P300 detection with application to brain-computer interfaces, IEEE Trans. Pattern Anal. Mach. Intell. 33 (3) (2011) 433–445.

[40] R. Schwartz-Ziv, N. Tishby, Opening the Black-Box of Deep Neural Networks via Information, arXiv:1703.00810v3, 2017.

[41] Y. Liu, J. Chen, L. Deng, Unsupervised sequence classification using sequential output statistics, in: Proc. NIPS, 2017.

[42] I. Goodfellow, Y. Bengio, A. Courville, Deep Learning, MIT Press, Cambridge, MA, 2016.

[43] A. Holzinger, B. Malle, A. Saranti, B. Pfeifer, Towards multi-modal causability with Graph Neural Networks enabling information fusion for explainable AI, Inform. Fusion 71 (2021) 28–37.

[44] M.D. Zeiler, R. Fergus, Visualizing and understanding convolutional networks, in: European Conference on Computer Vision, Springer, Cham, 2014, pp. 818–833.

[45] R.R. Selvaraju, M. Cogswell, A. Das, R. Vedantam, D. Parikh, D. Batra, Grad-cam: Visual explanations from deep networks via gradient-based localization, in: Proceedings of the IEEE International Conference on Computer Vision, 2017, pp. 618–626.

[46] C. Ieracitano, N. Mammone, A. Hussain, F.C. Morabito, A novel explainable machine learning approach for EEG-based brain-computer interface systems, Neural Comput. & Applic. (2021) 1–14.

[47] F.C. Morabito, C. Ieracitano, N. Mammone, An explainable Artificial Intelligence approach to study MCI to AD conversion via HD-EEG processing, Clin. EEG Neurosci. (2021). 15500594211063662.

[48] G.E. Hinton, N. Srivastava, A. Krizhevsky, I. Sutskever, Salakhutdinov, Improving Neural Networks by Preventing Co-adaption of Feature Detectors, 2012. arXiv:1207.0580v1.

[49] Y. Furusho, T. Kubo, K. Ikeda, Roles of pre-training in deep neural networks from information theoretical perspective, Neurocomputing (2017) 76–79.

[50] D. Labate, F. La Foresta, I. Palamara, G. Morabito, Bramanti, Z. Zhang, F.C. Morabito, EEG complexity modifications and altered compressibility in mild cognitive impairment and Alzheimer's disease, in: Proceedings of the 23rd Italian Workshop on Neural Networks (WIRN 2013), 2013.

13

Computational intelligence in cyber-physical systems and the Internet of Things

Cesare Alippi[a,b] and Seiichi Ozawa[c]

[a]POLITECNICO DI MILANO, MILAN, ITALY [b]UNIVERSITÀ DELLA SVIZZERA ITALIANA, LUGANO, SWITZERLAND [c]KOBE UNIVERSITY, KOBE, JAPAN

Chapter outlines

1 Introduction

Advances in embedded systems and communication technologies and the availability of low-cost sensors have paved the way to a pervasive presence of distributed applications in our everyday lives as well as in diversified segments of the market. In this direction, Cyber-Physical Systems (CPS), i.e., hardware/software systems interacting with the physical world are providing the technological framework to support such epochal shift in the human-machine interaction.

Artificial Intelligence in the Age of Neural Networks and Brain Computing. https://doi.org/10.1016/B978-0-323-96104-2.00001-4
Copyright © 2024 Elsevier Inc. All rights reserved.

A cyber-physical system is typically composed of a network of heterogeneous units strongly interacting with the physical environment they are deployed in. In CPS, individual units interact with the physical world, creating the basis for "smart solutions" which revolutionize scenarios from health to industry, from workplace to home, and from transportation to entertainment, ultimately leading to an enhanced quality of life. Designing such systems means actively participating in a new "digital revolution" that enables augmented interaction with the real world.

Cyber-physical systems are present at home, and at work, and provide the core technologies to design smart homes, buildings, and cities, enable the Internet of Things (IoT), support smart energy production, environmental protection, precise agriculture, management, and metering, facilitate smart transportation and healthcare just to provide a very concise list. The expected evolution of the field, as also perceived by the industry [1,2], will focus on the integration of hardware and software technologies to support application reconfiguration, enable autonomous operations, make native the access to the Internet, and extend the usage and operational models by introducing intelligent resources and application management mechanisms.

We all agree that addressing fundamental architectural, technological, and standards challenges, e.g., the energy consumption of the transistor, the communication level, and the IPV(6) protocol, will improve the units' efficiency and networking ability [3]. However, fundamental advances in highly performing hardware per se will not be enough to drastically change the way embedded applications impact our lives. In fact, we should also design methodologies that, by adaptively optimizing the use of existing embedded resources, provide the application with intelligent functionalities granting *adaptation abilities* to environmental changes, adaptive *fault detection and mitigation facilities*, and sophisticated adaptive *energy-aware modalities* to prolong the system lifetime [4]. Intelligence is also needed to prevent attacks from malicious software (malware) designed to steal sensitive information from users, take control of systems, impair or even disable the functionalities of the attacked devices, extort money from users, and so on. Recently, malware Mirai was shown to be able to take control of IoT devices and carry out a major cyber-attack [5]; this represents a vulnerability issue that has to be promptly addressed.

Current research addresses intelligent aspects mostly as independent research lines either without any functionality harmonization effort or with little emphasis on how to integrate the different—challenging—facets of these fields within a solid framework. Moreover, not rarely, strong assumptions are made to make derivations amenable at the cost of a high loss in performance, efficiency—and sometimes credibility—whenever real-world applications are taken into account. In particular, we assume *infinite energy availability,* in the sense that energy and power consumption is not an issue, *stationarity/time invariance,* implying that the process generating sensor data (the physical world and the interaction with the sensor transducer) is not evolving with time, *correct data availability* claiming that acquired data are complete and correct, and *secure* operations assuming that cyber-attacks are not carried out. By relaxing the above assumptions, we enter a new realm requesting the presence of intelligence in all computational architectures; these aspects are addressed in subsequent sections.

2 System architecture

The physical ICT architecture we consider here reflects those considered for CPS and IoT [6]. As such, it is a very variegated one composed, in its most general form, of heterogeneous hardware and software platforms. Endpoint units of the (Internet) connection communicate with servers (possibly also acting as gateways) in a star, field bus, or general topology depending on the particular application at hand. Computational complexity and hardware resources (e.g., memory capacity, energy availability) are application-specific, with units that, not rarely, are operating system-free. In other cases, units possess a simple operating system (e.g., RTOS), a more complex one (e.g., Android), or an operating system specifically developed for limited-resource devices, such as Contiki [7], ARMmbeb [8], or again, specifically targeted to IoT such as the Google Android Things [9].

An end unit can mount application-specific sensors and/or actuators, with the interesting case where humans can act both as sensors and actuators. Fog and cloud computing processing architectures can be elements of the overall architecture: the final architectural decision depends on the expected and the maximum response time tolerated by the application.

Where intelligence should be located in the architecture? This complex question receives a very simple answer: it depends on the energy availability and the computational and hardware/software resources needed by the application and the intelligent functionalities to carry out their tasks. Once intelligent functionalities are taken into account, we should consider hierarchical processing solutions with intelligence—for a given functionality—distributed along the processing architecture. Within this framework, low-performing end units provide (very) simple functionalities but lack a comprehensive, global view of the problem. As such, we should expect decisions taken hierarchically, with the effectiveness of the decision increasing with the availability of a larger set of data/features and the possibility to execute a more complex algorithm. In fact, more processing-demanding algorithms can be run, e.g., to identify a better solution to a specific problem, in systems where larger computational power/energy is available. Result outcomes from the processing stage are then sent back downward the communication chain to reach end units.

3 Energy harvesting and management

In cyber-physical systems where energy availability is an issue, an accurate and sound management of energy in addition to energy harvesting represents a major necessity. Due to its relevance, the aspect has been widely addressed in the related literature [4] that, however, leaves major investigation areas open.

The key point of harvesting is to maximize energy acquisition that, scavenged from an available source of power, is stored either in an energy accumulator (e.g., a battery or a super-capacitor) or directly consumed by the electronic system. Likewise, the major goal of energy management is to intelligently control energy consumption by acting at the hardware and software levels, with the most sophisticated decision strategies based both on available and forecasted energy availability. Machine learning and, more in general, computational intelligence techniques, are suitable methods to be considered here since physical descriptions of the harvestable energy are unavailable due to time variance of the environment, and accurate information about the current power consumption is available through measurements only.

3.1 Energy harvesting

In CPSs, energy can be harvested by relying on different technologies, e.g., from photovoltaic or Peltier cells to wind and flow turbines, and again, by relying on piezoelectric solutions. The optimal solution for a generic CPS application depends on the available—and harvestable—energy, no matter whether the available power is high or not. "We get what we have, and that has to be enough," says an old leitmotif. However, of particular relevance for the high-density power harvestable are solutions coming from small photovoltaic cells. They can be both deployed outdoors and indoors, with polymer flexible cells that, though less performing compared to the crystalline or amorphous counterparts, are foldable and assume any shape to fit with the available surface. This flexibility makes these harvesting solutions appealing to IoT since the cell can be designed to be deployed directly on the target object. Photovoltaic cells—but the same can be stated for wind and flow turbines—can greatly take advantage of intelligent solutions in the sense that we can maximize the acquired power through adaptation mechanisms. Adaptation is needed every time the energy source, here the light, provides a power density that evolves with time, e.g., due to the presence of clouds, dust, or water drops on the cell surface as well as due to varying incidence angles. Defined vp to be the controllable voltage imposed at the photovoltaic cell, the harvestable power depends, e.g., on the particular effective solar radiation as per Fig. 1A, where curve A is associated with a stronger power availability compared with case B. vp can be controlled over time using a Control Power Transfer Module (refer to Fig. 1B) that grants the harvester to maximize the extracted power to be sent to the storage mean. Details can be found in [4]. Adaptation can be seen as an online learning procedure where the optimal controlling parameters at time $k+1$ can be achieved through a gradient ascent algorithm as

$$v_{\mathrm{p}}(k+1) = v_{\mathrm{p}}(k) + \gamma \frac{\mathrm{d}(i_{\mathrm{p}} v_{\mathrm{p}})}{\mathrm{d}v_{\mathrm{p}}} = v_{\mathrm{p}}(k) + \gamma \left(i_{\mathrm{p}} + v_{\mathrm{p}} \frac{\mathrm{d}(i_{\mathrm{p}})}{\mathrm{d}v_{\mathrm{p}}} \right), \tag{1}$$

where γ is a small constant accounting for the step taken along the gradient descent direction. Such a solution requires the acquisition of the current ip and $\mathrm{v_p}$ over time through suitable sensors.

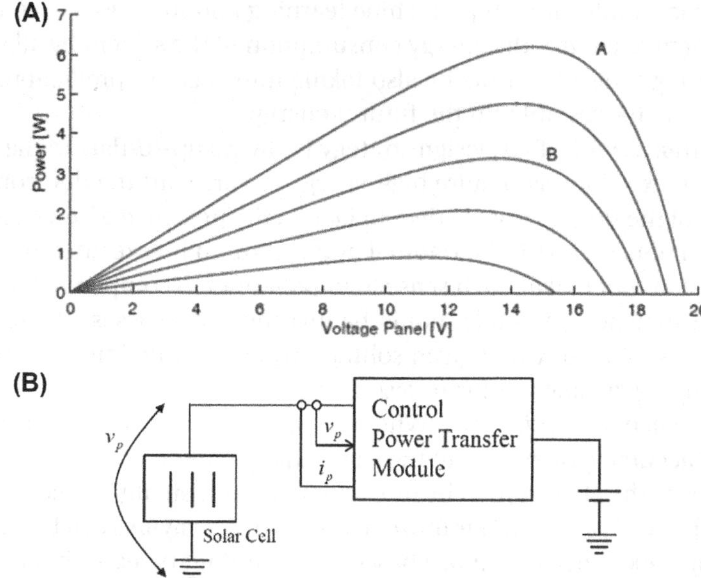

FIG. 1 (A) The characteristic curves for a photovoltaic cell: the acquired power depends on the applied controlling voltage v_p. (B) The Control Power Transfer Module identifies the optimal voltage according to (1) and applies it to the cell; other architectures can be considered, e.g., see [4].

3.2 Energy management and research challenges

Energy management is a very important issue in any cyber-physical and IoT system given the fact units are mostly battery-powered and need to be kept as simple as possible to reduce their cost.

Energy management can be carried out both at the hardware and software/application levels by leveraging on the following:

- *Voltage/frequency scaling.* By scaling power voltage and clock frequency, the power consumption of the device reduces. In fact, for CMOS technology, the power consumption scales quadratically with the voltage and linearly with the working frequency [4]. Machine learning and fuzzy logic techniques can be adopted, e.g., to profile the application at compile time and identify both at compile and run time when and how the control variables should be scaled. Evolutionary computation algorithms can also be considered at compile time to identify the optimal set of controlling parameters over execution time.
- *Adaptive sampling.* A great energy saving can be achieved by implementing an adaptive sampling strategy where the sampling frequency is adapted according to the current needs of the application. By reducing the sampling frequency—sometimes below the value granting signal reconstruction—we can also reduce the bandwidth

needed for communication [10]. Machine learning and fuzzy logic can be fruitfully considered here to control the energy consumption of the system by adaptively acting on the sampling rates of sensors by also taking into account predictions for both the residual and the harvestable (in the future) energy.

- *Keep the solution simple.* This design strategy is always up-to-date in the sense that, in general, complex solutions require high energy to carry out the due computation, which, most of the time, is not needed. In fact, in the presence of uncertainty affecting the measurements and with the optimal application to be executed on the CPS unknown, it does not make much sense to implement too complex solutions. Machine learning and statistical methods should be investigated to assess the loss in performance associated with a given solution by also taking into account existing uncertainty and available hardware resources.
- *Consider incremental applications.* Whenever performance accuracy is an issue, we can tradeoff accuracy for energy, in the sense that if a higher accuracy level is needed, then we tolerate the algorithm to be more complex and energy-eager. Identification of the tradeoff between accuracy performance and energy savings can be carried out with optimization algorithms, e.g., those based on evolutionary algorithms.
- *Duty cycling.* The more you sleep (i.e., the device enters low and deep power sleep modalities), the less energy you consume. By implementing duty cycling at the processor, sensor, and memory levels, we can significantly control energy consumption. Identification of timing to switch on and off different hardware elements as well as selection of the optimal sleep modality represents an application-dependent complex optimization problem whose optimal solution can be found at compile time with both machine learning and evolutionary computation algorithms.

4 Learning in nonstationary environments

In designing cyber-physical and IoT applications, we mostly assume that the process generating the sensor datastream is either stationary (i.e., data or features extracted from the signal are independent and identically distributed (i.i.d.) random variables) or time-invariant (the signal does not show an *explicit* dependency on time) [11]. However, such assumptions are hardly met in real applications and represent, in the best case, a first-order approximation of reality. In fact, sensors and actuators are naturally subject to aging and the environment evolves per se, e.g., think of seasonality, day-night cycles, or unpredictable effects affecting a plant. This problem is rarely addressed in existing CPS or IoT applications mostly due to the intrinsic difficulties and challenges that learning in nonstationary environments pose. In extreme cases where the changing intensity impairs the performance of the system, the designer implements strategies permitting the application to be remotely updated. However, adaptation to the change in stationarity should be anticipated and managed as early as possible to meet the expected quality of service.

In the literature, the difficult problem of detecting time-variance is generally transformed into the detection of changes in stationarity, through suitable transformations, with only a few studies addressing time-variance directly at the acquired datastreams level. As such, in the sequel, we focus on the change in the stationary problem.

The current literature about learning in nonstationary environments either proposes passive strategies, with the application undergoing a continuous adaptation (passive adaptation modality or passive learning), e.g., see [11,12], or active ones, with adaptation activated only once a trigger detects a change (active adaptation modality or active learning) [11,13].

Let us assume that the embedded application can be controlled through a vector of parameters θ so that the application code is described using the differentiable family function $f(x,\theta)$, x representing the input vector, e.g., containing sensors data. At time t, the vector of parameters θ_t, is associated with algorithm $f(x,\theta_t)$. The notation becomes easier to follow if we imagine that function $f(x,\theta_t)$ is a linear filter or a neural function. Differentiability is a convenient assumption to ease the presentation here but it is not strictly requested. In fact, we just require the application to be updated in response to a need.

Every time we are provided with output y_t (measurement) in correspondence with input x, the discrepancy $L(y_t, f(x,\theta_t))$ can be used to update the application. $L(. \, , .)$ is any appropriate figure of merit used to assess such discrepancy, e.g., a mean square, a Kullback-Leibler distance, etc. Passive and active approaches differentiate in the way the application update is carried out. The following paragraphs explain more in detail.

4.1 Passive adaptation modality

In passive solutions, the parameters describing the application are always updated following a compulsive update modality. The classic example is that of linear filters which update online the filter parameters based on the value of the discrepancy $(y_t, f(x,\theta_t))$, mostly based on a least square loss function. More in general, the updated parameters are

$$\theta_{t+1} = \theta_t - \gamma \left.\frac{\partial L(x,\theta)}{\partial \theta}\right|_{\theta_t}, \tag{2}$$

where γ is a small and application-dependent scalar value controlling the step taken along the gradient descent direction.

Passive solutions do not suffer from false positives and negatives in detecting a change in stationarity/time variance, since the learning-based system/application continuously updates parameters over time by integrating the available novelty content into the model. From this perspective, the partial derivative in (2) can be intended as the operator extracting the novelty information content from current data: if there is a novelty, the model needs to be updated. As a consequence, passive models are rather sensitive to noise in incoming data: after parameter convergence, the application continues to update the parameters to track the particular noise realization. A vast literature on passive approaches exists (also called online learning in the neural networks field) and the interested reader can focus on and implement those results in her/his CPS/IoT application [4,11,14]. However, the computational complexity of a passive approach might be inappropriate for embedded applications given the continuous need to update the model, operations which might end up in a prohibitive energy consumption and processing time whenever the update phase is energy/computation eager. Ensemble solutions and complex neural networks are examples in this direction where the cost we have to pay for high accuracy and flexibility is computational.

4.2 Active adaptation modality

In the active adaptation strategy, the presence of a change-detection trigger activates the due application reaction following the detected change in stationarity, e.g., by updating the learning-based system. This means that the application running on the embedded device undergoes an update/reconfiguration phase to track the change in stationarity only when triggered by the change detection module. The change detection module—or Oracle—operates by inspecting features φ extracted from the input data or preprocessed variables [4,13] to assess the presence of a change. In other terms, the Oracle ω acts as the indicator function

$$\omega(\varphi) = \begin{cases} 1, \text{if change in stationarity is detected} \\ 0, \text{otherwise} \end{cases}$$

and the update equation becomes

$$\theta_{t+1} = \theta_t - \gamma\omega(\varphi)\left.\frac{\partial L(x,\theta)}{\partial\theta}\right|_{\theta_t} \tag{3}$$

In its basic form, the Oracle is based on a threshold; in more sophisticated versions, the Oracle also relies on a confidence level—e.g., as it happens in statistical tests—or, it even, takes control of the occurrence of false positives by setting its expectation to a predefined value.

Adaptive strategies at cyber-physical systems following the active adaptation modality are known as "detect & react" approaches; such solutions have much focused on classifiers in the related literature, though results are more general [4].

It should be commented that if the computational load of passive solutions is negligible, they should be preferred over active ones unless the application is interested in knowing that a change in stationarity occurred (the change in stationarity might be associated with a faulty sensor for instance, as investigated in the next section). If the computational complexity of the update phase is not negligible, also in a relationship with the dynamics of the change, we might prefer active solutions. However, active approaches suffer from false alarms (false positives) introduced by the change-detection triggering mechanism hence inducing the application to update even though not strictly needed. Fortunately, in CPS applications, false positives do not negatively affect performance but only introduce an extra, not requested, computation.

One should expect that if the physical environment is changing with a low frequency, then an active approach might be more appropriate than a passive one. However, again, one should balance the application update phase with its computational complexity and the level of time-variance exposed by the environment the system interacts with. This problem becomes even more relevant and up-to-date in CPSs, IoT, and Smart-X technologies, producing high-dimensional datastreams where it is expected the computational load is high. Since active and passive solutions represent extreme strategies, current solutions are investigating hybrid approaches aiming at taking major advantage of them.

4.3 Research challenges

Several research challenges should be addressed to support a quick and effective design of cyber-physical and IoT technologies. Some of them encompass:

- *Design methodologies.* Neither investigations nor methodologies are available to shed light on the relationships among the effectiveness of active/passive approaches w.r.t. the speed/nature of the change and the computational complexity of involved methods. Such investigations are fundamental to permit embedded applications to detect possible changes in the environment and react accordingly to keep the quality of service at the appropriate level.
- *Design of distributed decision-making applications.* There are no computationally light change detection mechanisms for distributed embedded systems able to control the false positive rates. The challenge here is to provide distributed—possibly autonomous—decision-making strategies, reasonably based on machine learning methods.
- *Approximate computing.* What is largely needed are strategies permitting the harmonization of the learning in nonstationarity environment functionality for distributed embedded systems, possibly within an approximate computing framework. In this case, the approximation level introduced by the hardware as well as that introduced by the adoption of incremental software should be traded-off with accuracy performance as coming from active or passive learning strategies. It is expected that the optimization problem identifying the most suitable level of approximation over time can be carried out with evolutionary computation algorithms.
- *Addressing subtle changes.* Design of learning-based methodologies to detect and anticipate subtle drift changes is needed, e.g., to deal with aging at the sensor and actuators level. In fact, slowly developing changes are hard to detect in the sense their magnitude is small and can be detected by current change detection tests only over a long time period. However, it is expected that availability of datastreams should permit to run machine learning tools to estimate the current behavior of the features and build predictive models to assess the level of time variance.

5 Model-free fault diagnosis systems

Cyber-physical applications are mostly data-eager, in the sense that application decisions and behaviors are strongly driven by the information content extracted from a generally large platform of sensors. This dependency on sensor data can be however very critical, since sensors and real apparatus are prone to faults and malfunctioning that, in turn, negatively affect the information content carried by data and used by the application to make decisions [15,16]. The problem amplifies when low-cost sensors are considered and/or sensors are deployed in harsh and challenging environments (e.g., think of a body network where sensors, external buses, and connectors are subject to mechanical stress and environmental challenges). As such, faulty sensors detection (also including sensors working in suboptimal conditions) and mitigation are intelligent functionalities that must be included in the design of any CPS to prevent the propagation of erroneous information to the decisional level [17]. At the same time, we comment that a generic method designed to detect a fault occurrence will also detect any deviation in the information carried by data, e.g., caused by changes in the environment the sensor is deployed in (time variance), and react erroneously: a novel family of methods is hence requested to detect changes in the information content carried by data, disambiguate between faults and violation of the time-invariant hypothesis as well as identify, isolate, and possibly mitigate the occurrence of faults (Fig. 2). These tasks are carried out by Fault Diagnosis Systems (FDSs).

5.1 Model-free fault diagnosis systems

Since CPSs rely on a rich and diversified set of sensors produced by a plethora of companies, it is not possible to request an accurate physical model describing their modus operandi. In this direction, model-free Fault Diagnosis Systems are requested to detect, identify, and isolate the occurrence of faults without assuming that their signatures, the nature of uncertainty, and their ruling equations are available.

Research on standard (not model-free) FDSs has provided major breakthroughs in past decades by yielding several methodologies for detecting and diagnosing faults in several real-world applications, e.g., see [17,18]. However, the effectiveness of a traditional FDS is directly proportional to the available information and priors about the given system, in the sense that availability of (1) the equations ruling the interaction between the cyber system and the physical phenomenon, (2) information about the inputs and the system noise,

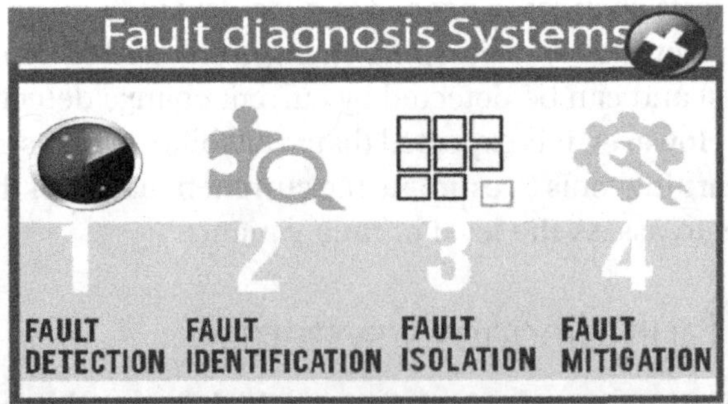

FIG. 2 A full fault diagnosis system is characterized by four phases: fault detection aiming at identifying the presence of a fault; fault identification characterizing the type and nature of the fault; fault isolation, localizing the fault; and fault mitigation, whose goal is to reduce the impact of the fault on the system.

and (3) the "fault dictionary" containing the characterizations of feasible faults, permits the FDS to operate in optimal conditions. Even though some information might become available in some very specific applications, in general, it is hardly usable in cyber-physical applications since the characterization of the CPS interaction, the nature of existing noise and uncertainty, and the signature of expected faults are missing. Moreover, we cannot spend huge efforts in designing an FDS for any CPS-based application if the requested procedure is too complex and articulated since costs and time-to-market are fundamental requirements in designing successful applications. Instead, we would appreciate a methodology able to automatically learn the FDS directly from the data the application receives (computational intelligence-based model-free approach: no available model for the system under investigation, no fault dictionary or fault signatures, no information about the nature of uncertainty). In other terms, all unknown needed entities are learned from available data through computational intelligence and machine learning techniques.

The particular computational intelligence technique depends on the information available to solve a specific subproblem. For instance, we can use machine learning and fuzzy systems to detect faults; the same technologies can be used to design a fault dictionary and identify the type of fault through a classifier or its magnitude through inference. Fault localization can take advantage of a statistical/probabilistic or fuzzy logic framework whereas mitigation can be based on machine learning and fuzzy systems.

Existing model-free FDSs automatically learn the nominal and the faulty states from sensor datastreams and take advantage of existing temporal and spatial relationships among sensors to detect a possible occurrence of faults. The learned relationships are then used to characterize the system's nominal state as well as detect any deviation from such a nominal behavior, diagnose the causes of the deviation, identify the nature of the faults, isolate faulty sensors, and—possibly—mitigate their effects. It must be pointed out that most existing solutions either apply the learning mechanism only to a particular aspect of the FDSs (e.g., the fault dictionary) or solve specific applications: very few—preliminary—model-free methodologies have been proposed in the literature, e.g., see [19]. Such solutions aim at characterizing the relationships present in the acquired datastreams to autonomously learn the nominal state and construct, whenever possible, the fault dictionary during the operational life of the system for fault detection, isolation, and identification purposes.

However, despite these encouraging results, major investigations must be accomplished to reach the maturity level needed to support an automatic design of a model-free FDS for networked cyber-physical applications that is automatic, effective, control false positives/negatives, and is computationally light.

5.2 Research challenges

To support the next generation of any cyber-physical application, we need to address some open research issues

- *Multiple faults.* The "single fault" assumption has to be relaxed to host multiple "concurrent" faults, possibly also of transient type, as is the case in cyber-physical/human applications. In fact, once a fault occurs, a domino effect will likely arise, and a subset of sensors affected. Graph-based machine learning techniques are expected to be the right tools to address this research topic.
- *Disambiguation module.* Once a change in stationarity is detected, we need to run powerful methods able to disambiguate among changes in the environment, faults, and false positives introduced by the change detection method. Given the nature of the problem and the type of information available, it is expected that machine learning and fuzzy tools should be the appropriate techniques to be applied here.
- *Unbalanced data.* Faults are rare events; as such, it is hard to have much data coming from the "faulty class." This implies that we need to provide machine learning methodologies to design effective FDSs starting from few and unbalanced data.
- *Modeling aspect.* We need to provide novel design methodologies for model-free FDSs. Such methodologies should be able to automatically configure the FDS for the given application after having profiled sensor data. It is expected that machine learning techniques should be the right tools to be used here to design such a system.

6 Cyber-security

As mentioned in the previous sections, CPS and IoT technologies will make our life easier and richer in opportunities. However, at the same time, such technologies are prone to cyber-attacks designed to steal precious information and harm people, companies, and governments. In late September 2016, botnets infected by the infamous IoT malware Mirai [5] caused a severe Distributed Denial of Service Attack (*DDoS*) that prevented major sites from correctly providing services to clients.

Cyber-attacks using IoT devices are expected to steadily increase by taking advantage of network scalability and vulnerability of IoT devices, an aspect that is far from being fixed. Moreover, malware Mirai that was originally designed to infect Linux-based IoT devices is still evolving, with its offspring targeting Windows computers and possibly, in the future, also Android smartphones.

Cyber-attacks on CPS are of deeper concern once applications target our daily life. Consider, for instance, an elderly care smart home with a solo senior person whose behavior is continuously monitored for safety purposes. The monitoring system consists of some surveillance cameras and various IoT sensors such as door locks and proximity sensors deployed in rooms and corridors. Once the monitoring system detects an emergency, an alert is issued and sent to caregivers and doctors. Following a malware infection, the system control is completely taken by the attacker who might decide to activate, e.g., a DDoS attack, hence leaving the person's safety issue unattended. Needless to say, CPS designed to protect the person will, in the best case, not work properly. It comes per se that smart cyber-security systems need to be considered to prevent such situations.

6.1 How can CPS and IoT be protected from cyber-attacks?

To effectively protect a given CPS or IoT device from cyber-attacks, we need to consider several cyber-security levels. The first security level should be designed to protect IoT sensor units and the second one has to shield the server where sensor data are processed and control signals issued to be delivered to actuators. Finally, the third level is designed to protect the whole CPS application by monitoring trends of cyber-attack activities on the Internet.

When thinking about the first level of security, we should keep in mind that the number of IoT units could be very large and heterogeneous in hardware and software. Here, given the constrained hardware resources, it is mostly unrealistic to implement a complex form of security such as installing antivirus software or embedding a network intrusion detection mechanism in hardware. The protection measures depend then on the computational resources of the end device. One solution here would be to utilize an anomaly (fault) detection mechanism as those used in fault diagnosis systems or an Oracle, as discussed in the learning in nonstationary environment sections.

Various software products are available to implement the second level of security. However, there is still plenty of room to design machine learning-based algorithms to identify malwares and detect unknown cyber-attacks using the zero-day vulnerability. Many approaches have been proposed so far in this direction, e.g., see [20,21] for details.

The third security layer is also very important and can be seen at the application level. Usually, the number of new malware victims gradually increases, the infection then rapidly spreads following some triggering events associated with malware evolution (the open source code of the malware is made available) and, finally, we end up in a pandemic situation. Early detection of malware can then mitigate the infection as presented in the next subsection case study.

6.2 Case study: Darknet analysis to capture malicious cyber-attack behaviors

To protect users from cyber threats, it is important to characterize malware behavior, with malware instances caught both within one's local network domain and the Internet as a whole. A classification system can then be designed to monitor the current system behavior to detect cyber-attacks. One way to observe large-scale events taking place on the Internet is to design a network probe inspecting activity in the *darknet*. The darknet is defined as the set of unused address-space of a computer network that should not be used and, as such, not have any normal communication with other computers. Following the definition, it comes out that almost all communication traffic along the darknet is therefore suspicious; by inspecting such traffic, we can grasp information related to cyber-attacks. Observable cyber-attacks are the main activities of random scanning worms and DDoS backscatter messages. However, since the darknet can receive packets from the whole Internet space, by operating in the darknet, we can monitor large-scale malicious activities on the whole Internet.

To grasp the groups of malware-infected hosts with similar scan activities, a source IP address and a destination port number (hereafter referred to as a port) are good information sources, which can be extracted from a TCP/SYN packet obtained by the darknet sensor. Since an individual service is assigned to a unique port, a port observed in darknet packets represents a service targeted by malware. Therefore, a set of such port features is associated with specific vulnerability scan activities by infected hosts. Such a set of ports is called *port-set* and clusters of infected hosts can be obtained based on the similarity among different port-sets.

(23/TCP, 2323/TCP) and (80/TCP, 8080/TCP) are common port pairs among related malware variants, exploiting network services hosted on similar but different ports. The similarity between the ports in these pairs is apparent due to the human convention to maintain some degree of likeness by keeping identifying morphemes, and consecutive digit sequences, in related numbers. Similar malware variants can be grouped by taking advantage of this fact. By applying FastText [22] to the port-sets, embedding vectors taking account of identifying morphemes in port numbers are obtained. This approach is called *Port-Piece Embedding* [23].

Fig. 3 shows the procedure to obtain port-piece embedding vectors. In Port-Piece Embedding, each port-set is taken as a statement in document analysis. First, port vectors, which are created from the original ports, are obtained. Then, each port is divided into *n*-grams (hereafter referred to as port-pieces). Then, port-piece vectors, which are created for the port-pieces contained in a port, are obtained. Then, the port-piece embedding vector is obtained by averaging the port number vectors and the port-piece (subwords) vectors. Then, the vector representation of a port-set is obtained by averaging the two types of port-piece embedding vectors in Fig. 3

To examine how scan activities are clustered, the port-set on February 15, 2020, was labeled as IoT malware *Mirai*. Fig. 4 shows the visualization results for FastText. Outliers refer to points that are neither the core point nor points assigned in clusters in DBSCAN [24]. The visualization using UMAP [25] results show Cluster 1, Cluster 2, and outliers, with

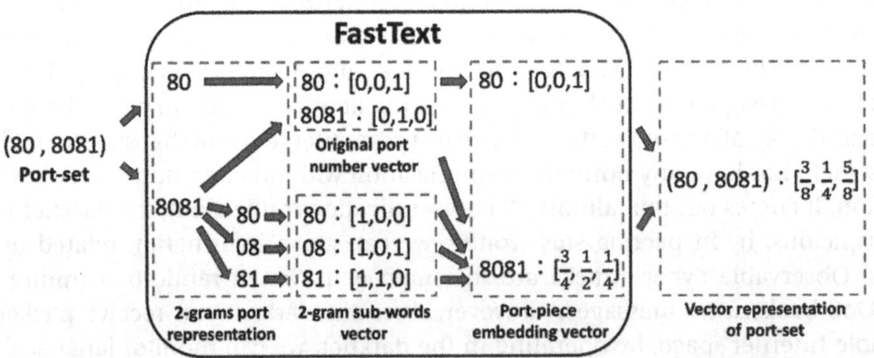

FIG. 3 An example of processing steps to obtain port-piece embedding vectors from a port-set using 2-gram FastText.

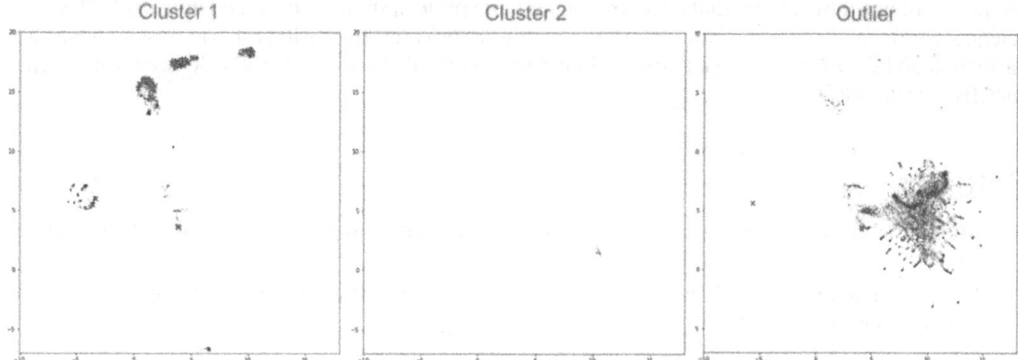

FIG. 4 Visualization of Mirai-featured (×: red (dark gray in print version)) and Mirai-benign (○: blue (gray in print version)) port-sets using FastText.

Mirai-featured port-sets shown in red. The visualization result in Fig. 4 also shows that most Mirai-featured port-sets are contained in Cluster 1. The Mirai-featured port-sets clustered in Cluster 2 contain 7547/TCP that is not included in the port-sets in Cluster 1, indicating the discovery of a major variant. From these results, we conclude that Port-Piece Embedding gives a good representation of IoT malware activities.

7 Conclusions

We are facing unprecedented times where the availability of sensors as well as cheap electronics and effective communication schemes are granting the spread of sensor networks permitting us to acquire huge information in a plethora of application domains. Embedded devices composing the measurement acquisition chain are, not rarely, inserted within an edge-cloud architecture collecting and processing data as well as controlling back sensor devices. Intelligent mechanisms proper of artificial intelligence give an extra axis to the technology, by shifting intelligent measurement and control systems to the next level. Intelligent mechanisms are integrated into the computational architecture and provide high value, notably, the possibility to deal with cyber-attacks, introduce adaptation mechanisms within a time-variant environment, and deal with energy harvesting and power management.

We shall expect more and more embedded intelligence in the next decade, as this is a natural evolution of these systems. Indeed, researchers and practitioners will guide the new path and bring this technology to the next level. Indeed, this is a call to your contributions.

Acknowledgment

The authors thank Dr. Ban Tao (National Institute of Information and Communications Technology) for providing darknet traffic data and their well-experienced expert knowledge of cyber-security. This chapter partially contains the experimental results of the research project, supported by the Ministry of Education, Science, Sports, and Culture, Grant-in-Aid for Scientific Research (B) 16H02874. The research was also partly funded by the International Partnership Program of the Chinese Academy of Sciences under Grant 104GJHZ2022013GC.

References

[1] International Data Corporation (IDC), Final Study Report: Design of Future Embedded Systems, 2012.

[2] D. Evans, The Internet of Things. How the Next Evolution of the Internet is Changing Everything, CISCO White Book, 2011.

[3] P. Marwedel, Embedded Systems Design, Springer, 2011, p. 241.

[4] C. Alippi, Intelligence for Embedded Systems: A Methodological Approach, Springer, Switzerland, 2014, p. 283.

[5] US-CERT, United States Computer Emergency Readiness Team, Alert (TA16-288A) - Heightened DDoS Threat Posed by Mirai and Other Botnets, November 2015. Tech. rep. URL: https://www.us-cert.gov/ncas/alerts/TA16-288A.

[6] C. Alippi, R. Fantacci, D. Marabissi, M. Roveri, A cloud to the ground: the new frontier of intelligent and autonomous networks of things, IEEE Commun. Mag. 54 (12) (2016) 14–20.

[7] Contiki, The Open Source OS for the Internet of Things. http://www.contiki-os.org.

[8] ARM, Introduction to the mbed OS 5 handbook. URL: https://docs.mbed.com/docs/mbed-os-handbook/en/latest.

[9] Google Inc., Android Things. https://developer.android.com/things.

[10] C. Alippi, G. Anastasi, M. Di Francesco, M. Roveri, An adaptive sampling algorithm for effective energy management in wireless sensor networks with energy-hungry sensors, IEEE-Trans. Instrum. Measur. 59 (2) (2010) 335–344.

[11] C. Alippi, R. Polikar, Guest editorial, IEEE Neural Networks and Learning Systems, Special issue on "Learning in nonstationary and evolving environments", Vol. 25, No. 1, pp. 9-11, January 2014.

[12] L.I. Kuncheva, Classifier ensembles for changing environments, in: Proceeding of 5th International Workshop Multiple Classifier Systems, 2004, pp. 1–15.

[13] C. Alippi, G. Boracchi, M. Roveri, Hierarchical change-detection tests, IEEE Trans. Neural Networks Learn. Syst. 28 (2) (2017) 246–258.

[14] J. Gama, I. Žliobaite, A. Bifet, M. Pechenizkiy, and A. Bouchachia, A survey on concept drift adaptation, ACM Comput. Survey, vol. 46, no. 4, pp. 1-44, April 2014.

[15] M. Basseville, I.V. Nikiforov, Detection of Abrupt Changes: Theory and Application, vol. 104, Prentice Hall, Englewood Cliffs, 1993. p. 529.

[16] R. Isermann, Fault-Diagnosis Systems: Introduction from Fault Detection to Fault Tolerance, Springer, 2006.

[17] V. Reppa, M.M. Polycarpou, C.G. Panayiotou, Distributed sensor fault diagnosis for a network of interconnected cyber-physical systems, IEEE Trans. Contr. Network. Syst. 2 (1) (2015) 15–23.

[18] C. Alippi, S. Ntalampiras, M. Roveri, Model-free fault detection and isolation in large-scale cyber-physical systems, in IEEE Trans. Emerg. Top. Comput. Intell., pp. 61-71, February 201.

[19] C.Alippi, M. Roveri, F. Trovo, A self-building and cluster-based cognitive fault diagnosis system for sensor networks, IEEE Trans. Neural Networks Learn. Syst., Vol. 25, No. 6, pp. 1021-1032, June 2014.

[20] R. Sommer, V. Paxson, Outside the closed world: on using machine learning for network intrusion detection, in: Proceedings of the 2010 IEEE Symposium on Security and Privacy, 2010, pp. 305–316.

[21] C. Sinclair, L. Pierce, S. Matzner, An application of machine learning to network intrusion detection, in: Proceedings of 15th Annual Computer Security Applications Conference, 1999, pp. 371–377.

[22] P. Bojanowski, E. Grave, A. Joulin, T. Mikolov, Enriching word vectors with subword information, Trans. Assoc. Comput. Linguist. 5 (2017) 135–146.

[23] S. Ishikawa, S. Ozawa, T. Ban, Port-piece embedding for darknet traffic features and clustering of scan attacks, in: Neural Information Processing, LNCS 12533, 2020, pp. 593–603.

[24] M. Ester, P.H. Kriegel, J. Sander, X. Xu, A density-based algorithm for discovering clusters in large spatial databases with noise, in: KDD '96: Proceedings of the Second International Conference on Knowledge Discovery and Data Mining, 1996, pp. 226–231.

[25] P. Bojanowski, E. Grave, A. Joulin, T. Mikolov, UMAP: Uniform Manifold Approximation and Projection for Dimension Reduction, arXiv: 1802.03426, 2018.

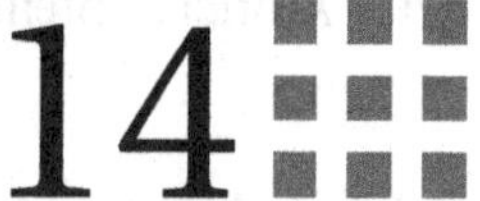

Evolving deep neural networks

Risto Miikkulainen[a,b], Jason Liang[b], Elliot Meyerson[b], Aditya Rawal[c], Dan Fink[b], Olivier Francon[b], Bala Raju[d], Hormoz Shahrzad[b], Arshak Navruzyan[e], Nigel Duffy[f], and Babak Hodjat[b]

[a]DEPARTMENT OF COMPUTER SCIENCE, THE UNIVERSITY OF TEXAS AT AUSTIN, AUSTIN, TX, UNITED STATES [b]COGNIZANT AI LABS, SAN FRANCISCO, CA, UNITED STATES [c]AMAZON AWS AI LABS, SANTA CLARA, CA, UNITED STATES [d]DEIVA AI, PALO ALTO, CA, UNITED STATES [e]LAUNCHPAD, INC., KIHEI, HI, UNITED STATES [f]CYNCH AI, SAN FRANCISCO, CA, UNITED STATES

Chapter outlines

1 Introduction

Large databases (i.e., Big Data) and large amounts of computing power have become readily available since the 2000s. As a result, it has become possible to scale up machine learning systems. Interestingly, not only have these systems been successful in such scale-up, but they have become more powerful. Some ideas that did not quite work before, now do, with million times more compute and data. For instance, deep neural networks

Artificial Intelligence in the Age of Neural Networks and Brain Computing. https://doi.org/10.1016/B978-0-323-96104-2.00002-6

Copyright © 2024 Elsevier Inc. All rights reserved.

(DNNs), that is, convolutional neural networks [1] and recurrent neural networks (in particular, long short-term memory [LSTM] [2]), which have existed since the 1990s, have improved state of the art significantly in computer vision, speech, language processing, and many other areas [3–5].

As DNNs have been scaled up and improved, they have become much more complex. A new challenge has therefore emerged: How to configure such systems? Human engineers can optimize a handful of configuration parameters through experimentation, but DNNs have complex topologies and hundreds of hyperparameters. Moreover, such design choices matter; often success depends on finding the right architecture for the problem. Much of the recent work in deep learning has indeed focused on proposing different hand-designed architectures for new problems [6–11].

The complexity challenge is not unique to neural networks. Software and many other engineered systems have become too complex for humans to optimize fully. As a result, a new way of thinking about such design has started to emerge. In this approach, humans are responsible for the high-level design, and the details are left for computational optimization systems to figure out. For instance, humans write the overall design of a software system, and the parameters and low-level code are optimized automatically [12]; humans write imperfect versions of programs, and evolutionary algorithms are then used to repair them [13]; humans define the space of possible web designs; and evolution is used to find effective ones [14].

This same approach can be applied to the design of DNN architectures. This problem includes three challenges: how to design the components of the architecture, how to put them together into a full network topology, and how to set the hyperparameters for the components and the global design. These three aspects need to be optimized separately for each new task.

This chapter develops an approach for the automatic design of DNNs. It is based on the existing neuroevolution technique of NEAT [15], which has been successful in evolving topologies and weights of relatively small recurrent networks in the past. In this chapter, NEAT is extended to the coevolutionary optimization of components, topologies, and hyperparameters. The fitness of the evolved networks is determined based on how well they can be trained, through gradient descent, to perform the task. The approach is demonstrated in the standard benchmark tasks of object recognition and language modeling, and in a real-world application of captioning images on a magazine website.

The results show that the approach discovers designs that are comparable to the state of the art, and does it automatically without much development effort. The approach is computationally extremely demanding—with more computational power, it is likely to be more effective and possibly surpass human design. Such power is now becoming available in various forms of cloud computing and grid computing, thereby making the evolutionary optimization of neural networks a promising approach for the future.

2 Background and related work

Neuroevolution techniques have been applied successfully to sequential decision tasks for three decades [16–20]. In such tasks, there is no gradient available, so instead of gradient descent, evolution is used to optimize the weights of the neural network. Neuroevolution is a good approach in particular to partially observable Markov decision process (POMDP) problems because of recurrency. It is possible to evolve recurrent connections to allow disambiguating hidden states.

The weights can be optimized using various evolutionary techniques. Genetic algorithms are a natural choice because crossover is a good match with neural networks: they recombine parts of existing neural networks to find better ones. CMA-ES [21], a technique for continuous optimization, works well on optimizing the weights as well because it can capture interactions between them. Other approaches such as SANE, ESP, and CoSyNE evolve partial neural networks and combine them into fully functional networks [22–24]. Further, techniques such as cellular encoding [25] and NEAT [15] have been developed to evolve the topology of the neural network, which is particularly effective in determining the required recurrence. Neuroevolution techniques have been shown to work well in many tasks in control, robotics, constructing intelligent agents for games, and artificial life [19]. However, because of the large number of weights to be optimized, they are generally limited to relatively small networks.

The evolution has been combined with gradient-descent-based learning in several ways, making it possible to utilize much larger networks. These methods are still usually applied to sequential decision tasks, but gradients from a related task (such as prediction of the next sensory inputs) are used to help search. Much of the work is based on utilizing the Baldwin effect, where learning only affects the selection [26]. Computationally, it is possible to utilize Lamarckian evolution as well, that is, encode the learned weight changes back into the genome [25]. However, care must be taken to maintain diversity so that evolution can continue to innovate when all individuals are learning similar behavior.

The evolution of DNNs differs from this prior work in that it is applied to supervised domains where gradients are available, and evolution is used only to optimize the design of the neural network. Deep neuroevolution is thus more closely related to bi-level (or multilevel) optimization techniques [27]. The idea is to use an evolutionary optimization process at a high level to optimize the parameters of a low-level evolutionary optimization process.

Consider, for instance, the problem of controlling a helicopter through aileron, elevator, rudder, and rotor inputs. This is a challenging benchmark from the 2000s for which various reinforcement learning approaches have been developed [28–30]. One of the most successful ones is single-level neuroevolution, where the helicopter is controlled by a neural network that is evolved through genetic algorithms [31]. The eight parameters of the neuroevolution method (such as mutation rate, probability, and amount; crossover probability; population and elite size) are optimized by hand. It would be difficult to include more parameters because the parameters interact nonlinearly. A large part of the parameter space thus remains unexplored in the single-level neuroevolution approach. However, a bi-level approach, where a high-level evolutionary process is employed to optimize these parameters, can search this space more effectively [32]. With bi-level evolution, the number of parameters optimized could be extended to 15, which resulted in significantly better performance. In this manner, evolution was harnessed in this example task to optimize a system design that was too complex to be optimized by hand.

Recently, several studies have applied this idea to optimizing DNNs. Originally, due to significant computational demands, they focused on specific parts of the design. For instance, Loshchilov and Hutter [33] used CMA-ES to optimize the hyperparameters of existing DNNs obtaining state-of-the-art results at the time on object recognition. Fernando et al. [34] developed a compositional pattern-producing network (CPPN) [35] to output the weights of an autoencoder neural network. The autoencoder was then trained further through gradient descent, forming gradients for the CPPN training, and its trained weights were then incorporated back into the CPPN genome through Lamarckian adaptation. A related approach was proposed by Zoph and Le [36]: the topology and hyperparameters of a deep network and LSTM network were modified through policy iteration. More recently, Such et al. [37] demonstrated the power of this approach in reinforcement learning tasks, and Real et al. [38] in image classification.

Building on this foundation, a systematic approach to evolving DNNs is developed in this chapter. First, the standard NEAT neuroevolution method is applied to the topology and hyperparameters of convolutional neural networks, and then extended to the evolution of components as well, achieving results comparable to state of the art in the CIFAR-10 image classification benchmark. Second, a similar method is used to evolve the structure of LSTM networks in language modeling, showing that even small innovations in the components can have a significant effect on performance. Third, the approach is used to build a real-world application of captioning images on an online magazine website.

3 Evolution of deep learning architectures

NEAT neuroevolution method [15] is first extended to evolving network topology and hyperparameters of deep neural networks in DeepNEAT, and then further to the coevolution of modules and blueprints for combining them in CoDeepNEAT. The approach is tested in the standard CIFAR-10 benchmark of object recognition, and found to be comparable to the state of the art at the time the experiments were run.

3.1 Extending NEAT to deep networks

DeepNEAT is a most immediate extension of the standard neural network topology-evolution method NEAT to DNN. It follows the same fundamental process as NEAT: first, a population of chromosomes (each represented by a graph) with minimal complexity is created. Over generations, structure (i.e., nodes and edges) is added to the graph incrementally through mutation. During crossover, historical markings are used to determine how genes of two chromosomes can be lined up. The population is divided into species (i.e., subpopulations) based on a similarity metric. Each species grows proportionally to its fitness and evolution occurs separately in each species.

DeepNEAT differs from NEAT in that each node in the chromosome no longer represents a neuron, but a layer in a DNN. Each node contains a table of real and binary-valued hyperparameters that are mutated through uniform Gaussian distribution and random bitflipping, respectively. These hyperparameters determine the type of a layer (such as a convolutional, fully connected, or recurrent) and the properties of that layer (such as number of neurons, kernel size, and activation function). The edges in the chromosome are no longer marked with weights; instead, they simply indicate how the nodes (layers) are connected together. To construct a DNN from a DeepNEAT chromosome, one simply needs to traverse the chromosome graph, replacing each node with the corresponding layer. The chromosome also contains a set of global hyperparameters applicable to the entire network (such as learning rate, training algorithm, and data preprocessing).

When arbitrary connectivity is allowed between layers, additional complexity is required. If the current layer has multiple parent layers, a merged layer must be applied to the parents in order to ensure that the parent layer's output is the same size as the current layer's input. Typically, this adjustment is done through a concatenation or element-wise sum operation. If the parent layers have mismatched output sizes, all of the parent layers must be downsampled to the parent layer with the smallest output size. The specific method for downsampling is domain dependent. For example, in image classification, a max-pooling layer is inserted after specific parent layers; in image captioning, a fully connected bottleneck layer will serve this function.

During fitness evaluation, each chromosome is converted into a DNN. These DNNs are then trained for a fixed number of epochs. After training, a metric that indicates the network's performance is returned back to DeepNEAT and assigned as fitness to the corresponding chromosome in the population.

While DeepNEAT can be used to evolve DNNs, the resulting structures are often complex and unprincipled. They contrast with typical DNN architectures that utilize the repetition of basic components. DeepNEAT is therefore extended to the evolution of modules and blueprints next.

3.2 Cooperative coevolution of modules and blueprints

Many of the most successful DNNs, such as GoogLeNet and ResNet are composed of modules that are repeated multiple times [5, 6]. These modules often themselves have complicated structure with branching and merging of various layers. Inspired by this observation, a variant of DeepNEAT, called Coevolution DeepNEAT (CoDeepNEAT), is proposed. The algorithm behind CoDeepNEAT is inspired mainly by hierarchical SANE [22] but is also influenced by component-evolution approaches ESP [39] and CoSyNE [24].

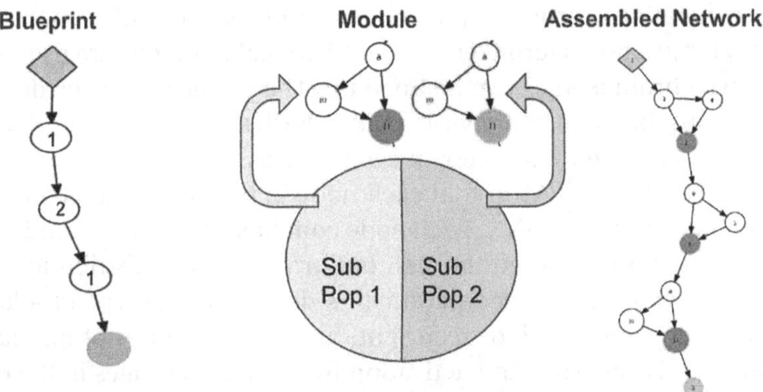

FIG. 1 A visualization of how CoDeepNEAT assembles networks for fitness evaluation. Modules and blueprints are assembled together into a network through the replacement of blueprint nodes with corresponding modules. This approach allows evolving repetitive and deep structures seen in many successful DNNs.

In CoDeepNEAT, two populations of modules and blueprints are evolved separately, using the same methods as described above for DeepNEAT. The blueprint chromosome is a graph where each node contains a pointer to a particular module species. In turn, each module chromosome is a graph that represents a small DNN. Both graphs and the nodes in them evolved. During fitness evaluation, the modules and blueprints are combined to create a larger assembled network (Fig. 1). Each node in the blueprint is replaced with a module is chosen randomly from the species to which that node points. If multiple blueprint nodes point to the same module species, then the same module is used in all of them. The assembled networks are evaluated in a manner similar to DeepNEAT, but the fitnesses of the assembled networks are attributed back to blueprints and modules as the average fitness of all the assembled networks containing that blueprint or module.

CoDeepNEAT can evolve repetitive modular structure efficiently. Furthermore, because small mutations in the modules and blueprints often lead to large changes in the assembled network structure, CoDeepNEAT can explore more diverse and deeper architectures than DeepNEAT. An example application to the CIFAR-10 domain is presented next.

3.3 Evolving DNNs in the CIFAR-10 benchmark

In this experiment, CoDeepNEAT was used to evolve the topology of a convolutional neural network (CNN) to maximize its classification performance on the CIFAR-10 dataset, a common image classification benchmark. The dataset consists of 50,000 training images and 10,000 testing images. The images consist of 32 × 32 color pixels and belong to 1 of 10 classes. For comparison, the neural network layer types were restricted to those used by Snoek et al. [40] in their Bayesian optimization of CNN hyperparameters. Also following Snoek et al., data augmentation consisted of converting the images from RGB to HSV color space, adding random perturbations, distortions, and crops, and converting them back to RGB color space.

CoDeepNEAT was initialized with population of 25 blueprints and 45 modules. From these two populations, 100 CNNs were assembled for fitness evaluation in every generation. Each node in the module chromosome represents a convolutional layer. Its hyperparameters determine the various properties of the layer and whether additional max-pooling or dropout layers are attached (Table 1). In addition, a set of global hyperparameters were evolved for the assembled network. During fitness evaluation, the 50,000 images were split into a training set of 42,500 samples and a validation set of 7500 samples. Since training a DNN is computationally very expensive, each network was trained for eight epochs on the training set. The validation set was then used to determine classification accuracy, that is, the fitness of the network. After 72 generations of evolution, the best network in the population was returned.

After evolution was complete, the best network was trained on all 50,000 training images for 300 epochs, and the classification error measured. This error was 7.3%, comparable to the 6.4% error reported by Snoek et al. [40]. Interestingly, because only limited training could be done during evolution, the best network evolved by CoDeepNEAT trains very fast. While the network of Snoek et al. takes over 30 epochs to reach 20% test error and over 200 epochs to converge, the best network from evolution takes only 12 epochs to reach 20% test error and around 120 epochs to converge. This network utilizes the same modules multiple times, resulting in a deep and repetitive structure typical of many successful DNNs (Fig. 2).

Table 1 Node and global hyperparameters evolved in the CIFAR-10 domain.

Node hyperparameter	Range
Number of filters	[32, 256]
Dropout rate	[0, 0.7]
Initial weight scaling	[0, 2.0]
Kernel size	{1, 3}
Max pooling	{True, false}
Global hyperparameter	**Range**
Learning rate	[0.0001, 0.1]
Momentum	[0.68, 0.99]
Hue shift	[0, 45]
Saturation/value shift	[0, 0.5]
Saturation/value scale	[0, 0.5]
Cropped image size	[26, 32]
Spatial scaling	[0, 0.3]
Random horizontal flips	{True, false}
Variance normalization	{True, false}
Nesterov accelerated gradient	{True, false}

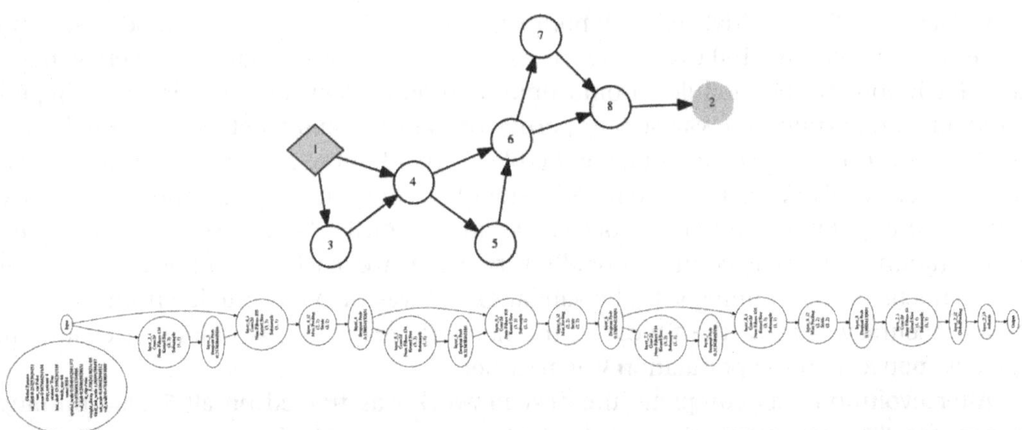

FIG. 2 *Top*: Simplified visualization of the best network evolved by CoDeepNEAT for the CIFAR-10 domain. Node 1 is the input layer, while Node 2 is the output layer. The network has a repetitive structure because its blueprint reuses the same module in multiple places. *Bottom*: A more detailed visualization of the same network.

4 Evolution of LSTM architectures

Recurrent neural networks, in particular those utilizing LSTM nodes, are another powerful approach to DNN. Much of the power comes from the repetition of LSTM modules and the connectivity between them. In this section, CoDeepNEAT is extended with mutations that allow searching for such connectivity, and the approach is evaluated in the standard benchmark task of language modeling.

4.1 Extending CoDeepNEAT to LSTMs

LSTM consists of gated memory cells that can integrate information over longer time scales (as compared to simply using recurrent connections in a neural network). LSTMs have been shown powerful in supervised sequence processing tasks such as speech recognition [41] and machine translation [42].

Recent research on LSTMs has focused in two directions: finding variations of individual LSTM memory unit architecture [36, 43–47], and discovering new ways of stitching LSTM layers into a network [48–50]. Both approaches have improved performance over vanilla LSTMs, with the best recent results achieved through network design. The CoDeepNEAT method incorporates both approaches: neuroevolution searches for both new LSTM units and their connectivity across multiple layers at the same time.

CoDeepNEAT was slightly modified to make it easier to find novel connectivities between LSTM layers. Multiple LSTM layers are flattened into a neural network graph that is then modified by neuroevolution. There are two types of mutations: one enables or disables a connection between LSTM layers, and the other adds or removes skip connections between two LSTM nodes. Recently, skip connections have led to performance improvements in deep neural networks, which suggest that they could be useful for LSTM networks as well. Thus, neuroevolution modifies both the high-level network topology and the low-level LSTM connections.

In each generation, a population of these network graphs (i.e., blueprints), consisting of LSTM variants (i.e., modules with possible skip connections), is created. The individual networks are then trained and tested with the supervised data of the task. The experimental setup and the language modeling task are described next.

4.2 Evolving DNNs in the language modeling benchmark

One standard benchmark task for the LSTM network is language modeling, that is, predicting the next word in a large text corpus. The benchmark utilizes the Penn Tree Bank (PTB) dataset [51], which consists of 929,000 training words, 73,000 validation words, and 82,000 test words. It has 10,000 words in its vocabulary.

A population of 50 LSTM networks was initialized with uniformly random initial connection weights within [−0.05, 0.05]. Each network consisted of two recurrent layers (vanilla LSTM or its variants) with 650 hidden nodes in each layer. The network was unrolled in time up to 35 steps. The hidden states were initialized to zero. The final hidden states of the current minibatch were used as the initial hidden state of the subsequent minibatch (successive minibatches sequentially traverse the training set). The size of each minibatch was 20. For fitness evaluation, each network was trained for 39 epochs. A learning rate decay of 0.8 was applied at the end of every six epochs; the dropout rate was 0.5. The gradients were clipped if their maximum norm (normalized by minibatch size) exceeded 5. Training a single network took about 200 min on a GeForce GTX 980 GPU card.

After 25 generations of neuroevolution, the best network improved the performance of the PTB dataset by 5% (test-perplexity score 78) as compared to the vanilla LSTM [52]. As shown in Fig. 3, this LSTM variant consists of a feedback skip connection between the memory cells of two LSTM layers. This result is interesting because it is similar to a recent hand-designed architecture that also outperforms vanilla LSTM [48].

The initial results thus demonstrate that CoDeepNEAT with just two LSTM-specific mutations can automatically discover improved LSTM variants. It is likely that expanding the search space with more mutation types and layer and connection types would lead to further improvements.

5 Application case study: Image captioning for the blind

In a real-world case study, the vision and language capabilities of CoDeepNEAT were combined to build a real-time online image-captioning system. In this application, CoDeepNEAT searches for architectures that learn to integrate image and text representations to produce captions that blind users can access through existing screen readers. This application was implemented for a major online magazine website. Evolved networks were trained with the open-source MSCOCO image-captioning dataset [53], along with a new dataset collected for this website.

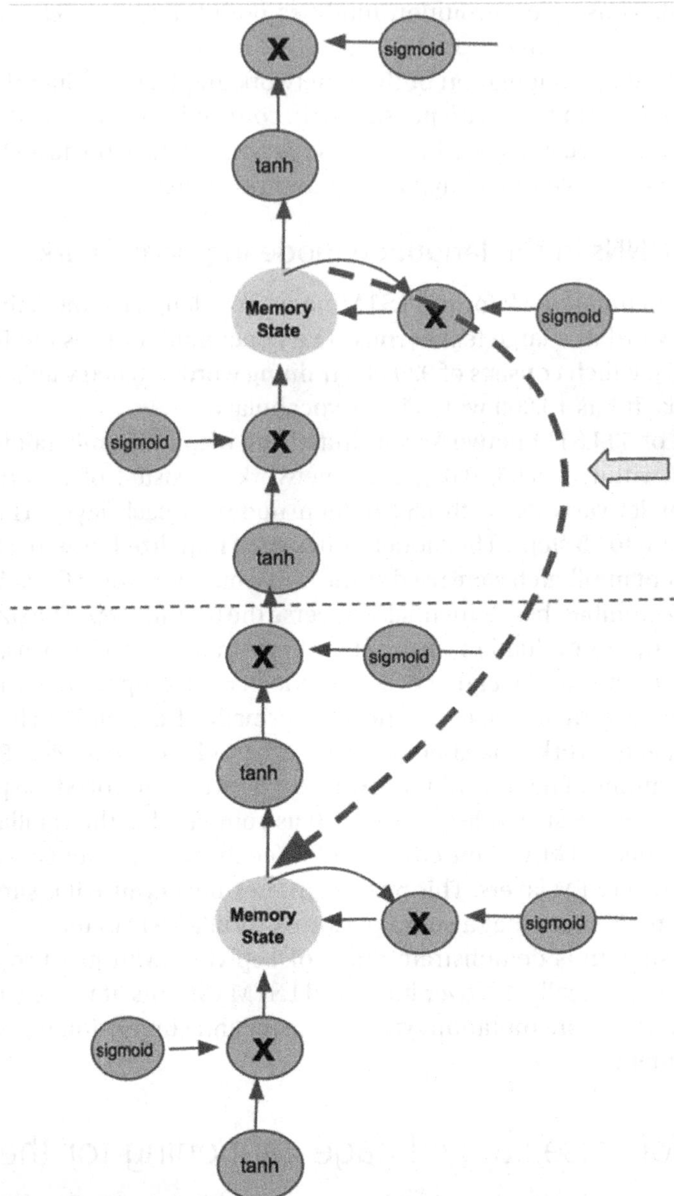

FIG. 3 The best-performing LSTM variant after 25 generations of neuroevolution. It includes a novel skip connection between the two memory cells, resulting in a 5% improvement over the vanilla LSTM baseline. Such improvements are difficult to discover by hand; CoDeepNEAT with LSTM-specific mutation searches for them automatically.

5.1 Evolving DNNs for image captioning

Deep learning has recently provided state-of-the-art performance in image captioning, and several diverse architectures have been suggested [54–58]. The input to an image-captioning system is a raw image, and the output is a text caption intended to describe the contents of the image. In deep learning approaches, a convolutional network is usually used to process the image, and recurrent units, often LSTMs, to generate coherent sentences with long-range dependencies.

As is common in existing approaches, the evolved system uses a pretrained ImageNet model [5] to produce initial image embeddings. The evolved network takes an image embedding as input, along with a one-hot text input. As usual, in training the text input contains the previous word of the ground-truth caption; in inference, it contains the previous word generated by the model [54, 56].

In the initial CoDeepNEAT population, the image and text inputs are fed to a shared embedding layer, which is densely connected to a softmax output over words. From this simple starting point, CoDeepNEAT evolves architectures that include fully connected layers, LSTM layers, sum layers, concatenation layers, and sets of hyperparameters associated with each layer, along with a set of global hyperparameters (Table 2). In particular, the well-known Show and Tell image-captioning architecture [54] is in this search space, providing a baseline with which evolution results can be compared. These components and the glue that connects them are evolved as described in Section 3.2, with 100 networks trained in each generation. Since there is no single best-accepted metric for evaluating captions, the fitness function is the mean across three metrics (BLEU, METEOR, and CIDEr) [53] normalized by their baseline values. Fitness is computed over a holdout set of 5000 images, that is, 25,000 image-caption pairs.

Table 2 Node and global hyperparameters evolved for the image-captioning case study.

Global hyperparameter	Range
Learning rate	[0.0001, 0.1]
Momentum	[0.68, 0.99]
Shared embedding size	[128, 512]
Embedding dropout	[0, 0.7]
LSTM recurrent dropout	{True, false}
Nesterov momentum	{True, false}
Weight initialization	{Glorot normal, He normal}
Node hyperparameter	**Range**
Layer type	{Dense, LSTM}
Merge method	{Sum, Concat}
Layer size	{128, 256}
Layer activation	{ReLU, Linear}
Layer dropout	[0, 0.7]

To keep the computational cost reasonable, during evolution the networks are trained for only six epochs, and only with a random 100,000 image subset of the 500,000 MSCOCO image-caption pairs. As a result, there is evolutionary pressure toward networks that converge quickly. The best-resulting architectures train to near convergence six times faster than the baseline Show and Tell model [54]. After evolution, the optimized learning rate is scaled by one-fifth to compensate for the subsampling.

5.2 Building the application

The images in MSCOCO are chosen to depict "common objects in context." The focus is on a relatively small set of objects and their interactions in a relatively small set of settings. The Internet as a whole, and the online magazine website in particular, contain many images that cannot be classified as "common objects in context." Other types of images from the magazine include staged portraits of people, infographics, cartoons, abstract designs, and *iconic* images, that is, images of one or multiple objects *out of context* such as on a white or patterned background. Therefore, an additional dataset of 17,000 image-caption pairs was constructed for the case study, targeting iconic images in particular. About 4000 images were first scraped from the magazine website, and 1000 of them were identified as iconic. Then, 16,000 images that were visually similar to those 1000 were retrieved automatically from a large image repository. A single ground-truth caption for each of these 17,000 images was generated by human subjects through MightyAI.[a] The holdout set for evaluation consisted of 100 of the original 1000 iconic images, along with 3000 other images.

During evolution, networks were trained and evaluated only on the MSCOCO data. The best architecture from evolution was then trained from scratch on both MSCOCO and MightyAI datasets in an iterative alternating approach: one epoch on MSCOCO, followed by five epochs on MightyAI until the maximum performance was reached on the MightyAI holdout data. Beam search was then used to generate captions from the fully trained models. Performance achieved using the MightyAI data demonstrates the ability of evolved architectures to generalize to domains toward which they were not evolved.

Once the model was fully trained, it was placed on a server where it can be queried with images to caption. A JavaScript snippet was written that a developer can embed in his/her site to automatically query the model to caption all images on a page. This snippet runs in an existing Chrome extension for custom scripts and automatically captions images as the user browses the web. These tools add captions to the "alt" field of images, which screen readers can then read to blind Internet users (Fig. 4).

5.3 Image-captioning results

Trained in parallel on about 100 GPUs, each generation took around 1 h to complete. The most fit architecture was discovered in generation 37 (Fig. 5). Among the components in

[a]See https://mty.ai/computer-vision/.

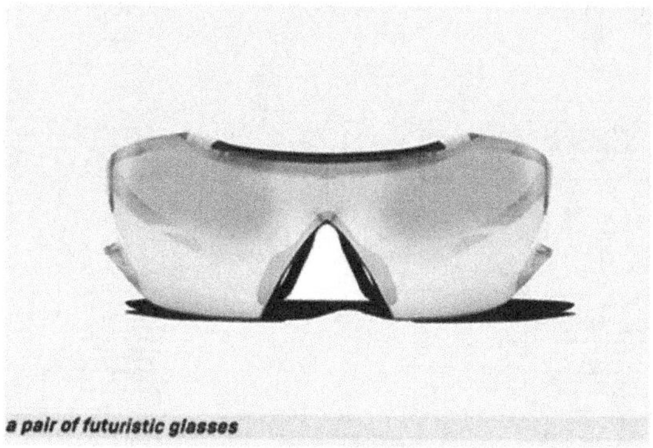

FIG. 4 An iconic image from an online magazine captioned by an evolved model. The model provides a suitably detailed description without any unnecessary context.

its unique structure are six LSTM layers, four summing merge layers, and several skip connections. A single module consisting of two LSTM layers merged by a sum is repeated three times. There is a path from the input through dense layers to the output that bypasses all LSTM layers, providing the softmax with a more direct view of the current input. The motif of skip connections with a summing merge is similar to residual architectures that are currently popular in deep learning [6, 59]. However, the high-level structure of multiple parallel pathways is an innovation of evolutionary search and is rarely seen in human-designed architectures. During the search, such parallel pathways provide robust performance as the architecture varies, and are thus likely to be discovered. During the performance, they possibly represent multiple parallel hypotheses that are combined to the most likely final answer. This architecture performs better than the hand-tuned baseline [54] when trained on the MSCOCO data alone (Table 3).

However, a more important result is the performance of this network on the magazine website. Because no suitable automatic metrics exist for the types of captions collected for the magazine website (and existing metrics are very noisy when there is only one reference caption), captions generated by the evolved model on all 3100 holdout images were manually evaluated as correct, mostly correct, mostly incorrect, and incorrect (Fig. 6). Fig. 7 shows some examples of good and bad captions for these images.

The model is not perfect, but the results are promising. The evolved network is correct or mostly correct on 63% of iconic images and 31% of all images. There are many known improvements that can be implemented, including ensembling diverse architectures generated by evolution, fine-tuning the ImageNet model, using a more recent ImageNet model, and performing beam search or scheduled sampling during training [60]; preliminary experiments with ensembling alone suggest improvements of about 20%. For this application, it is also important to include methods for automatically evaluation caption quality and filtering captions that would give an incorrect impression to a blind user. However, even without these additions, the results demonstrate that it is now possible to develop practical applications through evolving DNNs.

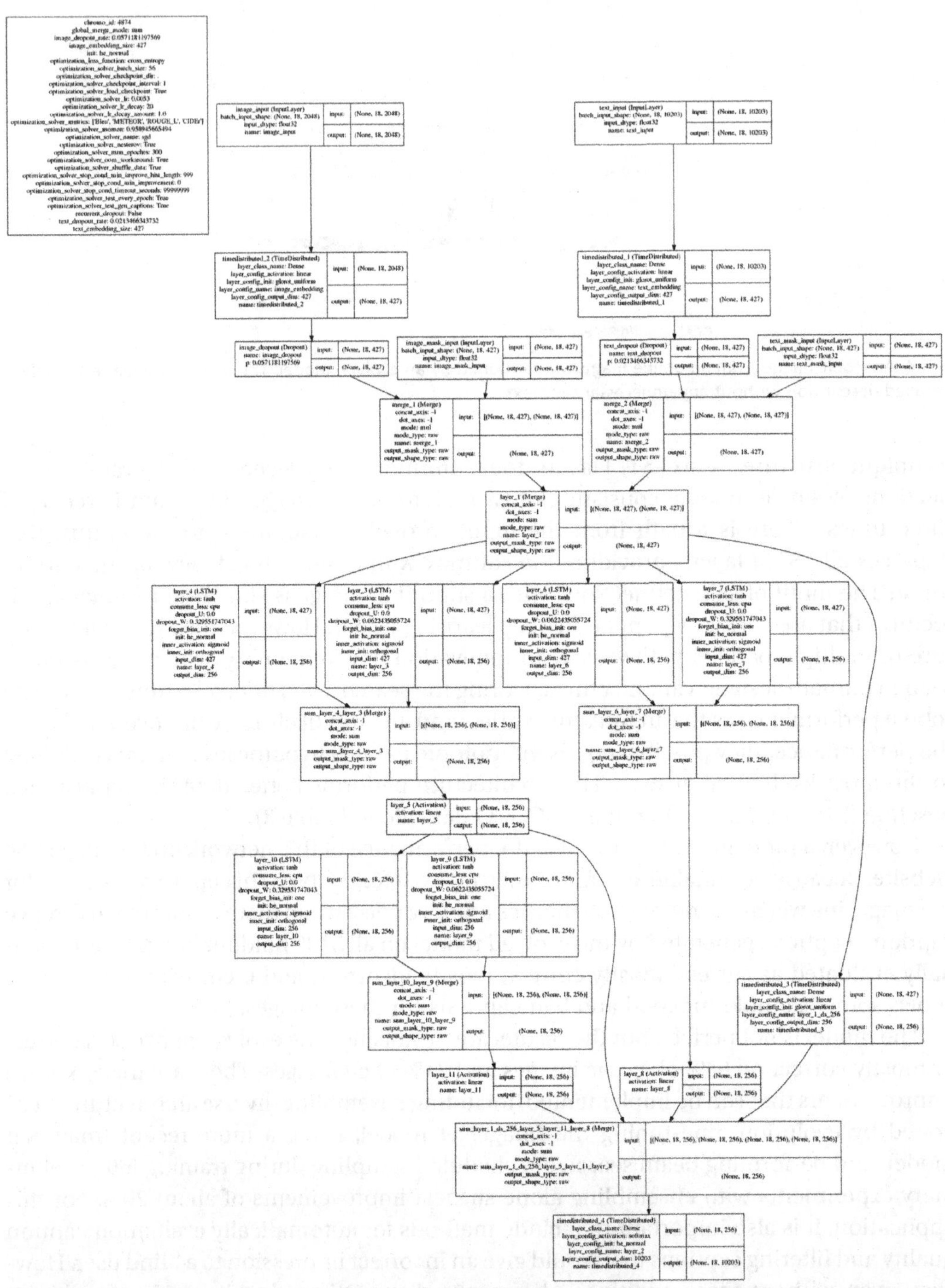

FIG. 5 The most fit architecture found by evolution. It consists of three LSTM-based modules as well as a parallel densely connected pathway. Multiple pathways are robust during search and can represent multiple hypotheses during performance. Such a high-level design is different from most hand-designed architectures and represents an innovation of evolutionary search.

Table 3 The evolved network improves over the hand-designed baseline when trained on MSCOCO alone.

Model	BLEU-4	CIDEr	METEOR
DNGO [40]	26.7	–	–
Baseline [54]	27.7	85.5	23.7
Evolved	**29.1**	**88.0**	**23.8**

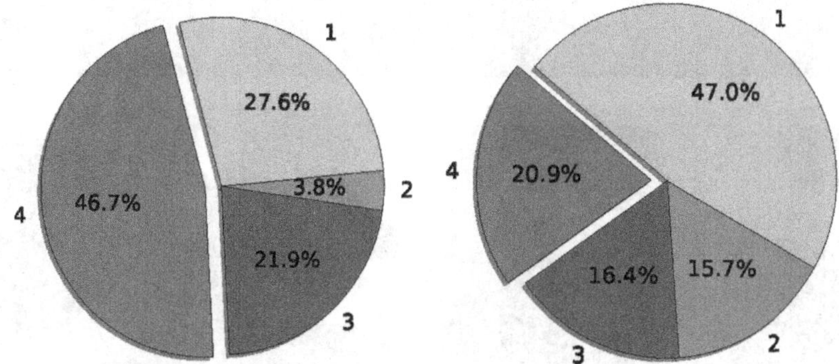

FIG. 6 Results for captions generated by an evolved model for the online magazine images rated from 1 to 4, with 4—correct, 3—mostly correct, 2—mostly incorrect, 1—incorrect. *Left*: On iconic images, the model is able to get about one-half correct. *Right*: On all images, the model gets about one-fifth correct. The superior performance on iconic images shows that it is useful to build supplementary training sets for specific image types.

6 Discussion and future work

The results in this chapter show that the evolutionary approach to optimizing deep neural networks is feasible: The results are comparable to hand-designed architectures in benchmark tasks, and it is possible to build real-world applications based on the approach. It is important to note that the approach has not yet been pushed to its full potential. It takes a couple of days to train each deep neural network on a typical GPU, and over the course of evolution, thousands of them need to be trained. Therefore, the results are limited by the available computational power.

Interestingly, since it was necessary to train networks only partially during evolution, evolution is biased toward discovering fast learners instead of top performers. This is an interesting result on its own: Evolution can be guided with goals other than simply accuracy, including training time, execution time, or memory requirements of the network. On the other hand, if it was possible to train the networks further, it would be possible to identify top performers more reliably, and final performance would likely improve. In order to speed up evolution, other techniques may be developed. For instance, it may be possible to seed the population with various state-of-the-art architectures and modules, instead of having to rediscover them during evolution.

Significantly more computational resources are likely to become available in the near future. Cloud-based services offer GPU computation at a reasonable cost, and they are

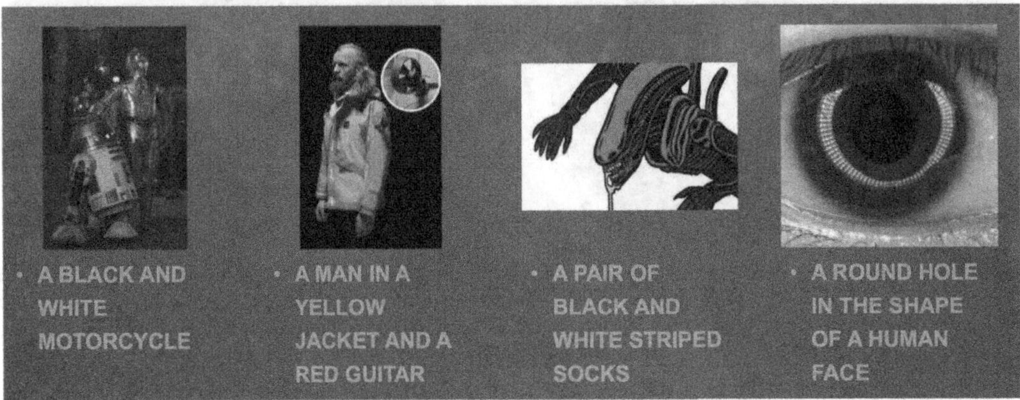

FIG. 7 *Top*: Four good captions. The model is able to abstract about ambiguous images and even describe drawings, along with photos of objects in context. *Bottom*: Four bad captions. When it fails, the output of the model still contains some correct sense of the image.

becoming cheaper. Not many approaches can take advantage of such power, but the evolution of deep learning neural networks can. The search space of different components and topologies can be extended, and more hyperparameters be optimized. While cloud services such as AutoML provide some such functionality and benefit from the increasing computing power as well, they currently represent brute-force approaches that are unlikely to scale as well. Given the results in this chapter, the evolutionary approach is likely to discover designs that are superior to those that can be developed by hand today; it is also likely to make it possible to apply deep learning to a wider array of tasks and applications in the future.

7 Conclusions

Evolutionary optimization makes it possible to design more complex deep learning architectures that can be designed by hand. The topology, components, and hyperparameters of the architecture can all be optimized simultaneously to fit the requirements of the task, resulting in superior performance. Such automated design can make new applications of deep learning possible in vision, speech, language, and other areas. The approach is computationally demanding and thus offers one way to put the anticipated increases in computing power to good use.

References

[1] Y. LeCun, L. Bottou, Y. Bengio, P. Haffner, Gradient-based learning applied to document recognition, Proc. IEEE 86 (1998) 2278–2324.

[2] S. Hochreiter, J. Schmidhuber, Long short-term memory, Neural Comput. 9 (1997) 1735–1780.

[3] R. Collobert, J. Weston, A unified architecture for natural language processing: deep neural networks with multitask learning, in: Proceedings of the 25th International Conference on Machine learning, ACM, 2008, pp. 160–167.

[4] A. Graves, A.-R. Mohamed, G. Hinton, Speech recognition with deep recurrent neural networks, in: 2013 IEEE International Conference on Acoustics, Speech and Signal Processing, IEEE, 2013, pp. 6645–6649.

[5] C. Szegedy, V. Vanhoucke, S. Ioffe, J. Shlens, Z. Wojna, Rethinking the inception architecture for computer vision, in: Proc. of CVPR, 2016, pp. 2818–2826.

[6] K. He, X. Zhang, S. Ren, J. Sun, Deep residual learning for image recognition, in: IEEE Conference on Computer Vision and Pattern Recognition, 2016, pp. 770–778.

[7] J.Y. Ng, M.J. Hausknecht, S. Vijayanarasimhan, O. Vinyals, R. Monga, G. Toderici, Beyond short snippets: deep networks for video classification, in: Proceedings of the IEEE Conference on Computer Vision and Pattern Recognition, 2015, pp. 4694–4702.

[8] Z. Che, S. Purushotham, K. Cho, D. Sontag, Y. Liu, Recurrent neural networks for multivariate time series with missing values, Sci. Rep. 8 (2018) 6085.

[9] G. Huang, Z. Liu, K.Q. Weinberger, Densely connected convolutional networks, in: Proceedings of the IEEE Conference on Computer Vision and Pattern Recognition, 2017.

[10] M. Tan, Q. Le, EfficientNet: rethinking model scaling for convolutional neural networks, in: International Conference on Machine Learning, 2019, pp. 6105–6114.

[11] J. Devlin, M.-W. Chang, K. Lee, K. Toutanova, BERT: pre-training of deep bidirectional transformers for language understanding, in: Proceedings of the 2019 Conference of the North American Chapter of the Association for Computational Linguistics: Human Language Technologies, Volume 1 (Long and Short Papers), Association for Computational Linguistics, Minneapolis, MN, 2019, pp. 4171–4186, https://doi.org/10.18653/v1/N19-1423.

[12] H. Hoos, Programming by optimization, Commun. ACM 55 (2012) 70–80.

[13] C.L. Goues, T. Nguyen, S. Forrest, W. Weimer, GenProg: a generic method for automatic software repair, ACM Trans. Softw. Eng. 38 (2012) 54–72.

[14] R. Miikkulainen, N. Iscoe, A. Shagrin, R. Cordell, S. Nazari, C. Schoolland, M. Brundage, J. Epstein, R. Dean, G. Lamba, Conversion rate optimization through evolutionary computation, in: Proceedings of the Genetic and Evolutionary Computation Conference (GECCO 2017), ACM, New York, NY, 2017, pp. 1193–1199.

[15] K.O. Stanley, R. Miikkulainen, Evolving neural networks through augmenting topologies, Evol. Comput. 10 (2002) 99–127.

[16] D.J. Montana, L. Davis, Training feedforward neural networks using genetic algorithms, in: Proceedings of the 11th International Joint Conference on Artificial Intelligence, 1989, pp. 762–767.

[17] D. Floreano, P. Dürr, C. Mattiussi, Neuroevolution: from architectures to learning, Evol. Intell. 1 (2008) 47–62.

[18] X. Yao, Evolving artificial neural networks, Proc. IEEE 87 (9) (1999) 1423–1447.

[19] J. Lehman, R. Miikkulainen, Neuroevolution, Scholarpedia 8 (2013) 30977.

[20] K.O. Stanley, J. Clune, J. Lehman, R. Miikkulainen, Designing neural networks through evolutionary algorithms, Nat. Mach. Intell. 1 (2019) 24–35.

[21] C. Igel, Neuroevolution for reinforcement learning using evolution strategies, in: Proceedings of the 2003 Congress on Evolutionary Computation, IEEE Press, Piscataway, NJ, 2003, pp. 2588–2595.

[22] D.E. Moriarty, R. Miikkulainen, Forming neural networks through efficient and adaptive coevolution, Evol. Comput. 5 (1997) 373–399.

[23] F. Gomez, R. Miikkulainen, Incremental evolution of complex general behavior, Adapt. Behav. 5 (1997) 317–342.

[24] F. Gomez, J. Schmidhuber, R. Miikkulainen, Accelerated neural evolution through cooperatively coevolved synapses, J. Mach. Learn. Res. 8 (2008) 937–965.

[25] F. Gruau, D. Whitley, Adding learning to the cellular development of neural networks: evolution and the Baldwin effect, Evol. Comput. 1 (1993) 213–233.

[26] G.E. Hinton, S.J. Nowlan, How learning can guide evolution, Complex Syst. 1 (1987) 495–502.

[27] A. Sinha, P. Malo, P. Xu, K. Deb, A bilevel optimization approach to automated parameter tuning, in: Proceedings of the Genetic and Evolutionary Computation Conference (GECCO 2014), Vancouver, BC, Canada, 2014, pp. 847–854.

[28] J. Bagnell, J. Schneider, Autonomous helicopter control using reinforcement learning policy search methods, in: Proceedings of the International Conference on Robotics and Automation 2001, IEEE, 2001.

[29] A.Y. Ng, H.J. Kim, M. Jordan, S. Sastry, Autonomous helicopter flight via reinforcement learning, in: Advances in Neural Information Processing Systems 16, 2004.

[30] P. Abbeel, A. Coates, M. Quigley, A.Y. Ng, An application of reinforcement learning to aerobatic helicopter flight, in: Advances in Neural Information Processing Systems 19, 2007.

[31] R. Koppejan, S. Whiteson, Neuroevolutionary reinforcement learning for generalized control of simulated helicopters, Evol. Intell. 4 (2011) 219–241.

[32] J.Z. Liang, R. Miikkulainen, Evolutionary bilevel optimization for complex control tasks, in: Proceedings of the Genetic and Evolutionary Computation Conference (GECCO 2015), July, 2015, pp. 871–878.

[33] I. Loshchilov, F. Hutter, CMA-ES for hyperparameter optimization of deep neural networks, in: International Conference on Learning Representations (ICLR-2016) Workshop Track, 2016.

[34] C. Fernando, D. Banarse, F. Besse, M. Jaderberg, D. Pfau, M. Reynolds, M. Lactot, D. Wierstra, Convolution by evolution: differentiable pattern producing networks, in: Proceedings of the Genetic and Evolutionary Computation Conference (GECCO 2016), ACM, New York, NY, 2016.

[35] K. Stanley, Compositional pattern producing networks: a novel abstraction of development, Genet. Program Evolvable Mach. 8 (2) (2007) 131–162, https://doi.org/10.1007/s10710-007-9028-8.

[36] B. Zoph, Q.V. Le, Neural architecture search with reinforcement learning, in: International Conference on Learning Representations, 2017.

[37] F.P. Such, V. Madhavan, E. Conti, J. Lehman, K.O. Stanley, J. Clune, Deep neuroevolution: genetic algorithms are a competitive alternative for training deep neural networks for reinforcement learning, arXiv:1712.06567 (2017).

[38] E. Real, A. Aggarwal, Y. Huang, Q.V. Le, Regularized evolution for image classifier architecture search, in: Proceedings of the AAAI Conference on Artificial Intelligence, 2019, pp. 4780–4789.

[39] F. Gomez, R. Miikkulainen, Solving non-Markovian control tasks with neuroevolution, in: Proceedings of the 11th International Joint Conference on Artificial Intelligence, Kaufmann, San Francisco, 1999, pp. 1356–1361.

[40] J. Snoek, O. Rippel, K. Swersky, R. Kiros, N. Satish, N. Sundaram, M.M.A. Patwary, M. Prabhat, R.P. Adams, Scalable Bayesian optimization using deep neural networks, in: Proc. of ICML, 2015, pp. 2171–2180.

[41] A. Graves, N. Jaitly, Towards end-to-end speech recognition with recurrent neural networks, in: Proc. 31st ICML, 2014, pp. 1764–1772.

[42] D. Bahdanau, K. Cho, Y. Bengio, Neural machine translation by jointly learning to align and translate, in: ICLR, 2015.

[43] J. Bayer, D. Wierstra, J. Togelius, J. Schmidhuber, Evolving memory cell structures for sequence learning, in: Artificial Neural Networks ICANN, 2009, pp. 755–764.

[44] R. Jozefowicz, W. Zaremba, I. Sutskever, An empirical exploration of recurrent network architectures, in: Proceedings of the 32nd International Conference on Machine Learning, 2015, pp. 2342–2350.

[45] K. Cho, B. van Merrienboer, Ç. Gulcehre, F. Bougares, H. Schwenk, Y. Bengio, Learning phrase representations using RNN encoder-decoder for statistical machine translation, in: Proceedings of the 2014 Conference on Empirical Methods in Natural Language Processing (EMNLP), 2014, pp. 1724–1734.

[46] K. Greff, R.K. Srivastava, J. Koutník, B.R. Steunebrink, J. Schmidhuber, LSTM: A Search Space Odyssey, IEEE Trans. Neural Netw. Learn. Syst. 28 (2017) 222–232.

[47] A. Rawal, R. Miikkulainen, Discovering gated recurrent neural network architectures, in: H. Iba, N. Noman (Eds.), Deep Neural Evolution—Deep Learning With Evolutionary Computation, Springer, 2020, pp. 233–251.

[48] J. Chung, C. Gulcehre, K. Cho, Y. Bengio, Gated feedback recurrent neural networks, in: Proceedings of the 32nd International Conference on Machine Learning, 2015.

[49] N. Kalchbrenner, I. Danihelka, A. Graves, Grid long short-term memory, arXiv:1507.01526 (2015).

[50] J.G. Zilly, R.K. Srivastava, J. Koutník, J. Schmidhuber, Recurrent highway networks, in: Proceedings of the 34th International Conference on Machine Learning, 2017, pp. 6346–6357.

[51] M.P. Marcus, M.A. Marcinkiewicz, B. Santorini, Building a large annotated corpus of English: the Penn Treebank, Comput. Linguist. 19 (2) (1993) 313–330.

[52] W. Zaremba, I. Sutskever, O. Vinyals, Recurrent neural network regularization, arXiv:1409.2329 (2014).

[53] X. Chen, H. Fang, T.Y. Lin, R. Vedantam, S. Gupta, P. Dollar, C.L. Zitnick, Microsoft COCO captions: data collection and evaluation server, arXiv:1504.00325 (2015).

[54] O. Vinyals, A. Toshev, S. Bengio, D. Erhan, Show and tell: a neural image caption generator, in: Proc. of CVPR, 2015, pp. 3156–3164.

[55] K. Xu, J. Ba, R. Kiros, K. Cho, A.C. Courville, R. Salkhutdinov, R.S. Zemel, Y. Bengio, Show, attend and tell: neural image caption generation with visual attention, in: Proc. of ICML, 2015, pp. 77–81.

[56] A. Karpathy, L. Fei-Fei, Deep visual-semantic alignments for generating image descriptions, in: Proc. of CVPR, 2015, pp. 3128–3137.

[57] Q. You, H. Jin, Z. Wang, C. Fang, J. Luo, Image captioning with semantic attention, in: Proc. of CVPR, 2016, pp. 4651–4659.

[58] R. Vedantam, S. Bengio, K. Murphy, D. Parikh, G. Chechik, Context-aware captions from context-agnostic supervision, in: The IEEE Conference on Computer Vision and Pattern Recognition (CVPR), 2017.

[59] C. Szegedy, S. Ioffe, V. Vanhoucke, A. Alemi, Inception-v4, inception-ResNet and the impact of residual connections on learning, in: Proceedings of the AAAI Conference on Artificial Intelligence, 2016.

[60] O. Vinyals, A. Toshev, S. Bengio, D. Erhan, Show and tell: lessons learned from the 2015 MSCOCO image captioning challenge, Trans. Pattern Anal. Mach. Intell. 39 (2016) 652–663.

15

Evolving GAN formulations for higher-quality image synthesis

Santiago Gonzalez[a,*], Mohak Kant[b], and Risto Miikkulainen[b,c]

[a]THE UNIVERSITY OF TEXAS AT AUSTIN, AUSTIN, TX, UNITED STATES [b]COGNIZANT AI LABS, SAN FRANCISCO, CA, UNITED STATES [c]DEPARTMENT OF COMPUTER SCIENCE, THE UNIVERSITY OF TEXAS AT AUSTIN, AUSTIN, TX, UNITED STATES

Chapter outlines

1 Introduction

Generative adversarial networks (GANs) have recently emerged as a promising technique for building models that generate new samples according to distribution within a dataset. In GANs, two separate networks—a generator and a discriminator—are trained in tandem in an adversarial fashion. The generator attempts to synthesize samples that the

*Current affiliation: Apple, Inc., Cupertino, CA, United States.

Artificial Intelligence in the Age of Neural Networks and Brain Computing. https://doi.org/10.1016/B978-0-323-96104-2.00014-2

Copyright © 2024 Elsevier Inc. All rights reserved.

discriminator believes are real, while the discriminator attempts to differentiate between samples from the generator and samples from a ground-truth dataset. However, GANs are challenging to train. Training often suffers from instabilities that can lead to low-quality and potentially low-variety generated samples. These difficulties have led many researchers to try formulating better GANs, primarily by designing new generators and discriminator loss functions by hand.

Neuroevolution may potentially offer a solution to this problem. It has recently been extended from optimizing network weights and topologies to designing deep learning architectures [1–3]. Advances in this field—known as evolutionary metalearning—have resulted in designs that outperform those that are manually tuned. One particular family of techniques—loss-function metalearning—has allowed for neural networks to be trained more quickly, with higher accuracy, and better robustness [4, 5]. Perhaps loss-function metalearning can be adapted to improve GANs.

In this chapter, such a technique is developed to evolve entirely new GAN formulations that outperform the standard Wasserstein loss. Leveraging the TaylorGLO loss-function parameterization approach [5], separate loss functions are constructed for the two GAN networks. A genetic algorithm is then used to optimize their parameters against two nondifferentiable objectives. A composite transformation of these objectives [6] is further used to enhance the multiobjective search.

This TaylorGAN approach is evaluated experimentally in an image-to-image translation benchmark task, where the goal is to generate photorealistic building images based on a building segment map. The CMP Facade dataset [7] is used as the training data and the pix2pix-HD conditional GAN [8] as the generative model. The approach is found to both qualitatively enhance generated image quality and quantitatively improve the two metrics. The evaluation thus demonstrates how evolution can improve a leading conditional GAN design by replacing manually designed loss functions with those optimized by a multiobjective genetic algorithm.

Section 2 reviews key literature in GANs, motivating the evolution of their loss functions. Section 3 describes the TaylorGLO metalearning technique for optimizing loss functions in general. Section 4 introduces the TaylorGAN variation of it, focusing on how the TaylorGLO loss-function parameterization is leveraged for evolving GANs. Section 5 details the experimental configuration and evaluation methodologies. In Section 6, TaylorGAN's efficacy is evaluated on the benchmark task. Section 7 places these findings in the general context of the GAN literature and describes potential avenues for future work.

2 Variations of GAN architectures

GANs [9] are a type of generative model consisting of a pair of networks, a generator, and discriminator that are trained in tandem. GANs are a modern successor to variational autoencoders (VAEs) [10] and Boltzmann machines [11], including restricted Boltzmann machines [12] and deep Boltzmann machines [13].

Table 1 GAN notation decoder.

Symbol	Description
$G(\boldsymbol{x}, \theta_G)$	Generator function
$D(\boldsymbol{z}, \theta_D)$	Discriminator function
$\mathbb{P}_{\text{data}}$	Probability distribution of the original data
$\mathbb{P}_z$	Latent vector noise distribution
$\mathbb{P}_g$	Probability distribution of $G(\boldsymbol{z})$
$\boldsymbol{x}$	Data, where $\boldsymbol{x} \sim \mathbb{P}_{\text{data}}$
$\widetilde{\boldsymbol{x}}$	Generated data
$\boldsymbol{z}$	Latent vector, where $\boldsymbol{z} \sim \mathbb{P}_z$
$\boldsymbol{c}$	Condition vector
λ	Various types of weights/hyperparameters

The following sections review prominent GAN methods. Key GAN formulations, and the relationships between them, are described. Consistent notation (shown in Table 1) is used, consolidating the extensive variety of notation in the field.

2.1 Overview

A GAN's generator and discriminator are set to compete with each other in a minimax game, attempting to reach a Nash equilibrium [14, 15]. Throughout the training process, the generator aims to transform samples from a prior noise distribution into data, such as an image, that tricks the discriminator into thinking it has been sampled from the real data's distribution. Simultaneously, the discriminator aims to determine whether a given sample came from the real data's distribution, or was generated from noise.

Unfortunately, GANs are difficult to train, frequently exhibiting instability, that is, mode collapse, where all modes of the target data distribution are not fully represented by the generator [16–22]. GANs that operate on image data often suffer from visual artifacts and blurring of generated images [18, 23]. Additionally, datasets with low variability have been found to degrade GAN performance [22].

GANs are also difficult to evaluate quantitatively, typically relying on metrics that attempt to embody vague notions of quality. Popular GAN image scoring metrics, for example, have been found to have many pitfalls, including cases where two samples of clearly disparate quality may have similar values [24].

2.2 Original minimax and nonsaturating GAN

Using the notation described in Table 1, the original minimax GAN formulation by [9] can be defined as

$$\min_{\theta_G} \max_{\theta_D} \mathbb{E}_{\boldsymbol{x}\sim\mathbb{P}_{\text{data}}}[\log D(\boldsymbol{x})] + \mathbb{E}_{\boldsymbol{z}\sim\mathbb{P}_z}[\log(1 - D(G(\boldsymbol{z})))]. \tag{1}$$

This formulation can be broken down into two separate loss functions, one each for the discriminator and generator:

$$\mathcal{L}_D = -\frac{1}{n}\sum_{i=1}^{n}[\log D(x_i) + \log(1 - D(G(z_i)))], \text{ and} \tag{2}$$

$$\mathcal{L}_G = \frac{1}{n}\sum_{i=1}^{n} \log(1 - D(G(z_i))). \tag{3}$$

The discriminator's loss function is equivalent to a sigmoid cross-entropy loss when thought of as a binary classifier. Goodfellow et al. [9] proved that training a GAN with this formulation is equivalent to minimizing the Jensen-Shannon divergence between $\mathbb{P}_g$ and $\mathbb{P}_{\text{data}}$, that is, a symmetric divergence metric based on the Kullback-Leibler divergence.

In the earlier formulation, the generator's loss saturates quickly since the discriminator learns to reject the novice generator's samples early on in training. To resolve this problem, Goodfellow et al. provided a second "nonsaturating" formulation with the same fixed-point dynamics, but better, more intense gradients for the generator early on:

$$\max_{\theta_D} \mathbb{E}_{\boldsymbol{x}\sim\mathbb{P}_{\text{data}}}[\log D(\boldsymbol{x})] + \mathbb{E}_{\boldsymbol{z}\sim\mathbb{P}_z}[\log(1 - D(G(\boldsymbol{z})))], \tag{4}$$

$$\max_{\theta_G} \mathbb{E}_{\boldsymbol{z}\sim\mathbb{P}_z}[\log D(G(\boldsymbol{z}))]. \tag{5}$$

Each GAN training step consists of training the discriminator for k steps, while sequentially training the generator for only one step. This difference in steps for both networks helps prevent the discriminator from learning too quickly and overpowering the generator.

Alternatively, unrolled GANs [17] aimed to prevent the discriminator from overpowering the generator by using a discriminator which has been unrolled for a certain number of steps in the generator's loss, thus allowing the generator to train against a more optimal discriminator. More recent GAN work instead uses a two-time-scale update rule (TTUR) [15], where the two networks are trained under different learning rates for one step each. This approach has proven to converge more reliably to more desirable solutions.

Unfortunately, with both minimax and nonsaturating GANs, the generator gradients vanish for samples that are on the correct side of the decision boundary but far from the true data distribution [19, 22]. The Wasserstein GAN, described next, is designed to solve this problem.

2.3 Wasserstein GAN

The Wasserstein GAN (WGAN) [20] is arguably one of the most impactful developments in the GAN literature since the original formulation by Goodfellow et al. [9]. WGANs minimize the Wasserstein-1 distance between $\mathbb{P}_g$ and $\mathbb{P}_{\text{data}}$, rather than the Jensen-Shannon divergence, in an attempt to avoid vanishing gradient and mode collapse issues. In the context of GANs, the Wasserstein-1 distance can be defined as

$$W(\mathbb{P}_g, \mathbb{P}_{\text{data}}) = \inf_{\gamma \in \Pi(\mathbb{P}_g, \mathbb{P}_{\text{data}})} \mathbb{E}_{(\boldsymbol{u},\boldsymbol{v})\sim\gamma}[\| \boldsymbol{u} - \boldsymbol{v} \|], \tag{6}$$

where $\gamma(\boldsymbol{u}, \boldsymbol{v})$ represents the amount of mass that needs to move from $\boldsymbol{u}$ to $\boldsymbol{v}$ for $\mathbb{P}_g$ to become $\mathbb{P}_{\text{data}}$. This formulation with the infimum is intractable, but the Kantorovich-Rubinstein duality [25] with a supremum makes the Wasserstein-1 distance tractable, while imposing a 1-Lipschitz smoothness constraint:

$$W(\mathbb{P}_g, \mathbb{P}_{\text{data}}) = \sup_{\|f\|_{L\leq 1}} \mathbb{E}_{\boldsymbol{u}\sim\mathbb{P}_g}[f(\boldsymbol{u})] - \mathbb{E}_{\boldsymbol{u}\sim\mathbb{P}_{\text{data}}}[f(\boldsymbol{u})], \tag{7}$$

which translates to the training objective

$$\min_{\theta_G} \max_{\theta_D \in \Theta_D} \mathbb{E}_{\boldsymbol{x}\sim\mathbb{P}_{\text{data}}}[D(\boldsymbol{x})] - \mathbb{E}_{\boldsymbol{z}\sim\mathbb{P}_z}[D(G(\boldsymbol{z}))], \tag{8}$$

where Θ_D is the set of all parameters for which D is a 1-Lipschitz function.

WGANs are an excellent example of how generator and discriminator loss functions can profoundly impact the quality of generated samples and the prevalence of mode collapse. However, the WGAN has a 1-Lipschitz constraint that needs to be maintained throughout training for the formulation to work. WGANs enforce the constraint via gradient clipping, at the cost of requiring an optimizer that does not use momentum, that is, RMSProp [26] rather than Adam [27].

To resolve the issues caused by gradient clipping, a subsequent formulation, WGAN-GP [21], added a gradient penalty regularization term to the discriminator loss:

$$GP = \lambda\, \mathbb{E}_{\hat{\boldsymbol{x}}\sim\mathbb{P}_{\hat{x}}}\left[(\| \nabla_{\hat{\boldsymbol{x}}} D(\hat{\boldsymbol{x}}) \|_2 - 1)^2\right], \tag{9}$$

where $\mathbb{P}_{\hat{x}}$ samples uniformly along lines between $\mathbb{P}_{\text{data}}$ and $\mathbb{P}_g$. The gradient penalty enforces a soft Lipschitz smoothness constraint, leading to a more stationary loss surface than when the gradient clipping is used, which in turn makes it possible to use momentum-based optimizers. The gradient penalty term has even been successfully used in non-Wasserstein GANs [22, 28]. However, gradient penalties can increase memory and compute costs [22].

2.4 Least-squares GAN

Another attempt to solve the issue of vanishing gradients is the least-squares GAN (LSGAN) [19]. It defines the training objective as

$$\min_{\theta_D} \frac{1}{2}\, \mathbb{E}_{\boldsymbol{x}\sim\mathbb{P}_{\text{data}}}\left[(D(\boldsymbol{x}) - b)^2\right] + \mathbb{E}_{\boldsymbol{z}\sim\mathbb{P}_z}\left[(D(G(\boldsymbol{z})) - a)^2\right], \tag{10}$$

$$\min_{\theta_G} \frac{1}{2}\, \mathbb{E}_{\boldsymbol{z}\sim\mathbb{P}_z}\left[(D(G(\boldsymbol{z})) - c)^2\right], \tag{11}$$

where a is the label for generated data, b is the label for real data, and c is the label that G wants to trick D into believing for generated data. In practice, typically $a = 0$, $b = 1$, $c = 1$. However, subsequently, $a = -1$, $b = -1$, $c = 0$ were found to result in faster convergence, making it the recommended parameter setting [21]. Training an LSGAN was shown to be equivalent to minimizing the Pearson χ^2 divergence [29] between $\mathbb{P}_{\text{data}} + \mathbb{P}_g$ and $2*\mathbb{P}_g$. Generated data quality can oscillate throughout the training process [22], indicating a disparity between data quality and loss.

2.5 Conditional GAN

Traditional GANs learn how to generate data from a latent space, that is, an embedded representation of the training data that the generator constructs. Typically, the elements of a latent space have no immediately intuitive meaning [30, 31]. Thus, GANs can generate novel data, but there is no way to steer the generation process to generate particular types of data. For example, a GAN that generates images of human faces cannot be explicitly told to generate a face with a particular hair color or of a specific gender. While techniques have been developed to analyze this latent space [32, 33], or build more interpretable latent spaces during the training process [30], they do not necessarily translate a human's prior intuition correctly or make use of labels when they are available. To tackle this problem, conditional GANs, first proposed as future work by Goodfellow et al. [9] and subsequently developed by Mirza and Osindero [34], allow directly targetable features (i.e., conditions) to be an integral part of the generator's input.

The conditioned training objective for a minimax GAN can be defined, without loss of generality, as

$$\min_{\theta_G} \max_{\theta_D} \mathbb{E}_{\boldsymbol{x}\sim\mathbb{P}_{\text{data}}}[\log D(\boldsymbol{x} \oplus \boldsymbol{c})] + \mathbb{E}_{\boldsymbol{z}\sim\mathbb{P}_z}[\log(1 - D(G(\boldsymbol{z} \oplus \boldsymbol{c})))], \tag{12}$$

where $\boldsymbol{z} \oplus \boldsymbol{c}$ is the basic concatenation of vectors. During training, the condition vector, $\boldsymbol{c}$, arises from the sampling process that produces each $\boldsymbol{x}$. This same framework can be used to design conditioned variants of other GAN formulations.

Conditional GANs have enjoyed great success as a result of their flexibility, even in the face of large, complex condition vectors, which may even be whole images. They enable new applications for GANs, including repairing software vulnerabilities (framed as a sequence to sequence translation) [35], integrated circuit mask design [36], and image-to-image translation [18]—the generation of images given text [37]—which is used as the target setting for this chapter. Notably, conditional GANs can increase the quality of generated samples for labeled datasets, even when conditioned generation is not needed [38]. Conditional GANs are therefore used as the platform for the TaylorGAN technique described in the following section.

2.6 Opportunity: Optimizing loss functions

The GAN formulations described earlier all have one property in common: the generator and discriminator loss functions have been arduously derived by hand. A GAN's performance and stability are greatly impacted by the choice of loss functions. Different regularization terms, such as the aforementioned gradient penalty can also affect a GAN's training. These elements of the GAN are typically designed to minimize a specific divergence. However, a GAN does not need to decrease a divergence at every step in order to reach the Nash equilibrium [28]. In this situation, an automatic loss-function optimization system may find novel GAN loss functions with more desirable properties. Such a system is presented in Section 4 and evaluated on conditional GANs in Section 6. The basic method for evolving loss functions, TaylorGLO, is reviewed in the following section.

3 Evolution of loss functions

Loss-function metalearning makes it possible to regularize networks automatically; TaylorGLO is a flexible and scalable implementation of this idea based on multivariate Taylor expansions.

3.1 Motivation

Loss-function metalearning for deep networks was first introduced by Gonzalez and Miikkulainen [4] as an automatic way to find customized loss functions that optimize a performance metric for a model. The technique, a genetic programming approach named GLO, discovered one particular loss function, Baikal, that improves classification accuracy, training speed, and data utilization. Intuitively, Baikal achieved these properties through a form of regularization that ensured the model would not become overly confident in its predictions. That is, instead of monotonically decreasing the loss when the output gets closer to the correct value, Baikal loss increases rapidly when the output is almost correct, thus discouraging extreme accuracy.

TaylorGLO [5] is a scalable reformulation of the GLO approach.[a] Instead of trees evolved through genetic programming, TaylorGLO represents loss functions as parameterizations of multivariate Taylor polynomials. It is then possible to evolve the parameters directly with CMA-ES, which makes it possible to scale to models with millions of trainable parameters and a variety of deep learning architectures.

3.2 Loss functions as multivariate Taylor expansions

Taylor expansions [39] represent differentiable functions within the neighborhood of a point using a polynomial series. In the univariate case, given a $C^{k_{\max}}$ smooth (i.e., first through $k_{\max}$ derivatives are continuous), real-valued function, $f(x)$: $\mathbb{R} \to \mathbb{R}$, a kth-order Taylor approximation at point $a \in \mathbb{R}$, $\hat{f}_k(x, a)$, where $0 \leq k \leq k_{\max}$, can be constructed as

[a]Open-source code for TaylorGLO is available at: https://github.com/cognizant-ai-labs/taylorglo.

$$\hat{f}_k(x,a) = \sum_{n=0}^{k} \frac{1}{n!} f^{(n)}(a)(x-a)^n. \tag{13}$$

This formulation can be extended to the multivariate case by defining an nth-degree multiindex, $\alpha = (\alpha_1, \alpha_2, \ldots, \alpha_n)$, where $\alpha_i \in \mathbb{N}_0$, $|\alpha| = \sum_{i=1}^{n} \alpha_i$, $\alpha! = \prod_{i=1}^{n} \alpha_i!$, $\mathbf{x}^\alpha = \prod_{i=1}^{n} x_i^{\alpha_i}$, and $\mathbf{x} \in \mathbb{R}^n$. Multivariate partial derivatives can be concisely written using a multiindex as

$$\partial^\alpha f = \partial_1^{\alpha_1} \partial_2^{\alpha_2} \cdots \partial_n^{\alpha_n} f = \frac{\partial^{|\alpha|}}{\partial x_1^{\alpha_1} \partial x_2^{\alpha_2} \cdots \partial x_n^{\alpha_n}}. \tag{14}$$

Thus, discounting the remainder term, the multivariate Taylor expansion for $f(\mathbf{x})$ at $\mathbf{a}$ is

$$\hat{f}_k(\mathbf{x},\mathbf{a}) = \sum_{\forall \alpha, |\alpha| \le k} \frac{1}{\alpha!} \partial^\alpha f(\mathbf{a})(\mathbf{x}-\mathbf{a})^\alpha. \tag{15}$$

The unique partial derivatives in $\hat{f}_k$ and $\mathbf{a}$ are parameters for a kth-order Taylor expansion. Thus, a kth-order Taylor expansion of a function in n variables requires n parameters to define the center, $\mathbf{a}$, and one parameter for each unique multiindex α, where $|\alpha| \le k$. That is,

$$\#_{\text{parameters}}(n,k) = n + \binom{n+k}{k} = n + \frac{(n+k)!}{n!\,k!}. \tag{16}$$

The multivariate Taylor expansion can be leveraged for loss-function parameterization [5]. Let an n-class classification loss function be defined as $\mathcal{L}_{\text{Log}} = -\frac{1}{n}\sum_{i=1}^{n} f(x_i, y_i)$. The function $f(x_i, y_i)$ can be replaced by its kth-order, bivariate Taylor expansion, $\hat{f}_k(x, y, a_x, a_y)$. For example, a loss function in $\mathbf{x}$ and $\mathbf{y}$ has the following third-order parameterization with parameters $\boldsymbol{\theta}$ (where $\mathbf{a} = \langle \theta_0, \theta_1 \rangle$):

$$\begin{aligned}\mathcal{L}(\mathbf{x},\mathbf{y}) = -\frac{1}{n}\sum_{i=1}^{n} \Big[& \theta_2 + \theta_3(y_i-\theta_1) + \frac{1}{2}\theta_4(y_i-\theta_1)^2 \\ & + \frac{1}{6}\theta_5(y_i-\theta_1)^3 + \theta_6(x_i-\theta_0) + \theta_7(x_i-\theta_0)(y_i-\theta_1) \\ & + \frac{1}{2}\theta_8(x_i-\theta_0)(y_i-\theta_1)^2 + \frac{1}{2}\theta_9(x_i-\theta_0)^2 \\ & + \frac{1}{2}\theta_{10}(x_i-\theta_0)^2(y_i-\theta_1) + \frac{1}{6}\theta_{11}(x_i-\theta_0)^3 \Big].\end{aligned} \tag{17}$$

As was shown by Gonzalez and Miikkulainen [5], the technique makes it possible to train neural networks that are more accurate and learn faster than those with tree-based loss-function representations. Representing loss functions in this manner guarantees that the functions are smooth, do not have poles, can be implemented through addition and multiplication, and can be trivially differentiated. The search space is locally smooth and has a tunable complexity parameter (the order of expansion), making it possible to find valid loss functions consistently and with high frequency. These properties are not necessarily held by alternative function approximators, such as Fourier expansions, Padé approximants, Laurent polynomials, and polyharmonic splines [5].

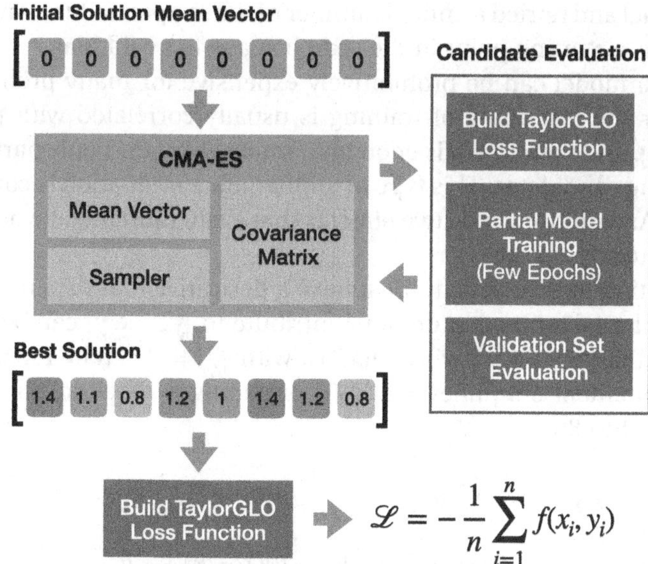

$$\mathcal{L} = -\frac{1}{n}\sum_{i=1}^{n} f(x_i, y_i)$$

FIG. 1 The TaylorGLO method [5]. Loss functions are represented by fixed-size vectors whose elements parameterize modified Taylor polynomials. Starting with a population of initially unbiased loss functions (i.e., vectors around the origin), CMA-ES optimizes their Taylor expansion parameters in order to maximize validation accuracy after partial training. The candidate with the highest accuracy is chosen as the final, best solution. This approach biases the search toward functions with useful properties, and is also amenable to theoretical analysis, as shown in this chapter.

3.3 The TaylorGLO method

TaylorGLO (Fig. 1) aims to find the optimal parameters for a loss function represented as a multivariate Taylor expansion. The parameters for a Taylor approximation (i.e., the center point and partial derivatives) are referred to as $\theta_{\hat{f}}$: $\theta_{\hat{f}} \in \Theta$, $\Theta = \mathbb{R}^{\#\text{parameters}}$. TaylorGLO strives to find the vector $\theta^*_{\hat{f}}$ that parameterizes the optimal loss function for a task. Because the values are continuous, as opposed to discrete graphs of the original GLO, it is possible to use continuous optimization methods.

In particular, covariance matrix adaptation evolutionary strategy (CMA-ES) [40] is a popular population-based, black-box optimization technique for rugged, continuous spaces. CMA-ES functions by maintaining a covariance matrix around a mean point that represents a distribution of solutions. At each generation, CMA-ES adapts the distribution to better fit evaluated objective values from sampled individuals. In this manner, the area in the search space that is being sampled at each step grows, shrinks, and moves dynamically as needed to maximize sampled candidates' fitness. TaylorGLO uses the $(\mu/\mu, \lambda)$ variant of CMA-ES [41], which incorporates weighted rank-μ updates [42] to reduce the number of objective function evaluations needed.

In order to find $\theta^*_{\hat{f}}$, at each generation CMA-ES samples points in Θ. Their fitness is determined by training a model with the corresponding loss function and evaluating the model on a validation dataset. Fitness evaluations may be distributed across multiple machines in parallel and retried a limited number of times upon failure. An initial vector of $\theta_{\hat{f}} = \mathbf{0}$ is chosen as a starting point in the search space to avoid bias.

Fully training a model can be prohibitively expensive for many problems. However, performance near the beginning of training is usually correlated with performance at the end of training, and therefore it is enough to train the models only partially to identify the most promising candidates. This type of approximate evaluation is common in meta-learning [43, 44]. An additional positive effect is that evaluation then favors loss functions that learn more quickly.

For a loss function to be useful, it must have a derivative that depends on the prediction. Therefore, internal terms that do not contribute to $\frac{\partial}{\partial \mathbf{y}}\mathcal{L}_f(\mathbf{x}, \mathbf{y})$ can be trimmed away. This step implies that any term t within $f(x_i, y_i)$ with $\frac{\partial}{\partial y_i} t = 0$ can be replaced with 0. For example, this refinement simplifies Eq. (17), providing a reduction in the number of parameters from 12 to 8:

$$\begin{aligned}\mathcal{L}(\mathbf{x},\mathbf{y}) = -\frac{1}{n}\sum_{i=1}^{n}\Big[&\theta_2(y_i-\theta_1)+\frac{1}{2}\theta_3(y_i-\theta_1)^2+\frac{1}{6}\theta_4(y_i-\theta_1)^3\\ &+\theta_5(x_i-\theta_0)(y_i-\theta_1)+\frac{1}{2}\theta_6(x_i-\theta_0)(y_i-\theta_1)^2\\ &+\frac{1}{2}\theta_7(x_i-\theta_0)^2(y_i-\theta_1)\Big].\end{aligned} \tag{18}$$

Building on this foundation, the method for evolving GAN formulations is described next.

4 The TaylorGAN approach

As GANs have grown in popularity, the difficulties involved in training them have become increasingly evident. The loss functions used to train a GAN's generator and discriminator constitute the core of how GANs are formulated. Thus, optimizing these loss functions jointly can result in better GANs. This section presents an extension of TaylorGLO to evolve loss functions for GANs. Images generated in this way improve both visually and quantitatively, as the experiments shown in Section 6.

TaylorGLO parameterization represents a loss function as a modified third-degree Taylor polynomial. Such a parameterization has many desirable properties, such as smoothness and continuity, that make it amenable for evolution [5]. In TaylorGAN, there are three functions that need to be optimized jointly (using the notation described in Table 1):

1. The component of the discriminator's loss that is a function of $D(\boldsymbol{x})$, the discriminator's output for a real sample from the dataset.
2. The synthetic/fake component of the discriminator's loss that is a function of $D(G(\boldsymbol{z}))$, the discriminator's output from the generator that samples $\boldsymbol{z}$ from the latent distribution).
3. The generator's loss, a function of $D(G(\boldsymbol{z}))$.

Table 2 Interpretation of existing GAN formulations.

Formulation	Loss *D* (real) $\mathbb{E}_{x \sim \mathbb{P}_{data}}$	Loss *D* (fake) $\mathbb{E}_{z \sim \mathbb{P}_z}$	Loss *G* (fake) $\mathbb{E}_{z \sim \mathbb{P}_z}$
GAN (minimax) [9]	$-\log D(\boldsymbol{x})$	$-\log(1 - D(G(\boldsymbol{z})))$	$\log(1 - D(G(\boldsymbol{z})))$
GAN (nonsaturating) [9]	$-\log D(\boldsymbol{x})$	$-\log(1 - D(G(\boldsymbol{z})))$	$-\log D(G(\boldsymbol{z}))$
WGAN [20]	$-D(\boldsymbol{x})$	$D(G(\boldsymbol{z}))$	$-D(G(\boldsymbol{z}))$
LSGAN [19]	$\frac{1}{2}(D(\boldsymbol{x}) - 1)^2$	$\frac{1}{2}(D(G(\boldsymbol{z})))^2$	$\frac{1}{2}(D(G(\boldsymbol{z})) - 1)^2$

These three components are all that are needed to define the discriminator's and generator's loss functions (sans regularization terms). Thus, TaylorGAN can discover and optimize new GAN formulations by jointly evolving three separate functions.

The discriminator's full loss is simply the sum of components (1) and (2). Table 2 shows how existing GAN formulations can be broken down into this tripartite loss.

These three functions can be evolved jointly. GAN loss functions have a single input, that is, $D(x)$ or $D(G(z))$. Thus, a set of three third-order TaylorGLO loss functions for GANs requires only 12 parameters to be optimized, making the technique quite efficient.

Fitness for each set of three functions requires a different interpretation than in regular TaylorGLO. Since GANs cannot be thought of as having accuracy, a different metric needs to be used. The choice of fitness metric depends on the type of problem and target application. In the uncommon case where the training data's sampling distribution is known, the clear choice is the divergence between such distribution and the distribution of samples from the generator. This approach will be used in the experiments here.

Reliable metrics of visual quality are difficult to define. Individual image quality metrics can be exploited by adversarially constructed, lesser-quality images [24]. For this reason, TaylorGAN utilizes a combination of two or more metrics and multiobjective optimization of them. Good solutions are usually located near the middle of the resulting Pareto front, and they can be found effectively through an objective transformation technique called composite objectives [6]. In this technique, evolution is performed against a weighted sum of metrics. Individual metrics are scaled such that their ranges of typical values match. Thus, if one metric improves, overall fitness will only increase if there is not a comparable regression along another metric.

5 Experimental setup

The technique was integrated into the LEAF evolutionary AutoML framework [45]. TaylorGAN parameters were evolved by the LEAF genetic algorithm as if they were hyperparameters. The implementation of CoDeepNEAT [46] for neural architecture search in LEAF was not used.

The technique was evaluated on the CMP Facade [7] dataset with a pix2pix-HD model [8]. The dataset consists of only 606 perspective-corrected 256×256 pixel images of building facades. Each image has a corresponding annotation image that segments facades into 12 different components, such as windows and doors. The objective is for the model to take an arbitrary annotation image as an input, and generate a photorealistic facade as output. The dataset was split into a training set with 80% of the images, and validation and testing sets, each with a disjoint 10% of the images.

Two metrics were used to evaluate loss-function candidates: (1) structural similarity index measure (SSIM) [47] between generated and ground-truth images and (2) perceptual distance, implemented as the L_1 distance between VGG-16 [48] and ImageNet [49] embeddings for generated and ground-truth images. During evolution, a composite objective [6] of these two metrics was used to evaluate candidates. The metrics were normalized (i.e., SSIM was multiplied by 17 and perceptual distance by -1) to have a similar impact on evolution.

The target GAN model, pix2pix-HD, is a refinement of the seminal pix2pix model [18]. Both models generate images conditioned upon an input image. Thus, they are trained with paired images. The baseline was trained with the Wasserstein loss [20] and spectral normalization [50] to enforce the Lipschitz constraint on the discriminator. The pix2pix-HD model is also trained with additive perceptual distance and discriminator feature losses. Both additive losses are multiplied by 10 in the baseline. Models were trained for 60 epochs.

When running experiments, each of the 12 TaylorGAN parameters was evolved within $[-10, 10]$. The learning rate and weights for both additive losses were also evolved since the baseline values, which are optimal for the Wasserstein loss, may not necessarily be optimal for TaylorGAN loss functions.

6 Results

TaylorGAN found a set of loss functions that outperformed the original Wasserstein loss with spectral normalization. After 49 generations of evolution, it discovered the loss functions

$$\begin{aligned}\mathcal{L}_{D_{\text{real}}} = {} & 5.6484\,(D(\boldsymbol{x}) - 8.3399) + 9.4935\,(D(\boldsymbol{x}) - 8.3399)^2 \\ & + 8.2695\,(D(\boldsymbol{x}) - 8.3399)^3,\end{aligned} \tag{19}$$

$$\begin{aligned}\mathcal{L}_{D_{\text{fake}}} = {} & 6.7549\,(D(G(\boldsymbol{z})) - 8.6177) + 2.4328\,(D(G(\boldsymbol{z})) - 8.6177)^2 \\ & + 8.0006\,(D(G(\boldsymbol{z})) - 8.6177)^3,\end{aligned} \tag{20}$$

$$\begin{aligned}\mathcal{L}_{G_{\text{fake}}} = {} & 0.0000\,(D(G(\boldsymbol{z})) - 5.2232) + 5.2849\,(D(G(\boldsymbol{z})) - 5.2232)^2 \\ & + 0.0000\,(D(G(\boldsymbol{z})) - 5.2232)^3.\end{aligned} \tag{21}$$

A learning rate of 0.0001, discriminator feature loss weight of 4.0877, and perceptual distance loss weight of 10.3155 evolved for this candidate.

Fig. 2 compares images for five random test samples that were generated with both the Wasserstein baseline and metalearned TaylorGAN loss functions. Visually, the TaylorGAN samples have more realistic coloration and details than the baseline. Baseline images all

FIG. 2 Five random samples from the CMP Facade test dataset, comparing Wasserstein and TaylorGAN loss functions. The loss functions are used to train pix2pix-HD models that take architectural element annotations (*top row*) and generate corresponding photorealistic images similar to the ground truth (*second row*). Images from the model trained with TaylorGAN (*bottom row*) have a higher quality than the baseline (*third row*). TaylorGAN images have more realistic coloration, better separation of the buildings from the sky, and finer details than the baseline.

have an orange tint, while TaylorGAN images more closely match ground-truth images' typical coloration. Note that color information is not included in the model's input, so per-sample color matching is not possible. Additionally, TaylorGAN images tend to have higher-quality fine-grained details. For example, facade textures are unnaturally smooth and clean in the baseline, almost appearing to be made of plastic.

Quantitatively, the TaylorGAN model also outperforms the Wasserstein baseline. Across 10 Wasserstein baseline runs, the average test-set SSIM was 9.4359 and the average test-set perceptual distance was 2129.5069. The TaylorGAN model improved both metrics, with an SSIM of 11.6615 and perceptual distance of 2040.2561.

Notably, the training set is very small, with fewer than 500 image pairs, showing how loss-function metalearning's benefits on small classification datasets also extend to GANs. Thus, metalearned loss functions are an effective way to train better GAN models, extending the types of problems to which evolutionary loss-function metalearning can be applied.

7 Discussion and future work

The results in this chapter show that evolving GAN formulations is a promising direction for research. On the CMP Facade benchmark dataset, TaylorGAN discovered powerful loss functions. With them, GANs generated images that were qualitatively and quantitatively better than those produced by GANs with a Wasserstein loss. This unique application showcases the power and flexibility of evolutionary loss-function metalearning, and suggests that it may provide a crucial ingredient in making GANs more reliable and scalable to harder problems.

At first glance, optimizing GAN loss functions is difficult because it is difficult to quantify a GAN's performance. That is, performance can be improved on an individual metric without increasing the quality of generated images. Multiobjective evolution, via composite objectives, is thus a key technique that allows evolution to work on GAN formulations. That is, by optimizing against multiple metrics, each with its own negative biases, the effects of each individual metric's bias will not deleteriously affect the path evolution takes.

There are several avenues of future work with TaylorGAN. First, it can naturally be applied to different datasets and different types of GANs. While image-to-image translation is an important GAN domain, there are many others that can benefit from optimization, such as image super-resolution and unconditioned image generation. Since TaylorGAN customizes loss functions for a given task, dataset, and architecture, unique sets of loss functions could be discovered for each of them.

There is a wide space of metrics, such as Delta E perceptual color distance [51], that quantify different aspects of image quality. They can be used to evaluate GANs in more detail and thus guide multiobjective evolution more precisely, potentially resulting in more effective and creative solutions.

8 Conclusions

While GANs provide fascinating opportunities for generating realistic content, they are difficult to train and evaluate. This chapter proposes an evolutionary metalearning technique, TaylorGAN, to optimize a crucial part of their design automatically. By evolving loss functions customized to the task, dataset, and architecture, GANs can be more stable and generate qualitatively and quantitatively better results. TaylorGAN may therefore serve as a crucial stepping stone toward scaling up GANs to a wider variety and harder set of problems.

References

[1] K.O. Stanley, J. Clune, J. Lehman, R. Miikkulainen, Designing neural networks through evolutionary algorithms, Nat. Mach. Intell. 1 (2019) 24–35.

[2] E. Real, A. Aggarwal, Y. Huang, Q.V. Le, Regularized evolution for image classifier architecture search, in: Proceedings of the AAAI Conference on Artificial Intelligence, AAAI, 2019.

[3] J. Liang, E. Meyerson, B. Hodjat, D. Fink, K. Mutch, R. Miikkulainen, Evolutionary neural AutoML for deep learning, in: Proceedings of the Genetic and Evolutionary Computation Conference (GECCO-2019), 2019.

[4] S. Gonzalez, R. Miikkulainen, Improved training speed, accuracy, and data utilization through loss function optimization, in: Proceedings of the IEEE Congress on Evolutionary Computation (CEC), 2020.

[5] S. Gonzalez, R. Miikkulainen, Optimizing loss functions through multivariate Taylor polynomial parameterization, in: Proceedings of the Genetic and Evolutionary Computation Conference (GECCO-2021), 2021.

[6] H. Shahrzad, D. Fink, R. Miikkulainen, Enhanced optimization with composite objectives and novelty selection, in: Artificial Life Conference Proceedings, MIT Press, 2018, pp. 616–622.

[7] R. Tyleček, R. Šára, Spatial pattern templates for recognition of objects with regular structure, in: Proceeding of the German Conference on Pattern Recognition (GCPR), Springer, Saarbrucken, Germany, 2013, pp. 364–374.

[8] T.-C. Wang, M.-Y. Liu, J.-Y. Zhu, A. Tao, J. Kautz, B. Catanzaro, High-resolution image synthesis and semantic manipulation with conditional GANs, in: Proceedings of the IEEE Conference on Computer Vision and Pattern Recognition (CVPR), 2018, pp. 8798–8807.

[9] I. Goodfellow, J. Pouget-Abadie, M. Mirza, B. Xu, D. Warde-Farley, S. Ozair, A. Courville, Y. Bengio, Generative adversarial nets, in: Z. Ghahramani, M. Welling, C. Cortes, N.D. Lawrence, K.Q. Weinberger (Eds.), Advances in Neural Information Processing Systems 27, Curran Associates, Inc., 2014, pp. 2672–2680.

[10] D. Kingma, M. Welling, Auto-encoding variational Bayes, in: Proceedings of the Second International Conference on Learning Representations (ICLR), December, 2014.

[11] G.E. Hinton, T.J. Sejnowski, Optimal perceptual inference, in: Proceedings of the IEEE Conference on Computer Vision and Pattern Recognition (CVPR), Citeseer, 1983, pp. 448–453.

[12] P. Smolensky, Information processing in dynamical systems: foundations of harmony theory, Colorado University at Boulder Department of Computer Science, 1986 (Technical Report).

[13] R. Salakhutdinov, G. Hinton, Deep Boltzmann machines, in: Artificial Intelligence and Statistics, 2009, pp. 448–455.

[14] J. Nash, Non-cooperative games, Ann. Math. 54 (1951) 286–295.

[15] M. Heusel, H. Ramsauer, T. Unterthiner, B. Nessler, S. Hochreiter, GANs trained by a two time-scale update rule converge to a local Nash equilibrium, in: I. Guyon, U.V. Luxburg, S. Bengio, H. Wallach, R. Fergus, S. Vishwanathan, R. Garnett (Eds.), Advances in Neural Information Processing Systems 30, Curran Associates, Inc., 2017, pp. 6626–6637.

[16] A. Radford, L. Metz, S. Chintala, Unsupervised representation learning with deep convolutional generative adversarial networks, arXiv:1511.06434 (2015).

[17] L. Metz, B. Poole, D. Pfau, J. Sohl-Dickstein, Unrolled generative adversarial networks, arXiv:1611.02163 (2016).

[18] P. Isola, J.-Y. Zhu, T. Zhou, A.A. Efros, Image-to-image translation with conditional adversarial networks, arXiv (2017) arXiv:1611.07004.

[19] X. Mao, Q. Li, H. Xie, R.Y.K. Lau, Z. Wang, S. Paul Smolley, Least squares generative adversarial networks, in: The IEEE International Conference on Computer Vision (ICCV), October, 2017.

[20] M. Arjovsky, S. Chintala, L. Bottou, Wasserstein generative adversarial networks, in: D. Precup, Y.W. Teh (Eds.), Proceedings of Machine Learning Research, Proceedings of the 34th International Conference on Machine Learning (ICML), 6–11 August, vol. 70, PMLR, International Convention Centre, Sydney, Australia, 2017, pp. 214–223.

[21] I. Gulrajani, F. Ahmed, M. Arjovsky, V. Dumoulin, A.C. Courville, Improved training of Wasserstein GANs, in: I. Guyon, U.V. Luxburg, S. Bengio, H. Wallach, R. Fergus, S. Vishwanathan, R. Garnett (Eds.), Advances in Neural Information Processing Systems 30, Curran Associates, Inc., 2017, pp. 5767–5777.

[22] X. Mao, Q. Li, H. Xie, R.Y.K. Lau, Z. Wang, S.P. Smolley, On the effectiveness of least squares generative adversarial networks, IEEE Trans. Pattern Anal. Mach. Intell. 41 (12) (2019) 2947.

[23] A. Odena, V. Dumoulin, C. Olah, Deconvolution and checkerboard artifacts, Distill (2016), https://doi.org/10.23915/distill.00003.

[24] A. Borji, Pros and cons of GAN evaluation measures, Comput. Vis. Image Underst. 179 (2019) 41–65.

[25] C. Villani, The Wasserstein distances, in: Optimal Transport, Springer, 2009, pp. 93–111.

[26] T. Tieleman, G. Hinton, Lecture 6.5-rmsprop: divide the gradient by a running average of its recent magnitude, COURSERA: Neural Netw. Mach. Learn. 4 (2) (2012) 26–31.

[27] D.P. Kingma, J. Ba, Adam: a method for stochastic optimization, CoRR abs/1412.6980 (2014).

[28] W. Fedus, M. Rosca, B. Lakshminarayanan, A.M. Dai, S. Mohamed, I. Goodfellow, Many paths to equilibrium: GANs do not need to decrease a divergence at every step, in: Proceedings of the Sixth International Conference on Learning Representations (ICLR), 2018.

[29] K. Pearson, On the criterion that a given system of deviations from the probable in the case of a correlated system of variables is such that it can be reasonably supposed to have arisen from random sampling, Lond. Edinb. Dublin Philos. Mag. J. Sci. 50 (302) (1900) 157–175.

[30] X. Chen, Y. Duan, R. Houthooft, J. Schulman, I. Sutskever, P. Abbeel, InfoGAN: interpretable representation learning by information maximizing generative adversarial nets, in: D.D. Lee, M. Sugiyama, U.V. Luxburg, I. Guyon, R. Garnett (Eds.), Advances in Neural Information Processing Systems 29, Curran Associates, Inc., 2016, pp. 2172–2180.

[31] A.B.L. Larsen, S.K. Sønderby, H. Larochelle, O. Winther, Autoencoding beyond pixels using a learned similarity metric, arXiv:1512.09300 (2015).

[32] V. Volz, J. Schrum, J. Liu, S.M. Lucas, A. Smith, S. Risi, Evolving Mario levels in the latent space of a deep convolutional generative adversarial network, in: Proceedings of the Genetic and Evolutionary Computation Conference (GECCO), ACM, 2018, pp. 221–228.

[33] M. Li, R. Xi, B. Chen, M. Hou, D. Liu, L. Guo, Generate desired images from trained generative adversarial networks, in: Proceedings of the IEEE International Joint Conference on Neural Networks (IJCNN), IEEE, 2019, pp. 1–8.

[34] M. Mirza, S. Osindero, Conditional generative adversarial nets, arXiv:1411.1784 (2014).

[35] J. Harer, O. Ozdemir, T. Lazovich, C. Reale, R. Russell, L. Kim, P. Chin, Learning to repair software vulnerabilities with generative adversarial networks, in: S. Bengio, H. Wallach, H. Larochelle, K. Grauman, N. Cesa-Bianchi, R. Garnett (Eds.), Advances in Neural Information Processing Systems 31, Curran Associates, Inc., 2018, pp. 7933–7943.

[36] M.B. Alawieh, Y. Lin, Z. Zhang, M. Li, Q. Huang, D.Z. Pan, GAN-SRAF: sub-resolution assist feature generation using conditional generative adversarial networks, in: Proceedings of the 56th Annual Design Automation Conference (DAC), ACM, 2019, p. 149.

[37] S. Reed, Z. Akata, X. Yan, L. Logeswaran, B. Schiele, H. Lee, Generative adversarial text to image synthesis, in: M.F. Balcan, K.Q. Weinberger (Eds.), Proceedings of Machine Learning Research, Proceedings of the 33rd International Conference on Machine Learning (ICML), 20–22 June, vol. 48, PMLR, New York, NY, 2016, pp. 1060–1069.

[38] A. van den Oord, N. Kalchbrenner, L. Espeholt, K. Kavukcuoglu, O. Vinyals, A. Graves, Conditional image generation with PixelCNN decoders, in: D.D. Lee, M. Sugiyama, U.V. Luxburg, I. Guyon, R. Garnett (Eds.), Advances in Neural Information Processing Systems 29, Curran Associates, Inc., 2016, pp. 4790–4798.

[39] B. Taylor, Methodus Incrementorum Directa & Inversa. Auctore Brook Taylor, LL. D. & Regiae Societatis Secretario, Typis Pearsonianis: Prostant apud Gul. Innys ad Insignia Principis in ..., 1715.

[40] N. Hansen, A. Ostermeier, Adapting arbitrary normal mutation distributions in evolution strategies: the covariance matrix adaptation, in: Proceedings of IEEE International Conference on Evolutionary Computation, IEEE, 1996, pp. 312–317.

[41] N. Hansen, A. Ostermeier, Completely derandomized self-adaptation in evolution strategies, Evol. Comput. 9 (2) (2001) 159–195.

[42] N. Hansen, S. Kern, Evaluating the CMA evolution strategy on multimodal test functions, in: International Conference on Parallel Problem Solving From Nature, Springer, 2004, pp. 282–291.

[43] J.J. Grefenstette, J.M. Fitzpatrick, Genetic search with approximate function evaluations, in: Proceedings of an International Conference on Genetic Algorithms and Their Applications, 1985, pp. 112–120.

[44] Y. Jin, Surrogate-assisted evolutionary computation: recent advances and future challenges, Swarm Evol. Comput. 1 (2011) 61–70, https://doi.org/10.1016/j.swevo.2011.05.001.

[45] J. Liang, E. Meyerson, B. Hodjat, D. Fink, K. Mutch, R. Miikkulainen, Evolutionary neural autoML for deep learning, in: Proceedings of the Genetic and Evolutionary Computation Conference (GECCO), 2019, pp. 401–409.

[46] R. Miikkulainen, J. Liang, E. Meyerson, A. Rawal, D. Fink, O. Francon, B. Raju, H. Shahrzad, A. Navruzyan, N. Duffy, et al., Evolving deep neural networks, in: Artificial Intelligence in the Age of Neural Networks and Brain Computing, Elsevier, 2019, pp. 293–312.

[47] Z. Wang, A.C. Bovik, H.R. Sheikh, E.P. Simoncelli, Image quality assessment: from error visibility to structural similarity, IEEE Trans. Image Process. 13 (4) (2004) 600–612.

[48] K. Simonyan, A. Zisserman, Very deep convolutional networks for large-scale image recognition, arXiv:1409.1556 (2014).

[49] O. Russakovsky, J. Deng, H. Su, J. Krause, S. Satheesh, S. Ma, Z. Huang, A. Karpathy, A. Khosla, M. Bernstein, A.C. Berg, L. Fei-Fei, ImageNet large scale visual recognition challenge, Int. J. Comput. Vis. 115 (3) (2015) 211–252, https://doi.org/10.1007/s11263-015-0816-y.

[50] T. Miyato, T. Kataoka, M. Koyama, Y. Yoshida, Spectral normalization for generative adversarial networks, in: Proceedings of the Sixth International Conference on Learning Representations (ICLR), 2018.

[51] A.R. Robertson, Historical development of CIE recommended color difference equations, Color Res. Appl. 15 (3) (1990) 167–170.

16

Multiview learning in biomedical applications

Angela Serra, Paola Galdi, and Roberto Tagliaferri

NEURONE LAB, DISA-MIS, UNIVERSITY OF SALERNO, FISCIANO, SALERNO, ITALY

Chapter outlines

1 Introduction

In the last decades, there has been a growing interest in applying data integration methods in the field of biomedical research, with the consequent proliferation of scientific literature devoted to this topic.

Multiview learning is the branch of machine learning concerned with the analysis of multimodal data, i.e., patterns represented by different sets of features extracted from multiple data sources. Classical examples of multiview medical data are the different clinical tests to which a patient can be subjected, such as magnetic resonance imaging, electrocardiogram, blood test, blood pressure, X-ray, and EEG (Fig. 1). These data are generally

Artificial Intelligence in the Age of Neural Networks and Brain Computing. https://doi.org/10.1016/B978-0-323-96104-2.00010-5

Copyright © 2024 Elsevier Inc. All rights reserved.

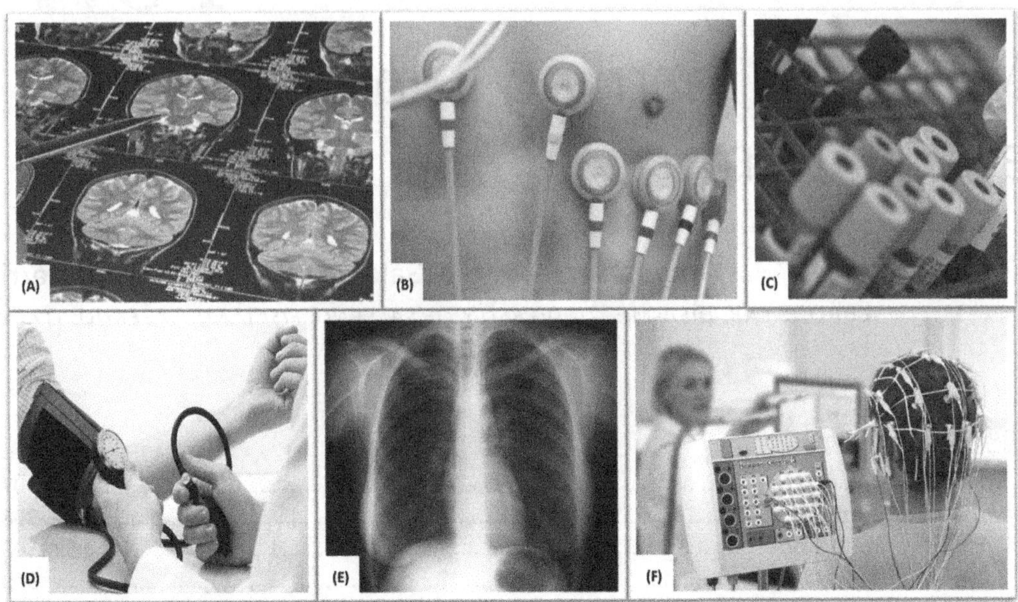

FIG. 1 Example of multiview data related to clinical tests. (A) Magnetic resonance imaging; (B) electrocardiogram; (C) blood test; (D) blood pressure; (E) X-ray; (F) EEG.

not homogeneous (for example, they can consist of images, signals, or text) but when analyzed together help to better understand the patient's medical condition.

The reasons for the fast spreading of this learning approach lie in the constant increase of real-world problems where heterogeneous data are available for describing the same phenomena. Bioinformatics and neurobiology are two prominent examples of fields of application that deal with multiview data: for the same set of samples, different kinds of measurements provide distinct facets of the same domain, encoding multiple biologically-relevant patterns. A model integrating different perspectives or views of the data can provide a richer representation of the underlying biological system than a model based on a single view alone.

The ability to combine different modalities assumes great relevance when trying to unravel complex phenomena such as the physiological and pathological mechanism governing the human neural system or the subtle molecular differences between subtypes of diseases, that are known to be the result of the interaction of several con-causes.

To achieve this goal, several tools provided by different disciplines are needed, including mathematical, statistical, and computational methods for the extraction of information from inhomogeneous data sources.

2 Multiview learning

These days, researchers working with data integration favor mainly two kinds of approaches: the first methodology implies the combination of complementary

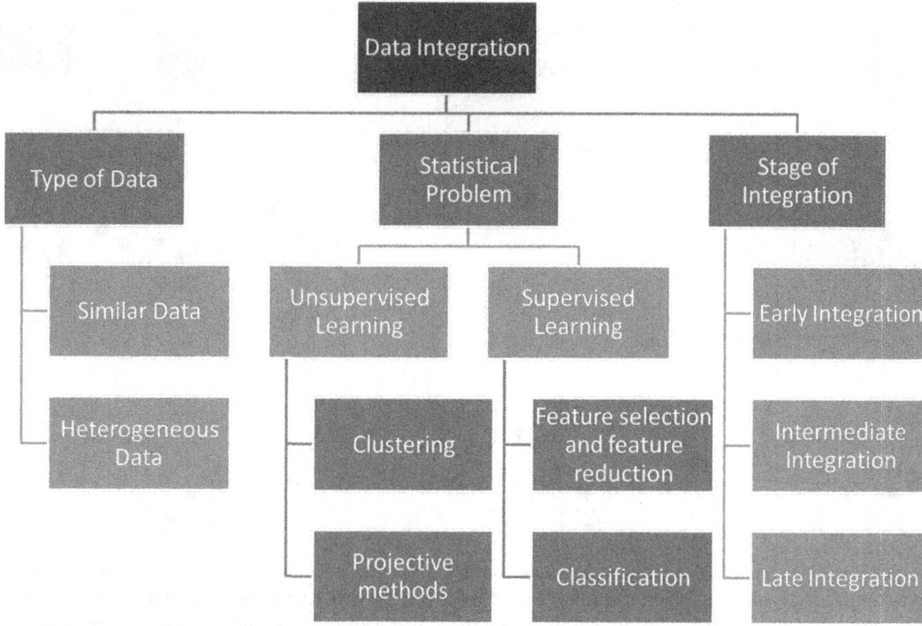

FIG. 2 Data integration taxonomy.

information coming from different sources describing complex phenotypes on the same set of samples (multiview learning); the second strategy, known as metaanalysis, tries to infer new knowledge integrating the information about the phenotypes of interest with prior knowledge regarding already known phenotypes by means of comparative methods. Fig. 2 reports a taxonomy of integration methodologies classified according to the statistical problem, the type of analysis to be performed, the type of data to be integrated, and the stage in which integration is accomplished.

2.1 Integration stage

When building up a workflow for data analysis, an investigator can choose to perform the integration step at different stages; we can then distinguish between early, intermediate, and late integration (Fig. 3). The choice of one method over another depends on aspects that are problem-specific, such as the heterogeneity of the input data and the statistical problem to be addressed.

Early integration is performed before any analysis step, directly manipulating the input data. This strategy consists in fact in concatenating all the variables from the multiple views to obtain a single feature space, but without changing the nature or general format of data. It is usually applied to combine data coming from multiple experiments in a bigger pool. The main drawback of this methodology is through the choice of a suitable distance metric: the

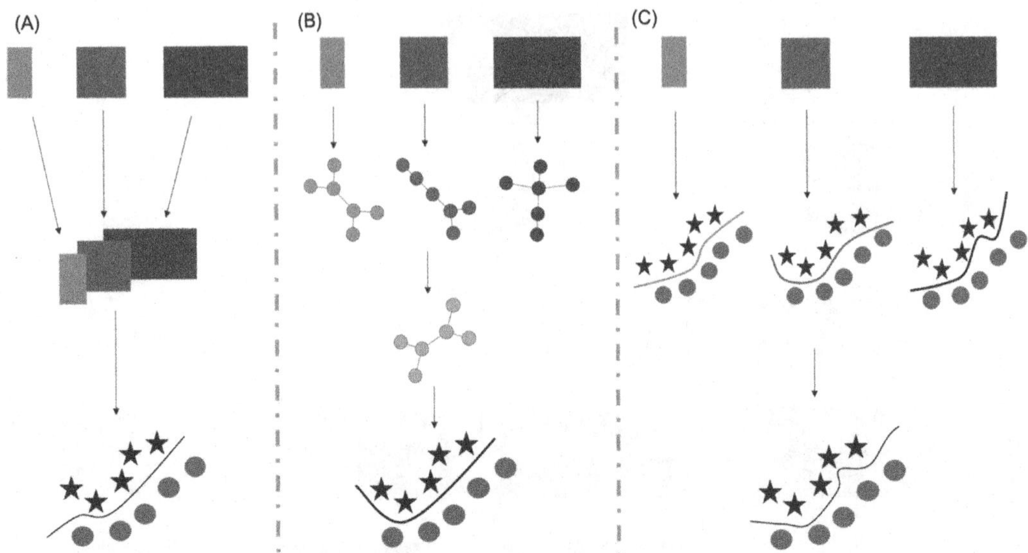

FIG. 3 Data integration stages as proposed by Pavlidis et al. They proposed an SVM kernel function to integrate microarray data. In early integration methodologies, SVMs are trained with a kernel obtained from the concatenation of all the views in the dataset (A). In intermediate integration, first a kernel is obtained for each view, and then, the combined kernel is used to train the SVM (B). In the late integration methodology, a single SVM is trained on a single kernel for each view and then the final results are combined (C).

concatenation of views translates in an increase of the dimensionality of the feature space, that in turn can affect the performance of classical similarity measures [1].

While early integration builds a new feature space concatenating different views, intermediate integration transforms each data view in a common feature space, thus avoiding the problem of increasing data dimensionality. For example, in classification problems every view can be transformed in a similarity matrix (or kernel) and these matrices can then be combined to obtain more accurate results.

Finally, in the late integration approach, a distinct analysis workflow is carried out separately for each view and only the results are integrated. The advantages of this methodology are that (1) the investigator can choose an ad hoc algorithm for each view to obtain the best possible result for each kind of data and (2) analyses on several views can be executed in parallel.

2.2 Type of data

Considering the nature of data that are the object of study, we can distinguish between the integration of homogeneous or heterogeneous data. In systems biology, data are said to be homogeneous if they assay the same molecular level, as for gene or protein expression or copy number variation. Conversely, heterogeneous data are derived from two or more different molecular levels. In the latter case, some challenges need to be tackled by the investigator. First of all, data may differ in format and structure, varying from discrete or continuous numerical values to more complex data such as sequences or graphs. Moreover, different data sources may be characterized by different noise levels depending on the platform and on the technologies used to generate the data. For this reason, during the integration phase, a step of batch effect removal needs to be included, to bring to comparable levels the noise and the random or systematic errors between the different views [2].

2.3 Type of analysis

The choice of the analysis to be performed is evidently determined by the type of data involved in the experiments and by the kind of integration that needs to be accomplished. Two broad categories of analyses can be identified: integrative analysis and metaanalysis. Metaanalysis is based on previous results, and in this sense it can be considered as a late integration approach. It consists of aggregating summary statistics from several studies, and therefore, it requires data to be homogeneous [3,4]. On the other hand, integrative analysis is a more flexible methodology, since it allows the fusion of different data sources to get more stable and reliable results.

Many methods have been developed that differ according to the type of data and the chosen stage for integration and span a landscape of techniques comprising graph theory, machine learning, and statistics.

3 Multiview learning in bioinformatics

3.1 Patient subtyping

One of the main difficulties in the treatment of complex diseases—such as cancer, neuropsychiatric diseases and autoimmune disorders—is the consistent variability in manifestations among affected individuals [5].

Precision medicine (Fig. 4) (or personalized medicine) is a new discipline that emerged in recent years and aims to solve this problem [6]. Its goal is that of individualizing the practice of medicine by taking into account individual variability in genes, lifestyle, and environment to predict disease progression and transitions between disease stages and target the most appropriate medical treatments [7].

Under these premises, the task of patients subtyping assumes a key role: in fact, once subpopulations of patients with similar characteristics are identified, more accurate diagnostic and treatment strategies can be developed for each of such groups. Moreover, the ability to refine the prognosis for a category of patients can reduce the uncertainty about the expected outcome of a clinical treatment on the individual.

The traditional approach to disease subtyping required the intervention of a clinician, whose role was to single out anomalies in patterns or groups of outlier patients based on previous clinical experience. This task was usually accomplished as an a posteriori analysis, and once a subgroup was selected a second retrospective or prospective study was necessary to confirm the hypothesis of the existence of a new class of patients.

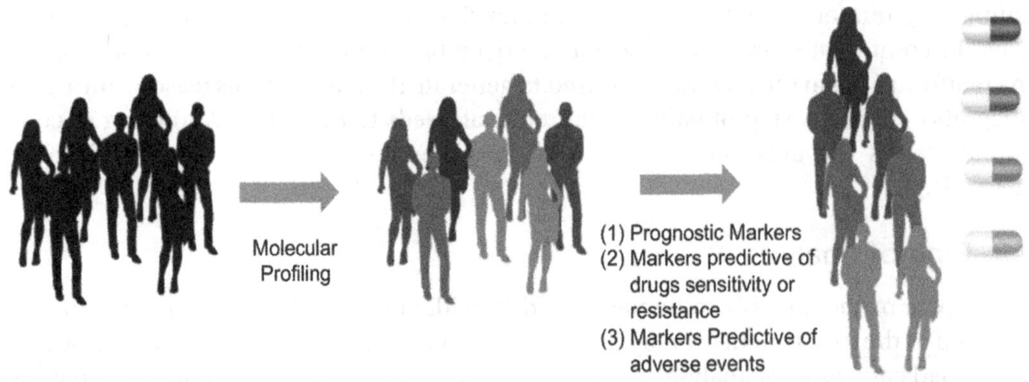

FIG. 4 Precision medicine.

Nowadays, thanks to the availability of high-throughput biotechnologies it is possible to measure individual differences at the cellular and molecular levels. Moreover, the application of unsupervised automated techniques for the analysis of high-throughput molecular data allows for unbiased biomedical discoveries. Statistical methods and machine learning approaches—such as nonnegative matrix factorization, hierarchical clustering, and probabilistic latent factor analysis [8,9]—have been applied to identify subgroups of individuals showing common patterns of gene expression levels.

Other omics data can be used in combination with gene expression to build more accurate models for patient stratification. For example, somatic copy number alterations have proved to be promising biomarkers for cancer subtype classification [10]. Other alternatives to be considered are microRNA expression and methylation data. Due to the variety of available data, data integration approaches to the problem of patients-subtyping have recently drawn the attention of the research community.

Nevertheless, the integration of heterogeneous omics data poses several computational challenges, since generally, a small number of samples is available for a relatively high number of variables and different preprocessing strategies need to be applied for each type of data source. In addition, data are usually redundant, so proper techniques are needed to extract only relevant information. Finally, care must be taken in defining a coherent metric for studying relations between samples described through heterogeneous modalities.

Several of the recently proposed data integration methods for patients subgroups discovery are based on supervised classification, unsupervised clustering, or bi-clustering [11–14]. A few approaches based on multiview clustering have been proposed for being used on omics data.

Similarity network fusion (SNF) [15] is an intermediate integration network fusion methodology able to integrate multiple genomic data (e.g., mRNA expression, DNA methylation, and microRNA expression data) to identify relevant patients' subtypes. The method first constructs a patients' similarity network for each view. Then, it iteratively

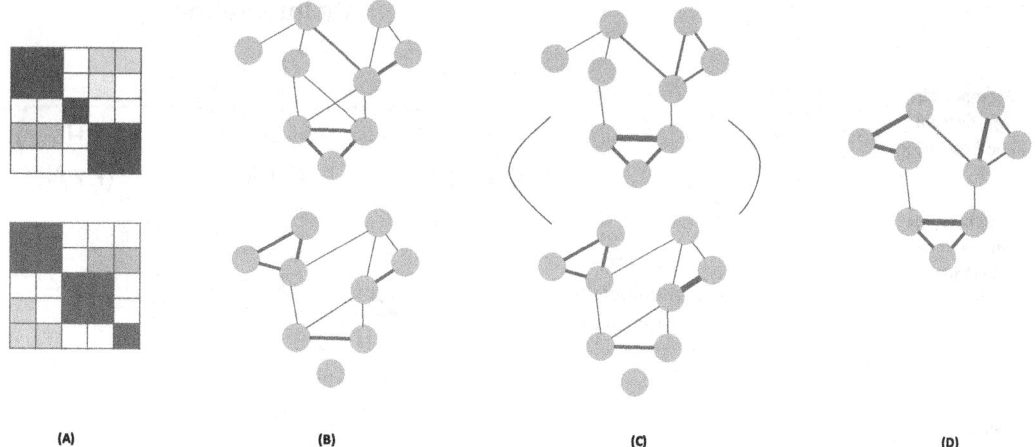

FIG. 5 SNF approach. The SNF tool first constructs the patients similarity matrices for each data type (A), then it computes the patient-by-patient similarity networks (B), the networks are then integrated in an iterative approach (C) the patients clusters are evaluated with a spectral clustering algorithm on the fused network (D).

updates the network with the information coming from other networks to make them more similar at each step. In the end, this iterative process converges to a final fused network (see Fig. 5).

MVDA, a multiview genomic data integration methodology [16], aims to combine dimensionality reduction, variable selection, clustering (for each available data type), and data integration methods to find patient subtypes, as described in Fig. 6. First, the feature number for each data type (genes, miRNAs, protein, etc.) is reduced by means of a cluster-based correlation analysis. Second, a ranked-based method is employed to select the features that best separate patients into subtypes. Third, clustering is used to identify patient subtypes independently from each reduced dataset. Fourth, integrative clustering methods are exploited to find more robust patient subtypes and assess the contributions of different data types used for the identification of all the patient subtypes.

Multi-Omics Graph cOnvolutional NETworks (MOGONET) [17] is a novel multiview learning tool that integrates multiomics data by using graph convolutional networks. MOGONET is able to perform patient classification and biomarker identification. The MOGONET pipeline first preprocesses each individual omic data type removing noise and redundant features. Afterward, patients' similarity networks are generated from each data view and used to train one graph convolution network for each view to perform patient class predictions. By following an intermediate integration approach, the predictions of each data layer are integrated in a unified tensor and given in input to a view correlation discovery network to obtain the final prediction. The authors demonstrated MOGONET efficacy by integrating mRNA expression data, DNA methylation data, and microRNA expression data. MOGONET has also the capability to identify biomarkers from the different omic data layers, which is an essential task to help understand the underlying biology in biomedical applications.

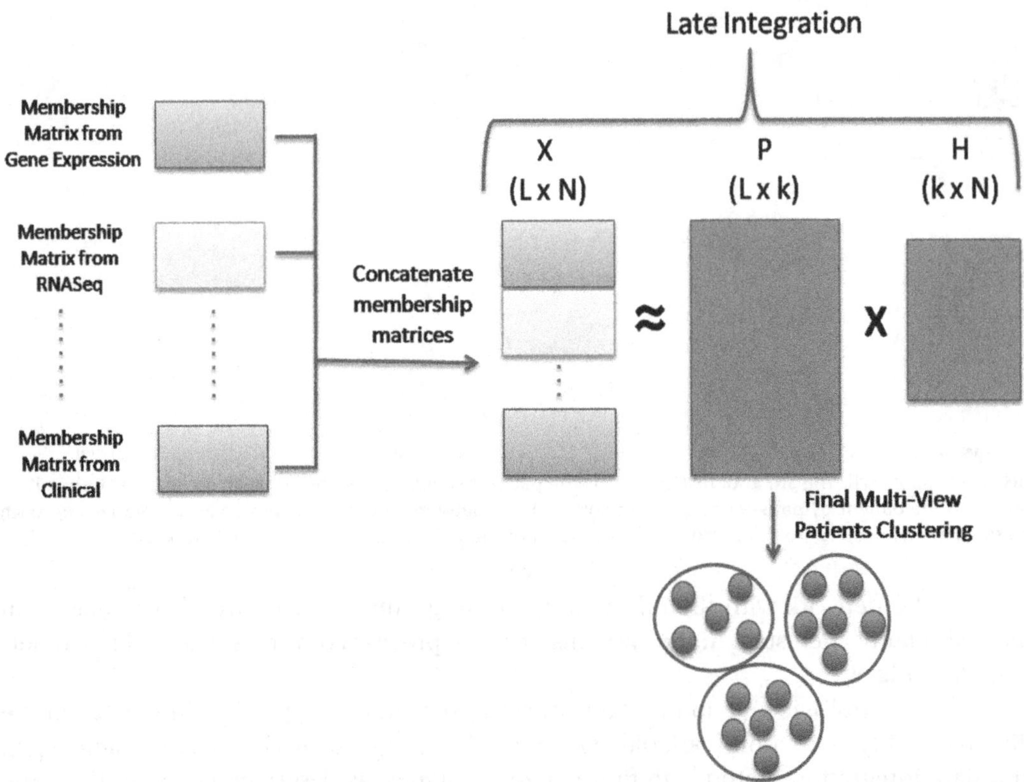

FIG. 6 The multiview genomic data integration methodology is composed of four steps. First, a dimensionality reduction is performed by clustering the features. A prototype is extracted for each cluster to represent it in the following steps. Second, the prototypes are ranked by the patient class separability and the most significant ones are selected. Third, single-view clustering methods are applied to each view to group patients and obtain membership matrices. Fourth, a late integration approach is used to integrate clustering results.

3.2 Drug repositioning

Drug repositioning is the process by which known drugs and compounds are used to treat new indications (i.e., a different disease from that for which the drug was placed on the market) [18].

The main advantage of drug repositioning over traditional drug development is that the risk of failure of adverse toxicology is reduced because the known drugs have already passed several toxicity tests. Moreover, the probability of drug failure during development is really high and is one of the higher costs in pharmaceutical development [19]. Drug repositioning tasks cut these costs from the production process.

This practice has therefore become increasingly attractive as it has the double benefit of making the production of the drug faster and decreasing the costs of production and marketing. Even more important is its ability to provide treatments for unmet medical needs [20].

Classical methods for drug repositioning rely on the response of the cell (at the level of the genes) after treatment, or on disease-to-drug relationships, merging several information levels [21–23]. However, these approaches encountered some limitations such as the noisy structure of the gene expression and the few amount of genomic data related to many diseases.

Multiview biological data (see Fig. 7) and their integration can significantly increase the ability of the scientific community to reposition existing drugs. Usually, these approaches use machine-learning or network theory algorithms to integrate and analyze multiple layers of information such as the similarity of the drugs based on how similar are their chemical structures, or on how close are their targets within the protein-protein interaction network, and on how correlated are the gene expression patterns after treatment.

For example, Iorio et al. [24], starting from transcriptomic data related to drugs treatment on human cells, constructed a network of interactions between drugs to characterize their mode of action. Each drug was represented by the ranked list of genes sorted by their differential expression values with respect to their control. The similarities between each couple of drugs, which become the weights of the edges of the network, were computed by using the inverse total enrichment score (TES) which is based on the Kolmogorov-Smirnov test [25]. Then, they scanned the network in search of communities, to identify groups of drugs with similar effects. Moreover, to reposition a new drug, the distances

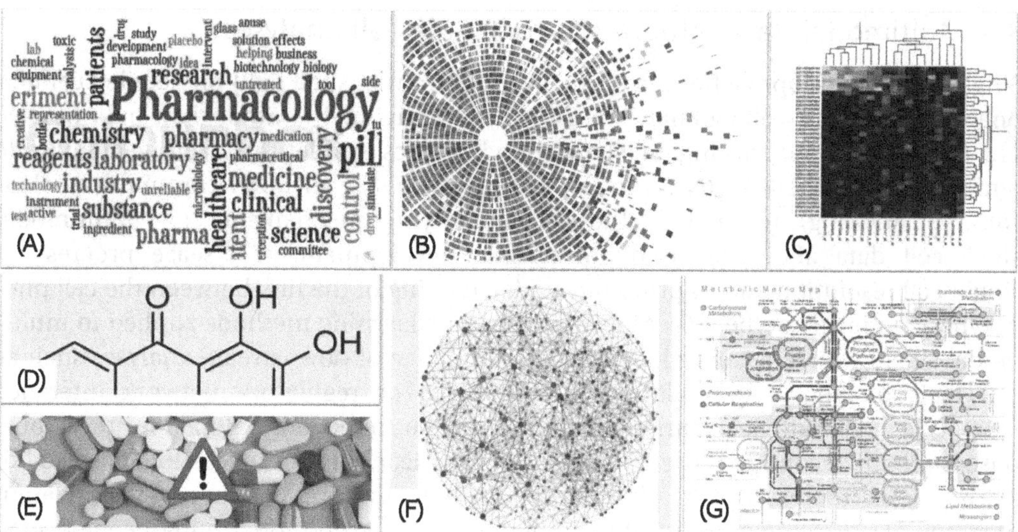

FIG. 7 Drug repositioning algorithms can integrate different kinds of information, such as text (A), genome-wide studies (B), gene expression (C), structural properties (D), adverse events such as drugs side effects (E), interactiome (F), pathways (G).

between its molecular alteration pattern and one of the drugs in the communities were calculated. Finally, the drugs were predicted to have the same behavior as those in the closest community.

Another example is the work of Napolitano et al. [26] that, for each drug, integrated three different omics views: genome-wide gene expression measures, chemical structure, and drug targets. They applied a kernel-based late integration approach where for each view they constructed a distance matrix and then they combined these matrices by creating a mean kernel. The first similarity matrix is the correlation between the gene expression patterns; the second depends on how similar are the drugs with respect to their chemical structure and the last one is the distance matrix between drug targets in their protein-protein interaction network. The combined matrix was used to train the multiclass SVM classifier to predict therapeutic classes. Their results show high accuracy in the classification task that allows for the re-positioning of systematically misclassified drugs.

Recently, an integrative network-based deep learning approach, deepDR, has been proposed [27]. deepDR integrates multiple networks, such as drug-disease, drug-side effect, drug-target, and drug-drug networks, to predict new connections between drugs and diseases. deepDR learns drug-related multimodal features from these networks by means of multimodal deep autoencoders. These new features are then concatenated and used to train a variational autoencoder that is subsequently used to infer new drug-disease connections. The results of the study show that this kind of approach outperforms other classical methods.

3.3 Multimodal data integration for single-cell analyses

Single-cell omics approaches are particularly relevant to shed light on detailed cellular phenotypes, as they allow analyzing single cell individually rather than bulk tissues. The fast advancement of single-cell multimodal omics enables the profiling of multiple omics layers (e.g., DNA, RNA, protein, methylated DNA, or open chromatin nucleosome positioning) to analyze the cell underlying mechanism [28]. Multimodal single-cell data allow the study of normal development or disease progress at single-cell resolution and improve our understanding of the link between the cell phenotypes and its genotype [29]. Multiview machine learning methods applied to multimodal single-cell data can enhance the performance of downstream analyses such as cell type labeling, subpopulation identification, or regulatory network inference [28,30]. Several multiview learning methodologies have been developed for these purposes and are becoming more and more popular. Examples of methodologies used to learn a joint representation of each cell include multimodal matrix factorization methods [31,32], k-nearest neighbor prediction [33], variational autoencoders [34], and canonical correlation analysis [35]. Particularly, some efforts have been done also to develop methods able to analyze single-cell CRISPR screenings to link gene perturbation to cell phenotypes [36,37].

4 Multiview learning in neuroinformatics

4.1 Support tools for automated diagnosis of neurodegenerative disorders

Magnetic resonance imaging (MRI) is a noninvasive imaging technique that exploits the magnetic properties of tissues to describe brain function at high temporal and spatial resolutions. The application of this method has brought great advances in neuroscience research, allowing for the investigation of the physiological and pathological mechanisms governing the human brain. Nevertheless, the knowledge transfer from research studies to clinical practice has been hindered by the limitations of standard analysis methods. For instance, commonly applied voxel-wise[a] generalized linear models are based on unrealistic assumptions (e.g., statistically independence of variables) that do not reflect the underlying neurological principles thus hampering the interpretation of the results.

In the past decade, the introduction of more sophisticated methods based on machine learning in the field of neuroscience has paved the way for the development of a framework for the automated decoding of variables of interest from MRI data. These methods have the potential to give significant insights about the causes of the phenomena under study and have already been successfully applied in practical applications such as single-subject classification.

However, machine learning models have to take up to the challenges that are intrinsic to the analysis of neuroimaging data, that are the extreme high dimensionality of the observations, the high redundancy present in the data, and the relatively small number of available samples. For this reason, existing methods need to be tailored to these applications.

In addition, the recent advances in MRI technologies have made available a wide range of modalities (or views) describing several aspects of the human brain, such as the representation of functional behavior through functional MRI, and the reconstruction of bundles of synaptic fascicles through diffusion tensor imaging. See Fig. 8 for one example.

Complementary neuroimaging modalities can then be combined together in a multiview learning approach to try to achieve a better understanding of the functioning of the brain as a whole. An example of application is the discrimination between different classes of neurogenerative diseases, based on the integration of functional and structural brain connectivity images. In a work by Fratello et al. published in 2017, multiview learning techniques based on random forests have been applied to discriminate groups of subjects affected by amyotrophic lateral sclerosis and Parkinson's disease. Both these pathologies affect the motor abilities of patients; however, they are characterized by high variable phenotypes thus making their diagnosis challenging. Since a definitive diagnostic test does not exist yet, a model able to discern the different pathological mechanisms underlying the neurophysiological signs by identifying reliable diagnostic and prognostic biomarkers

[a]A voxel is a volumetric pixel composing a 3D image of the brain.

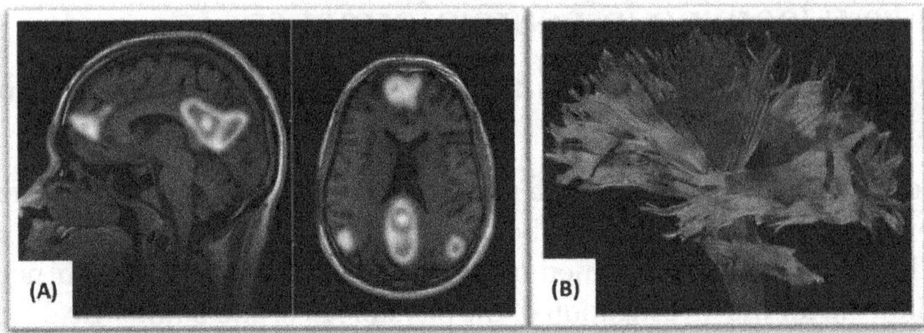

FIG. 8 Multiview neuroimaging examples: Panel (A) shows an example of fMRI imaging related to a working memory experiment; panel (B) shows the lateral views of a brain DTI tractogram.

would represent a substantial advance. The results of this work, showing classification accuracies significantly above chance, suggest that approaches based on the integration of multimodal brain images have the potential of bringing new insights in the investigation of neurodegenerative disease.

Recently, the availability of large-scale multimodal open datasets, such as data collected by the Alzheimer's disease neuroimaging initiative (ADNI), has prompted the development of multiview methods to improve the characterization of Alzheimer's disease progression. Structural MRI data have been used in combination with PET imaging to train support vector classifiers to discriminate between mild cognitive impairment and Alzheimer's disease to support early identification and allow targeted treatment [38,39]. Another work extended the multiclass support vector machine framework to incorporate features from MRI, PET, and cerebrospinal fluid biomarkers [40]. Chen and colleagues used functional networks derived from fMRI, morphological networks based on gray matter distribution, and anatomical network estimated from diffusion MRI to train a multiple kernel learning-support vector machine model to predict subjective cognitive decline [41]. All these works demonstrated that the fusion of multiview information led to more accurate models.

4.2 Multimodal brain parcellation

To better understand how the human brain works, it is often necessary to subdivide the brain in parcels to reflect its modular and hierarchical organization [42]. For decades now neuroscientists have been seeking a parcellation of the human brain consisting of spatially contiguous and nonoverlapping regions that showed homogeneous characteristics from both the anatomical and the functional points of view. The main limitation of existing anatomical atlas is that they might not adapt well to the signal of individual acquisitions, due to intersubject variability. On the other hand, parcellations that are based on individual brain activity can be difficult to compare or reproduce on new samples.

A great step forward in this context has been possible thanks to the introduction of a multiview late integration methodology proposed by Glasser et al. in 2016 [43]. In this work, multiple imaging modalities are used to derive several brain maps describing different properties: cortical myelin content, cortical thickness, pattern of activation from task fMRI, and functional connectivity from resting state fMRI. Considering sharp transitions in two or more of the above measures, a map of potential parcel borders is determined, and each parcel is described by a multimodal fingerprint, consisting of the set of features derived from the multiple views. Multimodal fingerprints are then used to train a classifier to identify parcels in individual subjects. In this way, the authors identified 180 regions per hemisphere. The great innovation introduced by this approach is the possibility to apply the parcellation to new subjects using the trained model, the only requirement being the availability of the same set of features for the new samples.

4.3 Brain imaging genomics

Brain imaging genomics is an emerging field that originated at the intersection of bioinformatics and neuroscience research aimed at elucidating the link between genetic variability and individual differences in brain structure and function, with the ultimate goal of improving our understanding of the genetic bases of neurological disorders [44]. It is based on the integration of genetic variations such as single nucleotide polymorphisms (SNPs) or copy number variations with quantitative traits derived from neuroimaging.

An exemplar application of this approach is provided in a work on data from the UK Biobank [45], where genome-wide association studies of 3144 functional and structural brain imaging phenotypes were carried out on a dataset of 8428 subjects. The imaging phenotypes included brain tissue volumes, cortical and microstructural properties, resting state fluctuations amplitudes, and signal strength in task-activated regions. The analyses revealed 1262 significant associations between SNPs and imaging-derived phenotypes, spanning all classes of imaging metrics, with the exception of task-related fMRI measures.

In 2020, Du and colleagues [46] proposed an extension of the imaging-genomics framework to combine genomics with multimodal imaging data in a single integrated model, by means of multitask sparse canonical correlation analysis. The proposed method can identify both single-modality and complex many-to-many relationships between SNPs and imaging metrics.

Further development of these techniques has the potential of enabling the discovery of causal pathways linking genetic variants to the phenotypic and molecular characteristics of the brain.

5 Deep multimodal feature learning

Classical machine learning methodologies strongly rely on data representation based on feature sets. The identification of the right features for a specific task can be challenging and is usually performed by experts. A new class of deep machine learning techniques are emerging able to cope with this problem. Deep learning models are composed of multiple processing layers able to represent data with a high level of abstraction [47]: each layer learns a representation of input data based on the output of the previous layer building a hierarchy of ever more abstract features. The ability of deep neural networks (DNNs) to learn a compressed representation of input data can be exploited to derive better features to train learning models. The underlying assumption is that observed data result from the contribution of multiple factors interacting at different levels. When more than a view is available, DNNs can be used to learn latent multimodal relationships.

5.1 Deep learning application to predict patient survival

The identification of stable and robust survival patients subgroups can improve the ability to predict specific prognosis. Many of the proposed machine learning techniques benefit from the availability of multimodality measures. One of the main problems in data integration is related to the fact that features from different views might not be directly comparable. Recently, Chaudhary et al. applied deep learning autoencoders to integrate multimodal omics data, in an early integration manner, with the purpose of extracting deep metafeatures to be used in further analyses [48]. Indeed, an autoencoder is an unsupervised feed-forward neural network that is able to learn a representation of the data by transforming them by successive hidden layers [49]. In particular, they performed a study to identify a subgroup of patients affected by hepatocellular carcinoma (HCC). The analyses were performed on 360 samples coming from the TCGA website for which RNASeq, miRNASeq, and DNA methylation data were available. After the preprocessing and normalization of each single view, they concatenated the data and applied a deep autoencoder to extract the new features. They implemented an autoencoder with three hidden layers (with 500, 100, and 500 nodes, respectively), the activation function between each couple of layers is the *tanh* and the objective function to be minimized is the *logloss* error between the original and the reconstructed data. Once the autoencoder was trained, they obtained 100 new features from the bottleneck layer. These features were used to execute k-means clustering to obtain the patient subgroups and perform survival analysis. The authors demonstrated the effectiveness of the dimensionality reduction performed with the autoencoder, by comparing the survival analysis obtained after a classical dimensionality reduction by using PCA and without using any dimensionality reduction techniques. They showed that the survival curves obtained in the last two cases were not significatively separated.

5.2 Multimodal neuroimaging feature learning with deep learning

Taking advantage of the multiple modalities available in neuroimaging, deep architectures have been used to discover complex latent patterns emerging from the integration of multiple views. In Ref. [50], stacked auto-encoders are used to learn high-level features from the concatenated input of MRI and PET data. The extracted features are then used to train a classifier for the diagnosis of Alzheimer's disease. Results showed that this approach outperformed traditional methods and shallow architectures. Similarly, in Ref. [51], MRI and

PET are used in combination to derive a shared feature representation using a restricted Boltzmann machine, once again for the classifications of patients affected by Alzheimer's disease. In Ref. [52], a framework based on deep convolutional neural networks is presented for infant brain segmentation that combines feature maps deriving from T1-, T2-, and diffusion-weighted MR images. The authors showed that the integration of multimodality images improved the performance compared to previous methods. One limitation for the applicability of this approach to neuroimaging data is the small quantity of available samples compared to the number of input features (curse of dimensionality). However, this problem can be alleviated with a preliminary feature selection step, that in this field is often attained by identifying regions of interest or by segmenting the brain in parcels and then deriving a single feature from each parcel.

6 Conclusions

The need to analyze the growing amount of biomedical multiview data, such as those made available by high throughput omics technology and brain imaging, substantially increases the importance of machine learning and data integration techniques. The first attempts to integrate data consisted in merging all views together and performing a joint data analysis. In the last years, data scientists started developing new methodologies that allow learning from multiple views by taking into account their diversity. In this work, we reviewed several integration methods that have been successfully applied to solve biomedical problems. The discussed methodologies were categorized based on three fundamental aspects of data integration: (I) the type of data under the analysis (homogeneous or heterogeneous), (II) the statistical problems to solve, and (III) the stage of the analyses when the integration is performed (early, intermediate or late).

Examples of how these methods can be applied to solve different research problems in bioinformatics and neuroinformatics were reported: we discussed the applications of multiview clustering and classification methodologies to drug repositioning and patient stratification; we reported an example of how both clustering and classification can be combined in a multiview setting for the automated diagnosis of neurodegenerative disorders; we discussed how multiple noninvasive imaging modalities can be exploited together to obtain more accurate brain parcellations. Moreover, we explained how the new emerging deep learning methodologies can be applied to the biomedical field for multimodal feature learning. Finally, we briefly introduced the two emerging fields of single-cell multiomics and brain imaging genomics, which since their conception have benefited from the application of multiview learning methods.

As shown in this work and in many others, significant work has been carried out in the field of multiview learning and data integration for biomedical applications. The main problem is the lack of a general criterion to choose a method among the others. Thus, it is becoming increasingly necessary to create a framework that allows us to perform different types of integrative analysis on different types of data. Such a tool would be of paramount importance, especially for those who initially want to approach these new techniques. A first attempt in this direction has been made in the context of independent subspace analysis in multimodal brain imaging data fusion [53]. In conclusion, even if there are some limitations, the results reached so far are encouraging. This suggests that the applications of multiview learning techniques to big data analysis in the biomedical field are really promising.

References

[1] C.C. Aggarwal, A. Hinneburg, D.A. Keim, On the surprising behavior of distance metrics in high dimensional space, in: International Conference on Database Theory, Springer, 2001, pp. 420–434.

[2] J. Luo, M. Schumacher, A. Scherer, D. Sanoudou, D. Megherbi, T. Davison, T. Shi, et al., A comparison of batch effect removal methods for enhancement of prediction performance using Maqc-ii microarray gene expression data, Pharmacogenomics J. 10 (4) (2010) 278–291.

[3] J.K. Choi, Y. Ungsik, S. Kim, O.J. Yoo, Combining multiple microarray studies and modeling interstudy variation, Bioinformatics 19 (Suppl. 1) (2003) i84–i90.

[4] D.R. Rhodes, Y. Jianjun, K. Shanker, N. Deshpande, R. Varambally, D. Ghosh, T. Barrette, A. Pandey, A.M. Chinnaiyan, Large-scale meta-analysis of cancer microarray data identifies common transcriptional profiles of neoplastic transformation and progression, Proc. Natl. Acad. Sci. U. S. A. 101 (25) (2004) 9309–9314.

[5] S. Saria, A. Goldenberg, Subtyping: what it is and its role in precision medicine, IEEE Intell. Syst. 30 (4) (2015) 70–75.

[6] L. Hood, S.H. Friend, Predictive, personalized, preventive, participatory (P4) cancer medicine, Nat. Rev. Clin. Oncol. 8 (3) (2011) 184–187.

[7] R. Mirnezami, J. Nicholson, A. Darzi, Preparing for precision medicine, N. Engl. J. Med. 366 (6) (2012) 489–491.

[8] J.-P. Brunet, P. Tamayo, T.R. Golub, J.P. Mesirov, Metagenes and molecular pattern discovery using matrix factorization, Proc. Natl. Acad. Sci. 101 (12) (2004) 4164–4169.

[9] C.M. Perou, T. Sørlie, M.B. Eisen, M. van de Rijn, S.S. Jeffrey, C.A. Rees, J.R. Pollack, et al., Molecular portraits of human breast tumours, Nature 406 (6797) (2000) 747–752.

[10] K. Vang Nielsen, B. Ejlertsen, S. Møller, J. Trøst Jørgensen, A. Knoop, H. Knudsen, H.T. Mouridsen, The value of Top2a gene copy number variation as a biomarker in breast cancer: update of Dbcg trial 89D, Acta Oncol. 47 (4) (2008) 725–734.

[11] R. Higdon, R.K. Earl, L. Stanberry, C.M. Hudac, E. Montague, E. Stewart, I. Janko, et al., The promise of multi-omics and clinical data integration to identify and target personalized healthcare approaches in autism spectrum disorders, Omics J. Integr. Biol. 19 (4) (2015) 197–208.

[12] G. Liu, C. Dong, L. Liu, Integrated multiple '-omics' data reveal subtypes of hepatocellular carcinoma, PLoS One 11 (11) (2016) e0165457.

[13] C.R. Planey, O. Gevaert, CoINcIDE: a framework for discovery of patient subtypes across multiple datasets, Genome Med. 8 (1) (2016) 1.

[14] E. Taskesen, S.M.H. Huisman, A. Mahfouz, J.H. Krijthe, J. de Ridder, A. van de Stolpe, E. van den Akker, W. Verheagh, M.J.T. Reinders, Pan-cancer subtyping in a 2D-map shows substructures that are driven by specific combinations of molecular characteristics, Sci. Rep. 6 (2016) 24949. Erratum in: Sci. Rep. 8 (1) (2018) 17304.

[15] B. Wang, A.M. Mezlini, F. Demir, M. Fiume, T. Zhuowen, M. Brudno, B. Haibe-Kains, A. Goldenberg, Similarity network fusion for aggregating data types on a genomic scale, Nat. Methods 11 (3) (2014) 333–337.

[16] A. Serra, M. Fratello, V. Fortino, G. Raiconi, R. Tagliaferri, D. Greco, MVDA: a multi-view genomic data integration methodology, BMC Bioinformatics 16 (1) (2015) 261.

[17] T. Wang, W. Shao, Z. Huang, H. Tang, J. Zhang, Z. Ding, K. Huang, MOGONET integrates multi-omics data using graph convolutional networks allowing patient classification and biomarker identification, Nat. Commun. 12 (1) (2021) 1–13.

[18] S.H. Sleigh, C.L. Barton, Repurposing strategies for therapeutics, Pharm. Med. 24 (3) (2010) 151–159.

[19] J.A. DiMasi, R.W. Hansen, H.G. Grabowski, L. Lasagna, Cost of innovation in the pharmaceutical industry, J. Health Econ. 10 (2) (1991) 107–142.

[20] K.A. O'Connor, B.L. Roth, Finding new tricks for old drugs: an efficient route for public-sector drug discovery, Nat. Rev. Drug Discov. 4 (12) (2005) 1005–1014.

[21] J.T. Dudley, M. Sirota, M. Shenoy, R.K. Pai, S. Roedder, A.P. Chiang, A.A. Morgan, M.M. Sarwal, P.J. Pasricha, A.J. Butte, Computational repositioning of the anticonvulsant topiramate for inflammatory bowel disease, Sci. Transl. Med. 3 (96) (2011) 96ra76.

[22] A. Gottlieb, G.Y. Stein, E. Ruppin, R. Sharan, PREDICT: a method for inferring novel drug indications with application to personalized medicine, Mol. Syst. Biol. 7 (1) (2011) 496.

[23] P. Sanseau, P. Agarwal, M.R. Barnes, J. Tomi Pastinen, B. Richards, L.R. Cardon, V. Mooser, Use of genome-wide association studies for drug repositioning, Nat. Biotechnol. 30 (4) (2012) 317–320.

[24] F. Iorio, R. Bosotti, E. Scacheri, V. Belcastro, P. Mithbaokar, R. Ferriero, L. Murino, et al., Discovery of drug mode of action and drug repositioning from transcriptional responses, Proc. Natl. Acad. Sci. 107 (33) (2010) 14621–14626.

[25] N. Smirnov, Table for estimating the goodness of fit of empirical distributions, Ann. Math. Stat. 19 (2) (1948) 279–281.

[26] F. Napolitano, Y. Zhao, V.M. Moreira, R. Tagliaferri, J. Kere, M. D'Amato, D. Greco, Drug repositioning: a machine-learning approach through data integration, J. Cheminformatics 5 (1) (2013) 30.

[27] X. Zeng, S. Zhu, X. Liu, Y. Zhou, R. Nussinov, F. Cheng, DeepDR: a network-based deep learning approach to in silico drug repositioning, Bioinformatics 35 (24) (2019) 5191–5198.

[28] M. Efremova, S.A. Teichmann, Computational methods for single-cell omics across modalities, Nat. Methods 17 (1) (2020) 14–17.

[29] Z. Jehan, Single-cell omics: an overview, in: Single-Cell Omics, Academic Press, 2019, pp. 3–19.

[30] A. Ma, A. McDermaid, X. Jennifer, Y. Chang, Q. Ma, Integrative methods and practical challenges for single-cell multi-omics, Trends Biotechnol. 38 (9) (2020) 1007–1022.

[31] S. Jin, L. Zhang, Q. Nie, ScAI: an unsupervised approach for the integrative analysis of parallel single-cell transcriptomic and epigenomic profiles, Genome Biol. 21 (1) (2020) 1–19.

[32] R. Argelaguet, D. Arnol, D. Bredikhin, Y. Deloro, B. Velten, J.C. Marioni, O. Stegle, MOFA+: a probabilistic framework for comprehensive integration of structured single-cell data, Genome Biol. 21 (2020) 111–117.

[33] Y. Hao, S. Hao, E. Andersen-Nissen, W.M. Mauck III, S. Zheng, A. Butler, M.J. Lee, et al., Integrated analysis of multimodal single-cell data, Cell 184 (13) (2021) 3573–3587.e29.

[34] A. Gayoso, Z. Steier, R. Lopez, J. Regier, K.L. Nazor, A. Streets, N. Yosef, Joint probabilistic modeling of single-cell multi-omic data with totalVI, Nat. Methods 18 (3) (2021) 272–282.

[35] T. Stuart, A. Butler, P. Hoffman, C. Hafemeister, E. Papalexi, W.M. Mauck III, Y. Hao, M. Stoeckius, P. Smibert, R. Satija, Comprehensive integration of single-cell data, Cell 177 (7) (2019) 1888–1902.

[36] B. Duan, C. Zhou, C. Zhu, Y. Yifei, G. Li, S. Zhang, C. Zhang, et al., Model-based understanding of single-cell Crispr screening, Nat. Commun. 10 (1) (2019) 1–11.

[37] L. Yang, Y. Zhu, Y. Hua, X. Cheng, S. Chen, Y. Chu, H. Huang, J. Zhang, W. Li, ScMAGeCK links genotypes with multiple phenotypes in single-cell Crispr screens, Genome Biol. 21 (1) (2020) 1–14.

[38] A. Ortiz, F. Lozano, J.M. Gorriz, J. Ramirez, F.J. Martinez Murcia, Alzheimer's Disease Neuroimaging Initiative, Discriminative sparse features for Alzheimer's disease diagnosis using multimodal image data, Curr. Alzheimer Res. 15 (1) (2018) 67–79.

[39] W. Shao, Y. Peng, Z. Chen, M. Wang, D. Zhang, Alzheimer's Disease Neuroimaging Initiative, Hypergraph based multi-task feature selection for multimodal classification of Alzheimer's disease, Comput. Med. Imaging Graph. 80 (2020) 101663.

[40] Y. Zhang, S. Wang, K. Xia, Y. Jiang, P. Qian, Alzheimer's Disease Neuroimaging Initiative, Alzheimer's disease multiclass diagnosis via multimodal neuroimaging embedding feature selection and fusion, Inf. Fusion 66 (2021) 170–183.

[41] H. Chen, W. Li, X. Sheng, Q. Ye, H. Zhao, X. Yun, F. Bai, Machine learning based on the multimodal connectome can predict the preclinical stage of Alzheimer's disease: a preliminary study, Eur. Radiol. (2021) 1–12.

[42] B. Thirion, G. Varoquaux, E. Dohmatob, J.-B. Poline, Which fMRI clustering gives good brain parcellations? Front. Neurosci. 8 (2014).

[43] M.F. Glasser, T.S. Coalson, E.C. Robinson, C.D. Hacker, J. Harwell, E. Yacoub, K. Ugurbil, et al., A multi-modal parcellation of human cerebral cortex, Nature 536 (7615) (2016) 171–178.

[44] L. Shen, P.M. Thompson, Brain imaging genomics: integrated analysis and machine learning, Proc. IEEE 108 (1) (2020) 125–162. Institute of Electrical and Electronics Engineers.

[45] L.T. Elliott, K. Sharp, F. Alfaro-Almagro, S. Shi, K.L. Miller, G. Douaud, J. Marchini, S.M. Smith, Genome-wide association studies of brain imaging phenotypes in UK Biobank, Nature 562 (7726) (2018) 210–216.

[46] L. Du, F. Liu, K. Liu, X. Yao, S.L. Risacher, J. Han, A.J. Saykin, L. Shen, Associating multi-modal brain imaging phenotypes and genetic risk factors via a dirty multi-task learning method, IEEE Trans. Med. Imaging 39 (11) (2020) 3416–3428.

[47] Y. LeCun, Y. Bengio, G. Hinton, Deep learning, Nature 521 (7553) (2015) 436–444.

[48] K. Chaudhary, O.B. Poirion, L. Liangqun, L. Garmire, Deep learning based multi-omics integration robustly predicts survival in liver cancer, Clin. Cancer Res. 24 (6) (2018) 1248–1259.

[49] Y. Bengio, Learning deep architectures for Ai, Found. Trends Mach. Learn. 2 (1) (2009) 1–127.

[50] S. Liu, S. Liu, W. Cai, H. Che, S. Pujol, R. Kikinis, D. Feng, M.J. Fulham, ADNI, Multimodal neuroimaging feature learning for multiclass diagnosis of Alzheimer's disease, IEEE Trans. Biomed. Eng. 62 (4) (2015) 1132–1140.

[51] H.-I. Suk, S.-W. Lee, D. Shen, Alzheimer's Disease Neuroimaging Initiative, Hierarchical feature representation and multimodal fusion with deep learning for AD/MCI diagnosis, NeuroImage 101 (2014) 569–582.

[52] W. Zhang, R. Li, H. Deng, L. Wang, W. Lin, S. Ji, D. Shen, Deep convolutional neural networks for multi-modality isointense infant brain image segmentation, NeuroImage 108 (2015) 214–224.

[53] R.F. Silva, S.M. Plis, T. Adalı, M.S. Pattichis, V.D. Calhoun, Multidataset independent subspace analysis with application to multimodal fusion, IEEE Trans. Image Process. 30 (2020) 588–602.

17

Emergence of tool construction and tool use through hierarchical reinforcement learning

Qinbo Li[a,b] and Yoonsuck Choe[a]

[a]DEPARTMENT OF COMPUTER SCIENCE AND ENGINEERING, TEXAS A&M UNIVERSITY, COLLEGE STATION, TX, UNITED STATES [b]META INC., SEATTLE, WA, UNITED STATES

Chapter outlines

1 Introduction

Tool use is often considered a key indicator of intelligence and complex cognition [1–3]. The most advanced form of tool use can be found only in humans. However, rudimentary tool-use behavior has been observed in multiple nonhuman species, ranging from insects to great apes [4]. In many cases, tool use in animals is limited to the manipulation of a single object (such as a stone or a stick), but tool construction (or manufacture) capabilities have also been documented. Apes (including chimpanzees, orangutans, and others) are well known for such capabilities, and there is extensive literature on the subject (see Chapter 6 in Ref. [4] for a comprehensive review). Such rich tool-use behavior is not restricted only to the species closest to humans. For example, New Caledonian crows can bend a wire to create a hook to retrieve food from a deep cylinder [5], they can also

Artificial Intelligence in the Age of Neural Networks and Brain Computing. https://doi.org/10.1016/B978-0-323-96104-2.00008-7

Copyright © 2024 Elsevier Inc. All rights reserved.

assess the "value" of the tool (e.g., hooked vs. straight) [6], and they can even construct compound tools by connecting multiple objects [7].

Compared to the large body of research on tool use in animals, there is relatively fewer works in the AI field. A quick search on Google Scholar turns up 44,600 results for animal tool use, but only about 8000 for tool use in artificial intelligence or robots (as of March 2022). An early paper on this topic by St. Amant and Wood raised the importance of tool use in the context of autonomous agents, where they introduced the "Tooling test," to replace the Turing test [2]. In follow-up work, we observed that investigating tool use in artificial agents can lead to a breakthrough in the field ("Tooling test rebooted") [3]. A more recent extension of these ideas can be found in Nair et al. ("Tool MacGyvering") [8] and Allen et al. ("The Virtual Tools Game") [9]. Finally, tool construction and use is especially interesting in the context of open-ended improvement in AI (see Ref. [10]), where the complexity of the tool and the cognitive capacity of the agent can form a coevolutionary relationship (see Ref. [11] on coevolution in neuroevolution).

Inspired by these works, we conducted a series of tool use and tool construction experiments in a simulated environment. The tasks in our prior works included the basic use of a stick for reaching [12–14], connecting two sticks for a longer reach (tool construction) [15], and grabbing a tool and dragging objects [16] using different tool types (I-, L-, and T-shaped) [17]. Different learning algorithms were used, depending on the task requirements. We started with neuroevolution (NEAT [18]), and gradually moved to deep reinforcement learning (e.g., ACKTR [19]), to fully utilize the visual input. In these works, we observed effective utilization of simple tools in the environment and rudimentary tool construction. Our trained agents also exhibited novel emergent behaviors such as sweeping, throwing, and hitting to achieve the goal [17], without those specific objectives prescribed in the learning algorithm.

In this chapter, we build upon our prior work to investigate tool construction and use in a realistic physics simulation environment. Although we have investigated primitive tool construction in Ref. [15] and tool use in a realistic physics simulation environment [16, 17], we have not combined these two aspects, so the combination of the two will be our main focus and contribution.

The rest of this chapter is organized as follows: in Section 2, we introduce some background on reinforcement learning, and some previous works related to learning to use tools, including our own previous work. We then introduce our proposed approach in Section 3, followed by our experiments and results in Section 4. The remaining sections are discussion (including future works) and conclusion in Section 5.

2 Background and related works

In this section, we briefly review existing works on tool use in AI and robotics, and provide some preliminaries on reinforcement learning.

2.1 Tool use in AI and robotics

Tool use has recently gained attention in artificial intelligence and robotics (for a review, see Ref. [2]); however, tool construction is a relatively unexplored area. The various existing works on tool use include (1) programmed, hard-coded behavior [20]; (2) learning through demonstration [21–25]; (3) learning affordances via random trial-and-error or body babbling [26–28]; (4) tool use based on tool-body assimilation [29, 30]; (5) Bayesian learning of tool affordances [31]; (6) evolved tool using behavior [32, 33] (cf. Ref. [34], where body morphology [not tools] was coevolved with the controller); and (7) deep reinforcement learning-based tool use, with dexterous manipulations [35].

However, most of the works listed above depended on some degree of designer knowledge regarding tool use and motor control, for example, fully hard-coded behavior, the tool being preattached to the limb, predefined tool features, predefined motor primitives, etc. Evolution-based approaches [32, 33] were relatively free of these constraints, but in those cases the tools were more or less simple markers, not something that can be manipulated with a limb-like structure of the agent.

AI-based work on tool construction has been very rare, with notable exceptions. Wang et al. [36] took a synthetic approach to construct tools, but their focus was more on understanding the various mechanistic and energetic needs of using the synthetically generated tools, not on tool construction by agents. In our own work [15], we demonstrated the construction and use of an extended stick in a reaching task. More recently, Yang et al. [37] used graph neural networks to construct tools, but in this work, the focus was only on construction, so the constructed tool was not used. Some works also appeared where environmental objects can be moved around to achieve a navigation goal. One example is by Choi et al. [38] who used a cognitive architecture called ICARUS to construct a bridge or a staircase using planks of different length. Another example is Baker et al. [39], who demonstrated emergent tool-use behavior in a multiagent competition environment. Perhaps the most advanced form of tool construction combined with tool use is the work by Nair et al., where they used a full pipeline to analyze the tool parts, construct the tool, and test them [8, 40]. The pipeline consisted of (1) workspace segmentation, (2) shape scoring, (3) attachment scoring, and (4) tool validation. The algorithm was implemented and tested on a physical robot.

2.2 Reinforcement learning

For sensorimotor tasks such as tool use and tool construction, reinforcement learning is the best fit. Reinforcement learning has seen rapid growth recently, with the emergence of deep reinforcement learning, utilizing deep neural networks [41]. Here, we only review some reinforcement learning algorithms that are suitable to our tool construction and use task, including policy gradient, actor-critic, trust region policy optimization (TPRO), proximal policy optimization (PPO), and deep Q network (DQN).

Policy gradient: There are many reinforcement learning algorithms that try to learn the value of the actions to select the actions. Policy gradient algorithms try to learn the policy directly without learning the value function [42]. Some policy gradient algorithms may still learn the value function, but the action selection is not based on the value function. As a result, policy gradient methods are ideal for problems where the state and action space are continuous. However, it is not straightforward to calculate the gradient because it depends on both the policy and the stationary distribution of the policy. The policy gradient theorem simplifies the calculation because it avoids the calculation of the partial derivatives of the stationary distribution [42].

Actor-Critic: To reduce the variance of the vanilla policy gradient method, Actor-Critic method learns a value function and uses it to assist the policy update. There are two roles in the Actor-Critic method: the actor, whose role is to maintain and update the policy to select an action and the critic, whose role is to estimate a value function with respect to the policy.

TRPO and PPO: Schulman et al. [43] proposed TRPO and demonstrated its robust performance. TRPO updates parameters by taking large steps, and at the same time it enforces a KL divergence constraint to avoid performance collapse. PPO [44] has the same intuition as TRPO while being less complicated by using a surrogate objective. Both TRPO and PPO are on-policy algorithms and can be used in discrete space problems and continuous space problems. Because of the state-of-the-art performance, we use PPO to train part of our model, which will be elaborated in the following section.

DQN: DQN is a value-based deep reinforcement learning algorithm that maps visual input sequence to the action value functions, using a convolutional neural network (CNN) front end, with a fully connected layer near the end [45]. DQN introduced experience replay and periodic update of the target network to achieve stability in learning. Since the model has a CNN frontend, it can deal with visual image sequences very well. The method has been used very successfully in domains such as video game playing, and related tasks that require the analysis of visual input. Several powerful variants of DQN were subsequently developed, including double DQN (DDQN) [46]. We also use DDQN to train a different part of our model. Details will be provided in the following section.

Hierarchical reinforcement learning: Many real-world tasks are very challenging, requiring multiple steps of decision-making, while the rewards are sparse. Learning to construct and use tools is one of these challenging problems. Hierarchical reinforcement learning decomposes the task into different levels of abstraction. Here, we briefly discuss recent advances in hierarchical reinforcement learning.

One of the most well-known formulation of hierarchical reinforcement is the concept of "options" introduced by Sutton et al. [47]. An option consists of a triplet $\langle I, \pi, \beta \rangle$, where π is a policy, β is a terminal condition, and I is an input set $I \subseteq S$. An option can be seen as an action at the higher level. The implementation of options is simple and it can increase the convergence speed of training. Parr and Russell [48] proposed an approach called hierarchical abstract machines (HAM). Similar to options, HAM investigates the theory of semi-Markov decision process. However, HAM is complex to implement and thus does not have many applications. MAXQ value function decomposition is another hierarchical reinforcement learning algorithm proposed by Dietterich [49]. MAXQ decomposes the value function into two components: one is the total expected reward of the action-state pair, and the other is the total reward expected parent task. Compared to options, MAXQ directly decomposes the task into subtasks and the policy for the subtasks can be reused. However, the learned hierarchical policy is not guaranteed to be optimal. Dayan and Hinton [50] proposed a framework called feudal reinforcement learning. In feudal reinforcement learning, there is a manager to assign subtasks to lower-level workers, and the workers learn to execute these subtasks. The manager observes the state of the environment at a higher level, while the workers focus on a subgoal in the original state space.

In our tool construction and use task, the agent needs to learn a sequence of steps to achieve the goal, for example, pick up the tools, construct the tool parts into a novel tool, and use the novel tool to achieve the goal. Each of the steps can be seen as a subtask. Therefore, we use the feudal reinforcement learning approach to train the agent. Here, we continue to discuss some recent approaches under the feudal reinforcement learning framework.

Kulkarni et al. [51] proposed to use two DQN [46] for the manager (the workers are trained using PPO). Learning policies at multiple levels at the same time leads to nonstationary training. To address this issue, Nachum et al. [52] proposed hierarchical reinforcement learning with off-policy correction (HIRO). Levy et al. [53] proposed hierarchical actor-critic (HAC) and claimed that HAC is more efficient than HIRO when learning multiple levels of policies. Vezhnevets et al. [54] proposed an end-to-end differentiable model called FeUdal Networks (FuNs) that use dilated LSTM for the manager. Their experiments showed that FuNs improved long-term credit assignment in ATARI games and in some memory tasks.

Curiosity: In addition to hierarchical reinforcement learning, we use curiosity reward to encourage exploration. In one of the related works, Burda et al. [55] proposed random network distillation to add an exploration bonus, where the bonus is the error of a neural network predicting the future states of the environment. They show that random network distillation achieves outstanding performance on hard exploration Atari games. For a more general treatment of the curiosity as an internal reward (intrinsic motivation), see Oudeyer and Smith [56].

3 Approach

Similar to Nguyen et al. [57], we created a physically simulated environment using OpenAI gym and PyBullet, illustrated in Fig. 1. The environment includes two robot arms, two tools, and one target. Note that this is the first time we are using two arms, since in all our previous works, we only had one arm in the simulation. The addition of the extra

FIG. 1 The tool construction environment builds with PyBullet and following the OpenAI gym protocol. The environment is surrounded by a rectangle arena (*black*). There are two robot arms (*blue cylinders [dark gray in print version]*), two tools (*green cylinders [light gray in print version]*), and one target (*red cube [dark gray in print version]*). The joints marked as *yellow spheres (light gray in print version)* are special joints that can be connected together upon contact. The goal of the agent is to move the object to the bottom of the environment.

arm allows us to conduct tool construction in the truest sense, by having the two arms pick up one object part each. Formally, we define the robot arm as the three-joint arm that directly belongs to the robot's body, and we define the tool as the sticks that can be picked up by the robot to achieve some goals. To simplify the problem, we add special joints (yellow spheres [light gray in print version] shown in Fig. 1) to the robot hand and the tool. The special joints can be connected to each other upon contact (like magnets). The goal of the agent is to move the target (red cube [dark gray in print version]) to the bottom of the environment.

3.1 Multimodal input

Instead of using only raw pixels of the image as input, we use both the image and proprioceptive feedback as input, similar to Nguyen et al.'s method [57]. To be specific, we use the following input:

- Vision input: RGB image of the entire environment.
- Proprioception input: the position and velocities of all the agent's joints.

3.2 Hierarchical reinforcement learning

In order to achieve the goal, the agent needs to complete a sequence of nontrivial subtasks, for example, pick up the tool on the left using the left hand, pick the tool on the right using the right hand, construct a "T" shape tool by connecting one end of a tool to the middle of another tool, and drag the target to the desired area. Nguyen et al. investigated simply using tools to drag the target with one arm, and they used manually designed multistep reward functions. Instead of such manually designed reward functions, reinforcement learning algorithms can be used directly with the final task goal as the reward, but the problem cannot be solved effectively because the exploration space is very large, and the reward is sparse.

We propose to use hierarchical reinforcement learning with curiosity reward. Specifically, our model consists of a manager and many workers. The manager learns to plan the "macrosteps" such as "pick up the two-joint tool," "pick up the three-joint tool," etc. The workers learn to execute the macrosteps generated by the manager. If the macrostep leads to a new state that the agent has not seen previously, then there will be some reward for the manager. Finally, there will also be a reward for the manager if the goal is reached. As for the macrostep, if we define them manually, we have to enumerate all the possible steps. In addition, if we were given a novel task, we might have to redefine those macrosteps. Therefore, we define the macrostep in a more general way: we define the macrostep as minimizing the distance between two salient objects (whatever they are), where the salient objects in our environment are the joints (yellow spheres [light gray in print version] shown in Fig. 1) and the target (the red cube [dark gray in print version] in Fig. 1). Because the final goal is to move the target to the bottom of the environment, reducing the distance between the target and the bottom is another macrostep. In addition, we add two macrosteps so that both the robot hands can release the tools they are holding.

The action space for the manager is all the pairs between all the salient objects, and the action space for the worker is the control of the two three-joint robot arm. We use DDQN [46] to train the manager and PPO [44] to train the worker. Algorithm 2 describes the details of training the manager with DDQN. In Algorithm 2, for each macrostep generated by the manager, a worker will be trained with PPO (Algorithm 1) to try to accomplish the macrostep. Fig. 2 illustrates the overall model architecture of our approach.

ALGORITHM 1 PROXIMAL POLICY OPTIMIZATION (PPO) ALGORITHM (PPO-CLIP VARIANT) [44].

Input: policy parameter θ, value function parameter ϕ, *clipping parameter* $\in$

For k in 0,1,2…:

Collect trajectories D_k using policy π

Compute rewards-to-go $\widehat{R}_t$

Compute advantage estimates $\widehat{A}_t$

$\theta_{k+1}=$

$\arg\max_{\theta} \frac{1}{|D_k|T} \sum_{\tau \in D_k} \sum_{t=0}^{T} \min\left(\frac{\pi_\theta(a_t|s_t)}{\pi_{\theta_k}(a_t|s_t)} A^{\pi_{\theta_k}}(s_t a_t), g(\in A^{\pi_{\theta_k}}(s_t a_t))\right)$, *where* $g(\in, A) =$

$(1-\in)A$ *if* $A<0$ *and* $(1+\in)A$ *otherwise.*

$\phi_{k+1} = \arg\min_{\phi} \frac{1}{|D_k|T} \sum_{\tau \in D_k} \sum_{t=0}^{T} \left(V_\phi(s_t) - \widehat{R}_t\right)^2$

End

ALGORITHM 2 PSEUDOCODE OF TRAINING THE MANAGER, USING DDQN [46].

```
Input: Visual and proprioceptive inputs
manager = DQN(observation, action_space)
target_manager = DQN(observation_space, action_space)
state = env.reset()
for i in (1, number_of_iterations) :
    action = manager.act(state)
    next_state, reward, done, info = env.step(action)
    replay_buffer.push(state, action, reward, next_state, done)
    state = next_state
    if done :
      state = env.reset()
    if len(replay_buffer) > batch_size :
      loss = compute_td_loss(batch_size)
    if i%100 == 0 :
      update_target_model(manager, target_manager)
```

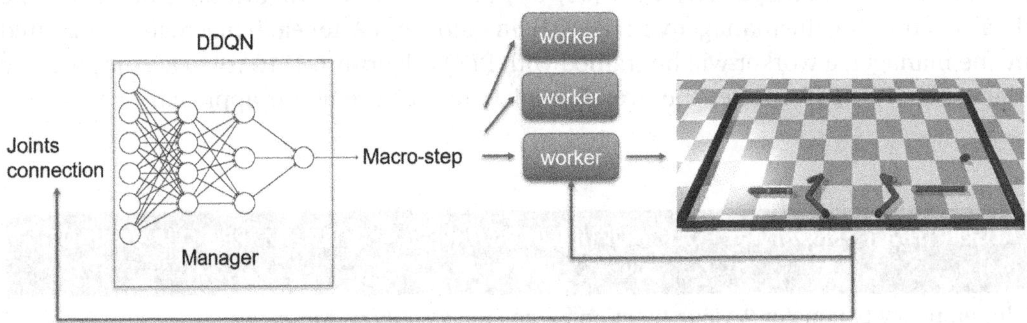

FIG. 2 The overall architecture of our approach.

There is one additional issue to be addressed for the macrostep: what should be the initial environmental state for the macrosteps? For the first macrostep, the initial state is the environment's initial state. But what is the initial state for the following macrostep? For example, if the first macrostep is "pick up the tool on the left side" and the second macrostep is "connect the end of one tool to the middle of another tool," then what should be the initial state of the second macrostep? To address this issue, we can save all the states of the environment (all positions of the objects, the joint's velocity, the joint's connection status, etc.) at the end of the previous step and use it to be the initial environmental state to train the next macrostep. However, the initial state from the previous macrostep is not fixed. For example, if the previous macrostep is "pick up the tool on the left side," then in the initial state of the next macrostep, the left hand should be holding the tool, but it could be at any position. Therefore, we run the previous macrostep for k times and save all the environment's state. When training the next macrostep, we randomly pick one environment's state to resume as the initial state. In our experiment, we set $k = 5$.

3.3 Neural network architecture

We trained the manager using the DDQN algorithm. The neural network structure for the manager is three fully connected layers with a hidden layer size of 128 for each hidden layer. A ReLU activation layer is followed by each layer except for the last layer. The input to the manager is the connection status of all the joints in the environment, for example, whether the left hand is holding a tool, whether two tools are connected to each other, and so on. The output of the manager is two joints to be connected, for example, the right hand of the agent and the tool on the right-hand side, the middle joint of one tool and the left joint of another tool, etc. These subtasks are distributed among the workers.

We trained the workers using the PPO algorithm. In PPO, we used the same network architecture for the actor and the critic. The overall network structure of the workers is illustrated in Fig. 3. We used the RGB image as well as the proprioceptive feedback as input.

We first used three convolutional layers to process the RGB image of the environment. The first convolutional layer consists of 32 kernels with a kernel size of 8 and stride of 4. The second convolutional layer consists of 64 kernels with a kernel size of 4 and stride of 2. The third convolutional layer consists of 64 kernels with a kernel size of 3 and stride of 1. Each of the convolutional layers is followed by a ReLU activation function. Then, we flatten the feature into a one-dimensional (1D) vector and concatenate it with the 1D proprioceptive input vector (joint angles and velocities).

The concatenated feature vector is then fed into two fully connected layers with a hidden layer size of 512 units. A ReLU activation layer is followed by the first fully connected layer. Both the actor and the critic share the same network architecture and parameters. The only difference is that the output dimension for the actor is 6, representing the control signal for the robot joints, while the output dimension for the critic is 1, representing the value. Fig. 3 shows the details of the actor network and the critic network.

4 Experiments and results

We implemented our approach in PyTorch [58]. We used the DDQN algorithm to train the manager and used the Adam optimizer [59] with default parameters ($\beta_1 = 0.9$, $\beta_2 = 0.999$, $\epsilon = 1 \times 10^{-8}$). The replay buffer size was set to 1000 and the batch size was set to 4. For every 100 iterations, the target model is synchronized with the current model.

We used the PPO algorithm to train the workers. The resolution of the image of the environment was (200, 360). We resized the image to (84, 84) and stacked four consecutive

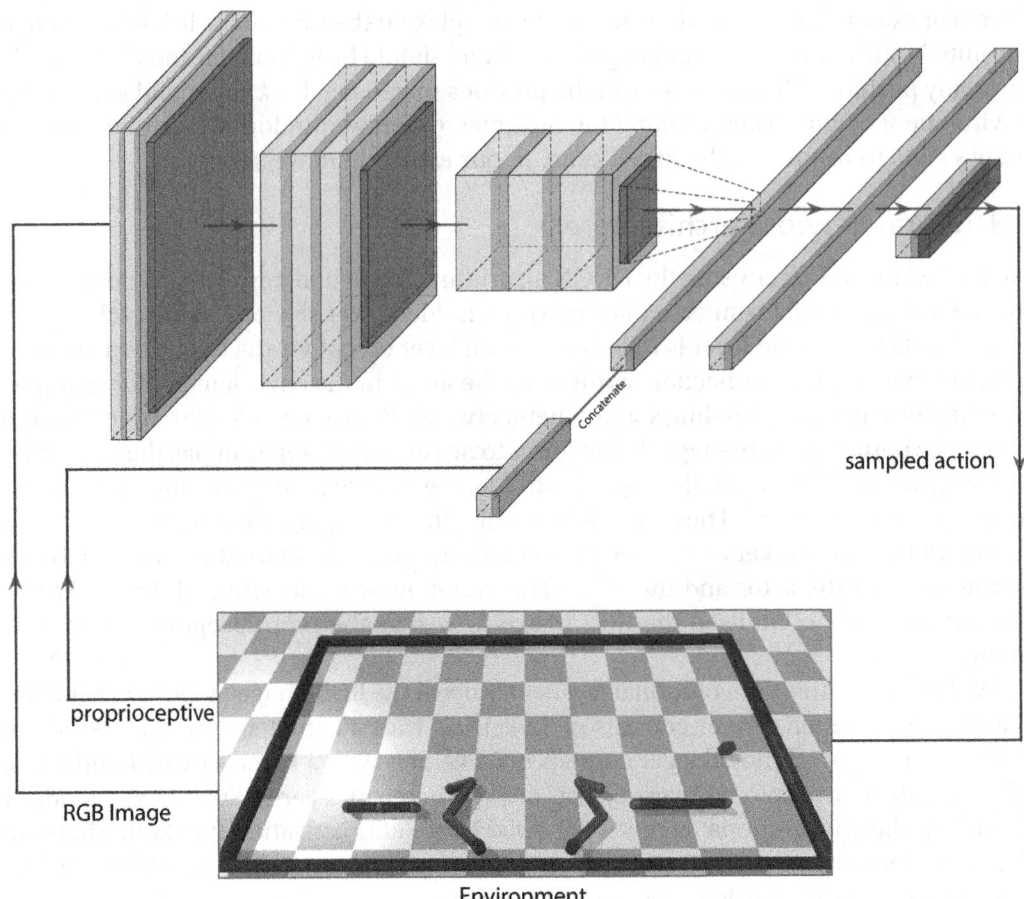

FIG. 3 The overall network architecture of the workers. This figure only shows the actor network of the workers. The critic network shares the same network architecture with the actor network, except the last output layer only has one-dimensional output.

frames before feeding them to the neural network. The maximum steps for each episode was 4000. We set the discount rate gamma to be 0.99 and used the Adam optimizer with default parameters.

We also evaluated the model using only RGB image sequences as input (i.e., no proprioceptive inputs). The network structure was the same as Fig. 3, except that the feature vector from the last layer of CNN was not concatenated with the proprioceptive input.

We ran all the training and evaluation on a machine with an NVIDIA GeForce RTX 2080 Ti GPU with 11G memory.

The manager successfully learned a sequence of subtasks to solve the task: (1) pick up the tool on the right; (2) pick up the tool on the left; (3) connect the two-joint tool with the middle joint of the three-joint tool to construct a "T"-shaped tool; and (4) use the

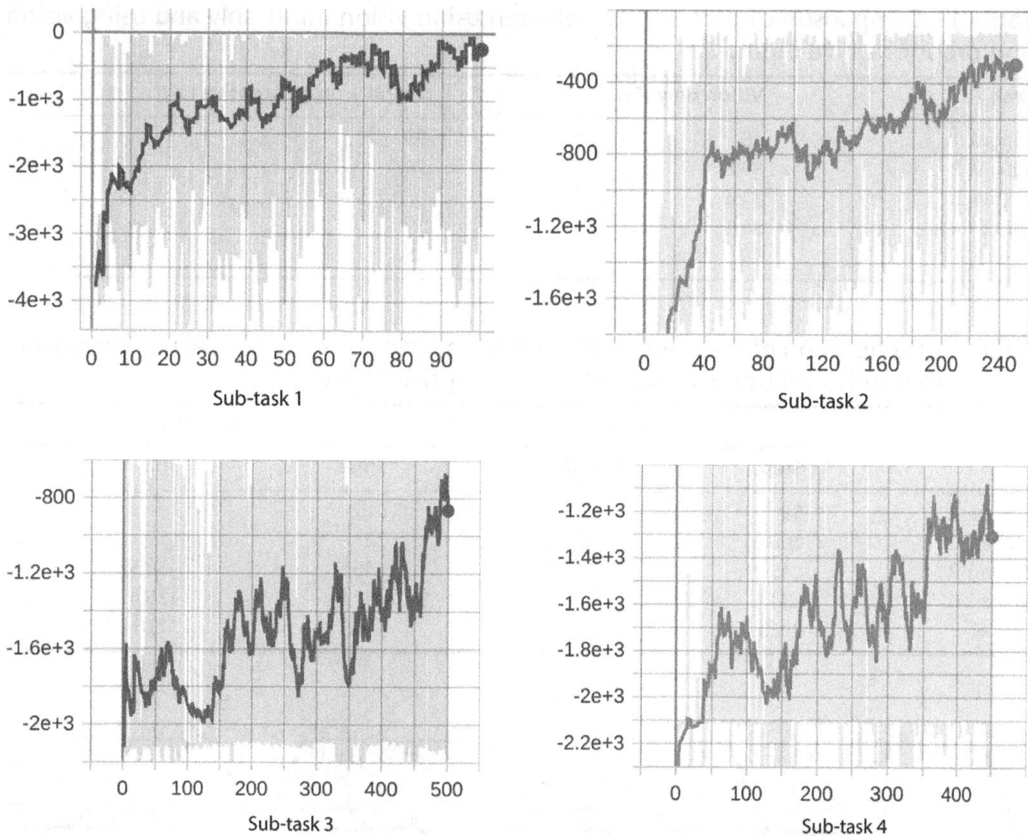

FIG. 4 The smoothed reward for each subtasks. The *Y*-axis stands for the reward and the *X*-axis stands for epochs.

"T"-shaped tool to drag the target to the bottom. Fig. 4 shows the smoothed reward for each subtasks. The overall success rate of our approach is 48%, while the success rate when using only RGB image as input (i.e., no proprioceptive input) is only 20%. Table 1 describes the success rate of the agent in finishing each of the subtasks. As it is can be seen from the table, the success rate using vision and proprioceptive input is much higher than the success rate using vision input only. Table 2 also shows the number of steps taken by the agent to achieve each of the subtasks. Similarly, the agent when using vision and proprioceptive input requires fewer steps to achieve the subtasks, except for the last subtask where a number of steps are similar.

Fig. 5 illustrates one of the successful trials of constructing a tool and dragging the target. As can be seen from the figure, without any predefined knowledge, the agent learned to construct a novel tool to drag the object. The agent first reaches the tool on the right side with its right arm (frame 3), and then reaches the tool on the left side with its left arm (frame 4), and then constructs a "T"-shaped tool (frame 6), and finally uses this tool to drag the object to the bottom of the screen (frames 7 and 8).

Table 1 Comparison of success rate between using vision input only and using vision and proprioceptive input.

Task	Vision only (%)	Vision + proprioceptive (%)
Subtask 1	76	99
Subtask 2	90.8	94.9
Subtask 3	82.6	92.6
Subtask 4	35.1	55.2
Overall	20	48

Table 2 Comparison of the number of steps needed to achieve the goal between using vision input only and using vision and proprioceptive input.

	Vision only		Full input	
Task	**Steps**	**Std**	**Steps**	**Std**
Subtask 1	53	113.6	21.3	1.5
Subtask 2	166.6	171.3	32	17.2
Subtask 3	245.3	197.5	145.5	138.5
Subtask 4	234.1	129	257.6	136.4
Overall	2923.2	2090.1	1488.5	1176.2

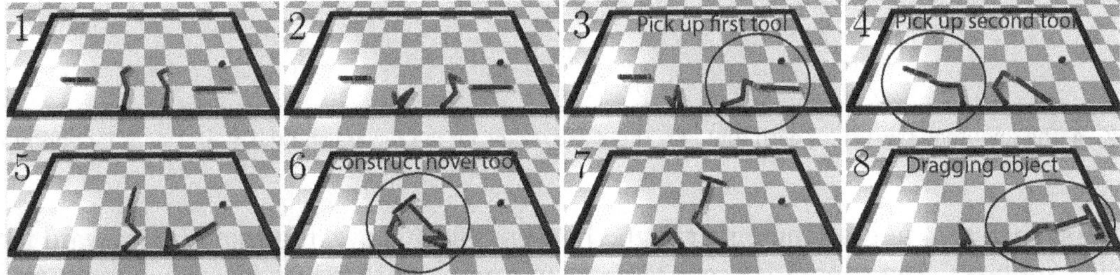

FIG. 5 Controlling two arms with joints to construct a "T"-shaped tool for dragging an object (*red cube [dark gray in print version]*) to the bottom of the screen.

Fig. 6 shows more results.

5 Discussion and conclusion

In this chapter, we introduced a physically simulated environment for tool construction and tool use. We proposed an approach to use raw pixel input as well as proprioceptive input to learn to construct and use a novel tool. Unlike our previous works [57], we did not use manually designed reward functions. We used hierarchical reinforcement learning with curiosity reward to avoid manually designed rewards and accelerate learning. In our approach, the manager proposes and assigns subgoals to workers and the workers

FIG. 6 (A) Successful trial using multimodal input. It took 1700 steps to complete the task for this trial. (B) Successful trial using vision input only. It took 3400 steps to complete the task for this trial. (C) Failed trial using multimodal input. The agent accidentally pushed the target away when constructing the "T"-shaped tool, making the task unsolvable. (D) Failed trial using vision input only. The agent struggles to construct the "T"-shaped tool without proprioceptive input.

then learn to achieve the subgoals. We designed the subgoals to be very general: minimizing the distance between some salient objects in the environment to encourage behaviors such as picking up tools, connecting two tools to build a new tool, and so on. Generally, such a definition of the subgoals allows us to explore the environment at a higher level: to reach and grab some objects and to construct some objects. We believe our strategy to generate general subgoals to encourage novel behaviors and to accelerate exploration can be used in other reinforcement learning tasks. Our experiments show that the agent can successfully learn a sequence of subtasks to construct a novel tool to achieve the goal. In addition, adding proprioceptive input can accelerate the training and lead to better performance. In future work, more immediately, we intend to include more realism and complexity to the task, for example, by introducing a gripper, requiring that tool parts be aligned and joined (rather than snapping on), and extending the task environment to a full three-dimensional (3D) space, as in the IKEA Furniture Assembly environment [60]. In the longer term, an important goal will be to further analyze the evolved or trained neural networks (continuing our own work [12, 13]), relate them to findings in neuroscience regarding tool use (e.g., Maravita and Iriki showed changes in the neural substrates due to tool use [61]), and investigate how tool use and tool construction and intelligence can coevolve in AI ("Triadic Niche Construction" [62]).

Acknowledgments

This chapter is largely based on the first author's Ph.D. dissertation [63]. Preliminary results of this work were presented at a workshop [64].

References

[1] J. Call, Three ingredients for becoming, in: Tool Use in Animals: Cognition and Ecology, Cambridge University Press, Cambridge, 2013, pp. 3–20.

[2] R.St. Amant, A.B. Wood, Tool use for autonomous agents, in: AAAI, 2005, pp. 184–189.

[3] Y. Choe, J. Yoo, Q. Li, Tool construction and use challenge: tooling test rebooted, in: AAAI-15 Workshop on Beyond the Turing Test, 2015. 2 p.

[4] R.W. Shumaker, K.R. Walkup, B.B. Beck, Animal Tool Behavior: The Use and Manufacture of Tools by Animals, JHU Press, 2011.

[5] C. Rutz, S. Sugasawa, J.E.M. Van der Wal, B.C. Klump, J.J.H.S.t. Clair, Tool bending in New Caledonian crows, R. Soc. Open Sci. 3 (8) (2016) 160439.

[6] B.C. Klump, J.J.H.S.t. Clair, C. Rutz, New Caledonian crows keep valuable hooked tools safer than basic non-hooked tools, Elife 10 (2021) e64829.

[7] A.M.P. von Bayern, S. Danel, A.M.I. Auersperg, B. Mioduszewska, A. Kacelnik, Compound tool construction by New Caledonian crows, Sci. Rep. 8 (1) (2018) 1–8.

[8] L. Nair, J. Balloch, S. Chernova, Tool Macgyvering: tool construction using geometric reasoning, in: 2019 International Conference on Robotics and Automation (ICRA), IEEE, 2019, pp. 5837–5843.

[9] K.R. Allen, K.A. Smith, J.B. Tenenbaum, Rapid trial-and-error learning with simulation supports flexible tool use and physical reasoning, Proc. Natl. Acad. Sci. 117 (47) (2020) 29302–29310.

[10] R. Wang, J. Lehman, J. Clune, K.O. Stanley, Poet: open-ended coevolution of environments and their optimized solutions, in: Proceedings of the Genetic and Evolutionary Computation Conference, 2019, pp. 142–151.

[11] K.O. Stanley, R. Miikkulainen, Competitive coevolution through evolutionary complexification, J. Artif. Intell. Res. 21 (2004) 63–100.

[12] Q. Li, J. Yoo, Y. Choe, Emergence of tool use in an articulated limb controlled by evolved neural circuits, in: Proceedings of the International Joint Conference on Neural Networks, 2015, https://doi.org/10.1109/IJCNN.2015.7280564.

[13] H. Wang, J. Yoo, Q. Li, Y. Choe, Dynamical analysis of recurrent neural circuits in articulated limb controllers for tool use, in: Proceedings of the International Joint Conference on Neural Networks, 2016, pp. 4339–4345.

[14] M. Freitag, Y. Choe, Analysis of tool use strategies in evolved neural circuits controlling an articulated limb, in: Proceedings of the International Joint Conference on Neural Networks, 2016, pp. 4331–4338.

[15] R. Reams, Y. Choe, Emergence of tool construction in an articulated limb controlled by evolved neural circuits, in: 2017 International Joint Conference on Neural Networks (IJCNN), IEEE, 2017, pp. 642–649.

[16] K.N. Nguyen, J. Yoo, Y. Choe, Speeding up affordance learning for tool use, using proprioceptive and kinesthetic inputs, in: 2019 International Joint Conference on Neural Networks (IJCNN), IEEE, 2019, pp. 1–8.

[17] K. Nguyen, Y. Choe, Emergence of different modes of tool use in a reaching and dragging task, in: International Joint Conference on Neural Networks (IJCNN), Shenzhen, China, 2021, pp. 1–8, https://doi.org/10.1109/IJCNN52387.2021.953377.

[18] K.O. Stanley, R. Miikkulainen, Evolving neural networks through augmenting topologies, Evol. Comput. 10 (2002) 99–127.

[19] Y. Wu, E. Mansimov, R.B. Grosse, S. Liao, J. Ba, Scalable trust-region method for deep reinforcement learning using Kronecker-factored approximation, in: Advances in Neural Information Processing Systems, 2017, pp. 5279–5288.

[20] R. Murphy, Introduction to AI Robotics, MIT Press, 2000.

[21] D. Lee, H. Kunori, Y. Nakamura, Association of whole body motion from tool knowledge for humanoid robots, in: IEEE/RSJ International Conference on Intelligent Robots and Systems, 2008. IROS 2008, IEEE, 2008, pp. 2867–2874.

[22] A.M. Arsenio, Learning task sequences from scratch: applications to the control of tools and toys by a humanoid robot, in: Proceedings of the 2004 IEEE International Conference on Control Applications, 2004, vol. 1, IEEE, 2004, pp. 400–405.

[23] R. Saegusa, G. Metta, G. Sandini, L. Natale, Developmental perception of the self and action, IEEE Trans. Neural Netw. Learn. Syst. 25 (1) (2014) 183–202.

[24] Y. Wu, Y. Demiris, Learning dynamical representations of tools for tool-use recognition, in: 2011 IEEE International Conference on Robotics and Biomimetics (ROBIO), IEEE, 2011, pp. 2664–2669.

[25] P. Pastor, H. Hoffmann, T. Asfour, S. Schaal, Learning and generalization of motor skills by learning from demonstration, in: IEEE International Conference on Robotics and Automation, 2009. ICRA'09, IEEE, 2009, pp. 763–768.

[26] A. Stoytchev, Behavior-grounded representation of tool affordances, in: Proceedings of the 2005 IEEE International Conference on Robotics and Automation, 2005. ICRA 2005, IEEE, 2005, pp. 3060–3065.

[27] D. Katz, O. Brock, Manipulating articulated objects with interactive perception, in: IEEE International Conference on Robotics and Automation, 2008. ICRA 2008, IEEE, 2008, pp. 272–277.

[28] D. Bullock, S. Grossberg, F.H. Guenther, A self-organizing neural model of motor equivalent reaching and tool use by a multijoint arm, J. Cogn. Neurosci. 5 (4) (1993) 408–435.

[29] S. Nishide, J. Tani, T. Takahashi, H.G. Okuno, T. Ogata, Tool-body assimilation of humanoid robot using a neurodynamical system, IEEE Trans. Auton. Ment. Dev. 4 (2) (2012) 139–149.

[30] K. Takahshi, T. Ogata, H. Tjandra, Y. Yamaguchi, Y. Suga, S. Sugano, Tool-body assimilation model using a neuro-dynamical system for acquiring representation of tool function and motion, in: 2014 IEEE/ASME International Conference on Advanced Intelligent Mechatronics (AIM), IEEE, 2014, pp. 1255–1260.

[31] R. Jain, T. Inamura, Learning of usage of tools based on interaction between humans and robots, in: 2014 IEEE 4th Annual International Conference on Cyber Technology in Automation, Control, and Intelligent Systems (CYBER), IEEE, 2014, pp. 597–602.

[32] B. Schäfer, N. Bergfeldt, M.J. Riveiro Carballa, T. Ziemke, Evolution of tool use behavior, in: Proceedings of the First IEEE Symposium on Artificial Life, Citeseer, 2007, pp. 31–38.

[33] J.R. Chung, Y. Choe, Emergence of memory in reactive agents equipped with environmental markers, IEEE Trans. Auton. Ment. Dev. 3 (3) (2011) 257–271.

[34] K. Sims, Evolving 3D morphology and behavior by competition, Artif. Life 1 (4) (1994) 353–372.

[35] A. Rajeswaran, V. Kumar, A. Gupta, G. Vezzani, J. Schulman, E. Todorov, S. Levine, Learning complex dexterous manipulation with deep reinforcement learning and demonstrations, arXiv:1709.10087 (2017).

[36] L. Wang, L. Brodbeck, F. Iida, Mechanics and energetics in tool manufacture and use: a synthetic approach, J. R. Soc. Interface 11 (100) (2014) 20140827.

[37] C. Yang, X. Lan, H. Zhang, N. Zheng, Autonomous tool construction with gated graph neural network, in: 2020 IEEE International Conference on Robotics and Automation (ICRA), IEEE, 2020, pp. 9708–9714.

[38] D. Choi, P. Langley, S.T. To, Creating and using tools in a hybrid cognitive architecture, in: AAAI Spring Symposia, 2018.

[39] B. Baker, I. Kanitscheider, T. Markov, Y. Wu, G. Powell, B. McGrew, I. Mordatch, Emergent tool use from multi-agent autocurricula, arXiv:1909.07528 (2019).

[40] L. Nair, N.S. Srikanth, Z.M. Erickson, S. Chernova, Autonomous tool construction using part shape and attachment prediction, in: Robotics: Science and Systems, 2019.

[41] K. Arulkumaran, M.P. Deisenroth, M. Brundage, A.A. Bharath, Deep reinforcement learning: a brief survey, IEEE Signal Process. Mag. 34 (6) (2017) 26–38.

[42] R.S. Sutton, D. McAllester, S. Singh, Y. Mansour, Policy gradient methods for reinforcement learning with function approximation, in: Advances in Neural Information Processing Systems 12, 1999.

[43] J. Schulman, S. Levine, P. Abbeel, M. Jordan, P. Moritz, Trust region policy optimization, in: International Conference on Machine Learning, PMLR, 2015, pp. 1889–1897.

[44] J. Schulman, F. Wolski, P. Dhariwal, A. Radford, O. Klimov, Proximal policy optimization algorithms, arXiv:1707.06347 (2017).

[45] V. Mnih, K. Kavukcuoglu, D. Silver, A.A. Rusu, J. Veness, M.G. Bellemare, A. Graves, M. Riedmiller, A.K. Fidjeland, G. Ostrovski, et al., Human-level control through deep reinforcement learning, Nature 518 (7540) (2015) 529–533.

[46] H. Van Hasselt, A. Guez, D. Silver, Deep reinforcement learning with double q-learning, in: Proceedings of the AAAI Conference on Artificial Intelligence, vol. 30, 2016.

[47] R.S. Sutton, D. Precup, S. Singh, Between MDPs and semi-MDPs: a framework for temporal abstraction in reinforcement learning, Artif. Intell. 112 (1–2) (1999) 181–211.

[48] R. Parr, S. Russell, Reinforcement learning with hierarchies of machines, in: Advances in Neural Information Processing Systems, Morgan Kaufmann Publishers, 1998, pp. 1043–1049.

[49] T.G. Dietterich, Hierarchical reinforcement learning with the MAXQ value function decomposition, J. Artif. Intell. Res. 13 (2000) 227–303.

[50] P. Dayan, G.E. Hinton, Feudal reinforcement learning, in: S. Hanson, J. Cowan, C. Giles (Eds.), Advances in Neural Information Processing Systems, vol. 5, Morgan-Kaufmann, 1993.

[51] T.D. Kulkarni, K. Narasimhan, A. Saeedi, J. Tenenbaum, Hierarchical deep reinforcement learning: integrating temporal abstraction and intrinsic motivation, in: Advances in Neural Information Processing Systems 29, 2016, pp. 3675–3683.

[52] O. Nachum, S.S. Gu, H. Lee, S. Levine, Data-efficient hierarchical reinforcement learning, in: Advances in Neural Information Processing Systems 31, 2018.

[53] A. Levy, G. Konidaris, R. Platt, K. Saenko, Learning multi-level hierarchies with hindsight, arXiv:1712.00948 (2017).

[54] A.S. Vezhnevets, S. Osindero, T. Schaul, N. Heess, M. Jaderberg, D. Silver, K. Kavukcuoglu, Feudal networks for hierarchical reinforcement learning, in: International Conference on Machine Learning, PMLR, 2017, pp. 3540–3549.

[55] Y. Burda, H. Edwards, A. Storkey, O. Klimov, Exploration by random network distillation, arXiv:1810.12894 (2018).

[56] P.-Y. Oudeyer, L.B. Smith, How evolution may work through curiosity-driven developmental process, Topics Cogn. Sci. 8 (2) (2016) 492–502.

[57] K.N. Nguyen, J. Yoo, Y. Choe, Speeding up affordance learning for tool use, using proprioceptive and kinesthetic inputs, in: 2019 International Joint Conference on Neural Networks (IJCNN), IEEE, 2019, pp. 1–8.

[58] A. Paszke, S. Gross, F. Massa, A. Lerer, J. Bradbury, G. Chanan, T. Killeen, Z. Lin, N. Gimelshein, L. Antiga, et al., PyTorch: an imperative style, high-performance deep learning library, in: Advances in Neural Information Processing Systems, 2019, pp. 8024–8035.

[59] D.P. Kingma, J. Ba, Adam: a method for stochastic optimization, in: International Conference on Learning Representations (ICLR), 2015.

[60] Y. Lee, E.S. Hu, J.J. Lim, IKEA furniture assembly environment for long-horizon complex manipulation tasks, in: IEEE International Conference on Robotics and Automation (ICRA), 2021.

[61] A. Maravita, A. Iriki, Tools for the body (schema), Trends Cogn. Sci. 8 (2) (2004) 79–86.

[62] A. Iriki, H. Suzuki, S. Tanaka, R.B. Vieira, Y. Yamazaki, The sapient paradox and the great journey: insights from cognitive psychology, neurobiology, and phenomenology, Psychologia 63 (2) (2021) 151–173.

[63] Q. Li, Exploring Multimodal Information in Deep Leaning (Ph.D. thesis), Department of Computer Science and Engineering, Texas A&M University, 2022.

[64] Q. Li, Y. Choe, Construction and use of tools through hierarchical deep reinforcement learning, in: 2021 IEEE/RSJ IROS Workshop on Human-Like Behavior and Cognition in Robots, 2021.

A Lagrangian framework for learning in graph neural networks

Marco Maggini, Matteo Tiezzi, and Marco Gori
DEPARTMENT OF INFORMATION ENGINEERING AND MATHEMATICS, UNIVERSITY OF SIENA, SIENA, ITALY

Chapter outlines

1 Introduction

Nowadays, neural networks have become a successful tool embedded in most of artificial intelligence-based systems. These models allowed us to attain state-of-the-art performances in many application domains, such as computer vision, natural language processing, bioinformatics, and robotics. In particular, deep learning principles [1] inspired the design of complex neural network architectures characterized by many computational layers, whose structure has been focused to solve a specific task [2, 3] or pushed the development of alternative techniques with respect to the existing models (e.g., the widespread use of attention-based models [4]). Neural network models are based on a distributed computational scheme in which signals are propagated among neurons through weighted connections. The topology of the connections defines the overall computation, both in the forward propagation of signals to compute the model outputs and in the error

https://doi.org/10.1016/B978-0-323-96104-2.00015-4
Copyright © 2024 Elsevier Inc. All rights reserved.

backpropagation to determine the weight gradients for the learning process. This same synchronous update scheme is applied to different varieties of neural architectures, designed to process fixed size vectors, temporal sequences, or graphs. In fact, even if the single computations are local to each neuron, the overall computation follows a precise flow driven by the neural network architecture and topology. The original feedforward neural network models, in particular multilayer perceptrons (MLPs) and their deep versions, have been devised to process inputs provided as real-valued vectors of features. Extensions of these architectures have been proposed to process temporal sequences (recurrent neural networks [RNNs] [5, 6]), pixels organized as two-dimensional (2D) rasters (convolutional neural networks [CNNs] [7]), directed acyclic graphs (DAG) (recursive neural networks [8, 9]), and general graph structures (graph neural networks [GNNs] [10]).

Backpropagation (BP) [11] is the learning mechanism exploited to optimize the neural network weights to solve a given task. BP provides an efficient way to compute the gradient of the loss function, which defines the learning objective, with respect to each connection weight. The original BP scheme proposed for MLPs has been extended also to complex architectures able to process structured inputs, such as backpropagation through time (BPTT) for RNNs and backpropagation through structure (BPTS) for recursive neural networks.

The chapter proposes an alternative view on the neural network computational scheme as the satisfaction of architectural constraints. The approach is inspired by the ideas of casting learning under the unifying notion of *constraint* [12, 13] and it is also related to the theoretical framework for BP formulated using Lagrangian optimization by LeCun et al. [14]. The introduction of the architectural constraints allows us to deliver a solution that is based on a truly local propagation (LP) of signals for the BP of the errors in the training phase. The Lagrangian formulation for constrained optimization is applied to derive a constraint-based representation of neural network architectures. In the most general setting, the LP algorithm casts learning in neural networks as the search for saddle points in the adjoint space composed of weights, neurons' outputs, and Lagrange multipliers. The chapter describes the implementation of popular shallow and deep neural models in the framework of LP, showing how the formulation also allows us to tolerate bounded violations of the architectural constraints that may favor robustness against noise. A related approach is proposed in Ref. [15], in which an inexact solution of the original learning problem is searched, followed by a postprocessing procedure that refines the last-layer connections. The approach proposed in Ref. [16] is based on closed-form solutions, but most of the architectural constraints are softly enforced, and additional variables are exploited to parameterize the neuron activations. Other proposals implement schemes based on constraints for block-wise optimization of neural networks [17].

Finally, the case of GNNs [18] is considered, for which the learning process of both the transition function and the node states is the outcome of a joint process, in which the state computation on the input graph is expressed by a constraint satisfaction mechanism that does not require an explicit iterative procedure and the network unfolding. The resulting training algorithm provides a nice trade-off between the flexibility introduced by the Lagrangian-based formulation of the graph diffusion and the addition of new variables. In fact, the only additional variables of the learning problem are associated with the nodes of the graph, whereas both the state transition function and the output function are classic BP-trainable models. This idea is also extended to the case of layered GNNs [19], in which multiple representations of each node are computed by a pipeline of constraints, that is related to a multilayer computational scheme.

2 Constraint-based models of neural networks

Neural networks implement a distributed computational scheme in which each one of simple interconnected units, the *neurons,* process a set of input signals, propagated through its incoming connections, to yield the output. The neuron's output x_n is obtained by a predefined (nonlinear) function that depends on a set of trainable parameters W_n and on the input signals $X_{in[n]}$, such that $x_n = f(X_{in[n]}, W_n)$. If the neural network contains N neurons, $X \in \mathbb{R}^N$ is the vector collecting all the units' outputs and $in[n]$ is the set of the units connected to the input of neuron n. A widely used implementation computes the neuron's output by applying a nonlinear function to the weighted linear combination of its inputs, as $x_n = \sigma(W'_n X_{in[n]} + b_n)$, where $W_n \in \mathbb{R}^{|in[n]|}$ is the vector of the neuron's weights and $b_n \in \mathbb{R}$ is the unit bias term. The activation function $\sigma(z)$ is a nonlinear mapping such as the *rectifier,* $ReLu(z) = \max(0, z)$, the *sigmoid,* $\sigma(z) = \frac{1}{1+e^{-z}}$, or the *hyperbolic tangent,* $\tanh(z) = \frac{e^z - e^{-z}}{e^z + e^{-z}}$.

The information flow characterizing neural architectures is completely driven by the topology of the neural connections and the nature of the input stimuli. The neuron functions are applied to the given input pattern to update the output vector X, following a predefined signal propagation scheme that depends on the specific architecture. The training process is aimed at finding an optimal value for the weights W to fit a set of target outputs provided for a given sample of inputs, the *learning set.* The weight update rule is based on a gradient-descent scheme that requires the computation of the derivatives of an objective function with respect to the connection weights. The *error BP* algorithm may be applied to compute the gradients by an efficient scheme that requires to propagate the error signals backward along the neuron's connections. This common scheme can be extended for any architecture and requires a synchronous flow of the error signals on the whole neural network. As shown before, neural network computation mainly requires two sets of variables, the neuron's outputs X and the connection weights W.

In the following, we show how the learning process can be made local by adding X as independent variables and by redefining the learning goal as a constrained optimization task. In particular, the newly obtained learning problem can be solved in the adjoint space of the neuron outputs X, the connection weights W, and the *Lagrangian multipliers.* The resulting algorithm is referred to as LP and it is shown to be effective for a complete parallelization of the learning process. The following sections describe the proposed framework when applied to popular neural network architectures, designed to process both flat and structured inputs. First, feed-forward multilayer neural networks are considered, remarking on how the proposed scheme can be applied to widely used models, such as CNNs [20] and residual neural networks (ResNets). Then, LP is described in the case of RNNs able to process sequences and GNNs applied to structured inputs encoded as generic graphs.

2.1 Multilayer perceptrons

The connection topology of an MLP is described by a DAG. In this case, neurons can be organized into H hidden layers and one output layer. Neurons in each layer receive connections only from neurons in the previous layer. The first layer consists of the external input, whereas the last layer, having not outgoing connections, represents the MLP output.

By $x_\ell \in \mathbb{R}^{N_\ell}$, we denote the output vector for a generic layer $\ell \in [0, 1, \ldots, H, H+1]$, where N_ℓ represents the number of neural units composing the layer. In particular, we denote with x_0 the external input vector and with x_{H+1} the MLP output. In order to distinguish the outputs when processing different external input patterns, we introduce an additional index p, such that $x_{0,p}$ is the specific pth input and $x_{\ell,p}$, with $\ell = 1, \ldots, H+1$, are the layer-wise neural outputs for the pth input pattern. The MLP processing scheme follows a forward flow through the layers. Starting with the first hidden layer ($\ell = 1$), the output vectors are computed by $x_{\ell,p} = \sigma(W_{\ell-1}x_{\ell-1,\,p} + b_\ell)$, where $W_{\ell-1} \in \mathbb{R}^{N_{\ell-1}\times N_\ell}$ collects the weights connecting layer $\ell - 1$ to layer ℓ, $b_\ell \in \mathbb{R}_\ell^N$ is the vector of bias terms, and $\sigma(\cdot)$ is the activation function that operates element wise on its vectorial argument.

We consider a supervised learning setting, in which a learning set is provided consisting of P pairs $(x_{0,p}, y_p)$, $p = 1, \ldots, P$, where $x_{0,\,p}$ is the input to the MLP and $y_p \in \mathbb{R}^{N_{H+1}}$ is the target vector for the MLP output. The output-target fitting for each example p is measured by a differentiable loss function $V\,(x_{H+1,\,p}, y_p)$. The training objective is to minimize the overall loss on all the learning set examples, with respect to the neural network parameters. In the classical formulation, the trainable parameters are just the connection weights collected in the matrices W_ℓ and b_ℓ, $\ell = 1, \ldots, H$. In the LP setting, we consider also the outputs at each hidden layer for each input sample, $x_{\ell,p}$, with $\ell = 1, \ldots, H$, as additional variables to parameterize the neuron activations. In order to cast the learning problem consistently with the neural network processing scheme, we need to add a set of (hard) *architectural constraints* that force the introduced free variables $x_{\ell,\,p}$ to be consistent with the computation performed by each layer, that is, $x_{\ell,p} = \sigma(W_{\ell-1}x_{\ell-1,p} + b_\ell)$. Hence, learning can be cast as a constrained optimization problem as

$$\begin{aligned} \min_{X,W,b} \quad & \sum_{p=1}^{P} V(x_{H+1,p}, y_p) \\ \text{subject to} \quad & \mathcal{G}(x_{\ell,p} - \sigma(W_{\ell-1}x_{\ell-1,p} + b_\ell)) = 0, \ \forall (p,\ell), \end{aligned} \tag{1}$$

where X collects all the $x_{\ell,\,p}$ output vectors for the hidden layers and input samples, W collects the connection weights $W_\ell, \ell=0,\ldots,H$, and b the neuron biases, $b_\ell, \ell=1,\ldots,H+1$. The constraints exploit the function $\mathcal{G}(\cdot)$, which is a generic function such that $\mathcal{G}(0)=0$. This function, as shown in the following (see Section 2.3 for further details), can be designed to differently weight the mismatch between each component of $x_{\ell,\,i}$ and the corresponding value of $\sigma(W_{\ell-1}x_{\ell-1,\,p}+b_\ell)$. In fact, the function is applied element-wise to each component of the argument, resulting in a set of N_ℓ constraints, each applied to one neuron of layer ℓ. To simplify the notation, $\mathcal{G}_{\ell,p} \in \mathbb{R}^{N_\ell}$ will be used to compactly indicate the left-hand side of the constraints in Eq. (1).

The constrained optimization problem of Eq. (1) can be reformulated as a unconstrained one in the Lagrangian framework [21], by introducing the Lagrange multipliers associated with each architectural constraint, $\lambda_{\ell,p} \in \mathbb{R}^{N_\ell}$. The Lagrangian function $\mathcal{L}$ is defined as

$$\mathcal{L}(X,W,b,\Lambda)=\sum_{p=1}^{P}\left(V(x_{H+1,p},y_p)+\sum_{\ell=1}^{H}\lambda'_{\ell,p}\mathcal{G}_{\ell,p}\right), \tag{2}$$

where Λ is the vector collecting all the Lagrangian multipliers $\lambda_{\ell,\,p}$. A squared L_2 norm regularizer on the network weights, scaled by a positive factor c, can be added to the Lagrangian $\mathcal{L}$ to favor the development of smooth functions.

In this formulation of the learning problem, the constraints describe the layered network architecture, by explicitly forcing the relationship between the inputs and the output of each neuron in each layer. Hence, the constraints force both the topology of the connections and the computation performed by each unit.

Fig. 1 shows an example of an MLP with one hidden layer with two neurons trained on the XOR problem. Each replica corresponds to the network fed with one of the four examples. The added free variables are represented as gray boxes and correspond to the hidden neurons' outputs for each of the four input examples. Hence, there are a total of eight additional variables. The introduction of these variables decouples the computation of the output neuron from the hidden layer updates but adds eight constraints with the corresponding Lagrange multipliers. In fact each $\lambda_{1,\,p}$, $p = 1, 2, 3, 4$ is a vector with two components, one for each hidden layer unit.

2.2 Local propagation

The optimization of the Lagrangian $\mathcal{L}$ of Eq. (2) can be cast as a *differential optimization* process [22] that converges toward a saddle point of this function. The process requires to minimize $\mathcal{L}$ with respect to W, b, and X and to maximize it with respect to Λ. Thus, the LP algorithm consists in a gradient-descent step to update W, b, and X, and in a gradient-ascent step to update Λ, until convergence to a stationary point.

The variables X and Λ are initialized to zero, whereas both the weights W and the biases b are randomly generated. With respect to the classical BP algorithm, the

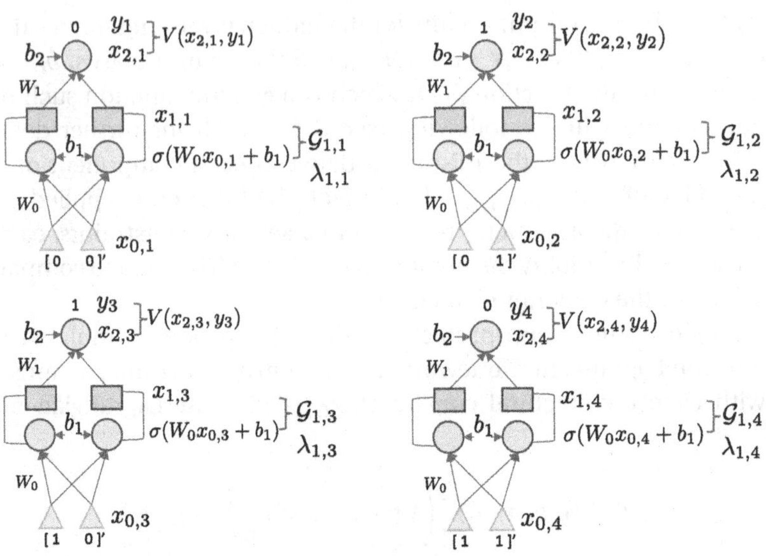

FIG. 1 LP for an MLP with one hidden layer trained on the XOR task.

variables in X are not set as the outcome of the forward step but in LP they evolve during the training process following the gradient-based optimization. At convergence, the architectural constraints of Eq. (1) are satisfied. In such optimality condition, the values in X correspond (or approximate, depending on the choice of $\mathcal{G}(\cdot)$) to the ones computed by the forward step of the BP-trained neural network. As a result, LP is exploited during training but the classical forward computation can be applied during inference.

A major advantage of LP is the *local* nature of gradient computation, meaning that each optimization step does not require any explicit propagation of signals but only relies on the variables directly connected to each neuron. This is different with respect to what is done by the BP algorithm, where the gradient exploits variables that are indeed local, but whose computation requires both a forward and a backward propagation of signals on the whole architecture. As shown in Fig. 2A, in order to compute the gradient of a given weight (the one highlighted in red), BP requires the complete forward propagation of the signals to compute the outputs of all neurons. Only afterwards, the errors can be computed at the output level, thereby the so-called *delta* terms can be propagated backwards through the layers to obtain the variables required to compute the local gradient. Hence, in the case of BP *locality* concerns only the propagation of signals among the connected units (both forward and backward) and the final computation of the gradient. By contrast, in LP, the variable updates require only values local to each unit and, hence, each step needs no explicit propagation of signals. The flow of information is indeed a consequence of the optimization process that drives the evolution of variables toward the satisfaction of the

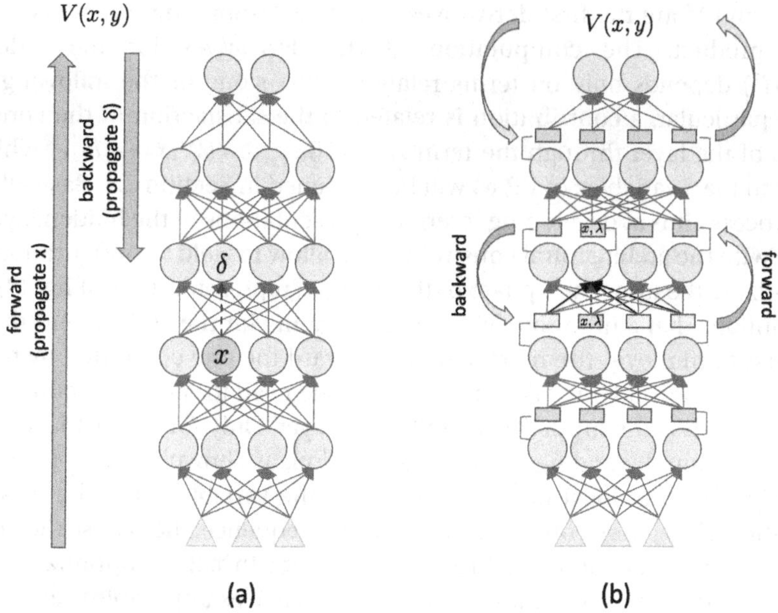

FIG. 2 Gradient computation in backpropagation (A) and local propagation (B).

constraints. In fact, the derivatives exploited in the optimization of the Lagrangian $\mathcal{L}$ are computed as follows:

$$\frac{\partial \mathcal{L}}{\partial W_\ell} = -\sum_{p=1}^{P} \Big(\lambda_{\ell+1,p} \odot \mathcal{G}'_{\ell+1,p} \odot \sigma'(W_\ell x_{\ell,p} + b_{\ell+1}) \Big) x'_{\ell,p}, \tag{3}$$

$$\frac{\partial \mathcal{L}}{\partial W_H} = \sum_{p=1}^{P} V'(x_{H+1,p}, y_p) \odot \sigma'(W_H x_{H,p} + b_{H+1}) x'_{H,p}, \tag{4}$$

$$\frac{\partial \mathcal{L}}{\partial b_\ell} = -\sum_{p=1}^{P} \Big(\lambda_{\ell,p} \odot \mathcal{G}'_{\ell,p} \odot \sigma'(W_{\ell-1} x_{\ell-1,p} + b_\ell) \Big) \mathbb{1}', \tag{5}$$

$$\frac{\partial \mathcal{L}}{\partial b_{H+1}} = \sum_{p=1}^{P} V'(x_{H+1,p}, y_p) \odot \sigma'(W_H x_{H,p} + b_{H+1}) \mathbb{1}', \tag{6}$$

$$\frac{\partial \mathcal{L}}{\partial x_{\ell,p}} = \lambda_{\ell,p} \odot \mathcal{G}'_{\ell,p} - W'_\ell \Big(\lambda_{\ell+1,p} \odot \mathcal{G}'_{\ell+1,p} \odot \sigma'(W_\ell x_{\ell,p} + b_{\ell+1}) \Big), \tag{7}$$

$$\frac{\partial \mathcal{L}}{\partial x_{H,p}} = \lambda_{H,p} \odot \mathcal{G}'_{H,p} + W'_H \Big(V'(x_{H+1,p}, y_p) \odot \sigma'(W_H x_{H,p} + b_{H+1}) \Big), \tag{8}$$

$$\frac{\partial \mathcal{L}}{\partial \lambda_{\ell,p}} = \mathcal{G}_{\ell,p}, \tag{9}$$

where $\mathcal{G}'$, σ', and V' are the first derivatives of the corresponding functions and $\odot$ is the Hadamard product. The computation of the derivatives for the hidden layers ($\ell \in [1, \ldots, H]$) depends only on terms related to the same or the following layer (see Fig. 2B). In particular, a contribution is related to the satisfaction of the constraints on the outputs of the layer through the term $\lambda_{\ell+1,p} \odot \mathcal{G}'_{\ell+1,p} \odot \sigma'(W_\ell x_{\ell,p} + b_{\ell+1})$ which plays a role similar to the δ variables in BP, as will be deepened in Section 2.4. Basically, the optimization process aims at developing internal representations in the hidden layers that are compatible with the architectural constraints and allow to yield a configuration in the last layer minimizing the loss. The update of the internal representations of Eq. (7) combines two contributions that aim to satisfying the constraints for the current and the following layer: the first term moves the representation toward the one computed by the previous layer, whereas the second one takes into account the need to satisfy the constraint for the representation that is the input for the following layer. Only for the last layer, there is an explicit contribution depending on the loss function, as shown in Eqs. (4), (6), (8).

The explicit effect of local updates is to move the variables onto the feasible region defined by the architectural constraints $\mathcal{G}_{\ell,p}$. As a consequence, they cause the flow of information from the loss function $V(\cdot, \cdot)$ through the network. In fact, the optimization of the last layer yields weights and representations in layer H for each example able to approximate the provided supervisions. The constraints on layer H force this layer to approximate such optimal representations and to select appropriate outputs for layer $H-1$. The interactions among layers due to such *architectural constraints* foster the flow of information in the neural network structure by means of the optimization process. The information generally flows through a large number of paths, such that many iterations could be required to keep the model inside the feasible region and efficiently learn the network weights. This represents a significant distinction of the LP algorithm with respect to BP: the search for internal representations and the way they are computed are somehow decoupled, such that the search space has more degrees of freedom during the optimization stages.

Additional constraints can be added to the Lagrangian function, in the search of solutions having specific properties. For instance, an L_1-norm regularizer (weighted by $\alpha > 0$) can be added for each $x_{\ell,\, p}$, in order to help the model to focus on sparse internal representations, reducing the search space.

2.3 Constraint functions

The definition of the constraints in Eq. (1) depends on the function $\mathcal{G}(\cdot)$. Overall, the final goal of the proposed formulation is the enforcement of architectural constraints, such that, when the optimality condition is met, they yield $x_{\ell,\, p} - \sigma(W_{\ell-1}x_{\ell-1,\, p} + b_\ell) = 0$. Instantiating the $\mathcal{G}(\cdot)$ function as the identity mapping (i.e., $\mathcal{G}(z) = z$) is the most simple solution that meets the requirement $\mathcal{G}(0) = 0$. Another possible approach is $\mathcal{G}(x) = x^2$, with the purpose of yielding a nonnegative codomain. Moreover, other functions may improve the convergence of the optimization algorithm or the numerical robustness of the solution. In particular, $\mathcal{G}(z)$ can be set to one of the following ϵ-insensitive functions

$$\text{eps}(z) = \max(|z| - \epsilon, 0), \tag{10}$$

$$\text{lineps}(z) = \max(z, \epsilon) - \max(-z, \epsilon). \tag{11}$$

Both these functions are continuous, assume a 0-value in $[-\epsilon, \epsilon]$, and they are linear out of this interval. Moreover, eps(z) is always positive, whereas lineps(z) is negative when $z < -\epsilon$. By setting $\epsilon = 0$, we impose the hard satisfaction of the constraint at hand. In particular, lineps(z) becomes the identity mapping.

When exploited in the architectural constraints of Eq. (1), these functions tolerate a bounded mismatch between the values of $x_{\ell,\,p}$ and $\sigma(W_{\ell-1}x_{\ell,\,p} + b_\ell)$, yielding ϵ-insensitive constraints. The introduced tolerance in the satisfaction of the constraint causes a kind of regularization mechanism in the network training since the solution is not influenced by small changes in the hidden layer representations. As a result, this mechanism fosters a more stable optimization process. For instance, if two examples p and q yield similar representations $\sigma(W_{\ell-1}x_{\ell,\,p} + b_\ell)$ and $\sigma(W_{\ell-1}x_{\ell,\,q} + b_\ell)$ at layer ℓ, then the same representation $x_{\ell,\,p} = x_{\ell,\,q}$ can be selected by the optimization algorithm for both of them, thus propagating the same signal to the upper layers. The effect is naturally limited to the training phase since inference is performed by a forward computation of the $x_{\ell,\,p}$'s, without taking into account the architectural constraints. Clearly, the value of ϵ should be chosen small enough to avoid a large difference between the setting in which the neural weights are learning and that in which they are exploited to compute the predictions. In some sense, the effect of the ϵ-insensitive constraints is somehow related to the application of the popular dropout [23] technique. Also, in this case, a too-large drop-unit factor may hinder the training process.

The main difference between eps$(\cdot)$ and lineps$(\cdot)$ is that the first is always positive, whereas the second can also be negative. This affects the development of the Lagrange multipliers, since from Eq. (9) it is evident that their variation is proportional to the function value. When the constraint is satisfied, the corresponding multiplier is left unchanged. Whereas in the case of $\mathcal{G}(z) > 0$, the multiplier increases, while it decreases for $\mathcal{G}(z) < 0$. Hence, when using eps$(\cdot)$ that is always positive, the multipliers can only increase or remain constant. In the case of lineps$(\cdot)$, the multipliers can either increase or decrease. In general, eps$(\cdot)$ yields more stable learning, where the violations of the constraints change more smoothly, even if the evolution of the Lagrangian multipliers has to be carefully checked to avoid too large values. A way to improve the numerical stability of the algorithm is to exploit the *Augmented Lagrangian* [21, 22], by adding the term $\rho \parallel \mathcal{G}_{\ell,p} \|^2$, for all p, ℓ to the Lagrangian $\mathcal{L}$ of Eq. (2).

2.4 Relationship between BP and LP

The complete locality of the LP allows a full parallelization of the algorithm. In fact, if we consider Eqs. (3)–(9), the computations for each layer ℓ can be distributed in different processing units (for instance, in GPU units that are designed to speed up matrix operations).

The only requirement is to share the memory with the units allocated for processing the $(\ell + 1)$-th and $(\ell - 1)$-th layers. The overall computation can then progress in parallel without the need global synchronization. As shown in Fig. 2, the LP computational scheme differs from that of BP in which a set of *sequential* steps are required to propagate signals through layers both in the forward and backward phases. In fact, in the forward propagation layer, ℓ can be updated only when all the previous layers have been processed. Indeed, the MLP output will be produced solely after a sequential update involving all the layers. Similarly, in the backward propagation, the gradients at layer ℓ can be computed only after the errors have been propagated through all the upper layers.

Even if the LP and BP algorithms approach the learning task with different strategies, they are strongly correlated. In fact, when the stationary conditions $\partial\mathcal{L}/\partial\lambda_{\ell,i} = 0$ and $\partial\mathcal{L}/\partial x_{\ell,i} = 0$ are imposed on the Lagrangian, the LP weight update rules collapse to those of the BP algorithm. Let us consider the case $\mathcal{G}(z) = z$, such that $\mathcal{G}'(z) = 1$. The stationary condition $\partial\mathcal{L}/\partial\lambda_{\ell,i} = 0$ implies that the architectural constraints are satisfied and, hence, the values of the layer outputs match those computed following the classical forward propagation rule $x_{\ell,\ p} = \sigma(W_{\ell-1}x_{\ell-1,\ p} + b_\ell)$ (see Eq. 9). If we define $\delta_{\ell,\ p} = \lambda_{\ell,\ p} \odot \sigma'$ $(W_{\ell-1}x_{\ell-1,\ p} + b_\ell)$, the weight update rules of Eqs. (3), (5) become

$$\frac{\partial\mathcal{L}}{\partial W_\ell} = -\sum_{p=1}^{P} \delta_{\ell+1,p} \cdot x'_{\ell,p},$$

$$\frac{\partial\mathcal{L}}{\partial b_\ell} = -\sum_{p=1}^{P} \delta_{\ell,p} \cdot \mathbb{1}',$$

whereas from the stationary condition $\partial\mathcal{L}/\partial x_{\ell,i} = 0$ and Eq. (7), we obtain the $\delta_{\ell,\ p}$ BP rule

$$\delta_{\ell,p} = \sigma'(W_{\ell-1}x_{\ell-1,p} + b_\ell) \odot W'_\ell \delta_{\ell+1,p}.$$

Finally, Eqs. (4), (6), (8) allow us to obtain the update rules for the last layer that involve the derivatives of the loss function. Hence, BP may be viewed as a special case of the LP algorithm when restricting the search to the subspace where the stationary conditions on $\lambda_{\ell,\ p}$ and $x_{\ell,\ p}$ hold.

2.5 Residual networks

ResNets [24] consists of a stack of residual layers that, in general, implement the following computation [25]:

$$x_\ell = z(h(x_{\ell-1}) + f(W_{\ell-1}x_{\ell-1})). \tag{12}$$

A widely used implementation sets $z(x) = ReLu(x)$, $h(x) = x$, and $f(x)$ to one of the nonlinear functions commonly used in neural network models. Hence, the layer output is obtained from a linear combination of the direct propagation of the input and its processing through a classical neural layer, which depends on a matrix of learnable weights. The residual connections limit the effect of the vanishing gradient problem, such that these units are exploited in deep neural networks yielding state-of-the-art results, for instance, in the case of deep convolutional neural nets [24].

The LP architectural constraint for residual layers can be obtained straightforwardly from Eq. (12), as

$$\mathcal{G}(x_{\ell,p} - z(h(x_{\ell-1},p) + f(W_{\ell-1}x_{\ell-1},p))) = 0, \tag{13}$$

for each input $p = [1, \ldots, P]$ in the learning set.

In order to compare the properties of the ResNet optimized with the classical BP and the proposed LP version, we assume that both $z(x)$ and $h(x)$ are identity mappings [25], such that

$$x_{\ell,p} = x_{\ell-1,p} + \sigma(W_{\ell-1}x_{\ell-1,p}), \tag{14}$$

where we redefined $f(\cdot) = \sigma(\cdot)$ to clarify that the second term implements a neural network layer as described before (see Fig. 3A). This specific setting for the residual connections makes it easier to analyze how the signals propagate through the layers both in the forward and backward steps [24]. In fact, it is easy to show that the signal propagates from layer ℓ to

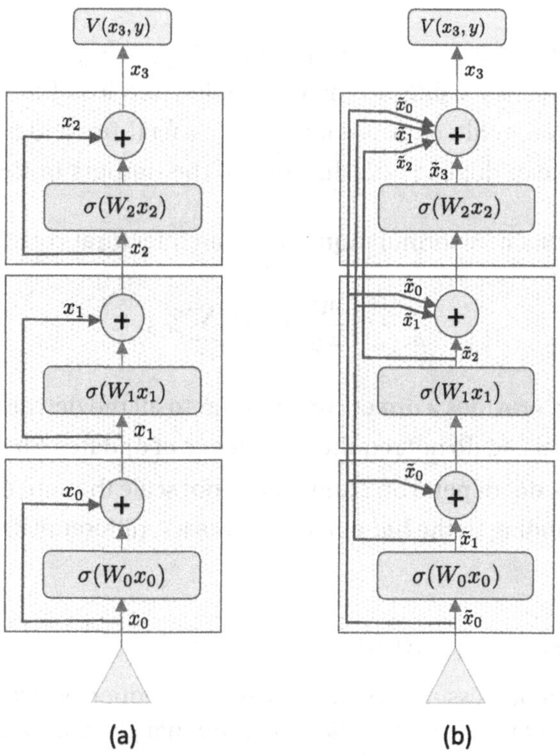

FIG. 3 (A) Residual network with three layers and (B) the same network after the change of variables ($x_\ell \rightarrow \tilde{x}_\ell$).

any layer $L > \ell$ by a sequence of sum operations, such that $x_{L,p} = x_{\ell,p} + \sum_{j=\ell}^{L-1} \sigma(W_j x_{j,p})$. Hence, the gradient with respect to x_ℓ of the loss function $V(W_H x_H, y)$ is

$$\frac{\partial V}{\partial x_{\ell,p}} = \frac{\partial V}{\partial x_{H,p}} \left(1 + \frac{\partial}{\partial x_{\ell,p}} \sum_{j=\ell}^{H-1} \sigma(W_j x_{j,p}) \right), \tag{15}$$

showing a direct contribution of the loss gradient to layer ℓ because of the term 1. In the case of the residual units of Eq. (14), the LP architectural constraints are the following:

$$\mathcal{G}(x_{\ell,p} - x_{\ell-1,p} - \sigma(W_{\ell-1} x_{\ell-1,p})) = 0. \tag{16}$$

Due to the locality of LP, the loss $V(W_H x_H, y)$ is considered only in the gradients for the last layer $H + 1$ (see, for instance, Eqs. 4, 8), that is, for the variables x_H and W_H. Due to the decoupling of the layer outputs, there is no direct contribution to the gradient computation for the other constraints/variables. However, if we define $\widetilde{x}_{\ell,p} = x_{\ell,p} - x_{\ell-1,p}$, Eq. (16) can be rewritten as

$$\mathcal{G}\left(\widetilde{x}_{\ell,p} - \sigma\left(W_{\ell-1} \cdot \sum_{j=0}^{\ell-1} \widetilde{x}_{j,p} \right) \right) = 0, \tag{17}$$

by exploiting the fact that $x_{\ell,p} = \widetilde{x}_{\ell,p} + x_{\ell-1,p}$ implies $x_{\ell,p} = \sum_{j=0}^{\ell} \widetilde{x}_{j,p}$ by repeating the substitutions up to $\ell = 0$.[a] By using the new variables, the loss function is computed as $V(W_H \cdot \sum_{j=0}^{H} \widetilde{x}_j, y)$. This architecture is equivalent to a feed-forward neural network, where the output of each layer depends on the sum of the outputs of the previous layers, as shown in Fig. 3B.

Hence, by using this new formulation for the architectural constraints, we have that

$$\frac{\partial \mathcal{L}}{\partial \widetilde{x}_{\ell,p}} = \frac{\partial V}{\partial \widetilde{x}_{\ell,p}} + \frac{\partial}{\partial \widetilde{x}_{\ell,p}} \sum_{j=\ell}^{H} \mathcal{G}_{j,p}, \tag{18}$$

showing that the loss provides a direct contribution to all the derivatives even if the computations are still local and do not require a sequence of updates. Since $V(W_H \cdot \sum_{j=0}^{H} \widetilde{x}_j, y)$, the derivative $\frac{\partial V}{\partial \widetilde{x}_\ell}$ does not depend on ℓ and it does not scale the sum of the gradients of the constraints corresponding to the hidden layers above ℓ, differently from what happens in Eq. (15).

2.6 Recurrent neural networks

RNNs are designed to process data organized as time sequences [26]. A neural module is exploited to implement the *state transition function* that given the current state and input

[a]We assume $\widetilde{x}_{0,p} = x_{0,p}$.

computes the new state vector. The resulting computational scheme corresponds to unroll this module in time to yield the *unfolded* network that allows the derivation of the BP through time algorithm to compute the weight gradients.[b] The unfolding procedure corresponds to add a new layer at each time step, whose input is the output of the previous layer and the current external signal. Hence, the RNNs can be viewed as a deep multilayer neural network, whose layers share the same weights. Moreover, in general, the state transition module can be implemented by multiple layers, such that the layer output variables (i.e., the states) will depend both on the layer and the time index as $x^t_{\ell,p}$. The architectural constraints can be directly written as

$$\mathcal{G}\left(x^t_{\ell,p} - \sigma(W_{\ell-1}x^t_{\ell-1,p} + U_{\ell-1}x^{t-1}_{\ell,p})\right) = 0,$$

where U_ℓ is the weight matrix exploited to propagate the state at the previous time step. For each input sample p, there is a constraint for each layer ℓ and time instant t. Hence, the variables of the optimization problem are the vectors $x^t_{\ell,p}$, the Lagrange multipliers $\lambda^t_{\ell,p}$, and the weight matrices W_ℓ and U_ℓ (notice that the weights do not depend on the index t since they are shared among all the time steps). The resulting LP optimization algorithm is local with respect to the layers and to the time steps, due to the decoupling of the variables. The only difference is due to the fact that the same weight matrices are shared among all time steps, and, hence, their derivative will depend on all the time steps for each input sequence, as

$$\frac{\partial \mathcal{L}}{\partial W_\ell} = -\sum_{p=1}^{P}\sum_{t=1}^{T_p}\left(\lambda^t_{\ell+1,p} \odot (\mathcal{G}^t_{\ell+1,p})' \odot \sigma'(W_\ell x^t_{\ell,p} + +U_\ell x^{t-1}_{\ell,p})\right)(x^t_{\ell,p})', \tag{19}$$

$$\frac{\partial \mathcal{L}}{\partial U_\ell} = -\sum_{p=1}^{P}\sum_{t=1}^{T_p}\left(\lambda^t_{\ell+1,p} \odot (\mathcal{G}^t_{\ell+1,p})' \odot \sigma'(W_\ell x^t_{\ell,p} + +U_\ell x^{t-1}_{\ell,p})\right)(x^{t-1}_{\ell,p})', \tag{20}$$

where T_p is the length of the pth input sequence.

3 Local propagation in graph neural networks

GNNs [10] are designed to extend the computational model of neural networks to process data organized as graphs. A graph is formally defined by a pair $G = (V, E)$, where V is a finite set of *nodes* and $E \subseteq V \times V$ contains the *arcs*. Hence, a graph is able to represent a set of entities as the nodes and binary relationships between them as the arcs. A GNN processes an input graph G by first computing an *encoding* for each node in V (*encoding* phase), and then by exploiting the computed latent node representations (also referred to as *node embeddings*) to yield the model output (*output/readout* phase). The overall processing scheme can compute an output for each node in the input graph (*node-focused* function)

[b]The description focuses on classical RNNs but can be extended also to widely used models such as the long short-term memories (LSTMs) [6].

or one single output for the whole graph (*graph-focused* function). An example of the first setting is the classification of documents by topics, taking into account the document (the node) content (the features) and the links or citations between them (the arcs). An example of the latter setting (graph-focused) can be found in the context of predicting the global properties of chemical compounds. Molecules are encoded as graphs where nodes represent the atoms and arcs encode the bonding between atoms, and the task is the prediction of the class of membership of the molecule.

3.1 The GNN model

The encoding phase in GNNs is based on a diffusion process among neighboring nodes in the graph. Let us consider a graph $G=(V, E)$. A feature vector $l_v \in \mathbb{R}^m$, the *node label*, may be provided for each node to represent node-related information. Similarly, an *arc label* $l_{(v, u)} \in R^d$ may be available for the arcs $(u, v) \in E$ to specify properties of the binary relationship between pairs of nodes. The *neighborhood* ne$[v]$ of a node $v \in V$ is defined as the union of the set of its *parent* nodes, $\mathrm{pa}[v] = \{u \in V: (u, v) \in E\}$ and the set of its *children*, $\mathrm{ch}[v] = \{u \in V: (v, u) \in E\}$, that is, $\mathrm{ne}[v] = \mathrm{pa}[v] \cup \mathrm{ch}[v]$. A GNN computes a state (encoding) $x_v \in \mathbb{R}^s$ for each node $v \in V$, given the labels assigned to the nodes and arcs, and the graph topology. We consider the original computational scheme proposed in Ref. [10], which will be referred to as GNN* [27].

The state x_v of each node in the input graph is computed by an iterative procedure based on the *state transition function* f_a that yields the updated state for each node v, given the current states of the nodes in its neighborhood and the available node and arc labels. Given the iteration index t, the new node state is computed as

$$x_v^{(t)} = f_a\left(x_{\mathrm{ne}[v]}^{(t-1)}, l_{\mathrm{ne}[v]}, l_{(v,\mathrm{ch}[v])}, l_{(\mathrm{pa}[v],v)}, x_v^{(t-1)}, l_v \mid \theta_{f_a}\right), \tag{21}$$

where $x_{\mathrm{ne}[v]}^{(t-1)}$ is the set of the states of the neighbors of node v at the previous iteration $t-1$, that is, $\{x_u^{(t-1)} : u \in \mathrm{ne}[v]\}$, $l_{\mathrm{ne}[v]}$ is the set of labels of the neighbor nodes, $l_{(v,\ \mathrm{ch}[v])}$ and $l_{(\mathrm{pa}[v],\ v)}$ are the sets of arc labels for the children and the parents of node v, and θ_{f_a} is a set of learnable parameters. The nodes in the graph may have different degrees $\mathrm{de}[v] = |\mathrm{ne}[v]|$, such that the number of arguments of f_a may vary among the nodes. In order to deal with a variable number of neighbors, different approaches have been proposed, based on the idea of aggregating the contribution of each node in ne$[v]$ by a permutation-invariant function, unless some predefined order is given for the neighbors of each node. In the original GNN* model, a function $h(\cdot)$ is applied to each arc and the resulting values are summed to yield the aggregated state as

$$x_v^{(t)} = \sum_{u \in \mathrm{ne}[v]} h(x_u^{(t-1)}, l_u, l_{(v,u)}, l_{(u,v)}, x_v^{(t-1)}, l_v | \theta_h), \tag{22}$$

where θ_h are the function parameters to be adapted by the training procedure. In particular, $h(\cdot)$ can be implemented by an MLP with $(2s + 2m + 2d)$ inputs and s outputs, such that θ_h collects the MLP weights. The node latent representations are computed by iterating Eq.

(22) for T steps. The iteration of the transition function $f_a(\cdot)$ allows the diffusion of information among the nodes through the arcs. In fact, by repeating t times the aggregation of 1-hop neighborhoods by $f_a(\cdot)$, the state of a node is propagated to the nodes distant up to t-hops. In the original GNN* model [10], the state transition function is iterated until convergence of the states, that is, until $x_v^{(t)} \simeq x_v^{(t-1)}, \forall v \in V$. The obtained latent representation corresponds to the *fixed point* of the state transition function $f_a(\cdot)$ computed on the input graph. The convergence of this computation is guaranteed if $f_a(\cdot)$ is a *contraction map*. In any case, in practical application, full convergence is not required, only a small number of iterations is sufficient to obtain informative node representations for the task at hand.

The iteration index t in the state computation can be seen as the *depth* of the GNN*, since a new *layer* (corresponding to $f_a(\cdot)$) is stacked to compute the states $x_v^{(t)}, v \in V$ from the outputs $x_v^{(t-1)}$ of the previous layer (iteration) of the GNN*. All these layers share the same $f_a(\cdot)$, and the resulting recurrent computational scheme can be described in the framework of RecGNN models [18]. Differently from more recent implementations, in GNN* the node states $x_v \in \mathbb{R}^s$ are initialized to zero and do not depend on the available node features $l_v \in \mathbb{R}^m$. However, $f_a(\cdot)$ exploits at each iteration both the available node labels (l_v) and arc labels ($l_{(u,\ v)}$). This avoids oversmoothing or the vanishing of the information available in the labels of the input graph [28].

Henceforth, the state transition function applied to a node $v \in V$ will be compactly denoted as

$$f_{a,v} = f_a\big(x_{\mathrm{ne}[v]}, l_{\mathrm{ne}[v]}, l_{(v,\mathrm{ch}[v])}, l_{(\mathrm{pa}[v],v)}, x_v, l_v \mid \theta_{f_a}\big). \tag{23}$$

Given this notation, the fixed-point problem is solved to compute the node state representations is defined by the *equality constraint*

$$\forall v \in V, \quad x_v = f_{a,v}. \tag{24}$$

When this constraint is satisfied, the states are node representations that potentially encode the whole graph.

Once the node states have been computed, the output of the GNN* is obtained by employing the *readout/output function,* denoted by the function y_v for the node-focused case, or y_G for graph-focused tasks, as follows:

$$y_v = f_r\left(x_v^{(T)} \mid \theta_{f_r}\right), \tag{25a}$$

$$y_G = f_r\left(\{x_v^{(T)}, v \in V\} \mid \theta_{f_r}\right). \tag{25b}$$

In the following, we will consider the GNN* state propagation scheme of Eq. (22), by applying the Lagrangian formulation to fulfill the constraint of Eq. (24). However, following the same approach that will be described in the following, the LP scheme can be applied to other models proposed in the literature, such as GIN [29], GCN [30], GraphSAGE [31], GAT [32], and in general models defined in the framework of message passing neural networks (MPNNs) [33–36].

3.2 Constraint-based node propagation

The GNN* learning algorithm requires an inference step at each training iteration, such that the fixed-point solution of Eq. (24) needs to be approximated at each epoch. This procedure requires to iterate the state transition Eq. (22) for T steps, which corresponds to the *unfolding* into T staked layers of the MLP implementing the transition function, as it happens for RNNs. Hence, the computational cost may become significant when the number of iterations T for convergence to the fixed-point increases (for instance in the case of large graphs).

The computation of the node states depends on the graph topology, which defines a set of constraints among the variables x_v, $v \in V$. In particular, Eq. (24) defines an equality constraint between the node state representation and its value computed by the state transition function. Hence, by adding free variables corresponding to the node states x_v, $v \in V$, the Lagrangian formulation of the learning problem can be cast by exploiting the constraint

$$\forall v \in V, \quad \mathcal{G}(x_v - f_{a,v}) = 0, \tag{26}$$

where $\mathcal{G}(\cdot)$ is a function characterized by $\mathcal{G}(0) = 0$, which can be selected as described in Section 2.3. The satisfaction of the constraints implies the solution of Eq. (24), such that the fixed-point computation is only defined by the constraints and does not require an explicit implementation.

To simplify the description of the LP problem formulation, we consider a node-focused task, in which a target output $\hat{y}_v$ is provided for some nodes $v \in S \subseteq V$ of the input graph G.[c] The learning task is defined by the following constrained optimization problem:

$$\begin{array}{ll} \displaystyle\min_{\theta_{f_a}, \theta_{f_r}, X} & \displaystyle\sum_{v \in S} L(f_r(x_v \mid \theta_{f_r}), \hat{y}_v) \\ \text{subject to} & \mathcal{G}(x_v - f_{a,v}) = 0, \quad \forall\, v \in V, \end{array} \tag{27}$$

where $L(f_r(x_v \mid \theta_{fr_r}), \hat{y}_v)$ is the loss function used to measure the target fitting for node $v \in S$. The variables considered in the optimization are the weights θ_{f_a} and θ_{f_r} of the MLPs implementing the state transition function and the output function, respectively, and the node state variables collected in $X = \{x_v : v \in V\}$. The solution to the optimization problem of Eq. (27) implicitly includes the definition of the fixed point of the state transition function, since any feasible solution satisfies the constraints and, consequently, the learned x_v are solutions of Eq. (24).

Fig. 4 shows how the GNN* computation is applied on an input graph. For each node of the graph, a replica of the state transition function f_a of Eq. (22) is instantiated. For each node, the state $x_v v \in 1, 2, 3, 4$ is a free variable as defined in the optimization problem of Eq. (27). The constraint forces the free state variable to approximate the result of the

[c] In case of node-focused tasks, if more graphs are provided in the learning set, they can be merged into a single graph containing the given graphs as disconnected components.

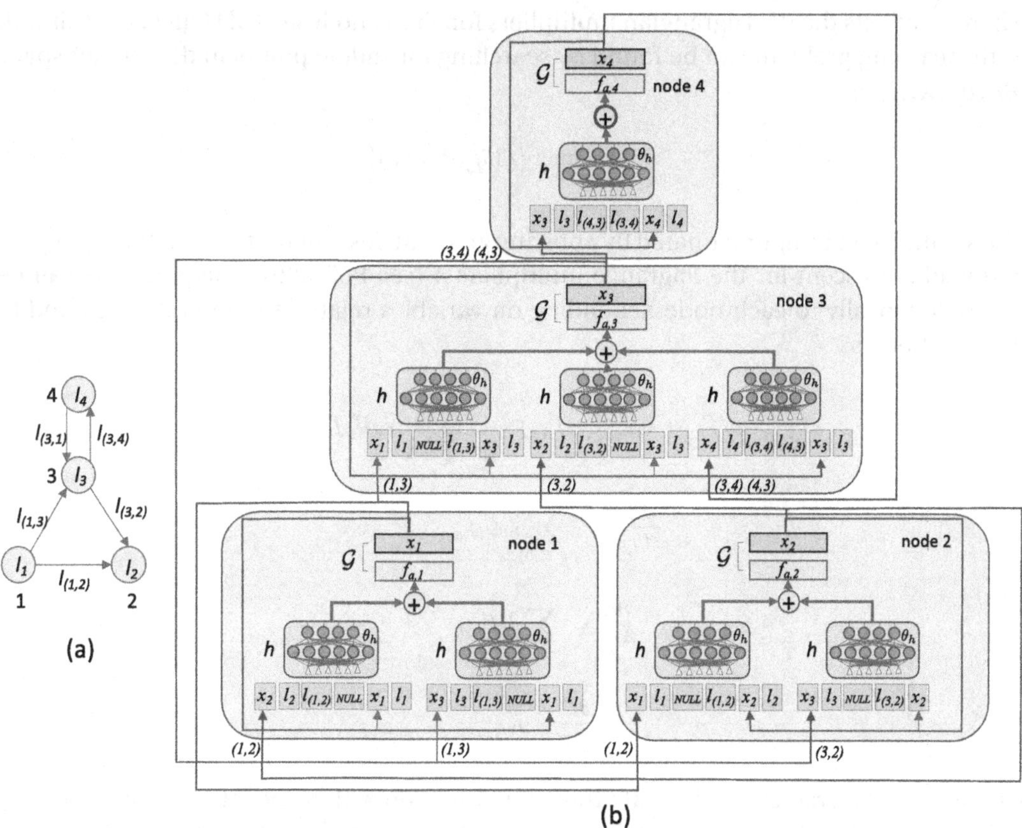

FIG. 4 (A) Input graph. (B) The GNN unfolded on the input graph. The node states x_1, x_2, x_3, x_4 are set as free variables and exploited as inputs to the replicas of the $h()$ function. The constraints between the free and computed variables are shown by the $\mathcal{G}$ symbol. The labels of the missing arcs are set to the special value *NULL*.

transition function computation for each node, as shown by the $\mathcal{G}$ symbol. Each node computes the output state by applying the function $h()$ to each neighbor of the node and, then, by summing all the contributions. The function $h(\cdot)$ has five inputs depending on the pair of connected nodes u and v: the state and label of the neighbor node u, the labels of the arcs (v, u) and (u, v) (the special value *NULL* is used when one of the arcs is missing), and the state and label of the node v. The function $h(\cdot)$ is implemented by an MLP with weights θ_h share among all its replicas.

As shown for MLPs in Section 2.2, we can derive the Lagrangian formulation of the constrained optimization problem of Eq. (27) by introducing a Lagrange multiplier λ_v for each constraint, yielding the following Lagrangian function:

$$\mathcal{L}(\theta_{f_a}, \theta_{f_r}, X, \Lambda) = \sum_{v \in S} L(f_r(x_v \mid \theta_{f_r}), y_v) + \sum_{v \in V} \lambda_v \mathcal{G}(x_v - f_{a,v}), \tag{28}$$

where Λ collects the $|V|$ Lagrangian multipliers for all the nodes $v \in V$. Hence, the solution to the learning problem can be found by searching for saddle points in the adjoint space $(\theta_{f_a}, \theta_{f_r}, X, \Lambda)$, as

$$\min_{\theta_{f_a}, \theta_{f_r}, X} \max_{\Lambda} \mathcal{L}(\theta_{f_a}, \theta_{f_r}, X, \Lambda). \tag{29}$$

The solution can be approximated by applying gradient descent for the variables $\theta_{f_a}, \theta_{f_r}, X$, and gradient ascent for the Lagrange multipliers Λ (see Ref. [22]). The gradients can be computed locally to each node depending on variables related to the node itself and to its neighbors, as

$$\frac{\partial \mathcal{L}}{\partial x_v} = L' f'_{r,v} + \lambda_v \mathcal{G}'_v (1 - f'_{a,v}) - \sum_{w:v \in \mathrm{ne}[w]} \lambda_w \mathcal{G}'_w f'_{a,w}, \tag{30}$$

$$\frac{\partial \mathcal{L}}{\partial \theta_{f_a}} = - \sum_{v \in V} \lambda_v \mathcal{G}'_u f'_{a,v}, \tag{31}$$

$$\frac{\partial \mathcal{L}}{\partial \theta_{f_r}} = \sum_{v \in S} L' f'_{r,v}, \tag{32}$$

$$\frac{\partial \mathcal{L}}{\partial \lambda_v} = \mathcal{G}_v, \tag{33}$$

where $f'_{a,v}$ is the gradient of the state transition function with respect to the same variable as in the partial derivative on the left side, $f_{r,v} = f_r(x_v \mid \theta_{f_r})$, $f'_{r,v}$ is its gradient with respect to θ_{f_r}, $\mathcal{G}_v = \mathcal{G}(x_v - f_{a,v})$ and $\mathcal{G}'_v$ is its first derivative, and, finally, L' is the first derivative of the loss function L. The functions f_a and f_r are implemented by MLPs and the required gradients can be computed by applying the classical BP algorithm. Despite the addition of the free state variables x_v and the Lagrange multipliers λ_v, $v \in V$, there is no significant increase in the memory requirements since the state variables also need to be memorized in the original formulation of GNN*, and there is just a single Lagrange multiplier for each node.

The diffusion mechanism of the state computation is enforced by means of the constraints, fostering a gradual evolution of state representations in order to satisfy the fixed-point condition. On the other side, the weights of the neural networks implementing the transition and output functions are efficiently updated by means of a BP scheme. In this process, the neural network weights and the node state variables are simultaneously updated, such that the learning proceeds by jointly updating the function weights and by diffusing information among nodes, through their state, up to a stationary condition where both the objective function is minimized, and the state transition function has reached a fixed point. The resulting computational scheme is referred to as Lagrangian propagation GNN (LP-GNN) [27].

3.3 Deep LP-GNNs

The implementation of the transition function f_a may exploit an MLP with any number of hidden layers. Adding layers to the MLP allows the model to learn more complex functions to diffuse the information on the graph, but the effect is still local to each node. Differently, a layered GNN* [19] adds layers to the state computation mechanism. In this case, a set of K states $\{x_{v,k}, k = 0, \ldots, K-1\}$ is computed for each node $v \in V$, where k is the layer index. The processing scheme considers the state representation computed for layer k as the node label to be processed by the GNN* at layer $k+1$. The states in the first layer, $x_{v,0}$, are computed by applying the state transition function of Eq. (22). Then for each layer $k > 0$, the states are updated by

$$x_{v,k}^{(t)} = f_a^k\left(x_{\mathrm{ne}[v],k}^{(t-1)}, l_{\mathrm{ne}[v]}, l_{(v,\mathrm{ch}[v])}, l_{(\mathrm{pa}[v],v)}, x_{v,k}^{(t-1)}, l_v, x_{v,k-1} \mid \theta_{f_a^k}\right), \tag{34}$$

where $\theta_{f_a^k}$ collects the weights of the MLP implementing the kth diffusion function. The final outputs are computed by the output function f_r using the node states $x_{v,K-1}$ at the last layer. A simplified version of the transition function for the layers $k > 0$ removes the dependence on the arc and node labels, such that $x_{v,k}^{(t)} = f_a^k\left(x_{\mathrm{ne}[v],k}^{(t-1)}, x_{v,k}^{(t-1)}, x_{v,k-1} \mid \theta_{f_a^k}\right)$. Finally, the model can be also extended by adding an output function f_r^k at each layer, such that the output $y_{n,k-1}$ at layer $k-1$ is concatenated to $x_{v,k-1}$ as input for the following layer. The available supervisions can be applied also to these added outputs [19].

In this architecture, the states need to be computed sequentially starting from the first layer. The computation at each layer k requires the relaxation procedure to compute the fixed point of the map f_a^k. During the iterations, the states computed by the previous layer $k-1$ are set as constant inputs. Hence, the computation cost of layered GNN* is increased by the need to compute the fixed point for each layer in the forward phase and to propagate the information through the resulting unfolding in the backward phase.

The LP-GNN local computation can be extended to layered GNN*s by considering the state variables $x_{v,k}$ at each node and layer as free variables. The fixed-point constraints of Eq. (26) are added for each layer, yielding the following constrained optimization problem for the case of multiple layers of GNN*s:

$$\begin{aligned} \min_{\Theta_{f_a}, \theta_{f_r}, X} \quad & \sum_{v \in S} L(f_r(x_{v,K-1} \mid \theta_{f_r}), \hat{y}_v) \\ \text{subject to} \quad & \mathcal{G}(x_{v,k} - f_{a,v}^k) = 0, \quad \forall\, v \in V,\ \forall\, k \in [0, K-1], \end{aligned} \tag{35}$$

where $\Theta_{f_a} = \left[\theta_{f_a^0}, \ldots, \theta_{f_a^{K-1}}\right]$ collects the weights of the MLPs implementing the transition function at each layer, and X the states $x_{v,k}$ for each node and layer. The notation $f_{a,v}^k$ extends that of Eq. (23) for Eq. (34), taking into account that $f_{a,v}^0$ corresponds to the original definition.

Fig. 5 shows a layered GNN with $K=3$ layers, in which the simplified version of the state transition function f_a is implemented. The input graph labels are fed as inputs only to the first layer $k=0$. The layers with $k>0$ use the state computed by layer $k-1$ in their input. The constraints force the free state $x_{v,k}$ at each layer k and node v to approximate the value computed by the transition functions f_a^k. The symbol $\mathcal{G}$ denotes these constraints.

As done for single-layer GNN*s, the constrained optimization problem can be transformed into a nonconstrained one, by introducing the Lagrangian function and the required Lagrangian multipliers $\lambda_{v,k}$, as

$$\mathcal{L}(\Theta_{f_a},\theta_{f_r},X,\Lambda)=\sum_{v\in S} L(f_r(x_{v,K-1}\mid\theta_{f_r}),\hat{y}_v)+\sum_{v\in V}\sum_{k=0}^{K-1}\lambda_{v,k}\mathcal{G}\left(x_{v,k}-f^k_{a,v}\right). \qquad (36)$$

The Lagrangian function can be optimized by searching saddle points, by gradient descent in Θ_{f_a}, θ_{f_r}, and X and gradient ascent in $\Lambda=\{\lambda_{v,k}\}$. The gradients can be obtained following the procedure described in the case of single-layer GNN*s. The Lagrangian approach allows both the optimization of the network weights of the networks and the diffusion of the information through the graph and the layers.

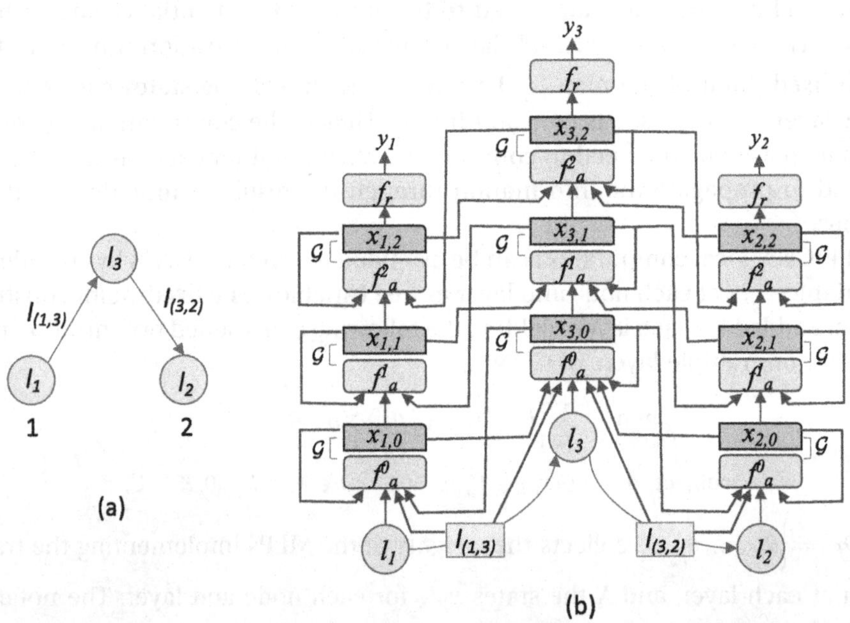

FIG. 5 (A) Input graph. (B) The layered GNN with $K=3$ layers unfolded on the input graph. The input graph labels are fed only to the first layer (simplified version of the transition function). The symbol $\mathcal{G}$ denotes the constraints between the transition function output and the corresponding state variables $x_{v,k}$.

4 Conclusions

The chapter introduced the idea of *architectural constraints* to cast neural network learning into a constrained optimization framework based on the Lagrangian framework. The Lagrangian formulation of the training process yields a fully local algorithm, referred to as LP that is based on the search of saddle points in the adjoint space constituted by the neural network weights, the neurons' outputs, and the Lagrange multipliers. LP requires additional variables but it is highly parallelizable. Furthermore, the satisfaction of the constraints may be based on ϵ-insensitive functions, allowing the development of robustness to noise. When injected into the convergence-based seminal GNNs, the described approach simplifies the learning procedure, avoiding the need to explicitly compute the fixed point of the state transition function during each epoch of the learning procedure. The extension to the case of layered GNNs shows that an appropriate implementation of the architectural constraints can be devised to deal with any neural network model.

Acknowledgments

We thank Alessandro Betti, Giuseppe Marra, and Stefano Melacci, who gave significant contributions to the work described in this chapter. The contents of this chapter are based on Refs. [27, 37, 38]. This work was partially supported by TAILOR, a project funded by the EU Horizon 2020 research and innovation program under GA No. 952215, and by HumanE-AI-Net, a project funded by EU Horizon 2020 research and innovation program under GA No. 952026.

References

[1] J. Schmidhuber, Deep learning in neural networks: an overview, Neural Netw. 61 (2015) 85–117.

[2] Z. Yang, X. He, J. Gao, L. Deng, A. Smola, Stacked attention networks for image question answering, in: IEEE Conference on Computer Vision and Pattern Recognition, June, 2016.

[3] H. Xu, K. Saenko, Ask, attend and answer: exploring question-guided spatial attention for visual question answering, in: European Conference on Computer Vision, Springer, 2016, pp. 451–466.

[4] A. Vaswani, N. Shazeer, N. Parmar, J. Uszkoreit, L. Jones, A.N. Gomez, Ł. Kaiser, I. Polosukhin, Attention is all you need, in: Advances in Neural Information Processing Systems, 2017, pp. 5998–6008.

[5] R.J. Williams, D. Zipser, A learning algorithm for continually running fully recurrent neural networks, Neural Comput. 1 (1989) 270–280.

[6] S. Hochreiter, J. Schmidhuber, Long short-term memory, Neural Comput. 9 (8) (1997) 1735–1780.

[7] Y. LeCun, Y. Bengio, Convolutional networks for images, speech, and time-series, in: M.A. Arbib (Ed.), The Handbook of Brain Theory and Neural Networks, MIT Press, 1995.

[8] C. Goller, A. Kuchler, Learning task-dependent distributed representations by backpropagation through structure, in: International Conference on Neural Networks, June, 1, 1996, pp. 347–352, https://doi.org/10.1109/ICNN.1996.548916. vol.

[9] P. Frasconi, M. Gori, A. Sperduti, A general framework for adaptive processing of data structures, IEEE Trans. Neural Netw. 9 (5) (1998) 768–786.

[10] F. Scarselli, M. Gori, A.C. Tsoi, M. Hagenbuchner, G. Monfardini, The graph neural network model, IEEE Trans. Neural Netw. 20 (1) (2009) 61–80.

[11] D.E. Rumelhart, G.E. Hinton, R.J. Williams, et al., Learning representations by back-propagating errors, Cogn. Model. 5 (3) (1988) 1.

[12] M. Gori, Machine Learning: A Constraint-Based Approach, Morgan Kaufmann, 2017.

[13] G. Gnecco, M. Gori, S. Melacci, M. Sanguineti, Foundations of support constraint machines, Neural Comput. 27 (2) (2015) 388–480.

[14] Y. LeCun, D. Touresky, G. Hinton, T. Sejnowski, A theoretical framework for back-propagation, in: Connectionist Models Summer School, vol. 1, Morgan Kaufmann, CMU, Pittsburgh, 1988, pp. 21–28.

[15] M. Carreira-Perpinan, W. Wang, Distributed optimization of deeply nested systems, in: Artificial Intelligence and Statistics, 2014, pp. 10–19.

[16] G. Taylor, R. Burmeister, Z. Xu, B. Singh, A. Patel, T. Goldstein, Training neural networks without gradients: a scalable ADMM approach, in: International Conference on Machine Learning, 2016, pp. 2722–2731.

[17] A. Gotmare, V. Thomas, J. Brea, M. Jaggi, Decoupling backpropagation using constrained optimization methods, in: Workshop on Efficient Credit Assignment in Deep Learning and Deep Reinforcement Learning, International Conference on Machine Learning, 2018, pp. 1–11.

[18] Z. Wu, S. Pan, F. Chen, G. Long, C. Zhang, P.S. Yu, A comprehensive survey on graph neural networks, IEEE Trans. Neural Netw. Learn. Syst. 32 (1) (2021) 4–24.

[19] M. Bianchini, G.M. Dimitri, M. Maggini, F. Scarselli, Deep neural networks for structured data, in: Computational Intelligence for Pattern Recognition, Springer International Publishing, 2018, pp. 29–51.

[20] Y. LeCun, L. Bottou, Y. Bengio, P. Haffner, Gradient-based learning applied to document recognition, Proc. IEEE 86 (11) (1998) 2278–2324.

[21] D.P. Bertsekas, Constrained Optimization and Lagrange Multiplier Methods, Academic Press, 2014.

[22] J.C. Platt, A.H. Barr, Constrained differential optimization, in: Neural Information Processing Systems, 1988, pp. 612–621.

[23] N. Srivastava, G. Hinton, A. Krizhevsky, I. Sutskever, R. Salakhutdinov, Dropout: a simple way to prevent neural networks from overfitting, J. Mach. Learn. Res. 15 (1) (2014) 1929–1958.

[24] K. He, X. Zhang, S. Ren, J. Sun, Deep residual learning for image recognition, in: IEEE Conference on Computer Vision and Pattern Recognition, 2016, pp. 770–778.

[25] K. He, X. Zhang, S. Ren, J. Sun, Identity mappings in deep residual networks, in: European Conference on Computer Vision, Springer, 2016, pp. 630–645.

[26] S. Hochreiter, Y. Bengio, P. Frasconi, J. Schmidhuber, et al., Gradient flow in recurrent nets: the difficulty of learning long-term dependencies, in: A Field Guide to Dynamical Recurrent Neural Networks, IEEE Press, 2001.

[27] M. Tiezzi, G. Marra, S. Melacci, M. Maggini, Deep constraint-based propagation in graph neural networks, IEEE Trans. Pattern Anal. Mach. Intell. (2021) 1, https://doi.org/10.1109/TPAMI.2021.3073504. 1.

[28] Q. Li, Z. Han, X. Wu, Deeper insights into graph convolutional networks for semi-supervised learning, in: AAAI Conference on Artificial Intelligence, 2018, pp. 3538–3545.

[29] K. Xu, W. Hu, J. Leskovec, S. Jegelka, How powerful are graph neural networks? in: International Conference on Learning Representations, 2019. https://openreview.net/forum?id=ryGs6iA5Km.

[30] T.N. Kipf, M. Welling, Semi-supervised classification with graph convolutional networks, in: International Conference on Learning Representations, 2017. https://openreview.net/forum?id=SJU4ayYgl.

[31] W.L. Hamilton, R. Ying, J. Leskovec, Inductive representation learning on large graphs, in: Advances in Neural Information Processing Systems, 2017.

[32] P. Veličković, G. Cucurull, A. Casanova, A. Romero, P. Liò, Y. Bengio, Graph attention networks, in: International Conference on Learning Representations, 2018.

[33] T.N. Kipf, et al., Deep Learning with Graph-Structured Representations (Ph.D. dissertation), University of Amsterdam, 2020.

[34] V.P. Dwivedi, C.K. Joshi, T. Laurent, Y. Bengio, X. Bresson, Benchmarking graph neural networks, CoRR abs/2003.00982 (2020). https://arxiv.org/abs/2003.00982.

[35] J. Gilmer, S.S. Schoenholz, P.F. Riley, O. Vinyals, G.E. Dahl, Neural message passing for quantum chemistry, in: International Conference on Machine Learning, PMLR, 2017, pp. 1263–1272.

[36] J. Gilmer, S. Schoenholz, P. Riley, O. Vinyals, D. George, Message passing neural networks, in: Machine Learning Meets Quantum Physics, Springer, 2020, pp. 199–214.

[37] G. Marra, M. Tiezzi, S. Melacci, A. Betti, M. Maggini, M. Gori, Local propagation in constraint-based neural networks, in: International Joint Conference on Neural Networks, IEEE, 2020, pp. 1–8.

[38] M. Tiezzi, G. Marra, S. Melacci, M. Maggini, M. Gori, A Lagrangian approach to information propagation in graph neural networks, in: ECAI 2020, IOS Press, 2020, pp. 1539–1546.

Index

Note: Page numbers followed by *f* indicate figures, *t* indicate tables, and *b* indicate boxes.

D

[illegible] in the United [illegible]
[illegible] Taylor Publisher Services

Printed in the United States
by Baker & Taylor Publisher Services